Introduction to
Investments and Finance
Theory and Analysis

FRED BLACKWELL RENWICK

New York University
Department of Finance
Graduate School of
Business Administration

Introduction to Investments and Finance

Theory and Analysis

THE MACMILLAN COMPANY, New York
COLLIER-MACMILLAN LIMITED, LONDON

The Macmillan Company
866 Third Avenue, New York, New York 10022
Collier-Macmillan Canada, Ltd., Toronto, Ontario

LIBRARY OF CONGRESS CATALOG CARD NUMBER: 73-115296

FIRST PRINTING

To M. Belle

This introductory text for the study of finance and investments is designed to help students understand the theoretical concepts and analytic foundations necessary for further study in the field.

It is an ambitious book for ambitious people. Those works which contribute to the refinement and growth of a subject are commonly addressed to an audience already versed in the basic concepts of its discipline. Beginning students, therefore, experience difficulty in comprehending the purport of controversial theories and professional debates. The importance of this understanding to the advancement of the profession and to more profitable investment decisions, and its dependence upon its effective communication, has provided the motivation for this new text.

It is the purpose of this presentation to strike the median level of rigor between a misleadingly simple descriptive and an overwhelmingly

Preface

theoretical treatment of the subject. After mastering the material it contains, students should be able to follow professional arguments in articles and journals to gain new insights into the subject; however, no introductory text should stand as a substitute for the reading of original sources. To delineate various key issues and concepts as basic to these sources and to arouse sufficient curiosity to attract new talent to these sources are this text's responsibilities.

Because the science of finance and investments consists of an interdisciplinary mixture, blending such substantive areas as price theory, aggregate economics, accounting, business policy, and quantitative methods in research and analysis, introductory material must contain the rudiments of theory and analysis.

The intent is that this text will in some part reflect those changes which have brought asset management closer to a scientific study and reduced the need for occasional reliance on that intuitive "feel" for the market which forms the mystique of experience.

It is expected that persons with diverse backgrounds and a variety of levels of experience will profit from this book. No particular expertise is assumed, other than an inquisitive spirit.

By focusing on the understanding of *fundamental principles* of financial analysis, rather than the *description* of institutional procedures, the book imbues the student with permanently valid knowledge which will not be affected by the transient qualities of practice and procedure. No "hot tips" are given, no rules of thumb. A conscientious attempt has been made to limit all explanations to the essential information for the development and strengthening of analytic skills. Discussions are kept to a minimum. Such descriptive material as adds perspective or substance to the analysis has been incorporated where it is relevant. Mathematical calculation gives way to verbal explanations and logical argument wherever possible; however, when its compact notation and precision avoid ambiguities that would otherwise arise, mathematics is used as an aid to clarity. Mathematics is never used compulsively to awe the reader or reviewer.

The book is divided into four major sections, according to subject matter, to facilitate teaching over several semesters. Parts I and II form a preface to financial analysis, Part III constitutes a basis for financial analysis and security evaluation, while Part IV develops a foundation for the profitable management of assets. The vital sections, Parts III and IV, each present material suitable for a one-semester course, should such a disposition be desired.

The first three chapters of Part I compromise a brief review of background material for the remainder of the book. These chapters present an introduction to Wall Street and the elements of finance and investments, with a summary of some prerequisite economics, differences between owning and financing with debt securities and common stocks, and some measures of the securities market. The next three chapters of Part II are crucial to the understanding of the book. They treat the fundamental concepts of the time value of money, internal rate of return, uniform annual revenue, and Fisher's rate of return over cost, and complete the foundation of other concepts used throughout the book. Analysis under conditions of risk and uncertainty is introduced.

All four parts of the book together constitute a thorough introduction to the science, theory, and methods of modern financial analysis. Advanced students, having completed courses in principles of accounting, corporation finance, and quantitative methods and entering on a course of security and analysis or portfolio management, may start directly with either Parts III or IV, although a quick review of the earlier portions is beneficial generally.

Acknowledgments

Many people have influenced the writing of this book. In particular, I am indebted to Professor Lawrence S. Ritter, New York University, for starting me on this text. Professor Ritter first suggested that a text-book such as this might be a worthwhile contribution to the education of students.

My former colleagues and teachers at New York University, Professors Eugene M. Lerner (now at Northwestern) and Willard T. Carleton (now at Dartmouth), have had a major impact on my framework for analysis. Also, Professor Henry C. McBay, during my undergraduate years at Morehouse College, instilled in me respect and admiration for the scientific method of analysis. Finally, I must mention the real experts and teachers: my many students in security analysis, portfolio analysis, and advanced topics in investments at G.B.A., New York University.

Mrs. Jule H. Broomhead cheerfully performed a heroic job of typing the drafts required in the preparation of this book. Mrs. Broomhead also keypunched and ran computer programs to analyze empirical data on General Electric's Mark I Time-Sharing System in Teaneck, New Jersey.

I acknowledge kind permission from *Industrial Management Review*, *The Journal of Finance*, and *Management Science* to reprint the substance of my articles: (1) "Economic Growth and Distributions of Change in Stock Market Prices," *Industrial Management Review*, vol. 9, no. 3, Spring 1968, pp. 39–67; (2) "Asset Management and Investor Portfolio Behavior: Theory and Practice," *The Journal of Finance*, vol. XXIV, no. 2, May 1969, pp. 181–206; and (3) "Theory of Investment Behavior and Empirical Analysis of Stock Market Price Relatives," *Management Science*, vol. 15, no. 1, September 1968, pp. 57–71.

Fred. B. Renwick

Contents

Part I

Background

Mr. Counsellor: What do you recommend, bonds or common stocks? I have heard that money can be doubled in the stock market, but which *particular* stock should I buy? Sir, my problem is not which stock to buy; my problem is *when to sell* the stocks I already hold. How much should I set aside today if I plan to retire in twenty years with an income of $400 per month for life? Never mind twenty years, I have $500 today and would like to have $100,000 by next year; how can I accomplish this objective?

In a different office, at a different location, the questions might be, Mr. Banker: I've just invented a new gadget which I call a Martian Landing Module, but I need $10 million to start production. Will you loan me the money? How much is the cost of raising $100,000 of new equity capital? Which alternative do you recommend for raising

Some Prerequisites for Financial Analysis and Asset Management 1

$500,000 of new capital: issue first-mortgage bonds, convertible debentures, preferred shares, or additional common stock? Are retained earnings in fact a cost-free source of financing? How do corporate and personal income taxes affect the risks and profitability of equity ownership?

These and similar question are asked every day of financiers and professional managers of investible dollars. Many of the questions are sensible; some are naive. Throughout this textbook we shall attempt to provide a rationale for arriving at answers to the sensible questions and at the same time show why the naive questions are naive.

The setting naturally focuses on Wall Street, on institutions that deal in money and credit, on the spending that creates the need for money and credit, and on prices which determine the amount of money and credit required. Hence, the journey through the why's and wherefore's of financial analysis and asset management begins logically with these preliminaries.

Background knowledge necessary for the successful study of finance and investments can be placed into two broad categories. One category contains core subjects such as fundamentals of economics, macro as well as micro; principles of accounting, national income accounting as well as managerial accounting; quantitative methods, including statistical inference; and methods for forecasting.

The second category of background knowledge includes institutional material and information concerning day-to-day practices and procedures used by firms in the financial community.

Much of the analytical material required for background is summarized in the first six chapters. Readers already familiar with this material may wish to skip directly to more advanced chapters of the text. Chapter 1 focuses attention on the setting for profitable finance and investments. The topics discussed are

1. The need for financing: Demand and supply of real goods and services
2. Finance vs. investments: Interacting decision elements
3. Financial resources: The money side of spending and some major pools of money and credit
4. Accounting statements: The "fact sheets" of financial analysis.

1.1 The Need for Financing

The need for financing starts with a desire to spend. Spending, and the desire to spend, by private individuals, businesses, and governments lies at the heart of economic, and thus financial, activity. Finance and economics are unalterably intertwined. Good finance decisions invariably are good economic decisions. Hence one crucial prerequisite for profitable financial analysis is uncluttered understanding of the economics of the situation: the economics of what is being financed and why. One strategic question is: Why this particular project instead of some alternative project?

Spending and human desires to spend can be studied in two ways:

1. Each unit of spending can be studied in isolation individually (i.e., the *micro*economic approach), or
2. All spending units can be lumped together and the resultant aggregation can be studied (i.e., the *macro*economic approach)

Both approaches are summarized briefly below, with the latter presented first.

AGGREGATE SPENDING. Consider all the spending for *new* goods and services produced in the total economy during the year. The sum total of this spending is known as *gross national product* (GNP).

$$\text{GNP} = C + I + G + F \tag{1.1}$$

where

GNP = gross national product (total spending in the nation)
  C = spending by individuals for personal consumption
   I = gross private domestic investment by business firms
  G = governmental purchases
  F = net foreign spending

Spending by private individuals and households to fulfill personal need and wants is called consumption (C). Personal consumption, as the name implies, includes all legal expenditures made by private individuals. Individuals can purchase items such as a new automobile, or major appliance, or new furniture for the home (that is, *consumer durable* goods) or items such as a better quality diet, or increased variety of entertainment, or greater quantity of clothing, or more leisure-time activities such as, vacations or a new boat (that is, *nondurable* items). Nondurable items include monetary services such as upstairs maids, haircuts, and doctors' bills but excludes nonmonetary services such as the priceless help of millions of housewives and mothers. The only exclusion of money outlays made legally by private individuals is for new houses. A new house is considered as an *investment* and is therefore included in I, not C. All illegal purchases (e.g., narcotics, prostitution, crime, etc.) are excluded entirely from GNP.

Gross private domestic investment (I) represents spending by business people and farmers for *new* productive facilities and inventories and by consumers for new homes. For example, business firms might spend money for new goods and services (such as added plant and equipment), or more labor, or additional education of employees, or for increasing the level of technology of plant operations, or for additional inventory. Money must be forthcoming to pay for these expenditures. The money value of these new goods and services is counted in the investment component of spending.

The investment component of GNP can be subdivided into three categories: (1) new construction, which includes commercial and industrial construction (factories, warehouses, stores, etc.), farm buildings of all types, and private nonfarm residential construction; (2) sale of producers' durable equipment, which includes items of business equipment and machinery such as trucks, turbines, and lathes; and (3) change in business inventories, which refers to the net increase or decrease in inventories of raw materials and of semifinished and finished goods in factories, in wholesale and retail establishments, and on farms. These are the components which constitute *real* investment, (I) in equation (1.1).

Governmental purchases (G) measures the *purchases* of goods and services (not total spending) by governments at all levels. Federal, state, and local governments might purchase new items such as national defense, urban renewal, turnpikes and highways, or public library facilities. In general, government purchases, state and local as well as federal, are for goods and services which benefit society at large but are not suitable for purchase by private individuals or corporations.

Net foreign spending (F) is a relatively small item (approximately 1 percent or less of total GNP) which consists of the excess of buying by foreigners over our buying from them. Stated differently, F represents that part of GNP which gets exported if exports exceed imports.

In total, all the spending by private individuals, businesses, and governments taken together constitutes aggregate employment of the factors of production in the nation. As stated in equation (1.1) GNP is the most comprehensive single measure of economic activity in the nation. The U.S. Department of Commerce defines GNP as the aggregate money value of all the new goods and services produced in a given period of time, valued at current prices. From an accounting viewpoint, the total dollar sum indicated by GNP includes everything from services in beauty parlors to the purchase of nuclear submarines.

The basis for finance and investments emanates from these spending elements within the overall economy. This is so because spending (in a money economy) implies availability of money to pay for the goods and services purchased. Successful financial analysis therefore begins with careful economic analysis. Economic analysis can begin by focusing on *aggregate* economic conditions or total spending as discussed above,[1,2,3] or these first considerations can be directed to the microlevel of economic activity by (isolated) individual spending units as discussed below.

INDIVIDUAL SPENDING. Finance and economic activity can be studied at the level of each individual decision to spend. Thousand of individual consumers together constitute the aggregate spending and

[1] Data on GNP are readily available in many widely distributed publications by the federal government. See, for example, "Statistical Tables Relating to Income, Employment and Production," which is an appendix to each annual *Economic Report of the President*, U.S. Government Printing Office, Washington, D.C. Also see *Business Conditions Digest*, a monthly publication, U.S. Government Printing Office, Washington, D.C.

[2] For a primer on the concept and accounting for GNP, see David H. McKinley, Murray G. Lee, and Helene Duffy, *Forecasting Business Contions*, The American Bankers Association, 1965, Chap. II.

[3] For a complete analysis of GNP, see any good textbook on aggregate economics. Two good texts are (1) Gardner Ackley, *Macroeconomic Theory*, The Macmillan Company, New York, 1961, and (2) Joseph P. McKenna, *Aggregate Economic Aanlysis*, 3rd. ed., Holt, Rinehart and Winston, Inc., New York, 1969.

corresponding need for financing. This aggregation was depicted in the paragraphs above. Now let us turn our attention to prices and individual spending units.

Economic activity is a phrase which means that forces of demand and supply in a marketplace are acting upon goods and services which are scarce. The study of economics is a study of scarcity. The study of finance and investments is a study of money to pay for economic goods. An *economic good* is usually a scarce item which people want, and human wants are virtually insatiable. There is never enough of an economic good. Most people always want more, now: more houses, more food, more education, more jobs, more leisure, more auto-mobiles—more everything. And more dollars with which to buy everything are almost always in demand. But because of the painful fact that the supply of economic goods and services is always limited, someone will always fail to have his or her demands satisfied.[4] Hence, in an economic system, there must be some generally accepted way of allocating scarce resources. In the United States, the system is the (free market) *price system*.[5] Through a structure of (free market) prices, one can determine

1. Which particular goods and services shall be produced: more facilities for individual transportation (e.g., more automobiles) or more facilities for mass transportation; more agricultural products or more industrial products; more lawyers or more nuclear scientists?
2. Which particular method shall be used in producing the goods and services: more labor and less capital equipment or more capital equipment and less labor?
3. Which particular persons will get the goods and services which are produced: the wealthy; the poor; racial, ethnic, or religious groups; everyone equally?
4. How much of the available economic resources will be saved and allocated to future production and how much will be allocated to consumption now: what proportion of total (current) income should be spent now instead of being saved for that rainy day tomorrow; how much should be reinvested into the means of production so as to assure a capability of generating income tomorrow and the year after next?

---

[4] By way of contrast, air for breathing, a necessity to sustain human life, is a *free* good (i.e., not an economic good), because the supply of air is unlimited. Only if air were to become scarce would people be willing to pay money for it.

[5] The phrase *free market* is set in parentheses because some prices in the United States are set by fiat. For example, prices of the products of a public utility corporation might be set by a U.S. Government (e.g., Congressional) hearing committee, not by the free market.

Prices determine the answers to all four questions. The answers to these questions in turn, in a roundabout way, determine prices of securities and profitability of investments.

Prices determine which particular goods and services will be produced. If consumers are willing to pay a higher price for item X than for item Y, then producers will be motivated, through expectations of higher profits,[6] to increase the supply of item X. That is, if consumers of labor are willing to pay higher salaries (price of labor) for lawyers than for nuclear scientists, then over a period of time the supply of lawyers will tend to rise at a rate faster than the supply of nuclear scientists, because employees are motivated by prospects of higher income.

Supply tends to increase as price increases. Supply varies directly with price. Conceptually, the relationship between the quantity supplied and the price bid can be stated as[7]

$$q_s = a_0 + a_1 p_s \qquad (1.2)$$

where

q_s = quantity of goods and services supplied per unit of time
p_s = price offered per unit quantity forthcoming
a_0, a_1 = positive constants
a_0 = value of q_s when p_s equals zero
a_1 = a multiplier of change in offering price per unit to calculate the corresponding change in quantity forthcoming

Statement (1.2) indicates that changes in bid price per unit (i.e., the price someone is willing to pay) causes corresponding changes in quantity forthcoming per unit time,

$$\Delta q_s = a_1 \, \Delta p_s; \qquad a_1 = (\Delta q_s)/(\Delta p_s) \qquad (1.3)$$

where the symbol Δ means "arithmetic change in," $\Delta q_s = q_2 - q_1$, and

---

[6] Note the underlying assumption that expectations of higher profits tend to motivate producers. This type of motivation is fundamental to economic analysis. In economics and finance, more money (i.e., profit) always leads to greater personal satisfaction. Observe that in a noneconomic system (e.g., a system that is concerned primarily with what is "right," or "just," or "moral") this assumption of motivation through higher profits might be violated; hence different conclusions might result. This text will be concerned with profitable decisions.

[7] In the real world, the relationship between price and quantity may be *nonlinear* (e.g., a quadratic or cubic relationship) instead of linear, as stated in (1.2). However, for purposes of conceptual analysis, the linear form will suffice because we are concerned more with functional relationship than with the precise form of the function. For a detailed discussion of the economic factors which determine the constants a_0 and a_1, see any good textbook on price theory.

$\Delta p_s = p_2 - p_1$. The constant multiplier a_1 can be interpreted as a measure of responsiveness of quantity supplied to a change in price. However, a better measure of responsiveness of quantity to change in price is *elasticity*. Elasticity is better because the value of a_1 depends upon the units of a particular variable under measurement (e.g., bushels of wheat in one situation vs. millions of automobiles in another situation). Elasticity, on the other hand, is a standardized measure, independent of the particular units involved. Elasticity of supply is a percentage change in quantity forthcoming for a given percentage change in unit price,

$$\epsilon_s = (\Delta q_s/q_s)/[(-\Delta p_s)/p_s] \tag{1.4}$$

where ϵ_s = coefficient of price elasticity of supply; other terms are the same as defined previously.

Three conditions of elasticity are important for the study of price behavior. By convention, when elasticity is greater than unity, supply is agreed to be *elastic*; the schedule stated in (1.2) is relatively horizontal in position. When elasticity equals unity, supply is agreed to be *unitary elastic*. When elasticity is less than unity, supply is agreed to be *inelastic*; the schedule stated in (1.2) is relatively vertical in position.

Prices determine the second item listed above—the particular method of producing goods and services—because producers always prefer higher profits instead of lower profits. That is, economic goods and services tend to be produced in the cheapest way possible because manufacturers are motivated by profits. Profits equal the difference between total revenues and total costs. Rising costs of production imply lower profits (assuming the increase in cost cannot be passed on to the consumer) and therefore tend to lower the demand by producers for the relatively expensive factors of production. For example, if labor is more expensive than capital equipment, then the production process will tend toward more intensive utilization of capital equipment instead of the relatively expensive labor factor of production. If the price of input-factor X is larger than the price of input-factor Y, then (other thing equal) a greater quantity of input-factor X will be demanded by producers instead of a greater quantity of factor Y.

Demand for goods and services tends to decline as ask prices rise. Demand varies inversely with price. As before, we can write[8]

$$q_d = b_0 - b_1 p_d \tag{1.6}$$

---

[8] Note that since demand varies inversely with price, an alternative specification for equation (1.6) might be a nonlinear relationship such as

$$q_d = b_0 + b_1/p_d \tag{1.5}$$

where p_d is always positive (i.e., $p_d > 0$) and b_0 and b_1 are positive constants used to scale q_d to the correct height and slope, respectively. Also,

where

q_d = quantity of goods and services demanded per unit of time
p_d = price bid by consumers per unit quantity offered
b_0, b_1 = positive constants
b_0 = value of q_d when p_d equals zero
b_1 = a multiplier of change in bid price per unit to calculate the corresponding change in quantity demanded

Statement (1.6) indicates that changes in ask price per unit (i.e., the price asked and required by current owners) cause corresponding changes in quantity demanded per unit time,

$$\Delta q_d = -b_1 \, \Delta p_d; \qquad -b = (\Delta q_d)/(\Delta p_d) \qquad (1.7)$$

where all symbols are the same as defined previously. The elasticity of demand is a percentage change in quantity demanded per unit time for a given percentage change in unit price,

$$\epsilon_d = [(\Delta q_d)/q_d]/[(-\Delta p_d)/p_d] \qquad (1.8)$$

where ϵ_d = coefficient of price elasticity of demand and other terms are the same as defined previously.

Prices determine the third item listed above—which particular persons will get the goods and services which are produced—because anyone who has sufficient money (or an acceptable substitute for money, such as credit) and is willing to pay the current price (or higher) can always purchase any available good or service in a free market economy. Therefore, for a given set of consumer tastes, preferences, and prejudices (given demand per unit quantity), for those goods and services which are available, those consumers who are both *able* and *willing* to pay the highest prices in the open market will get the goods and services which are produced.

In *equilibrium*, the quantity of goods and services demanded per unit of time equals the quantity supplied: bid price equals ask price, the market is cleared, and trading occurs.

$$q_{\text{supply}} = q_{\text{demand}} = q_{\text{equilibrium}} \qquad (1.9)$$

$$p_{\text{supply}} = p_{\text{demand}} = p_{\text{equilibrium}} \qquad (1.10)$$

---

as noted in footnote 7, an alternative nonlinear form could be specified. However, for simplicity of explanation and analysis, the functional relationships stated in the linear form, equation (1.6), is satisfactory. The fundamentals of analysis are equally applicable to more complex models.

Equilibrium price and quantity of goods and services in a free market economy can be calculated by substituting values from equations (1.2) and (1.6) into equation (1.9). Thus, we can write

$$a_0 + a_1 p_s = b_0 - b_1 p_d \tag{1.11}$$

$$p_{\text{equilibrium}} = (b_0 - a_0)/(a_1 + b_1) \tag{1.12}$$

$$q_{\text{equilibrium}} = (a_1 b_0 + a_0 b_1)/(a_1 b_1) \tag{1.13}$$

Equations (1.12) and (1.13) show that equilibrium prices and quantities are determined by the parameters of the economic system under analysis, a_0, b_0, a_1, and b_1.

An equilibrium price means a stable price. In equilibrium, there is no economic cause for price or quantity to move either up or down. The reasoning which underlies this statement is as follows. If actual price is set to exceed equilibrium price, then this exceptionally large price will cause supply to rise and demand to fall, causing chronic surpluses. Goods and services are available but at prices higher than consumers are willing (or able) to pay. Hence, with unsold goods, producers tend to decrease the rate of production so that supply tends to fall back down to equilibrium levels. If producers "overshoot" so that supply falls below equilibrium levels, then, with consumers bidding against one another for the available scarce goods and services, prices will tend to rise, restoring the profit incentive to increase the rate of production back to equilibrium levels.

Alternatively, if actual price is set (for example, by fiat) at levels below the equilibrium price, then chronic shortages will result because at these low prices, manufacturers will find high rates of production to be unprofitable. Demand will exceed supply. If the price controls are removed, then producers can profitably raise prices per unit, causing incentive to produce and sell more units. Supply increases and the shortage is removed. The process is self-halting because if producers try to raise prices to levels higher than the equilibrium level, then consumers are no longer willing (or able) to buy at these high prices, leaving goods unsold. In equilibrium, therefore, both price per unit and production per unit time tend to remain constant.

However, equilibrium values *can* change over time. Points of equilibrium can change because the parameters that determine equilibrium (i.e., a_0, a_1, b_0, b_1) can change over time. The structural parameters of the economic system can change over time. For examples, styles, technology, personal preferences, and the number of people in the nation all may change from one time period to the next.

Finally, the price system in a free market economy determines the fourth item listed above: the allocation between present consumption and future production. This can be seen as follows. Each business firm and each household, in deciding how much of its income to spend today (present consumption), simultaneously decides how much of its income to save now (consume in the future). Saving always equals total (after tax) income, minus consumption, as shown in equation (1.14). Stated differently, saving equals after-tax income not spent,[9]

$$S = (1 - T)Y - C \qquad \qquad \textbf{(1.14)}$$

where

S = current saving
T = current tax rate
Y = total current income
C = present consumption expenditures

All factors are taken per unit of time.

We have already shown that prices of real goods and services determine employment (income), Y, and consumption, C. These same prices inherently determine saving. However, there is an additional aspect to the determination of saving: the *financial* aspect. Interest is paid on savings accounts. *Ceteris paribus*,[10] high rates of interest cause an increase in the propensity to save because saving becomes relatively profitable; consuming becomes relatively expensive. Money received from savings accounts is equally spendable as money received from real employment. But there is a tradeoff. Given a fixed income today ($Y = Y_0$), a rise in the propensity to save *must be* accompanied by a corresponding decline in the propensity to consume. This must be so because money can only be spent (today) or saved (to be spent later), not both. In either case, as interest rates rise and fall, consumers have reasons to respond by changing their allocation between present consumption and future consumption.

In the ways described above, the overall price system—the price of spending vs. the relative profitability of saving vs. the price of money and credit vs. prices of real goods and services—determines not only what we buy and how much it costs but also the jobs we work at and how much of our income is saved instead of spent.

---

[9] An important distinction is the difference between desired or *ex-ante* savings and actual or *ex-post* savings. The two savings are not necessarily equal. Equation (1.14) refers to ex-post, or "after the accounting period" actual, savings. The concepts ex-post and ex-ante are crucial for analysis in later chapters.

[10] *Ceteris paribus* is a phrase used frequently in the study of finance and economics which means "holding all other relevant factors (i.e., everything else) equal and constant." The purpose is to study how variations in one explanatory variable *alone* will affect a dependent variable.

The preceding discussion implies that financial analysis and investments both rest heavily on the behavior of prices in the real sectors of the economy. This implication will be clarified as the text progresses.

Profitable investments imply that financial resources are allocated to assets and uses which promise large returns. Other factors being the same, more investment dollars are always forthcoming to sectors in the overall economy where profitability is relatively high.[11] We turn now to a closer examination of finance and investment decisions themselves.

1.2 Finance vs. Investments: Interacting Decision Elements

Investment decisions and finance decisions interact with each other. Like the two blades of a pair of scissors, the investment (and saving) decision interacts with the finance (and spending) decision to cut the pie (called total income) into mutually satisfactory (*optimal*) proportions.

On the one hand, optimal investment decisions can be made only after the source, and therefore the cost, of financing has been determined. This is so because total profits can be calculated only if total costs (including costs of financing) are known. On the other hand, since the cost of financing depends upon the expected profit and *risk* of the project to be financed, total costs can be determined only after the investment decision has been made. Therefore, the two decisions together, finance *and* investments, are required for a solution. Either one alone is insufficient for decision-making purposes. For this reason, we shall make no clear distinction between finance management and investment management. Both are parts of the same job.

ELEMENTS OF FINANCE AND INVESTMENT DECISIONS. For many years finance and investment have encompassed the three major areas of spending in the aggregate economy as stated in equation (1.1). One can study specific applications to (1) *business* or corporate finance and investments, (2) *government* (sometimes called public) finance and investments, or (3) *personal* finance and investments. After these

---

[11] This introduction to analysis of investment behavior will be continued in later chapters. For now, understanding the concepts of GNP and supply and demand in a free market economy is sufficient. For further reading on price theory, market structures, and behavior of the firm, see any good text on microeconomics. Three suitable ones are (1) Kalman J. Cohen and Richard M. Cyert, *Theory of the Firm: Resource Allocation in a Market Economy*, Prentice-Hall, Inc., Englewood Cliffs, N.J., 1965; (2) Paul Samuelson, *Economics, An Introductory Analysis*, McGraw-Hill, Inc., New York, 1969; and (3) A. W. Stonier and D. C. Hauge, *A Textbook of Economic Theory*, John Wiley & Sons, Inc., New York, 1964.

similarities, there are differences. Finance and investments traditionally have been viewed as separate and distinct disciplines.

Finance decisions have been concerned primarily with the *sources* of money. Three major questions must be answered. According to traditional views of finance, these are

1. How many dollars will be required?
2. During what span of time will the money be needed?
3. What is the cheapest source (or combination of sources) for obtaining the required sum of money?

Risk is included implicitly in all three parts of the finance decision.

Investment decisions, on the other hand, traditionally have been concerned primarily with *uses* or budgeting of money instead of with locating the cheapest source of money. Elements of typical investment decisions are

1. How much total to invest?
2. What should be the allocation between current consumption (e.g., dividend payout) and reinvestment (i.e., retained and reinvested earnings)?
3. What is the optimal rate of total investment (i.e., what should be the rate of increase in capacity for production or earning)?
4. What specific assets should be purchased?
5. What proportion of the total money available should be invested in each particular asset?
6. How often to evaluate the performance of the portfolio of assets?

During recent years, because of the interactions noted above, fewer clear-cut distinctions have been made between investments and finance. However, we may benefit and possibly gain additional insight into the differences (if any) between the two disciplines from the following closer study.

FINANCE DECISIONS. The first part of the finance decision —how many dollars are needed?—requires analysis of alternative *uses* of money. For example, suppose a firm wishes to expand its operations to include goods not now produced by that firm. One possible course of action is to purchase a new plant, new equipment and to hire additional labor and management. An alternative action is to purchase an existing company which is already in the desired line of business. In either case, analyses of real (not to mention financial) costs are required.

Answers to the question "How many dollars are needed?" frequently are, at best, an *estimate* of the actual dollar outlay required. The more complex the factors involved in preparing the estimate, the larger is the chance for error in the estimate.

Errors can enter in many possible ways. There can be (1) errors or faults of judgment, (2) errors or bias of raw data, or (3) errors or incorrect interpretation of raw data. [For example, equation (1.6) could be the wrong model to use. Equation (1.5) could be the "correct" model.] Also, there can be errors of prediction. Even though statement (1.6) can be the correct statement to use and the values b_0 and b_1 both correct, the calculated value of the dependent variable can be merely an approximation to the real-world value of the actual variable.

Chances for error in the estimates often are interpreted as risks. Thus risk is frequently involved in financial decision making. However, we hasten to add that one purpose of financial analysis is not necessarily to avoid risk altogether, but to find how much risk is present in a particular opportunity, try to reduce (not necessarily minimize) this risk, and then require adequate compensation for the actual risk which is finally borne.

The second part of the finance decision—"During what span of time will the money be needed?"—requires forecasting. Any look into the future for the purpose of financing today requires knowledge of economic conditions in the future. And since no one has yet been able to forecast the future without error, there exists some finite chance of being wrong when stating the span of time during which the money will be needed. The second part of the finance decision, like the first part, implicitly includes risk.[12] Risk is a topic which is all pervasive in financial analysis, yet not enough is known about it. Risk is discussed throughout the text but is introduced specifically in Chapter 6. Also, this second part of the finance decision implies analysis of *long-term* financing as compared with *short-term* financing. As we shall see in later chapters, long-term money may have a cost which is substantially different from short-term financing.

The third part of the finance decision—"Where is the money coming from? How much does the money cost?"—requires inquiry into alternative sources for financing. Assets can be financed from either of two sources: (1) owners can supply the money themselves, thereby providing ownership equity, or (2) owners can borrow the money, thereby going into *debt*. These are the two basic forms of finance, equity vs. debt, which comprise the basis for analysis, with intricacies far beyond the obvious.

Alternatively, for some purposes, the third part of this finance decision can be viewed as a choice between (1) obtaining the required

---

[12] Many alternative methods are used in forecasting the need for funds for business purposes. For two methods, the projected (pro-forma) *balance sheet method* and the *cash flow method* of forecast, see Pearson Hunt, Charles Williams, and Gordon Donaldson, *Basic Business Finance, Text and Cases*, 3rd ed., Richard D. Irwin, Inc., Homewood, Ill., 1967, pp. 160–167.

money from *inside the firm* (e.g., from depreciation allowances and other forms of capital consumption, or from prior earnings retained within the firm), or (2) obtaining the required money from *outside the firm* (e.g., from new borrowing or new equity ownership). From either point of view, debt vs. equity or inside financing vs. outside financing, the answers to part 3 of financial analysis require that attention be focused on concepts and issues such as

1. The cost of equity capital
2. The cost of debt capital
3. The overall or weighted average cost of capital
4. Marginal sequential costing
5. Capital structure
6. Risk exposure
7. Direct costs in short-term financing.

INVESTMENT DECISIONS. The first part of the investment decision—"How much total to invest?"—constitutes the capital budgeting decision. To illustrate what is involved in this part of the investment decision, consider total wealth to be the sum of consumption expenditure and investment.

$$W = C + I \qquad (1.15)$$

where

W = total wealth or present worth of all valuable things owned
C = total consumption or present worth of all spending
I = total investment or present worth of all income not spent

At one extreme, if the rate of investment is too large over the long term (e.g., investment equals 100 percent of wealth), then no money is available for present consumption. The results may be insufficient money to sustain life. For a going-concern and for well-fed families, consumption (C) must be a positive amount. Over the long run 100 percent investment of total wealth is impossible for individuals and corporations.

At the other extreme, if the rate of investment is too small over the long term (e.g., investment equals 0 percent of wealth), then life perhaps may be reduced to a hand-to-mouth existence. Each minor recession or slight decline in income could be catastrophic because of the lack of savings. With zero investment over the long run, misery and poverty could reign as predicted by Rev. Thomas Malthus.[13] One hundred percent consumption is not a rational alternative.

---

[13] See Thomas Robert Mathus, *An Essay on the Principle of Population as it Affects the Future Improvement of Society*, London, 1826.

Between the two extremes—no saving vs. 100 percent saving—lies a desired level or rate of saving. What should this level be? The answer involves a part of the investment decision: *opportunities* for profitable investment.

The second part of the investment decision—"What specific assets should be purchased?"—requires analysis and selection between alternative assets. Answers to this part of the investment decision depend mainly upon the characteristics of the assets themselves. For example, some assets are more risky than others, even though the expected returns are similar. The choice among alternatives for investment can be wide. To list a few, wealth can be held in the form of

1. Cash: Currency (either domestic or foreign) and demand deposits in commercial banks
2. Near cash: Savings account in commercial banks and savings and loan share certificates of deposit
3. Negotiable securities: Stocks, bonds, puts, calls, and commodity futures
4. Human capital: Health, education, and professional practices
5. Physical capital: Business operations, plant and equipment, and real estate.

However, the second part of the investment decision requires more specific choices concerning cash outlays. If negotiable securities are selected, then specific names of securities must be stated. Should the portfolio include shares of General Motors? Xerox? International Business Machines? Should the portfolio be limited to shares of these companies, or should bonds be included also? Perhaps the portfolio should include some "other" investment vehicle such as real estate, plant and equipment, human capital (i.e., education and technology), time deposits, or even cash. If so, then which particular ones? An extensive analysis can be performed using the tools and methods discussed throughout this text, beginning with Chapter 4 and continuing through Chapter 11.

The third part of the investment decision answers the question "How much should be the amount invested in each security named?" Of the total amount invested, what proportion should be allocated to each particular asset? What should be the diversification? Should there be an equal dollar amount invested in each security, or should there be more invested in some assets than in other assets? This part of the investment decision constitutes portfolio analysis and management. The methods of analysis applicable for portfolio decision making are presented in Chapters 12 and 13 of the book.

Finally, the fourth part of the investment decision provides the feedback necessary for improving the overall investment decision-making process. "What is the performance of the investment portfolio? Could performance have been better? Was actual performance better than anticipated? If so, *why* did performance exceed expectations? How often should the portfolio be reevaluated? Daily? Weekly? Every five years? How often should the portfolio be "turned over"? Every six months? Once each year? Never? Is a daily or weekly trading strategy more profitable than a strategy of buying and holding for, let us say, three years?

No universal answers or standards of investment performance have been adopted to date. Some investors act on the belief that high turnover of the portfolio is the key to superior performance, and some studies show that a strategy of "buy and hold" for three or four years can result in performance equivalent to that obtained from more frequent trading. In Chapter 14 we shall study some of the issues and evidence.[14]

1.3 Financial Resources: The Money Side of Spending

Spending for real goods and services is fine, but where is the money coming from? Who has the money and how did they get it?

In this section, some major pools of money and credit are discussed. Also considered are financial institutions and intermediaries, as well as markets for money, credit, equity, and negotiable securities.

THE EQUATION OF EXCHANGE. The demand for real goods and services as expressed in the preceding paragraphs implies availability of money (or credit) to pay for the goods and services purchased. More specifically, instead of accounting for total spending in terms of private, corporate, and government purchases as we did in equation (1.1), total spending can be exprsesed in terms of the total dollars exchanging hands. One popular way of stating total spending is (1.16), the *equation of exchange.*

$$MV = PT \qquad\qquad (1.16)$$

where

M = total stock (supply) of money

---

[14] For a more extensive discussion on corporate investment and finance decisions from the point of view of corporate financial management, see the following two references: (1) Ezra Solomon, *The Theory of Financial Management*, Columbia University Press, New York, 1963, and (2) Alexander A. Robichek and Stewart C. Meyers, *Optimal Financial Decisions*, Prentice-Hall, Inc., Englewood Cliffs, N.J., 1965. For additional reading on public finance, see Roland N. McKean, *Public Spending*, McGraw-Hill, Inc., New York, 1968.

V = velocity or number of times, per unit time, that money changes hands

P = average price per unit of all goods and services involved in the transactions consumated during the time interval under consideration

T = total physical volume of all sales transactions in which money changes hands

The equation of exchange is a truism which states that the total supply of money, multiplied by the turnover (i.e., the number of times per year that a dollar is "spent"), equals the average price per unit purchased times the total transactions or quantity of items purchased.

Observe from the equation of exchange that a *rise* in total spending in the aggregate economy [i.e., an increase in the product (PT)] can be accomplished by either an increase in the supply of money (M), or an increase in the number of times each dollar is spent (V). Viewing statement (1.16) from the left-hand side instead of the right-hand side, the equation says that an increase in the money supply is sufficient to enable a rise in aggregate spending—but it is not necessary. If the supply of money increases, then V can decrease so that the equation remains satisfied; more dollars in circulation are not necessarily accompanied by a rise in either P or T. More is said in Chapter 9 concerning this.

Equation (1.16) is useful in studying the influence of aggregate economic phenomena (e.g., the changes in the supply of money) on prices in securities markets. Price levels (P) and transactions (T) are partially determined by economic conditions in the real sector of the economy as explained (in part) in the preceding paragraphs. The money supply merely makes that (desired) level of spending possible. The equation of exchange as stated in (1.16) helps focus attention on the balance between factors in the financial sector of the economy and factors in the real sector of the economy. These two sets of factors interact to determine policies for optimal finance and investment. More is said in Chapter 9 concerning these factors. For now, (1.16) will be studied.

WHAT IS MONEY? The equation of exchange focuses attention on money, the uses of money, and the reasons for wanting money. Several comments are in order.

First, equation (1.16) can be interpreted to imply that money, and only money, is useful in exchange for goods and services. This implication is wrong. Some people accept credit (e.g., signature on an American Express card). Other people accept shares of common stock or rare paintings in exchange for goods and services. In other words, money is only *one* of many possible media of exchange, but, for purposes of financial analysis, money (and credit) will be considered as *the* media.

Within the context of equation (1.16), money is an asset (or economic good) which measures one's ability to buy.[15] More money implies a greater ability to purchase available goods and services. Thus, one dollar of purchasing power implies one dollar of earned income, which implies employment (of labor or capital) worth a market price of one dollar. Other (i.e., nonmoney) assets can be converted into money by selling (i.e., liquidating) them for a price in a marketplace.

WHERE DOES MONEY COME FROM? Second, equation (1.16) raises questions regarding which particular factors determine (i.e., cause) the supply of money (and credit)? The equation of exchange is *not* a behavioral statement in that the factors on the right-hand side (*PT*) do not "cause" or "explain" the factors on the left-hand side.

How then can the supply of money and credit (or, alternatively, the supply of *loanable funds*) increase or decrease? For answers here, the basic principles of banking, which involve the creation of money and credit, are important. For full understanding of these principles, the reader is referred to an appropriate textbook,[16] but a brief summary is given below.

Basically, money comes from the U.S. Treasury and the banking system. There are three kinds of money in use: (1) "checkbook money,"

---

[15] Milton Friedman and David Meiselman used two criteria for selecting assets to be included in the money supply: (1) those assets which together provide the largest correlation with income and (2) the larger correlation of the sum with total income than with any of the components separately. The second criterion ensures that an increase in correlation is attributed to the inclusion of a component in the money supply concept and not to the association between income and the particular component alone. Friedman and Meiselman find that the set of assets, including currency, demand deposits, and time deposits at commercial banks only, satisfies the criteria better than either a narrower concept, including only currency and demand deposits, or a broader concept, including also savings-type accounts at mutual savings banks, savings and loan associations, and post offices.

See (1) M. Friedman and D. Meiselman, "The Relative Stability of Monetary Velocity and the Investment Multiplier in the United States, 1897–1958," in Commission on Money and Credit, *Stabilization Policies*, Prentice-Hall, Inc., Englewood Cliffs, N.J., 1963, and (2) George G. Kaufman, "More on an Empirical Definition of Money," *The American Economic Review*, March 1969, pp. 78–87. Also see Phillip Cagan, *Determinants and Effects of Changes in the Stock of Money, 1875–1960*, National Bureau of Economic Research, New York, 1965.

[16] For the basic principles of how commercial banks create money and credit, see any good text on banking. Two recommended ones are (1) Charles L. Prather, *Money and Banking*, 9th ed., Richard D. Irwin, Inc., Homewood, Ill., and (2) Paul M. Horvitz, *Monetary Policy and the Financial System*, 2nd ed., Prentice-Hall, Inc., Englewood Cliffs, N.J., 1969.

demand deposits at commercial banks; (2) "pocketbook money," paper currency issued by the "central bank"—the Federal Reserve System—this money is called Federal Reserve Notes; and (3) "pocket money," coins for making change and operating automatic machines. Coin money is issued by the U.S. Treasury. Gold and silver have value as money also, but private persons in the United States are not allowed to hold and use gold as money. Gold must be sold to the U.S. Treasury at a fixed preestablished price. However, private persons *are* allowed to own shares in gold-mining companies.[17]

The federal government has the legal power to print and issue new money, *treasury money*. (For the mechanics of *how* this is done, see, e.g., Prather, footnote 16). The Federal Reserve Banks have the legal power to issue new money, *Federal Reserve Notes*. Commercial banks have the legal right and power to "create" their own money, *bank credit*. Limits and restrictions exist in all three cases. Since the major percentage of money currently in use today consists of checkbook money, and since one of our primary concerns in finance and investments is with sources and uses of money, a quick summary of what happens to money when it is deposited in a checking account may be helpful.

Suppose you deposit $1000 in your checking account. Your bank, which is one among a system of banks throughout the nation, is allowed by law to retain some percentage (X) of your $1000 and loan the remainder to someone who wishes to take out a loan. If X is 20 percent then your bank will be able to make new loans totaling $800. Suppose one person borrowed the entire $800, and made a purchase or paid a bill. Suppose the $800 is now deposited in another checking account in another bank. This second bank now has legal permission to make new loans totaling $(1 - X)\$800$ or, if X still equals 20 percent, $640. The process of deposit-loan-deposit can continue until the capacity for additional loans is exhausted. The end result is that your $1000 deposit enabled the creation of a series of new deposits (i.e., checkbook money). The series of loans can be stated

$$\$1000(1 - X) + \$1000(1 - X)^2 + \cdots + \$1000(1 - X)^n$$

$$= \$1000\left[\frac{1}{X} - 1 - \frac{(1 - X)^{n+1}}{X}\right] \qquad (1.17)$$

---

[17] Some listed gold-mining companies are Dome Mines (DM), Giant Yellowknife Mines (GYK), Benguet Consolidated (BE), Campbell Red Lake Mines (CRK), International Mining (IM), American South African (ASA), and Homestake Mining (HM). Also some important South African and Canadian gold-mining shares are sold on the Johannesburg Exchange and the Toronto Exchange, respectively.

After infinite time, if $X = 20$ percent, and all money was deposited in checking accounts, and loans were made, the total amount of money would be the original $1000, plus loans totaling $4000.[18]

$$\$1000\left(\frac{1}{.20} - 1 - 0\right) = \$4000 \qquad (1.18)$$

If the reserve requirements had been 25 percent instead of 20 percent, fewer loans could have been made. The precise amount is $3000.

$$\$1000\left(\frac{1}{.25} - 1 - 0\right) = \$3000 \qquad (1.19)$$

By raising and lowering the reserve requirements, therefore, the Federal Reserve System (i.e., the Central Bank) can control the ability of commercial banks to create new checkbook money.[19]

To summarize, the supply and availability of credit both depend on factors in the banking system of the nation. Newly created money, including credit, exists because the U.S. Treasury has the power to print new money and the Federal Reserve Banks and commercial banks have the (legal) power to create new money by making loans. Some of this newly created money may find its way into the securities markets (especially into margin accounts). Existing (i.e., old) money may be held by individuals and business firms in the form of savings—both current savings and past savings. Individuals may hold savings in the form of life insurance, pension funds, personal trusts, or advisory accounts. More familiar examples may be cash—either currency or demand deposits. These savings represent loanable funds. If the price is right, these funds may be offered for use in the money and credit markets. Corporate savings represent all undistributed profits, along with allowances for capital consumption. However, the total quantity of loanable funds available from this source might be relatively small,

---

[18] The series is a geometric progression whose first term is $a = 1000(1 - X)$ and common ratio is $r = (1 - X)$. Therefore the sum of the first n terms is

$$S = \frac{a(r^n - 1)}{r - 1} = \frac{1000(1 - X)[(1 - X)^n - 1]}{(1 - X) - 1} \qquad (1.20)$$

which simplifies to (1.17).

[19] Other ways are possible too. For example, inflows and outflows of gold and silver influence treasury money and Federal Reserve Money. Also Federal Reserve discount rates and moral suasion can influence the *willingness* as well as the *ability* of commercial banks to create new money. Also, "The Fed" can *sell* (buy) government securities in the open market, thereby *removing* (replacing) money from (into) circulation. See Prather or Horvitz, *op. cit.*

because business firms typically reinvest their savings into the operations of the business. If it were more profitable to provide loanable funds to money and capital markets than to reinvest available savings into the operations of the business, business would hardly have economic justification for its existence.

This, then, is where the money comes from for finance and investments.

REASONS FOR WANTING MONEY. Third, equation (1.16) raises questions regarding what happens to the money not involved in transactions. What do people do with money?

The demand for money and credit is important for financial analysis. The total demand for money and credit can be traced to three motives.

1. Transactions motive (income effect)
2. Precautionary motive (liquidity effect)
3. Speculative motive (price level anticipations effect)

The *transactions motive* was illustrated in previous paragraphs concerning the spending of income. The transactions motive for holding money stems from the need of households and businesses to pay for ordinary day-to-day purchases. Cash balances for transactions purposes, therefore, tend to vary directly with the level of income and with the propensity to consume. Put another way, holding other things constant, households and businesses which have higher incomes than their neighbors can spend more than those neighbors. To facilitate this higher spending on a day-to-day basis, cash balances must be relatively high. Then the transactions motive is one reason for holding *active* cash balances.

For money to be bid away from active balances held for transaction purposes into the money and capital markets, prospective profits on investment in these markets must be sufficiently high (i.e., security prices must be low enough) so as to at least compensate for the risks involved in the investment and for postponing consumption. Indications from the transactions motive for holding money are that in order to curb spending and encourage saving, security prices must be low (i.e., interest rates must be high). Conversely, to encourage spending and curb saving, security prices must be high. This kind of analysis is pursued in Chapter 9.

The *precautionary motive* for holding money and the wish for *credit reserves* is found in the desire of households and businesses to be financially able to meet (foreseen and unforeseen) contingencies. These contingencies can fall into several categories.

First, there can be a desire or need to synchronize income with expenditures. Excess liquidity in the form of cash balances or credit reserves can fulfill the requirement to bridge this span of time. So there is a precautionary demand for *active* cash balances. In the case of credit, the demand is a buffer between current credit transactions and future cash income.

Second, since liquidity permits one to avail oneself readily of any extraordinarily good buys or bargains encountered by chance, having one's assets in the most liquid form—as *idle* cash balances in bank checking accounts, instead of in the form of securities—may be a profitable convenience. Also, there are costs—brokerage fees and transfer taxes—in transferring from cash into securities and back again.

Third, there can be a desire or preference for liquidity to guard against rainy day contingencies which might arise. Particularly relevant may be those risks against which one cannot protect oneself by purchasing insurance policies: prolonged illness, unemployment, unfavorable shifts in consumer demand, or similar such events. In this category, the precautionary demand is for *idle* cash balances.

The precautionary motive for needing money and credit results in both active and idle balances. To bid dollars away from these active and idle precautionary balances one must either (1) remove the reason for holding such balances (e.g., provide a national guaranteed minimum wage to protect against the events listed in the third category above) or (2) make holding such active and idle balances relatively uneconomic by offering higher returns for alternative uses of those dollars.

The *speculative motive* for desiring cash balances and credit reserves stems from a basic desire to make profits (or avoid losses) by trading (speculating) in money and capital markets. For example, if investors believe that interest rates are abnormally high and will soon fall, the implication is that bond prices are currently low and will soon rise.[20] To make profits in the bond markets investors can reduce their current demand for cash balances and increase the demand for bonds, in anticipation of future capital gains. Conversely, if investors believe that interest rates are abnormally low (i.e., bond prices are abnormally high) and will soon rise (fall), then the demand for bonds will drop (to avoid capital losses) and the demand for cash balances will rise.

These three motives—transactions, precautionary, and speculative—constitute the demand for money. If the total demand for cash balances exceeds the supply, there *can be* a flow of funds away from the securities markets. Conversely, if the supply of money and credit exceeds the demand, these extra funds *can* flow into the securities

---

[20] The mechanics of these relationships are shown in detail in Chapter 4.

markets. In any case, the balance between supply and demand for money and credit is important for financial analysis.[21]

SOME MAJOR POOLS OF MONEY AND CREDIT. Financial institutions and intermediaries serve as buffers to help balance the supply of money and credit with the demand for money and credit. At times, these buffers may fill to near capacity. At other times they may be nearly depleted. At all times, their function is to help make savings readily available for investments.

The financial markets facilitate matching the supply of investable funds with the demand for investable funds. When business firms wish to raise new capital, they may turn to the financial markets. When investors have funds available for the purchase of equity or debt instruments, they may turn to the financial markets. On one hand we have the institutions and on the other hand we have the markets.

Financial institutions and intermediaries can be classified as belonging to either of two categories—deposit-type or contractual-type. *Deposit-type* institutions include profit-seeking businesses such as commercial banks (which accept demand deposits and create credit), mutual savings banks, savings and loan associations, and credit unions. *Contractual-type* institutions include profit-seeking businesses such as mutual funds; investment companies; finance, mortgage, and loan companies; life insurance companies; fire and casualty insurance companies; private noninsured pension funds; state and local government pension funds; corporate pension funds; and commercial banks (as investors of deposit funds and as trustees for private trust funds). Also, there are nonprofit-seeking institutions such as foundations and religious, educational, and charitable funds.

These institutions, both deposit type and contractual type, help to assure that savings (income not spent) can and will be available for investment. Money for finance and investment purposes often is funneled from thousands of individual, small savers through these institutions and intermediaries to the final user. Final users of money can look to these institutions and intermediaries as a potential source of funds.

Some names of banks and foundations are listed on Tables 1.1 and 1.2 for illustrative purposes.

---

[21] For further reading on these concepts and issues, see (1) John Maynard Keynes, *The General Theory of Employment, Interest, and Money*, Harcourt, Brace & World, Inc., New York, 1936, and (2) Lawrence S. Ritter, "The Role of Money in Keynesian Theory," in Deane Carson (ed.), *Banking and Monetary Studies*, Richard D. Irwin, Inc., Homewood, Ill., 1963.

Table 1.1   AN ILLUSTRATIVE LISTING OF BANKS THAT MANAGE TRUST PORTFOLIOS*

Total trust asset rank	Bank name	Total trust assets $ Billion	% of total
1	Morgan Guaranty Trust Company	16.8	6.7
2	The Chase Manhattan Bank	13.6	5.5
3	Bankers Trust Company	11.1	4.4
4	First National City Bank	10.9	4.4
5	United States Trust Company	8.4	3.4
6	Mellon National Bank and Trust Company	7.6	3.1
7	Manufacturers Hanover Trust Company	7.3	2.9
8	Wilmington Trust Company	5.6	2.3
9	The First National Bank of Chicago	5.4	2.2
10	Continental Illinois National Bank	5.1	2.1
11	Chemical Bank New York Trust Company	4.6	1.8
12	The Northern Trust Company (Chicago, Ill.)	4.5	1.8
13	Old Colony Trust Company	4.2	1.7
14	Harris Trust and Savings Bank	3.9	1.6
15	Bank of America National Trust and Savings Association	3.7	1.5
16	The Cleveland Trust Company	3.6	1.4
17	National Bank of Detroit	3.4	1.4
18	The Bank of New York	3.3	1.3
19	Girard Trust Bank (Philadelphia, Pa.)	2.9	1.2
20	The First Pennsylvania Banking & Trust Co. (Philadelphia, Pennsylvania)	2.7	1.1

* Source: *The Institutional Investor*, September 1968, pp. 30–31.

The markets for financial assets can be characterized and classified according to many possible schemes. Some possibilities are

1. Major users: Variety of types
2. Type of instrument or contract: Debt or equity
3. Maturity of instruments
4. Degree of centralization
5. Direct vs. open market transactions
6. Primary vs. secondary transactions

For purposes of introductory financial analysis, attention can be directed to the markets for equity securities and the markets for debt securities.

Table 1.2   AN ILLUSTRATIVE LISTING OF FOUNDATIONS
ACTIVE AS INSTITUTIONAL INVESTORS

1. Ford Foundation, New York City
2. Rockefeller Foundation, New York City
3. Duke Endowment, New York City
4. Lilly Endowment, Inc., Indianapolis, Indiana
5. Kresge Foundation, Detroit, Michigan
6. Alfred P. Sloan Foundation, New York City
7. Carnegie Corporation of New York, New York City
8. Charles Stewart Mott Foundation, Flint, Michigan
9. Pew Memorial Trust, Philadelphia, Pennsylvania
10. John A. Hartford Foundation, Inc., New York City
11. Longwood Foundation, Wilmington, Delaware
12. Rockefeller Brothers Fund, New York City
13. Danforth Foundation, St. Louis, Missouri
14. Moody Foundation, Galveston, Texas
15. Houston-Endowment, Houston, Texas
16. Howard Hughes Medical Institute, Miami Beach, Florida
17. Commonwealth Fund, New York City
18. Avalon Foundation, New York City
19. Richard King Mellon Foundation, Pittsburgh, Pennsylvania
20. Carnegie Institute of Washington, Washington, D.C.
21. Emily and Ernest Woodruff Foundation, Greensboro, North
    Carolina
22. Old Dominion Foundation, New York City
23. Sarah Mellon Scaife Foundation, Pittsburgh, Pennsylvania
24. Max C. Fleischmann Foundation, Reno, Nevada
25. Charles F. Kettering Foundation, Dayton, Ohio
26. Surdna Foundation, Inc., Yonkers, New York
27. El Pomar Foundation, Colorado Springs, Colorado
28. Robert A. Welch Foundation, Houston, Texas
29. Alcoa Foundation, Pittsburgh, Pennsylvania
30. Phoebe Waterman Foundation, Inc., Philadelphia, Pennsylvania
31. Charles Hayden Foundation, New York City
32. Callaway Foundation, LaGrange, Georgia
33. Louis and Maud Hill Family Foundation, St. Paul, Minnesota
34. Charles A. Dana Foundation, Inc., Greenwich, Connecticut
35. John Simon Guggenheim Memorial Foundation, New York City
36. Smith Richardson Foundation, Inc., Greensboro, North Carolina
37. Louis Calder Foundation, New York City
38. Eugene Higgins Trust, New York City
39. China Medical Board of New York, Inc., New York City

Debt markets can be classified as *money* and *capital markets.*
Money and capital markets are phrases which refer to the complex
of financial institutions and mechanisms where intermediate-term funds
(loans of up to 10 years' maturity) and long-term funds (longer-

maturity loans and corporate stocks) are pooled and made available to business, government, and individuals, and where instruments that are already outstanding are transferred. Traditionally, the money market has usually been described as the market for short-term debt (debt with a year or less to maturity). The money market provides facilities for the quick and dependable transfer of short-term debt instruments used to finance the needs of business, government, agriculture, and consumers. The capital market traditionally deals in long-term funds, both debt and equity. Transactions involving intermediate-term money, money represented by debt with from 1 to 5 or 10 years to maturity, are usually included in capital market activity.[22]

WALL STREET. The investment market, which is the primary concern of this text, refers to places where trading occurs in negotiable securities. The essence of the investment market can be summed up in two words: *Wall Street.*

Wall Street is a logical point of departure for the forthcoming journey through the why's and wherefore's of price behavior for stocks and bonds. Wall Street is the undisputed center of the money and capital market of the world. This famous street is almost synonymous with stock exchanges, big money, and business transactions involving millions of dollars. Few people will challenge Wall Street's leadership in the area of finance.

Aside from its well-known functional characteristics, this famous center for money has several outstanding physical characteristics.[23] Wall Street is one of many narrow oneway streets in New York's lower Manhattan. During working hours, the nine-to-five crowd usually spills over from the sidewalks onto the narrow roadway. The hustle and bustle of activity fills the noonday air everywhere. After business hours, the street becomes a desolate place. It is probably the only street in the world which begins in a graveyard, the Trinity Church graveyard, and ends in a river, the East River.

The institutions located along Wall Street constitute supermarkets for money, but shopping on the street is not limited to millionaires. Anyone can participate. The stock market is a public auction market. Buyers and sellers in middle-income as well as high-income categories

---

[22] For further reading about institutions and financial intermediaries, see (1) Murray E. Polakoff et al., *Financial Institutions and Markets*, Houghton Mifflin Company, Boston, 1969, and (2) Herbert E. Dougal and Jack E. Gaumnitz, *Capital Markets and Institutions*, Prentice-Hall, Inc., Englewood Cliffs, N.J., 1965.

[23] For an interesting pictorial history of Wall Street, see Leonard Louis Levinson, *Wall Street, New York*, Ziff-Davis Publishing Company, Chicago, 1961.

meet in the institutions of Wall Street to exchange dollars for negotiable securities. During the late 1960's, for example, over 20 million individual shareowners participated in profits (and losses) from trading in shares of common stocks. Of these 20 million shareowners, approximately one-third reside in small communities with population of 25,000 persons or less, and a majority had household incomes of less than $10,000 per year.[24] Easy budget plans are available for systematic investment that require as little as $4 every 3 months.[25] So one need not be a millionaire to exploit opportunities to put unspent cash to work in the securities markets. Wall Street indeed services small individual investors.

But this mighty fortress can and often does behave as a prime mover in the (efficient?) exchange between users and suppliers of huge sums of money. For example, referring to any ready reference of annual market statistics, we see that during the 1960's over 1 billion shares per year on average traded hands on the New York Stock Exchange alone.[26] Bond sales on the New York Stock Exchange, between 1963 and 1966, averaged over $2.5 billion per year. Using these figures and assuming that stocks sold for $50 per share on average, then, for the New York Stock Exchange alone (one of several markets for stocks), money exchanged hands at the rate of approximately $1 billion per week.

To reduce this astronomical sum to a more comprehensible level, $1 billion per week is equivalent to approximately three-fourths of the total sales of all manufacturing and trade in the United States during the time period observed. Related another way, $1 billion per week is approximately equivalent to 10 percent of all the goods and services (10 percent of the gross national product) produced in the nation during the time period observed.

One can conclude that large and small investors use the public auction markets of Wall Street frequently. Individual investors may act either alone, trading for their own personal portfolios, or they may act together by participating in professionally managed mutual funds, trust funds, or pension funds.

Shopping on the Street can be profitable. But shopping there can be expensive. Various kinds of securities can be bought or sold to the highest bidder. Instead of buying or selling securities directly, investors can buy options to buy and sell securities. If prices are low and investors believe that prices will rise soon, the order of the day might be to buy.

---

[24] Source: 1967 *Census of Share Owners, New York*, The New York Stock Exchange, New York, 1967.

[25] Such a plan is available through Merrill Lynch, Pierce, Fenner and Smith, members of the New York Stock Exchange and other principal exchanges.

[26] See *The Dow Jones Investor's Handbook*, published annually by Dow Jones and Company, Inc., New York.

Alternatively, if prices are high and investors believe there will be a decline in prices within the near future, the order might be to sell. Investors may even "sell short": investors may sell securities not yet owned, in anticipation of buying them at a later date for a lower price to cover the short sale. Profits are taken when selling price exceeds purchasing price. Losses are taken when investors buy high and sell low, as many often do. The direction of security prices, unlike the direction of the Street, is two-way.

Because security prices do go down as well as up, there are chances for loss as well as chances for gain. The markets are risky. Investors in the securities markets must be able and willing to suffer the consequences decreed by the marketplace when future prices fail to behave in accord with well-formulated expectations. Formulating correct expectations is part of the game—a crucial part of the stock market game. Later chapters in the book (chapters of Part III) are devoted to understanding the economic mechanisms that underlie the financial markets and the factors which must be considered in formulating expectations concerning future prices of bonds and stocks.

MARKETS FOR STOCKS AND BONDS. The principal markets for stocks and bonds in the United States consist of registered exchanges, exempt exchanges, and the over-the-counter market. These are listed on Table 1.3.

The registered exchanges consist of The New York Stock Exchange (NYSE) located at 11 Wall Street, the American Stock Exchange (AMEX) located at 80 Trinity Place, and several regional exchanges dispersed throughout the nation. The NYSE and the AMEX are the largest of all the registered exchanges. Access to trading on the exchanges is limited to "members only." Since 1875, the price of member-on the New York Stock Exchange has ranged from a low of $4000 to a high of over $500,000. In addition, there are other criteria for membership such as personal integrity, financial capability, and overall acceptance by existing members. These criteria are set forth by the Board of Governors of the exchange.

Membership on an exchange brings with it the right to buy and sell securities for the personal account of the member as well as for his customers. Members trade only with one another. If a nonmember investor wishes to buy and sell securities, he must "hire" a member to execute the order. The fee charged by the member is called a commission. Current schedules for commissions can be obtained from any member firm.

Orders to buy and sell securities are executed on the trading floor of the exchange. The agent who fulfills the order for the member firm is called a "specialist." The purpose of the specialist is to maintain an

Table 1.3 MARKET PLACE FOR SECURITIES IN THE UNITED
STATES

1. Registered exchanges
     American Stock Exchange
     Boston Stock Exchange
     Chicago Board of Trade
     Cincinatti Stock Exchange
     Detroit Stock Exchange
     Midwest Stock Exchange
     National Stock Exchange
     New Orleans Stock Exchange
     New York Stock Exchange
     Pacific Coast Stock Exchange
     Philadelphia-Baltimore-Washington Stock Exchange
     Pittsburgh Stock Exchange
     Salt Lake City Stock Exchange
     San Francisco Mining Exchange
     Standard Stock Exchange of Spokane
2. Exempt exchanges
     Colorado Springs Stock Exchange
     Honolulu Stock Exchange
     Richmond Stock Exchange
     Wheeling Stock Exchange
3. Over-the-counter market
   a. Security houses
        Investment banking houses
        Over-the-counter houses
        Exchange members
        Municipal bond houses
        Government bond houses
   b. Dealer banks (permitted by law to deal only in U.S. Government
      obligations and municipal issues). Dealer banks engage in
      regular banking business in addition to their over-the-counter
      activities.

orderly market in a particular security or a particular group of securities. Trading takes place at the trading post of the specialist on the floor of the exchange. The specialist maintains an inventory record book of buy and sell orders and bid and ask prices. If there are no buyers or no sellers, or if the spread is too great between bid price and ask price, the specialist has the duty and right to buy or sell for his own account. This is consistent with the stated duty of the specialist to maintain an orderly market for trading in the stock.

The over-the-counter (OTC) market is a "bargain" market, not an auction market. That is, prices of transactions are bargained or agreed upon between the buyer (or the seller) and the specialist. In an auction market, the specialist is the "auctioneer" who negotiates between the seller and the buyer.

Large block transactions by institutional and professional investors can cause problems of marketability. To sell 200,000 shares of Du Pont at $50 per share requires someone (or someones) willing (and able) to buy that amount at that price. Such large volume transactions have caused the emergence of a "third" and a "fourth" market. These markets consist of broker-dealers not necessarily members of an exchange who match buyers and sellers directly and negotiate instead of charging the fixed, established commission fee. For these transactions, listed prices of the securities traded are usually accepted by both buyer and seller as the market price.

These are some of the bare fundamentals necessary to begin a more analytical study of price behavior in securities markets.[27] We turn next to a brief summary of financial accounting statements.

1.4 Accounting Statements: The Fact Sheets of Financial Analysis

Accounting statements are the fact sheets of financial analysis. These statements lay bare the financial position of the person, firm, or government for whom they are prepared. Two particular accounting statements are important for introductory financial analysis and investments. They are (1) the *income statement* and (2) the *balance sheet*. There are many other accounting statements but these are the two most basic.[28] No matter which statement is under study, the primary purpose of the financial statement is the same—to provide factual answers, arrived at in a standard, uniform way agreed upon by the accounting profession, to the questions relevant for financial analysis. The form of the particular statement may vary from company to company. Statements from some companies may contain more information than other corresponding statements of other companies,

---

[27] For further reading on the mechanics of buying and selling securities and related topics, see (1) Louis Engel, *How to Buy Stocks*, 4th ed., Bantam Books, Inc., New York, 1968; (2) Robert Sobel, *The Big Board*, The Free Press, New York, 1965; (3) James E. Walter, *The Role of Regional Security Exchanges*, University of California Press, Berkeley and Los Angeles, 1957; (4) Sidney Robbins, *The Securities Markets: Operations and Issues*, The Free Press, New York, 1966; and (5) William J. Baumol, *The Stock Market and Economic Efficiency*, New York, Fordham University Press, New York, 1965.

[28] See Myron J. Gordon and Gordon Shillinglaw, *Accounting, A Management Approach*, 3rd ed., Richard D. Irwin, Inc., Homewood, Ill., 1964.

depending on the individual circumstances. But the goal is always the same; the underlying principles of accounting are applicable universally. Some characteristics of income statements and balance sheets are examined below.

STATEMENTS OF INCOME. The income statement presents a factual accounting of the earnings received during the reporting period If prepared by a member of the accounting profession in good standing, as it should be, then the income statement will be arranged and itemized in a standard, systematic way to indicate the cost of obtaining the current income as well as the source of that income. A representative statement of income is shown in Table 1.4. Observe the form and arrangement of items in the listing.

At the beginning of the income statement in Table 1.4, there is the heading. The heading consists of the name of the firm, the name of the statement, and the length of time covered by the statement. If any of these three items is omitted, the statement is incomplete.

Next, the first group of items specifies the sources of revenue (gross sales of $500,000) and discloses costs and expenses of operating the business (cost of goods sold plus operating expenses equal $380,000). Each item listed on the statement must be descriptive of its contents.

The next listing is the operating profit (or loss) from the primary operations of the business for the accounting period (net operating income equals $115,000).

Next is "other" revenue or income and "other" expenses. These are revenues and expenses which accrue because of the *financial* (in contrast with the *operational*) function of the business. "Other revenue" may include interest income, dividend income, rent income, royalties, commissions, etc. "Other expenses" may include interest expense, amortization of bond discount and expense, net loss on real estate properties, and miscellaneous expense items arising out of non-operating activities.

Total income before taxes is itemized ($120,000), as are federal income taxes ($60,000). Then net income after taxes ($60,000) is itemized for the accounting period.

If relevant, extraordinary gains and losses are listed. Extraordinary gains and losses accrue from special situations such as fire, flood, loss of property due to action by foreign countries, and losses on deposits in closed banks. Extraordinary gains and losses are "abnormal" items. On occasion, comparative data may be given for one or more of the preceding periods.

Finally, parenthetical statements, footnotes, explanatory notes, and detailed attached schedules will disclose additional information such as inventory pricing method, depreciation method, and the effect

Table 1.4   ILLUSTRATIVE INCOME STATEMENT

Universal International, Inc.
Income Statement
for the Year Ended December 31, 1985

Gross sales		$500,000
Less: Sales returns and allowances	$ 2,000	
Sales discount	3,000	5,000
Net sales		$495,000
Cost of goods sold:		
Finished goods inventory, January 1	$ 22,000	
Cost of goods manufactured*	310,000	
	332,000	
Finished goods inventory, December 31	32,000	300,000
Gross margin on sales		$195,000
Operating expenses:		
Selling expenses†	$ 50,000	
General and administrative expenses	30,000	
Total operating expenses		80,000
Operating income		115,000
Other revenue†		76,000
		$191,000
Other expense†		71,000
Income for the year before federal income taxes		$120,000
Federal income taxes		60,000
Net income for the year after federal income taxes		$ 60,000
Extraordinary gain†		10,000
		$ 70,000
Extraordinary loss†		5,000
Net income and extraordinary items		$ 65,000

* Cost of goods manufactured may be itemized in further detail on a separate schedule.

† These items may be specified in further detail on separate accompanying schedules, depending on the magnitude of the amounts involved.

on the net income of changes made in accounting practices during the period.[29]

The income statement, therefore, is designed to provide a reliable, factual answer to the question "How much is total income?" Also,

---

[29] For further reading in this area, see some good text in accounting such as Ralph D. Kennedy and Stewart Y. McMullen, *Financial Statements: Form, Analysis and Interpretation*, 4th ed., Richard D. Irwin, Inc., Homewood, Ill., 1962.

income statements such as the one described above can be useful in estimating *future* income of the business which is discussed in greater detail in Part III.

BALANCE SHEETS. The balance sheet provides answers to the questions "What is the worth of total assets?" and "Of the total investment in assets, how much represents borrowed funds (debt) and how much represents owner's funds (equity)?" The *balance* is between the (book) value of total assets (A) and the sum of total liabilities (L), with total equity (E). That is, the finance of any given asset (A) must be from either (1) debt sources, or (2) equity or ownership sources, or (3) some combination of (1) and (2). For future reference, we can file in memory the accounting tautology of the balance sheet:

$$A = E + L \qquad (1.21)$$

where

A = total assets (total dollar value of "things owned")
E = total equity (total dollars supplied by owners)
L = total liabilities (total dollars supplied by lenders)

Observe the form and arrangement of items on the balance sheet. A typical accounting form of a balance sheet is shown in Table 1.5. The arrangement of items in the account form is in agreement with practices of the accounting profession.

The arrangement of items on the balance sheet usually follows a standard format (listed in order of liquidity). On the asset side of the balance sheet we can have

1. Current assets
2. Long-term investments
3. Fixed assets
4. Intangible assets
5. Deferred charges
6. Other assets

On the side listing liabilities and equity ownership, we can have

1. Total liabilities
   a. Current (i.e., short-term) liabilities
   b. Long-term liabilities
2. Total ownership equity
   a. Capital stock
   b. Paid-in surplus
   c. Retained earnings
   d. Appropriated retained earnings
   e. Appreciation surplus

Total assets = Total liabilities + Total ownership equity.

Table 1.5   ILLUSTRATIVE BALANCE SHEET

Universal International, Inc.
Balance Sheet
for the Year Ended December 31, 1985

ASSETS

Current assets:		
Cash		$161,600
Accounts receivable, net		124,000
Notes receivable		27,000
Interest receivable		200
Merchandise inventories		333,900
Prepaid expenses		1,200
Total current assets		$647,900
Property and equipment:		
Building and equipment	$653,800	
Less: Depreciation to date	358,000	295,800
Land		26,300
Total assets		$970,000

LIABILITIES AND OWNERSHIP

Current liabilities:		
Accounts payable		$102,500
Taxes payable		29,000
Dividends payable		30,000
Interest payable		1,500
Advances from customers		10,000
Total current liabilities		$173,000
Other liabilities:		
Mortgage loan payable		120,000
Total liabilities		$293,000
Ownership equity:		
Capital stock	$500,000	
Retained earnings	177,000	
Total ownership equity		677,000
Total liabilities and ownership		$970,000

The assets are listed separately from the liabilities and the equity. Physically, the listings can be side-by-side, or in a single column as shown in Table 1.5, with assets at the head of the column, then liabilities, and last, owners' equity. For both assets and liabilities, the most liquid items are listed first. On the asset side, we start with cash, the most liquid of all financial assets and proceed through accounts receivable (i.e., credit sales from which payments are expected within a month or two), notes receivable, interest receivable, inventories, and prepaid expenses.

After current assets are listed, following in order of liquidity we have long-term investments, fixed assets, intangibles, deferred charges, and other assets.

A Word of Caution. A word of caution is needed at this point. Accounting statements published by corporations contain an accurate summary of the *past* financial condition of the company. For purposes of investment analysis, we are more concerned with the *future* financial condition of the company. Only to the extent that judgments concerning the future can be formulated on the basis of present and historical conditions is careful examination of historical records a worthwhile endeavor.

More specifically, analysis of published historical financial statements has value in two cases: (1) to explain historical prices and (2) to determine if historical corporate behavior sheds light on future corporate behavior.

It is apparent that the mere quotation of certain quantities does not guarantee the examiner that the figures are reliable. Some companies are aware of the analyst's skepticism and will be eager to detail many of the published figures. Also, when stock is listed on a reputable exchange, very stringent requirements are applied to prevent fraudulent listing of incorrect data. As a rule, an annual report will be audited by a reputable accounting firm—an independent firm that is legitimately concerned with its standing in the financial world. The requirements of this disclosure were created for the benefit of the investor to correct abuses that were prevalent in the past. For purposes of our analysis, we can assume that published figures are accurately represented.

Here is where the problem exists. Suppose we find an entry on a balance sheet that lists land at a value of $66,000,000. We can assume that this value corresponds to the value of the land in previous years (unless some note of a change is given), and we can assume that this is the same value that the company states on its income tax returns and other governmental reports. In one sense, this is the value of the land. However, this particular company may choose to list land at original values that do not reflect current values on the open market. As a matter of fact, many companies do choose to handle land value in this way on their balance sheets. Obviously, then, a $66,000,000 land value may be hiding a much greater potential asset, if the land is in the center of a rich urban area or at the site of proposed construction. Thus, though the listed land value of $66,000,000 may be much greater, the balance sheet will not necessarily tell us this important fact. An astute analyst will always question the reported numbers and uncover all relevant information.

QUESTIONS FOR STUDY

1. Why are securities markets needed?
2. If you want to buy fifty shares of stock, how must you do it? How much will the transaction cost?
3. Why do people invest in money assets?
4. Where does "money" come from?
5. Why isn't more money available?
6. Describe how commercial banks create credit.
7. If price is set by fiat at a level of 10 percent above the equilibrium (free market price), then how much of a surplus will result?
8. If price is set by fiat at a level of 20 percent below the equilibrium (free market) prices, then how much of a shortage will result?
9. What is "liquidity preference?"
10. Prepare a statement to account for your income over the past year.
11. Prepare a balance sheet to account for the worth of the assets which you own.
12. List and describe five alternative sources where current and historical corporate income statements and balance sheets can be obtained.
13. Write a five-page paper discussing the major foundations (charitable, educational, and religious foundations) in the United States today.
14. List the top twenty banks in the United States, ranked according to the total size of their trust assets.
15. How would you go about determining
    (a) the aggregate savings of households?
    (b) total mortgage debt?
    (c) the total sources and uses of funds of the federal government of the United States for last year?
16. Explain what is meant by "equilibrium price" and "equilibrium quantity."
17. Explain how the price system can be used to create
    (a) chronic shortages
    (b) chronic surpluses
18. Obtain and compare the income statements and balance sheets of a railroad company, a public utility, and an industrial firm. Explain any differences you may find.

What is the difference between owning bonds and owning shares of common stocks? If you have $50,000 available for investment, which should you buy: bonds or common stocks?

The answers depend upon many factors: your personal financial situation and individual preference as well as economic factors in the securities markets themselves. These factors are all discussed later in Parts III and IV. At that time, the answer possibly will be "diversify— buy some of each." But before leaping ahead to the final answer, we must understand the fundamental differences between owning stocks and owning bonds. These differences form the basis for complete analysis.

We should note here that many securities and transactions in finance involve neither "pure" bonds nor "pure" stocks. There are

Bonds vs. Common Stocks: Some Characteristics and Comparisons

2

various classes of hybrid securities such as convertible debentures, preferred stocks, warrants, puts, calls, straddles, spreads, strips, and straps. However, throughout this text we shall focus attention solely on the "pure" form of the security. Our discussions and analyses will be limited to bonds and common stocks. The concept of equity ownership is discussed first, then debt, and then some comparisons of each. Finally, some alternative classifications are presented for grouping stocks and bonds.

2.1 Equity

Common stocks are negotiable securities which represent ownership equity. Corporations are empowered by law to issue shares of common stock. The shares can be held and traded privately by the owners of a firm. If a firm meets the requirements established for trading over-the-counter or for listing on one of the registered exchanges, then ownership shares can be bought and sold by the public through registered stock brokers as described in Chapter 1.[1]

Investment in common stocks puts you, the investor, in the position of being part owner of the corporation. You own a proportionate part of the physical assets of the firm and share in the right of direction of the operations of that business. Share ownership carries with it the right, power, and duty to exercise managerial prerogatives. These prerogatives extend to exercising a vote in the formulation and enforcement of policy in corporate goals and objectives. As a shareholder and part owner of the firm, you have the right to receive a proportionate part of any residual profit.

Restated, equity represents that part of the corporate financial structure which absorbs the variability in the prospective flow of earnings from business operations. Total corporate income from operations must be allocated several ways *before* being divided among shareholders. Interest must be paid to bondholders, dividends must be paid to holders of preferred shares, and income taxes must be paid to the Internal Revenue Service. After these payments are made, shareholders have the right to a proportionate part of the remainder. Your part of the remainder can come as either dividend income, or capital gains, or both.

Under highly fluctuating business conditions in the overall economy, all the fluctuations in corporate income are passed on to shareholders. Because of all the prior claims equity ownership is risky. Money may, or may *not*, remain after all the fixed charges are paid. In fact, equity is often defined by money managers as risk or venture capital. Equity finance is crucial to economic growth—without it, many new firms could never begin and many existing firms could never expand.

The concept of equity need not be limited to shares in a corporation. Equity is also important in personal finance. Examples 2.1 and 2.2 will illustrate the behavior of equity ownership in a home that is purchased and held for five years.

EXAMPLE 2.1: Equity Ownership—The Purchase of a New House. Consider the purchase of a new home for your family. Suppose the total cost of all the transactions will be $50,000. Suddenly you need $50,000 in cash. How will you raise the money? There are several possibilities. Some are

---

[1] The Listing requirements on the NYSE or the AMEX can be obtained directly from the respective exchange. Also, see S.E.C. requirements for publicly traded corporations, Securities and Exchange Commission, Washington, D.C.

1. Debt
   a. Personal loan from a friend
   b. Conventional bank loan from your friendly neighborhood banker
   c. Mortgage loan insured by the Federal Housing Authority (FHA)
2. Equity
   a. Out of pocket (e.g., write a check for the full amount)
   b. Joint ownership with other members of your family

Your first consideration might be to borrow the $50,000. So you begin to shop for a $50,000 mortgage or loan. However, it soon becomes apparent that no one will loan you $50,000. It is impossible to obtain a mortgage loan for the total price of the home.

The point here is that assets cannot be financed with 100 percent debt. One hundred percent debt financing may be legitimate in theory but in practice, considering investor attitudes and behavior, some equity must always accompany a loan. If no equity is available, the person financing the home will become the owner[2] and as owner, he can, at his discretion, permit you to rent or lease from him.

The second consideration might be to withdraw $50,000 from your checking account, assuming that you do have $50,000 in your checking account. This is a workable though possibly expensive alternative. The immediate question is why do you have an idle balance of $50,000 in the first place? If banks pay 5 percent interest on savings accounts, you are foregoing .05 × $50,000 or $2500 in interest income per year by holding $50,000 in a checking account instead of in a savings account. Under these conditions, your *liquidity preference* appears to be relatively large. But if you do not own $50,000, either as idle cash balances in the form of currency, demand deposits, or as income producing near-cash assets in the form of savings accounts, certificates of deposit, or common stock, then this second alternative is not relevant.

The third consideration is to use a combination of sources of financing. Borrow as much as possible, obtaining a first mortgage (or even a second and third mortgage on the home), and then obtain the balance from personal sources. The second and third mortgages will cost higher rates of interest than a first mortgage because these additional loans are successively more risky. To compensate lenders for bearing this additional risk, greater return must be forthcoming. Personal alternatives for obtaining the required equity might be to sell your existing home and obtain the equity invested there, or to use existing savings, or to sell some securities which you own. This way of

---

[2] If an asset is financed primarily with debt, then, for tax purposes, the creditors qualify as owners.

financing is an alternative used extensively by corporations as well as by private individuals. Governments must finance with debt. No one can own an equity share in a federal, state or local government.

The maximum amount that you will want to borrow depends upon several factors which will be based upon a (subjective) evaluation made by the prospective lender. The lender will evaluate your economic ability as well as your personal willingness to repay the loan, plus interest. Of course, you must supply information on which he will render an opinion.

Suppose that the lender decides that you are a good credit risk and he will loan you $30,000, the maximum amount he considers appropriate for this house. You supply $20,000 from personal sources. Then, as of the time of the purchase, the total value of the house may be accounted for as follows:

Mortgage (liability)	$30,000
Equity (ownership)	20,000
Value (total assets)	$50,000

A more formal statement of financial position, that is, a balance sheet for the asset, is shown on Table 2.1. As per the balance sheet statement, the value of total assets always equals the sum of debt financing plus equity financing.

$$A = L + E \qquad \qquad (2.1)$$

where

A = dollar value of total assets
L = total liabilities (short-term and long term)
E = total equity financing

Table 2.1 THE FINANCE OF A HOME

Mr. and Mrs. Durant Worthy
Balance Sheet as of July 31, 197–

ASSETS

House and furnishings	$35,000	
Land	15,000	
Total assets		$50,000

LIABILITIES AND OWNERSHIP

Mortgage loan payable	$30,000	
Total liabilities		$30,000
Ownership equity		
Retained earnings (from savings account)	$20,000	
Total ownership equity		$20,000
Total liabilities and ownership		$50,000

The finance—the capital structure mix—of the home can be described and summarized as either of several ratios. Some of the more important ratios are (1) the proportion of equity finance, (2) the proportion of debt finance, and (3) the proportion of debt, relative to equity. Using the balance sheet in Table 2.1, the summary measures can be listed as follows:

1. Your $20,000 represents 40 percent ownership in the value of the house. The proportion of total equity relative to total assets is 40 percent.

$$E/A = \$20,000/\$50,000 = 40\% \qquad (2.2)$$

2. There is a 60 percent liability against the house. The proportion of debt relative to total assets is 60 percent.

$$L/A = \$30,000/\$50,000 = 60\% \qquad (2.3)$$

3. The proportion of debt relative to equity, another measure of financial position frequently used, is 1.5. Put another way, the house is financed with one and a half times more debt than equity.

$$L/E = \$30,000/\$20,000 = 1.5 \qquad (2.4)$$

The bank which made the loan of $30,000 holds the debt security, the mortgage. You are in debt to the bank. You are obligated to repay the $30,000, plus interest, no later than some mutually agreed upon date. This debt is for an amount of money—$30,000. It is not for a share in the ownership of the house.

The schedule for the mortgage payments (assuming 6 percent interest for 30 years) is shown on Table 2.2. Each annual (or monthly) payment is divided into two parts: interest and reduction of principal. The amount applied to reduction of principal increases as the loan approaches maturity. As the loan approaches maturity, the balance outstanding decreases at a rate faster than it does during the early years of the mortgage. If the mortgage is refinanced as of the end of 8 years, the balance which requires refinancing is $26,244.20, as shown in Table 2.2.

EXAMPLE 2.2: Equity Ownership—The Homeowner, Five Years Later. One important aspect of equity ownership is that as a shareholder and part owner of the firm you have the right to receive a proportionate part of any residual profit. Sometimes the profits are large; other times the profits can become losses. The same idea applies to personal finance. We illustrate this below.

Consider the house purchased in Example 2.1. Suppose that 5 years have elapsed since the house was purchased. Suppose also that conditions are different in the overall economy. Suppose that two events have occurred during the 5-year interim: (1) interest rates have increased,

Table 2.2 TIME SERIES OF MORTGAGE PAYMENTS

Interest and Principal Remaining on a $30,000 Mortgage
(interest $= 6\%$; $n = 30$ years;
capital recovery factor $= .0726489$)*

Year	Payment (R) ($)	Interest ($)	Principal ($)	Balance remaining ($)
0				30,000.00
1	2179.47	1800.00	379.47	29,620.50
2	2179.47	1777.23	402.24	29,218.30
3	2179.47	1753.10	426.37	28,791.90
4	2179.47	1727.52	451.95	28,340.00
5	2179.47	1700.40	479.07	27,860.90
6	2179.47	1671.65	507.81	27,353.10
7	2179.47	1641.19	538.28	26,814.89
8	2179.47	1608.89	570.58	26,244.20
9	2179.47	1574.65	604.81	25,639.40
10	2179.47	1538.37	641.10	24,998.30
11	2179.47	1499.90	679.57	24,318.80
12	2179.47	1459.13	720.34	23,598.40
13	2179.47	1415.90	763.56	22,834.80
14	2179.47	1370.09	809.38	22,025.50
15	2179.47	1321.53	857.74	21,167.50
16	2179.47	1270.05	909.42	20,258.10
17	2179.47	1215.49	963.98	19,294.10
18	2179.47	1157.65	1021.82	18,272.30
19	2179.47	1096.34	1083.13	17,189.20
20	2179.47	1031.35	1148.12	16,041.10
21	2179.47	962.46	1217.00	14,824.10
22	2179.47	889.44	1290.02	13,534.00
23	2179.47	812.04	1367.42	12,166.60
24	2179.47	730.00	1449.47	10,717.10
25	2179.47	643.03	1536.44	9,180.71
26	2179.47	550.84	1628.62	7,552.08
27	2179.47	453.13	1726.34	5,825.74
28	2179.47	349.54	1829.92	3,995.82
29	2179.47	239.75	1939.72	2,056.10
30	2179.47	123.37	2056.10	−.0025

* For a definition of capital recovery factor, see Chapter 4.

and (2) the demand for houses has increased, increasing the market value of the house from the original $50,000 to $75,000.

From Table 2.2, as of the end of the fifth year, the precise balance remaining on the original $30,000 mortgage is $27,860.90, showing a reduction of mortgage principal of $2139.10 ($30,000 − $27,860.90). For purposes of illustration, however, we shall round this amount off to an even $2000 and ignore depreciation. Then the balance sheet for the property looks as shown in the top half of Table 2.3. The mortgage outstanding represents approximately 37 percent of the value of the house. The owner's equity has increased to $47,000 or almost 63 percent of the current value.

Table 2.3 THE HOMEOWNER FIVE YEARS LATER

Mr. and Mrs. Durant Worthy
Balance Sheet as of July 31, 197– + 5

Situation 1:

ASSETS

House and furnishings	$40,000	
Land	35,000	
Total assets		$75,000

LIABILITIES AND OWNERSHIP

Mortgage loan payable	$28,000	
Total liabilities		$28,000
Ownership equity	$47,000	
Total ownership equity		$47,000
Total liabilities and ownership		$75,000

Situation 2:

ASSETS

House and furnishings	$25,000	
Land	10,000	
Total assets		$35,000

LIABILITIES AND OWNERSHIP

Mortgage loan payable	$28,000	
Total liabilities		$28,000
Ownership equity	$ 7,000	
Total ownership equity		$ 7,000
Total liabilities and ownership		$35,000

The increase in interest rates in the general economy has no effect on the original mortgage rate contracted at the time of purchase 5 years ago. This original rate is a fixed obligation over the life of the indenture, not modified or changed by fluctuations in rates established at future dates. Observe that if the situation is reversed so that you are the lender instead of the borrower, you may wish to have some protection against (opportunity) loss of income through rising interest rates after you have made long-term commitment.

Equity ownership participates in any residual profits or losses; debt ownership does not. If the market demand had turned in the other direction, lowering the value of the house to $35,000, instead of raising it to $75,000, the balance sheet for the property might be as shown in the bottom half of Table 2.3. That situation is summarized as follows:

Mortgage $28,000   (same assumption of $2000
                           reduction of mortgage principal)

Equity   7,000
Value $35,000

The owner's equity is now less than his original investment and is only 20 percent of the value. The bank's mortgage, now representing 80 percent of the value of the house, remains the same and continues to command the same interest rates. Please note that in this extreme case, the bank may become uneasy about its 80 percent debt financing of the house and require the owner to invest some additional equity in order to bring the financing proportions back into line.

In this example, the bank can be compared with a bond holder and the owner of the house may be compared with a stockholder.

2.2 Debt

Debt, as opposed to equity, denotes borrowing instead of ownership. Debt securities are called bonds. Bonds are certificates of indebtedness. Investment in bonds puts you, the investor, in the position of being a creditor of the company (or government) that issued the bond. The company (or government) owes money to you. You have a contractual (legal) right to collect interest and principal according to terms stated in contract when the bonds were issued. If the company fails to pay either the interest or principal, the bonds are said to be in default and you, the creditor, have a legal right to take the case to court and force the company to pay. At worse, you may force the company into bankruptcy. In any event, if any money is available to the firm (for example, through the liquidation of assets), then creditors rank at the head of the line of all investors waiting to be paid.

In general, bonds can be either secured or unsecured. Creditors often find it advantageous to have a legally enforceable lien on the property of a debtor, so that in case of default, the creditors have their prior rights secured by that property. There are many types of bonds which are secured. *Mortgage security* bonds represent debt securities where some or all of the property owned by the debtor is offered as security for the bond in the case of default. *Collateral security* bonds represent debt securities which are secured by deposit of other bonds and stocks. *Chattel security* bonds are equipment obligations, where the money is used to finance equipment such as locomotives, railway cars, aircraft, buses, or large trucks.[3] Bonds which are not secured by any kind of lien or pledge are called *debentures*. Example 2.3 will illustrate the principles involved in the ownership of debt.

E X A M P L E 2.3: Creditorship—The Purchase of a 10-Year Corporate Bond. Suppose that a particular corporate bond is listed in today's daily issue of the *Wall Street Journal*. The vital statistics for the listed bond are

1. Par (face) value: $1000
2. Date of maturity: 10 years from today
3. Coupon rate: 5 percent
4. Current price: $800

Suppose that you have $800 (plus transactions costs) available for investment purposes and, after thoughtful consideration,[4] conclude that the company issuing the bond is credit worthy. You decide to investigate the future financial return if you do in fact purchase the bond. The analysis could proceed as follows.

First, the coupon rate of 5 percent refers to the annual interest payments based on the face value of the bond at maturity. Given that the bond will be worth $1000 upon maturity (i.e., the face value), the corporation is obliged to pay the sum of (1) $50 = (.05 × $1000) each year during the coming 10 years, plus (2) $1000 in exchange for the physical possession of the bond as of the end of the tenth year. This stream of payments represents income (and capital gain) to you as holder of the bond. For illustrative purposes, this income stream is depicted on Figure 2.1. Note that your total income from the transaction (ignoring taxes and commissions) consisted of two parts: (1) 5 percent of the face value of the bond during each year of the life of the bond and (2) a capital gain of $200 realized after a 10-year period of waiting.

Second, how profitable is the transaction? What is the total return on your $800 investment? There are several ways to calculate an answer. Many analysts think in terms of the *current yield*.

---

[3] There are many legal and institutional aspects of bonds. See (1) Frederick Amling, *Investments*, Prentice-Hall, Inc., Englewood Cliffs, N.J. 1965, Chap. 4; (2) Ralph E. Badger and Paul B. Coffman, *Investment Analysis*, McGraw-Hill, Inc., New York, 1967, Chaps. 3 and 4; (3) John C. Clendenin and George A. Christy, *Introduction to Investments*, McGraw-Hill, Inc., New York, 1969; and (4) Jerome B. Cohen and Edward D. Zinbarg, *Investment Analysis and Portfolio Management*, Richard D. Irwin, Inc., Homewood, Ill., 1967.

[4] These "thoughtful considerations" consist of a thorough analysis of economic conditions in bond markets as described in Chapter 9.

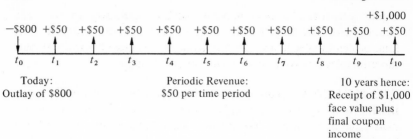

Figure 2.1.   Illustration of income flows from ownership of a bond.

Current yield equals current (annual) income ($50) divided by the dollar sum of the initial investment ($800), expressed as a percent. In this particular case the current yield equals 6.25 percent, ($50/$800) = .0625. In other words, a current yield of 6.25 percent on an $800 investment provides current (annual) income of $50, (.0625) ($800) = $50.

But current yield is only part of the total picture. Current yield ignores the $200 capital gain. For accounting purposes, the $200 could be prorated or allocated over the 10 years. Thus, we could view the appreciation of capital as $20 per year ($200/10 years). But this $20 is *not* actually received each year. The $20 comes in one lump sum at the end of 10 years. The $20 has some value, but its value is different from the $50 of current income. Groceries cannot be bought today with $20 to be received 10 years in the future. Thus the total analysis of this investment involves the notion of *time value of money*. The notion is that money to be received at some later date is less valuable than money received now. This concept is discussed and illustrated in Chapter 4.

The third financial consideration to be made before you invest your hard-earned $800 involves risk. Risk as used in this context involves liquidity.[5] Are you financially able to hold the bond until the maturity date 10 years hence? Or is it likely that you may have to raise cash, due to unforeseen circumstances and may have to sell the bond before its date of maturity? If the latter is likely, then you must investigate (i.e., analyze) the prospects for selling the bond at some future date. If you sell, someone must be there to buy. For every seller, there must be a buyer, and vice versa. Also, what will the selling price be? Why are you able to buy a $1000 bond today for only $800? Perhaps next year this same bond might have a market value of only $700, assuming that the bond will be marketable at all. But the market value of the bond could rise to $1200 by next year, in which case a nice

---

[5] Risk involves many dimensions. These are discussed in Chapter 6.

capital gain would be made. How can you know the answers? What are the prospects? What is the outlook? Some of the answers depend upon your own skills in financial analysis and on your personal financial situation. Other answers depend upon the firm which issued the bond under consideration, other companies that have bonds outstanding, and the overall economy. These relevant corporate and aggregate economic factors are discussed in Chapters 7, 8, and 9.

To summarize, the purchase of a bond entitles the owner to a specified stream of income during the life of the bond, plus a lump sum payment at the date of maturity. Assuming no default, the bond can be redeemed at face value upon maturity. If sold before maturity, capital gains or capital losses can be incurred, depending on the state of the markets.

2.3 Debt vs. Equity

The fundamental differences between equity ownership and creditorship are the basis of intricate studies. The most sophisticated techniques of security analysis (methods of asset valuation) rest on these fundamental differences.

In one sense, debt is secured capital. Interest charges paid by the firm to service the debt can be identified as that portion of investment income expected to be reasonably constant. For a constant level of corporate debt, interest charges will remain constant so that bondholders can anticipate steady income in future years. Barring default of interest or principal, there is little need for bondholders to be greatly concerned with fluctuations in the overall economy, if the bonds are held to maturity. As long as companies are able to pay the fixed interest expenses, bondholders enjoy guaranteed incomes.

Share ownership is more involved than ownership of bonds. The presence of creditors can impair the rights of ownership. Creditors have first rights to any assets and, under certain circumstances, can interfere with the direction and prerogatives of management: the larger the proportion of debt, the greater the impairment of ownership. If the proportion of debt is exceptionally large (e.g., 90 percent of total financing), debt holders can even participate in policy making along with management (see footnote 2). Complications can arise under a variety of circumstances. For example, one stockholder might hold a dominant portion or outright majority of stock and use this happy position to his own financial advantage. Another possibility occurs when an outside interest is trying to influence management policies by a takeover or a significant purchase of stock. These are special situations which investors must be constantly aware of if they are to avoid un-happy experiences in the securities markets.[6]

EXAMPLE 2.4: Owning Bonds vs. Owning Stocks—A Comparison.

To illustrate some operational differences between the investment characteristics of bonds and stocks, consider the following:

1. Mr. Alexander Scott bought a 5 percent bond issued by Universal International Corporation. Mr. Scott paid $1000 for the bond on its date of issue. The terms of purchase were (simplified for our purposes)

   a. Each year, the corporation will pay interest in the amount of $50

   b. 20 years from the date of issue, the corporation will return the original $1000.

   Upon redemption, the $50 annual interest payments will cease. The interest payments made to Mr. Scott every year are a part of the operating expenses of the corporation. These interest payments are tax-deductible legal obligations of the firm and *must* be made before any dividends are paid to shareholders.

2. At the same time that Mr. Scott bought his bond, Mrs. Ann Rice purchased 100 shares of common stock issued by Universal International. The purchase price of each share was $10. Her total purchase amounted to $1000, the same amount as the purchase made by Mr. Scott (ignoring transactions costs). Suppose that at the time of the purchase, Universal International was paying an annual dividend on its stock of 50 cents per share.

3. If the market price of the stock remains constant for 20 years, and if the dividend payments remain the same, the investment made by Mrs. Rice is equally profitable as the investment made by Mr. Scott. For each year of the 20 years, Mrs. Rice receives $50 in dividends and, at the end of the 20 years, the market value of her stock is $1000. During those 20 years, Mrs. Rice owns an equity in the corporation, while Mr. Scott is one of their creditors.

3. However, a situation of constant price and dividends for equity shares over a time span of 20 years is unusual. Ever since brokers gathered under the buttonwood tree and started a sidewalk market in securities, prices of stocks have fluctuated. Sometimes prices go up and sometimes prices go down, but prices rarely remain constant (especially for 20 years). It is quite plausible for the market price of a stock that was $10 a share to rise to $50 or

---

[6] In some cases, exercise of ownership over a corporation has been completely divorced from the ownership of a stock in that corporation. What ownership rights, for example, can be exercised by the individual stock-holders of the General Motors Corporation? The dubious significance of ownership rights has raised questions about the purely financial aspects of equity ownership and the relationship of equity to debt.

$60 per share, or even to $500 or $600 per share, considering split-ups, over a time period of 20 years—or to fall to $2.50 or $3.00 a share, or even become worthless, according to the fortunes of the company. Also, the dividend rate can vary over a period of time. In continuing prosperity, the company may choose to increase its dividend payments. The 50 cents per share in effect when Mrs. Rice originally purchased her stock could become 75 cents or $1.00 or even more per share. On the other hand, a series of less profitable years could cause the corporation to lower its dividend rate, and Mrs. Rice might receive 10 cents per year on each share of her stock or, under especially difficult circumstances, no dividend at all. There are never any guarantees that dividends will be paid.

The shareholder owns a part of the company and a part of the company's profits or losses. Shareholders have an equity in the company. Aside from the dollar returns over time, the owner of a share of stock may reap several personal benefits from his investment. For example, the stockholder has the right to exercise the power of control.

The bondholder has other advantages: (1) his investment entitles him to specific amounts of interest and the return of his investment principal and (2) interest income is paid to the bondholder even during times when the company is not profitable. On the negative side, the bondholder's return is not increased during the more profitable years of the company. The rates remain the same. And, if interest rates rise in the general economy, then bond prices will fall, and the bondholder may have cause to be disappointed in his choice of a security. The bondholder may be locked in. If he continues to hold the bond, and interest rates continue to go higher, the bondholder is forced to forego the higher rates of interest obtainable elsewhere. If he sells the bond to obtain cash to reinvest at higher interest rates, the bondholder can suffer capital losses due to the decline in bond prices. Thus, one can conclude that proper anticipation of the future course of interest rates is one of many crucial aspects relevant to the investment decision.

To summarize, debt and equity are the two basic ways of financing assets. Debt implies creditorship (or borrowing) whereas equity implies ownership. The securities issued to represent these two methods of financing are bonds for debt and common stock for equity. We turn next to a more detailed study of some alternative ways to classify bonds and stocks.

2.4 Classification of Securities

Securities, like many animals, vegetables, and minerals, can be listed in groups and subsets which have relatively homogeneous characteristics. The purpose of classifying securities is to assign an individual security to a population which has already been specified. Parameters of populations can be studied, established, and verified, and inferences can be drawn from samples in the universe (assuming universe parameters are finite). Understanding of the behavior of any particular security, then, can be enhanced if that security is assigned to a known population. For example, one can say that "all stocks tend to behave in the same way and all bonds tend to behave in the same way; but stocks tend to behave differently from bonds." Then, to classify a given (new) security in a category labeled either "bond" or "stock," one has immediate insight into the *probable* behavior of that new security.

There is no one classification of securities. The practice is generally to follow the definitions and groupings made by recognized, professional advisory services. Among the oldest professional advisory services are

1. Dow-Jones and Company, 30 Broad Street, New York, New York, 10004
2. Standard and Poor's Corporation, 345 Hudson Street, New York, New York, 10014
3. Moody's Investors Services, Inc., 99 Church Street, New York, New York, 10007
4. Value Line (Arnold Bernhard and Company, Inc.), 5 East 44th Street, New York, New York, 10017

Also, many brokers, institutional investors, and financial magazines devise their own definitions and groupings.[7] In any case, the rationale for any particular classification of securities rests on the relative homogeneity of characteristics (economic, financial, and legal) of the particular securities involved. Some widely used groupings are (1) type of security, (2) industry group, and (3) quality rating.

TYPE OF SECURITY. At the beginning we get the broadest grouping possible

1. Equity (common stocks)
2. Debt (bonds and some classes of preferred stocks)
3. Other (convertible securities and various options)

Looking within each group, the broad class of issuer can be identified as either

---

[7] See (1) *Fortune* and *Fortune*'s list of the 500 largest companies (classified on the basis of size) in the United States; (2) *Forbes* and *Forbes*' listing of some 23 broad groups of companies; *Forbes* is published twice monthly by Forbes Inc., 60 Fifth Avenue, New York, New York, 10011; and (3) *Wall Street Reports*, published monthly by Wall Street Reports and Intelligence Bulletin, Inc., 54 Wall Street, New York, New York, 10005.

1. Corporate (debt or equity)
2. Civil (federal, state, or municipal government securities)

If considering bonds, the *length of time to maturity* may be an important characteristic. Common stocks never mature. Ownership equity exists for the life of the firm, which is indefinite. Thus, for bonds, we can list

1. Short-term
2. Intermediate-term
3. Long-term
4. Perpetual (infinite or no maturity date)

INDUSTRY GROUP. If considering the types of economic markets which corporations service, *industry groups* can be the relevant factor. Within a category of industry groups we can list

1. Industrials
2. Utilities
3. Railroads
4. Air carriers
5. Insurance companies
6. Banks

Industrials can be subdivided further according to the degree of competition. There may be a large number of sellers of similar products, with each seller acting independently of all the others. In pure competition, individual firms are powerless to exert control over product price, because each firm produces such a small fraction of the total output of the industry. Increase or decrease in production by an individual firm can have little influence on the total supply of these particular goods and services. But some industrial firms operate under oligopoly or monopoly. Oligopoly is a market structure in which a few firms dominate the industry (e.g., three or four firms may control 70 or 80 percent of a market) with a group of smaller firms sharing the remaining market. For example, metal producers, automobile manufacturers, petroleum producers, and electronic computer manufacturers tend to have more control over prices of their products than do firms in purely competitive market structures. The result is that even within a homogeneous group such as "all industrial firms," there still is great heterogeneity.

Public utilities, railroads, and banks, by way of comparison, are regulated to some extent by an agency of the federal government. Each one tends to be monopolistic—the firm and the industry are virtually synonymous. The firm is the only producer of its particular product and the product is unique in that there are no good (or close) substitutes available. Consumers must buy the product from the monopolist or do without.

There are many other groupings in widespread use. The New York Stock Exchange lists 90 separate categories of major industrial activity.

These categories are shown in Table 2.4. *Fortune* lists 500 of the largest companies in the United States. The *Fortune* breakdown is based on the size of firm. *Forbes* lists 23 broad groups of companies.[8] *Forbes* uses the terms "agglomerates," "conglomerates," and "multi-industry." This emphasizes the fact that many businesses sprawl over many industrial categories. The *Forbes* listing is based on the extent of *diversification*, starting with nondiversified single-product companies

Table 2.4   MAJOR INDUSTRIAL ACTIVITY OF NEW YORK STOCK EXCHANGE FIRMS*

Aerospace
Air transport
Amusements
  Motion pictures
  Radio and TV Broadcasters
  Other
Auto parts
Automobiles
Baking and Milling
  Bread and cake
  Biscuit bakers
  Other
Banking, savings and loan
  Banking
  Savings and loan
Building
  Cement
  Heating and air conditioning
  Roofing and wallboard
  Other
Chemicals
Coal
Containers
  Metal and glass
  Paper
Drugs and cosmetics
  Cosmetics
  Drugs
  Other
Electronics and electrical
  Major diversified
  Electrical equipment
  Electronic products

Household appliances
Radio and TV equipment
Finance and small loan
  Finance
  Small loan
  Factoring
Food products
  Canned foods
  Packaged foods
  Corn refiners
  Other
Home furnishings
Investment companies
Leather and shoes
Liquor
  Brewers
  Distillers
Machinery, agricultural
Machinery, industrial
  Construction and materials
    handling
  Industrial machinery
  Machine tools
  Special machinery
  Steam generating
  Other
Meats and dairy products
  Meat packers
  Dairy products
Metal
  Aluminum
  Copper
  Fabricating

[8] See *Forbes*, vol. 103, no. 1, January 1, 1969, pp. 77–218. *Forbes* publishes the list periodically.

Table 2.4 (Continued)

Gold and silver	Variety chains
Lead and zinc	Other chains
Other	Retail trade, department stores
Miscellaneous (diversified)	Rubber fabricating
Miscellaneous (most titles indi-	Shipbuilding
cate major activity)	Shipping
Office equipment	Soaps and vegetable oils
Oil	Soft Drinks and candy
Crude producers	Candy and gum
Integrated domestic	Soft drinks
International	Steel
Oil well supplies	Sugar
Other	Telephone
Paper	Textiles and apparel
Printing and equipment	Apparel
Publishing	Synthetic fibers
Books	Textile products
Periodicals	Tobacco
Other	Cigarettes
Rail equipment	Cigars
Railroad and trucking	Other
Railroads	Utilities, electric
Trucking	Utilities, gas
Real Estate and hotels	Distributors
Retail Trade, chains	Pipeline companies
Food chains	Utilities, other

* Source: "Stocks on the Big Board," published by The New York Stock Exchange, February 1969.

and proceeding in complexity to multiproduct diversified conglomerates. The Dow-Jones 30 Industrials or Standard and Poor's 500 Stock Composite (both of which are discussed in Chapter 3) are selected and listed on the basis of *representativeness of the market*. These, then, are representative ways by which professional analysts classify securities within the category called "industry groups."

QUALITY RATINGS.   Securities are also classified according to their type and extent of risk exposure. For example, the phrase "blue chip" is used frequently to denote a *risk class*. Blue chip refers to the most stable corporations.

In considering the extent of risk and the quality rating, several alternative listings can be employed:

1. Quality ratings by, for instance, Moody's or Standard and Poor's
2. Length of time since a default
3. Length of time of dividend payments

4. Volatility of market price
5. Market where traded

Several professional investment services classify bonds and stock in a number of grades according to the "quality" or "investment risk" associated with the security. This system of grading uses the letters A, B, C, and D.

For bonds, the scheme of grading is described as follows. The highest-grade bonds (those with the least risk to the investor) are judged to be the best quality. They carry the smallest degree of investment risk and are generally referred to as "gilt edged." Interest payments are protected by a large (or exceptionally stable) margin and the principal is secure. The three highest grades of bonds (bonds with the smallest financial risk) are indicated by an A, followed by lowercase letters to distinguish between the three grades. In Moody's system, top-grade bonds have ratings of Aaa, Aa, and A, respectively. As the financial risk or likelihood of default of the bonds increases, the quality deteriorates, and the ratings may be indicated by the symbols B, C, or D. The D rating of Standard and Poor's refers to bonds already in default. In Moody's rating system, the Ba group is defined as "bonds which are rated Ba are judged to have speculative elements; their future cannot be considered as well assured. Often the protection of interest and principal payments may be very moderate and thereby not well safeguarded during both good and bad times over the future. Uncertainty of position characterizes bonds in this class."[9]

The common stock quality rating is described as follows. The different categories of stocks are indicated by letters followed by a plus or minus sign. Thus, we may have A+, A, A−, B+, B, B−, or C to indicate the quality of a given stock. The quality of a stock is interpreted by Standard and Poor's to mean the relative stability and growth of per share earnings and dividends. The Value Line Investment Survey takes the quality of a stock to mean the relative stability of its price over the past 10 years and the growth rate of the cash earnings of the company. Once again, there is no one established classification accepted by everyone.

QUESTIONS FOR STUDY

1. Suppose you have $25,000 available for investment. Outline and discuss at least five reasons why you would choose to invest the $25,000 in
   (a) shares of common stock
   (b) bonds

---

[9] Source: Moody's *Bond Record*. Also, see Standard and Poor's *Bond Guide* and Standard and Poor's *Stock Guide*.

2. Suppose you need $25,000 to finance a project. Outline and discuss at least five reasons why you would seek $25,000 in
    (a) debt financing
    (b) equity financing
3. Change the amount from $25,000 to $25 million; repeat questions 1 and 2 above.
4. Explain the difference between a bond and a share of stock.
5. Industrial corporations can be subdivided into several smaller categories. Explain several instances where these separations can occur.
6. Obtain an income statement and balance sheet from each of the following types of companies:
    (a) commercial business
    (b) air carrier
    (c) railroad
    (d) public utility
    (e) commercial bank
   Compare the form and content of these financial statements. What insights can you gain from this comparative analysis to aid in your job as a money manager? Write a short critique of your findings.
7. Using the financial statements obtained to answer question 6, calculate some measures of profitability, growth, and capital structure of the various groups of companies.
8. On the basis of your answer to question 6, explain how you might design an experiment to calculate measures of important financial variables for groups of companies. Is it possible to identify industries on the basis of their financial characteristics?
9. Obtain a copy of the industry listings of companies on a current version of Standard and Poor's Compustat® Tape. Compare this list with the listing made by the New York Stock Exchange as shown in Table 2.4. Explain the differences you find between the two listings.
10. Instead of trading in common stocks directly, what advantages (and risks) might there be in trading *options* (i.e., puts, calls, straddles)?

Stock market prices make news every trading day. The news announcer might report "Dow-Jones Industrials *UP* 1.65, 20 rails *UP* 1.16, utilities *UP* .19, 65 stock composite *UP* .88; average price on the Big Board up 14 cents; on the Amex up 6 cents." What does this mean? Almost everyone knows that prices in the securities markets fluctuate up and down like a yo-yo. But *not* almost everyone knows how these fluctuations are measured or how to profit from the measurements.

Our purpose in this chapter is to study some ways of measuring and expressing "What happened on Wall Street today?" Later these measurements will be used as a guide to formulate policy for investment and to calculate efficient portfolios. For now, we shall focus attention on some of the most popular answers to: "What's happening in the market today?" These answers consist of index numbers constructed,

Measuring the Market
Price Behavior of
Bonds and Common Stocks

3

maintained, and published periodically by investment counseling firms, financial news services, and the stock exchanges. Discussed below are indexes of the markets as maintained and published by Dow-Jones and Company, Standard & Poor's Corporation, Moody's Investors Service, Inc., The New York Stock Exchange, The American Stock Exchange, and The National Quotation Bureau, Inc.

3.1 The Dow-Jones Averages

The oldest and probably best-known answers to "How's the market?" involve the Dow-Jones Averages. The Dow-Jones Averages date back to October 7, 1896, when Dow-Jones and Company began the daily publication of average closing prices of active industrial stocks. The original list included only 12 stocks. The list was expanded in 1916 to include 20 stocks. As of 1969 the Dow-Jones Industrials have a total of 30 stocks, all blue chip companies trading on the New York Stock Exchange.

The list of names in the Dow-Jones Industrials has been stable at 30 since October 1, 1928. However, substitutions have been made within that list. New names are substituted for existing ones for several reasons. A company is replaced on the list if the trading in that stock becomes relatively inactive. If the price of a share falls to extremely low (or rises to extremely high) levels so that changes in price become so small (or large) as to have little (or great) effect on the average, then that particular stock is replaced. An extremely small or extremely large price per share can cease to be representative of the market average. Also, a stock may be replaced if the company ceases to represent a substantial sector of American industry.

THE SIXTY-FIVE STOCK COMPOSITE GROUP.   In addition to the 30 industrial common stocks, Dow-Jones and Company maintains and publishes daily indexes which are calculated from (1) 20 transport common stocks, (2) 15 utility stocks, and (3) a "composite" 65 stock group which consists of the total of the 30 industrials, 20 rails, and 15 utilities.

> 30 Industrials
> 20 Transportation companies
> 15 Public utilities
> --
> 65 Stock composite

The names of the 65 companies included in the four different indexes are published every Monday in *The Wall Street Journal*. The names of the companies currently included in these averages are shown in Table 3.1. Comparison of the listing in Table 3.1 with a current listing can show either the (1) name change of existing companies, or (2) substitution of different names for existing names. The business activities of the 30 companies in "The Dow" are shown in Table 3.2.

For the bond market, there are Dow-Jones averages of (1) 40 bonds, (2) 10 income railroad bonds, and (3) 20 U.S. cities bonds (Municipal Bond Yield Average). The 40-bond group is composed of 10 higher-grade railroads, 10 second-grade railroads, 10 public utilities, and 10 industrials.

The Dow-Jones securities averages, therefore, include four stock averages, six bond averages, and one average of yields on a group of bonds.

Calculation of the Dow-Jones Averages.   The original reason for a limited number of securities was speed and simplicity in computations. With the advent of high-speed computers this logic became outdated. However, since the Dow-Jones averages were (and still are) in such widespread use, their existence will probably continue for years to come.

Table 3.1 LIST OF COMPANIES USED IN COMPUTING THE
VARIOUS DOW-JONES STOCK MARKET
AVERAGES*

30 Industrial Stocks

Allied Chemical	General Electric	Standard Oil of
Aluminum Company	General Foods	California
of America	General Motors	Standard Oil of
American Brands	Goodyear	New Jersey
American Can	International	Swift and Company
American Telephone	Harvester	Texaco
and Telegraph	International Nickel	Union Carbide
Anaconda	International Paper	United Aircraft
Bethlehem Steel	Johns Manville	U.S. Steel
Chrysler	Owens Illinois	Westinghouse
Du Pont	Procter and Gamble	Electric
Eastman Kodak	Sears Roebuck	Woolworth

20 Transportation Stocks

American Airlines Inc.	Northwest Airlines	Seaboard Coast
Canadian Pacific	Pacific Intermoun-	Southern Pacific
Consolidated Freight	tain Express	Southern Railway
Eastern Airlines	Pan American World	Trans World Airlines
Great Northern Railway	Airlines	UAL Incorporated
Louisville and Nashville	Penn Central	Union Pacific Corp.
Norfolk and Western	Company	U.S. Freight
	St. Louis–San	Company
	Francisco	
	Santa Fe Industries	

15 Utility Stocks

American Electric	Consolidated	Pacific Gas and
Power	Natural Gas	Electric
Cleveland Electric	Detroit Edison	Panhandle Eastern
Illuminating	Houston Lighting	Pipe Line
Columbia Gas System	and Power	Peoples Gas
Commonwealth Edison	Niagara Mohawk	Philadelphia Electric
Consolidated Edison	Power	Public Service
		Electric and Gas
		Southern California
		Edison

* Source: *The Wall Street Journal*, Monday, February 2, 1970.

Table 3.2   BUSINESS ACTIVITIES OF THE THIRTY
DOW-JONES INDUSTRIAL COMPANIES

Name	Business*
1. Allied Chemical	Basic chemicals: plastics, fibers
2. Aluminum Company of America	Leading factor in U.S. industry: wholly integrated producer
3. American Can	Largest manufacturer metal containers
4. American Telephone and Telegraph	"Bell" system, electronics
5. American Brands	Cigarettes, cigars, biscuits
6. Anaconda	Copper producer, fabricator
7. Bethlehem Steel	Second largest steel company
8. Chrysler	Third largest auto maker
9. Du Pont	Largest chemical company: dominant position in synthetic fibers
10. Eastman Kodak	Photograph apparatus, chemicals
11. General Electric	Largest manufacturer of electrical equipment
12. General Foods	Food and grocery products
13. General Motors	Largest manufacturer automotive products: cars, trucks, buses; diesels; air engines; appliances
14. Goodyear	Largest rubber fabricator, tires
15. International Harvester	Truck manufacturer, farm machinery, construction
16. International Nickel	Nickel, platinum, copper
17. International Paper	World's largest paper maker, lumber, building material
18. Johns-Manville	Leader in asbestos products
19. Owens-Illinois	Glass containers, forest products, specialty glass, disposable paper products, plastic items
20. Procter and Gamble	Leading soap maker, foodstuffs from vegetable oils
21. Sears Roebuck	Largest retailer general merchandise
22. Standard Oil (California)	Integrated international oil
23. Standard Oil (New Jersey)	World's leading oil company
24. Swift and Company	World's largest meat packer
25. Texaco	Important factor world oil
26. Union Carbide	Ranks second in chemical industry
27. United Aircraft	Major manufacturer aircraft engines
28. U.S. Steel	Steel and cement, shipping
29. Westinghouse Electric	Oldest and second largest manufacturer electrical equipment and appliances
30. Woolworth	Largest variety chain, shoe stores

* Source: *Security Owner's Stock Guide*, published monthly by Standard and Poor's Corporation, 345 Hudson St., New York, New York 10014.

THE ORIGINAL METHODS.   The method of calculating Dow-Jones industrial averages has been altered several times over the years. When the service began in 1896, the price index was precisely what the name stated—the average daily closing prices of 12 active industrial stocks. To calculate the average of the 12 closing prices, one added all 12 prices and divided by 12.

$$P_{av} = \left(\sum_{i=1}^{12} p_i\right)\!\Big/12 \qquad\qquad (3.1)$$

where

P_{av} = average closing price for 12 stocks as of time t
p_i = closing price for stock i, $i = 1, 12$
$\sum_{i=1}^{12}$ = addition of all 12 closing prices

To know whether current (average) prices are high or low relative to some past (base) time, this current average was divided by the base period average. In this way a measure of the level of the market relative to a standard base period of time was obtained.

$$I = (P_{av})_{t=n}/(P_{av})_{t=0} \tag{3.2}$$

where

I = current value of price level index
$(P_{av})_{t=n}$ = average closing prices as of time $t = n$
$(P_{av})_{t=0}$ = average closing prices as of time $t = $ zero

But such a simple average was not good enough. The first adjustment was to account for stock splits. This was accomplished originally in a straightforward manner. When a stock was split, a multiplier was applied to the subsequent price, and this multiplier was thereafter an integral part of the index average calculation. To illustrate the original method of adjusting the price level index for split-ups, suppose there are 3 companies in the index (instead of 12) with closing prices of $P_1 = \$50$, $P_2 = \$70$, and $P_3 = \$60$. Then

$$P_{av} = (\$50 + \$70 + \$60)/3 = \$60 \text{ per share} \tag{3.3}$$

The average closing price before the split is $60. In this simplified illustration the divisor equals 3.

Suppose the $60 stock splits up, 3 shares for 1, so that the price per share becomes $20 instead of $60. Suppose also that the market rises so that the closing prices of the three stocks are $P_1 = \$53$, $P_2 = \$75$, and $P_3 = \$22$. Then without recognizing and adjusting for the 3-for-1 split-up, the average would be calculated (incorrectly) as follows:

$$P_{av} = (\$53 + \$75 + \$22)/3 = \$50 \text{ per share} \tag{3.4}$$

The average price is $50 per share despite the fact that the market rose! To correct this deficiency, the method first used was to multiply the price of each split share by the amount of the split. Thus

$$P_{av} = [\$53 + \$75 + 3(\$22)]/3$$
$$= (\$194)/3 = \$64.66 \text{ per share} \tag{3.5}$$

The market rise is now reflected. This method was used for computing Dow-Jones Averages until 1928.

64 Background

REFINEMENTS OF THE ORIGINAL METHOD. In 1928, a new method of adjusting for stock splits was introduced. It can be described in the following three-step sequence. On the night before the split, the following calculations are made:

1. The average for the three stocks is calculated before the split in the standard way:

$$(\$50 + \$70 + \$60)/3 = \$60 \text{ per share} \tag{3.6}$$

2. The total (aggregate) price of the three stocks is calculated *as if split has already taken place*:

$$\$50 + \$70 + \$20 = \$140 \tag{3.7}$$

3. A divisor is calculated so that the "after-split" level is forced to equal the level before split. That is, divide the after-split total by the true (calculated) average:

$$\$140/\$60 = 2\tfrac{1}{3} = 7/3 \tag{3.8}$$

The new divisor is $2\tfrac{1}{3}$. This new divisor is used to calculate the average price beginning the next day and thereafter until another split occurs.

Using the same example as before, the values on the day after the split are

$$\$53 + \$75 + \$22 = \$150 \tag{3.9}$$

This total of $150 is divided by the calculated divisor, $2\tfrac{1}{3}$, instead of the usual 3. The new stock price average, then, is $64.29.

$$\$150/2\tfrac{1}{3} = \$150/(\tfrac{7}{3}) = \$64.29 \tag{3.10}$$

Note that the $64.29 result is slightly different from the $64.66 obtained previously. Why?

The new divisor, calculated as described above, is used daily until another split occurs, an issue of rights takes place, other distribution takes place, or new stocks are substituted for existing names. The current divisor is published every day in the *Wall Street Journal*, under the tables on the next to last page where the statistics of the averages are listed.

The divisor remains unchanged if the stock split, distribution, issue of rights, or substitution causes a distortion of less than 5 points in the industrial average.

The simplicity of the method used by Dow-Jones and the small number of stocks used in the calculation makes it an extremely accessible index. The stocks included in the average are a matter of record, so it is possible for anyone to calculate the average. The 20-stock railroad average, the 15-stock utility average, the 65-stock composite, and the various bond averages are compiled in the same manner.

3.2 Standard and Poor's Indexes of the Markets

In 1923, Standard & Poor's Corporation (S & P) devised and began to publish a price level index of shares issued by leading industrial groups. At that time, 233 stock issues, representing 26 corporate subgroups were included in the index. As of April 28, 1969, the coverage is 500 stocks, representing 93 different groups.[1]

The major corporate categories contained in S & P's 500 stock composite are

> 425 Industrials
> 20 Railroads
> <u>55</u> Utilities
> 500 Stock composite

Within each of the three categories, there are subcategories. For example, each of the 425 industrial companies is assigned to one of many subgroups ranging from aerospace, air transport, and aluminum to tire and rubber goods, tobacco, and vegetable oil. The 55 public utilities are subdivided into four categories

> 35 Electric companies
> 11 Natural gas company distributors
> 7 Pipe line companies
> <u>2</u> Telephone companies
> 55 Utilities

In addition to the 500 stock composite, Standard & Poor's Corporation maintains price indexes of shares of banks, insurance companies, and investment companies,[2] and supplementary groups of companies.[3]

In the bond markets, S & P publishes records of weekly bond yields (in percent) for industrials—AAA, AA, A, BBB; railroads—AAA, AA, A, BBBB; utilities; governments—long-term, intermediate-term, short-term; and municipals.

---

[1] For a current listing of the stocks in the 500 composite group and for a summary of all the S & P indexes of the security markets, see any recent issue of *The Outlook*, published weekly by Standard & Poor's Corporation, 345 Hudson Street, New York, New York, 10014.

[2] The bank, insurance, and investment company group includes 9 New York City banks, 16 banks outside New York City, 16 fire and casualty insurance companies, 10 life insurance companies, and 9 investment companies (closed-end).

[3] There are four supplementary groups: 130 capital goods companies, 181 consumer goods companies, 25 high-grade common stocks, and 20 low-priced common stocks.

In addition to major groups of companies, Standard & Poor's maintains data files on individual companies. The data include pertinent items from the income statements and balance sheets as filed by the respective company. Income statistics include net sales, operating income as a percent of sales, operating income, depreciation and amortization, net income before taxes, net income, earnings per share, dividends, and share price data. Balance sheet statistics include total assets, gross property, cash items, inventories, receivables, current liabilities, net working capital, long-term debt, and book value per common share. Income statement and balance sheet data records are available in computer-readable form for the past 20 years on S & P's Compustat magnetic tape.

Calculation of the S and P Stock Market Averages. Standard & Poor's indexes of the security markets are calculated in the following way. First, the total current market value is calculated for all shares outstanding for the companies included in the index. Second, this total current value is divided by the aggregate average value of those shares during the base period (1941–1943). To adjust the scale, the quotient is multiplied by the arbitrary constant 10. Thus, the precise formula used to calculate S & P indexes is

$$\text{Index} = \left[\left(\sum_{i=1}^{N} p_1 q_1 \right) \Big/ \left(\sum_{i=1}^{N} p_0 q_0 \right) \right] 10 \tag{3.11}$$

where

p_1 = current market price of each stock in the index

q_1 = number of shares of each stock currently outstanding

p_0 = average price during the base period (1941–1943)

q_0 = number of shares outstanding during the base period (subject to adjustment of changes in capitalization)

$\sum_{i=1}^{N}$ = addition of all market values of the individual companies in the group

N = total number of stocks in the index

Equation (3.11) is a modification of the Paasche formula and is generally defined as a "base-weighted aggregative," expressed in relatives with the average value for the base period equal to 10. The price of each stock is weighted by the number of shares outstanding. This weighting scheme causes each stock to influence the index in proportion to its respective market importance. In other words, more valuable stocks cause greater changes in the S & P Indexes than do less valuable stocks. "Value" is used here as total market value of all stock outstanding (unit price times quantity). Since the base period market value is relatively constant, the S & P index number reflects only fluctuations in current market values.

Note that the S & P method of calculation implicitly adjusts for price changes due to issuance of rights, stock dividends, split-ups, and similar refinements. The method gives index numbers which have a relatively high degree of continuity. Continuity is especially important when comparisons are to be made over long spans of time.

CHANGES IN THE BASE VALUE. Whenever certain corporate actions are taken which cause arbitrary changes in the market price of the stock in the index, a compensating change is made in the base value of the index. For example, stock dividends and stock split-ups produce changes in stock prices, all of which are not true market fluctuations. Base changes are, then, proportional adjustments in value to offset arbitrary changes in the market value upon which the index is based. The procedure is as follows.

Suppose there is a change (e.g., the addition or deletion of a stock, a consolidation or acquisition, an issuance of stock rights) which causes the market value of the stock outstanding to increase by \$12 million. Also, assume that the aggregate market value of all stock after this increase is \$1590 million and that the base period value is 302.9. Then Standard & Poor's Corporation uses equation (3.12) to calculate a new base period value of 305.2.

$$\text{Old base value} \left(\frac{\text{New market value (new basis)}}{\text{Old market value (old basis)}} \right) = \text{New base value} \tag{3.12}$$

$$302.9 \left(\frac{1590}{1578} \right) = 305.2 \tag{3.13}$$

Note that the difference between the numerator and denominator in equation (3.13) is 12, the amount for which the adjustment is being made. Adjustments are always made in this manner. Reductions in base period values can occur if a stock is withdrawn or the substitution of a smaller company is made. In such case the numerator is, of course, smaller than the denominator.

On March 1, 1957, the current base (1941–1943 equal to 10) was adopted arbitrarily. Also in 1957, due to the availability of electronic computers, the four main group indexes could be computed at 5-minute intervals. The firm does not publish these frequent readings but does maintain a record of them. Indexes as of each hour are published in the Daily News Section of S & P's *Corporation Records*. Daily high, low, and closing indexes are published in their weekly *Outlook* and their monthly *Current Statistics*.

3.3 Moody's Averages

Moody's Investors Service, Inc. maintains and publishes several indexes of the securities markets. Moody's 200 common stock composite group consists of

125 Industrials
25 Railroads
24 Electric utilities
15 Bonds
<u>10</u> Insurance companies
<u>200</u> Common stock composite

The 125 industrial firms are selected subjectively to meet the following criteria:

1. The firm must represent a broad industrial sector of the economy. All major industries (as defined by the Federal Reserve Board's Index of Industrial Production) are represented in the group.
2. The firm must be typical of the various industry groups as listed on the New York Stock Exchange.
3. Within industries, the firm must be typical of companies with wide investment interest. Most of these firms are listed on the New York Stock Exchange.
4. Medium-sized as well as large companies are represented.

One particular firm is worthy of note—American Telephone and Telegraph. Because of its size, "Telephone" is excluded from the utilities group, but is included in the 200 common stock composite.[4]

In addition to index values for the major groups outlined above, Moody's maintains and publishes price averages for natural gas stocks, several financial sub-groupings (among them finance companies, life insurance companies, mutual fund management companies, savings and loan companies), and 55 industry subgroupings (steels, drugs, chemicals). Also, yields on preferred stock and bond averages are published.

Aside from major groups, Moody's maintains and publishes annual per share statistics on individual companies.[5]

---

[4] "Telephone" would dominate the group because with approximately 550 million shares outstanding at a market price of $50 per share, the aggregate value of Telephone shares is $27.5 billion. Telephone also has valuable debt outstanding.

[5] For each company included in Moody's *Industrial Stock Average*, the following data are available.
1. Sales ($)
2. Pretax profit ($)
3. Pretax margin (percent of sales) ($)
4. Net on common ($)

Historical monthly and annual data are published in the respective Moody's manuals. Current data are published in Moody's *Stock Survey*. Moody's averages appear regularly in the *Survey of Current Business*, a monthly publication of the U.S. Department of Commerce.

Calculation of Moody's Averages.   Moody's index of the market is a price average: the index is the price per share of the average. However, in calculating the index, the price per share of each company is weighted by the number of shares outstanding. An aggregate value for all stocks is calculated in this way and the results are divided by the adjusted number of shares outstanding. The precise formula for calculating Moody's Industrial average is

$$P_{av} = \left[\sum_{i=1}^{M} (P_i N_{\text{actual}}) \Big/ \sum_{i=1}^{M} (N_{\text{adj}}) \right] \qquad (3.14)$$

where

P_{av} = price per share of the average
P_i = price per share of stock i contained in the average
N_{actual} = actual number of shares outstanding
$\sum_{i=1}^{M}$ = addition of all stocks (M) included in the average
N_{adj} = number of shares, adjusted for stock splits and all stock dividends regardless of size

The adjusted number of shares (the divisor) holds the key position in the statistical computation of the averages. This adjustment allows the level of per share prices to remain unaffected by stock splits and stock dividends. The adjustment also facilitates substitutions in the list. To illustrate, suppose there is only a single company contained in the average and this company has 1 million shares outstanding, selling at $50 per share. Let there be a 2-for-1 split so that there are now 2 million shares outstanding, selling at $25 per share. The split has no effect on the value of the company—that value remains at $50 million. But the price per share is $25 instead of $50. To keep the average at the correct level, the market value ($50 million) is divided by the original number

---

5. Cash flow ($)
6. Dividend ($)
7. Dividend as percent of net income (%)
8. Dividend as percent of cash flow (%)
9. Price (at year-end) ($)
10. Price/cash flow ratio
11. Price/earnings ratio
12. Yield on cash dividend (%)
13. Book value ($)

of shares—1 million. A similar procedure is followed in the case of stock dividends.[6]

3.4 The New York Stock Exchange Indexes

The New York Stock Exchange's answer to the question "What's happening in the market?" consists of four group indexes and a composite index for a total of five separate indexes. The composite index includes every stock listed on the Exchange, some 1250 stocks as of the inception of the index (December 31, 1965), The group indexes are

1. *The Finance Index:* 75 issues of closed-end investment companies savings and loan companies, real estate holding and investment companies, and others in commercial and instalment finance, banking, insurance, and related fields
2. *The Transportation Index:* 76 issues, representing railroads, airlines, shipping, and motor transport
3. *The Utility Index:* 136 issues of operating, holding, and transmission companies in gas, electric, power, and communications.
4. *The Industrial Index:* the approximately 1000 stocks not included in the other three indexes
5. *The NYSE Common Stock Composite Index:* every stock listed on the exchange

The NYSE measures of the market are calculated up to the second by computers installed at the Exchange and are transmitted out over the Exchange's ticker network at half-hour intervals during the trading day. On the half hour, the ticker prints out items:

1. Time
2. NYSE Common Stock Index (e.g., 50.04 points), along with its net change (e.g., up .03 points) from the previous day's close
3. Change in the market: change in the average price of NYSE shares expressed in dollars and cents

On the hour, the computers in the Exchange transmit five items for print-out on the ticker:

1. Time
2. Approximate NYSE trading volume
3. Change in the market (e.g., up 30 cents)
4. NYSE Index with its net change
5. Industrial, transportation, utility, and finance indexes, with their net changes in points

---

[6] For further reading on Moody's averages and how they retain consistency during issuance of new shares through rights, conversions, acquisitions, mergers, breakups, and replacements, see Bodhan J. Kekish, "Moody's Averages," *Financial Analysts Journal*, May–June 1967, pp. 65–69.

At the end of the day, the ticker prints out a closing report for the entire day.

Calculation of the NYSE Index Values. All indexes calculated by the New York Stock Exchange indicate current market value, relative to market value in a base date. The base date is chosen (arbitrarily) as the close of the market on December 31, 1965. The formula used to calculate the New York Stock Exchange price level indexes is

$$\text{Current price level index} = \frac{\text{Current market value}}{\text{Base market value}} \times 50$$

(3.15)

where

$$\text{Current market value} = \sum_{i=1}^{n} (p_i q_i)$$

p_i = price per share of the ith stock

q_i = number of shares listed for stock i

n = total number of stocks in the index

$\displaystyle\sum_{i=1}^{n}$ = summing over-all stocks in the index

Base market value = aggregate value of all issues listed as of the base date, adjusted for changes in capitalization

The level of the index was set at 50.00 as of the base date (December 31, 1965) to reflect the fact that the average price at that time was approximately $50 per share. The adjusted base market values are calculated according to the formula

$$\text{Adjusted base market value} = \frac{\text{Current value after list change}}{\text{Current value before list change}} \times \text{Prior base value}$$

(3.16)

To illustrate how the index is calculated, suppose the current market value of all stocks listed on the NYSE equals $550 billion and the base market value equals $500 billion. Then, as indicated by equation (3.17), the current index equals 55.

$$\text{Current price level index} = (\$550/\$500) \times 50 = 55 \qquad \textbf{(3.17)}$$

For calculating the net change in average price of NYSE shares, equation (3.18) is used.

$$\text{Change in average price} = \left(\frac{\text{Average price of shares listed}}{\text{index value}}\right) \text{Change in index}$$

(3.18)

As an illustration of (3.18), suppose the index value is 79.20, down from 80.00. Then the change in the index is down .80. If the average price per share listed equals $50, then the change in average price is down 50 cents.

$$\Delta P = (50.00/80.00) \times .80 = 50 \text{ cents (down)} \qquad \textbf{(3.19)}$$

where ΔP = change in average price.

A decline of .80 in the NYSE Common Stock Index at current levels reflects a decline in the market of 50 cents. This change in the market is shown on the ticker tape.

Adjustment of base market values can be illustrated as follows. Suppose a rights financing adds $1.1 billion to total current market value in equation (3.17). Since the market value before the list change was $550 billion, the numerator of equation (3.16) becomes $551.1 billion. Also, since the prior base value was $500 billion, the adjusted base market value will be $501 billion and the level of the current index will be 55, the same level as before the list change.

$$\text{Adjusted base market value} = (\$551.1/\$550) \times \$500 = \$501 \text{ billion}$$
$$\textbf{(3.20)}$$

$$\text{Current index} = (\$551.1/\$501) \times 50 = 55 \qquad \textbf{(3.21)}$$

Base market values for December 31, 1965 are readjusted to compensate for subsequent changes in capitalization, new listings, and delistings. These readjustments are made daily. If an issue is delisted, the base market value must be decreased so that the current market value minus the delisted shares will not change the level of the index.[7]

3.5 The American Stock Exchange Index System

The American Stock Exchange (Amex) began publishing its index in June 1966. The index consists of three parts:

1. Price level index
2. Breadth of market index
3. Price-earnings index

The price level index is designed to answer the question "What is the current price level of issues traded on the American Stock Exchange,

---

[7] For further reading, see Stan West and Norman Miller, "Why the New NYSE Common Stock Indexes?" *The Financial Analysts Journal*, May–June 1967, pp. 49–54. This particular issue of the journal contains articles on various indexes.

and how has the level changed in the recent past?" In answering, the price level index shows the average price change of all common stocks and warrants traded on the American Stock Exchange. The index is issued hourly, at the close of trading each day, and is reported in dollars and cents.

The breadth of market index for the American Stock Exchange is designed to answer the question "To what extent are changes in price spread broadly across the market or concentrated in only a few issues?" The breadth of market index, therefore, provides information in addition to that provided by the price level index and helps to explain the cause of changes in the price level index. The breadth of market index is plotted as a histogram and shows how many issues advanced and declined (by different amounts) from their previous closing prices. On the vertical axis of the bar chart (histogram) is "number of issues traded" and on the horizontal axis is "price changes since previous close." Thus the bar chart shows how many stocks were up $\frac{1}{8}$ point, down $\frac{1}{4}$ point, up $1\frac{1}{2}$ points, down $\frac{3}{8}$ point, etc.

The price-earnings index for the American Stock Exchange is designed to answer the question "How many issues sell at different price/earnings ratios?" This index is also a bar graph. The vertical axis is labeled "number of issues traded" and the horizontal axis is labeled "price/earnings ratio." The chart gives the number of issues that sold between zero and five times earnings, etc., in progressive multiples of 5.

To calculate the AMEX price level index, first calculate the base price. The base price equals the average price of all stocks and warrants admitted to dealings on April 29, 1965. That price was $16.88. Second, add up the *changes* in price of each common stock and warrant since the previous close and divide that total by the number of these stocks and warrants. This result will give the average change in price and must be added to (or subtracted from) the previous index value. Suppose we have the following situation:

Index at close	$16.88
Price changes from previous close for all common stocks and warrants	$ 457.00
Number of common stocks and warrants	1050.00
Index change	$457/1050 = $ .34
New index value	$17.22

We see that the price level index shows the average change in price of all common stocks and warrants traded on the Exchange—up 34 cents. The index is reported in dollars and cents hourly and at the close of each day's trading.

3.6 The National Quotation Bureau

Indexes of activity in the over-the-counter securities markets are maintained and published by the National Quotation Bureau (NQB). The NQB Industrial Average contains shares of 35 industrial companies. The NQB Insurance Stock Average contains shares of 15 insurance firms.[8]

QUESTIONS FOR STUDY

1. As a measure of the market, the NYSE Index is superior to the Dow-Jones Industrial Average, because the NYSE contains all stocks traded on the exchange, while the Dow-Jones index contains only 30 blue chip stocks. True or false? Explain your answer.
2. Explain the weighting scheme for the Dow-Jones Industrial Index. Show how a high-priced stock will have greater effect in the index than a change of the same relative magnitude in a low-price stock.
3. The NYSE Index is technically superior to the AMEX Index as a true measure of the market, because the former weights each stock by the number of its shares outstanding, whereas the latter uses equal weights for all issues in the index. True or false? Explain your answer.
4. Write a short (10-page) paper on "How the bond market has performed over the years."
5. Do stock market prices tend to be more volatile than bond market prices? Present some evidence to substantiate your answer.
6. Explain how each one of the popular stock averages is adjusted for

    (a) Split-ups
    (b) Reverse splits
    (c) Stock dividends
    (d) Substitutions (new names substituted for old names)
    (e) Additions (expanded list of securities)

7. Why are indexes needed for bond and stock market prices?
8. Write a short (10-page) paper on the general construction of index numbers. Be sure to explain *what* you are trying to measure and *why* a particular index may or may not be a good measure of what you are trying to determine. Also, during the course of your discussion, suggest some tests to determine just how good a particular index may or may not be.
9. Obtain year-end data for each of the popular averages for the past 10 years and plot the data on a graph. Compare the behavior of each index with each other index. How do you interpret your findings?

---

[8] A current listing of the particular stocks included in the averages can be obtained from National Quotation Bureau, Inc., 116 Nassau Street, New York, New York, 10038.

10. Repeat question 9 above, this time using *average* data for the year instead of year-end. Are the results significantly different? Why or why not, as the case may be?

11. What might have motivated Professor Lawrence Fisher to say, "An index based on price alone is intrinsically uninteresting?" Reference: Lawrence Fisher and James H. Lorie, "Rates of Return on Investments in Common Stocks, 1926–1965," *The Journal of Business*, no. 1, part 2, January 1966.

Some Concepts and Methods Fundamental to Financial Analysis

Part II

Several important concepts form the foundation and framework for the profitable appraisal of alternative investment opportunities. The time value of money is one of these elementary concepts. Stated simply, the time value of money means that one dollar received today is worth more (now) than that same dollar if received 50 years hence.

Dollars have greater value if received now instead of later, because money can be put to profitable use during the intervening span of time. Money can be deposited in a savings account which is insured (up to a maximum limit) by the federal government. So, a lump sum deposited today, if left to collect interest over a period of time, is virtually guaranteed to grow larger. Since everyone has the opportunity to open an insured savings account, and since interest payments increase the balance in the account over time, we can say that money has a time

The Time Value of Money

4

value.[1] The longer the span of time, the larger the balance of the account at the end of that time. The difference between present value and future value is the total of interest dollars collected over that time span. The ideas discussed in these introductory paragraphs will be expanded in the chapter.

Since finance and investments *always* involve money outlays made in anticipation of corresponding returns at future points in time, then to evaluate and assess the investment merits of alternative projects, one must assess the value of dollars received (and/or paid out) at different points in time. As depicted in Figure 4.1, dollars can be received (or paid) and therefore evaluated in several ways.

First, dollars can be expressed as *lump sums* at two different points in time. In this case, two comparisons can be made:

---

[1] Insured accounts are taken as the example so that risk and uncertainty, two more important concepts, can be ignored. Later, in Chapter 6, risk and uncertainty are added to the analysis.

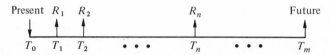

Figure 4.1.   Illustration of sums of money at different points in time.

1. Compound a present lump sum to an equivalent future value so as to compare two future lump sums.
2. Discount a future lump sum to an equivalent present value so as to compare two present lump sums.

Second, dollars can be expressed as *periodic revenues* to be received (or paid) at many different points in time. In this case, four comparisons can be made:

1. Compound a periodic revenue stream to an equivalent *future* lump sum so as to compare future lump sums.
2. Discount a periodic revenue to an equivalent *present* lump sum so as to compare present lump sums.
3. Compound a present lump sum to an equivalent future periodic revenue stream so as to compare uniform periodic revenues.
4. Discount a future lump sum to an equivalent periodic stream of revenue so as to compare uniform periodic revenues.

Third, in a case where the stated periodic revenues are *nonuniform*, compounding (or discounting) to an equivalent lump sum and then discounting (or compounding) back to an equivalent *uniform* periodic revenue stream may be appropriate. Also, since interest payments can be (and often are) paid more often than once per year, consideration must be given to effective annual interest rates and continuous compounding.

These then are the topics for discussion in Chapter 4. Some illustrative examples are presented in the Appendix at the end of this chapter.

4.1 Compound Interest

Compound interest is a wonderful phenomenon. Because interest income can be compounded, money grows more rapidly than it otherwise would. Dollars not only multiply; they multiply at an ever-increasing rate. Compound interest is one consideration in the concept of time value of money.

Time value of money is the most basic, the most fundamental, concept required to begin the study of investments. It involves two ideas:

1. Interest income can be received periodically over time. That is, wealth increases with time if money is put to productive use profitably instead of remaining as idle cash balances.
2. As a result of the addition to total income through interest payments, total wealth increases over time. The longer the money is in productive use, the larger the total income will be. Under these conditions, total income (total wealth) increases with time. Because wealth increases if profitable investments are made, one can say that money has a time value.

To illustrate the concepts of compound interest and the time value of money, let us consider several insured savings accounts. In the first case, suppose there are two accounts, both paying the same rate of interest and both containing a cash balance of $1000 today. Without further qualification, these two accounts *are equal*. The accounts are identical because they (1) pay the same rate of interest,[2] (2) have the same cash balance as of today, and (3) are insured (i.e., guaranteed). Given a choice between the two accounts, any rational investor will be indifferent about owning either account because of the identity.

In the next case, suppose two accounts have a cash balance today of $1000, but suppose one account pays interest amounting to 6 percent of the account balance once each year while the other account pays 20 percent interest each year. Then for the first account, since interest is paid (i.e., compounded) once per year (i.e., annually), the account balance at the end of the first year will be the original principal of $1000 plus interest equal to 6 per cent of $1000, or a total of $1060.

$$\$1000 + .06(\$1000) = \$1000(1 + .06) = \$1060 \qquad (4.1)$$

Assuming no additional deposits or withdrawals during the second

---

[2] Using the language of investment and anticipating subject material in later chapters, we can say that these two accounts have the same expected rate of growth.

year, 6 percent will be paid on $1060 to yield an account balance at the end of the second year of principal plus interest equal to $1123.60.

$$\$1060 + .06(\$1060) = \$1060(1 + .06) = \$1000(1 + .06)^2$$
$$= \$1123.60 \qquad (4.2)$$

The complete listing for each of the 10 years is shown in Table 4.1. For comparison, Table 4.1 also lists the state of the account if interest is 20 percent instead of 6 percent.

Table 4.1 TWO SAVINGS ACCOUNTS WITH
REINVESTMENT OF INTEREST

Savings Account I*

Interest period (T)	Principal (P) ($)	Interest (I = iP) ($)	Account balance as of end of interest period (S = P + I) ($)
1	1000.00	60.00	1060.00
2	1060.00	63.60	1123.60
3	1123.60	67.42	1191.02
4	1191.02	71.46	1262.48
5	1262.48	75.75	1338.23
6	1338.23	80.29	1418.52
7	1418.52	85.11	1503.63
8	1503.63	90.22	1593.85
9	1593.85	95.63	1689.48
10	1689.48	101.37	1790.85

* i = 6 percent, compounded annually for 10 years.

Savings Account II†

Interest period (T)	Principal (P) ($)	Interest (I = iP) ($)	Account balance as of end of interest period (S = P + I) ($)
1	1000.00	200.00	1200.00
2	1200.00	240.00	1440.00
3	1440.00	288.00	1728.00
4	1728.00	345.60	2073.60
5	2073.60	414.72	2488.32
6	2488.32	497.66	2985.98
7	2985.98	597.20	3583.18
8	3583.18	716.64	4299.82
9	4299.82	859.96	5159.78
10	5159.78	1031.96	6191.74

† i = 20 percent, compounded annually for 10 years.

The two accounts in Table 4.1 are *not equal*. Even though each account has a cash balance today of $1000, because larger interest accrues to the second account, the second $1000, will grow over 10 years to a total of $6191.74 where as over the same span of time, the first $1000 will grow to a total of only $1790.85. Given a choice between the two accounts, all rational investors (i.e., investors who obtain satisfaction from maximizing wealth) will prefer the second account.

Several conclusions can be drawn from the above illustration. First, note the difference between *equal* money values and *equivalent* money values. If 6 percent interest is compounded annually, then $1000 today has the same effect as $1790.85 to be received 10 years hence. Therefore $1000 today is *equivalent to* $1790.85 10 years hence. But if interest is compounded at the rate of 20 percent per year, then $1000 today is *equivalent to* $6191.74 10 years hence. One thousand dollars today is always *equal to* $1000 today, regardless of the interest payments. For analytical purposes, comparisons between two different sums of money are meaningful and correct only if the sums are equal or equivalent. If two or more different sums of money are to be compared, and if these sums are separated in time, then, for the comparisons to be meaningful and correct, these sums must be converted to equivalent values so that all sums are expressed as of the same point in time.

Second, the value (i.e., worth) of the account varies directly with the rate of interest payments. From Table 4.1, note that after the first interest payment and for all succeeding periods of time the account balance of the 20 percent account exceeds the account balance of the 6 percent account. This observation will be applied later in a context of maximizing wealth as of some future planning date. To do this, it is sufficient to maximize returns received during every time period between now and the target date. Also, in the context of assessing corporate dividend policy, a topic to be discussed in Chapter 8, this observation implies that (other things the same) a dollar retained and reinvested at relatively high rates of return (e.g., 20 percent) can be worth more today than a dollar paid out and reinvested at relatively low rates of return (e.g., 6 percent). In other words, since rational investors prefer the 20 percent account, how much would have to be paid for the investor to accept the 6 percent account?[3]

Also from Table 4.1, it is interesting to note that if 20 percent interest is compounded annually, then $1000 doubles in less than 4 years, triples in less than 7 years, and after 10 years is worth more than six times its original size. These numbers illustrate why compound interest is such a wonderful phenomenon!

_____

[3] Answer: In 10 years with the 6 percent account, the investor will have $4400.89 less than he would have had with the 20 percent account. The question is "If interest is 6 percent compounded annually, then what is the equivalent value today of $4400.89 10 years hence?" The answer is approximately $2456.83. That is, for the investor to be equally wealthy, he must be paid $2456.83 to accept the $1000, 6 percent account instead of the $1000, 20 percent account.

Third, we should note what happens if interest is paid but is withdrawn instead of being compounded. If interest income is withdrawn from the savings account immediately after each payment instead of remaining in the account (i.e., not reinvested) at the rate i, then the account will grow at a slower rate than before. The dollar sums are tabulated on Table 4.2. From the first line of Table 4.2 the $1000 principal is deposited in a savings account to earn interest during the first

Table 4.2 SAVINGS ACCOUNT WITH NO REINVESTMENT

A. $i = 6$ percent

Interest period (T)	Checking account balance as of end of interest period ($)	Principal (in savings) (P)($)	Interest on savings ($I = iP$)($)	Savings account balance as of end of interest period ($S = P + I$)($)
1	00.00	1000.00	60.00	1060.00
2	60.00	1000.00	60.00	1060.00
3	120.00	1000.00	60.00	1060.00
4	180.00	1000.00	60.00	1060.00
5	240.00	1000.00	60.00	1060.00
6	300.00	1000.00	60.00	1060.00
7	360.00	1000.00	60.00	1060.00
8	420.00	1000.00	60.00	1060.00
9	480.00	1000.00	60.00	1060.00
10	540.00	1000.00	60.00	1060.00

B. Simple interest added

Interest period	Principal	Interest	Total at end of interest period
1	P	iP	$P + iP = P(1 + i)$
2	P	iP	$P + iP = P(1 + i)$
3	P	iP	$P + iP = P(1 + i)$
4	P	iP	$P + iP = P(1 + i)$
5	P	iP	$P + iP = P(1 + i)$
6	P	iP	$P + iP = P(1 + i)$
7	P	iP	$P + iP = P(1 + i)$
8	P	iP	$P + iP = P(1 + i)$
9	P	iP	$P + iP = P(1 + i)$
10	P	iP	$P + iP = P(1 + i)$

time period. At this time, the balance in the checking account is zero. Immediately after interest is paid, the total interest payment of $60 is withdrawn from the savings account and deposited in the interest-free checking account. The process is repeated every year for the next 9 years. At the end of the 10-year span of time, the total wealth of the owner equals $540.00 in the checking account plus $1060 in the savings account. Total wealth therefore is $1600, which is $190.85 less than he would have had if he had permitted reinvestment and the compounding of interest. With no reinvestment, wealth accumulates at a slower rate.

The bottom half of Table 4.2 shows how a formula can be derived to express the future value (S) of a present lump sum (P), assuming simple interest. From the bottom half of Table 4.2, we have

$$S = P + \sum_{j=1}^{n} (iP)_j = P + (iP)_1 + (iP)_2 + \cdots + (iP)_n$$

$$= P(1 + ni)$$

(4.3)

where

$$S = \text{future lump sum of money}$$
$$P = \text{present lump sum of money}$$
$$i = \text{rate of interest (expressed as a percent per unit time)}[4]$$
$$n = \text{number of unit time intervals}$$
$$\sum_{j=1}^{n} = \text{summation (adding) over all time } n \text{ time intervals}$$

Therefore, using formula (4.3) we get

$$S = 1000[1 + (10)(.06)] = \$1000(1.60) = \$1600 \qquad \textbf{(4.4)}$$

One can conclude from this discussion that for evaluating alternative proposals for finance or investment, the ever-present time value of money always stands as one possible criterion for acceptance or rejection. This is a fundamental point in the theory of investment behavior.

4.2 Equivalent Lump Sums of Money: Compounding (Compound Amount Factor, given P)

In this section we shall focus attention on a systematic way of calculating the future value of present lump sums of money, assuming compound interest. That is, we shall calculate the compound amount factor (CAF), given a present lump sum of money (P). In Table 4.1 the balance of the savings account was tabulated as of the end of each time period. In actual practice, such tabulations are always possible but can be tedious. For example, suppose you want to know the future value of $452 485.02 as of the end of 42 years if interest is compounded at 12 percent per year. Preparation of a table similar to Table 4.1 for this example will be time-consuming and tedious. Therefore to expedite analysis, we shall resort to a faster but equally precise method. We shall develop analytical formulae similar to statement (4.3).

---

[4] The term "nominal rate of interest" is used to express i.

Table 4.3   PRESENT WORTH COMPOUND AMOUNT FACTOR (PWCAF)

1	P	iP	$P + iP = P(1 + i)$
2	$P(1 + i)$	$iP(1 + i)$	$P(1 + i)^2$
3	$P(1 + i)^2$	$iP(1 + i)^2$	$P(1 + i)^3$
$\vdots$	$\vdots$	$\vdots$	$\vdots$
n	$P(1 + i)^{n-1}$	$iP(1 + i)^{n-1}$	$P(1 + i)^n = S$

Using symbols to represent the dollar totals as listed in Table 4.1, we can write Table 4.3. The initial deposit is $P = \$1000$. The account balance as of the end of the tenth year is

$$S = P(1 + i)^n \tag{4.5}$$

where all symbols are the same as defined previously. Note the implicit assumption in the derivation of formula (4.5) that interest income is reinvested (i.e., allowed to accumulate) at the rate i percent per unit time period. This assumption of reinvestment is very important for later analyses.

The factor $(1 + i)^n$ is known as the compound amount factor and can be used to calculate the future value (S) for any given present lump sum (P). Standard tables of compound interest factors have been tabulated and are widely accessible.[5] Thus, consulting such a table, we find that if interest is compounded annually at 12 percent for 42 years, then the compound amount factor is 116.74452. Hence to calculate the future lump sum of any number of present dollars, one needs only to multiply P by 116.74452.

Next, consider situations where interest is paid and compounded several times per year. In what way is the present worth compound amount factor altered to accommodate this situation? The answer is best seen through illustrations with tables again.

Table 4.4 shows the behavior of the account if 6 percent is compounded twice per year and four times per year, respectively. In the first case, $1000 today grows to $1806.11 as of 10 years (20 compounding times) hence. In the second case, $1000 today grows to $1814.02 as of 10 years (40 compounding times) hence. If symbols as shown in Table 4.5 are used to represent the dollar values themselves, then, from the last line of Table 4.5, *any* present lump sum (P) will grow to a future value (S) of

$$S = P(1 + i/m)^{mn}, \qquad m \geq 1 \tag{4.6}$$

---

[5] One such table is included in the Appendix of this book.

where

    m = number of times per period that interest is compounded
    mn = total number of interest payment periods between the present and the future

and other symbols are the same as defined previously.

Table 4.4 SAVINGS ACCOUNTS WITH MULTIPLE PERIODS FOR COMPOUNDING

A. i = 6 per cent, compounded semiannually

Interest period (T)	Principal (P) ($)	Interest ($I = iP$) ($)	Account balance as of end of interest period ($S = P + I$) ($)
1	1000.00	30.00	1030.00
2	1030.00	30.90	1060.90
3	1060.90	31.83	1092.73
4	1092.73	32.78	1125.51
5	1125.51	33.77	1159.27
6	1159.27	34.78	1194.05
7	1194.05	35.82	1229.87
8	1229.87	36.90	1266.77
9	1266.77	38.00	1304.77
10	1304.77	39.14	1343.92
11	1343.92	40.32	1384.23
12	1384.23	41.53	1425.76
13	1425.76	42.77	1468.53
14	1468.53	44.06	1512.59
15	1512.59	45.38	1557.97
16	1557.97	46.74	1604.71
17	1604.71	48.14	1652.85
18	1652.85	49.59	1702.43
19	1702.43	51.07	1753.51
20	1753.51	52.61	1806.11

B. i = 6 per cent, compounded quarterly

Interest period (T)	Principal (P) ($)	Interest ($I = iP$) ($)	Account balance as of end of interest period ($S = P + I$) ($)
1	1000.00	15.00	1015.00
2	1015.00	15.23	1030.23
3	1030.23	15.45	1045.68
4	1045.68	15.69	1061.36
5	1061.36	15.92	1077.28
6	1077.28	16.16	1093.44
7	1093.44	16.40	1109.84
8	1109.84	16.65	1126.49
9	1126.49	16.90	1143.39
10	1143.39	17.15	1160.54
11	1160.54	17.41	1177.95
12	1177.95	17.67	1195.62

Table 4.4 (Continued)

Interest period (T)	Principal (P) ($)	Interest (I = IP) ($)	Account balance as of end of interest period (S = P + I) ($)
13	1195.62	17.93	1213.55
14	1213.55	18.20	1231.76
15	1231.76	18.48	1250.23
16	1250.23	18.75	1268.99
17	1268.99	19.03	1288.02
18	1288.02	19.32	1307.34
19	1307.34	19.61	1326.95
20	1326.95	19.90	1346.86
21	1346.86	20.20	1367.06
22	1367.06	20.51	1387.56
23	1387.56	20.81	1408.38
24	1408.38	21.13	1429.50
25	1429.50	21.44	1450.95
26	1450.95	21.76	1472.71
27	1472.71	22.09	1494.80
28	1494.80	22.42	1517.22
29	1517.22	22.76	1539.98
30	1539.98	23.10	1563.08
31	1563.08	23.45	1586.53
32	1586.53	23.80	1610.32
33	1610.32	24.15	1634.48
34	1634.48	24.52	1659.00
35	1659.00	24.88	1683.88
36	1683.88	25.26	1709.14
37	1709.14	25.64	1734.78
38	1734.78	26.02	1760.80
39	1760.80	26.41	1787.21
40	1787.21	26.81	1814.02

Table 4.5 PRESENT WORTH COMPOUND AMOUNT FACTOR (multiple compounding)

Interest period	Principal	Interest	Account balance as of end of interest period
1	P	$(i/m)P$	$P\left(1 + \dfrac{i}{m}\right)$
2	$P(1 + i/m)$	$(i/m)P(1 + i/m)$	$P(1 + i/m)^2$
3	$P(1 + i/m)^2$	$(i/m)P(1 + i/m)^2$	$P(1 + i/m)^3$
$\vdots$			
y	$P\left(1 + \dfrac{i}{m}\right)^{y-1}$	$(i/m)P\left(1 + \dfrac{i}{m}\right)^{y-1}$	$P\left(1 + \dfrac{i}{m}\right)^{mn}$
$\vdots$			
mn	$P\left(1 + \dfrac{i}{m}\right)^{mn-1}$	$(i/m)P\left(1 + \dfrac{i}{m}\right)^{mn-1}$	$P\left(1 + \dfrac{i}{m}\right)^{mn} = S$

Note that in the special case when $m = 1$, equation (4.6) is the same as (4.5). Therefore, (4.5) may be viewed as a special case of the more general formulation (4.6).

As an exercise, the reader should prepare tables similar to Table 4.4, letting 6 percent interest be compounded monthly ($m = 12$) and twice per month ($m = 24$).

CONTINUOUS COMPOUNDING. Conceptually, m from statement (4.6) can be indefinitely large. If interest is compounded each day for 365 days, then m equals 365. If interest is compounded each second of each minute of each day for 365 days, then, for practical purposes, m equals infinity; that is, interest is compounded continuously.

To know what happens to the compound amount factor as m approaches infinity, it is helpful to study the quantity

$$[1 + (1/Q)]^Q, \qquad Q > 0 \tag{4.7}$$

where $Q =$ any positive number, as Q increases without limit. It can be shown that the quantity stated in (4.7) approaches a constant, $e = 2.71828$, as Q becomes indefinitely large.[6]

$$\lim_{Q \to \infty} [1 + (1/Q)]^Q = 2.71828 = e \tag{4.8}$$

where $e =$ base of Naperian Logarithmic System.[7]

Now if Q is defined to be

$$Q = (m/i) > 0 \tag{4.9}$$

then statement (4.6) can be written as

$$S = P\{[1 + (i/m)]^{m/i}\}^{in} \tag{4.10}$$

Therefore, given that $i =$ constant, then as m increases indefinitely, Q proceeds toward infinity, and the quantity inside the brackets of (4.10) approaches e. Hence, for continuous compounding we get an exponential relationship between present and future values.

$$S = Pe^{in} \tag{4.11}$$

---

[6] For proof, see any text on advanced calculus. Intuitively, letting Q equal 1, 2, 4, 10, 100, and 1000, successively, corresponding values can be calculated for the quantity $[1 + (1/Q)]^Q$. These values are 2, 2.25, 2.4414, 2.5937, 2.7048, and 2.7169, respectively. As Q proceeds to take on values larger than 1000, the quantity proceeds to approach the limiting value 2.71828.

[7] That is, e is a number so that $\ln(e) = 1$. Then $e^1 = 2.71828$ and $1 = \ln(e) = \ln(2.71828)$.

where all terms are the same as defined previously. In other words, when compounding is continuous, the compound amount factor, $[1 + (i/m)]^n$, can be replaced by the exponential factor e^{in}.

To illustrate the calculations when interest is compounded continuously, suppose a nominal rate of 8 percent is compounded continuously for 1 year. Then $1.00 deposited today would grow to become $1.08 as of the end of the year.

$$
\begin{aligned}
S &= Pe^{in} \\
&= 1.00(2.71828)^{.08(1)} \\
&= 1.083287 \\
&= \$1.08
\end{aligned}
\qquad (4.12)
$$

Two comments are in order here. First, the exponential function, $e^{.08}$, must be calculated. This value is found in a standard table of exponential functions.[8] Second, the accuracy of the calculations (i.e., number of decimal places carried in the arithmetic) may be misleading. If we are dealing in dollars and cents, then fractions of a penny are ignored (or at best, rounded to the nearest penny). In later chapters, the dollar values may be subjective estimates, accurate in some cases only to the nearest $100. The interpretation of the results of any calculation therefore should proceed in the context of the input data to the analysis.

EFFECTIVE ANNUAL COMPOUNDING.   From Table 4.4 we observed that if interest is compounded more than once per year, say two times in one case and four times in another case, then for purposes of making comparisons between the two accounts, it is desirable to standardize both accounts. One way of standardizing is to express the rate of interest on each account as if it were compounded once per time period instead of several times per time period. In other words, to standardize nominal rates which are compounded many times per year, the nominal rate can be expressed as an *effective rate*.

Thus to calculate the effective rate, given m and the nominal rate, we can proceed as follows. If interest is compounded annually at the effective rate, then the future lump sum is

$$
S = P(1 + i_e)^n \qquad (4.13)
$$

where i_e = effective annual interest rate; other terms are the same as defined previously. But since interest is actually i, compounded m times

---

[8] In fact, the reader should be familiar with the standard mathematical tables. Two good references are (1) *C.R.C. Standard Mathematical Tables*, Chemical Rubber Publishing Company, 231 Superior Avenue, N.E. Cleveland, Ohio, and (2) *Handbook of Probability and Statistics with Tables*, Handbook Publishers, Inc., Sandusky, Ohio.

per year, then the future lump sum is stated by (4.13). Because use of the effective rate must yield results identical with the actual rate, we can write

$$P(1 + i/m)^{mn} = P(1 + i_e)^n \qquad (4.14)$$

Then the effective rate can be solved from (4.14) by dividing both sides by P, taking the nth root, and subtracting unity. Thus

$$i_e = (1 + i/m)^m - 1 \qquad (4.15)$$

To illustrate, suppose 8 percent is compounded quarterly. Then the effective rate is 8.24 percent:

$$\begin{aligned} i_e &= (1 + .08/4)^4 - 1 = (1.02)^4 - 1 \\ &= .0824 \quad \text{or} \quad 8.24 \text{ percent} \end{aligned} \qquad (4.16)$$

Stated differently, 8.24 percent compounded annually yields the same results as 8.00 percent compounded quarterly.

Taking another example, suppose 8 percent per annum is compounded continuously. Then the effective rate is 8.33 percent:

$$i_e = (2.71828)^{.08} - 1 = .083287 = 8.33 \text{ percent} \qquad (4.17)$$

That is, a nominal rate of 8 percent compounded continuously throughout the year is the same as 8.33 percent compounded once per year.

4.3 Equivalent Lump Sums of Money: Discounting (present worth factor, given S)

Thus far, all the analysis has been in terms of compounding: calculating values of future lump sums, given present lump sums. Now, we turn attention to discounting. We shall calculate the present worth factor (PWF), given a future lump sum of money (S).

Discounting is the reverse of compounding. For example, suppose that instead of opening the $1000 savings account today, you are guaranteed to receive $1000 in cash as of the end of 10 years hence. Then the question is "How much is that $1000 worth today?" That is, calculate the present value of a lump sum of money to be received at a specified time in the future.

As before, we can proceed to tabulate the balance of the account, by assuming a rate of interest and working backward. As of the end of the ninth year, assuming an interest rate of 6 percent, there must have been $943.40 on deposit to have an account balance of $1000 as of the end of the tenth year. ($943.40)(1 + .06) = $1000. Next, there must have been $890.00 on deposit to have an account balance of $943.40

as of the end of the ninth year. ($890.00)(1 + .06) = $943.40. Continuing in this manner and working backward to today, if 6 percent interest is compounded annually, and if no money is withdrawn from the account, then there must be $558.40 on deposit if the account balance 10 years hence is to be precisely $1000. Therefore, $1000 to be received at the end of 10 years is equivalent to $ 558.40 today if the rate of interest is 6 percent and compounding occurs annually. These data are shown on Table 4.6. For comparison, two alternative rates of interest are shown: 6 percent per year and 20 percent per year.

Because of the time value of money, $1000 to be received 10 years hence is worth less than $1000 to be received today. Precisely how much less depends on both the rate of interest and the frequency of compounding.

Table 4.6   FUTURE VALUE DISCOUNT FACTOR (FVDF)

Calculation of Equivalent Present Value
from a Given Future Value

A. i = 6 percent, compounded annually for 10 years

Interest period (T)	Principal (P)($)	Interest ($I = iP$)($)	Account balance as of end of interest period ($S = P + I$)($)
10	943.40	56.60	1000.00
9	890.00	53.40	943.40
8	839.62	50.38	890.00
7	792.09	47.53	839.62
6	747.26	44.84	792.09
5	704.96	42.30	747.26
4	665.06	39.90	704.96
3	627.41	37.64	665.06
2	591.90	35.51	627.41
1	558.40	33.50	591.90

B. i = 20 percent, compounded annually for 10 years

10	833.33	166.67	1000.00
9	694.44	138.89	833.33
8	578.70	115.74	694.44
7	482.25	96.45	578.70
6	401.88	80.38	482.25
5	334.90	66.98	401.88
4	279.08	55.82	334.90
3	232.57	46.51	279.08
2	193.81	38.76	232.57
1	161.51	32.30	193.81

The formula used to calculate the values listed in Table 4.6 can be derived from statement (4.6) because all factors in the formula are known, except P, and P is the value we are looking for. Hence

$$P = S/[(1 + i/m)^{mn}] \tag{4.18}$$

where all terms are defined previously.

The factor $1/[1 + (i/m)]^{mn}$ is called the present worth factor and is the reciprocal of the compound amount factor as shown in equation (4.6). The present worth factor is listed in the Table of Compound Interest Factors in the Appendix.

4.4 Periodic Sums vs. Equivalent Lump Sums

SITUATION 1: Compounding (compound amount factor, given R). In this section we shall calculate the compound amount factor (CAF), given periodic revenues (R).

Many times, opportunities for finance and investment involve periodic revenues (i.e., cash inflows and outflows) over time. In these situations, it might be expeditious to calculate an equivalent lump sum (present or future). In this section we shall consider a future lump sum of money which is equivalent to a periodic stream of deposits in a savings account.

Suppose a savings account is opened as of the beginning of the next interest period with a deposit of $1000. But this time, instead of leaving the money to accumulate with no additional deposits or withdrawals, suppose an additional $1000 deposit is made at the beginning of each of the next 9 consecutive years. Altogether, 10 deposits of $1000 each are made. The stream of periodic revenue is shown on the top half of Figure 4.2. The question is "What will be the size of the account as of the end of the tenth year?" That is, compute the equivalent future value of a specified periodic stream of revenue.

Conceptually, the answer can be determined by repeated application of statement (4.6). That is, compound each of the $1000 deposits to the future time (T_{10}) and add the 10 numbers. Thus, if that particular account pays a nominal rate of 6 percent, compounded semiannually then $m = 2$, $i = .06$, and as of time T_{10}, the balance in the account will be $14,042.70.

$$
\begin{aligned}
S &= R_0(1 + i/m)^{10m} + R_1(1 + i/m)^{9m} + R_2(1 + i/m)^{8m} \\
&\quad + \cdots + R_9(1 + i/m)^{1m} \\
&= \sum_{t=0}^{9} R_t(1 + i/m)^{(10-t)m} \\
&= \$1000 \sum_{t=0}^{9} (1 + .06/2)^{2(10-t)} \\
&= \$14,042.70
\end{aligned} \tag{4.19}
$$

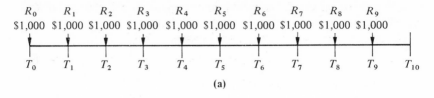

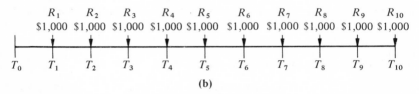

Figure 4.2. Ten periodic deposits, $1,000 each, into a savings account. (a) As of the beginning of the interest payment period. (b) As of the end of the interest payment period.

The calculations are straightforward, but can be tedious without mechanical help.[9]

If the 10 periodic deposits had been made as of the *end* of the year instead of the *beginning* of the year, then each deposit will earn interest for one time period less than it previously did, thereby causing the balance in the account to be less than it was before. Ten periodic deposits as of the end of the period are shown on the bottom half of Figure 4.2. Again, taking $m = 2$ and $i = .06$, as of T_{10}, the balance is $13,236.60.

$$S = R_1(1 + i/m)^{9m} + R_2(1 + i/m)^{8m} + \cdots$$
$$+ R_9(1 + i/m)^{1m} + R_{10}$$

$$= \sum_{t=1}^{10} R_t(1 + i/m)^{(10-t)m}$$

$$= \$1000 \sum_{t=1}^{10} (1.03)^{2(10-t)} \tag{4.20}$$

$$= \$13,236.60$$

Note that in the particular cases cited above, all of the deposits (R_t) are identical (i.e., $R_1 = R_2 = \cdots = R_{10} = \$1000$). In general, there is no need to restrict all revenues to be equal. In fact, most frequently, they will be unequal. The formulas presented above (i.e., compound each individual item up to time T_{10} and then add) always

---

[9] A desk calculator or time-shared computer terminal is useful in performing the calculations presented in this book. Some of the calculations contained herein were performed using a General Electric Company Model 235 time-sharing system.

hold. But in special cases when all the R_t's are equal, and one deposit is made, as of the end of each period of compounding (not merely annually as illustrated in the examples above), then the formulas can be simplified. The simplified formulas can be obtained as follows. Instead of depositing \$1000 once each year, let the deposit be (\$1000/m) m times each year. That is, if $m = 4$, then the deposits are \$250 four times each year. Then the lump sum future value equivalent to the periodic revenue stream can be stated as before.

$$S = [R_1(1 + i/m)^{mn-1}] + [R_2(1 + i/m)^{mn-2}]$$
$$+ \cdots + [R_{mn-1}(1 + i/m)^1] + R_{mn}$$
$$= R\{[(1 + i/m)^{mn-1}] + [(1 + i/m)^{mn-2}] \qquad \textbf{(4.21)}$$
$$+ \cdots + [(1 + i/m)^1] + 1\}$$
$$= R\left[\sum_{t=0}^{mn-1} (1 + i/m)^t\right]$$

Now, one can show that the term in the brackets of statement (4.21) simplifies in a way so that a standard table of compound interest factors can be used to calculate S, given R.[10]

$$S = R\{[(1 + i/m)^{mn} - 1]/(i/m)\} \qquad \textbf{(4.22)}$$

Using the tables in the Appendix to calculate the compound amount factor, given R, when $m = 2$, $i = .12$ and $n = 10$, we get

$$S = \$250\{[(1 + .12/2)^{20} - 1]/(.12/2)\}$$
$$= \$250(36.78752) \approx \$9198 \qquad \textbf{(4.26)}$$

That is, if \$250 is deposited every 6 months for 10 years (at the end of the period of compounding), and if the interest is 12 percent, compounded semiannually, then at the end of the tenth year the balance in the account will be approximately \$9198.

---

[10] The required simplification involves showing that

$$\left[\sum_{t=0}^{mn-1} (1 + i/m)^t\right] = \{[(1 + i/m)^{mn} - 1]/(i/m)\} \qquad \textbf{(4.23)}$$

To do so, proceed in three steps. First, multiply both sides of equation (4.21) by the factor $(1 + i/m)$ to obtain equation (4.24).

$$S(1 + i/m) = R[(1 + i/m)^{mn} + (1 + i/m)^{mn-1} + (1 + i/m)^{mn-2}$$
$$+ (1 + i/m)^{mn-3} + \cdots + (1 + i/m)^2 + (1 + i/m)]$$
$$\textbf{(4.24)}$$

Second, subtract equation (4.21) from (4.24) to obtain equation

$$S(i/m) = R[(1 + i/m)^{mn} - 1] \qquad \textbf{(4.25)}$$

Third, divide both sides of equation (4.25) by the factor (i/m) to obtain the simplified formula, equation (4.22). Equation (4.22) is useful (under the conditions assumed) for computing the equivalent future value of a periodic revenue stream, given the interest rate and the frequency of compounding.

Note: As an exercise, the reader should derive a formula equivalent to (4.22) when equal deposits are made at the beginning of the period instead of the end of the period.

SITUATION 2: Discounting (present worth factor, given R).   In this section we shall calculate the present worth factor (PWF), given periodic revenues (R).

This situation is the reverse of the preceding example. Situation 2 can be viewed as follows. Given a requirement to make periodic withdrawals in the future, what size lump sum today will meet these requirements?

As before, the answer involves repeated application of statement (4.18): one must discount each future withdrawal back to the present and add the 10 numbers. Thus, if withdrawals are made as of the end of the period, the following statement can be written:

$$P = [R_1/(1 + i/m)^m] + [R_2/(1 + i/m)^{2m}]$$
$$+ [R_3/(1 + i/m)^{3m}] + \cdots + [R_{10}/(1 + i/m)^{10m}] \quad \textbf{(4.27)}$$

Note that statement (4.27) is general in that each withdrawal (R_t) may be different from all other withdrawals. However, in a case where all withdrawals are the same size, statement (4.27) simplifies so that the Table of Compound Interest Factors can be used directly. Thus if

$$R_1 = R_2 = \cdots = R_n = R \qquad\qquad \textbf{(4.28)}$$

then [11]

$$P = \sum_{n=1}^{T} R_n/(1 + i/m)^{mn}$$
$$= R\{[(1 + i/m)^{mn} - 1]/[(i/m)(1 + i/m)^{mn}]\} \qquad \textbf{(4.29)}$$

Using the tables in the Appendix to calculate the present worth factor, given R, when $m = 2$, $i = .12$, and $n = 10$, we get

$$P = \$250[(1 + .12/2)^{20} - 1]/[(.12/2)(1 + .12/2)^{20}]$$
$$= \$250(11.46945) \approx \$2863 \qquad \textbf{(4.31)}$$

That is, if \$250 is withdrawn every 6 months for 10 years (at the end of each compounding period), and if interest is 12 percent compounded semiannually, then for the balance of the account to be precisely zero

---

[11] Statement (4.29) can be verified by setting the equivalent future value of the revenue stream, as stated in (4.22), equal to the equivalent future value of a present lump sum. Thus, we can write

$$S = P(1 + i/m)^{mn} = R[(1 + i/m)^{mn} - 1]/(i/m) \qquad \textbf{(4.30)}$$

By dividing both sides of (4.30) by the factor $(1 + i/m)^{mn}$, we get (4.29), Q.E.D.

as of the last withdrawal, $2863 must be on deposit today. The present worth factor, 11.46945, is obtained from the tables.

As a cross check with the problem in Statement (4.26), verify that a present lump sum of approximately $2863 is equivalent to a future lump sum of approximately $9198, if $i = .12$ and $m = 2$.

To calculate the present lump sum which is equivalent to a future periodic revenue, statement (4.27) or, in special cases, statement (4.29) can be applied. The fundamental principle of analysis here is that lump sums (dollar values) may be added or equated to each other only if they are measured *as of the same point in time*.

4.5 Lump Sums vs. Equivalent Periodic Sums

SITUATION 3: Compounding. Here we calculate the capital recover factor (CRF); we compound a present lump sum into an equivalent uniform periodic revenue stream.

Situation 3 is the reverse of situation 2. That is, if there exists a given lump sum in the account today, then what size periodic revenue can be withdrawn so that the balance of the account equals precisely zero as of the time of the last withdrawal?

The answer can be stated directly by solving equation (4.29) for the unknown value (R):

$$R = P\{[(i/m)(1 + i/m)^{mn}]/[(1 + i/m)^{mn} - 1]\} \qquad (4.32)$$

Thus, given P, one can use the capital recovery factor (CRF), as expressed in equation (4.32), to compute R. For example, if $100,000 is on deposit today[12] and interest is 8 percent, compounded annually, then $11,683 can be withdrawn as of the end of the year, each year for 15 years, before the account balance equals zero.

$$\begin{aligned} R &= \$100,000\{[(.08/1)(1 + .08/1)^{15}]/[(1 + .08/1)^{15} - 1]\} \\ &= \$100,000(.11683) \qquad\qquad\qquad\qquad\qquad (4.33) \\ &= \$11,683 \end{aligned}$$

If it is desired to spread the withdrawals equally over 30 years instead of 15 years, then each withdrawal can be $8883.

$$\begin{aligned} R &= \$100,000\{[(.08/1)(1 + .08/1)^{30}]/[1 + .08/1)^{30} - 1]\} \\ &= \$100,000(.08883) \qquad\qquad\qquad\qquad\qquad (4.34) \\ &= \$8883 \end{aligned}$$

SITUATION 4: Discounting. Here we calculate the sinking fund deposit factor (SFDF). The SFDF is useful for discounting a future lump sum into an equivalent uniform periodic revenue stream.

---

[12] If the maximum limit for federal insurance is $20,000 per account, then use five or more accounts for $100,000.

Situation 4 is the reverse of situation 1. That is, a target goal is often established for some future date, and it is necessary to know what size deposit, if made periodically, will amount to the target lump sum? For example, suppose $100,000 is required to pay for a purchase antici-pated 15 years hence. Then what size periodic payment is needed to accumulate the required future lump sum?

The answer can be stated directly by solving equation (4.22) for the unknown value (R):

$$R = S\{(i/m)/[(1 + i/m)^{mn} - 1]\} \tag{4.35}$$

Given S one can use the sinking fund deposit factor, as expressed in equation (4.35), to compute R. For example, if interest is 8 percent compounded annually, then annual deposits (at the end of the period) of $3683 will accumulate to a balance of $100,000 as of 15 years hence.

$$\begin{aligned} R &= \$100,000\{(.08/1)/[(1 + .08/1)^{15} - 1]\} \\ &= \$100,000(.03683) \\ &= \$3683 \end{aligned} \tag{4.36}$$

Note: As an exercise, the reader should answer the question "If $3683 is deposited annually (at the end of the year) into an account paying 8 percent compounded annually, then how many years must elapse before the account balance will be precisely $100,000?" The answer should be 15 years.

4.6 Present and Future Equivalent Values of Perpetual Revenues

In some cases (e.g., Consols), it may be required to evaluate the worth of an income stream which never terminates. In other words, the periodic revenue (R) continues forever. In this situation, when n approaches infinity, statement (4.32) simplifies to[13]

$$R = P(i/m) \tag{4.37}$$

Alternatively, we can write

$$\begin{aligned} P &= R(m/i) \\ &= R/(i/m) \end{aligned} \tag{4.38}$$

---

[13] This simplification can be seen as follows. Divide both the numerator and the denominator of (4.32) by the factor $(1 + i/m)^{mn}$ to obtain

$$R = P((i/m)/\{1 - [1/(1 + i/m)^{mn}]\}) \tag{4.41}$$

Then as n proceeds to become infinitely large, the last term in brackets on the right-hand side of (4.41) proceeds toward zero. Hence, in the limit, we get statement (4.37).

To illustrate, if interest is 16 percent, compounded quarterly, then a lump sum of $100 today is equivalent to a periodic stream of $4, four times per year—forever:

$$R = \$100(.16/4) = \$4 \tag{4.39}$$

Alternatively, a periodic stream of $4, four times per year (assuming the same interest and compounding) is worth a lump sum of $100 today:

$$P = \$4(4/.16) = \$100 \tag{4.40}$$

If an opportunity for investment is expected to pay an income of $60 twice per year forever, and if interest is 6 percent, compounded annually, then a rational investor would be willing to pay $P = \$60/.03 = \$2000$ today for that particular asset.

4.7 Summary

In Chapter 4 we have studied the time value of money. We have learned how to convert lump sums and periodic sums of money to equivalent values. Lump sums—present or future—can be converted to equivalent periodic streams. Likewise, periodic streams of income can be converted to equivalent lump sums (present or future). Nonuniform periodic streams can be converted to equivalent lump sums (present or future). And then these lump sums can be converted to uniform periodic streams. Thus two or more nonuniform periodic streams of revenue can be standardized and compared. Finally, interest can be compounded once per year or continuously—an infinite number of times per year. Effective annual interest rates can be computed and infinite income streams can be evaluated.

After having studied Chapter 4, one should be able to convert money values to either of the alternative forms which may be encountered in actual practice.

SOME ILLUSTRATIVE EXAMPLES

The purpose of this appendix is to illustrate the methods and concepts presented in Chapter 4. Five examples are presented.

A. Calculation of Total Wealth

Suppose you are to receive two lump sums of money—$1000 today and another $1000 10 years from today. How much is the total offer worth?

Answer: The worth of the offer today (or as of any other time, past or future) depends upon the interest rate and the frequency of compounding. If interest is 10 percent, compounded annually, then from the tables of compound interest factors, we find that $1000 10 years hence is worth only $385.53 today because that amount, put on deposit and left alone, will accumulate to $1000 in 10 years. Therefore the offer is worth $1000 plus $385.53 today.

Alternatively, using future values, the $1000 received today can be deposited to accumulate to a total of $1000(2.59386) or $2594 as of 10 years hence. So, assuming that the $1000 received today is deposited at 10 percent for 10 years, the offer is worth $1000 plus $2594 or $3594 as of 10 years hence.

The example illustrates that evaluation and comparison of dollar sums can be made as of any particular point in time—past, present, or future. However, no matter when the time, all dollars must be as of the *same* time. The computations are mechanical. The interpretation (the reason for performing the calculations) is far from mechanical. The interpretation is that alternative proposals for investment can always be evaluated in the context of the ever-present certain opportunity to receive at least the time value of money on the investment.

B. Present Worth of a Bond

Two questions are generally asked when a bond is purchased: (1) "How much should be paid for the bond?" and (2) "What will be the rate of return on the investment (i.e., the yield to maturity) if the bond is purchased at the quoted market price and held to maturity?"

The answer to the first question depends on the time value of money. What rate of interest can be received if, instead of purchasing the bond, the money is put to its more profitable alternative use?[14]

---

[14] For comparisons to be valid, alternative uses of money must be in the same risk class. Risk is discussed in Chapter 6.

If you have the opportunity to invest in a 6 percent savings account or else a bond with a face value of $1000 which pays 4 percent and is due to mature in 8 years, then the "fair" price to pay for the bond may be computed as follows.

Assuming that the 4 percent coupon is paid and reinvested (at 6 percent) twice each year, then

$$P = \frac{(c/m)F}{(1 + i/m)^1} + \frac{(c/m)F}{(1 + i/m)^2} + \cdots + \frac{(c/m)F}{(1 + i/m)^{mn}} + \frac{S}{(1 + i/m)^{mn}}$$

(4.42)

where

P = price paid for bond = unknown

F = face value or principal to be paid upon maturity of the bond = $1000

S = Sum to be realized upon sale or disposition of the bond = $1000

c = coupon (interest) rate specified in the bond = .04

m = number of interest payments per year = 2

n = number of years to maturity of the bond or redemption before maturity, measured from the date of purchase = 8

i = rate of return on the purchase price = opportunity rate of profit = .06

Thus,

$$P = \frac{\$20}{(1 + .06/2)^1} + \frac{\$20}{(1 + .06/2)^2}$$

$$+ \cdots + \frac{\$20}{(1 + .06/2)^{16}} + \frac{\$1000}{(1 + .06/2)^{16}}$$

$$= \$20(12.5611) + \$1000(.6232)$$ **(4.43)**

$$= \$874.39$$

To illustrate the fact that the stream of interest income from the bond, every 6 months for a period of 8 years, plus the $1000 to be received upon maturity, is worth only $874.39 today, consider the listing in Table 4.7. The student should work out the problem the alternative way (i.e., compound the periodic $20 to the future at 6 percent and then convert that future lump sum to the present). Observe that if the opportunity rate of profit had been higher than 6 percent, the present worth of the bond would be less than $874.39 because reinvestment of each $20 at 10 percent instead of 6 percent would cause the income stream to grow at a faster rate. The lesson here is that the present worth of a bond depends upon what opportunity rate of profit is assumed for reinvestment of the future income.

102   Concepts and Methods Fundamental to Financial Analysis

Table 4.7   PRESENT VALUE OF A BOND

At the end of	Interest paid ($)	Factor for present value	Amount of present value ($)
6 months	20	.9709	19.42
1 year	20	.9426	18.85
$1\frac{1}{2}$ years	20	.9151	18.30
2 years	20	.8885	17.77
$2\frac{1}{2}$ years	20	.8626	17.25
3 years	20	.8375	16.75
$3\frac{1}{2}$ years	20	.8131	16.26
4 years	20	.7894	15.79
$4\frac{1}{2}$ years	20	.7664	15.33
5 years	20	.7441	14.88
$5\frac{1}{2}$ years	20	.7224	14.45
6 years	20	.7014	14.03
$6\frac{1}{2}$ years	20	.6810	13.62
7 years	20	.6611	13.22
$7\frac{1}{2}$ years	20	.6419	12.84
8 years	20	.6232	12.46
Principal amount at maturity	1000	.6232	623.27
			874.49

To illustrate this example further, if interest had been paid and reinvested annually instead of semiannually, the present value of the bond would be

$$P = \$40/(1 + .06)^1 + \$40/(1 + .06)^2$$
$$+ \$40/(1 + .06)^3 + \cdots + \$40/(1 + .06)^8 + \$1000/(1 + .06)^8$$
$$= \$40(6.2098) + \$1000(.6274) \qquad (4.44)$$
$$= \$875.79$$

The movement of bond prices is almost always opposite to the movement of interest rates. Because of compound interest and the time value of money, income to be received at some future date must be discounted to calculate its present worth. Thus, because the purchase of a bond entitles the owner to periodic income at dates some time in the future, the present worth of the bond can be written as equation (4.42).

Observe that equation (4.42) is based solely on the time value of money. To assume that the current market price equals the present worth as defined in equation (4.42) implicitly assumes that the market can absorb any quantity of purchases and sales of these bonds without influencing the quoted price. Restated, direct use of the model (4.42) assumes that schedules of supply and demand in bond markets are perfectly elastic. If these assumptions are violated, then the present value model as expressed in equation (4.42) must be augmented to account for sloping schedules of demand and supply. Also, equation (4.42) omits *explicit* consideration of risk, even though some scholars might include risk implicitly in *i*, calling *i* a "risk-adjusted rate of discount." In the context of analysis in this text, however, we shall reserve the use of *i* to mean default-free yield and shall use *k* to mean risk-adjusted yield.

Both of the assumptions—perfectly elastic schedules of demand and supply and risk-free securities—may be tenable if we limit the analysis to long-term bonds issued by the U.S. Government which are purchased and held to maturity. The federal government is not likely to default on either interest or principal.

For a given bond, the face value (F), the coupon rate (c), the number of interest payments per year (m), and the number of years to maturity (n), as expressed in equation (4.42), are all specified and contractual. Each of these values may be taken as a known constant by the investor. From the viewpoint of the *issuer* of the bonds, however, these values are not given and constant, but must be calculated. This leaves P, S, and i. Consider S next. If there is no chance for default, as many investors are willing to assume in the case of bonds issued by the U.S. Government, the principal amount of the loan is virtually guaranteed to be repaid upon maturity. Under these conditions, if the bond is held to maturity, S will always equal F. This leaves P and i, bond price and yield to maturity. These two factors vary inversely with one another. As yields rise, prices decline. In the limit, if n equals infinity (e.g., the bond never matures, such as a British Consol), then equation (4.42) simplifies to

$$P = R/(i/m) \qquad \textbf{(4.45)}$$

where

$P =$ present worth of a future periodic revenue stream
$R =$ periodic future revenue to be received forever
$i =$ rate of interest
$m =$ number of times per year i is compounded

We see that price varies directly with the number of times per year interest is compounded and the coupon rate of interest varies inversely with the opportunity rate of return on risk-free investments.

C. Change in Present Worth of a Bond when the Rate of Profit on Reinvestment Changes: Same Maturity Dates

Holding the date of maturity constant, this case illustrates the effect on the market value of a bond when there is a change in the rate of discount.

Suppose a $1000 bond pays 4 percent and is due to mature in 15 years. (1) How much should you be willing to pay for the bond today if your goal is to realize 3 percent on your investment? (2) How much would you pay for the same bond if you needed to realize 10 percent on your investment? Interest is compounded semiannually.

Answers:

$$P = \frac{\frac{1}{2}(.04)\$1000}{(1 + .03/2)^1} + \frac{\frac{1}{2}(.04)\$1000}{(1 + .03/2)^2}$$
$$+ \cdots + \frac{\frac{1}{2}(.04)\$1000}{(1 + .03/2)^{30}} + \frac{\$1000}{(1 + .03/2)^{30}}$$
$$= \sum_{t=1}^{30} \frac{\$20}{(1.015)^t} + \frac{\$1000}{(1.015)^{30}} \tag{4.46}$$
$$= \$20(24.0158) + \$1000(.6398)$$
$$= \$1480.96$$

$$P = \frac{\frac{1}{2}(.04)\$1000}{(1 + .10/2)^1} + \frac{\frac{1}{2}(.04)\$1000}{(1 + .10/2)^2}$$
$$+ \cdots + \frac{\frac{1}{2}(.04)\$1000}{(1 + .10/2)^{30}} + \frac{\$1000}{(1 + .10/2)^{30}}$$
$$= \sum_{t=1}^{30} \frac{\$20}{(1.05)^t} + \frac{\$1000}{(1.05)^{30}} \tag{4.47}$$
$$= \$20(15.3725) + \$1000(.2314)$$
$$= \$538.83$$

Note: If the required rate of profit on investment (i.e., the rate of discount) is less than the coupon payments [e.g., in part (1), 3 percent is less than 4 percent], then a prudent investor would be willing to pay a price higher than the face value of the bond. That is, in this case, the bond is worth more than the face value. Note also that if the required rate of profit on investment is greater than the coupon payments [e.g., in part (2), 10 percent is greater than 4 percent], then the bond is worth less than the face value. Holding other things constant,[15] bond prices vary inversely with the time value of money. This fundamental point will be discussed in greater detail in Chapter 7.

D. Change in Present Worth of a Bond when the Rate of Profit on Reinvestment Changes: Different Maturity Dates

Consider three different 4 percent, $1000 bonds. Suppose that these three bonds have maturity dates 5 years, 10 years, and 30 years

[15] "Holding other things constant" is a phrase used frequently by economists for the purpose of examining the effects on a dependent variable by letting one explanatory variable change. In this context, the "other things" include risk class, date of maturity, supply, demand, and all other such factors which interact to determine ultimate price.

hence, respectively. Then calculate the present worth of each of the bonds assuming interest rates obtainable from equivalent risk class investment instruments are (1) 6 percent, (2) 8 percent, and (3) 4 percent.

Using the same formula as previously, we get

$$P = \sum_{mn=1}^{mt=J} \frac{(i)(1/m)(F)}{(1 + r/m)^{mn}} + \frac{F}{(1 + r/m)^{mt}} \tag{4.48}$$

$$= A_1 + A_2$$

where $J = 5$, 10, and 30 years, respectively, for each different bond, and other symbols are the same as defined previously.

Table 4.8 PRESENT VALUE VS. YIELD AND LENGTH OF TIME TO MATURITY

1. $r = 4$ percent, $i = 4$ percent, $m = 1$, $F = \$1000$

Bond	r	J	A_1 (\$)	+	A_2 (\$)	=	P (\$)	
1	.04	5	178.07		821.93		1000.00	
2	.04	10	324.44		675.56		1000.00	(4.49)
3	.04	30	691.68		308.32		1000.00	

2. $r = 6$ percent, $i = 4$ percent, $m = 1$, $F = \$1000$

Bond	r	J	A_1 (\$)	+	A_2 (\$)	=	P (\$)	
1	.06	5	168.50		747.26		915.75	
2	.06	10	294.40		558.40		852.80	(4.50)
3	.06	30	550.59		174.11		724.70	

3. $r = 8$ percent, $i = 4$ percent, $m = 1$, $F = \$1000$

Bond	r	J	A_1 (\$)	+	A_2 (\$)	=	P (\$)	
1	.08	5	159.71		680.58		840.29	
2	.08	10	268.40		463.19		731.60	(4.51)
3	.08	30	450.31		99.38		549.69	

The solutions are shown in Table 4.8. The following conclusions can be drawn from the solutions:

1. When the discount rate equals the coupon rate, bonds of all maturities (Solution 1 in Table 4.8) sell at face value. When the discount rate exceeds the coupon rate, then bonds sell below face value. The reader should verify that, if the discount rate is less than the coupon rate, the bonds sell above face value.
2. For a *decline* in discount rate (e.g., from .06 to .04, or a drop of $(.06 - .04)/.06$ equals $33\frac{1}{3}$ percent, the present values of the short-term, medium-term, and long-term bonds increased by 9.33 percent, 17.48 percent, and 38.27 percent, respectively. In terms of percentage, the rise in price for long-term bonds is greater than the corresponding rise for medium- to short-term bonds.

3. Similarly, for a *rise* in interest rates (e.g., from .06 to .08 in Solutions 2 and 3 above), the present values of the short-term, medium-term, and long-term bonds decreased by 8.41 percent, 14.45 percent, and 24.30 percent, respectively. As before, the percentage drop in price was much greater for long-term bonds than was the corresponding percentage drop in price for medium- to short-term bonds.

These are general characteristics of bonds with different maturity classes. For a given change in the market rate of discount, the corresponding change in price is greater for long-term bonds than for short-term bonds. In other words, as interest rates change in the aggregate economy, one would expect greater volatility in prices for long-term debt than in prices for short-term debt. Prices of 91-day treasury bills should be less sensitive to changes in interest rates than, for example, 30-year bonds.

E. Effect of a Change in the Period for Compounding

Using the same three bonds as in Section D one can show that a change in the compounding periods, e.g., from once per year to twice per year, will have little effect on the present value of the various maturities. Thus, we get results as tabulated in Table 4.9.

Table 4.9   PRESENT VALUE VS. PERIOD OF COMPOUNDING

1. $r = 4$ percent, $i = 4$ percent, $m = 2$, $F = \$1000$

Bond	r	J	A_1 ($)	+	A_2 ($)	=	P ($)	
1	.04	10	179.65		820.35		1000.00	
2	.04	20	327.03		672.97		1000.00	**(4.54)**
3	.04	60	695.22		304.78		1000.00	

2. $r = 6$ percent, $i = 4$ percent, $m = 2$, $F = \$1000$

Bond	r	J	A_1 ($)	A_2 ($)	P ($)	
1	.06	10	170.60	744.09	914.70	
2	.06	20	297.55	533.68	851.23	**(4.55)**
3	.06	60	553.51	169.73	723.24	

3. $r = 8$ percent, $i = 4$ percent, $m = 2$, $F = \$1000$

Bond	r	J	A_1 ($)	A_2 ($)	P ($)	
1	.08	10	162.22	675.56	837.78	
2	.08	20	271.81	456.39	728.19	**(4.56)**
3	.08	60	452.47	95.06	547.53	

To illustrate operation of the bond model, if

$$F = S = \$1000, \; i = 4 \text{ percent}, \; m = 2, \; n = 8, \text{ and } r = 6 \text{ percent}$$

$$\textbf{(4.52)}$$

then

$$P = \frac{\$20}{(1 + .06/2)^1} + \frac{\$20}{(1 + .06/2)^2}$$

$$+ \cdots + \frac{\$20}{(1 + .06/2)^{16}} + \frac{\$1000}{(1 + .06/2)^{16}}$$

$$= (\$20) \sum_{t=1}^{16} \frac{1}{(1.03)^t} + (\$1000) \frac{1}{(1.03)^{16}} \qquad (4.53)$$

$$= \$20(12.5611) + \$1000(.6232)$$

$$= \$251.2220 + \$623.20$$

$$= \$874.42$$

That is, assuming no restrictions or limitations on availability of either bonds or money, a rational investor would be willing to pay the present worth, $874.42, for the bond illustrated above. At the price of $874.42, the investor will be compensated at the rate of $r = 6$ percent of his investment. This 6 percent is the total compensation for use of the $874.42. It accounts for both risk and the time value of money. If either money or bonds (or both) become scarce, then additional and more powerful factors (supply and demand) enter the analysis. For simplicity, we shall assume that bonds can be purchased or sold in any quantity at the calculated present value. We recognize that a universally complete model would consider time, risk, demand, supply, investor preferences, and several other dimensions of complexity simultaneously. For purposes here, it is sufficient to focus attention on a few factors as a starting point and build up gradually to greater complexity.

Observe from the mathematical calculations, using the concept of time value of money, that it is possible to carry the arithmetic out to as many decimal places as one has the patience. However, more decimal places must not *under any circumstances* be interpreted to mean more accuracy.

In such an analysis, all the other factors which we hold constant (i.e., risk, demand, supply) interact with the time value of money to determine price. Therefore, all factors considered, any particular numerical value obtained using only time value of money as the criterion, as in the examples above, must necessarily be regarded as only an approximation (sometimes not a very close approximation) to actual observed market price. Hence, it may be pointless to carry the computations to fractions of a penny.

QUESTIONS FOR STUDY

1. $1000 invested 10 years ago at interest compounded semiannually now amounts to $2000.

    (a) What is the "nominal" annual interest rate? (*Ans.* 7.05 percent)

    (b) What is the "effective" annual interest rate? (*Ans.* 7.18 percent)

2. An investor owns a building on which there is a $100,000 mortgage which earns 6 percent per annum. The mortgage is to be paid for in 20 equal year-end payments. After making 8 payments, the investor wants to reduce his annual fixed charges by refinancing the balance of the debt with a 30-year mortgage at 5 percent, also to be retired by annual payments. By how much would the annual charges be reduced? (*Ans.* $3961)

3. Maintenance cost on a piece of equipment is $400 per year. What expenditure for a new machine is justified if no maintenance is required for the first five years, $100 per year for the next 10 years, and $400 per year thereafter? Assume money to cost 6 percent (*Ans.* $3335.02)

4. A company is licensed to manufacture a patented item on which the patent has 7 years to run. The company makes 7500 items per year and pays the inventor $100 per year, plus 5 cents per item. The inventor offers to sell the patent for $3000. If a return of 6 percent is desired on the investment, will it pay the company to buy the patent? (*Ans.* No. Present worth of the annual payments is less than $3000.)

5. What is the effective annual interest rate if 6 percent interest is compounded monthly? (*Ans.* 6.17 percent)

6. At what interest rate must a man invest $75.87 a year in order to have a balance of $1000 after his tenth payment? (*Ans.* 6 percent)

7. How long will it take money to double at 15 percent interest? (*Ans.* Approximately 5 years)

Chapter 4 presented some of the basic tools needed to compare alternative sums of money. Special attention was devoted to sums of money received at different points in time. In Chapter 5, we shall continue to study the time value of money. However, the emphasis will shift now to concepts and methods of analysis which will show how these methods can be used to improve the quality and, therefore, profitability of investment decisions.

Conditions of certainty are still assumed. We continue to recognize that the final investment decision depends at all times upon risk as well as upon potential or actual profit. But since one factor must be introduced at a time, in this chapter we shall assume risk to be zero and focus attention exclusively on investment returns. Here, all opportunities for investment under condition of certainty have cash flows which are

Analysis for Asset Selection Under Conditions of Certainty

5

known for certain. There is no doubt that the anticipated future income will be forthcoming.

The formal models and methods of analysis under conditions of certainty all focus attention on a single factor—profitability of the investment. To assess the investment merit of an available asset, we need to measure the profitability of investing in that asset. The greater the profitability, the more desirable the asset and vice versa. If money is guaranteed to be lost on the deal, the opportunity for investment is unequivocally rejected.

Under these conditions (in the absence of risk), the criterion for selection between alternative assets is to choose the most profitable asset.[1] Stated in more formal language, since the objective is to maximize wealth, choose that asset which will add the most (or make the largest contribution) to present wealth. In the absence of risk, this goal can be

---

[1] In the presence of risk, the goal is achieved by *diversifying*, using methods discussed in Chapter 13.

achieved by choosing that single asset which has the highest expected incremental return on investment.

To translate the theoretical objective stated above into workable methods of analysis, we can use any of four methods, depending upon the particular opportunity being analyzed. The models (methods) used for the formulation and measurement of expected profitability of investment under conditions of certainty are

1. Net present value (NPV)
2. Equivalent uniform net annual revenue (UAR)
3. Internal rate of return (IRR)
4. Fisher's rate of return over cost

As with any model or method of analysis, there are advantages and disadvantages. No single model or method may explain or accomplish everything. A part of being a superior analyst is the ability to use the right tool at the right time.

In the following sections we shall study each of the four methods for the analysis of investment opportunities under conditions of certainty. During the study, the reader should continually criticize and compare the different methods. Examples and illustrations are given to make the analysis clearer.

5.1 Criterion of Net Present Worth

Net present value (NPV), net present worth (NPW), and discounted cash flow (DCF) have the same meaning. The measure consists of calculating the total profit anticipated from investment in an income-producing asset. All dollar values and cash flows are evaluated as of the present time.

Net present value expresses the difference between total revenues (total dollar inflows) and total costs (total dollar outlays) evaluated as of the present point in time. The criterion is as follows. If the total dollar inflows exceed the total dollar outflows, the net present value of the investment is positive, indicating that the project is profitable and should be accepted. The larger the magnitude of net present value, the more profitable the investment. Hence an array of alternative investments can be ranked according to their net present value.

Alternatively, if the total dollar outflows (costs) exceed the total dollar inflows (revenues), then the net present value is negative (or at best, zero), indicating that losses (or at best, break even) will occur if the opportunity is accepted. If net present value is negative the investment is rejected on the grounds that losses on investment are undesirable.

Because the calculation of net present value requires all lump sums of money to be converted to equivalent present values, the notion of time value of money as discussed previously is critical to understanding net present value. Equation (5.1) is the general formula used for computing the present value of future stream of periodic revenue:

$$P = \frac{Y_1}{(1 + k)^1} + \frac{Y_2}{(1 + k)^2} + \cdots + \frac{Y_n}{(1 + k)^n} + \frac{S}{(1 + k)^n} \quad (5.1)$$

where

P = present dollar value of the future income

Y_i = anticipated future income forthcoming as of the end of the interest payment period (assumed to be known)

k = rate of discount of income stream (Y)

S = sale price or net revenue forthcoming upon disposition of the asset (assumed to be known)

n = number of years the asset is held (assumed to be known)

This formula is derived in the same way as was (4.27). For simplicity but without loss of generality, annual compounding is assumed in (5.1). To calculate net present value, the present dollar value (P) of the future periodic revenue stream is calculated first. Then this present worth of all expected revenues is compared with the present worth of all cash outlays. The difference between present value of revenues and present value of costs is the net present value of the investment.

For calculation of present value, the rate of discount (k) must be known in advance. All cash flows, Y_i, and terminal value (S), are assumed to be known. To illustrate the importance of these factors and to show how the criterion of net present value can be applied in actual situations, three specific examples are presented below.

5.2 Calculation of Net Present Worth of an Investment

SITUATION 1: Different Opportunity Rates of Profit. Consider the purchase of a particular asset where the present cost is $1000 and the expected net annual receipts are as shown in Figure 5.1. The particular asset is of secondary importance. The asset may be a machine, a building, or a negotiable security. Of importance is the stream of cash

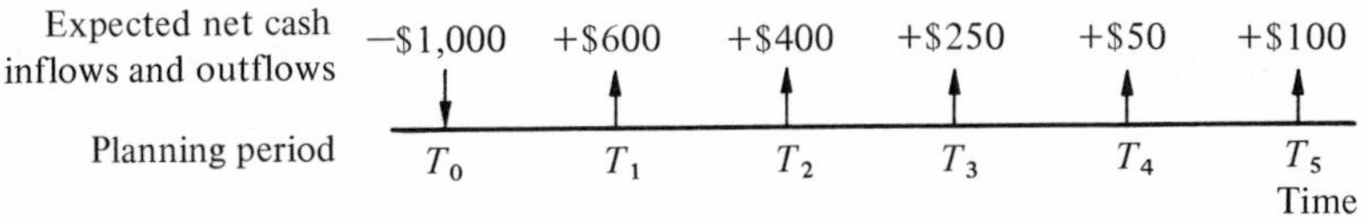

Figure 5.1. Expected costs and revenues associated with an asset. The $100 return at the end of t_5 includes a sales value of $50.

flow associated with the asset. The investment merit of the proposed asset can be calculated by applying the criterion of net present value. Now we can proceed to analyze the stream of cash flow.

Observe from equation (5.1) that to calculate equivalent present values of future revenue, the appropriate rate (or rates) of discount must be known in advance. To use the net present value method of analysis, the rate (or rates) of discount must always be known (i.e., estimated or determined in some manner) before hand. For the case at hand, let us consider the appropriate rate to be the same as the rate obtainable on an insured savings account.[2] Since k is an "opportunity rate of profit" or an "opportunity cost" incurred because of foregoing some alternative investment, use of the rate obtainable on an insured savings account can be justified. The assumption inherent in this selection for the value of k is that the asset and the savings account both have equal risks.

If a savings account pays 5 percent, then the present value of the future stream of revenue generated by the asset can be calculated and compared with the $1000 present outlay necessary to purchase the asset. The computational procedure is outlined below:

$$\begin{aligned}
\text{PV}_{\text{revenues}} &= \frac{\$600}{(1 + .05)} + \frac{\$400}{(1 + .05)^2} + \frac{\$250}{(1 + .05)^3} \\
&\quad + \frac{\$50}{(1 + .05)^4} + \frac{\$100}{(1 + .05)^5} \qquad \textbf{(5.2)} \\
&= \$571.43 \quad + \$362.81 \quad + \$215.96 \\
&\qquad\qquad\quad + \$41.14 \quad + \$78.35 \\
&= \$1269.69
\end{aligned}$$

$$\begin{aligned}
\text{NPV} &= \text{Inflows minus outflows} \\
&= \$1269.69 - \$1000.00 = \$269.69 \qquad \textbf{(5.3)}
\end{aligned}$$

Since the revenues exceed the costs by $269.69 (all evaluated as of the present point in time), the asset promises to be a profitable investment.

To standardize the results of the calculation, the present values can be expressed as an index:

$$I = \frac{\text{PV}_{\text{revenue}}}{\text{PV}_{\text{investment}}} = \frac{\$1269.69}{\$1000.00} = 1.27 \qquad \textbf{(5.4)}$$

USE OF FUTURE VALUES.   Alternatively, the analysis can cast all dollar sums as *future* values (or indexes thereof), instead of calculating net *present* values (and indexes thereof). The basic requirement is that all

---

[2] By using an insured savings account as the alternative, we avoid the complexities of considering risk at this time.

dollar sums be evaluated as of the *same point* in time (present *or* future). Thus

$$
\begin{aligned}
FV_{revenues} &= \$600(1 + .05)^4 + \$400(1 + .05)^3 + \$250(1 + .05)^2 \\
&\quad + \$50(1 + .05)^1 + \$100 \\
&= \$729.30 + \$463.05 + \$275.63 + \$52.50 \qquad (5.5) \\
&\quad + \$100 \\
&= \$1620.48
\end{aligned}
$$

$$
\begin{aligned}
FV_{investment} &= \$1000(1 + .05)^5 \\
&= \$1000(1.27628) \qquad\qquad\qquad (5.6) \\
&= \$1276.28
\end{aligned}
$$

$$
\begin{aligned}
NFV &= \$1620.48 - \$1276.28 \\
&= \$344.20
\end{aligned} \qquad\qquad (5.7)
$$

USE OF INDEXES OF PROFITABILITY.   The present value of revenues and costs (advantages vs. disadvantages) can be expressed as an index. Thus we can write

$$
I = \frac{FV_{revenues}}{FV_{investment}} = \frac{\$1620.48}{\$1276.28} = 1.27 \qquad\qquad (5.8)
$$

One can conclude from this analysis that because the net *present* value (or, alternatively, the net *future* value) is positive (i.e., the total income exceeds the total outlay), the asset promises to be a profitable investment. The investment decision, therefore, is to purchase the asset.

The decision to purchase the asset is equivalent to saying that investment of $1000 in the asset is more profitable than investment of $1000 in the reference alternative of a 5 percent savings account. By purchasing the asset, the investor ends up (presently) with $269.69 more than he would have had by placing his money in the savings account. The analysis assumes equal risks between the asset and the savings account.

UNIFORM PERPETUAL ANNUITY.   In theory, the comparison can continue over infinite time. At the end of the fifth year (i.e., at the end of the life span of the asset), the total proceeds can be reinvested for an infinite period of time, at the market rate of return. However, in this particular illustration, further analysis is not necessary, since the asset is expected to generate more wealth than the alternative savings account as of the end of the fifth year. Beyond the fifth year, the implicit assumption is that the savings account will be the only available investment opportunity because the asset will have been scrapped.

ALTERNATIVE RATES OF DISCOUNT.   The next important point to consider is that, other things equal, the final decision for investment depends upon the assumed opportunity rate of profit. For example, if a higher rate of discount had been used instead of 5 percent, the final decision might have been to not purchase the asset. To illustrate, if one has the opportunity to invest in a project expected to yield 20 percent over the next 5 years,[3] then, instead of using a discount rate of 5 percent, the appropriate rate of discount is now 20 percent. Then the present value, net present value, and index of profitability are all calculated as follows:

$$PV_{revenues} = \frac{\$600}{(1 + .20)} + \frac{\$400}{(1 + .20)^2} + \frac{\$250}{(1 + .20)^3}$$
$$+ \frac{\$50}{(1 + .20)^4} + \frac{\$100}{(1 + .20)^5} \qquad (5.9)$$
$$= \$500.00 + \$277.78 + \$144.68$$
$$+ \$24.11 + \$40.19$$
$$= \$936.75$$

$$NPV = \$986.75 - \$1000.00 = -\$13.25 \qquad (5.10)$$

$$I = \frac{PV_{revenues}}{PV_{investment}} = \frac{\$986.75}{\$1000.00} = .99 \qquad (5.11)$$

The conclusion now is that because the net present value of the proposed project is negative (i.e., the total outlay *exceeds* the present value of the expected income), the asset promises to be an unprofitable investment (relative to the alternative which is expected to yield 20 percent over the life of the asset) and should be rejected. Instead of purchasing the asset, the $1000 should be invested in the alternative project.

The lesson to be learned here is that the net present value of a proposed project (i.e., the expected profitability of the investment) varies inversely with the opportunity rate of profit. The higher the rate of profit obtainable from alternative investment projects (e.g. $k = 20$ percent instead of $k = 5$ percent), the smaller becomes the net present value (and the attractiveness) of any particular investment proposal.

SITUATION 2: Different Timing of Cash Flows. This example illustrates the criterion of net present value, assuming alternative investments with different timing and different life spans.

Observe from Situation 1 above that for comparing alternative projects, identical time durations were assumed for the investment and alternative projects. If two investment projects have different life spans, then returns available from reinvestment during the non-overlapping intervals of time must be considered; otherwise logical errors will result.

---

[3] Unless stated otherwise, equal risk and annual compounding are assumed.

To illustrate, suppose the alternative reference project from Situation 1 promises to pay 20 percent for only 3 years instead of 5 years. Suppose also that as of the end of 3 years, the best alternative investment for comparison is the 5 percent savings account. Using these assumptions, the timing considerations for analysis of the proposed investment in the machine may be as shown in Table 5.1.

Then the present value of future income from the asset is calculated using an opportunity rate of 20 percent for the first 3 years, and 5 percent thereafter:

$$PV_{revenues} = \frac{\$600}{(1.20)} + \frac{\$400}{(1 + .20)^2} + \frac{\$250}{(1 + .20)^3} + \frac{\$50}{(1 + .05)(1 + .20)^3}$$

$$+ \frac{\$100}{(1 + .05)^2(1 + .20)^3} \qquad (5.12)$$

$$= \$500 + \$277.78 + \$144.68 + \$27.56 + \$52.49$$

$$= \$1002.50$$

The $600, $400, and $250 are discounted at the rate of 20 percent per year, assuming that money invested today can earn 20 percent for a maximum of 3 years. After 3 years, only 5 percent can be obtained. Hence the $50 and $100 are discounted at 20 percent for 3 years each and then at the rate of 5 percent for 1 year and 2 years, respectively.

$$NPV = \$1002.50 - \$1000.00 = \$2.50 \qquad (5.13)$$

or, expressed as an index,

$$I = \frac{PV_{revenues}}{PV_{investment}} = \frac{\$1002.50}{\$1000.00} = 1.0025 \qquad (5.14)$$

The conclusion now is that the asset should be purchased, because it promises to be slightly more profitable than the combination of available alternatives.

Net future values can be used in the analysis. The preceding computations can be illustrated by using net future values instead of net present values, and the following equations can be written:

$$FV_{revenues} = \$600(1 + .20)^2(1 + .05)^2 + \$400(1 + .20)(1 + .05)^2$$
$$+ \$250(1 + .05)^2 + \$50(1 + .05)^1 + \$100$$

$$= \$952.56 + \$529.20 + \$275.63 + \$52.50 + \$100.00$$

$$= \$1909.89 \qquad (5.15)$$

$$FV_{investment} = \$1000(1 + .20)^3(1 + .05)^2$$
$$= \$1000(1.728)(1.1025) \qquad (5.16)$$
$$= \$1905.12$$

Table 5.1 AN INVESTMENT PROPOSAL AND THE OPPORTUNITY RATE OF PROFIT

Time	T_0	T_1	T_2	T_3	T_4	T_5	T_6	T_7
Machine	−$1000	+$600	+$400	+$250	+$50	+$100	$0	$0
Reference opportunity for investment	−$1000 ⟵———	$k = .20$	————⟶ ⟵	$k = .05$	———⟶ ⟵	+$100 ———⟶ ⟵	$k = .05$	⟶

By using net future values, the assumption is that $1000 can be invested at a 20 percent rate of return for 3 years and then at a 5 percent rate of return for 2 years to yield a future value of $1905.12. Similarly, $600, $400, $250, and $50 are assumed to earn 20 percent whenever possible and then 5 percent. The $100 is received at the end of the fifth year and earns no interest:

$$\text{NFV} = \$1909.89 - \$1905.12 = \$4.77 \qquad (5.17)$$

To standardize the results of the calculations, the future values can be stated as an index:

$$I = \frac{\text{FV}_{\text{revenues}}}{\text{FV}_{\text{investment}}} = \frac{\$1909.89}{\$1905.12} = 1.0025 \qquad (5.18)$$

One can conclude from the above analysis that under the conditions assumed, since the net present (or net future) value of expected revenues from operation of the asset is slightly positive, the asset should be purchased. Indications are that the increase in wealth of the investor is slightly greater by investing in the asset for 5 years instead of investing in the alternative opportunity at a 20 percent rate of return for 3 years and then a 5 percent savings account for the remaining 2 years.

SITUATION 3: Tradeoffs. This example illustrates how the criterion of net present value can be applied in a personal situation which involves tradeoffs between some money at one point in time or more money at a later point in time.

Suppose a wealthy relative offered to help finance a college education for your son. Instead of a gift today, however, suppose the relative offered you a choice. He will give you either $3000 3 years from now or $5000 5 years from now. Which alternative will you select?

One way to start toward the "correct" decision is to focus on alternative opportunities that will be available during the interim time after one proposal has reached maturity and the other opportunity is still continuing. Thus, the relative desirability of $5000 5 years from now vs. $3000 3 years from now depends upon (among other things) the rate of return obtainable on the $3000 if invested for 2 years. In other words—and this is a crucial point of theory—comparisons are valid between projects if and only if the projects are converted to the same point in time.

To illustrate, suppose that you choose the $3000 3 years from now and invest that amount immediately upon receipt, for a duration of 2 years. Then, if that investment returns more than 29 percent on average for those 2 years (ceteris paribus), the $3000 choice is worth more than the $5000 alternative. That is, indifference between the two offers exists when the forward 2-year rate for money is approximately 29 percent:[4]

$$\$3000(1 + r_4)(1 + r_5) = \$5000 \qquad (5.19)$$

$$\$3000(1 + r_{av})^2 = \$5000 \qquad (5.20)$$

$$\begin{aligned} r &= (\$5000/\$3000)^{1/2} - 1 \\ &= .29 \end{aligned} \qquad (5.21)$$

The decision, therefore, depends upon expectations regarding obtainable future rates of profit. If more than 29 percent can be obtained, then choose the $3000 3 years from now. If less than 29 percent can be obtained, then choose the $5000 5 years from now. If precisely 29 percent can be obtained, then choose either alternative.[5]

Observe that the required average rate of 29 percent can be obtained in a variety of ways. Thus, given a specified return for either of the 2 years, the required return for the other year may be calculated. For example, if r_4 is 10 percent, then r_5 must be approximately 51 percent. The 51 percent is calculated as follows.

$$(1 + r_4)(1 + r_5) = (1.29)^2 \qquad (5.22)$$

$$\begin{aligned} r_5 &= [(1.29)^2/(1 + r_4)] - 1 \\ &= (1.666/1.10) - 1 \\ &= .514 \end{aligned} \qquad (5.23)$$

These calculations are pertinent to the analysis of forward interest rates and to the management of bond portfolios as discussed in later chapters.

5.3 Criterion of Equivalent Uniform Net Annual Cash Revenues

Instead of calculating net present (or net future) value as illustrated in the preceding examples, we can calculate equivalent uniform annual net cash revenues for each proposed project. Instead of converting all dollar sums to equivalent lump sum values as of the present time (as shown in situation 1), the given nonuniform annual revenues

---

[4] A "forward rate" is defined as the interest rate today for money to be delivered (or invested) at some future date for a specified period of time. By way of comparison, a "spot rate" is defined as the rate today for money to be delivered (or invested) today. In either case, the time duration of the investment is specified. The starting or delivery date is the identifying feature.

[5] At 29 percent, a prudent investor might still prefer the $3000 3 years hence to avoid risks and uncertainties concomitant with those last 2 years. Your author's own personal choice is to ask for the $5000 now!

can be converted to either (1) equivalent uniform dollar values to be received over the life of the investment project (i.e., 5 years) or (2) equivalent uniform annuities to be received forever. Each of these two possibilities is discussed in Situations 4 and 5.

SITUATION 4: Equivalent Uniform Net Annual Revenue over the Life of the Projects.   First, the appropriate opportunity rate (or rates) of discount must be estimated. The estimation of an appropriate rate can proceed as follows.

What alternative use can be made of the $1000 during the time interval under consideration? Under the conditions assumed to exist, if $1000 is deposited in an account which receives 20 percent per year for 3 years and then 5 percent per year for 2 years, the value of the account at the end of the fifth year will be $1905.12.

$$\$1000(1 + .20)^3(1 + .05)^2 = \$1905.12 \qquad (5.24)$$

The *average* rate of return on the reference account over the 5-year span is approximately 13.8 percent. The calculations are shown below:

$$PV = \frac{FV}{(1 + k)^5} \qquad (5.25)$$

$$(1 + k) = \sqrt[5]{\frac{\$1905.20}{\$1000.00}} = [(1.20)^3(1.05)^2]^{1/5} = 1.13759 \qquad (5.26)$$

$$k = .13759 \qquad (5.27)$$

In other words, $1000 invested at 13.8 percent for 5 years is approximately equivalent to $1000 invested at 20 percent for 3 years and then at 5 percent for 2 years.

Using an average rate of return of 13.8 percent, one can proceed to the next step in the analysis and calculate that $1000 today is equivalent to a uniform income of approximately $291.28 per year for a 5-year time span (refer to section 4.5 in Chapter 4). These computations are listed below in equations (5.78) and (5.29). For convenience, 13.8 percent is rounded to 14 percent.

$$\$1000 = \frac{R}{1 + .14} + \frac{R}{(1 + .14)^2} + \frac{R}{(1 + .14)^3}$$

$$+ \frac{R}{(1 + .14)^4} + \frac{R}{(1 + .14)^5}$$

$$= \$R \sum_{n=1}^{5} \frac{1}{(1 + .14)^n} \qquad (5.28)$$

$$= \$R(.8772 + .7695 + .6750 + .5921 + .5194)$$

$$= \$R(3.4331)$$

$$R = \frac{\$1000}{3.4331} = \$291.28 \qquad (5.29)$$

The $291.28 is the uniform annual net cash revenue that can be obtained if the $1000 is invested in the reference project. The opportunity to purchase this income annuity must be compared with the opportunity to purchase an income annuity that would be forthcoming if the $1000 were used to purchase the available asset.

Next, consider investment in the asset. If the $1000 is invested in the asset, then a revenue stream of $600, $400, $250, $50, and $100 is anticipated during years 1 through 5, respectively. Computations outlined in equations (5.30), (5.31), and (5.32) below show that this revenue stream is equivalent to a uniform income of $292.01 per year, each year during the 5-year time interval. On the basis of uniform annual revenue, therefore, the asset promises to offer 73 cents per year more than the reference alternative 5-year investment. The decision is to purchase the asset. The asset promises to be slightly more profitable than the next best alternative use of the $1000.

$$\frac{\$600}{(1 + .20)} + \frac{\$400}{(1 + .20)^2} + \frac{\$250}{(1 + .20)^3} + \frac{\$50}{(1 + .05)(1 + .20)^3}$$
$$+ \frac{\$100}{(1 + .05)^2(1 + .20)^3} \tag{5.30}$$

$$= \frac{R}{1 + .14} + \frac{R}{(1 + .14)^2} + \frac{R}{(1 + .14)^3} + \frac{R}{(1 + .14)^4} + \frac{R}{(1 + .14)^5}$$

$$\$1002.50 = \$R(3.4331) \tag{5.31}$$

$$R = \frac{\$1002.50}{3.4331} = \$292.01 \tag{5.32}$$

SITUATION 5: Equivalent Uniform Net Annual Revenue over an Infinite Span of Time.   On the basis of an infinite annuity, if $1000 is deposited into an account which receives 20 percent per year for 3 years and then 5 percent per year for the remaining time, then the equivalent uniform annual income can be calculated as follows:

$$\$1000 = \frac{R}{(1 + .20)} + \frac{R}{(1 + .20)^2} + \frac{R}{(1 + .20)^3}$$
$$+ \frac{R}{(1 + .20)^3(1 + .05)} \tag{5.33}$$
$$+ \cdots + \frac{R}{(1 + .20)^3(1 + .05)^n}$$

Verbally, equation (5.33) states that R, the periodic annual income, when discounted as per the rules for compound interest, has a present value equal to $1000. Restated, if $1000 is deposited in a savings account today at interest of 20 percent per year for the next 3 years and then 5 percent per year thereafter, then R dollars can be withdrawn from the the account at the end of each year, *forever.*

Next, equation (5.33) must be examined to make sure that a realistic solution exists. When n is sufficiently large, $1/[(1.20)^3(1 + .05)^n]$ is sufficiently small so that the last term in the series is negligible. Stated mathematically, the infinite series *converges*, so that a finite sum is obtained. For example, if n equals 500, then $1/[(1.20)^3(1 + .05)^{500}]$ = 4.39435×10^{-11} or .0000000000439435, which, for many practical investment purposes, equals zero.

Thus, each successive term on the right-hand side of equation (5.33) can be added to the previous sum. Eventually, each new term will add a negligible amount to the previous sum. In this way, a unique solution can be obtained for R.

$$\$1000 = R\left[\sum_{t=1}^{3} \frac{1}{(1.20)^t} + \sum_{n=1}^{500} \frac{1}{(1.20)^3(1.05)^n}\right]$$

$$\$1000 = R\left[.8333 + .6944 + .5787 + \sum_{n=1}^{500} \frac{1}{(1.20)^3(1.05)^n}\right]$$

(5.34)

$$= R(2.1065 + 34.5600)$$
$$= R(36.6665)$$

$$R = \$1000/36.6665 = \underline{\underline{\$27.27}} \qquad (5.35)$$

Note: The reader should verify for himself that $1000 deposited today in a savings account which pays the stated interest rates is equivalent to an annual annuity of $27.27 forever.

Next, consider the asset. To assess the investment merit of the asset, the equivalent uniform annuity forthcoming from investing the $1000 in the asset can be calculated. The comparisons and computations are outlined below.

If the $1000 is used to purchase the asset, and the cash flows from the asset are reinvested, then at the end of the fifth year the balance of the account is $1909.89. The calculation is as follows:

$$600(1.20)^2(1.05)^2 + \$400(1.20)(1.05)^2 + \$250(1.05)^2$$
$$+ \$50(1.05) + \$100 = \$1909.89 \qquad (5.36)$$

As of this time (i.e., the end of the fifth year) the $1909.89 can be used to purchase an annuity of $95.50 per year for an infinite time interval. The calculations for this annuity are shown below:

$$\$1909.89 = \frac{R}{(1.05)} + \frac{R}{(1.05)^2} + \cdots + \frac{R}{(1 + .05)^n}$$

$$= R\left[\sum_{n=1}^{500} \frac{1}{(1.05)^n}\right] = 20.00R \qquad (5.37)$$

$$R = \frac{\$1909.89}{20.00} = \$95.50 \qquad (5.38)$$

Under the reinvestment conditions assumed, an annuity of $95.50 per year which begins at the end of 5 years hence, is equivalent to an annuity of $27.34 per year which begins at the end of the current year. These calculations are shown in equations (5.39), (5.40), and (5.41) below.

First, calculate the present value of $1909.89 to be received 5 years hence.

$$PV = \frac{\$1909.89}{(1.20)^3(1.05)^2} + \$1002.50 \tag{5.39}$$

Second, calculate an infinite annuity based on a present lump sum of $1002.50. Assuming 500 years (periods of compounding) to be sufficiently close to infinity, we get

$$\$1002.50 = R\left[\sum_{t=1}^{3} \frac{1}{(1.20)^t} + \sum_{n=1}^{500} \frac{1}{(1.20)^3(1.05)^n}\right] \tag{5.40}$$

$$= R(36.6665)$$

$$R = \frac{\$1002.50}{39.6665} = \$27.34 \tag{5.41}$$

Therefore, on the basis of uniform annual annuity for an infinite interval of time, investment in the asset promises to offer $27.34 − $27.27 or 7 cents per year more than the available reference alternative.

5.4 The Importance of Timing of Cash Flows

Observe that if the timing of the cash flows from the asset under consideration had been different, then the investment decision might have been different. For example, if instead of a cash flows timing as shown previously in Table 5.1, suppose the cash flows are reversed as depicted in Table 5.2, where the final lump sum received during T_5 includes the $50 sale price. In this case, the result of the analysis is not to purchase the asset. The analysis is presented below:

$$\begin{aligned} PV_{\text{revenues}} &= \frac{\$50}{(1 + .20)} + \frac{\$50}{(1 + .20)^2} + \frac{\$250}{(1 + .20)^3} \\ &\quad + \frac{\$400}{(1 + .05)(1 + .20)^3} + \frac{\$650}{(1 + .05)^2(1 + .20)^3} \\ &= \$41.67 + \$34.72 + \$144.68 + \$220.46 + \$341.19 \\ &= \$782.71 \end{aligned} \tag{5.42}$$

As before, the $50, $50, and $250 each are discounted at the rate of 20 percent per year under the assumption that money invested today can earn 20 percent during the next 3 years. After 3 years, however, only

Table 5.2 TIMING OF CASH FLOWS AND THE OPPORTUNITY RATE OF PROFIT

Time	T_0	T_1	T_2	T_3	T_4	T_5	T_6	T_7
Machine	−$1000	$50	$50	$250	$400	$650	$0	$0
Alternative investment opportunity	−$1000							$0

$$k = .20 \qquad k = .05 \qquad k = .05$$

5 percent can be obtained. The $400 and $650 are discounted at 20 percent for 3 years each and then at 5 percent for 1 year and 2 years, respectively.

$$NPV = \$782.71 - \$1000.00 = -\$217.29 \qquad (5.43)$$

Or, expressed as an index,

$$I = \frac{PV_{revenues}}{PV_{investment}} = \frac{\$782.71}{\$1000.00} = .783 \qquad (5.44)$$

The conclusion is that, since the net present value is negative, the cost exceeds the revenues. The asset should *not* be purchased. Instead, the reference alternative opportunity should be accepted because it promises larger profits.

5.5 Criterion of Internal Rate of Return

Computationally, internal rate of return is similar to net present value. Both methods use the same formula, equation (5.1). Instead of assuming a value for k and using this value to calculate P, a known value for P is given and then (5.1) is solved for k. Equation (5.1), therefore, is the general form useful in calculating either net present value or internal rate of return. Conceptually, however, internal rate of return is quite different from net present value. There are two ways to view internal rate of return. Both ways yield identical results.

First, instead of denoting total dollars of net profit (as does the net present value criterion), internal rate of return denotes total profits expressed as a percent of total investment outlays. As the name implies, IRR measures the average *rate* of return received on a total outlay (P). All dollar sums in the various cash flows are discounted (or compounded) to the same point in time (usually the present).

To illustrate the first view of IRR as an average rate of return received on investment, consider this elementary case. If a government bond is purchased today for $1000 and sold 1 year hence at the face value of $1000, then after receiving interest income of $60, the internal rate of return (the average rate of return on the total investment of $1000) is 6 percent. The $60 profit equals the rate of return multiplied by total present value of the investment outlays.

$$\$1000 = \$1060/(1 + k) \qquad (5.45)$$

$$k = (\$1060/\$1000) - 1 = .06 \qquad (5.46)$$

The second way to view internal rate of return is to equate IRR with the required rate of interest on a savings account—to view the cash outlays associated with the proposed investment as lump sum deposits into a savings account. Then view the cash revenues (receipts) from the investment project as withdrawals from that savings account. Then the internal rate of return is the rate of interest on a savings account required to provide a balance in the account (i.e., after all deposits and withdrawals) of precisely zero as of the end of the time period under consideration. Other things being equal, the higher the rate of interest, the larger the withdrawals for a given lump sum deposit and the more desirable the account. Ceteris paribus, larger IRR's are superior to smaller IRR's.

To illustrate this second view of IRR, consider the same bond as above. Instead of investing the $1000 in the bond, if the $1000 were to be deposited into a savings account, then what is the rate of interest required on the account to permit the owner to withdraw a total of $1060 (coupon plus face value) as of 1 year hence? The answer, 6 percent, is the required return. The calculations are

$$\$1000(1 + k)^1 = \$1060 \tag{5.47}$$

$$\begin{aligned} k &= (\$1060/\$1000) - 1 \\ &= .06 \end{aligned} \tag{5.48}$$

5.6 Calculation of Internal Rate of Return

The following five examples will show the proper application of IRR criterion to the evaluation of alternative projects for investment.

SITUATION 6: Calculation of Internal Rate of Return: Evaluation of an Asset.   Refer to the original set of cash flows and timing hypothesized in Figure 5.1. The internal rate of return method requires computation of the required discount rate which will equate the present value of all expected cash outlays with the present value of all expected cash revenues. Using the expected cash flow from Figure 5.1, we get

$$\$1000 = \frac{\$600}{(1 + k)} + \frac{\$400}{(1 + k)^2} + \frac{\$250}{(1 + k)^3} + \frac{\$50}{(1 + k)^4} + \frac{\$100}{(1 + k)^5} \tag{5.49}$$

The (internal) rate of return of investment in the asset therefore is that value of k which will equate the right-hand side of equation (5.49) with the left-hand side. In theory, the solution of the equation for k is straightforward. In practice the solution can be obtained with the aid of a computer.

To gain insight into the possible behavior of k, consider equation (5.49) in detail. This equation shows that if $k = 0$, then $600 + $400 + $250 + $50 + $100 = $1400. Thus, at one extreme, under conditions of zero return, the anticipated revenues exceed the expected cost by \$400. At the other extreme, if k exceeds zero by a very large amount, the present value of the anticipated revenues will not necessarily exceed the present value of the expected cost. For example, if k equals infinity, then all future sums of money are worthless today. As k varies from zero up to very large values, the right-hand side of equation (5.49) varies from \$1400 down to zero. At some (unique?) value for k, the equation must balance.

Table 5.3   RATE OF DISCOUNT VS. NET
PRESENT VALUE

$$\$1000 = \frac{\$600}{(1+k)} + \frac{\$400}{(1+k)^2} + \frac{\$250}{(1+k)^3} + \frac{\$50}{(1+k)^4} + \frac{\$100}{(1+k)^5}$$

k (%)	Revenue (\$)	Cost (\$)	Net (\$)
0	1400.00	1000	400.00
2	1345.05	1000	345.05
4	1293.93	1000	293.93
6	1246.27	1000	245.27
8	1201.76	1000	201.76
10	1160.10	1000	160.11
12	1121.06	1000	121.06
14	1084.39	1000	84.39
16	1049.90	1000	49.90
18	1017.41	1000	17.41
20	986.75	1000	−13.25
22	957.80	1000	−42.21
24	930.40	1000	−69.60
26	904.45	1000	−95.56
28	879.83	1000	−120.17
30	856.46	1000	−143.54
32	834.23	1000	−165.77
34	813.08	1000	−186.92
36	792.93	1000	−207.06
38	773.72	1000	−226.28
40	755.37	1000	−244.63

Some relevant relationships between k and net present value, for k varying between 0 percent and 40 percent, are shown in Table 5.3. From Table 5.3, for values of k between 18 percent and 20 percent the net present value of the investment project will equal zero. By trial and error (or by interpolation), the precise value of k can be calculated to be approximately 19.13 percent. For all values of k larger than 19.13 percent, the cost of the proposed investment will exceed the expected revenues. For all values of k smaller than 19.13 percent, the expected revenues will exceed the cost. The internal rate of return on investment in the asset, therefore, is 19.13 per cent.

SITUATION 7: Internal Rate of Return: Replacement of an Existing Oil Pump. Consider the possible replacement of an existing oil pump used to pump oil out of the ground.[6] Suppose that the existing pump can, without additional costs, provide revenues of $10,000 each year for the next 2 years and nothing thereafter. However, a new pump can operate faster than the existing pump and, for a present outlay of $1600, will produce revenues of $20,000 next year, after which time the oil will be depleted.

Decision: Should the new pump be purchased for a present cost of $1600 or should the existing pump be kept?

Solution: The correct solution using the criterion of internal rate of return requires correct formulation of the problem. Blind adherence to mathematical formulae can lead to wrong (or at best, ambiguous) conclusions.

To formulate the alternatives properly, let us apply the second interpretation of IRR. That is, recognize that the alternative use of the $1600 present outlay is a savings account. Then the analysis can proceed as follows.

STEP 1. Present outlay = $1600; return at the end of the first year = $20,000. This return is withdrawn and reinvested at some rate say (k_2) so that the total dollar sum at the end of the second year = $20,000 $(1 + k_2)$.

Section 5.2 instructs that projects with different life spans require standardization. The two different life spans can be standardized by taking either the longer of the two times or an infinite time for both. In either case, appropriate opportunity rates of profit must be assumed. In this instance, the simpler of the two standards is to compare both cash flows over a 2-year period. The assumed rate of profit on the reinvested $20,000 is k_2.

STEP 2. Opportunity use. Deposit $1600 in a savings account which pays a rate of interest (k_1). At the end of the first year, the balance of the account is interest and principal amounting to [1600(1 + k_1)$]. Also at that time $10,000 is received from operations of the existing pump. The total amount [$10,000 + 1600(1 + k_1)$] is reinvested (i.e., allowed to collect interest at the same rate k_1, so that at the end of the second year, the balance in the account is [$10,000$(1 + k_1)$ + 1600(1 + k_1)^2$]. Also, the account contains the final deposit of $10,000 which is received from the second year of operations of the existing pump.

---

[6] Many readers will recognize this as the celebrated "Lorie-Savage pump problem." See James Lorie and L. J. Savage, "Three Problems in Capital Rationing," *Journal of Business*, October 1955.

STEP 3. The internal rate of return on the $1600 investment is that rate of interest on the savings account required to provide a balance of precisely zero in the account if [$20,000(1 + k_2)] is withdrawn. Stated completely

$$\$20{,}000(1 + k_2) = \$10{,}000 + \$10{,}000(1 + k_1) + \$1600(1 + k_1)^2 \tag{5.50}$$

which reduces to

$$.16(1 + k_1)^2 + (1 + k_1) + 1 - 2(1 + k_2) = 0 \qquad \textbf{(5.51)}$$

Note that the resulting solution is quadratic in $(1 + k_1)$ (i.e., $n = 2$), implying that two solutions are possible. In the general case of equation (5.51), n can range anywhere from zero to infinity which implies a possible multiplicity of solutions. However, when the problem is formulated in terms of interest rates obtainable on a savings account, then the solutions have financial meaning. Negative and/or imaginary roots of the nth order equation are ignored.

Thus, using the standard quadratic formula to solve for $(1 + k_1)$ from (5.51) we get

$$
\begin{aligned}
(1 + k_1) &= \{-1 \pm [1 - 4(.16)(1 - 2 - 2k_2)]^{1/2}\}/2(.16) \\
&= [-1 \pm (1.64 + 1.28\,k_2)^{1/2}]/.32
\end{aligned}
\tag{5.52}
$$

Equation (5.52) shows that the rate of return on the $1600 investment varies directly with k_2, the rate of profit obtainable from reinvestment of the proceeds forthcoming from the new pump. If $20,000 is allowed to remain idle (i.e., not reinvested), then k_2 equals zero and a loss of approximately 12.19 percent is incurred.

$$
\begin{aligned}
(1 + k_1) &= (-1 + \sqrt{1.64})/.32 = (-1 + 1.281)/.32 \\
&= .8781
\end{aligned}
\tag{5.53}
$$

$$k_1 = .8781 - 1.000 = -.1219 \qquad \textbf{(5.54)}$$

Alternatively, if k_2 equals 10 percent, then the internal rate of return is approximately 121.6 percent.

$$
\begin{aligned}
(1 + k_1) &= (-1 + \sqrt{2.92})/.32 = (-1 + 1.709)/.32 \\
&= 2.216 \\
k_1 &= 2.216 - 1.000 = 1.216
\end{aligned}
\tag{5.55}
$$

For all positive rates of reinvestment of the 20,000, there is a unique IRR.

Observe the ambiguity and error that occur upon failure to show explicitly how the rate of return on investment depends upon the rate of profit assumed to be obtainable for future investable cash flows. If one assumes incorrectly that the rate of profit on reinvestment of the $20,000 is equal to the IRR of the $1600 outlay, then k_2 equals k_1 and we get[7]

$$1600(1 + k_1)^2 - 10,000(1 + k_1) + 10,000 = 0 \qquad (5.56)$$

$$(1 + k_1) = \frac{1 \pm \sqrt{1 - 4(.16)(1)}}{2(.16)} = \frac{1 \pm \sqrt{.36}}{.32} \qquad (5.57)$$

$$= \frac{1 \pm .6}{.32} = 5.00; \ 1.25$$

Two different apparently valid values of k will satisfy equations (5.57).

$$k_{1A} = 400 \ \text{percent}; \qquad k_{1B} = 25 \ \text{percent} \qquad (5.58)$$

Neither solution in (5.58) has financial meaning.[8] Such ambiguities can be avoided if reference is made to the savings account concept as shown previously in (5.50) through (5.55).

In summary, the above illustration pointed out several important ideas concerning IRR: (1) the internal rate of return method requires assumptions regarding rates of profit obtained on future cash revenues; (2) when more than two time intervals are included in the analysis, the computations can get tedious (there now exist computer algorithms and canned routines for solution); and (3) the internal rate of return is expressed as a percent of total investment and therefore can be misleading if used alone (e.g., 5 percent on $10,000,000 provides more dollars and therefore may be preferable to 5000 percent on $1.00).

SITUATION 8: Internal Rate of Return and the Timing of Cash Flows. As noted in Section 5.3, the time pattern of future cash flows is important for calculating the profitability of prospective investments. The timing of cash flows is equally important if IRR is used as the measure of profitability.

To illustrate the importance of timing to the investment decision using IRR, reconsider the example used in Section 5.3. But this time, instead of basing the investment decision on the net present value criterion, use the criterion of internal rate of return.

---

[7] This assumption is incorrect because we are solving for the IRR. The rate of profit (k_2) depends on the 1-year opportunities for investment available in the marketplace as of time T_1, not the IRR of the current project or $1600 outlay.

[8] See Ezra Solomon, "The Arithmetic of Capital Budgeting Decisions," *Journal of Business*, April 1956.

Using a present outlay of $1000 and revenue stream of $50, $50, $250, $400, and $650, respectively, as indicated previously in Table 5.2, we can write

$$\$1000 = \frac{\$50}{(1+k)} + \frac{\$50}{(1+k)^2} + \frac{\$250}{(1+k)^3} + \frac{\$400}{(1+k)^4} + \frac{\$650}{(1+k)^5}$$

$$(5.59)$$

As a question, equation (5.59) means, What must be the rate of interest if $50 to be received 1 year hence, plus another $50 to be received 2 years hence, plus $250 to be received at the end of 3 years hence,...all added together are equivalent to $1000 today? That rate of interest is the internal rate of return. Solution of equation (5.59) will provide that rate of return.

To solve equation (5.59) for the internal rate of return, one of several procedures may be used. Since equation (5.59) is a fifth-order equation, there exist five possible values of k which will provide a solution.[9] To show that equation (5.59) is in fact a fifth-order equation, one can rearrange it into the standard mathematical form for an equation and simultaneously use the standard convention of denoting dollar outlays by minus and cash revenues by plus. Thus, equation (5.59) can be written as

$$-\$1000(1+k)^5 + \$50(1+k)^4 + \$50(1+k)^3$$
$$+ \$250(1+k)^2 + \$400(1+k) + \$650 = 0$$

$$(5.60)$$

The relationships between alternative values for k and the net present values for this time pattern of cash flows is tabulated in Table 5.4. Observe from Table 5.4 that the present value of the revenue stream precisely equals the present value of the investment outlay if the rate of discount is between 8 percent and 10 percent. The precise value for k in this case is 8.64 percent.

An analytical solution for k from equation (5.60) can be obtained using a digital computer. Thus, if we use the General Electric Company Time Sharing Computer System Program, ROOTER***, we obtain the following five answers.

1. One positive real root:

$$(1+k) = 1.0864; \qquad k = 8.64 \text{ percent} \qquad (5.61)$$

---

[9] In general cases, an equation has as many solutions (i.e., roots) as the highest power of the variable. Thus, a quadratic equation has two roots, a cubic equation has three roots, a fourth-order equation has four roots, etc. However, not all the roots are required to be positive and/or real. Some roots can involve the square root of minus one and are therefore imaginary.

Table 5.4 RATE OF DISCOUNT VS. NET
PRESENT VALUE—DIFFERENT
TIMING

$$\$1000 = \frac{\$50}{(1 + k)} + \frac{\$50}{(1 + k)^2} + \frac{\$250}{(1 + k)^3}$$
$$+ \frac{\$400}{(1 + k)^4} + \frac{\$650}{(1 + k)^5}$$

k (%)	Revenue ($)	Cost ($)	Net ($)
0	1400.00	1000	400.00
2	1290.92	1000	290.92
4	1192.73	1000	192.73
6	1104.13	1000	104.13
8	1024.01	1000	24.01
10	951.41	1000	−48.59
12	885.48	1000	−114.52
14	825.50	1000	−174.50
16	770.82	1000	−229.18
18	720.88	1000	−279.12
20	675.19	1000	−324.81
22	633.31	1000	−366.69
24	594.87	1000	−405.13
26	559.53	1000	−440.47
28	526.98	1000	−473.02
30	496.95	1000	−503.05
32	469.22	1000	−530.78
34	443.57	1000	−556.42
36	419.82	1000	−580.19
38	397.78	1000	−602.22
40	377.31	1000	−622.69

2. Two pairs of complex conjugate (i.e., imaginary) roots:

$$(1 + k) = -.690739 \pm J(.482699) \quad \text{and}$$
$$(1 + k) = \quad .172538 \pm J(.90154)$$

(5.62)

Since only the positive real roots have significance in the financial
world, the internal rate of return is determined as 8.64 percent. This
answer agrees with the tabulations in Table 5.4.

To complete the analysis and arrive at an investment decision, the
calculated IRR of 8.64 percent must be compared with the opportunity
rate of profit on the $1000 investment. The original example in Section
5.3 stipulated that the alternative investment opportunity was assumed
able to provide a 20 percent return for the first 3 years and then a 5
percent return thereafter. Over a time span of 5 years, then, the average
opportunity rate of profit is expected to be 13.8 percent, and since the

IRR is less than that opportunity rate of profit, the decision is to reject the offer to purchase the machine.

$$[(1 + .20)^3(1.05)^2]^{1/5} = 1.13759 \tag{5.63}$$

Observe that a different timing pattern for the opportunity rate of profit can conceivably alter the decision. Thus, if the timing pattern for the opportunity rate of profit had been 5 percent for the first 2 years and 20 percent thereafter, then, without altering the average return of 13.8 percent over a 5-year time span, investment projects having higher cash flows near the end of the life of the project will be penalized less than they would in the case just illustrated. The student should work out an example to demonstrate this important fact. This principle will be used again later in the analysis of bond portfolios.

SITUATION 9: IRR and Cash Flows Involving Net Outlays: Multiple Roots. This example shows how the nonthoughtful discounting of future cash flows can lead to a wrong formulation of the internal rate of return.

Reconsider the cash flows from Situation 8. This time instead of having a *positive* cash flow of $650 at the termination of the project, let there be a *negative* net cash flow of $650 (e.g., suppose there are outlays such as the cost of contract termination, severance pay, and removal of equipment). Also, for purposes of the example, suppose the third receipt is anticipated to be $1250 instead of $250. Then, under these conditions, one might incorrectly formulate the internal rate of return for the project:

$$\$1000 = \frac{\$50}{(1 + k)} + \frac{\$50}{(1 + k)^2} + \frac{\$1250}{(1 + k)^3} + \frac{\$400}{(1 + k)^4} - \frac{\$650}{(1 + k)^5} \tag{5.64}$$

Mechanical solution of equation (5.64) indicates the following five roots.[10]

Three real roots—k_1, k_2, and k_3:

$$\begin{aligned}
(1 + k_1) &= 1.04637; & k_1 &= +4.64 \text{ percent} \\
(1 + k_2) &= .615312; & k_2 &= -38.47 \text{ percent} \\
(1 + k_3) &= -.754814; & k_3 &= -175.48 \text{ percent}
\end{aligned} \tag{5.65}$$

and one pair of complex conjugate (i.e., imaginary) roots—k_4 and k_5:

$$(1 + k) = -.428437 \pm J(1.07421) \tag{5.66}$$

---

[10] The solutions for all examples in this section were obtained by using the General Electric Time Sharing Computer System Program, ROOTER***.

Although the mathematics might be correct, the solution, $k_1 = 4.64$ percent, is incomplete from a financial viewpoint. The error in the formulation of (5.64) is conceptual. The $650 project termination cost should not be discounted as shown. Instead, the investment proposal should be viewed as follows:

1. The required cash outlays are $1000 today and $650 5 years from today.
2. The net cash revenues are $50, $50, $1250, and $400 as of the end of years 1, 2, 3, and 4, respectively.

The present value of the cash outlays depends upon the lump sum required today in order to have $650 at the end of 5 years, which, in turn, depends upon the opportunity rate of profit obtainable over the next 5 years. Thus, if the opportunity rate of profit over the next 5 years is assumed to be some value (r), then $650 5 years hence is equivalent to $650/(1 + r)^5$ today. In the particular case when r equals 6 percent, then $650 5 years hence is equivalent to $485.72 today.

$$\text{PV} = \$650/(1.06)^5 = \$485.72 \tag{5.67}$$

In this case, the present worth of the cash outlays associated with the proposed investment is $1000.00 + $485.72, or $1485.72. In general, the present worth of the cash outlays is as indicated in equation (5.68).

$$\text{PV}_{\text{outflows}} = \$1000 + [\$650/(1 + r)^5] \tag{5.68}$$

Then the internal rate of return equals that unique rate of interest on a savings account such that a lump sum of $1000 + [\$650/(1 + r)^5]$ deposited today will precisely permit withdrawals of $50, $50, $1250, and $400 at the end of each year, respectively, for the next 4 years. Withdrawal of the $400 will leave an account balance of zero. One may then write (by inspection) either of the following:

$$\left[\$1000 + \frac{\$650}{(1 + r)^5}\right] = \frac{\$50}{(1 + k)} + \frac{\$50}{(1 + k)^2} + \frac{\$1250}{(1 + k)^3} + \frac{\$400}{(1 + k)^4} \tag{5.69}$$

$$-\left[\$1000 + \frac{\$650}{(1 + r)^5}\right](1 + k)^4 + \$50(1 + k)^3 + \$50(1 + k)^2 \tag{5.70}$$
$$+ \$1250(1 + k) + \$400 = 0$$

Both equations are identical. They both show how the reinvestment assumption influences the IRR. In fact, the final solution for k must be in terms of r.

For purposes of analysis, two critical points can be examined:

1. If $r = 0$, then equation (5.70) reduces to equation (5.71) and the solution is $k = 1.89$ percent.

$$- \$1650(1 + k)^4 + \$50(1 + k)^3 + \$50(1 + k)^2 \tag{5.71}$$
$$+ \$1250(1 + k) + \$400 = 0$$

The four roots are

$$1.01892 \quad \text{and} \quad -.310404$$
$$-.339106 + J(.807157) \quad \text{and} \quad -.339106 - J(.807157)$$

$$(5.72)$$

2. If r equals infinity, then equation (5.70) reduces to equation (5.73) and the solution is $k = 19.7$ percent.

$$- \$1000(1 + k)^4 + \$50(1 + k)^3 + \$50(1 + k)^2$$
$$+ \$1250(1 + k) + \$400 = 0 \qquad (5.73)$$

The four roots are

$$1.19713 \quad \text{and} \quad -.314855$$
$$-.416139 + J(.942365) \quad \text{and} \quad -.416139 - J(.942365)$$

$$(8.74)$$

Note that if the error of assuming $r = k$ is made, then the solution is identical with the first incomplete formulation made at the beginning of the example. That is, if $r = k$, then equation (5.70) reduces to equation (5.75) and the solution is $k = 4.6$ percent.

$$-[\$1000(1 + k)^5 + \$650] + \$50(1 + k)^4 + \$50(1 + k)^3$$
$$+ \$1250(1 + k)^2 \qquad (5.75)$$
$$+ \$400(1 + k)^1 = 0$$

The five roots are

$$1.04637$$
$$.615312 \quad \text{and} \quad -.754814 \qquad (5.76)$$
$$-.428437 + J(1.07421) \quad \text{and} \quad -.428437 - J(1.07421)$$

Hence $k = 4.6$ per cent is a "correct" solution, but only under the assumption that 4.6 percent is the appropriate opportunity rate of discount for the $650.

Recall the definition that IRR is the same as the rate of interest received on a savings account so that a periodic sum (R) can be withdrawn at the end of each time period during the life of the project. This definition of internal rate of return means that a lump sum of $1000 can be deposited today and the stated cash flows can be withdrawn at the end of each year. At the end of the fifth year, a payment of precisely $650 will restore the balance of the account to zero. The cash flows in the account are tabulated in Table 5.5. Observe that this time pattern is equivalent to depositing $1000 today and withdrawing an equal amount of $228.66 each year for the next 5 years, or else $279.64 each year for the next 4 years. These results are tabulated in Table 5.5.

The internal rate of return can also be viewed as that rate of interest received on a savings account so that a periodic sum can be deposited (not withdrawn) at the end of each year during the life of the project.

This view of IRR means that $228.66 can be deposited as of the end of each year (or, deposits of $50, $50, $1250, and $400 and a withdrawal of $650, respectively) at an interest rate of 4.637 percent, and the account balance is precisely the future value of $1000.00 compounded at 4.63 percent. The student should work out these tabulations for himself.

Table 5.5 ANALOGY FOR INTERNAL RATE OF RETURN

Savings Account Deposit and Subsequent Withdrawal
(IRR = 4.637 percent)

Year	Principal ($)	Interest ($)	Deposit or withdrawal ($)	Balance ($)
		1. Nonuniform withdrawals and deposits		
1	1000.00	46.37	−50.00	996.37
2	996.37	46.20	−50.00	992.57
3	992.57	46.03	−1250.00	−211.40
4	−211.40	−9.80	−400.00	−621.21
5	−621.21	−28.81	+650.00	.01
		2. Uniform withdrawals for 5 years		
1	1000.00	46.37	228.66	817.71
2	817.71	37.92	228.66	627.00
3	627.00	29.07	228.66	427.37
4	427.37	19.82	228.66	218.53
5	218.53	10.13	228.66	.00
		3. Uniform withdrawals for 4 years		
1	1000.00	46.37	279.64	766.73
2	766.73	35.55	279.64	522.65
3	522.65	24.24	279.64	267.25
4	267.25	12.39	279.64	.00

In conclusion, for the particular timing of a stream of cash flows as stated in (5.64), the rate of return on the $1000 investment can be any amount between the limits 1.8 percent and 19.7 percent, depending upon how much an outlay of $650, to be made 5 years hence, is worth today. The final investment decision depends upon the rate of profit assumed to be available on interim cash flows.

SITUATION 10: Internal Rate of Return and the Opportunity Rate of Profit on Reinvestable Funds. In Situation 9, the final investment decision clearly depended upon the present worth of $650 5 years from now. Actually, another assumption was also implicit in the solution. The assumption is that the net cash flows received during the life of the project can in fact be reinvested at the internal rate of return. In practice, this may not always be true. The realities of investment may require reinvestment of the interim cash flows *not* at the internal rate, but instead at the market rate, which may be smaller (or larger) than the internal rate. That the internal rate of return depends upon the assumed rate of reinvestment can be illustrated as follows.

Consider the four cash flows associated with solution 2 in Situation 9, equation (5.73). That is, assume an infinite rate of discount for the future $650 outlay so that the inflow stream will consist of $50, $50, $1250, and $400, respectively, as of the end of each year for the next 4 years. Now suppose that there are three separate investment accounts paying 5 percent, 8 percent, and 6 percent, respectively. Now, if the income from the asset is deposited in these accounts, we can have, as of the end of the fourth year, a total of $1841.20.

$$
\begin{aligned}
\text{Account 1:} \quad & \$50(1 + .05)^3 && = \$57.88 \\
\text{Account 2:} \quad & \$50(1 + .08)^2 && = \$58.32 \\
\text{Account 3:} \quad & \$1250(1 + .06) && = \$1325.00 \\
& \text{Final Receipt} && = \$400.00 \\
\text{Total future value of the cash revenues} && = \$1841.20
\end{aligned}
$$

Then, the internal rate of return, by definition, is that rate of interest obtained on a savings account so that a deposit now ($1000 in this case) will grow to a future lump sum ($1841.20 in this case) during the time interval under consideration (4 years). Hence, with the reinvestment patterns hypothesized, the internal rate of return on the $1000 is approximately 16.5 percent, which is less than the 19.7 percent calculated using the implicit assumption of reinvestment at the internal rate.

$$\$1000(1 + k)^4 = \$1841.20 \tag{5.77}$$

$$1 + k = (\$1841.20/\$1000)^{1/4} \tag{5.78}$$

$$k = \sqrt[4]{1.84120} - 1 = .164864 \tag{5.79}$$

The internal rate of return method of analysis assumes that net cash flows received over the life of the project can be reinvested at the internal rate. This implicit assumption is often violated in the real world of economic and financial opportunities.

We see that individual investment projects can be analyzed and selected tentatively as potentially acceptable or classified as definitely not profitable on the basis of internal rate of return. Highly profitable investments will have a higher internal rate of return because, ceteris paribus, the larger the stream of net cash revenues, the larger the rate of discount required to equate the future revenues with the present outlays. Thus, when analyzing and selecting mutually exclusive investment projects with cash flows independent of one another, each potential investment can be ranked by its internal rate of return. This ranking indicates the ordering of expected profitability of the investment. Further analysis, as discussed in subsequent chapters, is required prior to the final decision of investing money.

5.7 Fisher's Marginal Rate of Return Over Cost

Fisher's rate of return over cost is a concept used to analyze two alternative investment options both at the same time and both relative to "the market rate of return." Fisher's measure is the difference in net present worth of the two investment options when each option is discounted at the same (market) rate of return. The rate which sets this difference equal to zero is defined as Fisher's marginal rate of return over cost.[11]

Fisher's concept for comparing two streams of cash flow in the manner described above can be expressed quantitatively:

$$\frac{(R_1 - R_2)_{t=0}}{(1 + k)^0} + \frac{(R_1 - R_2)_{t=1}}{(1 + k)^1} + \cdots + \frac{(R_1 - R_2)_{t=n}}{(1 + k)^n} = 0 \quad \textbf{(5.80)}$$

where

$(R_1 - R_2)_{t=i}$ = difference between net cash flows between two projects as of time period i

k = marginal rate of return over cost or "surplus of advantages over disadvantages"

The concept is illustrated below.

SITUATION 11: Comparison Between Two Alternative Investment Proposals. Suppose two available assets each require an immediate outlay of $1000. Suppose that asset 1 yields a receipt stream of $400 per year for the next 5 years, while asset 2 yields $100, $200, $400, $600, and $800, respectively, during the same 5-year span. Then the investment decision requires selection of either asset 1 or asset 2.

Proceed with the analysis using Fisher's marginal rate of return over cost as the decision criterion. Thus, the surplus of advantages over disadvantages for asset 1 vs. 2 can be calculated to be approximately

---

[11] See (1) Irving Fisher, *The Theory of Interest*, Kelley: New York, 1930, and reissued by Kelly and Millman, New York, 1954; (2) Armen A. Alchian, "The Rate of Interest, Fisher's Rate of Return over Costs and Keynes' Internal Rate of Return," *The American Economic Review*, December 1955; and (3) J. M. Keynes, *The General Theory of Employment Interest and Money*, Harcourt Brace & World: New York, 1936.

5.74 percent. Computations are shown in the equations below. The solution, 5.7 percent, is obtained from the final equation:

$$\frac{(\$400 - \$100)}{1 + k} + \frac{(\$400 - \$200)}{(1 + k)^2} + \frac{(\$400 - \$400)}{(1 + k)^3} + \frac{(\$400 - \$600)}{(1 + k)^4}$$

$$+ \frac{(\$400 - \$800)}{(1 + k)^5} + (\$1000 - \$1000) = 0 \qquad (5.81)$$

$$\$300(1 + k)^4 + \$200(1 + k)^3 + \$0(1 + k)^2 - \$200(1 + k)$$
$$- \$400 + \$0(1 + k)^5 = 0 \qquad (5.82)$$

$$3(1 + k)^4 + 2(1 + k)^3 - 2(1 + k) - 4 = 0 \qquad (5.83)$$

The four roots of equation (5.83) are

$$(1 + k) = 1.05739 \quad \text{and} \quad (1 + k) = -1.10645$$

and
$$(5.84)$$

$$(1 + k) = -3.08805 \pm J(1.02191)$$

The results of the computations can be interpreted as follows:

1. If the market rate of interest is approximately 5.74 percent, then an investor is equally wealthy with either option. That is, if $(1 + k) = 1.05739$, then assets 1 and 2 both have the same net present value, $696.98. NPV for asset 1 is

$$- \$1000 + \frac{\$400}{(1 + k)} + \frac{\$400}{(1 + k)^2} + \frac{\$400}{(1 + k)^3} + \frac{\$400}{(1 + k)^4}$$
$$+ \frac{\$400}{(1 + k)^5} \qquad (5.85)$$
$$= - \$1000 + \$378.29 + \$357.76 + \$338.34$$
$$+ \$319.98 + \$302.61 = \$696.98$$

NPV for asset 2 is

$$- \$1000 + \frac{\$100}{(1 + k)} + \frac{\$200}{(1 + k)^2} + \frac{\$400}{(1 + k)^3} + \frac{\$600}{(1 + k)^5}$$
$$+ \frac{\$800}{(1 + k)^5} \qquad (5.86)$$
$$= - \$1000 + \$94.57 + \$178.88 + \$338.34$$
$$+ \$479.97 + \$605.22 = \$696.98$$

2. At market rates of interest below 5.74 percent, say 2 percent, asset 2 is preferred to asset 1 because 2 has a net present value of $946.09 while asset 1 has a net present value of $885.38. These computations are shown below. NPV for asset 1 is

$$- \$1000 + \frac{\$400}{(1.02)} + \frac{\$400}{(1.02)^2} + \frac{\$400}{(1.02)^3} + \frac{\$400}{(1.02)^4} + \frac{\$400}{(1.02)^5}$$
$$= - \$1000 + \$392.16 + \$384.47 + \$376.93$$
$$+ \$369.54 + \$362.29 = \$885.38 \qquad (5.87)$$

NPV for asset 2 is

$$-\$1000 + \frac{\$100}{(1.02)} + \frac{\$200}{(1.02)^2} + \frac{\$400}{(1.02)^3} + \frac{\$600}{(1.02)^4} + \frac{\$800}{(1.02)^5}$$

$$= -\$1000 + \$98.04 + \$192.23 + \$376.93$$
$$+ \$554.31 + \$724.59 = \$946.09 \qquad \textbf{(5.88)}$$

3. At market rates of interest above 5.74 percent, asset 1 is preferred to asset 2 because 1 has a higher net present value at these high rates. For example, if the market rate of interest is 15 percent, then asset 1 has a net present value of \$340.86, whereas asset 2 has a net present value of only \$241.99. NPV for asset 1 is

$$-\$1000 + \frac{\$400}{(1.15)} + \frac{\$400}{(1.15)^2} + \frac{\$400}{(1.15)^3} + \frac{\$400}{(1.15)^4} + \frac{\$400}{(1.15)^5}$$

$$= -\$1000 + \$347.83 + \$302.46 + \$263.01$$
$$+ \$228.70 + \$198.87 = \$340.86 \qquad \textbf{(5.89)}$$

NPV for asset 2 is

$$-\$1000 + \frac{\$100}{(1.15)} + \frac{\$200}{(1.15)^2} + \frac{\$400}{(1.15)^3} + \frac{\$600}{(1.15)^4} + \frac{\$800}{(1.15)^5}$$

$$= -\$1000 + \$86.96 + \$151.23 + \$263.01$$
$$+ \$343.05 + \$397.74 = \$241.99 \qquad \textbf{(5.90)}$$

4. The choices above are correct although the internal rate of return for asset 1 is approximately 28.7 percent, while the internal rate of return for asset 2 is approximately 22.1 percent. Internal rate of return for asset 1 is 28.65 percent, as shown in (5.93).

$$\$1000 = \frac{\$400}{(1 + k)} + \frac{\$400}{(1 + k)^2} + \frac{\$400}{(1 + k)^3} + \frac{\$400}{(1 + k)^4}$$
$$+ \frac{\$400}{(1 + k)^5} \qquad \textbf{(5.91)}$$

$$-\$1000(1 + k)^5 + \$400(1 + k)^4 + \$400(1 + k)^3$$
$$+ \$400(1 + k)^2 + \$400(1 + k) \qquad \textbf{(5.92)}$$
$$+ \$400 = 0$$

The five roots of equation (5.91) are

$$(1 + k) = 1.28649; \qquad k = 28.65 \text{ percent}$$
$$(1 + k) = -.600358 \pm J(.400896) \qquad \textbf{(5.93)}$$
$$(1 + k) = .157112 \pm J(.756259)$$

Internal rate of return for asset 2 is 22.118 percent.

$$\$1000 = \frac{\$100}{(1 + k)} + \frac{\$200}{(1 + k)^2} + \frac{\$400}{(1 + k)^3} + \frac{\$600}{(1 + k)^4}$$
$$+ \frac{\$800}{(1 + k)^5} \qquad \textbf{(5.94)}$$

Solving equation (5.94) we get

$$-\$1000(1 + k)^5 + \$100(1 + k)^4 + \$200(1 + k)^3 \\ + \$400(1 + k)^2 + \$600(1 + k) \qquad \textbf{(5.95)} \\ + \$800 = 0$$

The five roots of equation (5.94) are

$$(1 + k) = 1.22118; \qquad k = 22.118 \; percent$$
$$(1 + k) = -.718863 \pm J(.478072) \qquad \textbf{(5.96)}$$
$$(1 + k) = .158271 \pm J(.924071)$$

A complete tabulation of the financial characteristics of the two proposed investments is listed in Table 5.6. Observe from Table 5.6 that the net present value of asset 1 becomes zero for k between 28 percent and 30 percent (the precise value, as was shown above, is $k = 28.7$ percent), the net present value for asset 2 becomes zero for k

Table 5.6 PROFITABILITY OF TWO ALTERNATIVE
INVESTMENTS

k (%)	NPV of Asset 1 ($)	NPV of Asset 2 ($)	Difference between Asset 1 and Asset 2 ($)
0	1000.00	1100.00	−100.00
2	885.38	946.09	−60.71
4	780.73	807.09	−26.36
6	684.95	681.25	3.70
8	597.08	567.08	30.01
10	516.32	463.27	53.05
12	411.91	368.69	73.22
14	373.23	282.35	90.89
16	309.72	203.37	106.35
18	360.87	131.00	119.87
20	196.25	64.56	131.69
22	145.46	3.46	142.00
24	98.15	−52.82	150.97
26	54.03	−104.74	158.77
28	12.80	−152.72	165.52
30	−25.77	−197.13	171.36
32	−61.92	−238.28	176.37
34	−95.84	−276.48	180.65
36	−127.71	−311.99	184.28
38	−157.69	−345.03	187.34
40	−185.93	−375.83	189.89
42	−212.58	−404.56	191.98
44	−237.73	−431.40	193.67
46	−261.52	−456.51	194.99
48	−284.02	−480.02	195.99
50	−305.35	−502.06	196.71

between 22 percent and 24 percent (the precise value is $k = 22.1$ percent), and the difference between the two net present values becomes zero for k between 4 percent and 6 percent (the precise value is $k = 5.7$ percent). Thus, if one has only $1000 to invest and must choose between these two alternatives (each of which is profitable in its own right), the choice depends upon the market rate of interest.

Ignoring differences in risk class, the existence of a market rate of interest less than the internal rate of return implies incomplete adjustment to competitive equilibrium. If the market rate of interest is 16 percent, then (from Table 5.6), the $1000 can be used to purchase asset 1, which then can be sold immediately at the market for a net present value of $309.72. Alternatively, the $1000 can be used to purchase asset 2, which then can be sold immediately (at the market) for a net present value of only $203.37, which is $106.35 less than the net proceeds from buying and selling asset 1. Under the assumed conditions, therefore, asset 1 is the more profitable of the two available alternatives.

5.8 Summary

Classical methods of investment analysis for capital budgeting have been studied in this chapter. The analysis assumed conditions of certainty. The questions to be answered are:

1. Given the cost of capital (k) what group of (independent) investment proposals should be selected?
2. Given a fixed lump sum for capital investment, what group of investment proposals should be undertaken?
3. Given a set of mutually exclusive investment opportunities which alternatives represent the best set?

The guiding principle for any investment decision is to accept proposals which promise to increase present wealth. In order of preference, those assets which offer the largest addition to total wealth will be adopted first. Those assets which offer the smallest addition to total wealth will be adopted last. Those assets which promise to reduce total wealth must be avoided.[12]

QUESTIONS FOR STUDY

1. Two investments are offered to a prospective buyer to provide a given service. The X investment has a first cost of $3000 and an estimated life of 6 years with no salvage value at the end of service life. Estimated average annual expenditures are labor, $300; power, $200; repairs,

---

[12] See James H. Lorie and Leonard J. Savage, "Three Problems in Rationing Capital," *Journal of Business*, October 1955.

$200; and taxes, $50. The Y investment has a first cost of $5000 and an estimated life of 8 years with $1000 salvage value at the end of that time. Estimated average annual expenditures are labor, $200; power, $175; repairs, $100; and taxes, $75. With interest at 6 percent, compare the two investments on the basis of

(a) Annual cost (Annual net revenue).
(b) Present worth.
(c) Capitalized annual cost.
(d) Show that the values computed under (a), (b), and (c) are equivalent.

2. Consider three alternative strategies for implementing a research design and development project. Assume the relevant data for analysis to be as listed in Table 5.7. The actual cash flows and cost of capital are assumed to be estimated elsewhere. Strategy 1 involves outlays of $15,000 per year for 3 years before the profits begin. Strategy 2 involves outlays of $24,000 per year for 2 years. Strategy 3 involves a single outlay of $50,000. Assume the cost of capital to be 40 percent. Which of the three strategies is most profitable?

Table 5.7 DATA FOR ANALYSIS OF THREE ALTERNATIVE STRATEGIES FOR IMPLEMENTING A DESIGN AND DEVELOPMENT PROJECT

Present Value Approach vs. Internal Rate of Return
(cost of capital = 40 percent)

	Expected cash flow		
Year end	Strategy 1 ($)	Strategy 2 ($)	Strategy 3 ($)
1971	0 (initial outlay)	0 (initial outlay)	0 (initial outlay)
1972	−15,000	−24,000	−50,000
1973	−15,000	−24,000	+40,000
1974	−15,000	+40,000	+40,000
1975	+40,000	+40,000	+40,000
1976	+40,000	+40,000	—
1977	+40,000	—	—

3. Compare the two bonds whose data are listed in Table 5.8. Which bond is more profitable?

Table 5.8 DATA FOR ANALYSIS OF TWO BONDS
(Cost of capital = 10 percent)

Bond	Face value ($)	Coupon (%)	Payments	Maturity (years)
1	1000	4	semiannual	3
2	1000	6	semiannual	5

Risk and uncertainty usually rage rampant in securities markets. Conditions of certainty as assumed in Chapters 4 and 5 are rare in the real world of finance because profits are difficult (often impossible) to forecast with certainty, present or future.

The notions of risk and uncertainty imply that a realized (ex-post) profit can in fact be different from the (ex-ante) profit expectations. If the chances are known for the possible deviations from expectations, then the situation is one of risk. If the chances for possible deviations from expectations are *not* known, then the situation is one of uncertainty.

These simple definitions of risk and uncertainty must be used with care, for they can be misleading. Risk and uncertainty both have many dimensions and are used in many different contexts. In this discussion,

Risk and Uncertainty in Asset Management
6

we shall study some alternative meanings of risk and then proceed with investment analysis, under conditions of risk and uncertainty.

6.1 Some Meanings and Measures of Risk

Phrases such as "business risk," "financial risk," "market risk," "interest rate risk," and "risk of inflation" are used daily by asset managers. As a rule, these terms are intended to imply likelihood of loss, probability of default, chances for bankruptcy, or possibility of failing to meet expectations.

Business risk is frequently used to mean the absence of certainty or the inability to predict future revenues and costs of business operations. Future business income can be forecast, but no one yet has been able to forecast the profits of a company without error. Financial risk is generally used to connote likelihood of default, probability of financial loss, or chance that part of the interest and/or principal repayment will fail to be forthcoming as anticipated. Financial risk occurs because of the inability to forecast financial returns precisely. Market risk implies that prices in money and capital markets move unpredictably up and down. Changes in the levels of securities markets are difficult (if not impossible) to predict.[1] Market risk emanates from this inability to precisely predict future conditions in the market place. Interest rate risk implies inability to precisely predict the future course of interest rates. Risk of inflation implies inability to predict whether the erosion rate of the purchasing power of money will increase (hence buy now to avoid higher prices later), or decrease (save now and buy later at lower prices), or remain the same (base decisions to purchase on utility for the particular commodity in question, not on prices because prices will be the same later as now).

Note that in all cases, the term risk implies that hazards are involved. Business risk infers the existence of chances that business income may differ from expectations. Income for any particular period of time (e.g. next year) may be unexpectedly high or unexpectedly low. Unforeseen fluctuations in product markets, factor markets, or financial markets (market risks or hazards in money, capital, labor, and/or product marketplaces) can cause business income to be exceptionally (and pleasantly) high or painfully (and catastrophically) low. Risks can emanate from structural changes in a dynamic economy. Consumer tastes change. Living habits change. Spending habits change. Past relationships between economic variables can lose validity for predicting the future course of the economy. There is a probability that the probabilities themselves will change. Risk sometimes carries over into uncertainty.

Risk and uncertainty are slippery and elusive concepts because of the many dimensions associated with them. To illustrate, consider the following factors:

1. Size of potential profit
2. Chances that (ex-post) realized profit will differ from (ex-ante) expected profit
3. Time

We shall begin with time, since it is easiest to illustrate. Time is an important dimension in the analysis of risk and uncertainty because dollar investments are usually made today, in anticipation of returns to be received at some future point. Because the future can rarely be forecast with certainty, we can say that risk increases with time. Other

---

[1] Over the short term, expected change for stock market price equals zero. See Chapter 10.

things equal, an investment committed for 10 years is more risky than a corresponding investment committed for 6 months to 1 year. Additional risk exists because greater variety and magnitude of errors (i.e., greater risks) are usually incurred in anticipating (forecasting) returns due 10 years hence than are incurred in anticipating returns due six months hence. Errors in predicting risks vary directly with time.

The first two of the three listed factors can be illustrated in the following game. Suppose either of two identical open containers is offered to you. You are required to choose one of the two. You look inside container 1 and see a prize of $1 million, tax-free. You look inside container 2 and see a prize of a trip to the guillotine.

No doubt your selection will be container 1 because you have seen the prize associated with both choices, and you believe that dollars are more pleasurable than decapitation. Your choice is made under conditions of certainty. You know the outcome of the choice. Visions of riches abound. Investments under conditions of certainty can be satisfying.

Now we change the game. Place a top securely on each container so that each prize must remain inside. Blindfold yourself and then let your competitor shuffle the two containers. With the blindfold still intact, choose one of the two containers. The prize (or penalty, as the case may be) is yours. You know the possible outcomes, but (ex-ante) you do not know which outcome will be yours. The "right" choice can be wonderful: the "wrong" choice can be disastrous. These conditions exemplify asset selection under risk.

Under risk, the alternative opportunities available for investment (i.e., the boxes) can be examined to note the possible payoffs as well as the chances associated with them. The final selection is made with full knowledge that one of the possible outcomes must result, but which particular outcome is not certain. With risk, the probabilities are certain. The chances involved in the game described above are 50:50.

Risk in one sense implies errors of estimate—inability to forecast precisely the particular return which will be realized on an investment. Many alternative returns may be possible, and each possibility has some finite chance of occurrence. The probability distribution of possible returns is known under conditions of risk.[2] The greater the inability to predict, the greater the risk. Other things the same, the wider the

---

[2] Probability distributions can be classified as either mathematical (theoretical) or empirical. Empirical distributions are used to describe and summarize empirical data and can take on any of several possible skewed or peaked forms. Some theoretical (mathematical) probability distributions encountered frequently in asset management are (1) normal (Gaussian), (2) triangular, (3) rectangular, and (4) stable paretian. For reference see any good text on elementary statistics and the appendixes for Chapter 6.

dispersion of possible returns around the expected return, the greater the risk.

Risk also implies perils or hazards associated with the possible prizes themselves. For example, in the game described above, one of the two possible outcomes was known to be extremely pleasurable ($1 million, tax-free) while the alternative outcome was known to be extremely displeasurable (beheading by guillotine). No matter what chances are involved, some investors would view the opportunity to choose one of the two containers as extremely risky. But other investors may be influenced by the chances involved, even considering the possibility of disaster. For example, instead of selecting one of *two* containers, suppose there are say 10,000 containers, 9999 of which are known to contain the "pleasant surprise" and only one of which contains the disaster. Many people will willingly take odds of 9999 to 1 of instant riches or disaster.[3] So the prize (or set of prizes) and probability are both important for analysis of risk.

In a third sense, risk is subjective. A given opportunity for investment can be assessed as "highly risky" by one investor and "slightly risky" by some other investor. For example, change the prizes in the two containers to more modest outcomes. Suppose the prize in container 1 is a certified check for $20,000 while the prize in container 2 is a bill to pay of $5000. To a wealthy person the game might be assessed as slightly risky, but well worth the chances involved, because a possible loss of $5000 is not crucial considering the chances of gaining $20,000. After playing the game many times the profits may outweigh the losses. The expected value of the game is $7500.[4] To a less wealthy person, the same game might be assessed as extremely risky and not worth the chances involved, since a loss of $5000 can mean bankruptcy. Even though the expected value of the game is $7500, there is the probability of ruin in the first round. Therefore, how much risk is (or is not) present in a given opportunity for investment is subjective.

Because of the several dimensions associated with risk and uncertainty, it is impossible to state unique, unambiguous, or single universally acceptable measures of risk. Looking at each dimension separately (i.e., holding other things equal) we see that

1. Larger expected profits are less risky than smaller expected profits.
2. Smaller dispersion about the expected value of profit is less risky than larger dispersion.
3. Profits expected sooner in time are less risky than profits expected later in time.

---

[3] Many criminals take chances even when the odds are stacked against them.
[4] $\frac{1}{2}($20,000$) - \frac{1}{2}($5000$) = 7500.

Of course, when potential projects differ in *all* dimensions, precise measurement of risk becomes complex. Several alternative measures of risk can possibly be required to state risk satisfactorily under these conditions. Several measures are listed in Table 6.1.

Table 6.1 SOME ALTERNATIVE MEANINGS AND MEASURES OF RISK

I. Probability Measures

    1. Probability of loss.
    2. Probability of profit.
    3. Probability that profits actually realized (ex-post) will exceed ex-ante expectations.
    4. Probability that profits actually realized (ex-post) will be less than ex-ante expectations.
    5. Probability that the realized returns will be less (or greater) than some (exogenously) specified required return.
    6. Probability of ruin (or fortune).

II. Profitability Measures

    7. Maximum possible profit (or loss) along with its chance of occurrence.
    8. Minimum possible profit (or loss) along with its chance of occurrence.
    9. Range of possible profits (and losses) (difference between the largest possible value and smallest possible outcomes).
   10. Expected value (mathematical expectation) of all possible returns.
   11. Mean (expected) value of possible losses (or profits).
   12. Modal (most likely value of all possible outcomes).
   13. Modal value of possible losses (or profits).
   14. Median (midpoint) value of all possible returns.
   15. Median value of possible losses (or profits).

III. Errors of Prediction

   16. Total dispersion of possible outcomes, centered on the expected outcome.
       a. variance
       b. standard deviation
   17. Partial dispersion (semivariance and/or semistandard deviation), e.g., mean deviation of possible profits (or losses) away from the expected return.
   18. Average absolute deviation of all possible outcomes, centered on the expected outcome.
   19. Relative dispersion.
       a. coefficient of variation
       b. relative variance

Table 6.1 (Continued)

20. Symmetry.
    a. skewness
    b. kurtosis

Uncertainty, compared with risk, formally means the lack of *any* knowledge, even subjective judgment, concerning the probabilities associated with the possible returns.[5] With uncertainty, the probabilities themselves are unknown. To illustrate uncertainty using the example of the containers, we can proceed as follows.

First, suppose that container 1, complete with its prize of $1 million tax-free is duplicated many times (say m times, where m is an unknown positive integer). Second, duplicate container 2 n times. Next, place all the $(m + n + 2)$ containers inside container 3. Here is the dramatic moment. If you are blindfolded and do not know how many containers are there (i.e., you do not know the size of m and n), then the outcome is uncertain. Under these conditions, there are many possibilities. For example, if m equals 100,000 and n equals unity, then there are 100,001 possibilities of selecting the $1 million out of a total universe of 100,003 items. The probability of "success" is .99997 (i.e., 100,001/100,003). But, at the other extreme, if m equals unity and n equals 100,000, then you might choose to forego the pleasure (?) of playing the game. (Why?).

The point of uncertainty, therefore, can be stated explicitly and precisely. You do not know the probabilities involved. Under uncertainty, the probabilities themselves are unknown.

Aside from probability, another dimension associated with uncertainty concerns the alternative possible payoffs themselves. To illustrate, we return to the containers. This time, instead of duplicating the containers, let the $m + n$ containers be filled with new, but unknown prizes. Now, we have conditions where the probabilities (m and n) are unknown and the possible payoffs are unknown as well. Under these conditions, let the blindfolded selection be made. Without doubt, certainty is absent. One of the "prizes" might be a bill to pay $100,000 (i.e., a $100,000 loss on investment).

Thus, even holding the (unknown) probabilities constant, risk and uncertainty can vary by changing the sign and/or the magnitude of the possible payoffs. Potential payoff (i.e., profit or loss), then, is one dimension of uncertainty.

In the minds of many people, uncertainty and risk are synonymous. Both terms are used frequently to denote the absence of certainty. As illustrated above, uncertainty can be viewed as an extreme case of risk. In either case, certainty is certainly absent.

---

[5] Subjective judgment can be used to specify a probability distribution of returns. See any good elementary statistics text.

The foregoing discussion can be summarized as

$$\text{Risk} = f(R,p,T,W) \qquad (6.1)$$

where

$R = $ expected return on investment (expectation of the payoff)
$p = $ probabilities associated with possible payoffs
$T = $ time
$W = $ current level of wealth

Equation (6.1) is a functional form used to denote the fact that the risk and uncertainty of a project are determined by four variables:

1. Expected return on investment
2. Probabilities involved
3. Time
4. Current level of wealth of the investor

The purpose of analysis under risk conditions is not necessarily to avoid risk altogether. Instead of avoiding risk, proper analysis and interpretation of risk will identify the "right" risks to take. In other words, the objective is not necessarily to eliminate risks; complete elimination of risk is impossible. Instead, the purpose of risk analysis is to identify which risks are present and in what amount. Then proper action can be taken to reduce risk, if possible, and adequate compensation for bearing these reduced risks can be demanded. In short, to evaluate and price risk, we must understand, specify, and measure risk.

6.2 Some Analytic Methods for Evaluation of Risk

SITUATION 1: Two Risky Projects, Both at the Present Time. We can start by using the same logic and methods of analysis established previously. In Chapter 5, the net present value (or IRR) was calculated under assumptions of certainty. These notions will be refined now to accommodate risk.[6]

---

[6] For some applications, there may be a question of how to form expectations or "best estimates" of return on investment. Expectations can be based on subjective expert judgment, econometric models, or other methods. See (1) William F. Butler and Robert A. Kavesh (eds.), *How Business Economists Forecast*, Prentice-Hall, Inc., Englewood Cliffs, N.J., 1966; (2) Henri Thiel, *Applied Economic Forecasting*, Rand McNally & Company, Chicago, 1966; (3) Arthur S. Goldberger, *Econometric Theory*, John Wiley & Sons, Inc., New York, 1964; (4) G. Tintner, *Econometrics*, John Wiley & Sons, Inc., New York, 1952; and (5) R. G. Brown, *Smoothing Forecasting and Prediction of Discrete Time Series*, Prentice-Hall, Inc., Englewood Cliffs, N.J., 1962.

The concept is simple. Instead of a point estimate of expected profit, provide an interval estimate, and specify the shape of the probability distribution of possible returns over that interval. In this way, additional information can be obtained for the prospects of profit (or loss) from a particular opportunity for investment. For a given level of return, the larger the dispersion of error about the expected value, the more risky the project. But, in general, in making comparisons between alternative projects, the levels of return may vary as well as the dispersion. Therefore, to make comparisons between two projects, both of which are risky, two probability distributions must be compared. The situations depicted in Figure 6.1 are possible. The two distributions can be independent or can be mutually correlated.[7]

Consider two available, independent investment projects, named I_1 and I_2, respectively. The probability distribution of expected returns from each project must be as per one of the five relationships shown in Figure 6.1.

At one extreme (the top panel), the smallest possible return from I_1 exceeds the largest possible return from I_2. In this situation, no matter how large the dispersion of I_1 about its expected value, I_1 promises returns larger than I_2. I_1 dominates I_2. At the other extreme (the bottom panel), the situation is reversed. I_2 dominates I_1 and is, therefore, not risky in comparison with I_1.

The second and fourth panels of Figure 6.1 illustrate situations where the left tail of one distribution overlaps the right tail of the other distribution. Here, the largest possible return from one potential investment exceeds the smallest possible return from an alternative opportunity. But other than this overlap, one opportunity offers returns superior to the alternative opportunity. In this type of situation, investors may want to *diversify* by spreading their money over both investments.

The third panel in Figure 6.1 illustrates situations where the returns from one potential investment (I_1) unconditionally cover a wider range and overlap the returns offered by an alternative investment (I_2). In this type of situation, I_1 is said to be more risky than I_2, and I_2 is less risky than I_1.

As an exercise, the student should compare I_1 and I_2 with the certain outcome for all five panels in Figure 6.1.

SITUATION 2: Cash Flows Distributed over Time.   In this section, we shall investigate net present value, considering risk.

The net present value criterion for accepting or rejecting proposed

---

[7] Correlation is a statistical term which denotes and measures covariance. These notions are explained in Appendix 2 of this chapter.

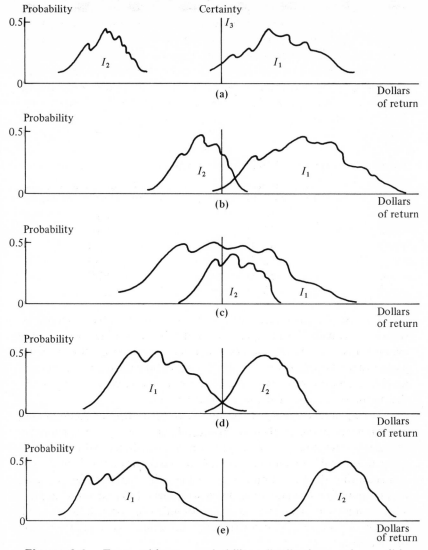

Figure 6.1. Two arbitrary probability distributions of possible returns.

investments can be refined to account for risk. The objective is to compute a probability distribution for net present value instead of computing single-point values, as illustrated previously in Situations 1–5 in Chapter 5. The necessary refinement can be accomplished by discounting both the mean and the variance of the probability distribution of each independently distributed future cash flow. The procedures are illustrated below.

ASSUMPTION: All Cash Flows are Statistically Independent.
Consider the cash inflows and outflows hypothesized previously in
Figure 5.1. At this level of analysis, however, permit more realism to
enter. Instead of assuming (as we did) that the dollar values stated for
each time period (T_0 through T_5) have a probability of unity (i.e.,
certainty), let there be a range of possible values which can occur during
each time period. A possible range is shown in Table 6.2. Observe that
Table 6.2 is the same as Table 5.1, except that one dimension is added—
risk.

Table 6.2   DATA FOR RISK ANALYSIS

Year	Expected net cash inflows and outflows ($)	Range for possible outcome (% of expected value)
0	−1000	±10
1	+60 0	±10
2	+40 0	±20
3	+25 0	±30
4	+5 0	±30
5	+10 0	±50

The expected net cash flows and range for possible outcome as
shown in Table 6.2 can be stated on the basis of objective analytic
experiments (e.g., pilot study, simulation, interview) or else on subjective (expert) judgment. For this example, take the data in Table 6.2
as given. The objective is to calculate the probability distribution for
the net present value of the investment project.

To expedite analysis, we can invoke the central limit theorem and
apply normal statistical theory.[8] From statistical theory, we can assume
that each flow is (approximately) normally distributed with mean (μ_i)
and variance (σ^2). In addition, because of the central limit theorem, we
can state that the (discounted) sum of the individual cash flows is also
(approximately) normally distributed with mean (R) and variance (σ_R^2).
This means that, ignoring time (for simplicity), for n different and
independent projects, we can write the total return (R) and the variance
of that return, σ_R^2.

$$R = \mu_1 + \mu_2 + \cdots + \mu_n \tag{6.2}$$
$$\sigma_R^2 = \sigma_1^2 + \sigma_2^2 + \cdots + \sigma_n^2 \tag{6.3}$$

where

R = total return from n different projects
μ_i = mean (expected) return from the ith project
σ_i^2 = variance of return expected from ith project

---

[8] See Appendix 2 at the end of this chapter for statements regarding the
statistics involved.

For a single project, distributed through n different and independent time periods, we can write:

$$R = \mu_1/(1 + k) + \mu_2/(1 + k)^2 + \cdots + \mu_n/(1 + k)^n \qquad (6.4)$$

$$\sigma_R^2 = \sigma_1^2/[(1 + k)]^2 + \sigma_2^2/[(1 + k)^2]^2 + \sigma_3^2/[(1 + k)^3]^2$$
$$+ \cdots + \sigma_n^2/[(1 + k)^n]^2 \qquad (6.5)$$

By applying the (exogenous) knowledge that for all normal distributions, 99.73 percent of all possible outcomes will fall within the range ± 3 standard deviations from the mean, and by using the data from Table 6.2, we can calculate standard deviations and variances as follows.

The stated range in Table 6.2 extends to the extreme limits ($\mu \pm 3\sigma$) of the probability distribution. Since the range and the expected value (μ) are known, and because normal distributions are always symmetrical, σ can be calculated. The results of these calculations are tabulated in Table 6.3.

Table 6.3   STANDARD ERROR OF EXPECTED RETURN*

Year	Expected net cash Inflows and outflows ($)	Range for possible outcome (%)	Standard deviation ($)	Variance
0	−1000	±10	100/3	$(100/3)^2$
1	+60 0	±10	60/3	$(60/3)^2$
2	+40 0	±20	80/3	$(80/3)^2$
3	+25 0	±30	75/3	$(75/3)^2$
4	+5 0	±30	15/3	$(15/3)^2$
5	+10 0	±50	50/3	$(50/3)^2$

* For the conditions assumed, upper limit = mean + 3(σ) = expected value + tolerance, Lower limit = mean − 3(σ) = expected value − tolerance.

$$\text{Upper limit} = \mu + 3\sigma = \mu(1 + e) \qquad (6.6)$$

Solution of (6.6) for the standard error of estimate yields

$$\sigma = \mu e/3 \qquad (6.7)$$

where e = tolerance error of estimate expressed as a decimal and other terms are the same as defined previously.

ASSUMPTION: The Process Is Unbiased; Mean Values Will Occur. Assuming the appropriate opportunity rate of discount to be 15 percent, the net present value of the proposed investment on Table

6.2 can be calculated in the usual manner to be an expected $66.88 profit. Under these conditions the project is accepted.

$$
\begin{aligned}
\text{NPV} = \sum_{j=0}^{n} \frac{R_j}{(1 + k)^j} = &-\$1000 + \frac{\$600}{(1 + .15)} + \frac{\$400}{(1 + .15)^2} \\
&+ \frac{\$250}{(1 + .15)^3} + \frac{\$50}{(1 + .15)^4} \\
&+ \frac{\$100}{(1 + .15)^5} \qquad\qquad (6.8) \\
= &-\$1000 + \$521.74 + \$322.46 \\
&+ \$164.38 + \$28.59 \\
&+ \$49.72 \\
= &\ \$66.88
\end{aligned}
$$

However, when risk is considered, enthusiasm might wane. Considering the risk of this proposed project, there are some 75 chances out of 1000 that money can be lost on this proposed project. The conclusion can be seen as follows.

First calculate the variance of the expected net present value. According to equation (6.3), the variance of a sum of independent random variables equals the sum of the variances of the individual components. And, since the individual expectations are separated in time, each future variance must be discounted to the present point in time as stated in equation (6.5).

Thus, we get

$$
\begin{aligned}
\sigma_R^2 = \text{var(expected return)} = &\sum_{i=0}^{n} \frac{\sigma_i^2}{(1 + k)^{2i}} \\
= (100/3)^2 + &\frac{(60/3)^2}{(1 + .15)^2} + \frac{(80/3)^2}{(1 + .15)^4} + \frac{(75/3)^2}{(1 + .15)^6} \\
+ &\frac{(15/3)^2}{(1 + .15)^8} + \frac{(50/3)^2}{(1 + .15)^{10}} \qquad (6.9) \\
= \$1111.11 + &\$302.46 + \$406.58 + \$270.21 + \$8.17 + \$68.66 \\
= \$2167.19
\end{aligned}
$$

$$
\begin{aligned}
\sigma = \text{Standard deviation (expected return)} &= \sqrt{\sigma^2} \\
= \sqrt{2167.19} &= \$46.55
\end{aligned} \qquad (6.10)
$$

Therefore, the probability distribution which specifies the net present value for the proposed investment is: mean = $66.88 and standard deviation = $46.55. This distribution is shown in Figure 6.2. Interpretation of the probability distribution on Figure 6.2 is as follows. Since an outcome (i.e., a net present value) can occur at any point within the range $66.88 ± 3($46.55), we see that larger net proceeds might be forthcoming from the investment ($66.88 + $139.65

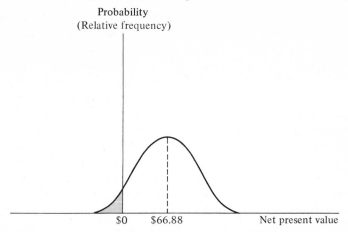

Figure 6.2. Probability distribution for net present value.

= \$206.55), but a net loss might be incurred (\$66.88 − \$139.65 = − \$72.79). This investment is risky.

Next analyze the extent of risk. What are the chances for loss? In this analysis, the chances for loss depend upon the area under the tail of the distribution to the left of a net present value of zero. In terms of standard deviation units, the relevant distance can be measured as

$$Z = \frac{\$0 - \$66.88}{\sigma} = \frac{-\$66.88}{\$46.55} = -1.43621 \Rightarrow \text{Area} = .4251 \quad \textbf{(6.11)}$$

That is, a net present value of zero lies 1.43621 standard deviations to the left of the expected value \$66.88. Referring to a table of areas under the normal curve, a distance 1.43621 standard deviation units encompasses approximately 42.51 percent of the total area under the left tail, and since each tail contains exactly 50 percent of the total area under the normal curve, the area that permits a negative net present value for this particular investment must be .0749 of the total possible area. This area corresponds to a probability of loss of .0749 or about 75 chances in 1000 to obtain a net present value of zero or less. As stated above, this investment is risky. Many real-world investments are risky.

$$\text{Total area under tail} = 50 \text{ percent} \qquad \textbf{(6.12)}$$

$$\text{Area between \$0 NPV and \$66.86 NPV} = 42.51 \text{ percent}$$
$$\textbf{(6.13)}$$

$$\text{Area between minus \$infinity and \$0 NPV} = 7.49 \text{ percent}$$
$$\textbf{(6.14)}$$

$$\text{prob(NPV} < 0|k = 15 \text{ percent}) = .0749 \qquad \textbf{(6.15)}$$

The above calculations are depicted in Figure 6.3.

ASSUMPTION: Nature Is a Malevolent Process—The Worst Possible Outcomes Will Occur: An Alternative Formulation. The analysis of risk for this particular project can proceed in a different way. Consider the following. By chance, suppose the combination of worst possible circumstances all occur at the appropriate time, so that the cost of the project happens to be near its upper limit and the revenue expected from the project happens to be near its lower limit. But instead of requiring each outcome to be precisely at its extreme possible value, permit a 5 percent chance that the cash flow will be somewhere near its extreme value. Now, from theory of normal probability distributions, we know that 5 percent of the area under a tail lies at a distance of approximately 1.645 standard deviations from the mean. Thus, under these conditions and still assuming a market rate of return of 15 percent, the net present value of the cash flow can be calculated to be minus $95.11. Equation 6.16 shows the calculation.

$$
\begin{aligned}
\text{NPV} &= \frac{-[1000 + 1.645(100/3)]}{1} + \frac{[600 - 1.645(60/3)]}{(1 + .15)} \\
&\quad + \frac{[400 - 1.645(80/3)]}{(1 + .15)^2} + \frac{[250 - 1.645(75/3)]}{(1 + .15)^3} \\
&\quad + \frac{[50 - 1.645(15/3)]}{(1 + .15)^4} + \frac{[100 - 1.645(50/3)]}{(1 + .15)^5} \quad \textbf{(6.16)} \\
&= \frac{-[1000 + 54.83]}{1} + \frac{[600 - 32.90]}{(1 + .15)} + \frac{[400 - 43.87]}{(1 + .15)^2} \\
&\quad + \frac{[250 - 41.13]}{(1 + .15)^3} + \frac{[50 - 8.23]}{(1 + .15)^4} + \frac{[100 - 27.12]}{(1 + .15)^5} \\
&= -\$1054.83 + \$493.13 + \$269.29 + \$137.34 \\
&\quad + \$23.89 + \$36.09 \\
&= -\$95.11
\end{aligned}
$$

What are the chances for incurring a loss of $95.11? The chances that each possible dollar value will actually fall within the 5 percent tail area of its distribution is 15.625×10^{-9} or about 16 times out of a billion. This is not very likely.

$$(.05)(.05)(.05)(.05)(.05)(.05) = 15.625 \times 10^{-9} \quad \textbf{(6.17)}$$

On the other hand, chances are plausible (75 out of 1000) that some loss will be sustained on the investment.

SITUATION 3: Internal Rate of Return, Considering Risk. The internal rate of return criterion for accepting or rejecting proposed investments can be refined to account for risk in a way quite similar to the illustration in Situation 2. To see this, consider the following.

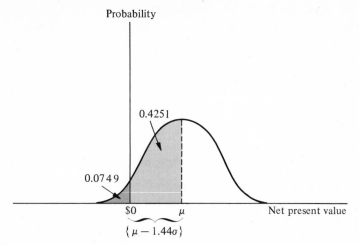

Figure 6.3.   Probability of loss on investment.

ASSUMPTION: All Cash Flows Are Statistically Independent.
Recall from Chapter 5 that the internal rate of return is defined as that
rate of reinvestment (i.e., discount) which equates a future revenue
stream with a present dollar outlay.

$$\text{NPV} = -Y_0 + Y_1/(1 + k) + Y_2/(1 + k)^2 + \cdots + Y_n/(1 + k)^n$$
$$\textbf{(6.18)}$$

where

$$\text{NPV} = \text{net present value of project}$$
$$Y_0 = \text{present net outlay, } Y_0 > 0$$
$$Y_1 = \text{net cash inflow one period hence, } Y_1 > 0$$
$$Y_2 = \text{net cash inflow two periods hence, } Y_2 > 0$$
$$k = \text{rate of discount}$$

Thus, if $k = \text{IRR}$, then the net present value, by definition, equals zero.

$$Y_0 = Y_1/(1 + k) + Y_2/(1 + k)^2 + \cdots + Y_n/(1 + k)^n \quad \textbf{(6.19)}$$

To calculate a probability distribution for IRR, we can proceed
as follows. First note that if k is greater than the IRR (k equals infinity),
then Y_0 exceeds $[Y_1/(1 + k) + Y_2/(1 + k)^2 + \cdots]$, causing net
present value to be negative. At the other extreme, if k is less the IRR
(k equals zero), then Y_0 may be less than $(Y_1 + Y_2 + \cdots)$, causing net
present value to be positive.

The probability that the internal rate of return is less than the
assumed rate of discount is the same as the probability that the net
present value is negative.

$$\text{prob}(\text{IRR} < k) = \text{prob}(\text{NPV} < 0|k) \quad \textbf{(6.20)}$$

For the case presented above, where k is taken to be 15 percent, the probability that the net present value is negative, using this rate of discount, was calculated to be .0749. Hence, the probability that the IRR is less than 15 percent is also .0749.

Finally, by assuming other values for k (e.g., by letting k vary in discrete steps from zero to infinity) and repeating the calculations outlined above, the complete probability distribution can be calculated for the internal rate of return.[9]

6.3 Simulation Methods for Analysis Under Risk

In the real world, investment projects often fail to pass the test of statistical independence as required in the preceding discussions. Cash flows during any given time period may be dependent upon (i.e., statistically correlated with) cash flows during some other time period. For example, more profits now might mean more dollars available for reinvestment later. Also, profit opportunities can be characterized by mixtures of various types of probability distributions. The distributions may not be Gaussian.

In these cases, analytic procedures are possible but, from a practical point of view, complex. When models become too complex for solution by analytic methods (as described in the preceding sections) then one can resort to *simulation*—Monte Carlo simulation. The Monte Carlo simulation method is a standard technique for mathematical analysis of multivariate distributions and for simulation of certain models that are analytically intractable.[10]

Application of the Monte Carlo method requires only two basic criteria. First, there must exist some model that represents reality. The model can be a probability distribution of the particular variable (or variables) under consideration. All that is required is a table or a graph of a cumulative probability distribution of the variable. This can be obtained either by direct observation or, indirectly, by the use of past records. There is no particular need to express the probability distribution explicitly in mathematical form.

The second thing needed for Monte Carlo simulation is a mechanism to simulate the model. The mechanism can be any random-number

---

[9] For further reading on dispersion of NPV and IRR, see Frederick S. Hillier, "The Deviation of Probabilistic Information for the Evaluation of Risky Investments," *Management Science*, vol. IX, April 1963, pp. 443–457.

[10] See David B. Hertz, "Risk Analysis in Capital Investment," *Harvard Business Review*, vol. 42, no. 1, Jan.–Feb. 1964, pp. 95–106, and Fred B. Renwick, "Economic Growth and Distributions of Change in Stock Market Prices," *Industrial Management Review*, Spring Issue 1968, pp. 39–67.

generator such as a pair of dice, a spinning pointer, a roulette wheel, a table of random digits, or a high-speed computer properly instructed. Each random number selected is considered a probability value. Repeated samplings (e.g., 100,000 times or more) will yield the desired distribution of probabilities necessary for risk analysis. The essence of Monte Carlo simulation can be illustrated as follows.

Consider the returns hypothesized in Table 6.4. Let I_2 be the probability distribution for present value of *revenues* to be received at

Table 6.4 PROBABILITY DISTRIBUTIONS FOR SIMULATION

Opportunity	Possible return ($)	Estimated Probability
I_2	400	.10
	200	.10
	150	.20
	100	.60
I_3	150	.05
	100	.70
	75	.20
	50	.05

the end of the coming planning period and let I_3 be the corresponding probability distribution for present value of *costs*. Then since profits equal the difference between revenues and costs (ignoring taxes, interest, and depreciation) the probability distribution for the present value of profits can be calculated using the technique of Monte Carlo simulation. The experiment can proceed as follows.

First, collect 100 chips (to represent a total probability of 1.00) and write the value $100 on 60 of them. That is, revenues of $100 will occur 60 percent of the time. Then continue labeling. Write the value $400 on each of 10 chips, $200 on each of 10 chips, and $150 on each of 20 chips, and place all 100 chips (i.e., the complete probability distribution) into a container.

Second, collect another 100 chips and write values of I_3 on the appropriate number of chips. Place these 100 chips into a second container.

Third, draw one chip from each container, the drawing mechanism may require the value of the second chip to be related to the value of the first chip. Calculate profit equals revenue minus cost; make a note of the difference so calculated, and replace each chip into its proper container.

$$E(\text{profit}) = E(\text{revenue}) - E(\text{costs}) \qquad (6.21)$$

Repeat step 3 several thousand times and plot a histogram to summarize the alternative values of profits so obtained. This histogram represents the desired probability distribution of possible profits.

$$\text{var(profit)} = \text{var(revenue)} + \text{var(costs)} - 2\,\text{cov(revenue, costs)}$$
$$(6.22)$$

Analytically, the Monte Carlo procedure yields all possible combinations of revenues and costs, keeping count of the resulting profits. For example, following from Table 6.4, with revenues of $400 ($p = .10$), costs could be (1) $150, $p = .05$; (2) $100, $p = .70$; (3) $75, $p = .20$; or (4) $50, $p = .05$. Then profit would be (1) ($400 − $150), $p = .005$; (2) ($400 − $100), $p = .070$; (3) ($400 − $75), $p = .020$; or (4) ($400 − $50), $p = .005$. Next, revenues could be $200 ($p = 0.10$), with costs being either of the four alternatives from I_3. The process of selection could continue until all possible combinations are exhausted. The results yield the desired probability distribution.[11]

6.4 Methods for Analysis Under Conditions of Uncertainty

As explained in the beginning of this chapter, uncertainty exists when the probability distribution of errors associated with (ex-ante) estimates of profit on investment is unknown. In actual practice, uncertainty should be rare because, according to the formal definition, uncertainty implies *complete* lack of knowledge, not even subjective judgment, concerning profit possibilities associated with a particular project. The implication for practical purposes, therefore, is that if uncertainty is present, then that particular opportunity for investment may be profitably avoided.

Under conditions where an array of possible profits can be estimated, assuming alternative states of the economy, but where the probability of occurrence of these alternative states is not known with certainty, then either of several methods of analysis can be applied. These methods are discussed below.

USE OF GAME THEORETIC TECHNIQUES AND DECISION THEORY IN ANALYSIS UNDER UNCERTAINTY FOR INVESTMENT DECISIONS. In cases where the probabilities themselves are known imperfectly (i.e., analysis under uncertainty), several criteria and corresponding methods of analysis are possible. Some relevant criteria and strategies for investment are:

1. Maximin: Maximize the minimum possible return.
2. Maximax: Maximize the maximum possible return

---

[11] The example assumes independence between revenues and costs, for simplicity. For further reading on Monte Carlo, see, e.g., J. Johnston, *Econometric Methods*, McGraw-Hill, Inc., New York, 1963.

3. Minimax: Minimize the maximum possible regret.
4. Criterion of rationality: Assume equal likelihood for all possible outcomes.
5. Mixed strategies.
6. Revise prior probabilities in the light of sample information.

Each of these methods is discussed below.

MAXIMIN CRITERION. This criterion exemplifies the pessimist. The rationale leading to the use of this criterion is: if things can go wrong, they will; therefore, the best action to take is that investment strategy which guarantees the best among all the worst possible returns. This is the maximin strategy.

To illustrate, suppose two securities are being considered for possible investment. Suppose also that both securities "move with the market" but security 1 moves by a larger amount than security 2. Some hypothetical percentages are listed in Table 6.5. If the market goes up, security 1 is anticipated to yield 40 percent, whereas security 2 is expected to yield only 10 percent. But, if the market goes down, security 2 promises 6 percent, whereas security 1 promises a loss of 20 percent.

Table 6.5 TWO HYPOTHETICAL INVESTMENTS

Security	The market Down	Up
1	−20%	40%
2	6%	10%

Under the conditions hypothesized, the pessimist will reason that, since bad things will happen if they possibly can, the market can be assumed to go down, causing the minimum possible payoff for security 1 of −20 percent and the minimum possible payoff for security 2 of 6 percent. The maximum of the minimum possible returns is 6 percent. The maximin choice between the two is security 2. Invest in security 2 to minimize possible losses.

MAXIMAX CRITERION. This criterion exemplifies the optimist. The optimist always assumes that the best outcomes will always occur and makes his selections accordingly. Thus, using the example from Table 6.5, the optimist would choose to ignore the fact that the market can go down and assumes that the market will go up. Then, if the market goes up, security 1 offers 40 percent return, whereas security 2 offers only 10 percent return. The maximum of the maximum possible returns is 40 percent. The maximax choice between these two is security 1. Invest in security 1 to make the maximum possible "killing."

MINIMAX CRITERION. This criterion exemplifies the paranoid. The paranoid believes that no matter what his (ex-ante) choice is, after the fact (ex-post), he will wish that a different choice had been made. The minimax strategy, therefore, is to examine all the possibilities, note the maximum possible regret for each available strategy, and then seek the smallest of the maxima.

To illustrate using the example on Table 6.5, if the market goes down, then the correct (no regret) choice is 6 percent. If the market goes down and security 1 has been chosen, then not only will the 6 percent be foregone, but a loss of 20 percent will be incurred to yield a regret of $[6 - (-20)]$ or 26 percent.

On the other hand, if the market goes up, then the correct (no regret) selection is security 1. If the market goes up and security 2 has been held, then the regret is the difference between the return that could have been obtained (i.e., 40 percent) and the return actually obtained (i.e., 10 percent). The regret matrix is shown in Table 6.6. The maximum

Table 6.6 REGRET MATRIX

| Security | The market | |
	Down	Up
1	26%	0
2	0	30%

possible regret for security 1 is 26 percent; for security 2 it is 30 percent. The minimax strategy to minimize the maximum possible regret, therefore, is security 1.[12]

CRITERION OF RATIONALITY. This criterion exemplifies the analyst who is compulsively rational. This analyst reasons that in the absence of any other information, the rational approach is to assume equal probabilities for each possible state of nature. Thus, this analyst would rationally assign probabilities of $\frac{1}{2}$ to each of the two possible states of the market. Then the expected return on investment from security 1 is 10 percent, whereas the expected return from security 2 is 8 percent. Since the larger expected return is 10 percent, security 1 is the choice for investment according to the criterion of rationality.

$$\tfrac{1}{2}(-.20) + \tfrac{1}{2}(.40) = .10 \qquad (6.23)$$

$$\tfrac{1}{2}(.06) + \tfrac{1}{2}(.10) = .08 \qquad (6.24)$$

---

[12] Note a possible alternative line of reasoning to select security 2. The reasoning is, I would rather "guess wrong" and obtain an opportunity loss of 30 percent than to "guess wrong" and incur actual losses.

USE OF PRIOR INFORMATION. Suppose you believe (subjectively) that under the present economic conditions the market is twice as likely to go down as it is to go up. That is,

$$\text{probability(down)} = 2 \ \text{probability(up)} \qquad (6.25)$$

Since

$$\text{probability(down)} + \text{probability(up)} = 1.00, \qquad (6.26)$$

equations (6.25) and (6.26) can be solved simultaneously to calculate

$$\text{probability(up)} = \tfrac{1}{3} \qquad (6.27)$$

$$\text{probability(down)} = \tfrac{2}{3} \qquad (6.28)$$

Then, the expected return on investment from security 1 is .00 percent, whereas the expected return from security 2 is 7.3 percent. Since the larger of the two expected returns is 7.3 percent, security 2 is the choice for investment.

$$\tfrac{2}{3}(-.20) + \tfrac{1}{3}(.40) = .00 \qquad (6.29)$$

$$\tfrac{2}{3}(.06) + \tfrac{1}{3}(.10) = .73 \qquad (6.30)$$

Table 6.7 MIXED STRATEGIES

Security	The market	
	Down	Up
A (long)	-20%	50%
B (short)	30%	-10%

MIXED STRATEGIES. Consider the two alternative strategies shown in Table 6.7. If the market goes up and you are long (holding) security A, returns are expected to be 50 percent; but if the market goes down, your investment in A will lose 20 percent. With the alternative strategy, if the market goes down and you are short (have sold) security B, returns are expected to be 30 percent. With B, you expect to lose 10 percent if the market rises.

Suppose you want to "hedge" against possibilities of the market moving in either direction. So instead of selecting either strategy (security) A or strategy B, you select some of each. That is, you invest X_A percent of your money according to strategy A and X_B percent according to strategy B. Observe the constraint:

$$X_A + X_B = 100 \text{ percent} \qquad (6.31)$$

If V_0 equals the total value or dollars invested, then $X_A V_0$ equals the total dollars invested in security A and $X_B V_0$ equals the total dollars invested in security B.

Then if the market goes down, $X_A V_0$ dollars will return -20 percent and $X_B V_0$ dollars will return 30 percent. That is, at the end of the time period, the total dollars in the portfolio will be

$$X_A V_0(1 + r_1) + X_B V_0(1 + r_2) =$$
$$X_A V_0(1.00 - .20) + X_B V_0(1.00 + .30) = (.80X_A + 1.30X_B)V_0$$

Alternatively, if the market goes up, then $X_A V_0$ dollars will return 50 percent, and $X_B V_0$ dollars will return -10 percent. As before, the total dollars in the portfolio as of the end of the time period will be

$$X_A V_0(1 + .50) + X_B V_0(1 - .10) = (1.5X_A + .9X_B)V_0 \quad \textbf{(6.33)}$$

Therefore, to obtain the same expected return regardless of which direction the market moves, set (6.32) equal to (6.33) and solve simultaneously with the constraint (6.31):

$$(.80X_A + 1.30X_B)V_0 = (1.5X_A + .9X_B)V_0 \quad \textbf{(6.34)}$$

Equation (6.34) simplifies to

$$.70X_A - .40X_B = 0$$
$$X_A + X_B = 1 \quad \textbf{(6.35)}$$

$$X_A = \tfrac{4}{11}; \qquad X_B = \tfrac{7}{11} \quad \textbf{(6.36)}$$

So \$4 of every \$11 invested will be allocated to going long security A, and the remaining \$7 will be allocated to going short security B. No matter which direction the market moves, the expected value of the return on the original investment (V_0) is 11.8 percent.

$$[(.80)\tfrac{4}{11} + (1.30)\tfrac{7}{11}]V_0 = (1 + .118)V_0 \quad \textbf{(6.37)}$$

Note that at 12 percent interest, money doubles approximately every 7 time periods; so such a strategy as the one hypothesized above (if exercised weekly or even monthly) can cause wealth to grow rapidly.

REVISION OF PRIOR PROBABILITIES. This method of analysis invokes Bayes theorem. The basic idea, is to calculate a set of posteriori probabilities on the basis of prior expectations and sample evidence. The method is illustrated as follows.

Suppose we do not know the direction of the next (ex-ante) change in the market for certain, but over the years we have kept records of observed (ex-post) changes. Suppose these records show that 51 percent of the changes were *up* and 49 percent of the changes were *down*. We might assess our prior probability distribution for the next change as .51 *up* and .49 *down*.

Next, suppose we consult an expert forecaster of the market, and this forecaster informs us that he expects the market to be down. Now, in the light of this sample information, how do we revise our prior probabilities?

The answer depends upon the track record (performance) of the expert forecaster. Suppose his record of forecasting is as shown in Table 6.8: when the forecast is for the market to be *up*, the market

Table 6.8 PERFORMANCE RECORD
OF EXPERT FORECASTER

Forecast	The market	
	Up	Down
Up	.60	.30
Down	.40	.70

actually goes *up* (i.e., the forecast turns out to be correct) 60 percent of the time but goes *down* 30 percent of the time. And when the forecast is for the market to be down, the market actually goes down 70 percent of the time but goes up 40 percent of the time.

Stated differently, when the market actually goes *up*, 60 percent of the time the forecast was *up* (correct), and the remaining 40 percent of the time the forecast was *down* (wrong). When the market actually goes down, the forecast is correct 70 percent of the time and incorrect 30 percent of the time.

Now, in light of a present forecast of down and the historical batting averages as shown in Table 6.8, we can revise our prior probabilities of .51 *up* and .49 *down* as follows:

From the theory of probability, we can write

$$Pr(F_D, M_D) = Pr(F_D) \cdot Pr(M_D | F_D) \tag{6.38}$$

where the symbol *Pr* means "probability of."
Then (6.38) can be solved to obtain

$$Pr(M_D | F_D) = \frac{Pr(F_D, M_D)}{Pr(F_D)}$$

$$= \frac{Pr(M_D) \cdot Pr(F_D | M_D)}{Pr(M_D) \cdot Pr(F_D | M_D) + Pr(M_U) \cdot Pr(F_U | M_U)} \tag{6.39}$$

Verbally, equation (6.38) states that the probability of both the forecast and the market being *down* equals the unconditional probability that the forecast will be *down*, multiplied by the probability that the market will be *down*, given that the forecast is for *down*. This latter quantity is the unknown to be solved for. Equation (6.39) is the solution.

Verbally, (6.39) states that the (revised) probability that the market will be *down*, given that the forecast is *down* equals a ratio of (1) the unconditional (prior) probability that the market will be down, multiplied by the (prior) probability that the forecast is down, given that the market is down to (2) the unconditional probability that the forecast is down. Note that the forecast can be *down* and the market could be either *up* or *down*. Equation (6.39) is known as the Bayes theorem.

Substituting numbers from Table 6.8 into (6.39), we get

$$Pr(M_D|F_D) = \frac{(.49)(.70)}{(.49)(.70) + (.51)(.40)} = \frac{.343}{.547} = .627 \quad \textbf{(6.40)}$$

Hence, our (revised) probability that the market will be down, given the forecast, is .627. Under these conditions, the (revised) probability of up is [1 − .627] or .373.

If the forecast had been up instead of down, then the revised probability of *up* is .676.

$$Pr(M_U|F_U) = \frac{(.51)(.60)}{(.49)(.30) + (.51)(.60)} = \frac{.306}{.453} = .676 \quad \textbf{(6.41)}$$

If the forecaster had been more accurate in his predictions, as indicated in Table 6.9, and the forecast was for *down*, then the revised probability that the market will be *down* is

$$Pr(M_D|F_D) = \frac{(.49)(.95)}{(.49)(.95) + (.51)(.90)} = \frac{.4655}{.5165} = .901 \quad \textbf{(6.42)}$$

**Table 6.9   PERFORMANCE RECORD
OF SUPER FORECASTER**

	The market	
Forecast	Up	Down
Up	.90	.05
Down	.10	.95

Under these same conditions, if the super forecaster had forecast *up*, then the revised probability that the market will actually rise is

$$Pr(M_U|F_U) = \frac{(.51)(.90)}{(.49)(.05) + (.51)(.90)} = \frac{.4590}{.4835} = .949 \quad \textbf{(6.43)}$$

If the forecaster is poor and is correct less than half the time, as in Table 6.10, and the forecast is for *up*, then the revised probability that the market will rise is

$$Pr(M_U|F_U) = \frac{(.51)(.40)}{(.49)(.80) + (.51)(.40)} = \frac{.204}{.596} = .342 \quad \textbf{(6.44)}$$

In other words, this forecaster is so "bad" that if he says the market will go *up*, the market is quite likely to go *down*. Hence, given that the forecast was for *up*, the probability that the market will actually go up is then revised from .51 down to .342, thereby causing the probability of *down* to be revised from .49 to [1 − .342] or .658.

Table 6.10 TRACK RECORD
OF "WRONG"
FORECASTER

	The market	
Forecast	Up	Down
Up	.40	.80
Down	.60	.20

Observe that, if the sample forecast is always correct (and it rarely is in actual practice), then the posteriori probability equals unity (i.e., you always believe the sample because the sample is always correct). Observe also that sample information which is always wrong is also useful, provided that it is consistently wrong. In this case, you believe just the opposite of what the sample indicates.

Some additional background information is summarized in the following two appendices.

The term *probability distribution* is used to convey information about every possible return from an opportunity for investment. For example, suppose the (ex-post) return on an investment in a particular asset depends upon the change in consumer spending habits. If consumer spending increases, suppose the return will be 40 percent. If consumer spending decreases or remains the same, suppose the return on an investment will be 10 percent. Then the probability distribution for the investment denotes the likelihood or chance of occurrence for each possible return.

Since there are only three possible acts by the consumer (increase, decrease, or no change) and a possible return is associated with each of those acts, then the probability distribution of possible returns depends upon the chances that the consumer will take one of the possible acts. If the consumer is not predictable and is equally likely to take any one of the three acts (i.e., chances of 1:3 for each of three possibilities), then, because a 40 percent return will result when one act is chosen (with probability 1:3) and a 10 percent return will result if either of two acts remaining is chosen (with probability 2:3), we can say that the probability of 10 percent is .666 (or two chances in three) and the probability of 40 percent is .333 (or one chance in three). The probability of some return other than 10 percent or 40 percent is zero.

These notions of probability as described above may appear to make sense intuitively. However, not everyone's intuition operates in the same way. Therefore, we must study probability in a more formal manner.

There are four different widely used concepts of probability.

1. Long-run relative frequency
2. Extended frequency
3. Relative proportion
4. Degrees of reasonable belief (sometimes called subjective betting odds)

Each notion is important for investment analysis under conditions of risk; therefore, each concept will be described briefly for reference in later chapters.

A. Long-Run Relative Frequency Concept

One concept views a probability as the limiting value of a long-run relative frequency. For example, reviewing the two containers used as illustrations at the beginning of the chapter, if one performs an experiment and selects a container (i.e., invest) repeatedly and keeps a record of the outcomes, then, considering the total number of experiments and the total number of different outcomes, one should find that out of

100,000 trials, approximately 50,000 or one-half resulted in the undesirable return. Using this concept of probability, a return of $1 million has a probability of 1:2 because after a large number of trials (i.e., in the long run) this return occurs approximately 50 percent or one-half of the time.

Coin tossing can be used as another illustration of the long-run relative frequency concept of probability. Here, the relative proportion of heads obtained on a large number of tosses of a fair coin is a measure of the probability of obtaining heads. If the coin is tossed 1 million times and a count is made of the number of heads, approximately 500,000 heads should occur if the coin is unbiased. The probability of obtaining a head, therefore, is the total number of heads obtained divided by the total number of tosses. As the number of tosses gets very large (approaches infinity) the probability of heads approaches .5. Results from such an experiment are expressed mathematically

$$Pr(H) = \lim_{n \to \infty} \left(\sum_{i=1}^{n} \text{Head} \right) \Big/ \left(\sum_{i=1}^{n} \text{Trials} \right) \qquad \textbf{(6.45)}$$

Considering that an investment must be made once (there is no opportunity for repeated chances many times in the real world), it may appear that the long-run relative frequency concept has limited usefulness in investments.

On the other hand, considering the thousands of opportunities in the securities markets as of any particular time (i.e., considering a cross section of the market), this long run relative frequency concept of probability can take on added meaning. Also, for studying the behavior of securities markets *through time*, this particular notion of probability is useful. Finally, even though the actual investment decision can be made only once, using simulation methods, probability distributions using the long-run relative frequency concept can be generated.

B. Extended Frequency Concept

The extended-frequency school of probability chooses the same observational starting point as the long-run relative frequency school. However, these scholars avoid postulating the existence of definite limits for the ratio of sums. Instead of postulating that the frequency ratio stated in equation (6.45) tends toward a definite limit as the number of tosses becomes very large, the extended-frequency school introduces the probability of an event simply as a number associated with that event. For example, if we were to perform a coin-tossing experiment, then the concrete meaning of the assertion that the probability of a head equals one-half is the following. In a long series of repetitious coin tossing, it is practically certain that heads will appear approximately half the time.

Observe that to define a probability using both concept 1 and concept 2, two items must be specified: the type of random experiment (e.g., coin tossing, throwing a die, or selecting a security out of a box), and the definition of "success" (e.g., a head, an ace, or a $1 million return). With both these items specified, then we can speak of the probability of success without ambiguity.

If success is impossible (i.e., the desired event can never occur during the performance of the specified experiment), then the probability of success is taken to be zero. For example, it is impossible to obtain an "ace" on a toss of a coin. Aces occur only on a throw of a die.

On the other hand, if it is known beforehand that the probability of success equals zero, then, according to probability concept 2, success is not necessarily an impossible event. That is, the extended-frequency interpretation of probability implies that the frequency ratio in equation (6.45) will be approximately equal to zero, so that in the long run, success (or failure) can occur in a very small proportion of the time.

For example, suppose we have a box the size of the earth filled with blue beads 1 centimeter (or inch) in diameter. Now add one red bead to the pile. Mix thoroughly and select a bead at random. Chances are that you will not get the red bead, but it is possible that you might. The probability of red (under these conditions) equals approximately zero; yet red is a possible event.

C. Probability Is a Relative Proportion

A third concept of probability dates back to the year 1812, when the mathematician LaPlace articulated the classical relative proportion concept of probability as,

"...a division in—equally possible—cases is conceivable in any kind of observations, and the probability of an event is the ratio between the number of cases favorable to the event, and the total number of possible cases...."

Stated mathematically,

$$\text{Probability of success} = \left(\frac{\text{Number of ways success can occur}}{\text{Number of possible outcomes}} \right) \quad \textbf{(6.46)}$$

Using the relative proportion concept of probability, the probability of a head on a toss of a coin equals 1:2, because on any particular toss there are two possible outcomes (heads or tails) and success can occur only one way (heads). Therefore, the probability of a head equals 1:2.

Using a different example, there are 36 possible ways to throw two dice (count the possible ways). Therefore, on a throw of two dice, the *probability* of a "7" is 6 out of 36 or 1:6.

D. Degrees of Reasonable Belief and Subjective Betting Odds

A fourth concept is that a probability distribution depicts the betting odds which a gambler is willing to accept (subjectively) regarding the outcome of a particular event. This concept is of particular importance in investment analysis.

The idea is that probability is subjective (dependent upon degrees of reasonable belief) instead of completely objective and deterministic by experiment as described with the first three concepts. Subjective probabilities have no direct connection with random experiments and, thus, no obvious frequency interpretation. To apply this concept, one must be able to express in numerical terms the degree of practical certainty one believes regarding the validity of future outcomes of an event.

When the ratio of the number of successes is unknown, one can establish a subjective basis of what would be the betting odds involved in the one-shot deal to come. That is, suppose you are to receive (win) W dollars if an outcome does not occur; suppose you are to pay (lose) L dollars if an outcome does occur. One can establish some sort of feeling or belief to accept or reject the stated odds (i.e., establish a relationship between returns so as to calculate a probability).

Now, if we assume a fair game, and if the game is to be played repeatedly, then, on average, the winning (W) will precisely equal the losses (L). That is to say, if p equals the probability of winning then $1 - p$ equals the probability of losing so that the expected value of winnings [$\$W(p)$] precisely equals the expected value of losses $\$L(1 - p)$, if the game is fair.

$$Wp = L(1 - p) \tag{6.47}$$

Solving equation (6.47) for p, the probability of winning, we get

$$p = L/(W + L) \tag{6.48}$$

and the probability of losing is

$$(1 - p) = \frac{(W + L)}{(W + L)} - \frac{L}{(W + L)} = W/(W + L) \tag{6.49}$$

The betting odds (the ratio of L to W) equal

$$L/W = p/(1 - p) \tag{6.50}$$

Equation (6.50) states that odds of 3 (pay) to 2 (receive) means that the probability of winning must equal $3:5$. Alternatively, betting odds of 2 (pay) to 3 (receive) implies that the *probability* of winning must be $2:5$.

Odds of $L = 1: W = 0$ imply probability of winning $= 1:1$ (certain winning). Likewise, odds of $L = 0: W = 1$ imply probability of winning $= 0:1 = 0$ (certain loss).

To summarize, *probability* has been stated and used in four essentially different ways (1) a long-run relative frequency, (2) extended frequency, (3) the number of possible successes as compared with the number of possible combinations of outcomes, and (4) a subjective assessment (e.g., betting odds) of the likely outcome of a future event. For purposes of investment analysis, this fourth view of probability is very important because, like a horse race, an investment is often a one-shot affair in which it is not possible to observe objective long-run relative frequencies.[13]

[13] For further reading on these alternative notions of probability distributions, see H. Cramer, *Mathematical Methods of Statistics*, Princeton, 1946.

REVIEW OF SOME THEOREMS FROM STATISTICS

The purpose of this appendix is to list in one place some statistical theorems which are important for understanding future subject material.

The Central Limit Theorem

Because of its widespread applicability, the central limit theorem is one of the most powerful and most important of all the theorems from statistics. The central limit theorem is important in financial analysis and investments because it tells us that normal probability distributions are applicable in a large number of cases in the real world. Use of the theorem permits us to simplify analyses using only two measurements, mean and variance, to define an entire probability distribution.

The central limit theorem can be stated as follows. Consider the random variables x's and y,

$$y = x_1 + x_2 + x_3 + \cdots + x_n \qquad (6.51)$$

where the x's are independent (i.e., statistically uncorrelated) and x_i has the mean value (μ_i) and the variance (σ_i^2) with each σ_i^2 finite. Then, subject to very lenient conditions and regardless of the amplitude (i.e., shape) of individual x_i distributions (i.e., the amplitude of the component distributions), the central limit theorem states that as the number of individual x_i becomes very large, the amplitude of the distribution of y approaches the normal or Gaussian distribution.

Put a different way, the central limit theorem tells us that although the sampling distributions for individual independent variables are different in shape, the probability distribution for a resultant large-size sample, obtained by taking observations at random from each of the component distributions, is normal in shape.

Generally there are only two conditions necessary to assure validity of the central limit theorem. They are that (1) the contribution of any particular individual component (μ_i) from equation (6.51) is small, compared with the total value of the sum (y) and (2) the variance of each individual component (σ_j^2) is finite.

For security prices, there is some doubt that this second requirement is met. Some scholars have presented evidence to indicate that the variance is infinite for probability distributions of successive price changes of risky securities.[14] Hence, financial analysts must be aware

---

[14] See (1) Benoit Mandelbrot, "The Variation of Certain Speculative Prices," *Journal of Business*, vol. 36, no. 4, October 1963, pp. 394–419;

that the limiting distribution of a sum of independent random variables can be non-Gaussian.

Tchebycheff's Theorem

Tchebycheff's[15] theorem is applicable for those cases in which the mean and variance are both finite but the particular shape of the probability distribution is unknown, and we do not wish to invoke the central limit theorem. Just as with the central limit theorem, Tchebycheff's theorem enables us to make probability statements concerning possible returns on investment. These probability statements can be made within definite, specified confidence intervals.

Consider an arbitrary probability distribution with mean (μ) and variance (σ^2) both finite. Then choose any arbitrary finite positive number δ and let δ be constant. Then the total area under the probability curve can be divided into four parts as shown in Figure 6.4. For all observations (x's) in the two areas adjacent to the mean (the areas marked A), we can write

$$|X_A - \mu| \leq \delta\sigma \tag{6.52}$$

For all x's in the two tail areas (the areas marked B) on Figure 6.4

$$|X_B - \mu| > \delta\sigma \tag{6.53}$$

Now, since we defined variance to be[16]

$$\sigma^2 = \sum_{i=1}^{N} Pr_i(X_i - \mu)^2 \tag{6.54}$$

the total variance of the distribution equals the sum of the variance in the tail areas plus the variance in the adjacent areas, or

$$\sigma^2_{\text{total}} = \sigma^2_A + \sigma^2_B \tag{6.55}$$

Therefore, since $\sigma^2_A > 0$, we can write

$$\sigma^2_{\text{total}} > \sigma^2_B = \sum_{i=1}^{m_1} Pr_i(X_i - \mu)^2 + \sum_{i=1}^{m_2} Pr_i(X_i - \mu)^2 \tag{6.56}$$

---

(2) Eugene Fama, "The Behavior of Stock Market Prices," *Journal of Business*, vol. XXVIII, no. 1, January 1965; and (3) Fred B. Renwick, "Theory of Investment Behavior & Empirical Analysis of Stock Market Price Relatives," *Management Science*, vol. 15, no. 1, September 1968.

[15] Tchebycheff is sometimes spelled Chebychev.

[16] This is an example of a discrete probability distribution (instead of continuous) so as to avoid using integrals.

Probability

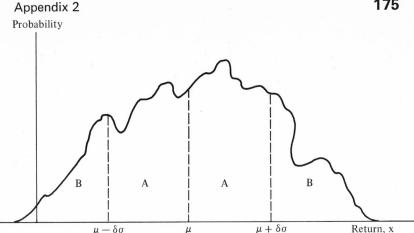

Figure 6.4. Arbitrary probability distribution of returns.

where

$\quad m_1$ = number of X_i's in the left-tail area.

$\quad m_2$ = number of X_i's in the right-tail area.

Squaring both sides of (6.53) and substituting into (6.56), we get

$$\sigma^2_{total} > \sum_{i=1}^{m_1} Pr_i(\delta^2\sigma^2) + \sum_{i=1}^{m_2} Pr_i(\delta^2\sigma^2) = \delta^2\sigma^2\left[\left(\sum_{i=1}^{m_1} Pr_i\right) + \left(\sum_{i=1}^{m_2} Pr_i\right)\right]$$

(6.57)

Dividing both sides of (6.57) by the positive constant $\delta^2\sigma^2$, we get

$$\left(\sum_{i=1}^{m_1} Pr_i\right) + \left(\sum_{i=1}^{m_2} Pr_i\right) < 1/\delta^2 \qquad (6.58)$$

Statement (6.58) is Tchebycheff's theorem. It says that for *any* probability distribution which has a mean and finite variance, the probability of differing from the mean by more than any chosen (constant) number of standard deviations (δ) is less than $1/\delta^2$. Tchebycheff's theorem is useful in situations where the distribution of possible returns is known to have a finite mean and variance, but where the *shape* of distribution is unknown.

If the shape is known to be normal, then more precise probability statements can be made. For example, the probabilities of outcomes falling in the tail areas 1, 2, 3 or more standard deviation units from the mean for normal and for Tchebycheff distributions are shown and compared in Table 6.11.

Bienayme—Tchebycheff Inequality

This inequality derived by Bienayme, in the middle of the nineteenth century, states that

$$Pr(|x - a| > \delta\sigma) \leq 1/\delta^2 \qquad (6.59)$$

where

$$E(x) = a$$
$$0 < E(x - a)^2 < \infty$$
$$\delta > 1$$

Table 6.11 PROBABILITY OF
DEVIATING BY A
SPECIFIED AMOUNT
$[Pr(|x - \mu| > \delta\sigma)]$

δ	**Distribution**	
	Normal	**Tchebycheff**
1	.3174	1.000
2	.0456	.250
3	.0026	.1111
4	.0000634	.0625
5	.0000005734	.0400

Verbally, (6.59) says the probability that a variate will differ from its mean by more than δ times its standard deviation is at most $1/\delta^2$, for any probability distribution. Stated differently, (6.59) means that for *any* shape distribution with finite mean and variance, at least $(1 - 1/\delta^2)$ 100 percent of the values are distributed in a range ($\pm \delta\sigma$) around the average. For example using the Tchebycheff values from Table 6.11, for any shape distribution, at least 25 percent of the observations which comprise the distribution are located within the range $\pm$ two ($\delta = 2$) standard deviations about the mean. The Tchebycheff limits may sound rather crude, but they can be quite useful (and profitable) when properly applied in portfolio analysis.

Tchebycheff Inequality

Tchebycheff's inequality states that for every possible return (R) greater than zero

$$Pr[G(R) > k] \le E[G(R)]/k \qquad \textbf{(6.60)}$$

where $G(R)$ is any nonnegative function of a random return, R. If $G(R) = (R - \mu)^2$, μ being the mean of R, and $k = \delta^2\sigma^2$, and σ^2 being the variance of R, then Tchebycheff's inequality reduces to the Bienayme-Tchebycheff inequality.

Bernoulli's Theorem

This theorem was propounded by James Bernoulli before his death in 1705 but was not published until 1713. In effect, the theorem states that when sampling from a universe with finite mean and variance, the proportion of "successes" in the sample will approach the proportion of "successes" in the universe as the size of sample increases. Redefined, Bernoulli's theorem states that the probability of deviating from the expected value of a proportion of events can be made as small as we wish by increasing the number of trials or observations sufficiently.

Bernoulli's theorem can be stated more precisely as follows. For a binomial distribution, the mean of the proportion k/n of successes is p, and the variance is pq/n. Applying Tchebycheff's inequality (6.59), we find that

$$Pr(|k/n - p| > \delta\sqrt{pq/n}) < 1/\delta^2 \qquad (6.61)$$

Now we choose any positive number ϵ so that

$$\epsilon = \delta\sqrt{pq/n} > 0 \qquad (6.62)$$

Then, if we choose $n > 1/(4\delta\epsilon^2)$, it is practically certain that, in one single series of n repetitions of the experiment, we shall have $|k/n - p| < \epsilon$. The particular value of δ we shall choose in order to realize a satisfactory degree of practical certainty depends on the risk that we are willing to run with respect to a failure of our predictions.

If ϵ is held fixed, then, as n changes, δ is to be changed appropriately, so that ϵ remains constant. Substituting (6.62) into (6.61) and noting that $1/\delta^2 = pq/(n\epsilon^2)$, we obtain

$$Pr(|k/n - p| > \epsilon) < pq/(n\epsilon^2) \qquad (6.63)$$

Equation (6.63) is Bernoulli's theorem. If we let n increase without limit, the right-hand side of (6.63) approaches zero; so the left-hand side is constrained to approach zero, regardless of how small we choose ϵ. In other words, increase the sample size and decrease the probability of deviating from the mean of the universe.

Bernoulli's theorem verifies our intuition. Nevertheless, while the probability of a deviation (no matter how small) approaches zero, no deviation (no matter how large) is impossible. There is a reason for this. To illustrate, consider the box discussed under the extended frequency concept of probability. The box is the size of the earth, filled with blue beads 1 inch (or centimeter) in diameter. Add one red bead to the box and stir thoroughly. Now draw one bead at random. The outcome will "certainly" be blue, because the probability of red is extremely small, about 10^{-27}, but the probability for the bead which was in fact selected is no larger.

Bernoulli's theorem, like Tchebycheff's, is strong enough to serve as a basis for mathematical statistics and to make inferences about the real world on the basis of probability theory. To apply the theory, there must be a sufficiently large number of observations. We shall use these theorems in the study of price behavior in securities markets and for selecting and evaluating performance of risky portfolios.

Some Elementary Theorems

Theorem 1. The expected value of a sum equals the sum of expected values

$$E(R_1 + R_2) = E(R_1) + E(R_2) \tag{6.64}$$

Proof. Let there be two universes, i.e., two bowls, designated R_1 and R_2, containing chips marked in the following manner

$$R_1: a_1, a_2, \ldots, a_N$$
$$R_2: b_1, b_2, \ldots, b_M$$

M and N may or may not be equal. Then,

$$
\begin{aligned}
E(R_1 + R_2) &= \sum_{i=1}^{(N+M)} \{R_{1i}[Pr(R_{1i})] + [R_{2i}Pr(R_{2i})]\} \\
&= \sum_{i=1}^{N} \{R_{1i}[Pr(R_{1i})]\} + \sum_{i=1}^{M} \{R_{2i}[Pr(R_{2i})]\} \tag{6.65} \\
&= E(R_1) + E(R_2)
\end{aligned}
$$

The results are true whether R_1 and R_2 are correlated or not.

Theorem. 2. The variance of a constant multiplied by a variable equals the square of the constant, multiplied by the variance of the variable.

$$\mathrm{var}(aR) = a^2\mathrm{var}(R) \tag{6.66}$$

where a represents any positive constant.

Proof.

$$
\begin{aligned}
\mathrm{var}(aR) &= E[aR - E(aR)]^2 = E\{a[R - E(R)]\}^2 \\
&= a^2E[R - E(R)]^2 = a^2\mathrm{var}(R). \tag{6.67}
\end{aligned}
$$

Theorem. 3. The variance of a sum of two variables equals the sum of variances of the two variables, plus twice the covariance between the two variables.

$$\mathrm{var}(R_1 + R_2) = \mathrm{var}(R_1) + \mathrm{var}(R_2) + 2\mathrm{cov}(R_1, R_2) \tag{6.68}$$

Proof.

$$
\begin{aligned}
\mathrm{var}(R_1 + R_2) &= E[(R_1 + R_2) - E(R_1 + R_2)]^2 \\
&= E\{[R_1 - E(R_1)] + [R_2 - E(R_2)]\}^2 \\
&= E[R_1 - E(R_1)]^2 + E[R_2 - E(R_2)]^2 \tag{6.69} \\
&\quad + 2E\{[R_1 - E(R_1)][R_2 - E(R_2)]\} \\
&= \mathrm{var}(R_1) + \mathrm{var}(R_2) + 2\mathrm{cov}(R_1, R_2)
\end{aligned}
$$

That is, the covariance of R_1 with R_2 [cov(R_1, R_2)], is the expected value or arithmetic mean of the cross products of deviations. Since the value of the covariance is influenced by the units in which the deviations are expressed, this influence is frequently eliminated by standardizing the covariance. Standardization is accomplished by expressing covariance in terms of correlation.

$$\rho_{R1,R2} = \frac{E\{[R_1 - E(R_1)][R_2 - E(R_2)]\}}{\sigma(R_1)\sigma(R_2)} = \frac{\text{cov}(R_1, R_2)}{\sigma(R_1)\sigma(R_2)} \quad (6.70)$$

This measure, (6.70), is an expression of the degree to which the variables R_1 and R_2 are linearly related. This measure is called ρ, the coefficient of linear correlation.

The coefficient of linear correlation, ρ, is a measure of the *degree of linear relationship* between two variables. For example, if two variables are related linearly to each other so that if the value of one variable increases then the value for the other variable also increases by a *determinate amount*, then the two variables are perfectly and positively correlated. In this situation, the coefficient of correlation is $+1$.

The covariance is a measure of the extent (if any) to which R_i will deviate from its expected value if R_j deviates from its expected value. Hence, given two mean values [$E(R_1)$ and $E(R_2)$], negative covariance implies that outcomes below the expected value of security 1 are usually accompanied by outcomes above the expected value for security 2 and vice versa.

Theorem. 4. The variance of a difference between two variables equals the sum of variances of the two variables, minus twice the covariance between the two variables.

Proof.

$$\begin{aligned}
\text{var}(R_1 - R_2) &= E[(R_1 - R_2) - E(R_1 - R_2)]^2 \\
&= E\{[R_1 - E(R_1)] - [R_2 - E(R_2)]\}^2 \\
&= E\{[R_1 - E(R_1)]^2 - 2[R_1 - E(R_1)][R_2 - E(R_2)] \\
&\qquad + [R_2 - E(R_2)]^2\} \quad (6.71) \\
&= \text{var}(R_1) - 2\text{cov}(R_1, R_2) + \text{var}(R_2)
\end{aligned}$$

Theorem. 5. The variance of a weighted sum of variables equals the square of each weight, times the variance of the associated variable, plus twice the weighted covariance between all possible pairs—all summed.

$$\text{var}(a_1 R_1 + a_2 R_2) = a_1^2 \text{var}(R_1) + a_2^2 \text{var}(R_2) + 2a_1 a_2 \text{cov}(R_1, R_2) \quad (6.72)$$

Proof.

$$\begin{aligned}
\text{var}(a_1 R_1 + a_2 R_2) &= E[(a_1 R_1 + a_2 R_2) - E(a_1 R_1 + a_2 R_2)]^2 \\
&= E\{a_1[R_1 - E(R_1)] + a_2[R_2 - E(R_2)]\}^2 \\
&= E\{a_1^2[R_1 - E(R_1)]^2\} + E\{a_2^2[R_2 - E(R_2)]^2\} \\
&\quad + E\{2a_1 a_2[R_1 - E(R_1)][R_2 - E(R_2)]\} \\
&= a_1^2 \text{var}(R_1) + a_2^2 \text{var}(R_2) + 2a_1 a_2 \text{cov}(R_1, R_2)
\end{aligned}$$

Theorem. 6. The expected value of the square of a random variable equals the square of the expected value, plus the variance of the variable.

$$E(R^2) = \text{var}(R) + [E(R)]^2 \tag{6.74}$$

Proof.

$$\begin{aligned}
\text{var}(R) &= E[R - E(R)]^2 \\
&= E\{R^2 - 2RE(R) + [E(R)]^2\} \\
&= E[R^2] - [E(R)]^2 \\
E[R_2] &= \text{var}(R) + [E(R)]^2
\end{aligned} \tag{6.75}$$

Theorem. 7. The coefficient of correlation (ρ) is related to the slope of a regression line (β).

$$\beta_{R1, R2} = \rho_{R1, R2}\sigma(R_1)/\sigma(R_2) \tag{6.76}$$

Proof. First, we can rewrite (6.70) as an average sum of cross products divided by the product of two calculated standard errors.

$$\begin{aligned}
\rho_{R1, R2} &= \frac{\dfrac{1}{N} \sum\limits_{i=1}^{N} [R_{1i} - E(R_1)][R_{2i} - E(R_2)]}{\sigma(R_1)\sigma(R_2)} \\
&= \frac{\text{cov}(R_1, R_2)}{\sigma(R_1)\sigma(R_2)}
\end{aligned} \tag{6.77}$$

Second, we can write the definition of a regression. A regression is a relationship between deviations from mean values.

$$[R_{1C} - E(R_1)] = \beta_{R1, R2}[R_2 - E(R_2)] \tag{6.78}$$

where R_{1C} denotes the calculated value of the dependent variable, R_1. Using the least-squares statistical procedure of minimizing the error of estimate, the slope, β, equals a sum of cross-product deviations divided by a sum of squared deviations.

$$\beta_{R1, R2} = \frac{\dfrac{1}{N} \sum\limits_{i=1}^{N} \{[R_{1i} - E(R_1)][R_{2i} - E(R_2)]\}}{\dfrac{1}{N} \sum\limits_{i=1}^{N} [R_{2i} - E(R_2)]^2} \tag{6.79}$$

Third, substituting the value of the numerator from (6.77) into (6.79) and simplifying, we get

$$\beta_{R1,R2} = \frac{\rho_{R1,R2}\sigma(R_1)\sigma(R_2)}{\text{var}(R_2)} = \rho_{R1,R2}\sigma(R_1)/\sigma(R_2) \qquad (6.80)$$

Theorem. 8. When two variables are correlated, the *coefficient of determination*, $\rho^2_{R1,R2}$ (rho squared), indicates the percent of dispersion of the dependent variable that is associated with (i.e., explained by) the explanatory variable. That is, the universe coefficient of correlation is called $\rho_{R1,R2}$ and the square of $\rho_{R1,R2}$ is called the universe coefficient of determination $[\rho^2_{R1,R2}]$. Then

$$\rho^2_{R1,R2} = \left[\frac{\text{cov}(R_1,R_2)}{\sigma(R_1)\sigma(R_2)}\right]^2 = \frac{\sum_{i=1}^{N}[R_{1Ci} - E(R_1)]^2}{\sum_{i=1}^{N}[R_{1i} - E(R_1)]^2} \qquad (6.81)$$

where $E(R_1)$ denotes the mean value for R_1.

Proof. First, write the total variation in the dependent variable. The total variation of the dependent variable is the sum of the squared deviations, written

$$\text{Total sum of squares} = \sum_{i=1}^{N}[R_{1i} - E(R_1)]^2 \qquad (6.82)$$

Then the sum of squares associated with calculated values (via linear regression) can be written

$$\text{Associated sum of squares} = \sum_{i=1}^{N}[R_{1Ci} - E(R_1)]^2 \qquad (6.83)$$

$$\text{Unassociated sum of squares} = \sum_{i=1}^{N}[R_{1i} - E(R_{1C})]^2 \qquad (6.84)$$

and

$$\text{Total sum of squares} = \text{Associated} + \text{Unassociated} \qquad (6.85)$$

Then the associated variation (relative to the total variation) expressed as a percent, by definition, is the coefficient of determination.

$$\rho^2_{R1,R2} = \frac{\sum_{i=1}^{N}[R_{1Ci} - E(R_1)]^2}{\sum_{i=1}^{N}[R_{1i} - E(R_1)]^2} \qquad (6.86)$$

The equality expressed in (6.81) can be shown as follows. From regression, equation (6.78)

$$R_{1C} - E(R_1) = \beta_{R1,R2}[R_2 - E(R_2)] \qquad (6.87)$$

so that

$$\rho_{R1,R2}^2 = \frac{\sum\limits_{i=1}^{N} [R_{1Ci} - E(R_1)]^2}{\sum\limits_{i=1}^{N} [R_{1i} - E(R_1)]^2} = \frac{\beta_{R1,R2}^2 \left\{ \sum\limits_{i=1}^{N} [R_{2i} - E(R_2)]^2 \right\}}{\sum\limits_{i=1}^{N} [R_{1i} - E(R_1)]^2}$$

(6.88)

If we substitute the value of $\beta_{R1,R2}$ as defined in (6.79) into the numerator of (6.88), we get

$$\rho_{R1,R2}^2 = \left(\frac{\sum\limits_{i=1}^{N} \{[R_{1i} - E(R_1)] [R_{2i} - E(R_2)]\}}{\sum\limits_{i=1}^{N} [R_{2i} - E(R_2)]^2} \right)^2 \left\{ \frac{\sum\limits_{i=1}^{N} [R_{2i} - E(R_2)]^2}{\sum\limits_{i=1}^{N} [R_{1i} - E(R_1)]^2} \right\}$$

(6.89)

Terms in the numerator and denominator of the right-hand side of (6.89) are equal and divide out, so (6.89) simplifies to

$$\rho_{R1,R2}^2 = \frac{\left(\frac{1}{N} \sum\limits_{i=1}^{N} \{[R_{1i} - E(R_1)] [R_{2i} - E(R_2)]\} \right)^2}{\left\{ \frac{1}{N} \sum\limits_{i=1}^{N} [R_{1i} - E(R_1)]^2 \right\} \left\{ \frac{1}{N} \sum\limits_{i=1}^{N} [R_{2i} - E(R_2)]^2 \right\}}$$

$$= \frac{[\text{cov}(R_1,R_2)]^2}{\sigma^2(R_1)\sigma^2(R_2)}$$

(6.90)

$$= \left[\frac{\text{cov}(R_1,R_2)}{\sigma(R_1)\sigma(R_2)} \right]^2$$

QUESTIONS FOR STUDY

1. Compare and contrast alternative methods of analysis for capital budgeting (investment selection) under certainty. List all necessary assumptions and illustrate the technique of analysis. How do the methods differ if risk and uncertainty are admitted?
2. Explain the nature of the investment decision under risk and/or uncertainty.
3. Explain and illustrate, with an example, the use of probabilistic information for the evaluation of risky investments.
4. Explain the application of Monte Carlo simulation in risk analysis in capital investment.
5. (a) What is risk?
   (b) How can risk best be measured?
6. In evaluating risk, it is sufficient to analyze dispersion about the mean. True or false? Defend your answer.
7. Various scholars disagree over the appropriate measure of risk for a share of common stock. Two yardsticks that we have studied are variance of expected return on investment and variance of expected

rate of growth of income. Many other measures are possible. What measure of risk would you recommend to a client and *why*?

8. Using data from Table 6.4, calculate the following measures of risk for the two investments I_2 and I_3:
    (a) Expected return
    (b) Variance of return
    (c) Standard deviation
    (d) Coefficient of variation
    (e) Skewness
    (f) Normalized third moment
    (g) Semistandard deviation

9. Generalize equation (6.68) to include n securities, where n might be any positive integer greater than 2.

10. *Given.* A $1000 corporate bond with interest income expected to be $60 each year for 2 years. At the end of the second year, after receiving interest, you expect to sell the bond for $1000. *Question.* If you expect the firm to default on either one or both of the interest payments, and if interest is 6 percent, then how much will you be willing to pay for the bond today?

11. Which investment would you choose, A or B, assuming each alternative requires an outlay of $100 today. In 2 years hence, A returns $150 with standard error $10. In 4 years hence, B returns $250 with standard error of $20.

12. For each of the following two alternatives, which investment is preferable [(a) or (b)] and *why*?
    (a) Invest $100 today and receive $106 with variance of $4, 12 months hence.
    (b) Invest $100 today and receive $115 with variance of $16, 8 months hence.

13. You are considering the purchase of common stock (today) for $800. Your forecast indicates that next year the shares will be worth $1100, with a variance of 48,400. If your opportunity cost of capital is 10 percent, should the investment be undertaken? (Note: $\sqrt{48,400} = 220$).

14. Consider the two alternative investments shown in Table 6.12. If the current rate of interest is 10 percent, which of the two alternative investments do you prefer? Why?

Table 6.12   DATA FOR ANALYSIS OF TWO ALTERNATIVE INVESTMENTS

Invest-ment	T_0 ($) μ	σ	T_1 ($) μ	σ	T_2 ($) μ	σ	T_3 ($) μ	σ	T_4 ($) μ	σ
A	−100	0	55	5	242	150	—	—	—	—
B	−100	0	11	1.10	—	—	200	60	440	140

15. A publishing house is considering the publication of a novel. Present information indicates equal likelihood that demand may be either 2000,

3000, or 4000 books. The books will cost $4.50 each and will sell for $10.50 each. Assume that any books left unsold by the end of the accounting period may be disposed of at a "bargain sale" of $3.50 each. *Question.* For a price of $1000 a consultant offers to make a market survey and reduce the risk associated with sales.
  (a) Explain why you would accept, reject, or be indifferent to the offer.
  (b) What price by the consultant will cause you to change your decision?

16. Assume that you have a budget of $100 available for investment and that you have either of two alternative opportunities: (a) invest $100 at 12 percent, compounded quarterly, for a period of 4 years, or (b) invest $100 at 8 percent, compounded semiannually, for a period of 2 years. *Question.* At what rate of reinvestment will you be indifferent to accepting either of the two alternative opportunities?

17. List and evaluate four methods of determining the relative profitability of alternative investment proposals. What assumptions do these methods make? What problems are involved?

18. When measuring the worth of investments under risk or uncertainty, ranking by an index of net present value will always equal an alternative ranking by internal rate of return. True or false? Explain.

19. The technique of Monte Carlo simulation is not applicable to investment analysis because no simulation can replace judgment. True or false? Explain.

20. Suppose that your employer agrees to pay you a salary of $12,000 per year; however, he also tells you that payday may come at the end of a week, at the end of a month, at the end of a quarter, or at the end of the year, depending on the level of sales and the state of accounts receivable at that time. This illustrates a case of uncertainty because you are uncertain as to precisely when payday may come. True or false? Explain.

21. The objective of good investment management is to maximize net present value. True or false? Explain.

22. (a) What are "models" as we have used them thus far? How can models be of use to the financial manager? What are the advantages and limitations of models?
  (b) What constitutes the role of the financial manager?

23. Suppose that you invest $100 in each of two securities. One security sells for $10 per share while the other security sells for $20 per share. Two years later, ignoring dividends, you sell the $10 security at a price of $5 per share, incurring a loss, and sell the $20 security at a price of $40 per share, taking a profit. *Question.* What is your rate of return on the two-stock portfolio?

24. Consider two alternative investments: (a) a 5 percent coupon, $1000 bond priced at face value, due to mature in three years, and (b) a $1000 bond, priced at face value, with a 10 percent coupon, due to mature in 5 years. The cash flows are depicted in Table 6.13. Which of the two alternative investments will you choose? Why?

Table 6.13 TIME DISTRIBUTION FOR TWO CASH FLOWS

Investment	T_0 ($)	T_1 ($)	T_2 ($)	T_3 ($)	T_4 ($)	T_5 ($)
A	−1000	50	50	1050	—	—
B	−1000	100	100	100	100	1100

25. Prove that the expectation of a product of two random variables equals the product of expectations, plus a second factor involving standard deviations and coefficient of correlation.

$$E[(R_1)(R_2)] = [E(R_1)][E(R_2)] + \rho_{R1,R2}[\sigma(R_1)][\sigma(R_2)] \quad \textbf{(6.91)}$$

where $\rho_{R1,R2}$ is by definition the Pearson correlation coefficient between R_1 and R_2. Explain the relevance of $E[(R_1)(R_2)]$ to asset management.

Elements of Security Analysis **Part III**

In studying the theory and practice of asset management, one point is unmistakable. Issues, opinions, and interpretations of facts are all surrounded by controversy. Rarely do financial analysts and scholars of capital theory come close to unanimous agreement on the causes of fluctuations in market prices for common stock and other risky assets. In this and the next two chapters, we shall study these issues and examine the writings of many of the experts and see what they have had to say on various points.

In long-term analysis, the controversies tend to be based on fundamental economic and corporate financial factors. At issue is the fundamental cause(s) of change in share price over the long term. Which particular fundamental factors cause security prices to behave as they do?

The Value of Assets
7

Some scholars believe that corporate *dividend payments* are extremely important in evaluating the worth of a share—with a dollar of current dividends being worth perhaps four times as much as a dollar of retained earnings. This dividend effect was observed by Graham and Dodd in 1934, with only slight alterations some 30 years later.[1] More recently, after extensive empirical tests, Friend and Puckett concluded that, in the stock market generally, except for unusual growth stocks, there is little basis for the customary view that a dollar of dividends has several times the impact on price of a dollar of retained earnings.[2]

At the other extreme, on this same issue of dividend policy, some scholars believe that corporate dividend payments are in no way

---

[1] Benjamin Graham and David L. Dodd, *Security Analysis*, 1st ed., McGraw-Hill, Inc., New York, 1934, and also *Security Analysis*, 4th ed., 1962.

[2] Irwin Friend and Marshall Puckett, "Dividends and Stock Prices," *American Economic Review*, vol. LIV, September 1964, pp. 656–682.

relevant to evaluating the worth of a share. So, at the date of this writing, the question remains, Are share prices in fact affected by corporate dividend policy, or are dividend payments merely an artifact which in no way affects the worth of equity ownership? The pros and cons of these viewpoints are discussed below in some detail.

Another controversial issue concerns the relevance (or nonrelevance) of *debt financing* to the market value of the firm and, therefore, to the market price of equity shares. As with dividend policy, there are sharp differences in opinion. These differences are also discussed in Chapter 7.

In short-term analysis, the major issue is whether changes in share price occur at random (nondeterministic) or whether changes in price are systematic and can be explained by nonrandom or deterministic factors. As a matter of empirical observation, day-to-day, week-to-week, and month-to-month fluctuations in price do appear to be indistinguishable from the characteristic random walk exhibited by an inebriated wanderer. Also, there is great concern over whether the distributions of changes in stock market prices have finite or infinite variances. If infinite, the implication is that most of the statistical methods currently used by most analysts—methods which *assume* that the variance of the population is finite—are rendered useless. Uselessness results because the underlying assumptions necessary for statistical inference are violated. If the variance of the population is infinite instead of finite, then statistical inferences made regarding the population (based on an observed sample from that population) are meaningless, no matter how large the size of sample. This is true even if the sample size increases toward the size of the population because there exists a finite (nonzero) probability that an observation (price change) of still larger magnitude (i.e., infinite magnitude) can possibly be obtained on the next draw. The theories and empirical evidence offered in support of these statements regarding price behavior of equity shares in the short run are presented and discussed in Chapter 10.

THE CRITICAL ROLE OF ASSUMPTIONS.   Underlying all of these controversies and debates is the critical role of assumptions. As we shall see, with a particular set of assumptions stated and accepted, logical arguments can lead to disturbing conclusions. Yet, the point of the analysis is to discover what will happen to price under a given set of conditions. If the assumptions are accepted, and if the arguments are sound, then the conclusions must be valid.

The following short outline serves as a guide for the journey.

1. Effects of debt finance on the market value of the firm
    a. Conventional view—*debt matters*
    b. Neoclassical view—*debt does not matter*

7.1 Effects of Debt Finance on the Market Value of the Firm

In this section, we shall discuss two opposing views to determine whether the proportion of debt in the financial structure of a firm affects the market value of equity ownership. One view, the "traditional" theory of finance, sets forth the proposition that corporate management is rightfully concerned with financial policy, including dividend rates as well as debt-equity proportions.

The opposite view, as set forth by capital theorists, the neoclassical view, regards problems such as the calculation of optimum capital structure and optimum dividend rate as nonsense, because the value of corporate assets rests on the earning power of the assets, not on the way assets are financed or on any particular split between retained earnings and dividend payout.

CONVENTIONAL THEORY OF FINANCE.   Consider the market value of the total assets of a firm.

$$A = B + S \tag{7.1}$$

where

A = total current market value of corporate assets
B = total market value of all bonds outstanding (debt financing)
S = total market value of ownership equity (aggregate dollar value of shares outstanding)

For simplicity and with no loss of generality, assume all liabilities to be bonds outstanding (i.e., no short-term borrowing or preferred shares outstanding). Then statement (7.1) indicates that the current market value of corporate assets equals the sum of the market values of assets financed from debt sources plus assets financed from equity sources.

The question is, for any given level of assets, does the relative proportion of debt finance (B/S, or alternatively, B/A), in any way affect S, the worth of equity ownership? According to conventional analysis, the answer is, yes. The rationale is set forth below.[3]

Conventional analysis of the effects of debt finance on the market

[3] Professor Ezra Solomon provides an excellent articulation of the traditional theory of finance in his monograph, *The Theory of Financial Management*, Columbia University Press, 1963, pp. 91–98. The treatment outlined partially follows Professor Solomon's original arguments.

value of the firm proceeds in three phases. The first phase is composed of firms that have little or no debt in their capital structure. Cost of additional debt, additional equity, overall cost of capital, and, the market value of the firm are calculated. The second phase is composed of firms that have moderate amounts of debt in their capital structure. The same calculations are repeated. Finally, the third phase is composed of firms that have ridiculously large amounts of debt in their capital structure, and the calculations are repeated a third time. Upon comparison of the three sets of calculations, the results show that the proportion of debt finance does affect the overall market value of the firm as well as the worth of equity ownership. The theory and calculations are outlined below.

PHASE 1.   All firms in phase 1 of finance have relatively small proportions of debt finance in their capital structure mix. Hence, let the asset valuation begin with zero leverage (i.e., no debt; $B = 0$) and let the total amount of debt increase from zero up to moderate levels, holding equity investment constant. Observe the assumption "holding equity investment constant." The overall result during phase 1 is that as leverage is increased from zero up to relatively moderate levels, the total market value of the firm will rise, as will the aggregate market value of the shares outstanding. The reasoning is as follows.

During phase 1, the explicit cost of borrowing, the interest paid on new added debt, is relatively constant, or else rises only slightly. This is true because creditors, potential as well as actual, consider the relatively small proportions of debt in this phase as being well within financially sound limits. The probability of default (i.e., the inability to meet contractual obligations to pay interest and repay principal) is small.

All firms with a relatively large proportion of equity financing are included in phase 1. Of these, the firms with relatively high income are considered as good credit risks. Being a good credit risk implies that debt financing can be obtained on very favorable (cheap) terms. Debt financing during the first phase, therefore, is conventionally viewed as being relatively cheap because of the relatively small financial risks involved in the loan. Recalling the simplified formula (4.37) from Chapter 4, the explicit cost of the ith increment of debt capital can be stated as [4]

$$k_i = I_i/B_i \qquad\qquad (7.2)$$

---

[4] If flotation costs and other expenses incurred in issuing the new debt are to be considered, then the analysis which follows must be refined to include these costs. Also, the *explicit cost* of debt capital tells only part of the story of total cost of debt financing. The *implicit cost* is considered to be negligible because, during phase 1, added debt causes little, if any, added financial risk.

where

k_i = explicit cost of new debt financing = market rate of discount on the future annual interest payments to be made on the new bonds to be issued (expressed as a decimal)

I_i = future periodic annual interest payments to be made on the new increment of debt (in dollars)

B_i = market value (present worth) of the new bonds to be issued (in dollars)

Therefore, since k_i for each new increment of debt increases slightly (if at all) during phase 1, an increase in the total quantity of bonds outstanding results in a rise in the market value of the aggregate debt outstanding.

$$B = I/k_B \qquad (7.3)$$

where

B = aggregate market value (present worth) of all bonds outstanding (in dollars)

I = total future annual interest payments to be made on all debt outstanding

k_B = cost of total debt capital = constant during phase 1

Next, examine what happens to the market value of outstanding equity during this phase. As more debt is added in phase 1, total interest payments rise, causing a rise in financial risks to equity owners, because income available after interest payments must absorb any and all fluctuations in net operating profit. However, offsetting this rise in risk is the added net earnings on equity which result from the profitable uses to which the relatively low-cost debt funds were put. In other words, during phase 1, additional debt causes relatively small increases in financial risk to share-owners, but these added risks are overpowered (perhaps dominated) by the rise in earnings which are forthcoming because of the added debt. Risks increase slightly, but the returns rise more than risks in this phase, so that the overall effect is equity values rise. The cost of equity capital (i.e., the rate of profit received on equity investment) remains approximately constant (or rises only slightly because of increased risks) with increased leverage during phase 1.

$$k_e = NI/S \qquad (7.4)$$

where

k_e = cost of equity capital = market rate of discount of the future annual net income for the firm

NI = annual net earnings on equity (net income)

S = aggregate market value of stock outstanding

Therefore, since S and B both rise during phase 1, the value of the firm must rise.

Observe the underlying assumption in the traditional theory of finance—that the assets of the firm are expanding because of added debt. Each additional increment of debt is added to the existing asset base, causing a rise in total assets, and therefore, a rise in total corporate earnings.

$$A + \Delta A = B + \Delta B + S \qquad (7.5)$$

where ΔA = change in market value of assets, ΔB = change in market value of bonds outstanding, and other values are constant, as defined previously.

Analysis under conditions of *increasing* assets differs from analysis under conditions of a *constant* asset base in which debt is being substituted for equity. For example, if we let total assets be constant

$$A = B + S \qquad (7.6)$$

where A = constant and the ratio B/S changes from zero toward some moderate proportion, then, an increase in the amount of debt means a decrease (by the same amount) in equity, so that not only is there an increase in total risk, there is a rise in risk per unit of equity because there is less equity. Also, under these conditions there is no additional income to offset this greater risk because total assets remained constant and precluded any additional income. This situation causes the firm to enter a different (higher) class of risk. Under these conditions, the worth of equity ownership will fall, offsetting any rise in the aggregate market value of the bonds outstanding and causing the market value of the firm to rise less rapidly (if at all) than the rise predicted under the assumption of constant equity.

To summarize, according to the conventional theory of finance, the overall effect of increasing corporate debt during phase 1 of increasing leverage is

1. A rise in aggregate market value of bonds outstanding ($B = I/k_B$), caused by a rise in aggregate income obligated to bondholders, with the cost of debt capital (k_B) relatively constant, resulting in
2. A rise in aggregate market value of stock outstanding ($S = NI/k_e$), caused by a relatively large rise in the annual net income (NI), with the small offsetting effect of a relatively slight rise in the rate of discount of the annual net earnings on equity (k_e), resulting in
3 A rise in the total market value of the firm ($V = S + B$).

Solomon notes that a rise in the total market value of the firm during phase 1 can be explained in a different way. That is, during this phase, the overall (weighted average) market rate of discount of net operating profits falls, causing the total market value of the firm to rise. The overall market rate of discount of net operating profits is written as

$$k_0 = k_e W_1 + k_B W_2 \qquad (7.7)$$

where k_0 = present spot market rate of discount of the future annual net operating profits and, W_1, W_2 = weights used for averaging the cost of existing equity capital (k_e) with the cost of existing debt capital (k_B).

The weight W_1 equals the total financing from equity sources, expressed as a percentage of the total financing. The weight W_2 equals the total financing from debt sources, expressed as a percentage of the total financing. The sum of the two weights equals 100 percent of total assets.

$$W_1 = S/(S + B); \qquad W_2 = B/(S + B); \qquad W_1 + W_2 = 1.00 \qquad (7.8)$$

The rationale underlying the formulation of equation (7.7) can be explained as follows. Ignoring corporate tax payments, the total annual net operating income (NOI) expected by the firm equals the sum of annual interest charges on debt outstanding (I) plus annual net earnings (NI) on existing equity.

$$\text{NOI} = \text{NI} + I \qquad (7.9)$$

where

    NOI = periodic net operating income received from operations of the firm

    NI = periodic net income available to common shareholders

    I = periodic interest payments to bondholders

Then the present value of the future stream of net operating income (by definition) equals the market worth of the firm.

$$V = \text{NOI}/k_0 \qquad (7.10)$$

where all terms are the same as defined previously. Expressing (7.10) in terms of k_0, we get

$$k_0 = \text{NOI}/V \\ = (\text{NI} + I)/(S + B) \qquad (7.11)$$

Further, substituting values from statements (7.4) and (7.3) into (7.11), we can write

$$k_0 = (k_e S + k_B B)/(S + B) \\ = k_e[S/(S + B)] + k_B[B/(S + B)] \qquad (7.12) \\ = k_e W_1 + k_B W_2$$

We see that equation (7.12) is identical to equation (7.7), stating that the average (overall) cost of capital to the firm is a weighted average of the cost of equity capital with the cost of debt capital.

Since the cost of additional debt is relatively low during phase 1, and because the corresponding adverse effect of added debt on the cost of equity is relatively small, additional low-cost financing tends to lower the weighted average of the two, causing the overall cost of capital to fall during this phase. Since the money obtained from the added debt is invested profitably by the firm, the net operating income rises. This rise, coupled with a decline in k_0, causes the aggregate market value of the firm to rise.

$$V = \text{NOI}/k_0 \qquad\qquad (7.13)$$

PHASE 2.   Phase 2 in the traditional theory of finance begins with a moderate amount of leverage. Debt is then increased from this moderate level up to a relatively "high" level, still holding equity investment constant. During phase 2, the aggregate market value of shares outstanding falls and, with rising debt, the total market value of the firm remains virtually constant. These results are rationalized as follows.

During phase 2 the cost of additional borrowing (k_i) rises with increasing debt because creditors no longer regard the total proportions of debt as being within the "sound limits" observed in phase 1. Added debt, therefore, causes a rise in financial risk incurred by all debt holders and shareholders of the firm. Even though there is a rise in the aggregate interest income forthcoming to bondholders, the concomitant rise in risk causes a rise in the required rate of return (i.e., the cost of debt capital), so that the total market value of bonds outstanding rises by an amount smaller than the corresponding rise during phase 1. The aggregate market value of the bonds outstanding (B) rises by only a moderate amount for firms in phase 2 of debt financing.

$$B = I/k_B \qquad\qquad (7.14)$$

Also, during phase 2, the cost of equity capital (k_e) rises as debt increases due to the added financial risks inherent in moderate to high fixed-interest payments. However, unlike phase 1, additional net earnings on the existing equity are no longer high enough to offset the added financial risks concomitant with the higher levels of debt. The overall result is that the aggregate market value of the shares outstanding fall as leverage rises during phase 2.

$$S = \text{NI}/k_e \qquad\qquad (7.15)$$

With the aggregate market value of the shares (S) falling and the market value of all bonds outstanding (B) rising during phase 2, the total market value of the firm depends upon the net balance. According to the conventional theory of finance, the balance is such that the total market value of the firm remains virtually constant as leverage is increased

$$V = (\text{NI}/k_e) + (I/k_B) \tag{7.16}$$

To summarize, net income, NI, rises during phase 2 because of additional investment in business operations; however, k_e also rises because of added financial risks. The rise in k_e is of such magnitude that it more than offsets the rise in NI, so that the ratio (NI/k_e) declines. But offsetting this decline is a rise in the ratio I/k_B. The cost of total debt (k_B rises, but more than offsetting the rise in k_B is a rise in total interest income to bondholders (I). The overall impact is that the decline in the ratio NI/k_e is offset by a rise in the ratio I/k_B, so that the market value of the firm (V) remains virtually constant. This also implies that during phase 2, the overall capitalization rate k_0 of operating profit remains virtually constant.

$$k_0 = k_e(S/V) + k_B(B/V) \tag{7.17}$$

PHASE 3.   Phase 3 in the traditional theory of finance begins with high levels of debt and proceeds up to ridiculously high levels. Equity investment is still held constant. Theoretical implications are drawn concerning the resultant impact on the market value of the firm. (Theoretical implications must be drawn because in actual practice members of the financial community will refuse to make additional credit available to firms with ridiculously high levels of existing debt.)

The theory indicates that during phase 3, leverage added beyond a critical level of debt will cause a rapid decline in the total market value of the firm. The reasoning is as follows.

During phase 3, the cost of additional borrowing (k_i) rises rapidly because creditors will make funds available only at very high interest rates, if at all, to compensate for the relatively high probability of default on the credit. The rise in k_B more than offsets the rise in interest income (I) so that the aggregate market value of bonds outstanding falls as additional bonds are issued.

$$B = I/k_B \tag{7.18}$$

Observe at this point that supply and demand can enter the analysis. Thus far, considerations have been limited to the dimensions of time and risk. With the supply of bonds increasing, given constant market demand, equilibrium price tends to fall. This decline in price caused by rising supply tends to reinforce the decline in price caused by added financial risks of the firm.

During phase 3, the cost of equity capital (k_e) rises rapidly because of the relatively high levels of fixed-interest payments. Interest payments have a prior claim and take precedence over payments to equity owners. Net operating profits, if any, are viewed as going mostly to bondholders during phase 3. The worth of equity ownership (S) declines for two reasons: (1) the added financial risks which cause k_e to rise and (2) the probable decline in NI due to high interest charges and a declining marginal efficiency of capital schedule facing the firm.

$$S = \text{NI}/k_e \qquad\qquad (7.19)$$

With both B and S falling during phase 3, the total market value of the firm declines rapidly. The three phases used by traditional finance theorists to explain the impact of debt finance on the market value of the firm can be summarized now.

The market value of the firm reacts in three discernible ways to increases in leverage: (1) with relatively small proportions of debt in the capital structure, further increases in debt will result in a rise in market value of total assets, (2) with moderate proportions of debt, further increases in leverage will have essentially no effect on the market value of the firm (the interacting forces tend to balance one another), and (3) with relatively large proportions of debt, further increases in leverage will cause a sharp decline in the total worth of the firm.

NEOCLASSICAL VIEW OF FINANCE. In this section we study the arguments set forth which lead to the conclusion that the proportion of debt finance in no way affects the total market value of the firm. This view is expressed most eloquently by Professors Modigliani and Miller, who are frequently referred to by the familiar form, "M & M."[5]

M & M argue that debt finance in no way affects the market value of the assets of the firm. The mechanism for balancing the market value of a levered firm is personal leverage and arbitrage. According to M & M, differences in total market value of corporate assets cannot exist between firms if the differences are due solely to differences in capital structure, for if such differences in value were to occur, then market mechanisms (specifically arbitrage) will come into action and remove any differences in value and restore equality and equilibrium. The mechanism for this market action can be explained as follows.

---

[5] F. Modigliani and M. H. Miller, "The Cost of Capital, Corporation Finance, and the Theory of Investment," *The American Economic Review*, vol. XLVIII, no. 3, June 1958, pp. 261–297. Also, see Merton H. Miller and Franco Modigliani, "Some Estimates of the Cost of Capital to the Electric Utility Industry, 1954–57," *The American Economic Review*, vol. LVI, no. 3, June 1966, pp. 333–391.

Consider two firms, identical in all respects except for finance mix.

$$V_1 = S_1 + 0 \qquad (7.20)$$

$$V_2 = S_2 + D_2 \qquad (7.21)$$

$$\text{NOI} = X_1 = X_2 = \bar{X} \qquad (7.22)$$

where

V_1, V_2 = the total market value of companies 1 and 2
S_1, S_2 = the market value of the common shares of companies 1 and 2
D_2 = the market value of the debts of company 2; by assumption, company 1 has all-equity financing
$\bar{X}$ = expected future periodic operating profits of the company (given the risk class), before deduction of interest and taxes

These two firms, by assumption, have the same probability distribution of expected net operating profits and consequently belong to the same risk class. M & M use risk class in the sense of business risk, not financial risk. Business risk can be measured by the coefficient of variation of expected net operating income.[6]

Then, M & M proceed to show that the market value of a firm depends upon the operating profits ($\bar{X}$), not upon the particular mix of equity (S) and debt (D). In other words, the market value of any asset (V_j) equals the present value of the periodic earnings expected from the operation of that asset. Refer to equation (4.38) in Chapter 4.

$$V_j = (\bar{X}_j / \rho_k) = S_j + D_j \qquad (7.23)$$

where

V_j = the total market value of any firm j
$\bar{X}_j$ = the expected future periodic profits of firm j before deduction of interest and taxes
ρ_k = the expected rate of return on the common stock of an unlevered company in risk class k; ρ_k is assumed constant for all firms in the homogeneous risk class k
S_j = the aggregate market value of the common shares of firm j
D_j = the market value of the aggregate debts of firm j

Equation (7.23) is the famous M & M Proposition I and can be proved as follows. First, from equations (7.21) and (7.20), suppose V_2 exceeds

---

[6] See Alexander Barges, *The Effect of Capital Structure on the Cost of Capital, a Test and Evaluation of the Modigliani and Miller Propositions,* 1962 Award Winner, The Ford Foundation Doctoral Dissertation Series, Prentice-Hall, Inc., Englewood Cliffs, N.J., 1963.

V_1 because of the existence of D_2. Then an equity investment in firm 2 will have the returns

$$Y_2 = \alpha(\bar{X} - rD_2) \tag{7.24}$$

where

Y_2 = return from a portfolio consisting of common stock from company 2

α = a fraction of the total outstanding stock (S_2) owned of company 2

$\bar{X}$ = expected net operating profit for the firm before deduction of interest and taxes

rD_2 = total interest payments made by the firm to creditors

Second, using personal credit in the amount αD_2, and at the same time using shares (αS_2), investors can use the total proceeds received from the sale of the equity shares along with the "homemade" leverage to purchase a proportion, $s_1 = \alpha(S_2 + D_2)$, of the outstanding shares of company 1. In this way, an investor can buy a fraction, $s_1/S_1 = \alpha(S_2 + D_2)/S_1$ of the shares outstanding, and the earnings of company 1. This equity investment in firm 1 will have the returns

$$\begin{aligned} Y_1 &= [\alpha(S_2 + D_2)/S_1]\bar{X} - r(\alpha D_2) \\ &= \alpha(V_2/V_1)\bar{X} - \alpha(rD_2) \end{aligned} \tag{7.25}$$

where Y_1 = return on the portfolio consisting of stock from company 1, $r(\alpha D_2)$ = interest payments on the personal debt made by the investor, and other terms are as defined previously.

Now compare the return from portfolio 2, equation (7.24), with the return from portfolio 1, equation (7.25). From (7.25), indications are that so long as V_2 exceeds V_1, Y_1 must exceed Y_2, with the consequence that it is profitable for holders of company 2's shares to sell their holdings, thereby depressing S_2 and subsequently V_2, and to acquire shares of company 1, thereby raising S_1 and thus V_1. In equilibrium, V_2 must equal V_1.

The implication is that differences in market value of total assets cannot occur because of differences in financing alone. In equilibrium the shares of the unlevered firm (S_1) sell for higher prices than do the shares of the levered firm (S_2). Rising leverage causes share prices to *fall* because the sum of total debt with total equity must remain constant. In contrast, during phase 1 under the conventional theory of finance, rising leverage causes the aggregate market value of stock outstanding to rise because of an increase in expected net income.[7]

---

[7] Observe the difference in assumptions underlying the two models.

Further, from Proposition I, M & M derived Proposition II. Proposition II follows directly as

$$i_j = \rho_k + (\rho_k - r)D_j/S_j \qquad (7.26)$$

where

i_j = the expected rate of return (or yield) on the stock of any company j

ρ_k = market rate of capitalization for a pure equity stream in the risk class

$(\rho_k - r)D_j/S_j$ = a premium (related to financial risk) which is equal to the debt/equity ratio times the spread between ρ_k and the interest rate, r

The proof of Proposition II is as follows. By definition, the yield or rate of return, on any investment equals the ratio of net profit to total investment.

$$i_j = (\bar{X}_j - rD_j)/S_j \qquad (7.27)$$

Now from Proposition I in equation (7.23), we can write

$$\bar{X}_j = \rho_k(S_j + D_j) \qquad (7.28)$$

Therefore, substituting (7.28) into (7.27), we get

$$i_j = \frac{\rho_k(S_j + D_j) - rD_j}{S_j} = \frac{\rho_k(S_j) + \rho_k(D_j) - r(D_j)}{S_j} \qquad (7.29)$$

$$i_j = \rho_k + (\rho_k - r)D_j/S_j$$

Proposition II states that the yield on the common stock issued by a company has two components:

1. The rate of return for an unlevered equity stream with the same business risk exposure, ρ_k
2. A premium related to financial risk

The risk premium rises with increasing leverage (D_j/S_j) and declines with increasing interest rates. ρ_k is determined by the business-risk class and is constant and equal for all firms within the class. At the extreme, if business risk equals zero, then ρ_k equals the pure rate of interest. In contrast, the traditional conclusions indicated that increasing leverage during phase 1 has a relatively slight (if any) effect on equity yields (see equation 7.4), because the added financial risks are small and more than offset by rising net income.

7.2 Alternative Methods for the Valuation of Assets

Two fundamentally different methods are discussed in the literature for calculating the worth of equity ownership and the market value of corporate assets. These methods are

1. Net operating income (NOI) method
2. Net income (NI) method

The essence of the two methods can be described as follows.[8]

THE NOI METHOD. The NOI method of asset valuation assumes that the total value of all bonds and stock outstanding is based solely on the net operating income for the firm. This assumption is made on the grounds that the firm has value because of its capacity to earn income, and since the income obtained on account of operating the business is the net operating income, then the NOI is the appropriate sum of money to discount.

Further, since the value of the firm emanates from the NOI, this value must always be the same—regardless of the proportion of bonds and stock. Thus, if the income statement and balance sheet for the firm are as shown in Table 7.1, then the worth of equity ownership according to the NOI method of valuation can be calculated as follows.

If the market rate of discount is 10 percent for all firms in the same business-risk class as Universal International, then based on a net operating income of $3 million, the total market value of the company equals $30 million.

$$V = \text{NOI}/\rho_k = \$3,000,000/.10 = \$30,000,000 \qquad (7.30)$$

The firm is worth $30 million regardless of the proportion of debt financing because the assets, when put into operation, can earn $3 million per year. And $3 million per year capitalized at the current market rate of 10 percent equals $30 million.

Then to calculate the market value of the shares, we subtract the (known) total bonded debt from the total value of the company to determine that the market value of equity ownership equals $26.80 per per share:

Total value of company	$30,000,000
Total bonded debt	3,200,000
Total value of common stock	$26,800,000
Value per share on 1,000,000 shares	$26.80

If there had been no bonds outstanding, the total value of common stock would have been $30 million. Under the NOI method of asset

---

[8] This presentation follows David Durand, "The Cost of Debt and Equity Funds for Business: Trends and Problems of Measurement," *Conference on Research on Business Finance*, National Bureau of Economic Research, New York, 1952; reprinted in Ezra Solomon, *The Management of Corporate Capital*, The Free Press, New York, 1964, pp. 91–116.

Table 7.1   INCOME STATEMENT OF THE UNIVERSAL
INTERNATIONAL MANUFACTURING COMPANY

Sales	$20,000,000
Cost of goods sold	17,000,000
Net operating income	3,000,000
Interest on debt	200,000
Taxes	1,300,000
Net income (after taxes)	$ 1,500,000

BALANCE SHEET OF THE UNIVERSAL INTERNATIONAL
MANUFACTURING COMPANY

ASSETS

Cash	$1,800,000	
Accounts and notes receivable	1,800,000	
Inventories	3,200,000	
Total current assets	6,800,000	
Real estate, plant and equipment, less depreciation	6,200,000	
Total		$13,000,000

LIABILITIES

Accrued items	$1,800,000	
Accounts payable	1,000,000	
Total current liabilities	2,800,000	
Bonded debt: 5 percent debentures	3,200,000	
Common stock: 1,000,000 shares at $6 per share	6,000,000	
Earned surplus	1,000,000	
Total		$13,000,000

valuation, the total value of common stock outstanding drops as the proportion (quantity) of bonds increases because the total investment value of the firm is based on NOI and therefore remains constant.

Proponents of NOI method argue that increasing the proportion of debt in the capital structure mix will in no way affect the total value of $30 million, because the totality of risk incurred by all security holders of a given company cannot be altered by merely changing the capitalization proportions. Such a change alters only the proportion of the total risk borne by each class of security holder.

THE NI METHOD.   The basic idea underlying the NI method is that the correct income to capitalize is that income available to shareholders (i.e., income after payment of taxes and all fixed charges). This assumption is made on the grounds that fixed charges such as contractual interest payment, allowances for capital consumption, and payment of taxes, should rightfully be subtracted from NOI before capitalization because this income, though earned by the firm, is not available to shareholders. The money available to shareholders is the residual amount remaining after all these mandatory payments have been made.

Hence, according to the NI method of asset valuation, the present worth of the shares is calculated by discounting net income and by adding this sum to the market value of the debt outstanding to calculate the market value of the firm.

If the appropriate rate of discount is 10 percent,[9] the worth of equity ownership according to the NI method of asset valuation can be calculated as follows. From Table 7.1, the net income equals $1.5 million, so, since the discount rate equals 10 percent, the total value of common stock equals $15 million or $15 per share.

$$\text{Total value of common stock} = \$1,500,000/.10 = \$15,000,000$$
$$\text{Value per share of 1,000,000 shares} = \$15.00$$

Because the total bonded debt equals $3.2 million, the total value of the company equals $18.2 million.

Under the NI method of valuation, the total investment value of the firm increases with the proportion of bonds in the capital structure. However, such an increase does not continue indefinitely. When phase 3 of debt financing is reached, the debt burden becomes so large that financial risk (probability of default) looms heavily in the background, causing the worth of equity ownership and the total investment value of the firm to fall.[10]

7.3 The Effects of Dividend Payout on the Market Value of the Firm

Leaving the issues of debt financing aside for now, consider corporate net income, a lump sum of corporate earnings available for distribution to shareholders. The management of a firm is (theoretically) free to distribute the money in any way it chooses: 100 percent can be retained and reinvested in the business, or 100 percent can be paid out as dividends to shareholders. The question is, What is the *optimal*

---

[9] Note this assumption. Explain its significance, also, comment on the $2.8 million of current liabilities.

[10] For additional reading, see John Lintner, "Dividends, Earnings, Leverage, Stock Prices and the Supply of Capital to Corporations," *The Review of Economics and Statistics*, vol. XLIV, no. 3, August 1962, pp. 243–244.

distribution of available income? Is there some proportion of payout (or retention) that will maximize the market value of the firm? Conventional financial analysts answer, yes; many capital theorists answer, no. Both views are presented below.

Conventional View: Dividends Matter. The "dividends definitely matter" school can be traced back to J. B. Williams. In 1938, Williams wrote[11]:

> A stock is worth only what you can get out of it.
> Even so spoke the old farmer to his son:
>
> > a cow for her milk,
> > a hen for her eggs,
> > and a stock, by heck,
> > For her dividends.
> >
> > an orchard for fruit,
> > Bees for their honey,
> > and stock, besides,
> > For their dividends.

Williams' prime contention is that the sole reason for an investor to purchase shares of common stock is to receive future income. Income to shareholders consists of dividends, capital gains, or losses upon sale of the shares. If dividends are forthcoming presently, then the value of equity investment is calculated on the basis of the discounted value of those future dividends and capital gains. According to Williams' views, the value of equity ownership depends directly on the level and time pattern of dividends. With anticipation of no income (dividends) or capital gains ever, equity ownership is worthless.[12] Put more directly, instead of investing in an opportunity where there is no hope of receiving future income, the money may as well be flushed down the drain.

Professor Myron Gordon, following Williams' line of reasoning, proceeded to extend the basic ideas. Following Gordon, we can write, as the worth of equity ownership,

$$P_0 = D_1/(1 + k_1)^1 + D_2/(1 + k_2)^2 + \cdots + D_t/(1 + k_t)^t + \cdots$$
$$(7.31)$$

where

P_0 = present worth of a share of common stock
D_i = dividends (income) forthcoming during time interval i
k_i = current (forward) market rate of discount

---

[11] John Burr Williams, *The Theory of Investment Value*, Harvard University Press, Cambridge, Mass., 1938; also reprinted in paperback by North-Holland Publishing Company, Amsterdam, 1964.

[12] Observe that these statements implicitly ignore the worth of the right to exercise managerial prerogatives in directing the future course of the business.

Then starting with two assumptions,

1. Aversion to risk
2. Increase in the uncertainty of a receipt with its time in the future

Gordon proceeded to show that there may be no change in share price (P_0) due to a time redistribution of dividends per se.[13] That is, instead of paying dividends D_1 at the end of the next time period [the present value of D_1 equals $D_1/(1 + k_1)$], suppose the company pays no dividends then and instead pays $D_1(1 + k)$ more than it would have otherwise paid at the end of the second time period. The present value of this second income equals $D_1(1 + k)/(1 + k)^2$ or $D_1/(1 + k)$ which is the same as before. Thus, assuming all k's to be equal, a time redistribution of dividends may not affect the price of a share of common stock.

However, Gordon notes that investors *will* change the rate of discount (k). That is, k actually equals an average of individual k_t. Instead of having a single k, as indicated in the following equation there may be a different k for each year.

$$P_0 = Y_1/(1 + k_1) + Y_2/(1 + k_2)^2 + \cdots + Y_t/(1 + k_t)^t + \cdots$$

$$(7.32)$$

where

P_0 = present worth of a share of stock
Y_t = income (dividends) forthcoming during time interval t
k_t = current market rate of discount for money to be received as of time t
k = an average of the k_i's from equation (7.31)

Then, recognizing the two assumptions which state that delaying income deeper in time implicitly causes risks to rise and realizing that investors must be paid for bearing risk, the k_i's get successively larger as dividend income is delayed further into time.

$$k_t > k_{t-1} \qquad \text{for all } t \qquad (7.33)$$

So if instead of paying D_1 at the end of the next time period, the company elects to pay no dividends then and pay $D_1(1 + k_1)$ more than it would have otherwise paid at the end of the second time period, then this dividend policy action would cause share price to fall because

---

[13] M. J. Gordon, "Optimal Investment and Financing Policy," *The Journal of Finance*, vol. XVIII, no. 2, May 1963, pp. 269.

$D_1(1 + k_1)/(1 + k_2)^2$ is less than $D_1/(1 + k_1)$. Hence, dividend policy influences share price.[14]

NEOCLASSICAL VIEW: DIVIDENDS DO NOT MATTER.

This view is articulated best by Miller and Modigliani. In 1961, M & M wrote, "...Thus, we may conclude that, given a firm's investment policy, the dividend payout policy it chooses to follow will affect neither the current price of its shares nor the total return to its shareholders."[15]

The crux of the M & M argument can be summarized as follows. So long as net income is available, and so long as there are profitable opportunities for the firm to reinvest the retained income, then the dividend policy decision reduces to "a mere detail" of no practical significance or consequence.

According to the M & M view, differences in market value cannot exist between firms with equal expected income because of differences in dividend payout policy alone. This is so because "dividend payments in no way affect the market value of the firm." To see why dividend policy is not relevant to the market value of the firm, we can proceed as follows. As before, equation (7.34) expresses the price of a share of common stock.

$$p_t = \frac{1}{1 + \rho_t}(d_t + p_{t+1}) \qquad (7.34)$$

where

p_t = price (ex-dividend in $t - 1$) of a share as of the start of period t

ρ_t = market rate of discount

d_t = dividends per share paid by the firm during period t

p_{t+1} = price per share as of the start of period $t + 1$.

To show the effects of dividend policy, consider what happens to the market value of all the shares outstanding under alternative policies. Since we are concerned with dividend policy and equity values, debt can be ignored. Then with all equity financing, the market value of equity equals the market value of the firm.

$$V = S \qquad (7.35)$$

---

[14] Gordon also established the proposition that the average rate of discount (k) is an increasing function of the rate of growth of dividends. The consequence of the theorem is that dividend policy per se influences the value of a share. See Gordon, *Ibid.* Also see Chapter 11.

[15] Merton H. Miller and Franco Modigliani, "Dividend Policy, Growth, and the Valuation of Shares," *The Journal of Business*, vol. XXXIV, no. 4, October 1961, pp. 411–433.

Also, the present market value of the firm equals the discounted future value of the firm.

$$V_t = \frac{1}{1 + \rho_t}(D_t + n_t p_{t+1}) \tag{7.36}$$

where

$V_t = n_t p_t =$ total value of the enterprise (assuming no debt) for simplicity

$\rho_t =$ market rate of discount

$D_t = n_t d_t =$ total dividends paid during t to holders of record at the start of time period t

$n_t =$ the number of shares of record at the start of time period t

$p_t =$ price per share at the start of time period t

Also, we can write

$$V_t = \frac{1}{1 + \rho_t}(D_t + V_{t+1} - m_{t+1}p_{t+1}) \tag{7.37}$$

where

$n_{t+1} = n_t + m_{t+1} =$ number of shares of record at the start of $t + 1$

$m_{t+1} =$ number of new shares (if any) sold during t at the ex-dividend closing price p_{t+1}

To evaluate the effects of dividend payout, we study (7.37). Current dividends (D_t) can affect the total value of the enterprise V_t in either of three possible ways:

1. Via the first term in parentheses (D_t). This is a clear, straightforward effect.
2. Via the seond term in the parentheses (V_{t+1}), the new ex-dividend market value. But since V_{t+1} must depend only on future and not on past events, such can be the case if and only if V_{t+1} is a function of future dividend policy and the current distribution (D_t) serves to convey some otherwise unavailable information as to what that future dividend policy will be.
3. Via the third term, $m_{t+1}p_{t+1}$, the value of new shares sold to outsiders during the period. The higher the dividend payout in any period, the more new capital that must be raised from external sources to maintain any desired level of investment.

Thus, M & M show "the dividend problem": the direct effect on value of the firm (V_t) via D_t and the *inverse* effect on the value of the firm via $m_t p_{t+1}$.

Further, M & M proceed to show that in an ideal world, the two dividend effects must always exactly subtract out so that the payout policy to be followed in t will have no effect on the price at t.[16]

QUESTIONS FOR STUDY

1. Explain how the existence of corporate taxes will (or will not) alter M & M's Propositions I and II. Reference: Franco Modigliani and Merton H. Miller, "The Cost of Capital, Corporation Finance and the Theory of Investment: Reply," *American Economic Review*, vol. XLIX, no. 4, September 1959, pp. 655–669.
2. Compare the rationale underlying the NI method of asset valuation with the rationale underlying the NOI method.
3. What is the real distinction between the pure earnings group of authors who assert that unlevered stock value depend on earnings (independent of dividends) and the dividend group?
4. Explain why some scholars and financial analysts might capitalize *current* corporate earnings, whereas others might capitalize *average future* earnings.
5. Compare the views of M & M with "conventional" views on the effects of (a) debt finance and (b) dividend policy.
6. How should depreciation be treated in valuing corporate assets?
7. What is M & M's "Homogeneous Risk Class"?
8. What are the basic assumptions underlying the M & M models for analysis of (a) capital structure mix and (b) dividend policy.
9. Gordon has presented theory and evidence which leads to the conclusion that a corporation's share price (or its cost of capital) is dependent upon the dividend payout rate. Modigliani and Miller have the opposite view in that they state "...the dividend payout policy it (i.e., the company) chooses to follow will affect neither the current price of its shares nor the total return to its shareholders." *Question.* Explain how these scholars have arrived at such vastly different conclusions

---

[16] *Proof.* Express $m_{t+1}p_t$ in terms of D_t.

$$m_{t+1}p_{t+1} = I_t - (X_t - D_t) \tag{7.38}$$

where I_t = the given level of the firm's investment or increase in its holding of physical assets in t and X_t = the firm's total net profit for the period. Then equation (7.38) expresses the amount of outside capital required. Substituting equation (7.38) into equation (7.37), the D_t subtract out, and we get

$$V_t = n_t p_t = \frac{1}{1+\rho_t}(X_t - I_t + V_{t+1}) \tag{7.39}$$

Since D_t does not appear directly among the arguments, and since X_t, I_t, V_{t+1}, and ρ_t are all independent of D_t, it follows that the current value of the firm must be independent of the current decision.

regarding the importance of dividend policy for the determination of share price.

10. The Universal International Manufacturing Company belongs to a risk class for which the appropriate capitalization rate is 10 percent. The firm currently has 100,000 shares outstanding selling at $50 each. Management is contemplating the declaration of a $4 dividend at the end of the current fiscal year, which just began. Answer the following questions based on the Modigliani and Miller Model. Ignore taxes.

   (a) What will be the price of the stock at the end of the year if a dividend is not declared? What will it be if a dividend is declared?

   (b) Assuming that the firm pays the dividend, has net income of $1 million, and makes new investments of $2 million during the period, how many new shares must be issued?

How much is a share of common stock worth? At $50 per share, is equity ownership in Avon Products, Inc. a "bargain" while at that same price, an equal number of dollars invested in Crown Zellerbach Corp. is "expensive"?—Or is it the other way around? Fifty dollars per share may be some 40 times current earnings for Avon Products and only some 17 times earnings for Crown Zellerbach.[1]

Is the market behaving irrationally when earnings of one firm are capitalized at a rate different from corresponding earnings of another firm? Or is the market correct and is telling us that there is some fundamental difference between the value of these two firms?

These and related questions are examined in this chapter. But before proceeding, it may be worthwhile to step back for a moment and formulate some perspectives on what we are trying to accomplish by

Fundamental Analysis of Securities 8

fundamental analysis. What is the nature of the job of the financial analyst? What is his function? What is the analyst supposed to do?

8.1 The Jobs of Asset Management and Financial Analysis

Asset management is a two-sided phenomenon. On one side of the asset is the investor—the potential investor as well as the current investor. Investors usually view the asset from an external situation

---

[1] These are actual data for the year 1964. Three years later, in 1967, the shares of Avon Products sold as high as $142, giving a price/earnings ratio of 63. Not only did the share price rise from $50 to $142, the P/E multiple rose from 40 to 63. Three years later, in 1967, the shares of Crown Zellerbach Corporation sold between $41 and $55, giving P/E ratios in the range 13 to 17. Thus, over the 3-year span of time, Crown Zellerbach shares hardly moved in either price or (P/E) multiple. Reference: *Standard & Poor's Stock Market Encyclopedia*, Standard & Poor's Corporation, 345 Hudson Street, New York, New York, 10014, 1969.

and then decide whether to buy, sell, or hold securities associated with the asset (or the asset itself).

On the other side is corporate management. Management is inside the firm—viewing the market prices of securities issued by the firm on the one hand, and viewing profitable opportunities for additional business spending on the other hand. Management must decide whether to increase, decrease, or hold constant the variables which define the economic character of the business. These variables include capital budgeting, growth, finance, credit policy, product pricing, and a host of similar items, all of which constitute the character of the business. Shareholders have the right and duty to participate in these managerial decisions. What should the answers be?

To reach the required decision, corporate management, as well as private investors, on occasion may seek advice from professional financial analysts. Analysts can be called upon to render opinions not only on the optimal *sources* of money, the lowest-cost source of funds, but also the optimal *uses* of money. Some possible uses can include items such as policy decisions on how much dividend to pay, whether to purchase some of the shares outstanding, or whether to retire some of the existing debt. Of major concern in the optimal use of corporate income is the determination of the proper rate of expansion or growth of physical plant and equipment and the optimal rate of investment in the labor force and technology for present and future growth of production.

The job of the financial analyst, therefore, can be described as embracing three interrelated areas. The functions are:

1. To guide and advise corporate management on optimal managerial decisions within the firm (e.g., capital budgeting decisions, finance policy, and dividend policy)
2. To specify and/or state the terms (i.e., costs) of floating new equity issues or new debt financing for the firm
3. To estimate expected return on investment and risk associated therewith as input information and data to a portfolio manager

First, there is the appraisal or valuation of individual securities. The analyst may be called upon to render opinions on, How much is a share of stock worth? In what way will the value of the shares change if the firm adopts a different target rate of growth? In what way will finance policy and dividend payout affect the worth of equity ownership and the value of the firm?

Second, the financial analyst is instrumental in the pricing of new issues. When corporate management issues new equity or debt, the analyst can be called upon to render opinions regarding the worth of these new securities. What should be the offering price? Frequently, the analyst is confronted with an enormous amount of data. The analyst has indexes, annual reports, market statistics, industry statistics, formulas, and theories by the truckload. The need always is for clarity and simplicity.

Third, the financial analyst is a source of input data for the portfolio manager. The analyst reduces risk in investing by providing superior information concerning the asset under analysis. The manager of a portfolio is concerned with questions such as, Which stock should I include in my portfolio, General Motors or I.B.M.? Should I buy some of each? If so, how much of each? Possibly I should buy some of each, but in addition hold some cash in reserve. What is the best timing? When should I sell? What factors are relevant? Is the current market price too high, or is the price too low? What is the correct price for this particular stock? Is the price likely to increase sharply or only moderately in the near future? What are the prospects for the stock over the long run? What are the risks involved?

The security analyst provides expert knowledge and information so that these questions can be answered with increasing certainty. As an advisor to the portfolio manager, the security analyst can be called upon to render opinions on issues such as, Why does a share of General Motors stock sell for $50 while a share of stock in I.B.M. may cost $500? Over the next few years, which of the two stocks is likely to have the highest appreciation in price? What makes prices rise? Why do prices fall?

In the end, almost always, investment analysis comes to the same point, separating the fundamental data from the surrounding "noise." The analyst must define the mechanism that causes the shares of one company to sell at 50 times earnings while the shares on a different company sell at 10 times earnings. The analyst must remove much of the risk and uncertainty associated with the investment decision-making process.

8.2 Some Factors for Analysis

From the viewpoint of either the investor/analyst outside the firm looking in or the manager/analyst inside the firm making policy decisions from within, the focal point is the market price of the securities outstanding. So we ask What *are* the relevant relationships between share price behavior and corporate economic-financial performance? What *are* the determinates of stock market prices? Actually, nobody knows—for sure. There are many conflicting theories, the most important of which were discussed in Chapter 7, and much empirical data, some of which shall be discussed in Chapters 10 and 11. In the final analysis, however, *all* assets, including bonds and shares of common stocks, are worth the amount someone else is willing to pay for the privilege of their ownership. If someone is willing to pay $100 for the privilege of owning an asset, then $100 is the worth of that asset. If someone is willing to pay $1000, then $1000 is the worth of the asset.

According to the fundamental notions developed previously in Chapters 4, 5, and 6, rational investors are *always* willing to pay the (risk-adjusted) present value of any valuable asset. Hence, the market value of corporate assets equals the risk-adjusted present value of the income obtained from owning and operating those assets. We can write the fundamental (conceptual) model used for calculating market value of any asset.

$$P = Y_1/(1 + k) + Y_2/(1 + k)^2 + \cdots + Y_n/(1 + k)^n \qquad (8.1)$$

where

P = present market price of any asset
Y_t = net periodic income received from owning and operating the asset
k = market rate of (risk-adjusted) discount
n = number of time periods of useful life of the asset

Statement (8.1) says that the present (market) value of any asset varies directly with three factors and inversely with two factors. Present worth varies with:

1. The level (magnitude) of periodic income anticipated (expected) to be forthcoming from the operation of that asset (i.e., the level of Y_t).
2. The timing (i.e., rate of growth) of the periodic revenue, a growing stream such as

$$Y_1 < Y_2 < \cdots < Y_{a-1} < Y_n \qquad (8.2)$$

   is superior to a declining stream such as

$$Y_1 > Y_2 > \cdots > Y_{n-1} > Y_n \qquad (8.3)$$

3. The time duration of the stream of income (n). Other things the same, uniform periodic revenue for n = infinity is worth more than uniform periodic revenue for n = 2.
4. The present (market) value of any asset varies inversely with yields obtainable on alternative assets having equivalent predictability (k).[2]

---

[2] Throughout these analyses the discount rate (k_i) is conceptually determined by two components, (1) the marginal rate of interest obtainable from an alternative risk-free investment (i.e., compensation for the time value

5. The error of forecast (i.e., risk exposure) of the anticipated future income. The premium for bearing risk is included implicitly in k.

Then fundamental analysis consists of a study of the five factors listed above.

But complications arise. In Chapter 7 we noted the lack of general agreement among experts on many fundamental issues. There are issues such as (1) which income, net operating income or net income? (2) which income, dividend income or corporate earnings per share? (3) can debt financing cause asset value to rise? Since capital structure is not stated explicitly in (8.1), is capital structure included implicitly?

Let us consider these issues separately, from the viewpoint of present value, using a corporate income statement and balance sheet for reference. Analysis of each item alone is no trivial task; all five combined is nearly impossible. But that is the nature of the job of the security analyst.

Since much of the analysis involves use of accounting forms such as income statements and balance sheets, we shall use these two items as a guide for discussion. An illustrative income statement and balance sheet are presented in Table 8.1.

The topics for discussion can be outlined as follows:

1. Analysis of profit
2. Profit and growth
3. Financing growth
4. Dividend payout and investment value

---

of money) and (2) the marginal return required to compensate for bearing risk.

Scholars have proposed several competing methods for determining numerical values of k_i for investments having varying degrees of risk. For example, aside from the possibility that the individual components (1) and (2) may combine either additively or multiplicatively to determine any particular series for k_i, component (2) may or may not be considered explicitly as a function of (1). That is, many economists take high risk-free interest rates themselves to be relatively risky in that this higher cost of liquidity will probably soon cause increased demand and hence higher prices for bonds, thus causing market yields on fixed-income investments to drop. According to this reasoning (1) which incorporates the level and structure of yields on government securities, will directly contribute a relatively large proportion to the total explanation of (2). Alternatively, many financial analysts explain component (2) primarily in terms of subjective risk aversion preferences of investors acting collectively along with some measure of the relative likelihood that the expected-equivalent return will fail to be obtained. Therefore, component (1) will influence (2) only indirectly and via some ill-understood intermediate mechanism. For purposes of analysis, the conceptual relationship is sufficient.

Table 8.1   UNIVERSAL INTERNATIONAL, INC.
Consolidated income account, Year Ending December 31, 197–

		$ Millions*
1. Net sales		20,026
2. Cost of sales	15,401	
3. Selling, general and administrative expenses	906	
4. Depreciation and obsolescence	713	
		17,020
5. Operating profit (net operating income from operations)		3,007
6. Equity in unconsolidated subsidiaries	57	
7. Interest received	96	
8. Miscellaneous income	21	
		174
9. Total income		3,181
10. Interest and amortization on debt $3\frac{1}{4}$'s	1	
11. Other interest and debt charges	35	
12. Miscellaneous	24	
13. Bonus and stock option plan	107	
		167
14. Balance (net income before taxes)		3,013
15. Foreign income taxes	129	
16. U.S. income taxes	1,257	
		1,386
17. Net income (after taxes)		1,627
18. Retained earnings beginning of year		7,209
19. Preferred dividends	13	
20. Common dividends	1,084	
		1,097
21. Retained earnings end of year		$ 7,739

Consolidated Balance Sheet as of December 31, 197–

ASSETS

	$ Millions*
22. Cash	403
23. Government securities, cost	1,400
24. Accounts and notes receivable	1,834
25. Inventories	3,210
26. Total current assets	6,847

* Totals may not add precisely because of rounding.

TABLE 8.1 (Continued)

	$Millions*
27. Subsidiary companies not consolidated	647
28. Other security investments and miscellaneous	43
29. Miscellaneous assets	65
30. Treasury stock	149
31. Real estate, plants and equipment	11,234
32. Reserve for depreciation	6,428
33. Net property	4,806
34. Unamortized special tools	527
35. Goodwill, patents, etc.	63
36. Prepaid expenses and deferred charges	126
37. Total	$13,273

LIABILITIES

38. Accounts payable	1,168
39. Taxes, payroll, etc., accrued	1,141
40. U.S. and foreign income & excess profits taxes	528
41. Accrued preferred dividends	3
42. Total current liabilities	2,840
43. Debenture 3¼'s, 1979	43
44. Foreign subsidiary debt	302
45. Employees benefit plans reserve	26
46. Credits under stock option plan	38
47. Sundry miscellaneous liabilities	448
48. Reserve for deferred income	24
49. Reserve for deferred investment credit	141
50. Other reserves	7
51. General reserve—foreign operation	142

EQUITY

52. $5 preferred stock	184
53. $3.75 preferred stock	100
54. Common stock ($1.66-2/3)	479
55. Capital surplus	760
56. Retained earnings	7,739
57. Total Stockholders Equity	9,261
58. Total (Liabilities and Equity)	$13,273

* Totals may not add precisely because of rounding.

8.3 Analysis of Profit

Other things the same, more profitable firms are worth more than firms not so profitable. This is true because rational investors always prefer larger profits to smaller profits. Corporate profitability, therefore, is one of the important determinants of the worth of equity ownership and the market value of corporate assets.

In this section we shall examine the question, How profitable is the firm? What factors contribute to and cause firms to be profitable? As we shall see, financial analysts usually investigate three different "profits": (1) current profits, (2) future expected profits, and (3) "normal" expected profits.

CURRENT PROFITS. The factors affecting corporate profitability are shown directly in the income statement published by the firm. For purposes of illustration, let us take actual data for a well-known firm as shown in Table 8.1.[3] The income statement in Table 8.1 shows two different "profits" for the firm: (1) line 5, net operating profit, and (2) line 17, net income. A third important item is "income available for common" (i.e., income after payment of preferred dividends, line 19).

Net operating income (NOI) is the residual remaining after subtracting total operating costs from total revenues.

$$NOI = (R_0 - C_0) \tag{8.4}$$

where

    NOI = net operating income from operations
      R_0 = total revenues (net sales) forthcoming to the firm because of business operations
      C_0 = total cost incurred in obtaining the revenue (R)

Operating costs (C_0) include depreciation and obsolescence (i.e., capital consumption and depletion) as well as labor, maintenance, and expenses directly associated with production and selling. Total revenues for operations (R_0) consists of net sales. From Table 8.1 net operating profit for the year reported equals $3.007 billion.

Net income (NI) is the amount of money available for all shareholders. Net income is the residual remaining after *all* costs and legally obligated payments are subtracted from *all* revenues.

$$NI = (1 - T)\pi = (1 - T)(R_t - C_t) \tag{8.5}$$

where

    NI = net income
     T = tax rate on corporate income
     π = total pre-tax profits earned by the firm
     R_t = total revenues forthcoming to the firm, including item 1 and items 6–8 in Table 8.1
     C_t = total costs of the firm, including items 2–4 and 10–13 in Table 8.1

---

[3] Data are actually for General Motors Corporation for the year ending December 31, 1967. Source: Moody's *Industrial Manual*, July 1968.

Note the difference between R_0, total revenues forthcoming to the firm because of business operations, and R_t, total revenues forthcoming to the firm. Total revenues (R_t) includes "other" income not derived directly from business operations. Similarly, total costs (C_t) include interest charges and "other" fixed expenses as listed in items 10–13 in Table 8.1. Total tax payments are subtracted to arrive at after-tax income. From Table 8.1 net income for the year reported equals \$1.627 billion.

Income available for holders of common shares (AVC) equals the residual remaining after subtracting preferred dividend payments from after-tax net income.

$$\text{AVC} = \text{NI} - \text{Pfd} = (1 - T)(R_t - C_t) - \text{Pfd} \qquad (8.6)$$

where AVC = income available for common shareholders, Pfd = preferred dividend payments, and other symbols are the same as defined previously. This residual income (AVC) is the amount of corporate profit (or loss) which accrues to common equity owners. All common shareholders are entitled to their proportional part of this money. Managers inside the firm and shareholders in the aggregate have the right to decide whether this money should be paid out in the form of dividends to shareholders or else retained and reinvested in the business operations of the firm. The correct decision is the choice which benefits everyone, if possible. The possibilities are examined later in this chapter.

From the considerations outlined above, the following factors are relevant to the analysis of current profits of the firm:

1. Net sales
2. Cost of sales
3. Selling, general and administrative expenses
4. Depreciation and obsolescence
5. A composite of items 6 through 8; these can be labeled "miscellaneous" or "other" income
6. A composite of items 10 through 13; these can be labeled "fixed charges"
7. Total taxes including foreign, federal, state, and local

The residual income after item 7 above is money available for distribution to holders of preferred shares and to holders of common shares. Hence, the overall profits of the firm can be stated as the difference between total revenues and total costs.

Other items from the balance sheet in Table 8.1 are included implicitly in the list of relevant factors. For example, consider the rate of production of goods and services vs. the rate of sales. These two rates can be (and frequently are) unequal. Inventories (item 25 on Table 8.1) take up the slack. Hence, inventory policy is relevant for the investigation of corporate profits. Too little inventory of finished goods can result in relatively long lead times for delivery and, therefore, the possibility of lost sales. Competitors with sufficient inventory on hand can make the sale instead. Too much inventory can mean money unnecessarily and unprofitably tied up. Inventory costs money to store, insure, and keep on hand.

Cash balances (item 22 in Table 8.1) also influence total profits. Too little cash on hand can mean panic borrowing, perhaps at unnecessarily high interest rates, to pay bills due. On the other hand, too much cash on hand can mean idle balances that are causing opportunity losses. Idle cash balances mean foregoing some available return on investment. In one sense, the total amount of cash on hand can be viewed as an inventory—a buffer whose purpose is to match the rate of expenditures to the rate of inflows. Finally, the time series pattern of all these factors is important for the analysis of corporate profits.

We turn next to a consideration of *relative* profits. In other words, is $3.007 billion reported on line 5 of Table 8.1 large, or is $3.007 billion small for this particular firm? Is $1.627 billion from line 17 in Table 8.1 large, or is $1.627 billion small? How profitable is the firm?

PROFIT MARGINS VS. RETURN ON INVESTMENT.   Unfortunately, traditional measurement of corporate profits and answers to the question "How profitable is the firm?" usually focus attention on profit margins instead of on total rate of return.

Profit margin equals net operating profit divided by net sales, expressed as a percent. (Note: some analysts use net income instead of net operating profit.) In the case of the data from Table 8.1, profit margin equals approximately 15 percent.

$$\text{Profit margin} = \text{Net operating profit/Net sales} \qquad (8.7)$$
$$= \$3007/\$20{,}026 = 15 \text{ percent}$$

The implication of using profit margin as the relevant measure of corporate profitability is: a profit margin of 15 percent is superior to smaller profit margins of 10 percent. With a margin of 15 percent, the operating profit on sales of $20,026 is approximately $3000, whereas, if the margin is: only 10 percent, then total dollars of profit on the same level of sales is only $2003. Or, solving equation (8.7) for net operating profit, we get

$$\text{(Profit margin)(Net sales)} = \text{Total profit}$$
$$.15(\$20{,}026) = \$3007 \qquad (8.8)$$
$$.10(\$20{,}026) = \$2003$$

The use of profit margins is unfortunate because many analysts measure corporate profitability by profit margins alone. Profit margins tell only a part of the total story. There is a very important second part to total profits which can be explained as follows.

Corporate management has at its disposal a total lump sum of money (A) which was obtained from both equity owners and creditors.

$$A = S + L \qquad (8.9)$$

where

A = total assets
S = total equity finance (common stock)
L = total liabilities (debt) finance

Because of investment of total assets into the operations of the business, total profits (π) are received. The total rate of profit (before taxes) on the corporate investment, therefore, is the percentage return received on total assets, *not* profit margins.

$$r_t = \pi/A \qquad (8.10)$$

where r_t = rate of return on assets and other terms same as defined previously.

The rate of profit (before taxes) on business operation (r_0) can be expressed as profit margin, multiplied by turnover of total assets.

$$\begin{aligned} r_0 &= \text{(Profit margin)(Turnover)} \\ &= \text{(NOI/Net sales)(Net sales/Total assets)} \end{aligned} \qquad (8.11)$$

Thus equation (8.11) shows that profit margin is but one factor in the total picture of corporate profitability. Total profitability of the firm rises if either profit margin or turnover rises. Profit margin can rise or else turnover can rise to cause a rise in profits. Low profit margins can be offset by high turnover of production. Conversely, low turnover can be offset by high profit margins.

To illustrate, consider two firms: a retailer specializing in expensive items where the turnover is low but when a sale *is* made, profit margins are high, and a discount store where turnover is high, but profit per item sold is relatively low. Then if the particular ratios are as shown in equation set (8.12), the two firms are equally profitable, even though profit margins for firm 1 are 8 times larger than profit margins for firm 2.

$$\begin{aligned} \text{Profit margin} \times \text{Turnover} &= \text{Rate of return on assets} \\ \text{Firm 1: } .40 \times \quad .75 &= .30 \\ \text{Firm 2: } .05 \times 6.00 &= .30 \end{aligned} \qquad (8.12)$$

In other words, a profit margin of 5 percent on a turnover of 6 times per year is equally as good, in terms of profitability, as a profit margin of 40 percent on a turnover of less than 1 time per year. If a person compares the two firms based on profit margin alone, firm 1 will be considered superior. If the same person compares the two on the basis of turnover ratio alone, firm 2 will be favored. Hence, we have two different decisions based on the same set of data. The lesson is that looking at a single component of profitability can lead to wrong conclusions.

Of course, if profit margins and turnover both are high relative to other firms, then perhaps we have the best of all possible worlds. But do not jump to conclusions too quickly. Ambiguous results can still creep in. To illustrate, suppose the turnover rate is high. A high rate of turnover of assets can be the result of efficient aggressive management. In this case, high turnover is "good." But the high turnover rate can be caused by the use of old equipment which is almost fully depreciated. A low value in the denominator of equation (8.11) gives a high turnover ratio. But a high turnover which is achieved in this particular way must be interpreted differently from a high turnover which is achieved because of a high value in the numerator (i.e., large sales). We must look behind the factors to determine why the rate is high. We may take investment action for the wrong reason.

What happens to profit if sales rise? Rising sales can cost money. Can sales be increased without increasing assets? Equation (8.11) fails to indicate the relationship between net operating profits and net sales. Equation (8.7) indicates only that profit margin is a ratio of NOI to net sales. There will almost always, be some interaction between sales and assets. If sales increase and assets increase, the resulting profit will depend on the relative change between these two causal factors. Also, equation (8.11) fails to be of help in evaluating the effect on corporate profitability if sales rise, because net sales are included as a factor in both the numerator and denominator and, therefore, divide out.

Finally, we should note that formulation (8.11) fails to indicate the influence of a change in capital structure on the profitability of the firm. If corporate profitability is independent of the method of finance (as some scholars believe), then formulation (8.11) is indeed satisfactory and, therefore, free of this particular criticism. But, if the method of finance *is* relevant, then formulation (8.11) is unsatisfactory.

To show the relationship between total net profit and financing, we can write [4]

$$\mathrm{NI} = r_0 A - iL - T(r_0 A - iL) \tag{8.13}$$

where

$$\mathrm{NI} = \text{net income}$$
$$r_0 A = \text{net operating income}$$
$$iL = \text{total interest payments}$$
$$T(r_0 A - iL) = \text{total tax payments}$$

---

[4] To be precise, statement (8.11) should be refined to account for "other" costs, items 6–8 and 10–13, respectively, in Table 8.1.

Expression (8.13) notes that net income equals net operating income, less total interest payments and total tax payments. Since interest is tax deductible, the tax rate (T) is applied to ($r_0 A - iL$). Then to show the relationship between return per dollar of equity invested and the profitability of the firm, we can proceed as follows.

First, factor (8.13) into (8.14) and then substitute (8.9) into (8.14). Thus we can write

$$\text{NI} = (1 - T)(r_0 A - iL) \qquad \textbf{(8.14)}$$

But since $A = S + L$, we can write

$$
\begin{aligned}
\text{NI} &= (1 - T)[r_0(S + L) - iL] \\
&= (1 - T)[r_0 S + r_0 L - iL] \\
&= (1 - T)[r_0 S + (r_0 - i)L] \\
&= (1 - T)[r_0 + (r_0 - i)L/S]S
\end{aligned}
\qquad \textbf{(8.15)}
$$

Statement (8.15) shows that the net income per dollar of equity investment involves four factors: (1) the tax rate (T), (2) the rate of profit on business operations (r_0), (3) the price of credit (i), and (4) the proportion of total liabilities, relative to total equity (L/S).[5] Dividing both sides of (8.15) by S, we can write

$$\text{NI}/S = (1 - T)[r_0 + (r_0 - i)L/S] \qquad \textbf{(8.16)}$$

Statement (8.16) implies that so long as the rate of return on corporate operations exceeds the rate of interest paid on debt outstanding ($r_0 > i$), then net income rises as the relative amount of debt rises.

However, there is more to the analysis. Note that the variation of per share net income with capital structure (i.e., risk) depends upon the interrelationship between the four factors: i, L/S, r_0 and T. That is, the rate of interest paid on debt capital, the relative size of total debt, corporate profitability, and taxes (i.e., government fiscal policy) all can be interrelated with one another. For example, ceteris paribus, interest charges can vary directly with the proportion of debt already in the capital structure and inversely with corporate profitability (r). This is true because potential lenders may view large proportions of debt as relatively risky and large rates of return on business operations as relatively safe. Therefore, whether earnings per share can be maximized with respect to capital structure depends upon whether interest (i) is a quadratic (or higher order) function of capital structure. A linear

---

[5] These relationships are noted by Lerner and Carleton. See E. Lerner and W. Carleton, *A Theory of Financial Analysis*, Harcourt, Brace & World, Inc., New York, 1966, pp. 20–32.

function leaves the question of maximization unanswered.[6] Hence, to verify the precise form of the functional relationships between the five variables stated in (8.16), empirical data are needed for the particular situation under analysis. In any case, the important point for analysis is that profit margin alone is an unfortunate choice for a measure of corporate profit ability. More appropriate measures are rate of return on assets as stated in (8.10) and after-tax per share earnings as stated in (8.16).

We turn next to considerations of the time series of corporate profitability.

FUTURE PROFIT VS. CURRENT PROFIT. Traditional security analysis places much emphasis on the careful study of current and/or historical income statements and corporate balance sheet. Again, this allocation of emphasis is unfortunate. Current and/or historical data often fail to tell the required story for assessing the worth of equity ownership. Referring to equation (8.1), all the required information concerns future profits. All five items listed in statement (8.1) are associated with future values, not current profits. For purposes of security analysis, we need to know how much profits will be. Note use of the future tense; the importance of accurate predictions can never be over emphasized.

Reconsidering (8.1), take the first item listed, next year's income. How much will be corporate income over the next reporting period?... and the period after that? How can the required predictions be made?

Many analysts use current and historical financial statements (income statements and balance sheets) published periodically by the firm as a guide to estimating profits for next year. Historical values are often extrapolated into the future. Other analysts sometimes use direct interviews with the corporate executives in charge. In this case, estimates can be based primarily on expert judgment. Still other analysts often use a combination of the two procedures mentioned above; but, no matter what the particular method used, forecasts of the future are required. How far into the future are forecasts made? As a matter of practice, some analysts use an average of estimates over the next 5 or 8 years. Other analysts use 1 year. There is no standard procedure. The theory, in equation (8.1), requires estimates over the operating life of the firm.

Given the requirement to forecast future profit, what factors are relevant for analysis? From the preceding discussions, three primary factors can be listed: (1) estimates of future total revenues, (2) estimates of future total cost, and (3) risks or probability of error in the forecasts. Each of these factors is discussed below.

---

[6] If the function is linear, then the second derivative equals zero, and the test for maximization fails.

Since profit equals the difference between total revenues and total cost, any forecast of future profit implicitly requires inquiry into changes in both total cost and total revenues.

$$\pi_1 = \pi_0 + \Delta\pi = \pi_0 + \Delta R - \Delta C \qquad (8.17)$$

where

π_1 = total pre-tax profits accrued at the end of one time period hence

π_0 = total pre-tax profits at the end of the current time period

$\Delta\pi$ = change in total pre-tax profits

ΔR = change in total revenues

ΔC = change in total costs

Equation (8.17) states that any change in profits must emanate from either changes in total revenues, or changes in total costs, or both.

$$\Delta\pi = \Delta R - \Delta C \qquad (8.18)$$

The expected value of the estimate of future profits depends upon the expected change in revenue and the expected change in costs.

$$\begin{aligned} E(\pi_1) &= E(\pi_0 + \Delta R - \Delta C) \\ &= \pi_0 + E(\Delta R) - E(\Delta C) \end{aligned} \qquad (8.19)$$

Statement (8.19) says that if expected revenues rise and expected costs (1) remain constant, (2) decline, or (3) rise but by a smaller amount than expected revenues, then, by (8.18), expected profits will rise for next year. Alternatively if expected revenues fall and expected costs fall by more than the fall in revenues, then profits can be expected to rise higher than current levels. Otherwise profits can be expected to decline, or at best, remain constant. Next, consider risk.

Revenues and costs are interrelated and forecasts are rarely without error. The mean square error (i.e., risk) of the estimate is[7]

$$\begin{aligned} \text{var}(\pi_1) &= \text{var}(\pi_0 + \Delta R - \Delta C) \\ &= \pi_0 + \text{var}(\Delta R) + \text{var}(\Delta C) - 2\text{cov}(\Delta R, \Delta C) \end{aligned} \qquad (8.20)$$

The interdependency (covariance) between total revenues and total costs can be either of two basic types.

1. If a firm can increase both total production and the volume of sales while at the same time reducing total costs (e.g., through economies of scale, increased intensity of utilization of existing plant and equipment, and/or application of technological innovations) then total revenue can vary inversely with total cost.

$$\frac{\partial R}{\partial C} < 0 \qquad (8.21)$$

---

[7] Refer to Appendix 2 in Chapter 6 for a review of the statistics of taking expectations and variance of correlated random variables. Specifically, see equation (6.71).

In this case the total error of estimate as stated in (8.20) will include a *positive* contribution from the covariance term, thereby causing (ceteris paribus) *larger* risks for firms in this category than for firms in the category discussed below. Put a different way, (8.20) states that small firms who can profit through economies of scale, intensity of utilization of existing plant and equipments, and technology, are more risky than firms not able to operate in this way. Hence, the return on investment in shares of these firms ought to include a premium to pay for this risk.[8]

2. At the other extreme, if increased output and increased sales can be achieved only at the expense of rising total costs (e.g., new plant and equipment, diseconomies of scale, obsolete methods of management, additional advertising, and price cutting), then total revenue varies directly with total cost.

$$\frac{\partial R}{\partial C} > 0 \qquad (8.22)$$

In this case, the total error of estimate as stated in (8.20) includes a *negative* contribution from the covariance term, thereby causing (ceteris paribus) *smaller* risks (i.e., greater predictability) for firms in this category than for firms in the category discussed above. Therefore, stockholder return on investment in shares of these firms ought to be smaller than the return on investment in shares of firms characterized by (8.21).

Considering taxes, we can write after-tax expected income and risk as

$$\begin{aligned} E[(1 - T)\pi_1] &= (1 - T)E(\pi_1) \\ &= (1 - T)[\pi_0 + E(\Delta R) - E(\Delta C)] \end{aligned} \qquad (8.23)$$

and

$$\text{var}[(1 - T)\pi_1] = (1 - T)^2\text{var}(\pi_0 + \Delta R - \Delta C) \qquad (8.24)$$

Since the tax rate (T) is always less than 100 percent, the variance of after-tax expected profits is always less than the variance of pre-tax

---

[8] Note that statement (8.20) does not say that small firms are more profitable than large firms. W. J. Baumol has put forth the proposition that large firms can be and are more profitable than small firms because increased money capital puts the large firms into a higher echelon of competing capital groups so as to increase their earnings per dollar of investment. Baumol's hypothesis was tested and confirmed by M. Hall and L. Weiss. See W. J. Baumol, *Business Behavior, Value, and Growth*, The Macmillan Company, New York, 1959; and Marshall Hall and Leonard Weiss, "Firm Size and Profitability," *The Review of Economics and Statistics*, vol. LIX, no. 3, August 1967, pp. 319–331.

expected profits. However, if the variability of expected profits is standardized by using relative variation (i.e., coefficient of variation), then taxes divide out and, therefore, have no influence on variation per dollar of expected income. The coefficient of variation is written as

$$\frac{\sigma[(1 - T)\pi_1]}{E[(1 - T)\pi_1]} = \frac{(1 - T)[\text{var}(\pi_0 + \Delta R - \Delta C)]}{(1 - T)[\pi_0 + E(\Delta R) - E(\Delta C)]} \qquad \text{(8.25)}$$

Equation (8.25) is an interesting statement. For example, note that after dividing out taxes in the numerator and denominator and holding the total dispersion constant, a rise in expected incremental costs $[E(\Delta C)]$ without an equal offsetting rise in expected incremental return $[E(\Delta R)]$ can cause the relative variation (i.e., shareholder risk) to rise. This means that since total cost includes fixed charges and the cost of debt financing, any additional interest charges must be offset by adequate additional revenues; otherwise risk of equity ownership will rise with additional debt in the capital structure mix. Future examination of (8.25) shows that if the expected increase in revenues more than offsets the expected rise in costs, then (other things the same) risk will fall, causing equity ownership to become more valuable. Therefore, the total impact of increased costs (including the explicit cost of debt financing) on the value of equity ownership must be evaluated in the light of corresponding changes in expected revenues and possible dispersion about those expectations.

If we drop the artificial assumption of holding the total dispersion constant and permit the numerator of (8.25) to vary along with the denominator, then the situation becomes more complex but, at the same time, moves closer to reality. The factors in the numerator of (8.25) can cause changes in the relative variation of expected profits as well as factors in the denominator. All these interacting factors point to one reason for the complexity of security analysis.

8.4 Concept of Normal Profit

The concept of "normal earnings" gives recognition to the fact that earnings realized in any particular year can be abnormally high or abnormally low. Labor strikes, equipment malfunction, fire, and floods rank among the factors that can cause abnormally low earnings. Earnings can be abnormally high on account of fads, temporary changes in consumer tastes, and similar phenomena.

Put a different way, a complete analysis of a single set of financial statements (i.e., analysis as of one point in time) is always incomplete because any one particular year can be exceptionally good or exceptionally bad, by chance. What is required is analysis over time. For example, to smooth out historical profits, one can calculate a weighted average of current and prior years earnings.

$$\pi_{\text{normal}} = (a_0 \pi_t) + (a_1 \pi_{t-1}) + \cdots + (a_n \pi_{t-n}) \qquad (8.26)$$

where π_{normal} = normal profits, π_t = reported profits in year t, and the coefficients (a_i) are weights, not necessarily equal, $\sum_{i=0}^{n} a_i = 1.00$. Alternatively, one can calculate a linear (or nonlinear) time series trend. That is, hypothesize a "naive" model—profits equal some function of time.

$$\pi_{\text{normal}} = f(\text{time}) \qquad (8.27)$$

Special specific methods are available for calculation[9]; however, the main point for analysis is to avoid the trap of using reported earnings as "normal" earnings.

8.5 Profit and Growth

How profitable *can* the firm be? If sales increase, will profits rise? Other things the same, since high growth is worth more than low growth, why not set production at the highest levels possible so that maximum growth can be achieved? Why not maximize growth?

In the real world of business opportunities, constraints exist. Constraints in product and factor markets as well as constraints in financial markets enforce upper bounds on how high growth can go— how profitable the firm can be—and how valuable the worth of equity ownership can become.

Considering that total profits equal the difference between total revenues and total costs,

$$\text{Total profits} = (\text{Total revenues} - \text{Total costs}) \qquad (8.28)$$

where

   Total profits $= \pi$
   Total revenues $= f(\text{unit price, credit policy, quantity sold} \ldots)$
      Total costs $= f(\text{labor, capital, overhead, quantity produced} \ldots)$

The upper limit on how big profits *can be* is determined by the functional relationship between total revenues and total costs. At the margin, profits are maximum when $\Delta R = \Delta C$.

Should the firm maximize profits (with respect to price, quantity, credit policy,...)? The answer is yes; only if maximum profits result in maximum share price. Most likely maximum profits today will not

---

[9] See, for example, Irwin Friend and Marshall Puckett, "Dividends and Stock Prices," *American Economic Review*, vol. LIV, September 1964, pp. 656–682; and Robert G. Brown, *Smoothing, Forecasting and Prediction of Discrete Time Series*, Prentice-Hall, Inc., Englewood Cliffs, N.J., 1963.

maximize share price because, as stated along with (8.1), a growing stream of income is more valuable than a declining (or fluctuating) stream. Therefore, maximum share price will result by maximizing profits only if that profit is successively larger in every succeeding future period of time. Market constraints may prevent this.

For profits to rise in every successive period of time, the increment in expected revenues must exceed the increment in expected costs for every future successive period of time.

$$E(\Delta R) > E(\Delta C) \qquad (8.29)$$

What are some actions that can cause a large increase in revenues? From Table 8.1, operating revenues come primarily from sales. Hence, rising sales can cause rising revenues. An increase in sales can occur in a variety of ways: (1) advertising and sales promotion campaigns; (2) price cutting (product pricing policy); (3) new, better, and/or different products, product differentiation; and (4) easier credit policy. However, given a constant size market for the goods and services being produced and sold, saturation will set in at some point in time and will limit further growth.

On the cost side, constantly rising sales over the long term will ultimately cause costs to rise. Advertising and sales promotion campaigns must be paid for. Additional goods and services will ultimately require additional labor and more plant and equipment. In the long run, costs will tend to rise. Hence, because of limitations in product markets and factor markets, growth cannot continue without limit. In the long run, as the rate of growth rises, total revenues tend to decline and total costs tend to rise, thereby causing profit to fall.

Growth means rising sales, rising production and, over the long run, a rising level of assets to produce those goods sold. In the long run, therefore, we can write

$$g = \frac{\Delta \text{Sales}}{\text{Sales}} = \frac{\Delta \text{Assets}}{\text{Assets}} \qquad (8.30)$$

Since

$$\pi = rA = r\frac{(\Delta A)}{g} \qquad (8.31)$$

we get a tautology which implies that at the margin, additional assets (ΔA) can cause profits to rise (e.g., through additional profitable sales). But a rise in the long-term average rate of growth of output (g), ceteris paribus, tends to cause total profits to fall.

From an economic point of view, a long-term permanent rising rate of growth means that at some point in time, the rate of production of goods and services will approach the rate of growth of the market (demand). If supply exceeds demand, ceteris paribus, prices will fall (see Chapter 1), causing total revenues to fall. In the factor markets, at some point, the rising rate of production necessary to sustain those rising sales will exceed the rate of growth of the supply of labor and producers' durable equipment, thereby causing a rise in the cost of factors of production.

If the above argument is continued to its logical conclusion, then with secular rising costs and falling revenues, profits (the difference between total revenues and total costs) must fall. Profits and long-term growth rates, therefore, tend to vary inversely as stated in (8.31). And since total profits are related directly to the rate of return on total assets, the return on assets must be related inversely with the level of long-term rate of growth.

After having considered fundamental factors that cause profit-ability and the relationship between the rate of profit and the rate of growth, we now turn to considerations of the influence of finance (if any) on the worth of equity ownership.

8.6 Financing Growth

Suppose the management of the firm comes to you—the financial analyst and holder of the purse strings of all nongovernment financing— and requests financing for a new asset.

Suppose that with the added money from finance, total assets are increased, $(A_1 = A_0 + \Delta A)$, so that expected profits next year are larger than profits would be without the added finance.

$$E_{\text{after}}(\pi_1) = E_{\text{before}}(\pi_1) + E(\Delta\pi)_{\text{new}} \tag{8.32}$$

That is to say, without the new financing, $E(\Delta\pi)_{\text{new}}$ will be foregone. Then the question is, Does it matter whether the new financing comes from new debt (ΔL) or new equity (ΔE)?

$$\Delta A = \Delta L + \Delta E \tag{8.33}$$

We shall examine all possibilities.

Recall from Chapter 1 that additional financing must basically come from one of two places: either *inside* the firm or else from *outside* the firm. Alternatively, the available sources can be viewed as either *debt* sources or else *equity* sources. If debt is considered, then the credit is classified as either short-term or else long-term (for some purposes, intermediate-term borrowing can be considered). If equity sources are considered, then the cash is obtained from (1) depreciation, (2) retained earnings, or (3) new shares of common stock. Preferred shares, by convention, are treated as a form of debt. For purposes of analysis here, hybrid securities (convertibles, preferred shares, warrants, options, and rights) are assigned to one of the pure categories, either debt or equity, as appropriate.

In any case, we wish to examine the relationship between the finance of growth and the worth of equity ownership. The question is, Can the finance of corporate assets affect the worth of equity ownership? Is there an "optimal" capital structure?

Our approach is as follows. First recognize that growth must be financed. Second, consider the overall impact on profits when the increment in assets is financed with additional debt. Third, repeat the analysis assuming equity financing for the additional assets. Finally, compare asset values and the worth of equity ownership using the two pure methods of financing and combinations thereof. The analysis is outlined below.

SITUATION 1: Financing with Additional Debt. The analysis requires study of both expected return and risks to share-owners as well as debt-holders, because the market value of shares plus the market value of debt constitutes the market value of the firm.

The existing debt (L) is being serviced with total interest payments (I_0) per year. The *rate* of profit to existing debt-holders is (I_0/L). The *risk* to existing debt-holders is (1) probability of default on interest, (2) marketability, in the event of sale prior to maturity, and (3) probability of default on redemption.

The relevant probability of default depends upon the willingness and ability of the firm to pay interest charges and redeem the debt. The ability of the firm to pay depends upon the location of the probability distribution of expected net operating income, relative to certain (i.e., for sure) fixed charges. For example, situation 1 in Figure 8.1 implies no risk (probability) of default because the smallest possible net operating profit more than covers the contractual fixed charges (I_0). Situation 2 in Figure 8.1 implies probability of default because the left

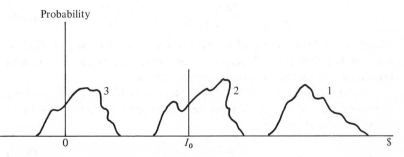

Figure 8.1. Probability distributions for expected net operating income vs. fixed charges.

tail of the probability distribution of expected net operating income lies below the level of fixed charges. If the actual realized profit happens to fall in this left-tail area, as it is likely to do for situation 2, then fixed charges can exceed operating profits. Situation 2 is risky. Situation 3 is default for sure. (*Note*: Review Figure 6.1 in Chapter 6 in the context of Figure 8.1).

Suppose the existing situation is 2 in Figure 8.1, and let the new debt increase total debt from L_0 to $(L_0 + \Delta L)$. Also let the investment of the proceeds from the new debt issue cause an increase in expected net operating income from $(NOI)_0$ to $[(NOI)_0 + \Delta(NOI)]$, with no change in risk [var(NOI)]. We now wish to examine risk and return for bondholders and shareowners.

Before financing, the business risk, or relative variation in expected profits (i.e., standard error of estimate per dollar expected), is

$$\frac{\sigma_0(NOI)}{E_0(NOI)} = \frac{\sigma_{before}(NOI)}{E_{before}(\pi_1)} \tag{8.34}$$

After financing, the same statistic is

$$\frac{\sigma_0(NOI)}{E_0(NOI + \Delta NOI)} = \frac{\sigma_0(NOI)}{E_{before}(\pi_1) + E(\Delta\pi)_{new}} \tag{8.35}$$

Since the risk for bondholders in situation 2 of Figure 8.1 consists of probability of default, that risk can decline under any combination of two conditions: (1) the probability distribution of NOI shifts further to the right than the rightward shift in total fixed charges or (2) the dispersion about the expected net operating income decreases sufficiently so as to decrease the area under the left tail which lies below the new larger fixed charges.

Since we invoked a simplifying assumption of no change in var (NOI), we can say that riskwise, for bondholders to be as well-off after financing as before, the new relative variation (after finance) must be *at most* equal to the original relative variation (without financing). Therefore we write (8.36) from (8.35) and (8.34).

$$\frac{\sigma_0(NOI)}{E_{before}(\pi_1) + E(\Delta\pi)_{new}} \leq \frac{\sigma_0(NOI)}{E_{before}(\pi_1)} \tag{8.36}$$

Statement (8.36) is satisfied for any positive value of $E(\Delta\pi_{new})$. That is, risk for bondholders will decline if the expected increase in revenues exceeds the expected increase in interest payments.

In terms of return, for bondholders to be as well off after financing as before, their rate of profit must be *at least* equal to their original rate of profit. Stated precisely,

$$\frac{(I_0 + \Delta I)}{(L_0 + \Delta L)} \geq \frac{I_0}{L_0} \tag{8.37}$$

Statement (8.37) can be solved for the explicit cost of additional debt, assuming risks remain constant. Multiplying both sides of (8.37) by $(L_0 + \Delta L)$, we get

$$I_0 + \Delta I \geq \frac{I_0}{L_0}(L_0 + \Delta L) \qquad (8.38)$$

Then

$$\Delta I \geq \frac{I_0}{L_0}(\Delta L) \qquad (8.39)$$

After dividing both sides of (8.39) by ΔL, we can write the explicit cost of the additional debt as

$$(\Delta I)/(\Delta L) \geq I_0/L_0 \qquad (8.40)$$

The incremental cost of new debt is at least as great as the cost of debt outstanding.

But how about existing stockholders? If the worth of equity ownership declines because of the added debt, then the explicit cost of debt is illusory because share price will fall, thereby tending to decrease the overall market value of the firm. In a situation such as this, there is an *implicit* cost of debt financing as well as an explicit cost. This implicit cost of the added debt must be added to the explicit cost to calculate total cost of debt financing.

Before financing with additional debt, the expected income available to shareholders in the aggregate is

$$\begin{aligned} E_{\text{before}}(\text{NI}) &= E[(1 - T)(\pi_1 - I_0)] \\ &= (1 - T)[E_{\text{before}}(\pi_1) - I_0] \end{aligned} \qquad (8.41)$$

Statement (8.41) assumes no preferred shares outstanding, so that 100 percent of the net income is available for distribution to holders of common shares. The error of estimate (risk) per dollar of income expected is

$$\frac{\sigma_0(\text{NI})}{E_{\text{before}}(\text{NI})} = \frac{[(1 - T)^2 \text{var}(\pi_1)]^{1/2}}{(1 - T)[E_{\text{before}}(\pi_1) - I_0]} \qquad (8.42)$$

After financing with additional debt, the expected income available to shareholders is

$$\begin{aligned} E_{\text{after}}(\text{NI}) &= E[(1 - T)(\pi_1 + \Delta\pi_{\text{new}} - I_0 - \Delta I)] \\ &= (1 - T)[E(\pi_1 + \Delta\pi_{\text{new}}) - (I_0 + \Delta I)] \end{aligned} \qquad (8.43)$$

The error of estimate (risk) per dollar of income expected is

$$\frac{\sigma_{\text{after}}(\text{NI})}{E_{\text{after}}(\text{NI})} = \frac{\{(1 - T)^2[\text{var}(\pi_1) + \text{var}(\Delta\pi) + 2\text{cov}(\pi_1, \Delta\pi)]\}^{1/2}}{(1 - T)[E(\pi_1 + \Delta\pi_{\text{new}}) - (I_0 + \Delta I)]}$$

$$(8.44)$$

Then for equity owners to be equally well-off (or better) after new debt financing as before, their risk-return combinations must at least remain constant. Comparisons are outlined below.

$$E_{\text{after}}(\text{NI}) \geq E_{\text{before}}(\text{NI}) \tag{8.45}$$

$$(1 - T)[E(\pi_1 + \Delta\pi_{\text{new}}) - (I_0 + \Delta I)] \geq (1 - T)[E_{\text{before}}(\pi_1) - I_0] \tag{8.46}$$

$$E(\Delta\pi_{\text{new}}) - \Delta I \geq 0 \tag{8.47}$$

That is, for the return of equity owners to be no worse off because of the new debt financing, the expected increment of new profit must more than cover the increased interest charges. Also, the risk of equity ownership after financing must be no larger than the corresponding risk before financing.

$$\frac{\sigma_{\text{after}}(\text{NI})}{E_{\text{after}}(\text{NI})} \leq \frac{\sigma_{\text{before}}(\text{NI})}{E_{\text{before}}(\text{NI})} \tag{8.48}$$

$$\frac{\{(1 - T)^2[\text{var}(\pi_1) + \text{var}(\Delta\pi) + 2\text{cov}(\pi_1,\Delta\pi)]\}^{1/2}}{(1 - T)[E(\pi_1 + \Delta\pi_{\text{new}}) - (I_0 + \Delta I)]}$$
$$\leq \frac{[(1 - T)^2\text{var}(\pi_1)]^{1/2}}{(1 - T)[E_{\text{before}}(\pi_1) - I_0]} \tag{8.49}$$

The risk of equity ownership in statement (8.49) can be examined further as follows. First observe that taxes divide out of both sides of (8.49).

$$\frac{[\text{var}(\pi_1) + \text{var}(\Delta\pi) + 2\text{cov}(\pi_1,\Delta\pi)]^{1/2}}{E(\pi_1) + E(\Delta\pi) - I_0 - \Delta I} \leq \frac{[\text{var}(\pi_1)]^{1/2}}{E(\pi_1) - I_0} \tag{8.50}$$

If the increment in profits ($\Delta\pi$) can be predicted with certainty, then, with $\text{var}(\Delta\pi) = 0$, the covariance between π_1 and $\Delta\pi = 0$, and (8.50) simplifies to

$$\frac{\sigma(\pi_1)}{E(\pi_1) + E(\Delta\pi) - I_0 - \Delta I} \leq \frac{\sigma(\pi_1)}{E(\pi_1) - I_0} \tag{8.51}$$

Since (8.51) has the same numerator both before and after financing, then the sufficient condition for (8.51) to be true is for the denominator of the left-hand side to exceed the denominator of the right-hand side.

$$E(\pi_1) - I_0 \leq E(\pi_1) + E(\Delta\pi) - I_0 - \Delta I \tag{8.52}$$

or

$$E(\Delta\pi) > \Delta I \tag{8.53}$$

If the expected increase in profits exceeds the increment in interest, then condition (8.53) is met, and the market value of equity will rise, causing the real cost of debt to be less than the explicit cost. If condition (8.53) is not met, the market value of equity will fall due to added risk, causing the real cost debt financing to exceed the explicit cost.

However, if the increment in profits ($\Delta\pi$) cannot be predicted with certainty as with many real-world investments, then var($\Delta\pi$) does not equal zero and (8.50) does not simplify to (8.51). In other words, if the incremental profit cannot be predicted for certain, then for shareholders to be equally well off after financing as before, expected increase in profit must exceed the increment in interest payment.

The market value of equity depends upon expected net income and risk (i.e., error of expectation) as stated in (8.46) and (8.50).

SITUATION 2: Financing with Additional Equity. Consider the same problem as above, but this time, let the added profit ($\Delta\pi$) be financed from new equity sources instead of debt ($S_{\text{after}} = S_{\text{before}} + \Delta S$).

$$A + \Delta A = L + S + \Delta S \qquad (8.54)$$

Also retain situation 2 in Figure 8.1.

Then, before financing, expected net operating profits and net income are

$$E_{\text{before}}(\text{NOI}) = E(\pi_1) \qquad (8.55)$$

$$E_{\text{before}}(\text{NI}) = E[(1 - T)(\pi_1 - I_0)] \qquad (8.56)$$

and corresponding risks are:

$$\frac{\sigma_{\text{before}}(\text{NOI})}{E_{\text{before}}(\text{NOI})} = \frac{[\text{var}(\pi_1)]^{1/2}}{[E(\pi_1)]} \qquad (8.57)$$

and

$$\frac{\sigma_{\text{before}}(\text{NOI})}{E_{\text{before}}(\text{NOI})} = \frac{[(1 - T)^2 \text{var}(\pi_1)]^{1/2}}{(1 - T)[E(\pi_1) - I_0]} \qquad (8.58)$$

After financing, the two expected profits are:

$$E_{\text{after}}(\text{NOI}) = E(\pi_1 + \Delta\pi) \qquad (8.59)$$

and

$$E_{\text{after}}(\text{NI}) = E[(1 - T)(\pi_1 + \Delta\pi - I_0)] \qquad (8.60)$$

and the corresponding risks are

$$\frac{\sigma_{\text{after}}(\text{NOI})}{E_{\text{after}}(\text{NOI})} = \frac{[\text{var}(\pi_1) + \text{var}(\Delta\pi) + 2\text{cov}(\pi_1, \Delta\pi)]^{1/2}}{E(\pi_1 + \Delta\pi)} \qquad (8.61)$$

and

$$\frac{\sigma_{\text{after}}(\text{NOI})}{E_{\text{after}}(\text{NI})} = \frac{\{(1 - T)^2[\text{var}(\pi_1) + \text{var}(\Delta\pi) + 2\text{cov}(\pi_1, \Delta\pi)]\}^{1/2}}{(1 - T)[E(\pi_1) + E(\Delta\pi) - I_0]} \qquad (8.62)$$

In terms of risk, for existing bondholders to be equally well off, after the additional new equity financing

$$\frac{\sigma_{\text{after}}(\text{NOI})}{E_{\text{after}}(\text{NOI})} \leq \frac{\sigma_{\text{before}}(\text{NOI})}{E_{\text{before}}(\text{NOI})} \qquad (8.63)$$

$$\frac{\{[\text{var}(\pi_1) + \text{var}(\Delta\pi) + 2\text{cov}(\pi_1, \Delta\pi)]^{1/2}}{E(\pi_1) + E(\Delta\pi)} \leq \frac{[\text{var}(\pi_1)]^{1/2}}{E(\pi_1)} \qquad (8.64)$$

Otherwise, the bonds outstanding will become more risky, causing existing market value of bonds to fall. However, observe that in the case of certainty, (8.64) is always true for any positive $E(\Delta\pi)$ because, certainly, the two numerators are equal and the denominator on the left-hand side of (8.64) exceeds the denominator on the right-hand side.

For the stockholders (in the aggregate) to be equally well-off after the new financing as before, the expected return per unit of equity investment must be at least as great after the new financing as before. That is, the total return per dollar of equity investment after finance must be at least as large after the new financing as before the new financing.

$$\frac{E_{\text{after}}(\text{NI})}{S + \Delta S} \geq \frac{E_{\text{before}}(\text{NI})}{S} \tag{8.65}$$

and

$$\frac{(1 - T)[E(\pi_1 + \Delta\pi - I_0)]}{S + \Delta S} \geq \frac{(1 - T)[E(\pi_1 - I_0)]}{S} \tag{8.66}$$

Therefore, from (8.66) we can state the minimum expected increment in profits necessary to merit additional equity financing. Proceed by multiplying both sides of (8.66) by $(S + \Delta S)$ and dividing by $(1 - T)$.

$$E(\pi_1) + E(\Delta\pi) - I_0 \geq \frac{(S + \Delta S)}{S}[E(\pi_1) - I_0]$$

$$= (1 + \frac{\Delta S}{S})[E(\pi_1) - I_0] \tag{8.67}$$

Then solving (8.67) for the smallest worthwhile increment in profit, we get

$$E(\Delta\pi) \geq \frac{\Delta S}{S}[E(\pi_1) - I_0] \tag{8.68}$$

Statement (8.68) shows that the cost of the increment of equity financing at least equals the existing returns to equity

$$\frac{E(\Delta\pi)}{\Delta S} \geq \frac{[E(\pi_1) - I_0]}{S} = \frac{E_{\text{before}}(\text{NI})}{S} \tag{8.69}$$

Otherwise, given the conditions and assumptions stated above, the aggregate market value of stock outstanding will fall, because the overall returns to equity shall be lowered.

Considering risk, for shareholders to be equally well-off after the new equity financing as before, the risk per unit of equity investment after financing must be no greater than the risk prior to the new financing.

$$\frac{\sigma_{\text{after}}(\text{NI})}{(S + \Delta S)[E_{\text{after}}(\text{NI})]} \leq \frac{\sigma_{\text{before}}(\text{NI})}{S[E_{\text{before}}(\text{NI})]} \tag{8.70}$$

Statement (8.70) expands as follows

$$\frac{\{[var(\pi_1) + var(\Delta\pi) + 2cov(\pi_1,\Delta\pi)]\}^{1/2}}{(S + \Delta S)[E(\pi_1) + E(\Delta\pi) - I_0]} \le \frac{[var(\pi_1)]^{1/2}}{S[E(\pi_1) - I_0]}$$

(8.71)

and then the maximum allowable error of estimate of the increment in profit $[var(\Delta\pi)]$ can be calculated by solving equation (8.71). Hence, sufficient conditions are stated for additional equity financing to be profitable.

COMPARISONS: ADDITIONAL DEBT VS. ADDITIONAL EQUITY. In this section, we consider the question, Which is more profitable for shareholders—additional debt financing or additional equity financing?

To answer the question, let us first summarize the results given above for debt financing and equity financing and then proceed with the comparisons.

SUMMARY OF DEBT FINANCING. In the case of debt financing analyzed above, the returns to equity at least increased from

$$\frac{E_{before}(NI)}{S} = \frac{(1 - T)[E_{before}(\pi_1) - I_0]}{S}$$

(8.72)

to

$$\frac{E_{after}(NI)}{S} = \frac{(1 - T)[E(\pi_1 + \Delta\pi_{new}) - (I_0 + \Delta I)]}{S}$$

(8.73)

For the debt financing to be profitable to shareholders,

$$\frac{E_{after}(NI)}{S} \ge \frac{E_{before}(NI)}{S}$$

(8.74)

Risks per unit of equity before and after the new financing are

$$\frac{\sigma_{before}(NI)}{S[E_{before}(NI)]} = \frac{[var(\pi_1)]^{1/2}}{S[E_{before}(\pi_1) - I_0]}$$

(8.75)

and

$$\frac{\sigma_{after}(NI)}{S[E_{after}(NI)]} = \frac{[var(\pi_1) + var(\Delta\pi) + 2cov(\Delta\pi,\pi)]^{1/2}}{S[E(\pi_1 + \Delta\pi) - (I_0 + \Delta I)]}$$

(8.76)

For the risk of equity ownership not to rise on account of the new financing, the risk after finance is no greater than the risk before finance.

$$\frac{\sigma_{after}(NI)}{S[E_{after}(NI)]} \le \frac{\sigma_{before}(NI)}{S[E_{before}(NI)]}$$

(8.77)

SUMMARY FOR EQUITY FINANCING. In the case of equity financing analyzed above, the returns to equity increased from at least

$$\frac{E_{\text{before}}(\text{NI})}{S} = \frac{(1 - T)[E(\pi_1) - I_0]}{S} \tag{8.78}$$

to

$$\frac{E_{\text{after}}(\text{NI})}{(S + \Delta S)} = \frac{(1 - T)[E(\pi_1 + \Delta \pi) - I_0]}{S + \Delta S} \tag{8.79}$$

For the new equity financing to be profitable to shareholders

$$\frac{E_{\text{after}}(\text{NI})}{(S + \Delta S)} \geq \frac{E_{\text{before}}(\text{NI})}{S} \tag{8.80}$$

Risks per unit of equity before and after the new financing are

$$\frac{\sigma_{\text{before}}(\text{NI})}{S[E_{\text{before}}(\text{NI})]} = \frac{(1 - T)[\text{var}(\pi_1)]^{1/2}}{S\{(1 - T)[E(\pi_1) - I_0]\}} \tag{8.81}$$

and

$$\frac{\sigma_{\text{after}}(\text{NI})}{(S + \Delta S)[E_{\text{after}}(\text{NI})]}$$
$$= \frac{(1 - T)[\text{var}(\pi_1) + \text{var}(\Delta \pi) + 2\text{cov}(\Delta \pi, \pi)]^{1/2}}{(S + \Delta S)\{(1 - T)[E(\pi_1) + E(\Delta \pi) - I_0]\}} \tag{8.82}$$

Risk after financing is at most equal to the risk before financing. Otherwise the added risk will cause the worth of equity ownership to fall.

COMPARISON: DEBT FINANCE VS. EQUITY FINANCE. To compare risks after financing with debt to risks after financing with equity, it is sufficient to compare statement (8.76) with (8.82). But since the numerators are the same for both equations, it is sufficient to compare denominators. Hence, we can compare

$$S[E(\pi_1 + \Delta \pi) - (I_0 + \Delta I)] \quad \text{vs.} \quad (S + \Delta S)[E(\pi_1 + \Delta \pi) - I_0] \tag{8.83}$$

Statement (8.83) implies that any positive increment in interest payments (ΔI) assures that added debt will cause a rise in the risk of equity ownership. Put a different way, debt financing is always more risky than equity financing. The right-hand side of (8.83) will always exceed the magnitude of the left-hand side of (8.83) for positive increments of ΔI or ΔS. Rewriting (8.83), we get

$$|S(Q) - S(\Delta I)| \quad \text{vs.} \quad |S(Q) + \Delta S(Q)| \tag{8.84}$$

where $Q = [E(\pi_1 + \Delta\pi) - I_0]$ and other items are the same as defined previously. Equation (8.84) is similar to

$$|A - B| \quad \text{vs.} \quad |A + C| \qquad \textbf{(8.85)}$$

where A, B, and C are all positive numbers.

Then for any positive C and any positive B, the right-hand side of (8.85) will exceed the left-hand side, causing the relative variability of returns on equity to be larger for debt financing than for equity financing. But even if debt financing is more risky than equity financing, the relative returns on equity must be examined before a conclusion regarding optimal finance is reached. The relative returns may increase sufficiently to offset the added risks, but then they may not.

To compare expected returns to equity after financing with new debt and expected returns after financing with new equity, it is sufficient to compare (8.73) with (8.79). Thus we can write

$$\underset{\text{new debt}}{\frac{(1 - T)[E(\pi_1 + \Delta\pi) - (I_0 + \Delta I)]}{S}} \quad \underset{\text{vs.}}{\text{vs.}} \quad \underset{\text{new equity}}{\frac{(1 - T)[E(\pi_1 + \Delta\pi) - I_0]}{(S + \Delta S)}}$$

$$\textbf{(8.86)}$$

Statement (8.86) can be rearranged as follows

$$\frac{E(\pi_1 + \Delta\pi)}{S} - \frac{(I_0 + \Delta I)}{S} \quad \text{vs.} \quad \frac{E(\pi_1 + \Delta\pi)}{(S + \Delta S)} - \frac{I_0}{(S + \Delta S)}$$

$$\textbf{(8.87)}$$

$$\frac{E(\pi_1 + \Delta\pi)}{S} - \frac{(I_0 + \Delta I)}{S} > \frac{E(\pi_1 + \Delta\pi)}{(S + \Delta S)} - \frac{I_0}{(S + \Delta S)} \qquad \textbf{(8.88)}$$

That is, solving the inequality (8.88) we get insights concerning the relationships between expected profits, increment in interest (if additional debt finance is used), and increment in equity investment (if additional equity finance is used). Proceed by multiplying both sides of (8.88) by the factor $S(S + \Delta S)$ and simplifying.

$$(S + \Delta S)[E(\pi_1 + \Delta\pi)] - (S + \Delta S)(I_0 + \Delta I)$$
$$> S[E(\pi_1 + \Delta\pi)] - S(I_0)$$
$$\textbf{(8.89)}$$

$$\Delta S[E(\pi_1 + \Delta\pi)] - S(\Delta I) - \Delta S(I_0 + \Delta I) > 0 \qquad \textbf{(8.90)}$$

Condition (8.90) can occur if the new total expected profit exceeds the new total interest payments plus some percentage of the total equity already invested. In other words, for (8.90) to be true, the magnitude of the positive factors must exceed the magnitude of the negative factors. Thus, we can write

$$\Delta S[E(\pi_1 + \Delta\pi)] > S(\Delta I) + \Delta S(I_0 + \Delta I) \qquad \textbf{(8.91)}$$

and by dividing both sides of (8.91) by ΔS, we get

$$[E(\pi_1) + E(\Delta\pi)] > S\left(\frac{\Delta I}{\Delta S}\right) + (I_0 + \Delta I) \tag{8.92}$$

We stated previously that the expected increase in profits should exceed the increment and interest, if debt financing is used, and the expected net operating profit (without additional financing) should exceed the initial interest payments.

$$E(\Delta\pi) > \Delta I \qquad \text{and} \qquad E(\pi_1) > I_0 \tag{8.93}$$

However, there is no guarantee that condition (8.92) will be true because of the additional factor on the right-hand side of (8.92), $S(\Delta I/\Delta S)$. The condition depends upon expected profits $[E(\pi_1)]$ and increment due to additional financing $[E(\Delta\pi)]$ in relation to the factors on the right-hand side of (8.92). Not only is the increment in interest (ΔI) important but so is the increment in interest, relative to the percentage increase in equity investment $[(\Delta S)/S]$.

If statement (8.92) is true, then debt financing of expected increases in growth will cause greater returns to equity, per dollar of equity invested, than will equity financing of that expected increase in growth.

On the other hand, equity financing will cause higher returns to equity than will debt financing, if the condition stated in (8.88) or (8.92) is reversed.

$$\frac{E(\pi_1 + \Delta\pi)}{(S + \Delta S)} - \frac{I_0}{(S + \Delta S)} > \frac{E(\pi_1 + \Delta\pi)}{S} - \frac{(I_0 + \Delta I)}{S} \tag{8.94}$$

That is,

$$S[E(\pi_1 + \Delta\pi)] - S(I_0) > (S + \Delta S)[E(\pi_1 + \Delta\pi)] \\ - (S + \Delta S)(I_0 + \Delta I) \tag{8.95}$$

$$0 > \Delta S[E(\pi_1 + \Delta\pi)] - S(\Delta I) - \Delta S(I_0 + \Delta I) \tag{8.96}$$

Condition (8.96) is true, if the new total expected profits is less than the new total interest payments plus some percentage of the total equity already invested in the firm.

$$S(\Delta I) + \Delta S(I_0 + \Delta I) > \Delta S[E(\pi_1 + \Delta\pi)] \tag{8.97}$$

$$(I_0 + \Delta I) + S\left(\frac{\Delta I}{\Delta S}\right) > E(\pi_1 + \Delta\pi) \tag{8.98}$$

If the additional interest payments (ΔI) are large relative to the additional required equity $[(\Delta S)/S]$, so that (8.98) is true, then additional equity, not additional debt, can cause a relatively larger increase in expected net income per dollar of equity investment than can additional debt.

SITUATION 3: How About Both Debt and Equity Financing Together? Is there some "optimal" mix of debt and equity investment that will maximize the total returns to equity or the total market value of the firms?

Let us examine the situations possible. Begin by admitting additional finance from both debt and equity sources. In other words, let ΔA consist of some equity (ΔS) and also some debt (ΔL).

$$A + \Delta A = S + \Delta S = L + \Delta L \qquad (8.99)$$

Then, before the new finance, the expected returns and risks are

$$E_{\text{before}}(\text{NOI}) = E(\pi_1) \qquad (8.100)$$

$$E_{\text{before}}(\text{NI}) = E\{(1 - T)[E(\pi_1) - I_0]\} \qquad (8.101)$$

$$\frac{\sigma_{\text{before}}(\text{NI})}{S\{E_{\text{before}}(\text{NI})\}} = \frac{\{(1 - T)^2[\text{var}(\pi_1)]\}^{1/2}}{S\{(1 - T)[E(\pi_1) - I_0]\}} \qquad (8.102)$$

After the new finance, the corresponding risks and returns are

$$E_{\text{after}}(\text{NOI}) = E(\pi_1 + \Delta\pi) \qquad (8.103)$$

$$E_{\text{after}}(\text{NI}) = E\{(1 - T)[E(\pi_1 + \Delta\pi) - (I + \Delta I)]\} \qquad (8.104)$$

$$\frac{\sigma_{\text{after}}(\text{NI})}{(S + \Delta S)[E_{\text{after}}(\text{NI})]}$$
$$= \frac{\{(1 - T)^2[\text{var}(\pi_1) + \text{var}(\Delta\pi) + 2\text{cov}(\pi_1,\Delta\pi)]\}^{1/2}}{(S + \Delta S)\{(1 - T)[E(\pi_1 + \Delta\pi) - (I + \Delta I)]\}} \qquad (8.105)$$

For the added finance to be totally profitable on all counts, the risks after must be no larger than the risks before the new investment was undertaken.

$$\frac{\sigma_{\text{after}}(\text{NI})}{(S + \Delta S)[E_{\text{after}}(\text{NI})]} \leq \frac{\sigma_{\text{before}}(\text{NI})}{S[E_{\text{before}}(\text{NI})]} \qquad (8.106)$$

Also, for the new investment to be profitable, the returns after finance must exceed the returns before finance.

$$\frac{E(_{\text{after}}\text{NI})}{(S + \Delta S)} \geq \frac{E_{\text{before}}(\text{NI})}{S} \qquad (8.107)$$

If the standard errors on both sides of (8.106) do not change appreciably, then for the project to be a profitable investment, it is sufficient that

$$\frac{E_{\text{after}}(\text{NI})}{(S + \Delta S)} \geq \frac{E_{\text{before}}(\text{NI})}{S} \qquad (8.108)$$

Expanding (8.108), we get a statement of the total returns per dollar of equity investment.

$$\frac{(1 - T)[E(\pi_1 + \Delta\pi) - (I_0 + \Delta I)]}{(S + \Delta S)} \geq \frac{(1 - T)[E(\pi_1) - I_0]}{S} \qquad (8.109)$$

Then (8.109) can be used to examine the profitability of the new finance mix. We can proceed as follows. First, multiply both sides of (8.109) by the factor $S(S + \Delta S)$, and divide by $(1 - T)$.

$$S[E(\pi_1 + \Delta\pi)] - S(I_0 + \Delta I) \geq (S + \Delta S)[E(\pi_1) - I_0] \quad (8.110)$$

statement (8.110) simplifies as follows

$$S[E(\pi_1)] + S[E(\Delta\pi)] - S(I_0) - S(\Delta I) \geq S[E(\pi_1)] \\ - S(I_0) + \Delta S[E(\pi_1)] - I_0] \quad (8.111)$$

$$S[E(\Delta\pi)] - S(\Delta I) \geq \Delta S[E(\pi_1) - I_0] \quad (8.112)$$

$$E(\Delta\pi) - (\Delta I) \geq \frac{\Delta S}{S}[E(\pi_1) - I_0] \quad (8.113)$$

Equation (8.113) states that for the new project to be profitable, the net increment in profit $[E(\Delta\pi) - (\Delta I)]$ must at least equal the percentage increase in equity $[(\Delta S)/S]$ multiplied by the net profit anticipated without the new project $[E(\pi_1) - I_0]$.

Now, since the total increment in finance $(\Delta S + \Delta L)$ is fixed as stated in (8.99), then as the increment is equity (ΔS) increases, ΔI decreases. As ΔI increases, ΔS decreases. If $\Delta S = 0$, then ΔI is maximum, and the increase in assets is 100 percent debt financed.

$$\Delta I = f(\Delta L) \quad (8.114)$$

and

$$E(\Delta\pi) \geq (\Delta I) \quad (8.115)$$

As the increment in equity (ΔS) rises, the increment in debt (ΔL) falls so that $(A + \Delta A)$ remains constant.

$$A + \Delta A = S + \Delta S + L + \Delta L = A_1 \quad (8.116)$$

But what about an optimal mix of new finance—a mix that will maximize the after-finance return to equity? What particular mix of ΔS and ΔL will maximize U as defined below?

$$\frac{(1 - T)[E(\pi_1 + \Delta\pi) - (I_0 + \Delta I)]}{(S + \Delta S)} = U \quad (8.117)$$

In other words, we wish to maximize U with respect to (say) the proportion of total debt financing,

$$(L + \Delta L)/A_1 \quad (8.118)$$

subject to the constraint that the total finance from all sources is fixed,

$$(L + \Delta L) + (S + \Delta S) = A_1 = \text{Constant} \quad (8.119)$$

and the fact that the total dollars of interest paid is related to the rate of interest and the total liabilities incurred,

$$(I_0 + \Delta I) = i(L + \Delta L) \tag{8.120}$$

Then, substituting the constraints (8.119) and (8.120) into the objective function (8.117) we get

$$U = \frac{(1 - T)[E(\pi_1 + \Delta\pi) - i(L + \Delta L)]}{A_1 - (L + \Delta L)} \tag{8.121}$$

Dividing both numerator and denominator by A_1, we get

$$U = \frac{(1 - T)[(1/A_1)E(\pi_1 + \Delta\pi) - i(L + \Delta L)/A_1]}{1 - (L + \Delta L)/A_1} \tag{8.122}$$

which is the same as (8.121). A necessary condition for maximizing U is that the first derivative must equal zero. Thus differentiating (8.122) with respect to proportion of total debt financing, we get

$$\frac{dU}{d(L + \Delta L/A_1)} = \frac{[1 - (L + \Delta L)/A_1][-(1 - T)i] - (Z)(-1)}{[1 - (L + \Delta L)/A_1]^2} = 0 \tag{8.123}$$

where $Z = (1 - T)[(1/A_1)E(\pi_1 + \Delta\pi) - i(L + \Delta L)/A_1]$.
Equation (8.123) is satisfied when

$$(1 - T)\{-i + [i(L + \Delta L)/A_1] + [(1/A_1)E(\pi_1 + \Delta\pi)]$$
$$- [i(L + \Delta L)/A_1]\} = 0 \tag{8.124}$$

But note that equation (8.124) is independent of the proportion of total debt finance because the two terms involving $i(L + \Delta L)/A$ subtract out. That is, for (8.124) to be true, it is sufficient that the total expected profits equal a percentage of total assets.

$$E(\pi_1 + \Delta\pi) = iA \tag{8.125}$$

So, under the conditions assumed in taking the derivatives (8.123), i.e., the rate of interest (i) is constant for small increments in debt, then equation (8.125) is independent of the particular finance mix.

The conclusion is that the optimal finance of new projects depends upon the expected returns from the opportunity for corporate investment and on the asociated costs as discussed in the preceding sections; not upon any optimal target ratio of debt to equity.

8.7 Dividend Payout and Investment Value

We turn now to the question, "Is there some optimal split between retention of earnings and dividend payout so that share price can and will be maximized?"

Consider a lump sum of money (NI) as the residual remaining in the firm after payment of all costs of business operations, finance, and after payment of all federal, state, local, and foreign taxes. Introduce *one* exception—payment to shareholders. The relevant question is, What is the optimal way to pay the shareholders? Two ways of payment are possible: (1) current dividends (now) or (2) capital gains (later). Of course, there can be some combination of the two.

The question then becomes one of trade-off. Which alternative provides larger value: (1) current income or (2) capital appreciation? Is there some optimal combination of the two?

The analysis can proceed in either of two ways: (1) in terms of a sequence of short-term periodic decisions or (2) in terms of a long-run average value of payout.

At the margin, the optimal allocation of money available depends upon all the available opportunities for investment. One opportunity is for the firm to pay out the money in dividends. Other alternatives most likely involve the decision to reinvest within the business.

The optimal allocation of available money earned by the firm depends upon the alternative incremental profit to the shareholder. Put in the form of a question, Is the shareholder better off by receiving the current dividends and reinvesting them himself, or is the shareholder better off by letting the firm retain the money and reinvest in the business? To arrive at an answer, we can proceed as follows.

If dividends are paid and the shareholder reinvests this (after-tax) money at the market, then the future value of these dividends is

$$S_S = (1 - T_p)D_t(1 + k_m)^n \qquad (8.126)$$

where

S_S = future value of the current dividend payment to shareholders
T_p = personal tax rate facing the individual investor
D_t = total current dividends paid out to shareholders
k_m = market rate of return available to individual shareholders
n = number of time periods the account is held

The risk is in predicting the value of k_m.

$$\text{Risk} = \text{var}(k_m) \qquad (8.127)$$

If dividends are not paid but are retained and reinvested at the corporate rate of return, then the future value of these dividends is

$$S_f = D_t(1 + k_f)^n \qquad (8.128)$$

where S_f = future value of the dividends that would have been paid out, k_f = corporate rate of return, and other symbols are the same as stated above. The risk is in predicting the value of k_f.

For retention to be more profitable to shareholders than payout, reinvestment by the firm must be more valuable than reinvestment by private individuals.

$$S_f \geq S_S \tag{8.129}$$

Substituting values from (8.128) and (8.126) into (8.129), we get

$$D_t(1 + k_f)^n \geq (1 - T_p)D_t(1 + k_m)^n \tag{8.130}$$

Statement (8.130) can be solved to show the minimum required return on corporate reinvestment if retention is to be more profitable to shareholders than payout.

$$(1 + k_f) \geq \sqrt[n]{(1 - T_p)}(1 + k_m) \tag{8.131}$$

The risk can be stated as

$$\text{Risk}(S_f) \geq \text{Risk}(S_S) \tag{8.132}$$

To illustrate, suppose the personal marginal tax rate is 50 percent, and the time horizon (n) is 10 years. Then

$$(1 + k_f) \geq (.5)^{1/10}(1 + k_m) = .931(1 + k_m) \tag{8.133}$$

$$k_f \geq .931k_m - .069 \tag{8.134}$$

If the market rate (k_m) equals 9 percent, then, assuming equal risks, the shareholders are better off for retention and reinvestment within the firm for all rates of profit exceeding approximately 1.5 percent.

$$\begin{aligned} k_f &\geq .931(.09) - .069 \\ &= .08379 - .069 \\ &= .01479 \end{aligned} \tag{8.135}$$

If the personal marginal tax rate is zero, and k_m equals 9 percent, then the corporate rate must be at least 9 percent also.

$$k_f \geq (1)(1 + k_m) - 1 = k_m = .09 \tag{8.136}$$

The above analysis can be refined to account for capital gains taxes and income taxes on the interest received in (8.128) and (8.126) respectively.

We can conclude, therefore, that shareholder tax rate and need for additional current income (k_p) both are relevant for calculating lower bound on k_f. If shareholders need current income for transactions purposes instead of reinvestment in money assets, then k_p is not equal to k_m but, instead, can be very large. For example, if income is needed today to pay for living expenses, then the personal rate of discount k_p can be very large (the investor has no intention of reinvesting at k_m). Under these conditions, money received next year may be worthless today in the mind of the shareholder.

To summarize, if there are not sufficient projects profitable enough for equity financing, then the earnings can be distributed to the shareholders (i.e., to give or not to give depends upon the profitable investment opportunities facing the firm). If the opportunities are large in number and high in profit, then the firm will be paying no dividends and issuing new shares. If the opportunities are small in number (or nonexistent) and are not so profitable, then the firm will approach 100 percent payout of net income.

A share of stock, like any asset, is worth the present value of the income expected to be forthcoming as a result of operating and owning that share. The shares of Avon Products, Inc. may be a bargain at $50 each, because of the high (and perhaps rising) rate of return on money reinvested by the firm and the relative predictability of further increases in the rate of future growth. Crown Zellerbach Corp., on the other hand, may be expensive at $50 per share, because of its relatively low and steady (or declining) rate of return on reinvested money within the firm and the relatively low rate of increase of growth.

In Chapter 11 some specific models for equity valuation shall be discussed.

DEPRECIATION

As depicted in Table 8.1, depreciation contributes to (or subtracts from) corporate profitability. Depreciation itself can be viewed as the reduction in value of property due to a decline in the ability or capacity to perform present and future service. Alternatively, depreciation can be viewed as the consumption of investment in property, or the loss in service capacity of property because of use, wear and tear, physical deterioration, current action of the elements, obsolescence, inadequacy, or the demands of public authority. Depreciation results from forces and conditions which limit the service life of property and cause retirement. For purposes of analysis, then, depreciation can be considered from three viewpoints:

1. Physical depreciation
2. Economic depreciation
3. Accounting depreciation

Salient aspects of each of these is discussed below:

A. Physical Depreciation

Physical depreciation can be viewed as the actual (or true) decrease in value of assets as determined from a physical inspection of the property by qualified valuation experts. Physical depreciation results from the passage of time and the wear and tear caused by continual use of the asset. An extreme example of physical depreciation is the collapse of the one-horse shay.

B. Economic Depreciation

Economic depreciation can be viewed as the decline in value of an asset because the products produced by that asset no longer command the value in the market place that they once did. The concept of economic depreciation is broader and more inclusive than the concept of physical depreciation in that assets may become technologically obsolete and, therefore, command lower prices in the marketplace even though relatively little physical deterioration has occurred.

CALCULATION OF ECONOMIC DEPRECIATION.

Economic depreciation occurs because the earning power of the asset declines. Whereas physical depreciation is directly related with the age and the wear and tear of the asset, economic depreciation is related to the ability of the asset to produce income.

As an asset ages, that asset may no longer be capable of producing the quantity or quality of products that it formerly did. Hence, the value of the asset can decline in accordance with its rate of physical depreciation. Alternatively, the value of the asset may decline over time because the tastes and preferences of the community have changed. That is, consumers may prefer or have access to newer products that can substitute for those goods produced by the asset. The rate of economic depreciation tends to rise, ceteris paribus, as the quantity, quality, and variety of capital, labor, and knowledge increases.

If one assumes that there is no change in investment opportunities for an asset during the time period under consideration (i.e., no rightward or leftward shift in the schedule of investment opportunities) and also assumes continuous discounting (i.e., the inverse of continuous compounding), then the rate of economic depreciation (W) can be calculated, given the initial market value of the asset (A_0), the current market value of the asset (A_t), and the interval of time (t).

$$A_t = A_0 e^{-(Wt)} \qquad (8.137)$$

Note that statement (8.137) assumes continuous discounting. With this particular form of representing economic depreciation, assets will drop to about $\frac{1}{2}$ of 1 percent of their initial value after five time constants ($e^{-5} = .006738$).

The constant irrational number e equals 2.7128 and is used as the base for the Naperian or "natural" logarithm system. It arises from the formulation of compound interest. Recall from Chapter 4, equation (4.11), that if interest (i) is compounded at m intervals during the year, $1 invested will grow to $(1 + i/m)^{mt}$ dollars by the end of t years. If interest is compounded continuously during the year, then it can be shown that the following is true.

$$\lim_{m \to \infty} [(1 + i/m)^{(m/i)}]^{it} = (e)^{it} \qquad (8.138)$$

That is,

$$\lim_{m \to \infty} (1 + 1/m)^m = 2.71828\ldots \qquad (8.139)$$

For continuous depreciation instead of growth, the exponent takes on a negative sign as denoted above in equation (8.137).

To illustrate the operation of equation (8.137), assume that a new machine capable of generating profits of $3300 per year sold for $22,000. Ten years later, assume that the machine is capable of generating profits of only $330 per year. The economic value of the machine would have declined proportionally to $2200 (i.e., assuming a constant rate of return on assets, $r = \pi/A = \$3300/\$22,000 = .15 = \$300/X$, so that $X = \$300/.15 = \$2200$). That is, 10 years later, the machine would command a price of $2200 in the market place. Then, the amount of economic depreciation is ($22,000–$2200) or $19,800. However, the rate of economic depreciation (W) is determined from the formula

$$e^{-10W} = \$2200/\$22,000 = .100 \qquad \textbf{(8.140)}$$

Solution of equation (8.140) for W may be obtained by taking logarithms.

$$-10W = \log_e(.100)$$

$$\textbf{(8.141)}$$

$$W = [\log_e(.100)]/(-10) = (-2.3)/(-10) = 23 \text{ percent}$$

$$\textbf{(8.142)}$$

Hence, the solution indicates that return on investment in the machine is 15 percent, and the economic value of the machine is declining at a rate of 23 percent per year continuously over the 10-year period of time.[10]

C. Accounting Depreciation

Accounting depreciation can be defined as the decrease in the value of assets as determined by the application of some systematic method generally agreed upon for accounting purposes. That is, accounting depreciation can be taken as the rate at which depreciation charges are entered in the corporation's books. In theory, accounting depreciation should provide a close approximation to economic value over the life of the asset.

In practice, accounting depreciation can differ from economic depreciation. This is especially true for firms dealing in highly techno-logical products and innovations, because a sudden "breakthrough" can make production equipment obsolete which still has many years of serviceable life available, if viewed according to physical condition or accounting write-off. If the rate of economic depreciation differs from the rate of accounting depreciation, then corporations may have (financial) incentive to add to or subtract from their stock of assets. For example, if the rate of economic depreciation is less than the rate of accounting depreciation, the firm will have incentive to expand because the rate of return on assets will exceed the market rate of dis-count of the income from those assets. The particular methods used to calculate economic and accounting depreciation determine whether these incentives will or will not exist.

---

[10] For a discussion of the relationship between accounting and economic depreciation see Eugene M. Lerner and Willard T. Carleton, *A Theory of Financial Analysis*, Harcourt, Brace & World, Inc., New York, 1966, Chap. 4.

The actual magnitude of the difference between economic depreciation and accounting depreciation can be determined by the particular
method chosen to compute accounting depreciation.

Several alternative methods are listed for computing accounting
depreciation: straight-line, declining-balance, sum-of-the-years-digit,
and sinking-fund. The U.S. Treasury Department has established
policies and guide lines concerning which of these methods are acceptable for purposes of income tax.

CALCULATION OF ACCOUNTING DEPRECIATION. This section of the study
will outline and illustrate four methods currently used to compute
accounting depreciation.

STRAIGHT-LINE DEPRECIATION (SLD). The straight-line
method of depreciation allocates an equal proportion of the depreciable value of an asset to each time period included in the life of the
asset. Stated precisely,

$$D_t = (P - L)/N \tag{8.143}$$

where

D_t = amount of depreciation during time period (t)
P = initial price of the asset being depreciated
L = liquidation value (salvage value) of the asset
N = total number of time periods (e.g., years) of service life of
the asset
$(P - L)$ = total depreciable value of the asset

The cumulative (total) depreciation to the end of any time can be
computed as

$$D_n = nD_t = n(P - L)/N$$
$$= (n/N)(P - L) \tag{8.144}$$

where D_n = total (cumulative) depreciation to the end of any time,
n = number of time periods since the beginning of depreciation, and
other terms are the same as defined above. The appraisal value of the
asset at the end of any year (n) can be calculated as

$$B_n = P - D_n = P - (n/N)(P - L)$$
$$= P[1 - (n/N)] + (n/N)L \tag{8.145}$$

where B_n = book or appraisal values as of time n and other terms are the
same as defined previously.

ILLUSTRATION 1—Straight-Line Depreciation. Suppose we
have an asset whose purchase price is $2200, whose salvage value is
$200, and whose useful life is 10 years, then we can list

$$P = \$2200 \qquad L = \$200 \qquad N = 10 \text{ years}$$

Compute.

    (1) Annual depreciation (D_t)
    (2) Total depreciation to the end of the eighth year (D_8)
    (3) Book value of the asset at the end of the second year of useful life.

Solution.

    (1) Use equation (8.143) to compute annual depreciation.

$$D_t = \frac{\$2200 - \$200}{10} = \frac{\$2000}{10} = \$200 \text{ per year}$$

    (2) Use equation (8.144) to determine D_8.

$$D_8 = (8/10)(\$2000) = \$1{,}600$$

    (3) Use equation (8.145) to compute book value.

$$B_2 = P - (n/N)(P - L) = \$2200 - (\tfrac{2}{10})(\$2000) = \$1800$$

FIXED-PERCENTAGE DEPRECIATION. This method of depreciation is also known as diminishing-value depreciation, reducing-balance
depreciation, and declining-balance depreciation. When used for income
tax purposes, the maximum value of the allowable fixed percentage is
twice the rate computed by the straight-line method. This is the rule
implied by the phase "double-declining balance."

    To compute depreciation using the fixed-percentage method, one
takes the annual depreciation (D_t) to be a percentage (f) of the value of
the property as of the beginning of the particular year. The percentage
value (f) remains constant but the annual depreciation (D_t) decreases
with the age of the property. Equation (8.146) is the formula for computing the fixed percentage (f) when L, P, and N are given.

$$f = 1 - (L/P)^{1/N} \qquad \text{(8.146)}$$

where f = fixed percentage of the value of the property being depreciated and other terms are the same as defined previously. Then the
amount of depreciation during any time period (t) can be stated.

$$D_t = fB_{t-1} \qquad \text{(8.147)}$$

where

    D_t = periodic depreciation occurring during any time period (t)
    f = fixed percentage rate of depreciation
    B_{t-1} = book value of the asset at the beginning of the time period
        under consideration

The total (cumulative) depreciation to the end of any time (n) can be
stated as

$$D_n = P[1 - (L/P)^{n/N}] \qquad \text{(8.148)}$$

where all terms are the same as defined previously.

Substitution of the value of D_n from equation (8.148) into the definition of book value, equation (8.145), yields results for fixed-percentage depreciation

$$B_n = P - D_n = P - P[1 - (L/P)^{n/N}] = P(L/P)^{n/N}$$
$$= P(1 - f)^n \qquad \text{(8.149)}$$

ILLUSTRATION 2—Fixed-Percentage Depreciation. Suppose we have the same asset as in illustration 1 above, but now we wish to use fixed-percentage depreciation instead of straight-line depreciation. That is

Given. $P = \$2200$, $L = \$200$, and $N = 10$ years.
Problem.

1. Compute the value of the fixed percentage (f)
2. Tabulate for each year the value of D_t, ΔD_t, and B_t
3. Show by using equation (8.148) and equation (8.145) that values of D_n and B_n at the end of the fifth year are the same as those in Table 8.2

Solution.

1. $f = 1 - (L/P)^{1/N} = 1 - (\$200/\$2200)^{1/10}$
   $= 1.0000 - .7868 = .213$ or   21.3 percent
2. $D_5 = P[1 - (L/P)^{n/N}] = \$2200[1 - (\$200/\$2200)^{5/10}]$
   $= \$2200[1 - \sqrt{(1/11)}] = \$1537$
3. $B_5 = P - D_5 = \$2200 - \$1537 = \$663$

The calculated values of D_5 and B_5 are same as underlined values in Table 8.2.

SUM-OF-THE-YEARS-DIGITS DEPRECIATION. This is an accelerated method of depreciation and can be summarized as follows.

$$\sum n = 1 + 2 + 3 + \cdots + (N - 2) + (N - 1) + N$$
$$= N(N + 1)/2 \qquad \text{(8.150)}$$

where $\sum n =$ the sum of the years digits over the useful life of the depreciable property.

Then the periodic amount of depreciation during any period (t) can be written

$$D_t = [(N + 1 - n)/(\sum n)](P - L) \qquad \text{(8.151)}$$

and the total (cumulative) depreciation is

$$D_n = \{[n(2N + 1 - n)]/[N(N + 1)]\}(P - L) \qquad \text{(8.152)}$$

where all terms are the same as defined previously.

Table 8.2 FIXED PERCENTAGE DEPRECIATION
(values calculated to nearest $1)

Year n	Value at start of year ($) B_{T-1}	Annual depreciation ($) $D_t = (f)B_{T-1}$	Value at end of year ($) $B_T = B_{T-1} - D_t$	Total depreciation to end of year ($) $D_T = \sum (D_t)$
1	2200	469	1731	469
2	1731	369	1362	838
3	1362	290	1072	1128
4	1072	229	843	1357
5	843	180	663	1537
6	663	141	522	1678
7	522	111	411	1789
8	411	88	323	1877
9	323	69	254	1946
10	254	54	200	2000

The periodic depreciation (D_t) is proportional to the remaining life of the property as of the beginning of the specific year (n). Then the sum of the years digits depreciation can be calculated.

ILLUSTRATION 3—Sum-of-the-Years-Digits Depreciation. A machine which costs $1500 will have a salvage value of $300 at the end of an estimated life of 5 years. What are the annual depreciation and the book value at the end of the third year?

Given. $P = \$1500$, $L = \$300$, $N = 5$ years, and $n = 3$ years

Problem. Compute the periodic depreciation (D_t) and the book value (B_n) of the asset as of the end of the third year.

The total depreciable value of the asset is $1200.

$$P - L = \$1500 - \$300 = \$1200$$

The sum-of-the-years-digits for a total of 5 years is 15.

$$\sum n = \{N(N+1)/2\} = \{5(6)/2\} = 15$$

Then the periodic depreciation for the third year is $240.

$$D_t = [(N+1-n)/(\sum n)](P-L)$$
$$= [(5+1-3)/15]\$1200 = \$240$$

Total depreciation to the end of the third year is $960.

$$D_n = \{[n(2N+1-n)]/[N(N+1)]\}(P-L)$$
$$= \{3(10+1-3)/[5(6)]\}\$1200 = \$960$$

The book value of the asset at the end of the third year is $540.

$$B_n = P - D_n = \$1500 - \$960 = \$540$$

COMPARISON OF ALTERNATIVE METHODS OF DEPRECIATION. Consider the following data:

Given.

1. Cost of asset $= \$10,000$
2. Life of asset $= 5$ years
3. Salvage value of asset $= \$1500$

Exercise for students.

1. Show that the diminishing balance rate (i.e., fixed-percentage rate) that satisfies these conditions is approximately 31.6 percent.
2. Show that the economic rate of depreciation (assuming continuous depreciation) that satisfies these conditions is approximately 38 percent.
3. Verify that the values shown in Table 8.3 are correct.
4. Discuss the implications for corporate growth, given the data from Table 8.3.

Table 8.3 COMPARISON OF ALTERNATIVE METHODS OF DEPRECIATION

Year	Straight-line		Diminishing-balance		Sum-of-the-years-digits		Economic rate	
	Beginning balance ($)	Period change ($)	Beginning balance ($)	Period change ($)	Beginning balance ($)	Period change ($)	Beginning balance ($)	Period change ($)
1	10000	1700	10000	3160	10000	2833	10000	3161
2	8300	1700	6840	2161	7167	2267	6839	2162
3	6600	1700	4679	1479	4900	1700	4677	1478
4	4900	1700	3200	1011	3200	1133	3199	1012
5	3200	1700	2189	692	2067	567	2187	691
Balance	1500		1497		1500		1496	
Total amortized		8500		8503		8500		8504

To summarize, depreciation is relevant to financial analysis and can contribute to corporate profitability for several reasons. (1) Assets (capital) consumed in the process of production must be replaced if the asset base is to remain intact. Replacement of depreciated assets costs money. The money is removed from the income stream. Only those assets which never wear out, which never have to be replaced, or which never become obsolete are free of depreciation. All other assets are subject to depreciation. (2) If the rate of accounting depreciation exceeds the rate of economic depreciation, then the firm can undergo profitable expansion by reinvesting the sum of money calculated by the accounting method. Since this (accounting) sum exceeds the alternative sum calculated using the economic rate, the economic value of the firm is enhanced. In other words, reinvested depreciation can be internal source of financing growth and expansion.

SINKING-FUND DEPRECIATION (SFD.) The periodic depreciation is that sum (D_t) which, invested at the end of each year at interest (i) compounded annually, will accumulate to the depreciable value $P - L$ of the property at the end of the service life (n) of the property. (Remember: $m = 1$, i.e., interest is assumed to be compounded annually.) The sinking-fund method of depreciation is designed to accumulate a lump sum of money at some specified future date by periodic investments. The magnitude of the lump sum equals the depreciable value of the asset.

$$D_t = (P - L)\left[\frac{i}{(1 + i)^N - 1}\right] = (P - L)(\text{SFDF}) \qquad (8.153)$$

where

D_t = periodic depreciation or lump sum amount to be invested in an account drawing interest (i), so that at the end of the useful life of the asset, the value of the account precisely equals the depreciable value of the asset

SFDF = sinking-fund deposit factor (refer to Chapter 4)

other terms are the same as defined previously.

$$D_n = (P - L)\left[\frac{(1 + i)^n - 1}{(1 + i)^N - 1}\right] \qquad (8.154)$$

where all terms are the same as defined previously.

$$B_n = P - D_n = P - (P - L)\left[\frac{(1 + i)^n - 1}{(1 + i)^N - 1}\right] \qquad (8.155)$$

ILLUSTRATION 4—Sinking-Fund Depreciation. Suppose we have the same asset discussed previously and interest is 6 percent.

Given. $P = \$2200$, $L = \$200$, $N = 10$ years, and $i = .06$.
Problem. Compute:

1. Total depreciable value $(P - L)$
2. Annual depreciation (D_t), using sinking-fund depreciation
3. Total depreciation (D_n) to the end of 6 years
4. Book value of the asset at end of 6 years (B_t)

Solution.

1. The total depreciable value of the asset is $2000.

$$P - L = \$2200 - \$200 = \$2000$$

2. The annual depreciation is $151.80.

$$D_t = (P - L)(\text{SFDF}) = \$2000(.0759) = \$151.80$$

3. The total depreciation to the end of 6 years is $1058.

$$D_6 = \$2000\left[\frac{(1.06)^6 - 1}{(1.06)^{10} - 1}\right]$$

$$= \$2000\left[\frac{1.4185 - 1}{1.7908 - 1}\right] = \$1058$$

4. The book value of the asset at the end of 6 years is $1142.

$$B_6 = P - D_6 = \$2200 - \$1058 = \$1142$$

AVERAGE INTEREST AS USED IN CONNECTION WITH DE-PRECIATION. When money is obtained to make the initial purchase, there exists a financing cost. If the money is obtained from equity sources (owner capital), then the financing is received at the cost of equity. If the funds are obtained by borrowing (e.g., commercial bank loan, bond issue), then the financing is received at the cost of debt. In practice, large corporations frequently purchase assets with funds obtained from both equity and debt sources. In this case, financing cost can be viewed as the cost of capital without specific reference to the source of the capital funds.

For purposes of this study, consider the financing cost to be some rate of interest (i). A typical agreement is to pay interest at the rate of i percent per annum of the unpaid balance of the loan. Illustration 5 may best explain the fundamentals involved.

ILLUSTRATION 5—Interest on Investment.
Given. $P = \$1200$, $L = \$200$, $i = .06$, and $N = 5$ years.

For these data Table 8.4 indicates the allocation of funds in each of the 5 years. Straight-line reduction of principal is assumed. Results of the calculations are shown in Table 8.4. The unpaid principal at the end

Table 8.4 STRAIGHT-LINE DEPRECIATION AND AVERAGE
INTEREST (paid at end of year)

Year ending n	In reduction of principal $D_t = (P - L)/N$ ($)	Interest on unpaid balance ($)	Unpaid amount of principal ($)
0	—	—	1200
1	200	72	1000
2	200	60	800
3	200	48	600
4	200	36	400
5	200	24	200

of 5 years is equal to the salvage value which could be used to pay off the balance due. Regarding annual interest, the average for the 5-year period can be computed as follows:

$$\text{Average interest} = \frac{\$72 + \$24}{2} = \$48 \text{ per year}$$

The $48 per year denotes the average annual interest paid over the 5-year interval of time for the asset. Note that this method of computing charges does not accumulate cash as did the sinking fund method. Rather, it aids the determination of the total cost of the asset. For example, using straight-line depreciation as shown in the previous table, the depreciation charges were computed to be $200 per year. But with an average interest of $48 per year, the total cost of the asset is $200 + $48 or $248 per year, on the basis of 6 percent interest charge.

Formulas can be derived for computing average annual interest. Equation (8.156), for example, is applicable when the concept of average interest is coupled with straight-line depreciation.

$$I_a = (P - L)\left(\frac{i}{2}\right)\left(\frac{n + 1}{n}\right) + Li \qquad (8.156)$$

Where

I_a = Average annual interest in dollars, during service life (n) in years

To illustrate the operation of equation (8.156), one can substitute the values given above in Illustration 5. Thus,

$$I_a = (P - L)\left(\frac{i}{2}\right)\left(\frac{n + 1}{n}\right) + Li$$

$$= (1200 - 200)\left(\frac{.06}{2}\right)\left(\frac{6}{5}\right) + (\$200 \times .06) = \$48$$

QUESTIONS FOR STUDY

1. Why do market prices fluctuate?
2. As a measure of corporate profitability, would you recommend use of (a) profit margin, (b) rate of return on assets, or (c) rate of return on equity? Explain the advantages of the method you recommend and the disadvantages of the two methods you would not recommend.
3. If each of two stocks is paying $1 per share dividends (currently), but the price of stock B is expected to grow at twice the 4 percent rate anticipated for stock A, then, if investors require a return of 10 percent, stock B would currently sell for three times the price of stock A. True or false? Explain.
4. If accounting depreciation exceeds economic depreciation, then it is likely that current market prices exceeds the present worth of the shares because the earnings per share indicated in the annual reports will be overstated. True or false? Explain.
5. Corporate growth can be financed from one of four components:
    (a) Retained earnings
    (b) New equity issues
    (c) New debt issues
    (d) Excess of accounting depreciation over economic depreciation.
   Which method would you recommend to a client who comes to you for advice?
6. Share prices can change because there is a change in either
    (a) Expected future income
    (b) The rate at which the future is discounted
    (c) The ownership represented by a share (i.e., change in the quality and variety of output-producing physical assets).
   True or false? Explain.
7. Explain how you would expect corporate profitability to change if the firm diversified in a way so that the long-run average cost curve shifted in rightward direction and the demand curve simultaneously became more elastic.
8. Beta Manufacturing Company has earnings of $20 million after taxes and interest. The chief executive officer is considering retaining $10-million for expansion of plant and equipment and paying a cash dividend of $10 million. The chief financial officer disagrees. He recommends that instead of paying a cash dividend of $10 million, the company should purchase shares of its own stock on the open market. There are currently 1 million shares outstanding selling for $100 per share. *Question.* As an expert investment counselor, would you recommend (a) firing or (b) promoting the financial officer. Support your recommendation.
9. If the demand schedule for the company's output shifts in a rightward direction and simultaneously the cost curve does not shift but becomes more inelastic, the optimal rate of corporate growth will rise, causing maximum obtainable share prices to reach new higher levels. True or false? Explain.

10. Explain the following event in analytical terms. A company in a declining industry has consistently paid a high percentage of its earnings in dividends. It decides to buy a firm operating in a different but growing market area. To accumulate the funds for the purchase of this firm, the firm cuts its dividends. The price of the stock promptly fell and, before the acquisition could be consummated, an outside firm bought control over the company.

11. Fixed-percentage depreciation is similar to economic depreciation in that both concepts recognize that assets can decline in value at a nonlinear rate. True or false? Explain.

12. Accounting depreciation and economic depreciation generally tend to equal each other in the short run but not in the long run. True or false? Explain.

13. It has been said that prolific technology causes income to rise, which causes a rightward shift in the demand schedule and a decrease in the elasticity of demand for electric power. Would you expect an increase, a decrease, or no change in the rate of return that electric power companies earn on their assets as they expand output to meet the rising demand? Why? *Note.* For simplicity, you may assume that the supply schedule and ratio of capital-to-output both will remain constant.

14. In establishing the capital budget for the forthcoming period, Corporation Alpha discounts the anticipated cash flow from each proposed investment project and ranks the projects by their respective internal rate of return. Corporation Beta apparently ignores depreciation because they rank each proposed investment project by a simple ratio of a single year's profits to assets. What modifications would you make in order to compare the budget of Corporation Beta with the budget of Corporation Alpha? What are your underlying assumptions?

15. Using as a guide the analyses outlined above in situation 1 (financing with additional debt) and situation 2 (financing with additional equity), show how financing with preferred shares will (or will not) affect the risks and profitability of owning common shares.

16. Using the data in Table 8.5, outline some reasons why the price of Avon Products ranged from $3 to $76 while the price of Crown Zellerbach ranged from $39 to $60.

17. *Exercises in Computing Depreciation on Fixed Assets and the Return on Investment.*

   (a) Calculate the appraisal value at the end of 6 years of a $20,000 asset that has a useful life of 10 years and a salvage value of 10 percent of its first cost at that time. Assume straight-line depreciation.

   (b) A $60,000 building has a life of 80 years and no salvage value at the end of that time. Using the sinking-fund method of depreciation and 8 percent interest, compute the value of the building at the end of 20 years.

   (c) Using the sum-of-the-years-digit method, compute the book value at the end of 4 years of an asset that costs $40,000 new and

Table 8.5 SOME STATISTICS FOR TWO FIRMS*

Crown Zellerbach Corporation

	Gross revenues ($ million)	Profit margin (%)	Earnings per share ($)	Dividends per share ($)	Price range high	low
1958	475.5	13.3	2.11	1.64	53	39
1959	528.6	14.2	2.51	1.64	54	45
1960	554.5	13.3	2.55	1.64	49	36
1961	563.9	12.7	2.33	1.64	60	46
1962	570.4	13.0	2.47	1.80	59	37
1963	616.6	12.5	2.50	1.80	60	45
1964	663.8	12.7	2.98	1.85	66	51
1965	700.4	11.2	3.03	2.00	60	47

Avon Products, Inc.

	Gross revenues ($ million)	Profit margin (%)	Earnings per share ($)	Dividends per share ($)	Price range high	low
1958	120.1	18.4	0.37	0.16	10	3
1959	141.9	21.6	0.50	0.22	19	9
1960	168.2	22.5	0.61	0.30	27	16
1961	185.1	24.3	0.72	0.38	37	26
1962	210.8	25.3	0.88	0.47	36	19
1963	248.6	24.7	1.03	0.63	47	29
1964	299.4	26.9	1.38	0.73	56	43
1965	352.0	25.5	1.66	0.90	76	52

* Source: Moody's *Quarterly Manual of Industrials*.

261

      has a serviceable life of 8 years and a salvage value of $5000 at the end of that time.

(d) Calculate the depreciation charge for each year, using the fixed-percentage method, of an asset that costs $100,000, has a life expectancy of 6 years, and an estimated salvage value of $900.

(e) Given equipment that has a first cost of $150,000, an estimated life of 9 years, and a salvage value of $2500.

    (1) What uniform annual payment must be made into a fund at the end of the year in order to replace the equipment (assuming replacement cost equals initial cost), if the fund earns 12 percent?

    (2) What is the appraisal value of the equipment at the end of the fifth year, based on straight-line depreciation?

(f) An office building which cost, exclusive of its elevators, and mechanical equipment, $5 million has an estimated useful life of 40 years and no salvage value. Its elevators and mechanical equipment, which cost $400,000, have an estimated useful life of 20 years and a salvage value of $10,000.

    (1) Using the straight-line method of depreciation, determine the value of the building and its equipment at the end of 10 years' service.

    (2) What is the annual cost of amortizing the initial purchase of equipment and of providing a sinking fund to replace the equipment at the end of 20 years? Assume interest to be 10 percent.

In the early fall of 1929, shares of U.S. Steel were selling at approximately $216. By June of 1932, those same shares were selling at approximately $22. During the decade following 1958, shares of Avon Products showed a price appreciation of some 20 times their initial value. From early 1962 to mid-1965, the Dow-Jones Industrial Average ranged from a low of approximately 550 to a high of about 995, a rise of some 80 percent of its original value. But 5 years later, by mid-1970, the Dow had dropped some 300 points down to the 700 level.

Some questions that come to mind are, What are the *causes* of these variations in price level? Can all the causes be associated with the economic performance of each firm individually?

In light of the empirical facts, factors associated with the economic performance of the individual firm—and these factors alone—are

Bond and Stock Market Prices vs. Aggregate Economic Conditions 9

relatively unsatisfactory as causal explanations because, intuitively, it seems unlikely that the share price for a major producer of a basic metal (such as U.S. Steel) can fall by a factor of 10 (i.e., 1000 percent) in a time span of three or four years solely because of company economics. Hence, by reason alone, we can infer that other factors—factors in addition to corporate economic and finance factors—can cause fluctuations in price in the securities markets.

These other factors are broad in overall scope. Industry events and the state of the overall economy both tend to influence prices in bond and stock markets. Bond and stock market prices do fluctuate with activity in the overall economy.

Bond market prices almost always move inversely with interest rates. That is, when interest rates rise, prices for bonds generally fall. Conversely, when interest rates fall, then prices for bonds generally rise. The longer the time to maturity of the bond, the larger the percentage change in bond price, for a given change in the rate of interest. An illustration of these facts was presented in Chapter 4. (Refer to Table 4.8.)

Stock market prices, on the other hand, tend to signal forthcoming changes in business expansions and contractions. The observed relationship between changes in stock market prices and forthcoming changes in GNP is sufficiently stable that the National Bureau of Economic Research, the authority on cycles in economic activity in the United States, uses changes in Standard and Poor's index of price of 500 common stocks as one of the most important of 36 indicators that tend to lead movements in Gross National Product.[1] To illustrate the power of this relationship, the 1966 List of Indicators (shown in Moore and Shiskin's Table 6) includes a total of 88 series which are correlated in some manner with GNP for the United States. Of these 88 series, 36 series lead GNP, 25 are roughly coincident, 11 series tend to lag GNP, and 16 are unclassified by timing. Each of the 88 series is scored according to six separate criteria: (1) economic significance, (2) statistical adequacy, (3) historical conformity to business cycles, (4) cyclical timing record, (5) smoothness, and (6) promptness of publication. The scoring was designed to reflect a desire not only to make as explicit as possible the criteria for selection of indicators but also to increase the amount of the information available to the user to aid in evaluating the current behavior of the indicators. According to each of these six criteria, Standard and Poor's index of prices of 500 common stocks scores very high within the group of 36 leading series.

Benjamin King found that a "market factor" accounts for (i.e. explains) approximately 50 percent of the variability in stock market prices. King noted that "The very fact that we have averages of industrials, rails, and utilities, not to mention indexes founded on narrower classifications of securities, implies that many investors think of stocks as falling into groups based on similarity of performance."[2] Indeed, the Department of Commerce tabulates National Income by industry groups. See Table 9.1.

One possible observation from and comment on King's study is that if approximately 50 percent of the variability in share prices can be explained by an aggregate market factor, then approximately 50 percent of the study of security analysis ought to be allocated to studying the market. Such an allocation of attention is opposite from conventional security analysis. Traditionally, security analysts have allocated the greater part of their attention to forecasting earnings of the firm over the next few years. If King's study is correct, then the time and attention

---

[1] See Geoffrey H. Moore and Julius Shiskin, *Indicators of Business Expansions and Contractions*, Occasional Paper 103, National Bureau of Economic Research, New York, 1967.

[2] Benjamin F. King, "Market and Industry Factors in Stock Price Behavior," *The Journal of Business*, vol. XXXIX, no. 1, Part II, January 1966.

Table 9.1 NATIONAL INCOME BY INDUSTRY (BILLIONS OF DOLLARS)*

	1963	1964	1965	1966	1967†
Agriculture, forestry, and fisheries	18.6	18.0	21.0	22.5	21.4
Mining	6.0	5.9	6.1	6.5	6.4
Contract construction	24.2	26.5	29.1	32.0	33.2
Manufacturing	143.8	155.6	172.6	191.8	196.6
Nondurable goods	57.5	61.9	66.5	73.2	75.8
Durable goods	86.3	93.6	106.1	118.6	120.8
Transportation	20.0	21.2	23.2	25.0	26.1
Communication	9.8	10.5	11.2	12.5	13.1
Electric, gas, and sanitary services	10.3	11.0	11.4	12.2	12.9
Wholesale and retail trade	73.4	79.3	84.3	91.5	96.8
Finance, insurance, and real estate	53.6	57.1	61.9	67.1	70.9
Services	54.1	59.1	64.1	71.0	77.0
Government and government enterprises	64.7	70.0	75.2	85.0	93.6
Federal	25.3	31.9	28.5	32.6	35.8
State and local	32.9	38.1	39.3	43.9	49.0
Rest of the world	3.4	4.0	4.2	4.2	4.6
All industries, total	481.9	518.1	564.3	620.8	652.9

* Source: *Survey of Current Business*, Department of Commerce, Office of Business Economics.
† NOTE: This table is for illustration purposes only. The precise years and data have no special meaning here.

ordinarily spent projecting corporate earnings can possibly be spent more profitably by examining the broad aggregate economic and financial factors, over which individual firms may have little or no control.

We can conclude, therefore, that there is some relationship between the empirical behavior of bond and stock market prices and aggregate employment. As an expert security analyst, it is necessary to understand the mechanisms underlying this observed relationship. Toward this end we shall study some relationships between aggregate economic conditions and prices in bond and stock markets.

THE TASK AT HAND.   Suppose you have $100,000 available for investment in negotiable securities and are properly concerned regarding opportunities for profit over the long-term in the securities markets. Most people know that prices in bond and stock markets respond to economic conditions in the nation generally. Government spending, corporate and personal income tax rates, interest rates, unemployment, inflation, war, peace, consumer spending, availability of money and credit, business spending, and corporate profits all influence prices in bond and stock markets. Therefore, the behavior of these factors over the long term will affect long-term opportunities for profit in the markets for securities.

Being a hard-nosed investor, knowledge that prices in the securities markets respond to everything in the aggregate economy is hardly satisfying. What you would like to know is not only what factors influence opportunities for profit on your $100,000, but also in what way is this influence exhibited and by how much will price be affected? Chapter 9 is addressed to these questions.

The job confronting us now is to study the factors in the overall economy that determine bond yields and rates of return on equity investment. For example, between the years 1860 and 1965, yields on long-term bonds issued by the U.S. Federal Government ranged from a low of 1.95 percent (1941) to a high of 5.32 percent (1920).[3] In early 1970, the yield on Treasury Bonds reached 7.00 percent. For purposes of investment analysis, the question is, Why? What keeps yields within this range? Why don't bond yields go higher (or lower)? Under what condition could bond yields go higher (or lower)? Also, given the variability in bond yields, in what way is profitability in equity investment (common stocks) influenced? In other words, if you have a lump sum of money, possibly $100,000, available for investment in the money,

---

[3] Source: U.S. Department of Commerce, Bureau of the Census, *Long-Term Economic Growth*, 1860–1965, series B73, U.S. Government Printing Office, Washington, D.C., pp. 202–203.

capital, or equities markets, then how will changes in the overall economic environment influence the risks and returns you can expect on the investment?

Since bond prices are simpler than prices of equity shares to analyze, let us start with bonds and then discuss stocks in relation to bonds.

9.1 Analysis of Bond Market Yields

Factors Influencing Bond Yields. Starting with the fundamental precepts of risk-adjusted present value, we can write the determinants of bond market prices.

$$P = Y_1/(1 + k_1) + Y_2/(1 + k_2)^2 + \cdots + Y_n/(1 + k_n)^n \quad \textbf{(9.1)}$$

where

P = present market worth of any income-producing asset
Y_i = periodic income to be received from the asset
k_i = market rate of discount, including a premium for risk
n = number of time periods included in the useful life of the asset
Y_n = the sale price of the asset, plus the final periodic payment of income

In the case of bonds, periodic income equals coupon income received from the bonds

$$Y_1 = Y_2 = \cdots = Y_{(n-1)} = (c/m)F \quad \textbf{(9.2)}$$

$$Y_n = [(c/m)F] + S \quad \textbf{(9.3)}$$

where

c = coupon or nominal annual rate of interest paid on the bond (usually specified as a percent of the face value)
m = number of times per year for payment of interest (e.g., $m = 2$)
F = face value or principal to be paid upon maturity
S = sale price or sum to be realized upon maturity

Statement (9.1) is a general formulation which can be applied to specific assets. In the case under consideration now, the aggregate market price of bonds, the periodic income can be considered as the aggregate coupon payments on all bonds outstanding in the marketplace, and P can be considered as an index of price levels in bond markets.

In the special case when n equals infinity, then (9.1) simplifies to

$$P = [(c/m)F][m/k] = (cF)/k \quad \textbf{(9.4)}$$

where all terms are the same as defined above.

In either case, (9.1) or (9.4), all factors in the function must be known and stated as of any particular time, *except one*. That is, F, S, c, m, and n can all be known and stated so that any stated price (P) implicitly states *yield* (k).[4] Alternatively, any stated yield (k) implicitly states price (P). Hence, the study and analysis can proceed in terms of either prices or yields. Knowledge of yields is equivalent to knowing prices, and vice versa.

The study of factors influencing bond market prices, therefore, reduces to a study of the factors influencing bond yields. This is stated precisely in (9.4). More generally, as stated in (9.1), the relevant factor is "yield to maturity" because n can, and frequently does, take on finite values instead of being infinite. We shall start with the notion yield and end with the extension, yield to maturity.

At first glance, the relationship between bond price (P) and yield (k) might appear to be similar to the chicken and the egg; which one comes first? Which one causes the other? Do bond prices determine yields or do yields determine bond prices? Our argument shall be that yields are formulated first, according to supply and demand in economic and financial marketplaces. Supply and demand in both the real and money sectors of the economy interact with investor expectations, regarding the future course of the overall economy, and, also, with consumer preferences, regarding the division of income between saving and spending. (Refer to Chapter 1 for review.) These interactions together determine bond market yields.

From (9.1), bond market yields for a given maturity (n) are influenced by:

1. Level and change in level of periodic interest payments, Y_i
2. Term structure of interest rates, k_i
3. Risk premiums, included in k_i

Yield as the Price of Credit.   Since bonds are securities which represent debt, bond yields represent (at a minimum) an opportunity cost for making credit available to the issuer of the bonds. Stated simply, a bond is a security which represents a loan. The yield is the income received by the lender. Applying the criterion of time value of money, this income must be at least as large as the alternative income that can be received from a savings account (assuming equal risks); otherwise the

---

[4] This statement assumes that the bonds are already issued and are available for trading in the markets. Before the bonds are issued, F, S, c, m, and n are all unknown and have to be determined. For some insights into the issues involved in calculating these values from the viewpoint of the issuer, see Kalman J. Cohen and Frederick S. Hammer, "Optimal Coupon Schedules for Municipal Bonds," *Management Science*, vol. 12, no. 1, September 1965, pp. 68–82.

savings account is more profitable, thereby causing the demand for the bond to decline. Hence, with a decline in demand, bond prices will tend to fall, implying that yields will tend to rise to levels that are competitive with returns on savings accounts. Bond yields are, therefore, at least equal to alternative (equivalent risk) rates of interest on credit in the overall economy.

Observe there is no such thing as *the* interest rate. The phrase "interest rate" is applied (and misapplied) in many contexts. Some alternative meanings of the interest rate are:

1. The borrowing rate (price of credit)
2. The lending rate (profit on loans)
3. Price of liquidity (income foregone by holding cash, i.e., the rate paid on a savings account)
4. The Prime Rate (the rate the Federal Reserve Bank charges member banks for loans)
5. The mortgage rate (e.g., the rate charged on a 30-year F.H.A. mortgage)
6. The rate levied by a department store on delinquent charge accounts
7. The nominal rate (i.e., the profit on an investment in government bonds)
8. The real rate (i.e., the profit on an equity investment in physical plant and equipment)

These represent a few alternative notions of what the phrase "interest rate" can mean.[5] For some purposes, no distinction is necessary between the alternative meanings. For other purposes, distinctions are crucial. In the analysis to follow, the relevant distinction will be made in the context of the analysis.

Note also that interest rates (i.e., bond yields) generally stay within a relatively narrow range. That is, from statement (9.4), a doubling of the interest rate, from 6 percent to 12 percent, will cause prices of consols to drop by 50 percent.[6] A decline of 50 percent in price, in any market for securities, is of catastrophic proportions and arouses much consternation in political as well as economic circles. Hence, if current rates are in the neighborhood of 6 percent, it is unlikely that rates will soon rise to 30 percent or 40 percent.

---

[5] Note that we did not say that interest is the price of money. The price of money is the reciprocal of the price level. See, for example, Milton Friedman, "Factors Affecting the Level of Interest Rates," *Savings and Residential Financing*, 1968 Conference Proceedings sponsored by the U.S. Savings and Loan League, 221 North LaSalle Street, Chicago, Illinois, 60601.

[6] If $P_0 = (CF/i_0)$ and $P_1 = CF/(2i_0)$, then
$P_1/P_2 = 1/2$,   so that $P_1 = .5 P_0$.

At the other extreme, considering the lower limits, it is unlikely that yields will approach zero or lower. A yield of zero means that credit is available for free. So long as demand (for any good) exceeds supply, the price mechanism comes into action; hence, free credit is unlikely. Negative yields imply that borrowers (instead of lenders) will be paid for accepting credit. This also is unlikely because few lenders would be willing to pay someone to take a loan from them.[7] Therefore, when considering bond yields, the probabilities are that future yields will be in the neighborhood of current yields.

9.2 Equilibrium Levels of Interest Rates

What causes yields to be at current levels? Why do yields fluctuate around 6 percent instead of around 36 percent or 136 percent? What causes yields to rise and fall? Answers to these questions imply answers to the questions, "What makes bond prices and why do these prices vary?"

Loanable Funds Analysis. One can argue that the price of credit, like the price of any economic good, is determined by demand and supply of that good—demand and supply of loanable funds. To study interest rates and bond price behavior, therefore, we can consider the factors that determine the demand and supply of credit and of financial instruments created for making loanable funds. Consider equations (9.5) and (9.6).

$$\dot{L}_S = a_0 + a_1 i \qquad\qquad (9.5)$$

$$\dot{L}_D = b_0 - b_1 i \qquad\qquad (9.6)$$

where

$\dot{L}_S$ = the supply or quantity of loanable funds forthcoming (for a given risk class) per unit time

i = the interest rate (i.e., price of credit)

$\dot{L}_D$ = the quantity of loanable funds demanded per unit time at interest rate (i)

a_1, b_1 = positive constants

$a_0, b_0 \geq 0$

The constants (a_0, b_0) and (a_1, b_1) are the parameters of the system, and their values determine the position and slope, respectively, of the supply and demand schedules. The two schedules are depicted in Figure 9.1.

---

[7] Stated differently, negative interest implies a negative price. In this case, the government will pay for the removal of the bonds from the marketplace. Price will be negative. The price of garbage is negative. People are willing to pay for removal of garbage.

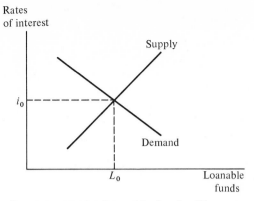

Figure 9.1. Interest rates vs. loanable funds. (For convenience, the schedules are pictured as straight lines.)

In the real world, the schedules can be non-linear; but (9.5) and (9.6) will suffice as a framework for analysis.

The components of demand and supply for loanable funds can be stated as follows:[8]

$$\dot{L}_S = S + M \tag{9.7}$$

$$\dot{L}_D = H + I \tag{9.8}$$

where

$S =$ supply of loanable funds forthcoming from planned private and business savings, per unit time

$M =$ supply of loanable funds forthcoming from net credit creation through the banking system

$H =$ hoarding demand for loanable funds

$I =$ investment demand for loanable funds

$\dot{L}_S$ and $\dot{L}_D =$ defined above

Then in equilibrium, demand equals supply and the interest rate is determined by the parameters of the system, a_0, a_1, b_0, and b_1.

$$\dot{L}_S = \dot{L}_D \tag{9.9}$$

$$S + M = I + H \tag{9.10}$$

$$a_0 + a_1 i = b_0 - b_1 i \tag{9.11}$$

---

[8] For discussion and listing of some factors contributing to the demand for and supply of both short-term and long-term credit, see J. M. Culbertson, "The Interest Rate Structure: Towards Completion of the Classical System," in F. H. Hahn and F. P. R. Brechling (eds.), *The Theory of Interest Rates*, St. Martin's Press, Inc., New York, 1965, pp. 173–205.

Solving equation (9.11) for i, we get the equilibrium rate of interest stated in terms of the system constants.

$$i = (b_0 - a_0)/(a_1 + b_1) \qquad (9.12)$$

Also, since interest can be expressed in terms of S, M, I, and H, we can write

$$\dot{L}_S = a_0 + a_1 i = S + M; \qquad i = (S + M - a_0)/a_1 \qquad (9.13)$$

$$\dot{L}_D = b_0 - b_1 i = H + I; \qquad i = (b_0 - H - I)/b_1 \qquad (9.14)$$

We can write the three equations, all of which must be satisfied under conditions of equilibrium.

$$\begin{aligned} i &= (b_0 - a_0)/(a_1 + b_1) \\ &= (S + M - a_0)/a_1 \\ &= (b_0 - H - I)/b_1 \end{aligned} \qquad (9.15)$$

or

$$\frac{(b_0 - a_0)}{(a_1 + b_1)} = \frac{(S + M - a_0)}{a_1} = \frac{(b_0 - H - I)}{b_1} \qquad (9.16)$$

We can conclude that the interest rate depends upon and varies with the relative height and slope of the schedules for demand and supply of loanable funds.

Income-Expenditures Analysis.   According to Hicks' interpretation of Keynes, the overall phenomena contributing to the formation and formulation of interest rates can be described and explained in terms of economic activity in the product and factor markets (i.e., the "real" sector of the economy) interacting with financial activity in the financial sector of the economy.[9]

The equilibrium level of interest rates in the overall economy is determined by the intersection of a schedule representing equilibrium conditions in the "real" sector of the economy—the investment-saving (I-S) schedule—with a schedule representing equilibrium conditions in the monetary sector of the economy—the liquidity preference for money (L-M) schedule.

The overall mechanism starts with the fundamental notion that aggregate spending equals aggregate income and is determined by four

---

[9] See (1) J. R. Hicks, "Mr. Keynes and the 'Classics': A Suggested Interpretation," *Econometrica*, vol. 5, no. 2, April 1937, pp. 147–159; (2) Joseph P. McKenna, *Aggregate Economic Analysis*, 3rd ed., Holt Rinehart and Winston, Inc., New York, 1969; and (3) Gardner Ackley, *Macroeconomic Theory*, The Macmillan Company, New York, 1963.

component parts: (1) personal consumption, (2) business spending, (3) government purchases, and (4) net foreign spending.

$$Y = C + I + G + F \tag{9.17}$$

where

$Y =$ money value of all legal goods and services purchased as of any particular time in the nation

$C =$ aggregate expenditures made by private individuals

$I =$ aggregate business investment (including purchases of houses by private individuals)

$G =$ total purchases made by federal, state, and local governments

$F =$ net foreign spending

Then the *I-S* and *L-M* schedules and the corresponding determination of interest rates are explained as follows.

THE *I-S* SCHEDULE. The *I-S* schedule describes equilibrium conditions in the overall economy when planned investment equals planned savings. Equilibrium occurs in the real sector of the economy, i.e., in product and factor markets, when planned savings equals planned investment.

Planned savings equals expected income, not spent. Therefore, if plans for consumer spending are related to after-tax expected income, then we can write[10]

$$C = a_0 + a_1(1 - T)Y \tag{9.18}$$

where a_0, a_1 both are positive constants, $T =$ personal tax rate, and C and Y are defined above. Then, using the definition that planned savings equal unspent, after-tax income, we can write

$$S = (1 - T)Y - C \tag{9.19}$$

where all terms are the same as defined above. Substituting equation (9.18) into (9.19), we get the following equation, which indicates that, as of any particular time, planned saving is determined by after-tax expected income:

$$\begin{aligned} S &= (1 - T)Y - [a_0 + a_1(1 - T)Y] \\ &= -a_0 + [(1 - a_1)(1 - T)]Y \end{aligned} \tag{9.20}$$

If taxes (T) equal zero, then the savings function simplifies to

$$S = -a_0 + (1 - a_1)Y \tag{9.21}$$

---

[10] See Milton Friedman, *A Theory of the Consumption Function*, Princeton University Press, Princeton, N.J., 1957.

Note that neither taxes nor income affect a_0, the minimum consumption necessary to sustain life. Statement (9.21) is the savings function.

Turning to planned investment, this model hypothesizes interest rates as the primary determinant of business investment. If interest rates are expected to be high, then plans for aggregate investment will show relatively small investment. Under conditions of high interest rates, new investment will be postponed until a later time when new financing can be obtained on more favorable terms. Alternatively, if interest rates are expected to be low, then plans will be made for relatively large business investment because money for financing can be obtained at relatively low rates. Hence, the theory tells us that planned investment and expected rates of interest tend to vary inversely together.

$$I = b_0 - b_1 i \tag{9.22}$$

where

$$I = \text{level of total business investment}$$
$$b_0, b_1 = \text{positive constants}$$
$$i = \text{the rate of interest}$$

Alternatively, because interest rates and aggregate investment are hypothesized to vary inversely with each other, we can write, instead of of (9.22),

$$I = \beta_0 + \beta_1/i \tag{9.23}$$

Both (9.22) and (9.23) let aggregate investment and interest rates vary inversely with each other.

However, we should note that equations (9.22) and (9.23) both appear to be an oversimplification of the real-world determinants of business investment. It is true that business investment depends to some extent on interest rates, but many other factors are also important. Hammer, for example, proposes the following model[11]:

$$I_t = \alpha_0 + \alpha_1 W_t + \alpha_2 (\rho_k - r)_t + \alpha_3 K_t + u_t \tag{9.24}$$

where

$$I_t = \text{aggregate gross investment expenditures by business firms}$$
$$\text{on new plant and equipment during year } t$$

---

[11] Frederick S. Hammer, *The Demand for Physical Capital: Application of a Wealth Model*, Prentice-Hall, Inc., Englewood Cliffs, N.J., 1964. Also see J. L. Hexter, "A Test of Hammer's Demand for Physical Capital Model Using Firm Data," *The Journal of Finance*, vol. XXIII, no. 1, March 1968, pp. 105–112.

W_t = wealth (net worth) of firms at the beginning of year t

ρ_{k_t} = the expected return on real capital investment during year t

r_t = the rate of interest during year t

K_t = the aggregate capital stock of business firms at the beginning of year t

α_i = regression coefficients

u_t = a stochastic error term

Equation (9.24) states that aggregate business investment is determined primarily by a linear combination: (1) initial wealth of the firm, (2) the difference between the expected rate of profit on corporate investment and the interest rate, and (3) the initial stock of capital on hand. For purposes of analysis here, we shall continue the analysis with the simpler Keynesian formulation (9.22).

At equilibrium, planned savings equals planned investment, so we can set planned investment, from equation (9.22), equal to planned saving, from equation (9.20), to give

$$-a_0 + [(1 - a_1)(1 - T)] Y = b_0 - b_1 i \qquad \textbf{(9.25)}$$

Statement (9.25) shows the relationship which must exist between expected interest rates (i) and expected income (Y) if planned savings are to equal planned investment. Equation (9.25) is the *I-S* schedule.

If the equality of statement (9.25) fails to hold, then planned savings will exceed (or fall short of) planned investment, thereby causing an excess (or deficiency) in the supply of funds available to finance new assets. This excess (or deficiency) in supply, in turn, causes interest rates to fall (or rise) back to equilibrium levels. At equilibrium, there is no cause for change.

The *I-S* schedule can be expressed analytically as the relationship between levels of aggregate income (Y) and corresponding equilibrium rates of interest.

$$\begin{aligned} i &= [(a_0 + b_0)/b_1] - \{[(1 - a_1)(1 - T)]/b_1\} Y \\ &= \beta_0 - \beta_1 Y \end{aligned} \qquad \textbf{(9.26)}$$

where β_0 is a positive constant = $(a_0 + b_0)/b_1$ and β_1 is a positive constant = coefficient of Y in (9.26). Statement (9.26) says that aggregate income and equilibrium interest rates move inversely with one another. This is the *I-S* schedule, a restatement of (9.25).

THE *L-M* SCHEDULE.   The liquidity preference for money (*L-M* schedule) describes a set of equilibrium conditions in the overall economy which occurs when the total demand for money equals the total supply of money.

As of any particular point in time, the supply of money is exogenous and constant.[12]

$$M_{\text{supply}} = M_0 = \text{Constant} \tag{9.27}$$

The demand for money (cash balances) consists of (1) transactions demand and (2) liquidity-preference demand (including demand for precautionary and speculative reasons). The transactions demand is hypothesized as depending upon expected income as stated in (9.28). Liquidity-preference demand is hypothesized as depending upon expected interest rates as stated in (9.29).

$$M_{\text{trans}} = f(Y) = p_0 + p_1 Y \tag{9.28}$$

$$M_{\text{liq.pref}} = f(i); \qquad i = q_0 - q_1 M_{\text{liq.pref}} \tag{9.29}$$

where p_0, p_1, q_0, and q_1 all are positive constants and are parameters of the financial system. In financial equilibrium, the supply of money equals the demand for money

$$M_{\text{supply}} = M_{\text{trans}} + M_{\text{liq.pref}} \tag{9.30}$$

Therefore, substituting (9.28) and (9.29) into (9.30), we derive conditions which state the relationship between aggregate income (Y) and corresponding equilibrium rates of interest (i).

$$M_0 = (p_0 + p_1 Y) + \left(\frac{q_0 - i}{q_1}\right) \tag{9.31}$$

Solving (9.31) for i, we get

$$i = [q_0 + q_1(p_0 - M_0)] + p_1 q_1 Y \tag{9.32}$$

Equation (9.32) shows a relationship between aggregate income (Y) and interest rates (i). Equation (9.32) is the L-M schedule. The I-S and L-M schedules are depicted together in Figure (9.2).

OVERALL EQUILIBRIUM.   At overall equilibrium, the I-S schedule intersects the L-M schedule to determine a unique equilibrium aggregate income (Y_0) and corresponding interest rate (i_0). One can solve the two equations, (9.26) and (9.32), simultaneously in terms of Y,

$$\begin{aligned} i &= [(a_0 + b_0)/b_1] - \{[(1 - a_1)(1 - T)]/b_1\} Y \\ i &= [q_0 + q_1(p_0 - M_0)] + (p_1 q_1) Y \end{aligned} \tag{9.33}$$

---

[12] Refer to Chapter 1 for a summary discussion of the money supply. For general reading on the subject of aggregate income, money, and interest, see M. G. Mueller (ed.), *Readings in Macroeconomics*, Holt, Rinehart and Winston, Inc., New York, 1966. In particular see reading number 12 therein: Lawrence S. Ritter, "The Role of Money in Keynesian Theory."

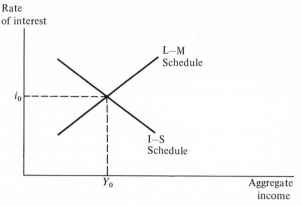

Rate
of interest

i_0

L–M
Schedule

I–S
Schedule

Y_0

Aggregate
income

Figure 9.2.   I-S and L-M schedules. (For convenience, the schedules are pictured as straight lines.)

or else in terms of i

$$Y = \left[\frac{(a_0 + b_0)}{(1 - a_1)(1 - T)}\right] - \left[\frac{b_1}{(1 - a_1)(1 - T)}\right]i$$

$$Y = -\left[\frac{q_0}{p_1 q_1} + \frac{(p_0 - M_0)}{p_1}\right] + \left(\frac{1}{q_1 p_1}\right)i \qquad (9.34)$$

Choosing the latter, we can write a relationship between equilibrium rates of interest and the exogenous money supply (M_0). Thus, from (9.34) we get

$$\left[\frac{(a_0 + b_0)}{(1 - a_1)(1 - T)}\right] - \left[\frac{b_1}{(1 - a_1)(1 - T)}\right]i$$

$$= -\left[\frac{q_0}{p_1 q_1} + \frac{(p_0 - M_0)}{p_1}\right] + \left(\frac{1}{p_1 q_1}\right)i \qquad (9.35)$$

Equation (9.35) simplifies to

$$\left\{\left[\frac{b_1}{(1 - a_1)(1 - T)}\right] + \left(\frac{1}{p_1 q_1}\right)\right\}i$$

$$= \left[\frac{q_0}{p_1 q_1} + \frac{(p_0 - M_0)}{p_1}\right] + \left[\frac{a_0 + b_0}{(1 - a_1)(1 - T)}\right] \qquad (9.36)$$

or

$$i = \alpha - \beta M_S \qquad (9.37)$$

where α and β both equal positive constants and other terms are the same as defined previously.

Note that one must take care in the interpretation of (9.37). At first glance, it might appear that since (9.37) shows an inverse relationship between the supply of money and the equilibrium rate of interest, ceteris paribus, an increase in the supply of money will cause a decline in interest rates, thereby causing prices in bond markets to rise. But, as a matter of empirical fact, a rise in the supply of money is not always accompanied by a rise in the price of bonds. The indications are, therefore, that the model (9.37) oversimplifies the relationships between the real-world variables.[13] We shall proceed with additional analysis.

A Monetary Analysis: Interest Rates and the Supply of Money. Professor Milton Friedman has set forth the following analysis of the relationship between changes in the supply of money and corresponding changes in interest rates.

Interest rates are determined by a mixture of interacting (counterbalancing) forces. Some of the forces tend to pull interest rates downward, but other forces tend to push interest rates upward. The final equilibrium level of interest rates depends upon the magnitude of the counterbalancing forces.[14]

Three effects need to be noted:
1. Liquidity effect
2. Income-and-price-level effect
3. Price-anticipations effect

The liquidity effect is straightforward: the larger the quantity of money available, the lower the interest rate will have to be to induce people to hold money. In times of high liquidity (large supply of money), excess cash can be converted into securities, causing increased demand (hence price) for securities, causing interest rates to fall. The liquidity effect indicates that interest rates vary inversely with the real quantity of money via the mechanism of the securities (i.e., bond) markets. Through the liquidity effect, a rise in the quantity of money causes a decline in interest rates. This effect increases not only the supply of loanable funds but also increases the rate of purchase of securities.

The income-and-price-level effect can be summarized as follows.

---

[13] Ever since Keynes put forth his brilliant treatise on aggregate employment, economists have debated its usefulness. Some monetary economists believe that the entire Keynesian framework is not necessary. Other economists argue equally vigorously that the Keynesian framework is not only necessary but provides useful insights that probably never would be discovered otherwise.

[14] This view and analysis of interest is consistent with notions developed and used by many economists. See Milton Friedman, "Factors Affecting the Level Rates," *Savings and Residential Financing 1968 Conference Proceedings*, U.S. Savings and Loan League, Chicago, Illinois, 1968. Also see Milton Friedman, "A Theoretical Framework for Monetary Analysis," *Journal of Political Economy*, vol. 78, no. 2, March/April 1970, pp. 193–238.

An increase in the money supply is synonymous with larger cash balances. Larger cash balances motivate people to increase spending, which causes (1) a rise in business investment for increased production to satisfy the new higher consumer demand and (2) a rise in prices. A rise in business investment causes a rise in the demand for loanable funds and, hence, a rise in interest rates. A rise in the general level of prices is synonymous with price inflation. However, given price inflation of 2 percent more than usual, with a slower rate of growth of money supply, the amount of real balances that people want to hold will be smaller with inflation than they would be without inflation. Increased spending in the attempt to acquire other assets raises the price of those assets and tends to drive interest rates down, thereby tending to offset the rise caused by an increase in the demand for loanable funds. The net result of the income-and-price-level effect is that as the supply of money increases, spending increases, thus causing a rise in the demand for investment funds (which tends to raise the rate of interest and increase total employment and aggregate income). But this rise is more than offset by an increase in the overall propensity to spend (caused by a rising rate of inflation which was due to the hypothesized increase in the supply of money). The rise in the propensity to spend tends to increase prices for real goods and services generally (because of increased demand). This spending, assuming that increased revenues exceed increased costs, causes the market value of assets to rise which means that interest rates fall.

The price-anticipations effect can be summarized as follows. When prices are rising at 2 percent per year, and people start anticipating this 2 percent as a normal increase, the cost of holding cash has increased. Consequently, under these conditions, people will want to hold smaller balances relative to income. The higher the rate of change of prices, the higher the velocity of money. What matters most for the bond market is not the ex-post yield but the ex-ante yield. Thus we can write

$$i_B = i_r + \left(\frac{1}{P}\frac{dP}{dt}\right) \tag{9.38}$$

where

i_B = nominal interest rate (on bonds)
i_r = real interest rate (on capital equipment)
$\left(\frac{1}{P}\frac{dP}{dt}\right)$ = anticipated percentage rate at which prices are changing at time t

If the real rate of return stays the same but the anticipated rate of price change goes up, the nominal interest rate will also go up. Equation (9.38) expresses the price-anticipations effect. In economies where the anticipated rate of inflation is very high, interest rates tend to be high and bond prices tend to be low. [For further reading see William E. Gibson, "Interest Rates and Monetary Policy," *Journal of Political Economy*, vol. 78, no. 3, May/June 1970, pp. 431–455.]

In this way, interest rates are determined and bond market prices react accordingly. Overall, an increase in the supply of money and loanable funds will have mixed (counterbalancing) interacting forces exerted on the rates of interest and on bond market prices.

9.3 Bond Yield Curves and Term Structure of Interest Rates

Given the overall level of interest rates, bond yields, and fluctuations of that level, we can expand our horizon by adding the time dimension. That is, we can turn attention next to a study not only of equilibrium yield but of yield to maturity.

Yield curves are graphs of yield to maturity plotted as a function of length of time until maturity. Yield curves can be plotted in two dimensions (yield to maturity vs. length of time until maturity) or in three dimensions (the third dimension is the coupon rate). An example of a yield curve is shown in Figure 9.3.

To illustrate a yield curve, suppose we have three bonds. Suppose the first bond matures 1 year hence, the second bond matures 5 to 10 years hence, and the third bond matures 30 or 40 years hence. Let the bonds be identical in every respect except in time to maturity. Should all three bonds be priced to provide the same yield? As a matter of empirical fact and theory, the answer is Not necessarily. Either of four general situations can occur. During periods in our nation's history, each situation has occurred.

1. Flat yield curves
2. Downward-sloping yield curves

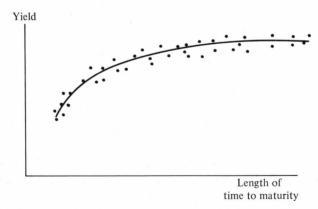

Figure 9.3. Illustrative upward-sloping yield curve.

3. Upward-sloping yield curves
4. Humped yield curves

Flat yield curves occur when short-term, intermediate-term, and long-term interest rates are all equal to each other.

$$i_1 = i_2 = \cdots = i_n \qquad (9.39)$$

A flat yield curve is perfectly horizontal in shape. That is, instead of the upward-sloping shape as illustrated in Figure 9.3, flat yield curves lie perfectly horizontal.

Downward-sloping yield curves occur when short-, intermediate-, and long-term interest rates become successively smaller.

$$i_1 > i_2 > \cdots > i_n \qquad (9.40)$$

For example, reconsider the fundamental equation (4.29) expressing the time value of money.

$$P = Y_1/(1 + i_1) + Y_2/(1 + i_2)^2 + \cdots + Y_n/(1 + i_n)^n \quad (9.41)$$

where

P = present worth of a future stream of income
Y_t = periodic revenue stream; all Y_t may be different
i_t = the interest rate; all i_t may be different

Then a downward-sloping yield curve represents a set of yields to be used in (9.41) which are denoted by (9.40).

Upward-sloping yield curves occur when short-, intermediate-, and long-term rates become successively larger.

$$i_1 < i_2 < \cdots < i_n \qquad (9.42)$$

Humped yield curves occur when intermediate-term yields are larger than either short-term or long-term yields.

The shape of the yield curve is important for asset management because the shape expresses the relative profitability investing in bonds with different dates of maturity.

Why should the yield curve sometimes be upward-sloping, with longer-term rates successively larger than shorter-term rates, and at other times be downward-sloping with shorter-term rates exceeding longer-term rates?

The shape of the yield curve can be explained in terms of the supply and demand for long-term funds as compared with the supply and demand for short-term funds. Relevant also are expectations of borrowers and investors over the long and short terms. Expectations can be very important. If investors think that interest rates generally will rise, then short-term loans will tend to be favored over long-term loans in anticipation of being liquid in the near future to exploit the new higher rates when the rates do in fact rise. Conversely, if investors believe that long-term rates will decline in the near future, then long-term investments will be favored over shorter-term investments to exploit capital gains in bond markets when the rates do in fact decline thereby causing bond prices to rise.

Several theories have been put forth to explain the observed term structure of interest rates. The most important of these theories are[14]

1. Expectations hypothesis
2. Liquidity premium theory
3. Combination of expectations—liquidity premium
4. Segmented markets theory

The Expectations Hypothesis. The expectations hypothesis implies that the term structure of interest rates constitutes at one moment of time a set of predictions of short-term rates at various moments of time in the future. The expectations theory holds that long-term rates are an average of short-term rates. The holder of a long-term security will earn, on average, the same return as the holder of a sequence of short-term securities over any specified time period.

To illustrate, consider three bonds with different maturity dates.

1 year	at 4 percent
2 years	at 5 percent
3 years	at 6 percent

If indeed the long-term interest rate is composed of a series of short-term rates, one can hypothesize what must be the rate today for money delivered one year in the future. That is, the yield curve implicitly states forward rates.[15] If the 2-year rate (today) is 5 percent, and the 1-year rate (today) is 4 percent, then the forward 1-year rate must be approximately 6 percent.

$$(1.05)^2 = (1.04)(1 + i) \qquad\qquad\qquad \textbf{(9.43)}$$

$$(1 + i) = (1.05)^2/(1.04) = 1.06 \qquad\qquad \textbf{(9.44)}$$

If the forward 1-year rate exceeds 6 percent, then investment in two 1-year bonds will be more profitable than investment in one 2-year

---

[14] See Frederick M. Struble "The Current Debate on the Term Structure of Interest Rates," *Monthly Review*, Federal Reserve Bank of Kansas City, January-February 1966. Reprinted in Lawrence S. Ritter (ed.), *Money and Economic Activity*, Houghton Mifflin Company, Boston, 1967, pp. 187–193.

[15] "Spot rate" is a term used to denote today's price for loans to be made today. By way of comparison, "forward rate" is a term used to denote today's price for loans to be made starting at some specified date in the future.

bond. Conversely, if the forward 1-year rate is less than 6 percent, then investment in one 2-year bond will be more profitable than investment in two 1-year bonds.

Similarly, for the 3-year bond at 6 percent, the expectations theory tells us that the forward 1-year rate for money to be delivered two years hence is approximately 8 percent.

$$(1.06)^3 = (1.05)^2(1 + i) \tag{9.45}$$

$$(1 + i) = (1.06)^3/(1.05)^2 = 1.08 \tag{9.46}$$

This is so because if the rate of profit on 1-year money as of two years hence exceeds 8 percent, then one 2-year bond and then a 1-year bond will be more profitable than one 3-year bond. Conversely, if the rate of profit on 1-year money as of 2 years hence is less than 8 percent, then one 3-year bond will be more profitable than a 2-year bond and then a 1-year bond.

The forward 2-year rate is also implied in the data stated above. The 2-year rate is approximately 7 percent.

$$(1.06)^3 = (1.04)(1 + i)^2 \tag{9.47}$$

$$(1 + i) = [(1.06)^3/(1.04)]^{1/2} = 1.07 \tag{9.48}$$

If the 2-year rate as of 1 year hence is some value other than 7 percent, then through the arbitrage mechanism, profits can be taken in the futures markets for interest rates.[16]

The Liquidity Preference Hypothesis. This hypothesis asserts that, since risks and term to maturity are positively related, a long-term bond should return more to its holder than a corresponding sequence of shorter maturities. Put another way, the liquidity preference theory

---

[16] David Meiselman tested the hypothesis:

$$_{(t+m)}E_t - {}_{(t+m)}E_{(t-1)} = b[{}_tR_t - {}_tE_{(t-1)}] \tag{9.49}$$

where

        E = expected rates

        R = spot rates

Presubscripts = a year of calendar time

Postsubscripts = the moment a rate is either inferred from the term structure or observed as an actual spot rate

See David Meiselman, *The Term Structure of Interest Rates*, Prentice-Hall, Inc., Englewood Cliffs, N.J., 1962. Also, see (1) Reuben A. Kessel, *The Cyclical Behavior of the Term Structure of Interest Rates*, Columbia University Press (NBER), New York, 1965; (2) Joseph W. Conard, *The Behavior of Interest Rates—A Progress Report*, NBER, Columbia University Press, New York, 1966; and (3) Burton Malkiel, *The Term Structure of Interest Rates*, Princeton University Press, Princeton, N.J., 1966.

hypothesizes that liquidity premiums exist, and these premiums increase monotonically at a decreasing rate as a function of term to maturity. In other words, using the same data as before, a 2-year rate of 5 percent will exceed two successive 1-year rates because of the additional risks inherent in investing for a 2-year period instead of getting your money back at the end of 1 year and having it available for reinvestment for an additional year.

$$(1.05)^2 > (1.04)(1 + i) \qquad\qquad \textbf{(9.50)}$$

$$(1 + i) < 1.06 \qquad\qquad \textbf{(9.51)}$$

The empirical evidence on the term structure of interest rates appears to support the notion that both theories, the expectations hypothesis and the liquidity preference notion, must be used in combination to adequately explain all the possible shapes of yield curves.[17]

The Segmented Markets Theory. The remaining theory is that the market for default-free securities is segmented because of institutional habits and restrictions. This theory holds that some institutions have constraints (legal or otherwise) which limit their buying and selling to one class of maturities. Hence, this theory instructs that arbitrage is not a workable mechanism, that movements of yields in one maturity range bear little or no relationship to yield movements in other maturity ranges, and that securities of different maturities are poor substitutes for each other. However, there appears to be little empirical evidence to support this view. The primary view among experts at the time of this writing is the combined notions of expectations and liquidity preference.

9.4 Risk Premiums in Bond Yields

Up to now, the analysis has included bonds all of equal risk. Yields were calculated under the assumptions that (1) the bonds are at all times marketable in any quantity at the stated price (i.e., the demand and supply schedules for the bonds are perfectly elastic) and (2) the probability of default is zero (i.e., both coupon income and redemption at face value will occur for sure). If these assumptions are violated, then the bond becomes risky and a risk premium is required to induce investors to purchase the bond.

In other words, the explicit cost of borrowing equals the sum of three items: (1) the pure rate of interest, (2) the risk premium, and (3) the cost of floating the debt issue. The risk premium is defined as the difference between market yield to maturity and the corresponding pure rate of interest. The corresponding pure rate of interest is defined as the

---

[17] See Kessel, *Ibid.*, and Malkiel, *Ibid.*

market yield on a riskless (default-free) bond maturing on the same day as the bond under consideration.

Lawrence Fisher proposed the following model for the determination of risk premiums on corporate bonds.[18]

$$x_0 = a_0 + a_1 x_1 + a_2 x_2 + a_3 x_3 + a_4 x_4 + \varepsilon \qquad (9.52)$$

where

$x_0 =$ average risk premium = difference between the market yield to maturity of the bond and the corresponding pure rate of interest

$x_1 =$ coefficient of variation of the firm's net income over the last 9 years (after all fixed charges and taxes)

$x_2 =$ length of time the firm has been operating without forcing its creditors to take a loss

$x_3 =$ ratio of the market value of the equity in the firm to the par value of the firm's debt

$x_4 =$ market value of all the publicly traded bonds the firm has outstanding

$\varepsilon =$ stochastic error term

The first three variables (x_1, x_2, and x_3) constitute what Fisher calls "the risk of default." The fourth variable, x_4, is intended to measure the marketability of a firm's bonds. If the value of x_4 is relatively large, then the implication is that the bonds are highly marketable. Hence, considering the coefficients in the model, a_2, a_3, and a_4, all should be negative to show that risk premiums decline as these factors rise, and a_1 should be positive to show that risk premium varies directly with the relative variability of corporate net income. Empirical results are consistent with the theory as put forth by Professor Fisher.

9.5 Return on Investment in Common Stocks vs. Aggregate Employment

In this section we shall discuss market value of common stocks vs gross national product (GNP). The analysis is primarily empirical.

In the context of the preceding paragraphs, common stocks are more complex to analyze than are bonds, because risks are different (and more intensive) for stocks than for bonds. There are two reasons for this added complexity:

---

[18] Lawrence Fisher, "Determinants of Risk Premiums on Corporate Bonds," *The Journal of Political Economy*, vol. LXVII, no. 3, June 1959, pp. 217–237.

1. Stocks never mature; hence no "face value" redemption exists.
2. Dividend income is not a contractual obligation; periodic revenues from common stocks are a function of corporate dividend policy.

With no guarantees of either periodic income or capital gains, common stocks can be viewed as risky, relative to bonds. Therefore, the risk premiums generally should be larger for stocks than for bonds. The question is, How much larger?

Several analytical approaches are possible. Since we now know that bond and stock portfolio yields both are correlated with (i.e., determined in part by), GNP, then one can measure the amount and stability of this correlation for various historical periods of time.[19] Several equivalent functional models can be stated.

$$V_t = f(\text{GNP}_{t+\tau}) \tag{9.53}$$

$$\Delta V_t = f(\Delta \text{GNP}_{t+\tau}) \tag{9.54}$$

$$k_t = f(\text{GNP}_{t+\tau}, V_t) \tag{9.55}$$

where

V_t = market value of a portfolio of common stocks as of time t
$\text{GNP}_{t \times \tau}$ = gross national product as of some future time $t + \tau$
k_t = rate of return on a portfolio of common stocks
Δ = "change in"

Estimates can be made of the change in stock market yield for a given change in GNP using either of the three forms stated above. For any stated level of GNP, a probability distribution of possible stock yields can be calculated.[20] The location of this probability distribution can be compared with the level of yield on long-term, default-free bonds. The difference between the expected yield on a portfolio of common stocks and the expected yield on a portfolio of long-term government bonds, therefore, is the risk premium paid on stocks.

---

[19] This basic idea was set forth in 1955 by Solomon and again in 1956 by Weston. (1) Ezra Solomon, "Economic Growth and Common Stock Value," *The Journal of Business*, vol. 28, no. 3, July 1955, pp. 213–221; and (2) J. Fred Weston, "The Stock Market in Perspective," *Harvard Business Review*, vol. 34, no. 2, March-April 1956, pp. 71–80. Both articles are reprinted in H. K. Wu and A. J. Zakon (eds.), *Elements of Investments, Selected Readings*, Holt, Rinehart, and Winston, Inc., New York, 1965.
[20] Note that the time lags (τ) in (9.53), (9.54), and (9.55) need verifying empirically because no one knows the precise time lapse between a rise in aggregate spending and a corresponding rise in aggregate dividends.

Such an experiment was performed with the following results.[21]

Description of the Experiments. A total of 15 portfolios were studied. Of the 15 portfolios, 10 were equity portfolios and 5 were bond portfolios.

Of the 10 equity portfolios, 5 consist of the Dow-Jones Industrial Average. The other 5 consist of the Standard & Poor's 500 Stock Composite Group.

The 5 bond portfolios consist of default-free, long-term government bonds. For simplicity, we assume that long-term institutional investors will be both willing and able to hold the bonds to maturity, so that the realized rate of return on the bond portfolio will, in fact, be the yield to maturity on the bonds.[22] In this way, we avoid several needless complexities that would otherwise be introduced into the analysis. That is, we avoid the need to consider the probability of default, as well as the need to consider capital gains and losses in the bond markets. These considerations are quite relevant for short-term investors.

As a baseline for comparing profitability of investment in common stocks with profitability from investing in bonds, one must use a time interval common to both alternative investments.[23] In the cases studied here, this time interval is determined by the date of purchase and the date of maturity of the bonds.

If we assume that a bond portfolio is purchased in each year, 1950, 1951, 1952, 1953, and 1954, and in each case the date of maturity is 10 years hence (i.e., 1960, 1961, 1962, 1963, and 1964), then the rate of profit on the bond portfolios will be as shown on the first line in Table 9.2. These rates are yields to maturity and are taken directly from published sources as indicated on the table.

For the 10 equity portfolios, the rate of return on investment must be computed. For these cases, the rate of return on investment is taken to be dividend yield plus percentage change in price. The rates of profit

---

[21] The following results are from an unpublished study performed by Fred B. Renwick and presented at the Third Annual Conference for Public Pension Fund Administrators, New York City, May 1, 1968. Comments and discussion of the paper were delivered by Professor Murray E. Polakoff.

[22] This, indeed, is a simplifying assumption. If the portfolio manager, for example, is concerned with minimum levels within the interim time period, then the model would have to be refined to accommodate this additional constraint. Also, recall from Situation 10 in Chapter 5 that the yield to maturity of bonds assumes reinvestment of coupon income at the internal rate of return.

[23] Refer to Chapters 4 and 5 for a review of the fundamental principles underlying this statement.

Table 9.2 DATA FOR STUDY OF YIELDS AND RISKS ON MIXED PORTFOLIOS

Portfolios	Return on investment (in percent)					
	1950–1960	1951–1961	1952–1962	1953–1963	1954–1964
Bonds					
Long-term (10-yr)					
U.S. Govt. Bonds* (yield to maturity)	2.32	2.57	2.68	2.94	2.55
Stocks					
Standard and Poor's 500 Stock Composite† (reinvesting dividends at current prices)	16.81	16.18	14.16	15.07	14.49
Dow-Jones Industrial Average‡ (reinvesting dividends at current prices)	16.07	15.38	13.10	14.59	13.46

* Data obtained from time series, published in *Long-Term Economic Growth : 1860–1965*, U.S. Department of Commerce, Bureau of the Census.
† Data obtained from time series, published in *Long-Term Economic Growth : 1860–1965*, U.S. Department of Commerce, Bureau of the Census; *Standard and Poor's Daily Stock Price Indexes : 1926–1960*, Standard and Poor's Corporation.
‡ *Dow-Jones Investors Handbook*, Dow-Jones and Company.

for the stock portfolios are shown on lines 2 and 3 of Table 9.2. These numbers indicate the average rate of return on investment over the 10-year period, assuming annual compounding, and assuming that dividends are reinvested at current prices during the year in which they were received.[24]

Notice that each of the stock portfolios provides a rate of return of more than ten percentage points higher than the rate of return on the bond portfolios. So, given perfect hindsight (i.e., complete certainty) a rational choice in every case would have been 100 percent investment in common stocks. (Why)?

However, the decision to buy or not to buy must be made before the fact, not after. This condition is examined in the next phase of the study.

Statistical Estimation of Return on Investment in Common Stock.   The ex-ante investment decision requires knowledge of future values of alternative portfolios. This knowledge must be obtained from forecasts of future levels of share prices and of dividend payments. Forecasting stock prices appears to be fair sport for amateurs and professionals alike.

For purposes of this study, the required estimates can be obtained by using the interdependence between levels of stock values and levels of gross national product. In other words, since the stock market is frequently taken to be a good predictor of aggregate economic conditions, we can use the dependence between those two variables to compute a statistical regression. We can regress the current value of the stock portfolio on the actual value of GNP for the coming year. These regression equations are listed in Table 9.3. All the R-squares are quite high, indicating a relatively good fit, for each portfolio.[25]

In Table 9.3, perhaps a statistic more meaningful than the standard error of estimate (as stated in the third column) is the percentage reduction in the standard error of the dependent variable. That is, using future levels of GNP to explain current values of stock portfolios accounts for some of the variability associated with the value of those portfolios and reduces the error associated with the estimates of what those values should be. The standard error of 3.88 shown in the first row in Table 9.3 represents a reduction of 83.5 percent of the error obtained

---

[24] For a derivation of the formulas used to compute the average annual compounded rate of return on investment, see Kalman J. Cohen and Bruce Fitch, "The Average Investment Performance Index," *Management Science*, vol. 12, no. 6, February 1966, pp. B195–B215. The actual computations for the values of the portfolios are shown in Appendix 1 for Chapter 9.

[25] *Note:* The analytic method is of importance here; not numerical results or the fact that data are taken for the years 1950–1964.

without the regression. The second regression equation (standard error of 3.64) reduces standard error of the dependent variable by 85.1 percent of its original value. On average, all the regressions for the Standard & Poor's portfolios reduce the standard errors by 82.5 percent.

$$.835281, .851754, .805591, .807719, .824442$$
$$\text{Average} = .824957$$

Use of the regression equations for the Dow-Jones portfolios reduce the standard errors of estimate by 79.8 percent of what they would have been without using the regression.

$$.845199, .862487, .751255, .75314, .775904$$
$$\text{Average} = .797597$$

To be able to reduce one's error of prediction by approximately 80 percent appears to make the effort of computing a regression worthwhile.

We can now use the regression models stated in Table 9.3 to compute the expected return on investment for the stock portfolios. These expected values, complete with upper and lower limits (i.e., the usual three-sigma limits), are shown in Table 9.4. For comparison, actual realized returns are listed alongside the theoretical (computed) returns. Notice that in every case, the minimum probable return on stocks exceeds the guaranteed return on bonds. A rational investor will choose

Table 9.3   REGRESSION EQUATIONS

	Standard error of estimate (adjusted for degrees of freedom)	Index of determinati (adjusted f degrees o freedom)
A. Standard and Poor's 500 Stock Composite portfolio vs. GNP		
1950–1960: $V_t = -106.23 + .37341\ GNP_{t+1}$	3.88	.97
1951–1961: $V_t = -105.11 + .363279\ GNP_{t+1}$	3.64	.98
1952–1962: $V_t = -\ 90.66 + .322061\ GNP_{t+1}$	4.59	.97
1953–1963: $V_t = -\ 78.17 + .288208\ GNP_{t+1}$	4.47	.97
1954–1964: $V_t = -\ 74.48 + .275136\ GNP_{t+1}$	4.25	.97
B. Dow-Jones Industrial Average portfolio vs. GNP		
1950–1960: $V_t = -1166.13 + 4.12409\ GNP_{t+1}$	40.228	.98
1951–1961: $V_t = -1128.87 + 3.94722\ GNP_{t+1}$	36.652	.98
1952–1962: $V_t = -\ 912.34 + 3.35809\ GNP_{t+1}$	61.856	.94
1953–1963: $V_t = -\ 760.33 + 2.95564\ GNP_{t+1}$	59.515	.95
1954–1964: $V_t = -\ 722.78 + 2.82788\ GNP_{t+1}$	56.224	.95

Table 9.4 RISKS USING KNOWN REGRESSION MODEL*

	Bond portfolio	Standard and Poor's stock portfolio				Dow-Jones Industrial stock portfolio			
		min.	expected	max.	actual	min.	expected	max.	actual
1950–1960	2.32	15.3	16.9	18.4	16.8	14.6	16.1	17.5	16.1
1951–1961	2.57	14.6	16.0	17.2	16.2	14.2	15.4	16.6	15.4
1952–1962	2.68	13.3	15.0	16.5	14.2	12.3	14.5	16.3	13.1
1953–1963	2.94	13.8	15.4	16.8	15.1	13.0	15.0	16.7	14.6
1954–1964	2.55	12.9	14.3	15.5	14.5	11.4	13.1	14.6	13.5

* Return on Investment (in per cent, compounded annually)

stocks in every case. No investment will be made in bonds. The stock portfolios dominate the bond portfolios.[26]

Statistical Estimation Using Only Known Data.   The next step in the study permits entry of an operational model. Up to this point, we have been using information not available at the date of investment decision. In practice, the investment manager knows neither the exact regression equation tò use nor the appropriate value to use for future GNP. Hence, he must be provided with a guide for satisfying both of these two requirements.

How can we obtain a proxy for the desired exact regression relationship? One approach is to utilize existing information regarding historical regression relationships between changes in GNP and corresponding changes in value of common stock portfolios.

A regression equation using all available data as of the date of the investment decision (1950), is shown at the top of Table 9.5. The time period over which this data was taken represents a variety of economic conditions: wars, severe inflation, severe depression, built-in economic stabilizers (both with and without), and a host of other important economic and financial factors.

Now, if we are willing to assume that the slope of the regression line computed for the past 40 years, complete with its relatively larger standard error of estimate, will not change significantly over the next 10 years, then we have provided a proxy for the desired exact relationship between changes in GNP and changes in values of common stock portfolios.

Expected results using this proxy are shown in Table 9.5. The wider limits about expected values indicate a rise in the relative risk of obtaining precisely the expected value.

Note, however, that the minimum probable return (even assuming 4 sigma deviations instead of the customary 3), still exceeds the guaranteed return from bonds. Again, rational investors averse to risk will choose 100 percent investment in common stocks.

Finally, we impose the ultimate deterioration on the quality of the input data. In the absence of known data regarding future levels of GNP, we formulate a rational opinion regarding those future levels.

Given the slope and standard error of a historical regression line, we ask the question, How far wrong can we estimate future changes in

---

[26] One implication here is, if we enrich the bond portfolios to include higher yielding corporates and possibly even 6 percent or 7 percent mortgages, the lowest probable return from the stock portfolios will still exceed the return from the fixed-income portfolio. The (risky) stock portfolios dominate the guaranteed returns. [on dominance, see p. 399.]

Table 9.5 RISKS USING ASSUMED REGRESSION MODEL

Regression equation (S and P portfolio 1908–1950):
$V_t = 4.4109 + .467823 (GNP) \pm 3 (17.0526)$;
reduction in standard error = 56.04 percent; index of determination = .81

Years	Bond	Standard and Poor's 500 stock Composite Portfolios			
		Minimum	Expected	Maximum	Actual
1950–1960	2.32	12.0	19.4	24.1*	16.8
		(8.0)	(19.4)	(25.4)†	
1951–1961	2.57	12.4	18.6	22.8	16.2
		(9.4)	(18.6)	(23.9)	
1952–1962	2.68	12.4	18.6	22.2	14.2
		(9.7)	(18.2)	(23.3)	
1953–1963	2.94	14.8	19.7	23.3	15.1
		(12.6)	(19.7)	(24.3)	
1954–1964	2.55	14.1	18.5	21.8	14.5
		(12.2)	(18.5)	(22.7)	

* Numbers without parentheses refer to 3σ limits
† Numbers with parentheses refer to 4σ limits
NOTE: All numbers refer to return on shareholder investment (in percent, compounded annually)

GNP before we alter the original decision to invest 100 percent of the
fund in common stocks? These results are shown in Table 9.6.

Table 9.6 MINIMUM POSSIBLE CHANGE IN GNP FOR
REALIZATION OF MINIMUM RETURN ON EQUITY
TO EQUAL RETURN FOR BONDS
Five Standard and Poor Portfolios (1950–1954)

Year	Minimum (%)	Actual (%)	Difference (%)
1950	3.63856*	5.83747	62.3311
	3.15181†	4.70528	66.9845
1951	3.52137	6.21789	56.6329
	3.06283	4.95411	61.8241
1952	3.43417	6.19622	55.4237
	2.99618	4.94008	60.6504
1953	3.48426	7.31472	47.6336
	3.03451	5.6432	53.7729
1954	3.20448	7.11747	45.0227
	2.8187	5.52223	51.0428

* Average simple rate of growth of GNP over 10 years.
† Average compound rate of growth of GNP over 10 years.
NOTE: Comment on the number of decimals of computer printout vs. data
accuracy.

Table 9.6 shows the minimum average annual rate of change in
GNP which, according to our assumed regression model in Table 9.5,
will cause the minimum probable return from common stocks to exactly
equal the guaranteed return from bonds. Under these conditions, we
would still prefer all equity.

Considering that the minimum change required is approximately
half of the actual change (on average) the implication is as follows: if the
decision maker can have firm convictions that the aggregate economy
will grow at a rate at least half as large as the actual rate of growth,
then he will decide on 100 percent investment in common stocks!

Implications. One implication of the above study concerns the thinking
of fund managers. Are stocks actually much more risky than bonds?
Table 9.5 indicates that over the time period of study, the 1950's to the
1960's, stocks were not risky at all. Stocks were not risky relative to
bonds because of the high cause and effect relationship between stock
price indexes and GNP. Equity values rise with real output.

Another implication concerns the appropriate allocation of investment funds. Why hold any bonds under these conditions? Why hold
governments, corporates, mortgages, or any other security that offers
less than the minimum return possible from common stocks?

A third implication is that if returns from stock portfolios are not
risky, relative to bonds, then there are fewer reasons for risk premiums

on common stocks, which implies a future decline in the difference between yield to maturity on bonds and the rate of return on equity investment over comparative time periods. As the historical record now shows, over the next few years, after 1964, there was a rise in the cost of issuing fixed income securities; bond yields rose sharply causing bond prices to fall. Stock prices dropped severely, narrowing the structural gap.

As an exercise, the student should repeat the experiments described above, using current data, and make forecasts for the coming 10 years.

This appendix contains computer listings to support the values shown in Tables 9.2 and 9.4. Tables 9.7 and 9.8 support Table 9.2 while Tables 9.10 and 9.11 support Table 9.4.

The following equations are used to compute return on investment in the common stock portfolios for Table 9.2.

$$V_t = (P_t + D_t)N_t \tag{9.56}$$

where

V_t = total value of portfolio as of time t
P_t = price level (per unit) as of time t
D_t = dividends (per unit) as of time t
N_t = total number of units held as of time t

$$N_{t+1} = (1 + D_t/P_t)N_t \tag{9.57}$$

$$V_t(1 + R_1)^1 = V_{t+1} \tag{9.58}$$

$$R_1 = (V_{t+1}/V_t) - 1 \tag{9.59}$$

where R_1 = rate of return on investment for 1 year.

$$V_t(1 + R_{av})^\tau = V_{t+\tau} \tag{9.60}$$

$$R_{av} = (V_{t+\tau}/V_t)^{1/\tau} - 1$$

$$= \sqrt[\tau]{(1 + R_1)(1 + R_2)(1 + R_3) \cdots (1 + R_\tau)} - 1 \tag{9.61}$$

where R_{av} = average rate of return on investment over τ years.

Tables 9.7 and 9.8 contain the data and results of calculations using the above equations.

Data tabulated on Tables 9.10 and 9.11, for each year, fit into the cells of the 3 × 6 matrix depicted on Table 9.9.

Table 9.7 STANDARD and POOR'S PORTFOLIO RETURNS

Year	(Price)$_t$	Dividends	N	V_t	R
1950	18.4	0	1	18.4	16.8099 *
	22.34	1.41	1	23.75	29.0761
	24.5	1.41	1.06312	27.5453	15.9803
	24.73	1.45	1.1243	29.4341	6.8571
	29.69	1.54	1.19022	37.1706	26.2839
	40.49	1.64	1.25196	52.7449	41.8996
	46.62	1.74	1.30267	62.9969	19.4369
	44.38	1.79	1.35128	62.3888	−.9653
	46.24	1.75	1.40579	67.4637	8.1343
	57.38	1.83	1.45899	86.3868	28.0493
	55.85	1.95	1.50552	87.0191	.7320

*Average return over 10-year period as computed from (9.61)

Table 9.7. *(Continued)*

Year	(Price)$_t$	Dividends	N	V_t	R
1951	22.34	0	1	22.34	16.1722
	24.5	1.41	1	25.91	15.9803
	24.73	1.45	1.05755	27.6867	6.8571
	29.69	1.54	1.11956	34.9638	26.2839
	40.49	1.64	1.17763	49.6135	41.8996
	46.62	1.74	1.22533	59.2569	19.4369
	44.38	1.79	1.27106	58.6849	−.9653
	46.24	1.75	1.32233	63.4585	8.1343
	57.38	1.83	1.37237	81.2581	28.0493
	55.85	1.95	1.41614	81.8529	.7320
	66.27	2.02	1.46559	100.085	22.2739
1952	24.5	0	1	24.5	14.1619
	24.73	1.45	1	26.18	6.8571
	29.69	1.54	1.05863	33.0611	26.2839
	40.49	1.64	1.11354	46.9136	41.8996
	46.62	1.74	1.15865	56.0322	19.4369
	44.38	1.79	1.20189	55.4913	−.9653
	46.24	1.75	1.25037	60.0051	8.1343
	57.38	1.83	1.29769	76.8361	28.0493
	55.85	1.95	1.33908	77.3986	.7320
	66.27	2.02	1.38583	94.6383	22.2739
	62.38	2.13	1.42807	92.1249	−2.6558
1953	24.73	0	1	24.73	15.0694
	29.69	1.54	1	31.23	26.2839
	40.49	1.64	1.05187	44.3153	41.8996
	46.62	1.74	1.09447	52.9288	19.4369
	44.38	1.79	1.13532	52.4179	−.965
	46.24	1.75	1.18111	56.6817	8.1343
	57.38	1.83	1.22582	72.5805	28.0493
	55.85	1.95	1.26491	73.1118	.7320
	66.27	2.02	1.30907	89.3967	22.2739
	62.38	2.13	1.34898	87.0225	−2.6558
	69.87	2.28	1.39504	100.652	15.6621
1954	29.69	0	1	29.69	14.4871
	40.49	1.64	1	42.13	41.8996
	46.62	1.74	1.0405	50.3188	19.4369
	44.38	1.79	1.07934	49.8331	−.9653
	46.24	1.75	1.12287	53.8866	8.1343
	57.38	1.83	1.16537	69.0015	28.0493
	55.85	1.95	1.20254	69.5065	.7320
	66.27	2.02	1.24452	84.9884	22.2739
	62.38	2.13	1.28246	82.7312	−2.6558
	69.87	2.28	1.32625	95.6887	15.6621
	81.37	2.5	1.36952	114.862	20.0372

Table 9.8 DOW-JONES PORTFOLIOS: RETURNS

Year	(Price)$_t$	(Dividends)$_t$	N	V_t	Return
1950	219.233	0	1	219.233	16.0687 *
	257.743	16.43	1	274.173	25.0601
	276.58	15.43	1.06375	310.624	13.295
	273.268	16.11	1.12309	324.998	4.6272
	350.473	17.5	1.1893	437.63	34.6565
	454.025	21.58	1.24868	593.881	35.7037
	494.823	22.99	1.30804	677.318	14.0494
	467.523	21.61	1.36881	669.529	−1.1499
	510.17	20	1.43208	759.245	13.3998
	639.088	20.74	1.48822	981.968	29.3349
	611.81	21.36	1.53652	972.875	−.9260
1951	257.743	0	1	257.743	15.3803
	276.58	15.43	1	292.01	13.295
	273.268	16.11	1.05579	305.522	4.6272
	350.473	17.5	1.11803	411.405	34.6565
	454.025	21.58	1.17386	558.292	35.7037
	494.823	22.99	1.22965	636.729	14.0494
	467.523	21.61	1.28678	629.407	−1.1499
	510.17	20	1.34626	713.746	13.3998
	639.088	20.74	1.39904	923.123	29.3349
	611.81	21.36	1.44444	914.575	−.9260
	698.233	22.71	1.49487	1077.71	17.8377
1952	276.58	0	1	276.58	13.1037
	273.268	16.11	1	289.378	4.6272
	350.473	17.5	1.05895	389.666	34.6565
	454.025	21.58	1.11183	528.792	35.7037
	494.823	22.99	1.16468	603.084	14.0494
	467.523	21.61	1.21879	596.149	−1.1499
	510.17	20	1.27512	676.032	13.3998
	639.088	20.74	1.32511	874.345	29.3349
	611.81	21.36	1.36811	866.248	−.9260
	698.233	22.71	1.41588	1020.77	17.8377
	624.828	23.3	1.46193	947.517	−7.1760
1953	273.268	0	1	273.268	14.5859
	350.473	17.5	1	367.973	34.6565
	454.025	21.58	1.04993	499.353	35.7037
	494.823	22.99	1.09984	569.51	14.0494
	467.523	21.61	1.15094	562.961	−1.1499
	510.17	20	1.20413	638.396	13.3998
	639.088	20.74	1.25134	825.669	29.3349

*Average return over 10-year period as computed from (9.11).

Table 9.8. *(Continued)*

Year	(Price)$_t$	(Dividends)$_t$	N	V_t	Return
1953	611.81	21.36	1.29195	818.023	−.9260
	698.233	22.71	1.33705	963.94	17.8377
	624.828	23.3	1.38054	894.768	−7.1760
	721.235	23.41	1.43202	1066.35	19.176
1954	350.473	0	1	350.473	13.4592
	454.025	21.58	1	475.605	35.7037
	494.823	22.99	1.04753	542.425	14.0494
	467.523	21.61	1.0962	536.187	−1.1499
	510.17	20	1.14687	608.035	13.3998
	639.088	20.74	1.19183	786.402	29.3349
	611.81	21.36	1.23051	779.12	−.9260
	698.233	22.71	1.27347	918.097	17.8377
	624.828	23.3	1.31489	852.215	−7.1760
	721.235	23.41	1.36392	1015.64	19.176
	848.573	31.24	1.40819	1238.94	21.987

Table 9.9 KEY TO LISTING OF PORTFOLIO RISK

Risk of portfolios using known 10-year regression equation (from Table 9.3) for estimation

(For use with Tables 9.10 and 9.11)

(1)	(2)	(3)	(4)	(5)	(6)
Year	$V_{minimum}$	$V_{expected}$	$V_{maximum}$	V_{actual}	—
	$R_{minimum}$	$R_{expected}$	$R_{maximum}$	R_{actual}	R_{bonds}
	σ_1	σ_2	σ_2/σ_1	σ_2^2/σ_1^2	—

where

σ_1 = Standard error of estimate (adjusted for degrees of freedom) from regression equations

σ_2 = maximum tolerable standard error of estimate so that minimum probable return from stock portfolio exactly equals guaranteed return from bond portfolio

If $V_{minimum} = (V_{expected} - 3\sigma)$, then $V_{minimum} = (V_{expected} - 3\sigma_2)$, so that

$$\sigma_2 = (V_{expected} - V_{minimum})/3$$

and

$$\sigma_2 = [V_{expected} - V_0(1 + R_{bonds})^{10}]/3$$

Table 9.10 STANDARD and POOR'S PORTFOLIOS RISK

(1)	(2)	(3)	(4)	(5)	(6)
1950	76.3392	87.9819	99.6246	87.0191	
	.1529	.1694	.1840	.1681	.0232
	3.8809	21.6129	5.5690	31.0143	
1951	87.5195	98.4429	109.366	100.085	
	.1463	.1599	.1721	.1618	.0257
	3.6411	23.2166	6.3762	40.6564	
1952	85.7545	99.5218	113.289	92.1249	
	.1335	.15047	.1655	.1416	.0268
	4.5891	22.5349	4.9105	23.1131	
1953	90.4701	103.893	117.316	100.652	
	.1385	.1544	.1685	.1507	0.294
	4.4743	23.617	5.27837	27.8612	
1954	100.193	112.944	125.695	114.862	
	.1293	.1430	.1552	.1449	.0255
	4.25039	24.9175	5.8624	34.3678	

Table 9.11 DOW-JONES PORTFOLIOS RISK

(1)	(2)	(3)	(4)	(5)	(6)
1950	858.16	978.844	1099.53	972.875	
	.1462	.1614	.174979	.1607	.0232
	40.228	234.366	5.82593	33.9415	
1951	972.896	1082.85	1192.8	1077.71	
	.142057	.154352	.16557	.1538	.0257
	36.6515	250.219	6.82698	46.6076	
1952	885.063	1070.63	1256.2	947.517	
	.1234	.1449	.1634	.1310	.0268
	61.8557	236.772	3.82782	14.6522	
1953	928.237	1106.78	1285.32	1066.35	
	.130074	.1501	.167461	.1459	.0294
	59.5145	247.221	4.15397	17.2555	
1954	1034.93	1203.6	1372.27	1238.94	
	.11436	.1313	.146248	.1346	.0255
	56.224	250.924	4.46293	19.9178	

QUESTIONS FOR STUDY

1. Explain the difference between the following terms or concepts:
   (a) Spot rate vs. forward rate
   (b) Liquidity premium vs. liquidity preferences
   (c) Continuous compounding vs. yield curve
   (d) Corporation finance vs. investment analysis
   (e) Common stock vs. bond
2. What determines the price (yield) that a lump sum of money ($100,000) can command in the market place?
3. (a) Explain how interest rates are determined in the aggregate economy.
   (b) Explain the relationship between investment analysis and question (a).
4. If the marginal efficiency of capital schedule is relatively elastic, then a relatively small increase in personal income taxes will ultimately cause a relatively large decline in the equilibrium level of share prices. True or false? Explain.
5. Assume an aggregate economy in equilibrium. If government spending increased (because of a war on poverty), and taxes decreased (because of fiscal policy), and interest rates increased (because of monetary policy), explain how you would expect share prices to behave.
6. The expectations theory contends that differences in yields on loans with different maturities are established not because the market expects to receive a higher return on one security than on another, but because the market expects the rates of return on the two securities to be the same over an equal period of time. Thus, two loans with 1 and 2 years to maturity that are selling to yield 6 percent and 7 percent, respectively, implies that the market is expecting the yield on a 1-year loan to be approximately 8 percent 1 year in the future. True or false? Defend your answer.
7. Using equation (9.16), explain what happens to bond yields and prices if:
   (a) b_0 increases
   (b) a_0 increases
   (c) a_1 declines
   (d) b_1 delcines
   (e) M increases
   (f) H decreases
   (g) I increases
8. List and explain the differences between three alternative theories that have been offered as a guide toward understanding the term structure of interest rates. How does this relate to security analysis?
9. Explain what should happen to security prices (and why) if each of the following events occur:
   (a) The aggregate consumption function, equation 9.18, shifts in a rightward direction.

    (b) The aggregate marginal efficiency of capital schedule, equation 9.22, shifts in a leftward direction.

    (c) The speculative demand for money, equation 9.29, increases.

    (d) The supply of money, equation 9.27, increases by 20 percent.

    (d) The rate of inflation increases.

    (e) The Federal Reserve System raises the discount rate.

10. Discuss the plausibility of Hammer's model, equation (9.24), in light of Modigliani and Miller's proposition II, Chapter 7, equation (7.26).

11. Comment on the following statement: "Common stocks are a good hedge against inflation."

What's happening in the market? That familiar question was examined in Chapter 3. Now, after having studied that security prices behave in accordance with the economic performance and finance of the individual companies, the industries in which these companies do business, and the overall economy at large, we return to the question. But this time we shall introduce a slight alteration. Instead of asking, "What's happening in the market today?" ask, "Given what's happening in the market today—and yesterday—and the day before—and all previous days—then, what is *going to* happen in the market tomorrow—and the day after—and the day after that?" In other words, given today's prices, what will be tomorrow's price?

You can probably guess the answer. Day-to-day fluctuations in stock market prices are indistinguishable from random numbers

The Random-Walk Theory of Stock Market Price and Short-Run Analysis

10

produced and served-up by some demon of chance. If prices, and changes in price, are studied on a day-to-day, week-to-week, or even month-to-month basis, we find that any particular change is uncorrelated with any other change which has occurred previously. This apparent randomness in the behavior of stock market prices has been cause for concern among both theoreticians and practicioners. In this chapter, we shall delve into some of the pertinent theories and study some of the underlying issues.

The questions for analysis are, Do share prices behave randomly over the short run, or do prices behave systematically? Can valuable information be obtained from reading charts of historical price movements? Do historical changes in price contain any information which will help enable us to do a better job of predicting future price, $P_{t+\tau}$? The primary issues at hand are:

1. Are stock market "patterns" predictable?

2. Do systematic trends exist; or do prices behave as a random-walk drunk?
3. Can future changes in price be explained by past changes in price?
4. Are the observed highs and lows local maxima and minima resulting from a nonrandom trend; or do these peaks and valleys occur at random?

The answers to all initial parts of the questions, unfortunately, appear to be no! There is a wealth of evidence, theoretical as well as empirical, to substantiate that answer. We shall turn next to a study of that evidence beginning with some preliminary considerations of precisely what is a random walk.

Theoretical considerations and empirical evidence assert that short-term change in share price is a random variable: a random walk. There is much evidence to substantiate this belief.[1] Conceptually, a random walk can be considered as the path traversed by a particle that moves in steps, each step being determined by chance, in regard to direction or in regard to magnitude, or both. For example, visualize an inebriated wanderer who takes steps both forward and backward at random, each step being of variable length, with some specified probability of moving in either the forward or the backward direction. Then, after the wanderer takes a total of *n* steps, there are finite probabilities associated with his various possible displacements from the origin. This wanderer illustrates, in its simplest form, the notion of a random walk.

The path of the random walk need not be limited to a single dimension. Expanded to three dimensions and drawing an illustration from a physical science, the random-walk theory has been used to describe the motion of certain particles that move freely in space. Each particle has some specified probability of moving to any of the nearest neighboring locations.

Applied to price behavior in risky markets, the random-walk model dates historically to a doctoral dissertation written by Louis Bachelier in 1900.[2] However, not much attention was devoted to the

---

[1] See (1) Paul A. Samuelson, "Proof that Properly Anticipated Prices Fluctuate Randomly," *Industrial Management Review*, Spring 1965, pp. 41–49; (2) Benoit Mandelbrot, "Forecasts of Future Prices, Unbiased Markets, and Martingale Models," *Journal of Business*, vol. XXXIX, supplement, January 1966, pp. 242–255; (3) The first sixteen articles reprinted in Paul Cootner (ed.), *The Random Character of Stock Market Prices*, The MIT Press, Cambridge, Mass., 1964; and (4) Eugene Fama, "The Behavior of Stock Market Prices," *Journal of Business*, vol. XXXVIII, January 1965, pp. 34–105.

[2] Louis Bachelier, *Theorie de la Speculation*, Gauthier-Villars, Paris, 1900; reprinted in Cootner, *Ibid.*, pp. 17–78.

model until the later 1950's when the underlying theory was rediscovered by Osborne.[3]

10.1 The Random-Walk Model of Share Price Behavior

The random-walk model emanates from considerations of short-term change in share price. To illustrate, suppose we wish to know tomorrow's price for common stocks. How profitable this knowledge would be!

To know's tomorrow's price, it is sufficient to know what particular increment (Δ) to add to (or subtract from) today's price.

$$P_{t+\tau} = P_t + \Delta \tag{10.1}$$

where

$$P_{t+\tau} = \text{price as of time } t + \tau$$
$$P_t = \text{price as of time } t$$
$$\Delta = \text{increment or change in price}$$

Statement (10.1) depicts price behavior in economic auction markets such as the trading floor of the New York Stock Exchange. The reasoning which underlies (10.1) can be put forth as follows.

On the listed stock exchanges, prices are set by buyers and sellers.[4] The price of each transaction is called out in a voice which is loud and clear and is simultaneously transmitted out over the ticker tape for all to see. There are no secret deals. Under these conditions, with the price (P_t) being set in a free market, and with all interested parties knowing P_t, then that price (P_t) is used easily as a starting point for negotiation of price of the next trade, $P_{t+\tau}$. It is the change and not the absolute value, which constitutes the fundamental element in price determination in the short run. If the change (Δ) is known and is constant, then since P_t is always known; tomorrow's price ($P_{t+\tau}$) is known. If Δ equals a constant of $+3$, then every succeeding price will be \$3 larger than the previous price. If Δ equals zero, then the price as of the next transaction is the same as the previous price. Therefore, to predict $P_{t+\tau}$ it is sufficient to predict Δ.

---

[3] M. F. M. Osborne, "Brownian Motion in the Stock Market," *Operations Research*, vol. VII, March–April 1959; reprinted in Cootner, *Ibid.*, pp. 100–128.

[4] The role of the specialist on the floor of the exchange is to keep an orderly market, not to set prices. Prices in the over-the-counter (OTC) market, in contrast, are set by "bargaining;" not auction. Also, volume data for transactions made over the counter are less readily available than volume data for transactions on the NYSE and the AMEX.

But to know the magnitude and direction of change in price for tomorrow is easier said than done. However, some insights into the behavior of stock market prices can be obtained through a systematic study of Δ.

Some Alternative Ways of Measuring Price Change.   Price change (Δ) can be expressed in several different ways. Scholars have used four alternative measures for price change. The measures are: (1) simple arithmetic differences, (2) percentage changes, (3) ratios, and (4) logarithmic differences.

1. Simple arithmetic change:

$$\Delta = P_{t+\tau} - P_t \qquad\qquad (10.2)$$

2. Percentage change:

$$\Delta = (P_{t+\tau} - P_t)/P_t = (P_{t+\tau}/P_t) - 1 \qquad (10.3)$$

3. Relative change:

$$\Delta = (P_{t+\tau}/P_t) \qquad\qquad (10.4)$$

4. Logarithm of relative change:

$$\begin{aligned}\Delta &= \log(P_{t+\tau}/P_t)\\ &= \log(P_{t+\tau}) - \log(P_t)\end{aligned} \qquad (10.5)$$

The reader should outline some possible reasons for preferences among these four alternatives. For example, the latter measurement, (10.5), the difference between logarithms of successive price, is the yield received for holding the asset for one time period, assuming continuous compounding. This equality between yield and difference between log of successive price can be shown as follows.

From (4.11) in Chapter 4, we can write

$$S = Pe^{i\tau} \qquad\qquad (10.6)$$

where

$$\begin{aligned}S &= \text{future value} = P_{t+\tau}\\ P &= \text{present value} = P_t\\ i &= \text{yield per unit time}\\ \tau &= \text{one}\\ e &= \text{base of naperian logarithm system}\end{aligned}$$

Then dividing both sides of (10.6) by P and taking logs, we get[5]

$$\log(S/P) = i \qquad\qquad (10.7)$$

---

[5] See Fama, *op. cit.*, p. 45.

or

$$i = \log(P_{t+\tau}/P_t) \qquad \textbf{(10.8)}$$

Hence the assertion is proved.

Concerning the length of the differencing interval (τ) several alternatives are possible. We can have

1. Daily changes
2. Weekly changes
3. Monthly changes

If longer spans of time are studied, then adjustments must be made for possible secular (causal) trend.

Concerning particular securities, the analysis can be a cross section or a time series (or both) on

1. Market indexes
2. Industry group indexes
3. Individual stocks

Empirical results are usually the same, no matter what the particular length of differencing interval or the particular securities. In any case, knowledge of the change, Δ, is the same as knowledge of price as of the next transaction. So we shall focus attention on the Δ, where Δ can take on meaning as stated in either (10.2), (10.3), (10.4), or (10.5).

10.2 The Hypotheses Underlying Random Walk

The general random-walk model involves three distinct hypotheses:

1. Any given set of changes in price conforms to some probability distribution. The particular shape of the distribution is not specified by the theory but is taken by many scholars to be normal in shape.[6]
2. The probability distribution is stationary (i.e., time invariant).
3. Successive changes are independent (i.e., uncorrelated) with each other.

These three hypotheses are discussed below.

Stationarity. Stationarity implies no trend in either mean or variance of the distribution of changes over time. To illustrate, start at any time (t) and observe one small increment in price,

$$\Delta = P_t - P_{t-1} \qquad \textbf{(10.9)}$$

---

[6] Some scholars have challenged the assumption of normality with the result that there are now two competing hypotheses concerning the shape of the distribution of change in price of risky securities, the Gaussian hypothesis and the stable paretian hypothesis. Both hypotheses are discussed later.

Then a *total* difference in price over some longer time span $(t - \tau)$ must equal the sum of the individual small differences over that span.

$$P_t - P_{t-\tau} = \sum_{j=t-\tau+1}^{t} \Delta_j \qquad (10.10)$$

By stationarity we mean the following. If the process generating the observed changes in price is stationary, then neither the particular starting time (t) nor the span of time $(t - \tau)$ is of particular significance in determining either the mean or the variance of the distribution of changes so observed. Any particular point in time and any (sufficiently long) span of time over which the small increments are observed will always produce an identical result.

Further examination of statement (10.10) shows that if the process is a random walk (i.e., a purely random number generator), then the expected value of the total net change in (10.10) must equal zero.

$$E(P_t - P_{t-\tau}) = E\left(\sum_{j=t-\tau+1}^{t} \Delta_j \right) = 0 \qquad (10.11)$$

where $E(P_t - P_{t-\tau})$ = mean value of the sequence of successive changes. Statement (10.11) must be true if the process is purely random because, if the net change is some value other than zero, then the process is not random; under these conditions, the process is deterministic.

In other words, statement (10.11) says that if stock market prices do change in a purely random way, then the average change over some time interval (τ) will be zero.

Also, the variance of the distribution of changes stated in (10.10) is independent of time and must be the same as the expected average squared change itself.

$$E(P_t - P_{t-\tau})^2 = E\left\{ \sum_{j=t-\tau+1}^{t} [\Delta_j - E(\Delta_j)]^2 \right\} \qquad (10.12)$$

where $E(P_t - P_{t-\tau})^2$ = variance of the distribution of changes in price. That is, if the process generating the observed changes in price is stationary, then the variance of the distribution of change as stated in (10.12) will be the same value, no matter when the particular starting time (t). Also, since the average change over the entire time interval is zero, the variance as stated in (10.12) simplifies to the mean value of the squared short-term changes themselves.

$$E(P_t - P_{t-\tau})^2 = E\left(\sum_{j=t-\tau+1}^{t} \Delta_j^2 \right) \qquad (10.13)$$

where all terms are the same as defined above.

The general consensus among scholars is that empirical distributions of short-term changes in price of risky securities are in fact approximately stationary.[7] Little, if any, controversy appears on the subject.

Hypothesis of Independence. Independence means that, just as with the inebriated wanderer visualized above or as in an unbiased coin-tossing experiment, knowledge of the sequence of past steps or past changes is of *no* help in learning the direction or the size of the step to come during the next time period. For example, if successive steps are independent, then the probability that the next change will equal $+3$, for example, is is no way influenced by any previous changes. The probability that $\Delta_{t+\tau}$ equals $+3$, given all historical prices and changes therein, is the same as the unconditional probability that $\Delta_{t+\tau}$ equals $+3$.

$$pr(\Delta_{t+\tau} = +3 | \Delta_t, \Delta_{t-1}, \ldots, \Delta_{t-n}) = pr(\Delta_{t+\tau} = +3) \quad \textbf{(10.14)}$$

Equation (10.14) is a precise statement of independence.

The theoretical Bachelier-Osborne argument used to support the independence hypothesis for successive changes in the price of common stocks is as follows: if successive bits of new information arise independently across time and if noise or uncertainty concerning intrinsic values fails to follow any consistent pattern, then successive changes in price of common stock will be independent.[8] In other words, independence means no serial correlation between successive changes in price. Successive steps are independent increments. Just as with the inebriated wanderer, i.e., given any particular level (location), the probability is always the same, $1:2$, that the next step will be either forward or backward (up or down). Continuing the reasoning from the preceding section, if the distribution of $(P_t - P_{t-\tau})$ has zero mean for all t, then if the sequence P_t represents daily closing prices and if the sequence $P_{t-\tau}$ represents daily opening prices, then the theory and the hypothesis of independence both say that daily opening and closing prices on the stock exchange must be independent of one another.

Empirical evidence to support the assumption of independence has been presented by many scholars. Fama, for example, applied three different experimental techniques to examine independence between successive price changes for each of the 30 stocks contained in the Dow-Jones Industrial Average. For each individual stock and for the group

---

[7] See M. D. Godfrey, C. W. J. Granger, and O. Morgenstern, "The Random-Walk Hypothesis of Stock Market Behavior," *Kyklos*, vol. XVII, 1964, pp. 1–30; and B. Mandelbrot, "The Variation of Certain Speculative Prices," *Journal of Business*, vol. 36, no. 4, October 1963, pp. 394–419.

[8] See Fama, *op. cit.*

as a whole, Fama studied differencing intervals of 1, 4, 9, and 16 days, using methods of (1) serial correlation measures, (2) runs analysis, and (3) Alexander's filter technique. (The methods of testing are described at the end of this section.)

M. G. Kendall studied time series of various Δ_t by applying standard statistical procedures which consist of decomposing the time series into a maximum of four component parts:

1. Linear trend
2. Seasonal components
3. Cyclical components
4. Irregular (random) components

$$U_t = C_t + I_t + S_t \qquad (10.15)$$

where

U_t = unadjusted time series of change in price (or logarithm of price relative)
C_t = trend-cycle component
S_t = seasonal component
I_t = irregular component

Kendall writes: "It is customary to analyze an economic time-series by extracting from it a long-term movement, or trend, for separate study and then scrutinize the residual portion for short-term oscillatory movements and random fluctuations. The assumption latent in this procedure is that the long-term and short-term movements are due to separate causal influences and therefore that the mathematical process of analysis corresponds more or less roughly to a real distinction of type in the generative system."[9] Kendall used 22 different industry aggregate price series, taken at weekly intervals from 486 to 2387 terms, to study the behavior of short-term change in price. The overall results were that there appear to be no measurable trends, no seasonal components, and no cyclical components. Only irregular components are evident. Kendall concludes that there is no reason to hope to be able to predict price movements on the exchange for a week ahead, using historical prices alone.

Several scholars have used spectral methods for studying the behavior of short-term changes in share price (as well as other variables from economics and finance).[10]

---

[9] M. G. Kendall, "The Analysis of Economic Time Series—Part I: Prices," *Journal of the Royal Statistical Society*, vol. 96, part 1, 1953, pp. 11–25, in Cootner, *op. cit.*, pp. 85–99.

[10] See C. Granger and O. Morgenstern, "Spectral Analysis of New York Stock Market Prices," *Kyklos*, vol. XVI, 1963, pp. 1–27. Also, the following

Spectral methods enable a series of prices (or changes in price) to be studied in the *frequency domain* instead of the time domain. That is to say, instead of measuring variance, covariance, coefficients of serial correlation, and similar time-series statistics, the entire time series can be transformed into a linear combination of sine and cosine terms (called a Fourier transform, after a French mathematician). Then the sine and cosine terms are analyzed with respect to amplitude, phase, and frequency. The frequency spectrum, spectral density, power spectrum, phase diagram, and coherance can be calculated. One can think of the power spectrum of a time series as distributing the total variance of the series over the frequency or period domain. For two series, jointly, the cospectrum distributes their covariance. The coherence essentially displays a correlation coefficient squared or coefficient of determination. Phase indicates the timing relationship between the two series. Lead or lag, each is noted as a function of frequency. One can draw an analogy by producing wavelengths in a light source.

The spectrum of a time series can be thought of as a decomposition of the variance at different frequencies. If successive values of Δ_t are independent, then all the autocovariances except at $\tau = 0$ will be zero, and the spectrum of Δ_t will be flat. If Δ_t is a Gaussian time series and has a flat spectrum, successive values of Δ_t are independent.

In general, empirical results of studies of stock market prices, no matter what the particular method of analysis, all agree: short-term changes in price of risky securities behave as independent increments. For all tests and for all differencing intervals, the amount of dependence in the data for the Dow-Jones 30 Industrials appears to be extremely slight or else nonexistent. Fama found some evidence of bunching of large values in the daily differences; however, the extent of bunching seemed to be only slightly greater than would be expected in a purely

---

references may be helpful for a review of the fundamentals of spectral analysis. (1) G. M. Jenkins, "A Survey of Spectral Analysis," *Applied Statistics, Journal of the Royal Statistical Society, Series C,* vol. XIV, no. 1, 1965, pp. 2–32; (2) R. B. Blackman and J. W. Tukey, *The Measurement of Power Spectra,* John Wiley & Sons, Inc., New York, 1958; (3) G. S. Fishman, "Spectral Methods in Econometrics," *Rand Report R-453-PR,* Santa Monica, 1968; (4) C. W. J. Granger and M. Hatanaka, *Spectral Analysis of Economic Time Series,* Princeton University Press, Princeton, N.J., 1964; (5) C. W. J. Granger and H. J. B. Rees, "Spectral Analysis of the Term Structure of Interest Rates," *Review of Economic Studies,* vol. 35, January 1968, pp. 67–76; (6) G. M. Jenkins and D. G. Watts, *Spectral Analysis and Its Applications,* Holden-Day, Inc., San Francisco, 1968; (7) H. F. Karreman, *Computer Programs for Spectral Analysis of Economic Time Series, Princeton University Econometric Research Program, Research Memo. No. 59,* Princeton, N.J., 1963; and E. Malinvaud, *Statistical Methods of Econometrics,* Chicago University Press, Chicago, 1966.

random model.[11] We can conclude that on the basis of all the tests he performed, the independence assumption of the random-walk model seems to be an adequate description of reality.

Before proceeding further to discuss the controversial part of the random-walk theory—the shape of the probability distribution of change in price—it may be worthwhile to summarize briefly some of the statistical methods (mentioned above) used to test the hypothesis of independence.

Serial correlation measures the amount of covariation between successive changes in price. Recall from Appendix 2 for Chapter 6, equation (6.76), that, if two variables, Δ_t and $\Delta_{t-\tau}$, are correlated, knowledge of one variable, $\Delta_{t-\tau}$, will aid in the prediction of the other variable, Δ_t. Hence, given a time sequence (p_t) representing daily closing prices on the stock exchange and another sequence (p_{t-1}), representing daily opening prices, then nonzero serial correlation between changes in these two series means that changes in one series can be predicted (with error of course) from changes in the other series.

$$\Delta_t = f(\Delta_{t-\tau}) \qquad (10.16)$$

As a matter of empirical fact, for all differencing intervals (τ), for any starting time (t), and for group indexes as well as for individual securities, serial correlation measures are *not* significantly different from zero.[12] Serial correlation measures therefore confirm independence.

Runs analysis measures the number of steps (or changes) taken in the same direction and compares this observed number with the number that would have occurred if the process is purely random. For example, taking the sequence

$$+ + - - - + - + - - - + + + + +$$

and starting from left to right, there is a " + " run of two, then a " − " run of 3, then a " + " run of 1, ..., out to finally a " + " run of 5. The total number of steps in the sequence is 16. Now, we can ask and calculate, for an unbiased coin-tossing experiment (e.g., a purely random sequence), how many runs are expected for length 1, length 2, length 3, ..., length n? If the process is purely random, out of 16 tosses of a coin, several runs of length 1 or 2 or 3 would hardly be surprising; but a run of length 15 or 16 would be surprising for a random process.

As a matter of empirical fact, for all differencing intervals (τ), for any starting time (t), and for group indexes as well as individual

---

[11] See Fama, *op. cit.* Also, see Eugene F. Fama, Lawrence Fisher, Michael C. Jensen, and Richard Roll, "The Adjustment of Stock Prices to New Information," *International Economic Review*, vol. 10, no. 1, February 1969, pp. 1–21.

[12] See the many articles in Cootner, *op. cit.*

securities, the number of runs for any particular length for any particular measurement is *not* significantly different from the runs that would be obtained from a purely random process.[13] Runs analysis therefore confirm independence.

Alexander proposed and tested various filter rules which can be described as follows. If the market moves up by X percent, then go long and stay long until it moves down by X percent, at which time sell and go short until it again moves up by X percent. Ignore moves of less than X percent. The more stringent the filter, the fewer losses are made, but the smaller the gain from any move that exceeds the filter of size. Thus the filter can be X equal 5 percent, 10 percent, 2 percent, etc. Alexander tested filters ranging from 5 percent to 50 percent, over time periods from 1897 to 1959.[14] Alexander's conclusion was consistent with beliefs held by technical analysts of the market and some specialists on the trading floor of the exchange: trends *do* exist and, once started, tend to persist. However, Mandelbrot and Fama both challenge the ability of traders to make profits by applying Alexander's rules.[15]

Market technicians believe that trends do exist.[16] Further, technicians believe that trends, once started, persist in the same direction until a change in direction occurs. One can use an analogy of an automobile traveling at high speed. It is impossible for the auto to reverse its direction of motion before slowing down and coming to a halt. In a similar way, a stock price trend, once started in one direction, either down or up, is believed to slow down before reversing its direction. Of course, common stocks are not automobiles; but some technicians use the analogy anyway.

Joel Owen[17] has presented evidence that local trends *do* exist in the Standard & Poor's index. Owen presented three major conclusions:

---

[13] See the articles in Cootner, *op. cit.*

[14] See (1) Sidney S. Alexander, "Price Movements in Speculative Markets: Trends or Random Walks," *Industrial Management Review*, vol. 2, no. 2, May 1961, pp. 7–26; and (2) Sidney S. Alexander, "Price Movements in Speculative Markets: Trends or Random Walks, No. 2," in Cootner, *The Random Character of Stock Market Prices*, The MIT Press, Cambridge, Mass., 1964.

[15] Fama, *op. cit.*, pp. 81–85, and Mandelbrot, "The Variation of Certain Speculative Prices," *Journal of Business*, vol. XXXVI, October 1963, pp. 394–419.

[16] See Robert D. Edwards and John Magee, *Technical Analysis of Stock Trends*, John Magee, Springfield, Mass., 1964; and *The Paflibe Chartbook*, a weekly publication of Dines Chart Corporation, 37 Wall Street, New York, 10005.

[17] Joel Owen, "Analysis of Variance Tests for Local Trends in the Standard and Poor's Index," *The Journal of Finance*, vol. XXIII, no. 3, June 1968, pp. 509–514.

1. There is no evidence to suggest that the rises and falls in the index reflect anything more than one long underlying trend.
2. There is evidence to support the notion that local trends exist when the numerical values of weekly differences are used.
3. There is evidence to support the notion that local trends, when they occur, persist no longer than one year.

However, even if local trends do exist and may persist for periods up to one year, there remains the problem of *predicting* the beginning, duration, and end of the trend, if profits are to be made.

The Shape of the Probability Distributions. The shape of the probability distribution is not specified for the general theory of random walks. However, under most conditions for which the number of steps is very large, the standard procedure is to invoke the central limit theorem and assume that the distribution is normal or Gaussian. (See p. 173.)

The theoretical Bachelier-Osborne argument used to support the Gaussian distribution hypothesis underlying the random-walk theory is as follows. If transactions are spread uniformly across time; and if the distribution of change in price from transaction to transaction has finite variance; and if the number of transactions per day, week, or month is very large, then price changes across these differencing intervals will be sums of many independent variables. Under these conditions, the central limit theorem leads us to expect that the daily, weekly, and monthly price changes for large-size samples will each have normal or Gaussian distributions.

Many empirical studies have been made of the frequency distribution of change in price for risky securities. In general, when the shape of an empirical frequency distribution of change in share price is compared with the shape of a theoretical normal probability distribution (i.e., when the central limit theorem is invoked), three distinct characteristics emerge. These characteristics are (1) peakedness, or a relative excess of observations within the interval centered on the mean, (2) a relative deficiency or too few observations at distances moderately removed from the mean (e.g., two to three standard deviations away), and (3) thick tails, or a significantly large proportion of observations at distances beyond three standard deviations from the mean.[18] These

---

[18] The observations in the tail areas are frequently called "outliers" or "mavericks." Their presence is so strong and troublesome that Osborne was motivated to record a typical comment, "The differences $|\Delta P|$ are not $\simeq 0$ at the extrema, as one learned in sophomore calculus that well behaved analytic functions tend to be and as is observed by the physicist in nature. In fact, the values of $|\Delta P|$ are rather larger than usual dispersion, in the neighborhood of the extrema. Thus, the concepts of continuity and analyticity both tend to break down." See M. F. M. Osborne, "The Dynamics of Stock Trading," *Econometrica*, vol. 33, no. 1, January 1965, pp. 88–113.

characteristics appear to be consistent regardless of which particular measure is taken for price change. [See equations (10.2) through (10.5)].

But conclusions from the previous experiments and studies include two severe shortcomings. First, scholars typically invoke the central limit theorem without specific evidence of its applicability. In practice, the assumption of normality is frequently resorted to and is generally valid, so long as the underlying processes creating the phenomenon are relatively linear. However, since it is well known that nonlinear generic processes will often produce deviations from the ideal Gaussian form,[19] one should expect (suspect?) a large sample of price relatives for common stocks or commodities to contain some mavericks. Examination of the reasons underlying this expectation constitutes part of the theme for analysis presented in the appendix for Chapter 10.

The second shortcoming in results of previous study concerns the lack of a satisfactory fundamental explanation for the occurrence of extremely large changes in price. Because applicability of the central limit theorem went unchallenged until 1963, there was no attempt to explain the observed deviations from normality. The usual practice, prior to Mandelbrot's suggestion to scrap the Gaussian hypothesis completely, was either to discard thé outliers from the sample and proceed with the experiment or else to ignore the outliers entirely.[20] In 1963, Mandelbrot asserted that scholars should cease ignoring the thick tails of the empirical distributions and proposed a new model of price behavior in speculative markets (see Cootner and Fama[21]). Mandelbrot's model is based on a noncentral limit theorem where the Gaussian distributions are replaced throughout by the more general family of stable paretian

---

[19] For a derivation of the necessary and sufficient conditions to assure validity of the central limit, see W. Feller, *An Introduction to Probability Theory and Its Applications*, vol. II, John Wiley & Sons, Inc., New York, 1966. A relevant example of a nonlinear process in financial analysis is the discounting of anticipated future income from a risky security in order to compute a present value.

[20] For example, M. G. Kendall (in P. Cootner, *The Random Character of Stock Market Prices*, The MIT Press, Cambridge, Mass., 1964, p. 87) discarded outliers from his sample with the assertion, "There are seven widely outlying values in the whole series, and it did not seem to be sophisticating the data to omit them from calculation of Moments." Osborne originally tended to ignore the outliers and emphasized the approximate normality of the distributions. Osborne recorded (in Cootner, *Ibid.*, p. 110), "Figures 7 and 8 support, *at least approximately*, (emphasis by the author) the conclusion of normality for $y(\tau)$, at least for intervals $\tau = 1$ month and 1 year."

[21] (1) Cootner, *Ibid.*, pp. 307–337, and also (2) Eugene Fama, "Portfolio Analysis in a Stable Paretian Market," *Management Science*, vol. II, no. 3, January 1965.

distributions. Thus, if the stable paretian hypothesis is accepted in place of the Gaussian hypothesis,[22] statistical analyses of price behavior will properly employ theoretical distributions with thick tails.

Observe that these techniques of analysis are mostly statistical in content. This means that understanding and rationalization of the behavior of stock market prices on fundamental economic and financial grounds is still lacking. Attempts must be made to increase this understanding and bridge the existing gap between theory and experiment. One such attempt was made by Renwick.[23] The key point of the Renwick paper is the suggestion that price be viewed as a ratio of two terms, each subject to error, with both numerator and denominator normally distributed. If this viewpoint is adopted, the implications are (1) one will expect the frequency distribution of price relatives for the shares of some companies to be bimodal in form instead of unimodal Gaussian and (2) growth of income and variance of growth of income can be used to discriminate between those distributions which have very thick tails and those distributions which have relatively thin tails. The main arguments from the Renwick paper are reprinted in the Appendix for Chapter 10.

---

[22] The key difference between the Gaussian hypothesis and the stable paretian hypothesis concerns the value of the characteristic exponent, α. The Gaussian hypothesis asserts that $\alpha = 2$, whereas the stable paretian hypothesis indicates a range for possible values of α: $0 < \alpha \leq 2$. Both hypotheses assume independence (i.e., no serial correlation between successive changes) and stationarity (i.e., no trend over time for either mean or variance). Then the general notion of the theory of random walks in share prices is that the changes in price conform to some probability distribution, either Gaussian or stable paretian. See, Fama (in Cootner, *Ibid.*, pp. 297–306) and E. Fama, "The Behavior of Stock Market Prices," *Journal of Business*, vol. XXVIII, no. 1, January 1965.

[23] Fred B. Renwick, "Theory of Investment Behavior and Empirical Analysis of Stock Market Price Relatives," *Management Science*, vol. 15, no. 1, September 1968.

THE DISTRIBUTION OF CHANGE IN PRICE

Some Theoretical Considerations

ASSET VALUATION. Following Lintner's exposition of generalized neo-classical capital markets,[24] we can begin the analysis of price with the assertion that capital values (including prices of corporate equity and commodities) are equal to the present value of the expected future returns as judged by traders in the marketplace.[25] Thus, if initial income (y) is received at the end of the year, and if g_j is the positive annual rate of growth of initial income during the jth future year, then the spot price any rational investor would pay (or receive) for a security can be expressed as

$$P_t = y/(1 + k_1) + y(1 + g_1)/(1 + k_2)^2$$
$$+ \cdots + y(1 + g_{n-1})^{n-1}/(1 + k_n)^n$$

$$(10.17)$$

where the k_i represent rates of discount.

Evaluation of (10.17) is expedited without loss of generality if mean values, g' and k', are substituted for the individual g_j and k_i. Also, for the convenience of eliminating an additional factor involving future sale price, the time horizon is taken to be infinite.[26] These two conditions

---

[24] John Lintner, "Dividends, Earnings, Leverage, Stock Prices, and the Supply of Capital to Corporations," *The Review of Economics and Statistics*, vol. XLIV, no. 3, August 1962.

[25] As noted by M. J. Gordon, *The Investment, Financing and Valuation of The Corporation*, Richard D, Irwin, Inc., Homewood, Ill., 1962, p. 36, instead of applying present value theory explicitly, many security analysts follow highly pragmatic and subjective methods for arriving at a share's value. However, inasmuch as these methods typically employ ratios of estimates of financial variables (e.g., price-earnings estimates), results using these methods are still subject to the findings of this study.

[26] Three observations should be made here. First, results will be unaffected whether continuous or discrete compounding is used. Discrete terms are used here to emphasize the fact that the various g_j and k_i may all be different, depending on the economic environment and money market conditions. Second, a single unique long-term average rate of discount (k') can be rationalized by combining two theories: liquidity preference and the expectations hypothesis. See R. A. Kessel, *The Cyclical Behavior of the Term Structure of Interest Rates*, Columbia University Press (NBER), New York, 1965 and Chapter 9, section 9.3. Third, in order for price to be nonnegative and finite, the series [equation (10.17)] must converge, which implies that

enable us to rewrite the convergent infinite series (10.17) as

$$P_t = [y/(k' - g')]_t \qquad (10.18)$$

where subscripts denote the time at which the components are evaluated.

Recognizing that a compound interest factor can be used to equate future income with present income, we can write

$$y_{t+\tau} = y_t \exp(r\tau) \qquad (10.19)$$

where r equals the continuously compounded nominal rate of growth of y_t over the time interval $t, t + \tau$. Then either one of the forms usually used by investigators for studying price behavior can be derived using (10.18) and (10.19). Thus, (10.20) states a simple arithmetic difference in price while (10.21), or log of both sides of (10.21), states relative price, or log of relative price, respectively. Observe that both (10.20) and (10.21) are ratios.

$$\begin{aligned} C_1 &= P_{t+\tau} - P_t = [y/(k' - g')]_{t+\tau} - [y/(k' - g')]_t \\ &= y_t[(k' - g')_t \exp(r\tau) - (k' - g')_{t+\tau}] \ / \ [(k' - g')_t(k' - g')_{t+\tau}] \end{aligned}$$
$$(10.20)$$

$$\begin{aligned} C_2 &= P_{t+\tau}/P_t = [y/(k' - g')]_{t+\tau}[(k' - g')/y]_t \\ &= [(k' - g')_t/(k' - g')_{t+\tau}] \exp(r\tau) \end{aligned} \qquad (10.21)$$

A more succinct statement of (10.20 or 10.21) is conceptually possible if one recognizes that both the numerator and denominator of either equation in fact express a best estimate selected from a range of likely values. That is, starting at any particular time (t or $t + \tau$), the marketplace estimate for both k' and g' as of that time is subject to error (due at least to the unforeseeable uncertain future). Also, investors may view income as consisting of two parts: a relatively stable permanent component and a relatively volatile transitory component.[27] Thus, a composite price change (C) can be expressed in the abstract form

$$C = (n + U)/(s + V) \qquad (10.22)$$

---

k' must always exceed g'. The requirement $k' > g'$ avoids the well-known growth stock paradox (see Section 11.1 and also D. Durand, "The St. Petersburg Paradox and Growth Stock Valuation," *Journal of Finance*, vol. 12, no. 3, September 1957, pp. 348–363) and the constraint $g' > 0$ eliminates shrinking or drying firms from further rational consideration for long-term investments.

[27] Many economists analyze income in this manner. See Friedman's permanent income hypothesis. Also, inability to perfectly forecast an uncertain infinite future is a frequent criticism of the usefulness of the present value theory for security analysis. This inability, however, in no way negates the theory. See Milton Friedman, *A Theory of the Consumption Function*, Princeton University Press, Princeton, N.J., 1957.

where n and s are constants (expected values) determined by the stable components of (10.20) and (10.21), and U and V are positive Gaussian variates (forecast errors), distributed with correlation ρ and with means μ_1 and μ_2, and standard deviations σ_1 and σ_2, respectively.

Therefore, for analysis of empirical distributions of change in price for securities which promise to pay income in the uncertain future, one relevant mathematical probability distribution appears to be the distribution of a ratio of normally distributed variates, (10.22). We now examine the mathematical and statistical properties of distributions of this type to determine the implications for financial analysis.

PROBABILITY DENSITY FOR PRICE CHANGE.   Ratios and sums of ratios are employed extensively in analyses for financial decisions. However, the explicit use of a probability density function for a ratio of a sum of ratios is rare, even though the relevant formulations are developed and documented in the literature. For example, as early as 1930, Geary[28] derived the formulation for the density of (10.22) for the particular case when n, s, μ_1, and μ_2 all equal zero, and noted that for this case the distribution has a finite mean but infinite variance.

Marsaglia[29] has updated and expanded Geary's findings. Marsaglia shows that given (10.22), the density of $(n + U)/(s + V)$ can be expressed as[30]

$$f(t) = \frac{\exp[-.5(n^2 + s^2)]}{\pi(1 + t^2)}\left(1 + \left[\frac{q}{\Phi(q)}\right]\int_0^q \Phi(V)\,dV\right) \qquad \textbf{(10.23)}$$

where

$$q = (s + nt)/(1 + t^2)^{1/2}$$
$$\Phi = \text{standard normal density}$$
$$\pi = 3.14$$

[28] R. C. Geary, "The Frequency Distribution of the Quotient of Two Normal Variates," *Journal of the Royal Statistical Society*, vol. 93, 1930.

[29] George Marsaglia, "Ratios of Normal Variables and Ratios of Sum of Uniform Variables," *Journal of the American Statistical Association*, vol. 60, no. 309, March 1965, pp. 193–204.

[30] It should be noted that Marsaglia's ratios differ slightly from Geary's in that Marsaglia uses

$$P = (n + U)/(s + V) \qquad \textbf{(10.24)}$$

where the definitions are different from those of (10.22). For (10.24), U and V are independent standard normal and $n \geq 0$, $s \geq 0$. Marsaglia (*Ibid.*) indicates that it is sufficient to study the distribution of (10.24) because translations, transformations, and/or changes of scale are always possible in order to accommodate correlation between U, V and/or negative values for n, s.

Formula (10.23) is but one of three alternative forms of the density derived by Marsaglia. This particular form is derived from both the extensively studied Nicholson's V function[31] and the bivariate normal distribution and is expressed in terms of the Cauchy density and the normal density and integral. Tables and computational procedures for these functions are readily available.[32]

The vital characteristic of (10.23) in terms of price theory is that the density of $(n + U)/(s + V)$ is unimodal or bimodal according to the region of Figure 10.1 where the point (n,s) lies, implying that as (n,s) moves away from (0,0) toward (∞,∞), the shape is altered for the probability density for change in price. The shape changes from a unimodal spike with infinite variance and moves toward a bimodal form. Marsaglia established the empirical curve that determines the two regions. The curve is asymptotic to $n \simeq 2.257$, and the rate of approach to the second mode after leaving (0,0) depends on the magnitude of n relative to s.

Now, given the formulation for price change, (10.20) or (10.21), as represented conceptually by (10.22), and given the characteristics of the density (10.23), we can proceed to develop a hypothesis for test.

Hypothesis for Test.   Consider (10.20) or (10.21) in the abstract form (10.22). The theory outlined above indicates that the density function for price change will be either unimodal or bimodal, depending on whether the point (n,s) lies to the left or to the right of the asymptote shown in Figure 10.1. But since empirical distributions of price changes for risky securities generally appear to be strongly unimodal, one can infer that the second mode, if present, is insignificant relative to the primary mode. Nevertheless, if a second mode *is* present, it may be the key to explaining price changes that lie far beyond three standard deviations from the mean. Recall from the experimental literature that the proportion of outliers contained in a large sample of price changes is also insignificant, relative to the total sample size. (Note that this is different from the prior assertion that the proportion of outliers is significantly large when compared with the tails of a theoretical normal distribution.)

If the outliers *do* constitute the second mode, then, for reasons indicated in the discussion earlier, there should exist a positive correla-

[31] C. Nicholson, "The Probability Integral for Two Variables," *Biometrika*, vol. 33, 1943, pp. 59–72; also, see N. L. Johnson, "Systems of Frequency Curves Generated by Methods of Translation," *Biometrica*, vol. 149, p. 36, 1949.

[32] National Bureau of Standards, "Table of the Bivariate Normal Distribution and Related Functions," Applied Mathematics Series 50, Government Printing Office, Washington, D.C., 1950; and Nicholson, *Ibid.*

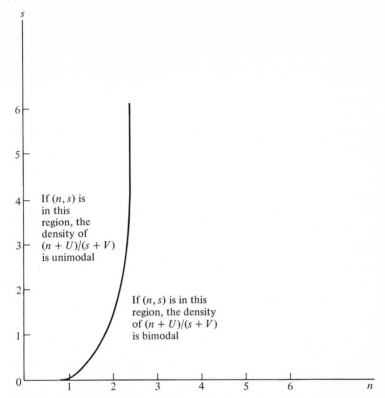

Figure 10.1. Probability density for change in price: regions for unimodal and bimodal density.

tion between the proportion of outliers and the fundamental economic factors that tend to cause a rise in n and/or a decline in s. In other words, one can test the hypothesis that the tail area for thick-tailed distributions of share-price relatives is directly proportional to factors explaining the numerator of (10.22) and is inversely proportional to factors explaining the denominator of (10.22).

Next, we proceed to refine the hypothesis into a form suitable for empirical verification. Observe from (10.21) that the numerator (n) can be taken as directly proportional to $\exp(r\tau)$, the ex-post rate of growth of income over the time interval $t,(t + \tau)$. Then for n to be large, so as to move the point (n,s) toward the bimodal region in Figure 10.1, the ex-post rate of growth of income over the period must be large. But for small values of τ (e.g., if daily changes in price are being examined), $\exp(r\tau)$ is necessarily small (how much growth can General Motors experience in one day?), thus inhibiting n from being large and nullifying the effects to be measured empirically. Hence, for empirical verification of the hypothesis, an additional measure must be obtained.

Even though indications from the model are that the proportion of mavericks varies directly with ex-post growth (along with other factors), no special statistical significance should be expected to be observed from the experiments if τ is small.

Again from (10.21), observe that the denominators can be taken as directly proportional to the change in $(k' - g')$ over the time interval t, $(t + \tau)$, assuming $(k' - g')_{t+\tau} = (k' - g')_t(F)$, where F represents some as yet unspecified factor which determines the change under consideration. Then (10.21) becomes (10.25).

$$C_2 = [\exp(r\tau)]/F = n/s \qquad\qquad (10.25)$$

Now to reduce the magnitude of s so as to move the point (n,s) toward the bimodal region in Figure 10.1, we must reduce the magnitude of the ratio $F = (k' - g')_{t+\tau}/(k' - g')_t$, which requires one of four conditions to occur. The ratio F is reduced if (1) g' rises during the time interval,[33] (2) the riskless component of k' declines over τ, (3) the risk component of k' declines over τ, or (4) some combination of the three foregoing effects occurs. To establish some specific quantities for measurement, these four possibilities can be studied further. One analysis is outlined below.

Since a rise in ex-post growth (r) is likely to cause a rise in expected future growth (g)[34] and because an increase in either r or g will give the same desired effect on s (i.e., it will tend to decrease s and shift the probability density function toward its bimodal form), empirical measurements of growth to verify the hypothesis can be made without compulsive separation into past, present, and future time categories.

---

[33] Note that any rise in g' is constrained by the growth-stock paradox so that $|g'| < |k'|$, which implies that it is necessary for k' to be a rising function of g'. Indeed, Gordon recognized a requirement for cost of capital (i.e., rate of discount) to be a *linear* function of rate growth. See Myron J. Gordon, *The Investment, Financing and Valuation of the Corporation*, Richard D. Irwin, Inc., Homewood, Ill., 1962, pp. 65–66.

However, Lerner and Carleton went a step further and asserted that a necessary condition for price maximization is that shareholders must discount growth at a faster rate than the growth rate itself (i.e., Lerner and Carleton propose that k' is a *quadratic* function of g'). For a review of some competing specifications, including one which holds that cost of capital is constant for a given class of financial risk and is, therefore, independent of growth, see Eugene M. Lerner and Willard T. Carleton, *A Theory of Financial Analysis*, Harcourt, Brace and World, Inc., New York, 1966, Chaps. 7 and 8.

[34] Indeed, many analysts forecast future growth by extrapolating the trend line representing average growth over the recent past and proceed to formulate investment decisions accordingly. Hence, it appears reasonable to use r as one determinant of growth.

But, on the other hand, there exists the risk that past or present rates of growth will fail to persist into the future. Future growth can be either higher or lower than current growth and can persist for either a long or a short time. By invoking the assumption of stationarity,[35] we can take the relevant measure of risk to be variance of growth [var(g)]. Relatively large var(g) implies relatively high probability that actual growth will deviate from the expected value. Finally, we can eliminate from further consideration alternative (2), the riskless component of k', because we are examining differences in behavior between share prices and, under the assumption of perfect capital markets, all prices of risky securities are influenced in a similar manner by changes in the risk-free market rate of interest.

In summary, the foregoing theory lends itself directly to a testable hypothesis: in making comparisons across firms, the proportion of outliers contained in the distribution of share price relatives should be directly proportional to the rate of growth of income and also should be inversely proportional to the variance of the rate of growth.

Empirical Results

The hypothesis developed above is confirmed by testing linear regressions for statistical significance.

$$\text{Mavericks} = M = a_1 + b_1(g') \qquad\qquad \textbf{(10.26)}$$

$$\text{Mavericks} = M = a_2 + b_2[1/\text{var}(g)] \qquad\qquad \textbf{(10.27)}$$

$$\text{Mavericks} = M = a_3 + b_3[g'/\text{var}(g)] \qquad\qquad \textbf{(10.28)}$$

The theory as outlined above indicates that (10.28) should exhibit the strongest relationship, (10.27) should be the next strongest, and (10.26) should be the weakest. Also, if the hypothesis set forth is true, one should be able to use the explanatory variables in (10.26), (10.27), and (10.28) to discriminate between the thick-tailed distribution and the thin-tailed distributions of change in share price. Empirical results substantiate both these predictions. Some evidence is presented below.

Regressions. Data for the dependent variable (M) are taken for the thirty stocks included in the Dow-Jones Industrial Average as published by Fama.[36] As shown in Table 10.1, Fama computed empirical

---

[35] The assumption of stationarity is conventional and enables a positive analysis. Special techniques must be applied to the probability structure of nonstationary data.

[36] Eugene Fama, "The Behavior of Stock Market Prices," *Journal of Business*, vol. XXVIII, no. 1, January 1965.

Table 10.1 EMPIRICAL FREQUENCY DISTRIBUTIONS*

The Dow-Jones 30 Industrials

Stocks					Intervals				
	0.5σ (1)	1.0σ (2)	1.5σ (3)	2.0σ (4)	2.5σ (5)	3.0σ (6)	4.0σ (7)	5.0σ (8)	> 5.0σ (9)
Unit normal	.3830	.6826	.8664	.9545	.9876	.9973	.999938	.9999994	.0000006
Allied Chemical	.4595	.7449	.8782	.9550	.9755	.9869	.996729	.9983647	.0016353
Alcoa	.4378	.7260	.8706	.9420	.9765	.9941	1.000000	1.0000000	.0000000
American Can	.4938	.7695	.8983	.9491	.9672	.9844	.995078	.9985390	.0024610
A.T. and T.	.5824	.8162	.9237	.9582	.9795	.9860	.992617	.9950779	.0049221
American Tobacco	.5394	.7818	.8893	.9462	.9704	.9844	.994544	.9968823	.0031177
Anaconda	.4300	.7075	.8785	.9522	.9757	.9933	.999162	1.0000000	.0000000
Bethlehem Steel	.4792	.7350	.8850	.9483	.9750	.9875	.996667	.9991667	.0008333
Chrysler	.4350	.7264	.8794	.9486	.9781	.9905	.997636	.9994090	.0005910
DuPont	.4336	.7257	.8825	.9469	.9775	.9936	.997586	.9991955	.0008045
Eastman Kodak	.4410	.7472	.8780	.9467	.9733	.9895	.998384	.9983845	.0016155
General Electric	.4631	.7460	.8771	.9427	.9775	.9870	.997047	.9994093	.0005907
General Foods	.4489	.7493	.8871	.9467	.9751	.9844	.997869	.9992898	.0007102
General Motors	.4716	.7455	.8859	.9571	.9792	.9910	.995851	.9979253	.0020741

Goodyear	.4638	.7487	.8898	.9509	.9854	.9914	.996558	.9982788	.0017212
International Harvester	.4408	.7450	.8967	.9475	.9750	.9875	.996667	.9991667	.0008338
International Nickel	.4722	.7635	.8833	.9413	.9686	.9871	.995173	1.0000000	.0000000
International Paper	.4444	.7498	.8742	.9433	.9758	.9869	.996545	1.0000000	.0000000
Johns Manville	.4365	.7377	.8730	.9485	.9809	.9909	.997510	.9991701	.0008299
Owens Illinois	.4778	.7389	.8909	.9466	.9717	.9838	.997575	.9991916	.0008084
Procter and Gamble	.5017	.7706	.8887	.9378	.9710	.9862	.995853	.9986178	.0013822
Sears	.5388	.7856	.9021	.9490	.9701	.9830	.993528	.9959547	.0040453
Standard Oil (Calif.)	.4584	.7348	.8724	.9439	.9764	.9917	.997047	.9994093	.0005907
Standard Oil (N.J.)	.5035	.7751	.8953	.9559	.9766	.9896	.997405	.9982699	.0017301
Swift and Co.	.4647	.7476	.8817	.9405	.9703	.9875	.997234	1.0000000	.0000000
Texaco	.4599	.7282	.8697	.9517	.9750	.9879	.998274	1.0000000	.0000000
Union Carbide	.4168	.7191	.8783	.9401	.9785	.9946	.999106	1.0000000	.0000000
United Aircraft	.4583	.7483	.8858	.9500	.9808	.9908	.997500	.9991667	.0008333
U.S. Steel	.4125	.6933	.8758	.9508	.9817	.9933	.999167	1.0000000	.0000000
Westinghouse	.4392	.7320	.8847	.9503	.9765	.9903	.997928	.9986188	.0013812
Woolworth	.4969	.7668	.8844	.9474	.9737	.9841	.996540	.9986159	.0013841
Averages	.4667	.7469	.8847	.9478	.9756	.9886	.996959	.9988358	.0011632

* Source: Fama, *Ibid.*

325

frequency distributions of daily changes in price from 1956 to 1962,[37] has compiled areas under the curve for selected intervals (measured in standard deviation units from the mean) for each of the 30 stocks (Table 10.1), and has compared these empirical distributions with the unit normal distribution, by subtracting the area under the normal curve (line 1 in Table 10.1) from the corresponding area under the empirical curve (Table 10.2). The dependent variable (M) was taken from Table 10.2, column 9, which is the excess area under the empirical curve beyond five standard deviations from the mean.[38] Observe the three identifying characteristics of the distribution of the averages (Table 10.2).

Data for the explanatory variables $[g'$ and $\mathrm{var}(g)]$ are taken for the respective corporations from the Compustat tape, using the following formulas:[39]

$$g_j = (E_{j+1} - E_j)/|E_j| \tag{10.29}$$

$$g' = \left[\prod_{j=1}^{T} (1 + g_j)\right]^{1/T} - 1 \tag{10.30}$$

$$\mathrm{var}(g) = (1/T) \sum_{j=1}^{T} (g_j - g')^2 \tag{10.31}$$

where E represents corporate earnings available for distribution to shareholders and j goes from 1956 to 1962, annually. Results are tabulated in Table 10.3.

Observe from Table 10.3, columns (1) and (3), that three companies (United Aircraft, Bethlehem Steel Corporation, and U.S. Steel Corporation) have negative rates of growth over the time period studied. Since the model requires positive values of n and s,[40] these three companies were eliminated from the sample, leaving a total sample size of 27. Summary statistics are listed at the bottom of Table 10.3 for the sample of 27 firms.

---

[37] The exact time period varies from stock to stock, but there are between 1200 and 1700 observations for each one of the 30 stocks.

[38] The numerical values are scaled by a factor of 10^4 for computational purposes.

[39] For a discussion of the theoretical implications of alternative methods of computing mean values for compound rates of discount and, by implication, growth, see H. Ben-Shahar and M. Sarnat, "Reinvestment and the Rate of Return on Common Stocks," *The Journal of Finance*, vol. XXI, no. 4, December 1966, pp. 737–742; and Reuben A. Kessel, *The Cyclical Behavior of the Term Structure of Interest Rates*, Columbia University Press (NBER), New York, 1965.

[40] Rather than complicate the experiments by changes of scale, it is judged acceptable to omit these three firms and examine a sample of size 27 instead of size 30.

Regression coefficients, relevant statistics, and tests of significance are summarized in Table 10.4. Observe that the order of significance of the regression equations is as predicted. Equation (10.28), with a correlation coefficient of .3811, is significant at the 5 percent level, according to the robust t-test, (Table 10.4, lines 6 and 7). Equation (10.27) is significant at the 10 percent level and (10.26) is not particularly significant. Thus, based on a sample of 27 firms for the years 1956 through 1962, equation (10.28) would be useful 95 percent of the time, if one were explaining the excess proportion of price changes that lie beyond five standard deviations from the average change. The inference for the market, in general, is that randomness might be important for explaining daily fluctuations in price, but significantly large changes in price can be accounted for at least in part by fundamental factors: growth and variability in growth.

Further Analysis: Identification. The second part of the hypothesis developed above indicates that it should be possible to use the explanatory variables [g', $1/\text{var}(g)$, and $g'/\text{var}(g)$] to discriminate between the thick-tailed distributions and the thin-tailed distributions of change in share price. This implication was tested and verified in two different ways. First, new regression equations were examined for a subsample consisting of only those distributions that exhibit very thick tails [i.e., the largest outliers selected from Table 10.2, column (9)].[41] The objective was to confirm that new t-tests show increased significance between the relationships hypothesized. The second set of tests involved computing the chi-square statistic with the objective of rejecting the hypothesis that all 27 samples could possibly come from the same population. The results of both tests are presented below.

For the new regressions, empirical data were extracted from Tables 10.2 and 10.3 and listed in Table 10.5. Regression coefficients and other statistics are computed and summarized in Table 10.6. Observe that, compared with Table 10.4, the significance of equation (10.28) increased from the 5 percent level to the 1 percent level. The index of multiple determination (Table 10.6, line 10) indicates that over one-half of the total variability in the excess relative frequency beyond five standard deviations is accounted for by the relatively simple statistic $g'/\text{var}(g)$. These results appear to be highly significant and confirm the

---

[41] Careful examination of the numbers in Table 10.2, column (9), reveals a "natural" grouping of the numbers. There are 8 names with thin-tailed distributions (i.e., negative values), 10 names with thick tails (i.e., positive values less than 9, after scaling as indicated in footnote 38), and 12 names with very thick-tails (positive values greater than 9). The 12 companies that constitute the very-thick-tails category were chosen for test purposes.

Table 10.2 COMPARISON OF EMPIRICAL FREQUENCY DISTRIBUTIONS WITH UNIT NORMAL*

Stocks					Intervals				
	0.5σ (1)	1.0σ (2)	1.5σ (3)	2.0σ (4)	2.5σ (5)	3.0σ (6)	4.0σ (7)	5.0σ (8)	>5.0σ (9)
Allied Chemical	.0765	.0623	.0118	.0005	−.0121	−.0104	−.003209	−.0016347	.0016347
Alcoa	.0548	.0434	.0042	−.0125	−.0111	−.0032	.000062	.0000006	−.0000006
American Can	.1108	.0669	.0319	−.0054	−.0204	−.0129	−.004860	−.0024604	.0024604
A.T. and T.	.1994	.1336	.0573	.0037	−.0081	−.0112	−.007321	−.0049215	.0049215
American Tobacco	.1564	.0992	.0229	−.0083	−.0172	−.0129	−.005394	−.0031171	.0031171
Anaconda	.0470	.0249	.0121	−.0023	−.0119	−.0040	−.000776	.0000006	−.0000006
Bethlehem Steel	.0962	.0524	.0186	−.0062	−.0126	−.0098	−.003271	−.0008327	.0008327
Chrysler	.0520	.0438	.0130	−.0059	−.0095	−.0068	−.002302	−.0005904	.0005904
Du Pont	.0506	.0431	.0161	−.0076	−.0101	−.0037	−.002351	−.0008039	.0008039
Eastman Kodak	.0580	.0646	.0116	−.0078	−.0142	−.0078	−.001553	−.0016149	.0016149
General Electric	.0801	.0634	.0107	−.0118	−.0100	−.0103	−.002891	−.0005901	.0005901
General Foods	.0659	.0667	.0207	−.0078	−.0125	−.0129	−.002069	−.0007096	.0007096
General Motors	.0886	.0629	.0195	.0026	−.0083	−.0063	−.004037	−.0020749	.0020741

Goodyear	.0808	.0661	.0234	−.0035	−.0022	−.0059	−.003380	−.0017206	.0017206
International Harvester	.0578	.0624	.0303	−.0070	−.0126	−.0098	−.003271	−.0008327	.0008327
International Nickel	.0892	.0809	.0169	−.0132	−.0190	−.0102	−.004765	.0000006	−.0000006
International Paper	.0614	.0672	.0078	−.0112	−.0118	−.0104	−.003393	.0000006	−.0000006
Johns Manville	.0535	.0551	.0066	−.0059	−.0067	−.0064	−.002428	−.0008293	.0008293
Owens Illinois	.0948	.0563	.0245	−.0078	−.0159	−.0135	−.002363	−.0008078	.0008078
Procter and Gamble	.1187	.0880	.0223	−.0167	−.0166	−.0111	−.004084	−.0013822	.0013822
Sears	.1558	.1030	.0537	−.0055	−.0175	−.0143	−.0064.1	−.0040447	.0040447
Standard Oil (Calif.)	.0754	.0522	.0060	−.0106	−.0112	−.0056	−.002891	−.0005901	.0005901
Standard Oil (N.J.)	.1204	.0925	.0289	.0014	−.0109	−.0077	−.002533	−.0017295	.0017295
Swift and Co.	.0817	.0650	.0153	−.0140	−.0173	−.0097	−.002704	.0000006	−.0000006
Texaco	.0769	.0456	.0033	−.0028	−.0126	−.0094	−.004664	.0000006	−.0000006
Union Carbide	.0338	.0365	.0119	−.0144	−.0091	−.0027	−.000832	.0000006	−.0000006
United Aircraft	.0753	.0657	.0194	−.0045	−.0068	−.0065	−.002438	−.0008327	.0008327
U.S. Steel	.0295	.0107	.0094	−.0037	−.0059	−.0040	−.000771	.0000006	−.0000006
Westinghouse	.0562	.0494	.0183	−.0042	−.0111	−.0070	−.002040	−.0043806	.0043806
Woolworth	.1139	.0842	.0180	−.0071	−.0139	−.0132	−.003398	−.0013835	.0013835
Averages	.0837	.0636	.0183	−.0066	−.0120	−.0086	−.002979	−.0011632	.0011632

* Source: Fama, *Ibid.*

Table 10.3   EXPLANATORY VARIABLES

	Company	g' (1)	$1/(\text{var}\,(g))$ (2)	$g'/(\text{var}\,(g))$ (3)
1	Allied Chemical Corp.	.087	24.310	2.106
2	Aluminum Company of America	.000	13.036	.000
3	American Can Company	.053	32.670	1.725
4	American Tel. and Telegraph	.101	814.090	82.541
5	American Tobacco	.053	525.031	27.957
6	Anaconda Company	.077	9.739	.747
7	Bethlehem Steel Corp.	−.008	19.024	−.161
8	Chrysler Corporation	.425	.133	.056
9	Dupont (Excluding GM)	.049	36.631	1.803
10	Eastman Kodak Company	.123	59.540	7.337
11	General Electric Co.	.046	43.442	1.997
12	General Foods Corp.	.086	1293.640	111.716
13	General Motors Corp.	.088	14.567	1.288
14	Goodyear Tire and Rubber	.069	111.976	7.761
15	International Harvester	.118	5.991	.708
16	International Nickel	.036	5.321	.190

17	International Paper	.016	62.067	.998
18	Johns-Manville Corp.	.088	37.966	3.347
19	Owens-Illinois Inc.	.062	39.307	2.446
20	Procter and Gamble Co.	.092	346.533	31.866
21	Sears, Roebuck and Co.	.091	195.626	17.807
22	Standard Oil Co. of Calif.	.036	211.876	7.724
23	Standard Oil Co. of N.J.	.032	47.617	1.522
24	Swift and Company	.043	6.337	.273
25	Texaco Inc.	.085	254.512	21.551
26	Union Carbide Corp.	.063	41.755	2.613
27	United Aircraft Corp.	−.008	4.162	−.031
28	U.S. Steel Corp.	−.055	15.529	−.857
29	Westinghouse Electric	.059	11.541	.676
30	Woolworth (F. W.)	.066	105.370	6.995

Summary: Number of observations—27			
Mean	.0794	161.1342	12.8056
Standard error	.0750	292.3729	26.1007
Variance	.0056	85481.9150	681.2478
Coefficient of variation	.9445	1.8145	2.0382

Table 10.4 REGRESSION RESULTS

Statistic	Eq (10.26)	Regression Eq (10.27)	Eq (10.28)
1. Constant term	11.53263	9.82840	9.95350
2. Standard error	2.46003	2.30143	2.27816
3. Regression coefficient	9.68003	.01535	.18334
4. Standard error	33.42545	.00802	.08895
5. Simple correlation coefficient	.0578	.3574	.3811
6. Students t-statistic (calculated)	.28960	1.91321	2.06127
7. Students t-statistic (book, $df = 25$)	10%: 1.708	5%: 2.060	1%: 2.787
8. Variance of residuals	163.39772	143.00742	140.13022
9. Standard error of estimate	12.78271	11.95857	11.83766
10. F-Statistic for regression equation	.0000	1.27903	1.56194
11. Index of multiple determination	.0000	.09282	.11108
12. Multiple correlation coefficient	.0000	.30467	.33328

Table 10.5 EMPIRICAL DATA FOR SUBSAMPLE
REGRESSIONS

Company	M (Excess area × 10⁴)	g′	1/(var(g))	g′/(var(g))
1. Allied Chemical	16.347	.087	24.310	2.106
2. American Can Co.	24.604	.053	32.670	1.725
3. American Tobacco	31.171	.053	525.031	27.957
4. A.T. and T.	49.215	.101	814.090	82.541
5. Eastman Kodak	16.149	.123	59.540	7.337
6. General Motors	20.741	.088	14.567	1.288
7. Goodyear	17.206	.069	111.976	7.761
8. Procter and Gamble	13.822	.092	346.533	31.866
9. Sears	40.447	.091	195.626	17.807
10. Standard Oil (N.J.)	17.295	.032	47.617	1.522
11. Westinghouse	13.806	.059	11.541	.676
12. Woolworth	13.835	.066	105.370	6.995

Table 10.6 REGRESSION RESULTS

Statistic	Eq (10.26)	Regression Eq (10.27)	Eq (10.28)
1. Constant term	15.68582	16.38322	17.08240
2. Standard error	3.43186	2.36640	2.33047
3. Regression coefficient	94.53842	.03410	.36739
4. Standard error	141.97433	.00986	.10331
5. Simple correlation coefficient	.2061	.7381	.7434
6. Students t-statistic (calculated)	.66586	3.45902	3.55630
7. Students t-statistic (book, $df = 10$)	10%: 1.812	5%: 2.228	1%: 3.169
8. Standard error of estimate	11.88832	8.19743	8.07298
9. F-Statistic for regression equation	.00000	4.98400	5.29421
10. Index of multiple determination	.00000	.49920	.51429
11. Multiple correlation coefficient	.00000	.70654	.71714

hypothesis that outliers can be explained on theoretical grounds as developed above.

Finally, the sample of 27 stocks was partitioned into two categories (thick tails and thin tails) and, on the basis of the statistic $g′/\text{var}(g)$ as tabulated in Table 10.3, a chi-square test of significance was made to determine whether samples in both categories come from the same

Table 10.7 TEST OF WHETHER 27 STOCKS CAME FROM THE SAME POPULATION

Category	Sample statistic		Total row frequency (n_i)
	$[g'/(\mathrm{var}(g)] > 1$	$[g'/(\mathrm{var}(g)] \leq 1$	
1. Thick tails (positive excess tail area)	Allied Chem. Corp.	Chrysler Corp.	20
	American Can Co.	International Harvester	
	American Telephone	Westinghouse Electric	
	American Tobacco		
	Dupont (Excluding GM)		
	Eastman Kodak Company		
	General Foods Corp.		
	General Electric Co.		
	General Motors Corp.		
	Goodyear Tire and Rubber		
	Johns-Manville Corp.		
	Owens-Illinois Inc.		
	Procter and Gamble		
	Sears, Roebuck and Co.		
	Standard Oil of Calif.		
	Standard Oil of N.J.		
	Woolworth (F. W.) Co.		

334

	Texaco Inc. Union Carbide Corp.	Aluminum Co. of America Anaconda Co. International Nickel International Paper Swift and Company	
2. Thin tails (negative excess tail area)			7
Total column frequency (n_j)	19	8	27

Chi-square:

$$\chi^2 = \left[\sum_{ij} (v_{ij} - n_j p_i)^2 / n_j p_i \right] = 7.92$$

$$df = (2 - 1)(2 - 1) = 1$$

$$\chi^2_{\text{book}} \ (df = 1): \quad \begin{array}{ccc} .05 & .01 & .001 \\ \overline{3.841} & \overline{6.635} & \overline{10.827} \end{array}$$

Conclusion: at the 1% level of significance, it is unlikely that the 27 stocks came from the same population.

population. The larger the computed value of chi-square, the less likely that the shares all come from the same population. As indicated in Table 10.7, the computed value of chi-square ($= 7.92$) indicates that, using $g'/\text{var}(g) = 1$ as the dividing point,[42] there is less than one chance in a hundred that the thin-tailed and the very thick-tailed distributions came from the same population.

Summary

Empirical distributions of price relatives for risky securities appear to be characterized by the probability density of a ratio of two terms. For empirical analysis, each term in the ratio was treated as being subject to error, with both the numerator and denominator normally distributed. Experimental data and conventional statistical tests support the hypothesis that deviations from normality can be predicted on a probability basis. The empirical evidence was developed from a non-random sample of 27 of the 30 names included in the Dow-Jones Industrial Average for the years 1956 through 1962. The chi-square test rejects, at the 1 percent level of significance, the hypothesis that the very thick-tailed and the relatively thin-tailed distributions observed in the sample both come from the same population of securities. For distinguishing between the two apparently different types of distributions, two corporate attributes were found to be significant: rate of growth of income (including both anticipated future rate of growth and realized historical rate of growth) and variance of growth. Inferences concerning the securities market as a whole perhaps could be made with greater confidence and/or increased precision if a larger-size random sample is examined.[43]

---

[42] This particular dividing point was determined subjectively by inspection of the data. The precise point, however, is not relevant to the central argument of the paper. The crucial idea is that such a point does exist and can be used to obtain results that are statistically significant.

[43] The empirical foundation for this study was chosen from Fama (*op. cit.*) for three reasons. First, Fama's work serves as a control or independent standard for verifying the shape of the empirical distributions for New York Stock Exchange prices. Second, though the 30 stocks contained in the Dow-Jones Industrial Average represent a nonrandom selection of common stocks traded, if we recognize that Fama's distributions do include at least some 36,000 data points, it becomes apparent that both the time and cost of preparing and processing a larger randomly selected sample becomes significant. Third, even a larger-size or random sample would provide no increase in precision of the statistical inference, if the assumption of stationarity is not valid. Consequently, perhaps better results could be obtained by further examination and verification of the underlying assumptions rather than by further examination of larger size sample.

On the practical level, it may prove profitable for some purposes to investigate an entirely different approach to the analysis made here. For example, it may prove worthwhile to investigate the fidelity with which other well-known mathematical distributions (e.g., Pearson's type IV or Johnson's type *Su* distributions)[44] can approximate empirical distributions of change in price.

QUESTIONS FOR STUDY

1. Explain the random-walk theory of stock market price.
    (a) What evidence (if any) is there to support the random-walk theory of stock market prices?
    (b) What are the arguments against the theory?
2. Outline and explain the evidence that historical data on the price of a stock will (or will not) enable us to improve our forecasts of the future profit from trading in the stock.
3. The articles in Cootner's book of readings show that stock prices can be simulated using random numbers; hence, it is futile to try to forecast prices. (True or false?) Explain.
4. The random-walk hypothesis is fallacious because price is a present value which is not random at all. True or false? Explain.
5. An analyst claiming to possess clairvoyant powers correctly identified the direction of change of price of seven out of nine securities drawn at random from the listings on the NYSE. What is the probability that this analyst can do at least this well if he is merely guessing and possesses no supernatural ability?
6. Can you reconcile the evidence of randomness with the fundamental theories of share price determination?
7. It has been said that the theory of random walks presents a challenge to the proponents of fundamental analysis as well as to the chartists (Eugene F. Fama, "What 'Random Walk' Really Means," *The Institutional Investor*, April 1968, pp. 38–40.) Explain why the above statement is true (or false).
8. Spectral analysis indicates that there exists high autocorrelation among changes in stock prices. True or false? Explain.

---

[44] Pearson's type IV distribution is characterized by unlimited range in both directions and is unimodal. A systematic account of the technique of fitting Pearson curves is given by Elderton. If a transformation of the variate is applicable, then the Johnson type *Su* distribution might be relevant. For a discussion of both types of distributions, see Sir W. P. Elderton, *Frequency Curves and Correlation*, 3rd ed., Cambridge University Press, London, 1938; and Maurice G. Kendall and Alan Stuart, *The Advanced Theory of Statistics*, vol. 1, Hafner Publishing Company, New York, 1961, Chap. 6.

9. Theil and Leenders use information theory to measure the success of models for prediction.

$$I(q:p) = \sum_{i=1}^{n} q_i \log_2 (q_i/p_i) = \sum_{i=1}^{n} q_i (\log_2 q_i - \log_2 p_i) \qquad \textbf{(10.17)}$$

where

$I(q:p)$ = information content of an indirect message which tells us that the odds have changed

p_i = original (prior) probability

= forecast (ex-ante) proportion of stocks advancing, declining or remaining constant

q_i = new (posteriori) probability i.e., the odds have changed after receipt of the message

q_i = actual (ex-post) proportion of shares advancing, declining or remaining constant.

If the prediction p_i is perfectly correct, then the actual outcome will provide no information, $I(q:p) = .00$. If the prediction p_i is far wrong, then the actual outcome will provide much information, $I(q:p) > 1$. Explain the rationale underlying the design of formula (10.17) and its possible application to asset management. *Note.* Theil and Leenders conclude that the long-run average proportion, $\bar{q}_i$, is a good estimate of tomorrow's proportion (p_{it}). H. Theil and C. T. Leenders, "Tomorrow on the Amsterdam Stock Exchange," *Journal of Business*, vol. 38, no. 3, July 1965; and E. Fama, "Tomorrow on the New York Stock Exchange," *Journal of Business*, vol. 38, no. 3, July 1965, pp. 285–299.

Models come in assorted sizes, shapes, types, and colors. Analogue models (e.g., slide rules) are useful in solving some problems by analogy (but slide rules cannot add). Scale or prototype models (e.g., for experimental air and spacecrafts) are useful for gaining insights into the possible behavior of the actual real-life item. Mathematical models (e.g., models of stock market price behavior) can be useful for gaining insights into the phenomena which they represent.

Models can be quite valuable—if used within the scope of their limitations. All models have some limitations; no single model is useful for everything. Even when a model is properly designed and put into actual real-life operation, unforeseen catastrophes (random fluctuations) can occur and cause disaster. To illustrate, consider, for a moment, the careful work of designing a ship. The angles are measured carefully,

Some Particular Models for Equity Valuation and Asset Selection 11

comparisons are made with designs previously successful, and artisanship at its highest is exhibited. Finally, the ship is launched and tested in the calm waters of the bay. Even in high winds, performance is excellent. The captain and the crew are delighted.

One bright morning, the captain, crew, and ship all put to sea. Within an hour, a tidal wave sweeps in from the horizon and sends the fine new ship to the bottom of the sea. All hands are saved. Back to the drawing boards.

Step away from the analogy and consider a few points:

1. There may have been nothing wrong with either the ship or the crew; the model ship may have been well constructed.
2. The condition of the sea and the presence of impending storms must be of major concern for any mariner; the condition of the market and its reaction to unforeseen events must be of major concern for any investor.
3. A ship does not always sail in calm waters of a bay; a ship fulfills

its meaning while sailing on the sea. Price of common stock is made in the market.

So it is, often enough, on the raging seas of the stock market. Models are constructed carefully. Plans are drawn and carried out with mathematical precision. But, the model does not behave. Apparently, for reasons of its own, the market can push the price of the stock up and down in seemingly uncontrollable surges. Yet, there may have been nothing wrong with the model; the model may have been well-constructed. And while no model takes all possible economic events into account, an actual price may respond to all possible economic events. After all, the worth of a stock has its meaning in the actual trading of the market: how many buyers and sellers are there, and what prices are these buyers and sellers willing to pay or receive?

With due caution, therefore, we can proceed with a thumbnail sketch of some of the models that have appeared in the literature during recent years. The object here is to present *representative models* which exhibit identifiable characteristics. The aim is to study these characteristics and learn principles and methods of analysis. From these fundamental methods, principles, and characteristics, we can learn some desirable attributes to build into our own models.

Many of the models discussed below have proved useful, not because they lead to instant riches, but rather because of they are able to provide rational and verifiable explanations of the real-world phenomenon of price behavior in money and capital markets. One important purpose of these models, therefore, is to provide insights into market mechanisms so as to enable investors to establish a more efficient and, therefore, profitable policy for selection among alternative assets.

Some models are constructed with the objective of predicting future price (or yield) so that a selection can be made among securities. Which security to pick? Other models are designed not to predict but to explain the existing structure of share price. These models are often used as a normative guide not only for investment policy but also for managerial policy within the firm (e.g., setting capital budgets, dividend policy, growth, and capital structure mix). The models discussed below focus attention on predicting and/or explaining the structure of share prices. Why are some shares $500 per share (priced at 50 times earnings) while other shares sell for $50 per share (priced at 8 times earnings) and still other shares sell for $5 per share (priced at 20 times earnings)?

The models discussed in this chapter can be classified as either logical (i.e., theoretical) or empirical. Some of the models try to be both. The logical models are developed to explain the structure of share price. The primary function of the empirical models is to describe the observed structure of share price. In one sense, the two types of models should be coincident, because a good theoretical model will in fact explain the observed structure of share price, while a good empirical model will contain the sound theoretical factors that cause the observed effect.

During the course of the discussion, it may be well for the reader to assess the strengths and weaknesses of the empirical and theoretical models in the terms of the investment uses for which they are designed.

SOME MODELS FOR ASSET VALUATION AND SELECTION.

1. Dividend-capitalization
2. Dividends vs. earnings
3. Price equals a multiple of earnings
4. Calculation of price/earnings and earnings/price ratios
5. Growth stock

11.1 The Dividend-Capitalization Model

The dividend-capitalization model dates back to J. B. Williams and a doctoral dissertation at Harvard.[1] The model was updated and subjected to additional testing by Gordon and Shapiro.[2]

The logic underlying the dividend-capitalization model can be stated simply. The (present) worth of *any* asset (including equity shares of common stock) equals the (risk-adjusted) discounted future income forthcoming because of owning that asset. In the case of common stocks, that income consists solely of dividends plus the sale price upon disposition of the stock. Corporate earnings are relevant only to the extent that earnings allow for and contribute to dividends. If earnings are retained and reinvested by the firm, then these retained earnings will grow to become dividends at some future date. These larger dividends are properly discounted from the future date to the present point in time. If the shares are sold before the new, higher dividends are in fact realized, then the future sale price will properly reflect the anticipated higher dividends still to be received. In any case, the market price is determined by the size of future dividends forthcoming, the time value of money for waiting patiently to receive those dividends, and a risk premium to compensate for the bearing of risk associated therewith. This is the straightforward logic underlying the dividend-capitalization model. An analytical presentation follows.

---

[1] John Burr Williams, *The Theory of Investment Value*, Harvard University Press, Cambridge, Mass., 1938.

[2] M. J. Gordon and Eli Shapiro, "Capital Equipment Analysis: The Required Rate of Profit," *Management Science*, October 1956; and M. Gordon, *The Investment, Financing, and Valuation of the Corporation*, Richard D. Irwin, Inc., Homewood, Ill., 1962.

The price of a stock is defined as the present value of its future stream of dividends.

$$P = \frac{D_0}{1 + k} + \frac{D_0(1 + g)}{(1 + k)^2} + \frac{D_0(1 + g)^2}{(1 + k)^3} + \cdots \tag{11.1}$$

$$+ \frac{D_0(1 + g)^{n-1}}{(1 + k)^n} + \frac{S}{(1 + k)^n}$$

where

P = present worth = market price of equity shares
D_0 = initial dividend payment expected as of the end of the next time period
g = expected rate of growth of dividends = constant
k = market rate of discount (including risk premium)
n = number of time periods in the planning horizon of the market
S = (future) market price of the shares as of the end of the planning horizon of the market

Statement (11.1) is the unconditional market price of equity shares. By applying some arithmetic, (11.1) can be simplified to

$$P = \frac{D_0}{(k - g)}\left\{1 - \left[\frac{(1 + g)}{(1 + k)}\right]^n\right\} + \frac{S}{(1 + k)^n} \tag{11.2}$$

In the special case when n equals infinity, (11.2) simplifies further to

$$P = D/(k - g) \tag{11.3}$$

where all terms are the same as stated above. Equation (11.3) is the well-known dividend capitalization model.

The simplification from (11.1) to (11.3) can be seen as follows. First, multiply both sides of (11.1) by the factor $[(1 + k)/(1 + g)]$ to obtain

$$P\frac{(1 + k)}{(1 + g)} = \frac{D_0}{(1 + g)} + \frac{D_0}{(1 + k)} + \frac{D_0(1 + g)}{(1 + k)^2} + \cdots + \frac{D_0(1 + g)^{n-2}}{(1 + k)^{n-1}}$$

$$+ \frac{S}{(1 + g)(1 + k)^{n-1}} \tag{11.4}$$

Now subtract (11.1) from (11.4) and simplify to obtain

$$P\frac{(1 + k)}{(1 + g)} - P = \frac{D_0}{(1 + g)} - \frac{D_0(1 + g)^{n-1}}{(1 + k)^n} \tag{11.5}$$

$$+ S\left[\frac{1}{(1 + g)(1 + k)^{n-1}} - \frac{1}{(1 + k)^n}\right]$$

$$P(1 + k) - P(1 + g) = D_0 - \frac{D_0(1 + g)^n}{(1 + k)^n} + \frac{S}{(1 + k)^{n-1}}$$

$$- \frac{S(1 + g)}{(1 + k)^n}$$

(11.6)

$$P(k - g) = D_0 \left\{ 1 - \left[\frac{(1 + g)}{(1 + k)} \right]^n \right\} + S \left[\frac{(k - g)}{(1 + k)^n} \right]$$ (11.7)

$$P = \frac{D_0}{(k - g)} \left\{ 1 - \left[\frac{(1 + g)}{(1 + k)} \right]^n \right\} + \frac{S}{(1 + k)^n}$$ (11.8)

Under the conditions, (1) the average rate of discount in the market (k) must exceed the long-term rate of growth (g), and (2) as n approaches infinity, then (11.8) reduces to (11.3).

Mathematically, as n becomes very large, the term

$$S/(1 + k)^n$$ (11.9)

becomes very small. In other words, money received many years into the future has little value today, regardless of the amount (S) to be received—so long as the rate of discount (k) is positive.

Model (11.8) states that if k exceeds g, then as n proceeds to become sufficiently large, the value of the expression, (11.10) approaches zero, so that (11.8) reduces to (11.3).

$$[(1 + g)/(1 + k)]^n$$ (11.10)

Examine what happens if the rate of long-term growth (g) exceeds the rate of discount (k). If g exceeds k, then, as n becomes infinite, the model, (11.3), becomes invalid. No shares ever sell at negative or infinite prices. Hence, when using the dividend-capitalization model, care must be taken to avoid the growth-stock paradox.[3]

Note that long-run average values are used for both g and k. In the short run, g can exceed k without invalidating the model so long as the long-run average growth exceeds the long-run average rate of discount.

To calculate price, D_0, k, g, n, and S all must be known. It may be of interest to estimate how long the holding period (n) must be to ignore the future sale price as expressed above in (11.8). To calculate a value for n, we can proceed as follows.

First, suppose that future price (S) is proportional to the rate of growth of the overall economy, as hypothesized in Chapter 9, and also to current price (P). Then

$$S = [a(1 + G)^n]P$$ (11.11)

---

[3] The growth-stock paradox is explained below, in detail, on page 346.

where a = constant of proportionality, G = average rate of growth of GNP over the planning horizon of the market, and other terms are the same as defined previously.

Next, assume that a present worth of one dollar or less is sufficiently small to ignore.

$$\frac{S}{(1 + k)^n} < \$1.00 \tag{11.12}$$

Then, substituting S from (11.11) into (11.12), we get

$$aP\left[\frac{(1 + G)}{(1 + k)}\right]^n < \$1.00 \tag{11.13}$$

The time horizon, n, can be solved from (11.13).

$$[(aP)/\$1.00] < \left(\frac{1 + k}{1 + G}\right)^n \tag{11.14}$$

and

$$n > \frac{\log[(aP)/\$1.00]}{\log[(1 + k)/(1 + G)]} \tag{11.15}$$

Some values for n for various values of P, k, and G are calculated and listed in Table 11.1. For convenience, the proportionality constant (a) is assumed to equal unity.

Table 11.1 CALCULATION OF TIME HORIZON

P ($)	k	G	n
50	.09	.02	58.9
50	.09	.04	83.3
50	.09	.06	140.2
50	.09	.08	424.5
100	.09	.02	69.4
100	.09	.04	98.1
100	.09	.06	165.0
100	.09	.08	499.7
500	.09	.02	93.6
500	.09	.04	132.4
500	.09	.06	222.7
500	.09	.08	674.3

If the time horizon is of the order of magnitude of 60 periods or longer, then the sale price of the shares can be ignored today, even considering the growth rate of the economy. Otherwise S must be estimated in some way if present work for the shares is to be calculated.

Concerning the required relationship between k and g, Gordon and Gangolli proved that k must be an increasing function of g. Their evidence can be summarized as follows.[4] Let k_t increase with time in any manner so long as $k_{t+1} > k_t$ for all t. Then, calculate a generalized average for the k's, taking care to avoid the growth stock paradox which is explained below. Analysis of this average shows that k turns out to be a function of g; k always has a positive rate of change with respect to g. Therefore, the inference is that k must be an increasing function of g.

The dividend-capitalization model assumes efficiency of the stock market in that shares are equal to the present value of the income (including capital gains) received from owning those shares. Prices fluctuate because present value fluctuates. The precise timing of the fluctuations is either ignored or else assumed to be instantaneous. That is, the elapsed time between change in present value and change in actual market price is assumed to be zero. Of course, this is an over-simplification of reality because information requires (finite?) time for dissemination. In reality investors who first get knowledge of a rise (fall) in present value recognize the increase (decrease) in value and imme-diately begin to increase (decrease) demand; hence, they start to bid prices up (down). As prices move in a direction toward their new present value levels, the activity of buying (selling) may cause overshoots. If shares become over- (under-) priced, then reverse action enters. Selling (buying) demand tends to push prices back to equilibrium, present value levels.

The dividend-capitalization model is concerned with equilibrium levels of price. Any rational investor is always willing to pay the (risk-adjusted) present worth, not a penny more, and sell for not a penny less. Price, therefore, equals present value. That present value is the present worth of the dividend stream forthcoming.

The assumptions and conditions for the meaning of the dividend-capitalization model as stated in (11.3) can be summarized as follows:

1. The discount rate (k) is an average value of the spot rates for money invested over the various length of time included in the planning horizon.
2. The rate of growth of current dividends (g) is the average value of all short-term rates of growth expected in the future.
3. The discount rate (k) for every security always exceeds the rate of growth (g)
4. The time horizon (n) equals infinity.

---

[4] Myron J. Gordon, "The Savings Investment and Valuation of a Corpora-tion," *Review of Economics and Statistics*, vol. XLIV, February 1962.

To illustrate the model using hypothetical figures, let

$$D = \$2.00, \qquad g = 5 \text{ perecnt}, \qquad \text{and} \qquad k = 9 \text{ percent}$$

Then the price per share is $50.

$$P = \frac{\$2}{.09 - .05} = \frac{\$2}{.04} = \$50 \qquad (11.16)$$

Shifting these figures slightly, let us imagine that we do not know what the future rate of growth will be. Actually, we do not know what that rate will be. The 5 percent is a postulated number, and it must inevitably be a postulated number in every real case as well. If the rate of discount is 9 percent, then a stock selling at $50 has an anticipated growth rate of 5 percent, if its dividend is $2. If we find good reason to believe that that company's growth rate ought to be 7 percent instead of 5 percent, then we can calculate that the stock of the company should be selling for $100 instead of $50 and we might buy the stock as being undervalued at a current price of $50. Many is the investor who has followed a formula to financial disaster!

The Growth-Stock Paradox. An interpretation of the dividend-capitalization model can be made in the context of the celebrated growth-stock paradox. The question is, How much more is a share of a growth stock worth as compared with a nongrowth share? In what way does growth affect the worth of an asset?

The growth-stock paradox tells us that no share of stock is worth an infinite price—no matter how large the rate of growth of the firm. Restated, the fundamental notion embodied in the growth-stock paradox is that investors must take care to avoid placing an excessively large value on shares of companies that have excessively high rates of growth. As a question, one can ask, "Is it possible that the market, at times, can pay too much for growth?" For an answer, Durand[5] resurrects a classic paper on probability that Daniel Bernoulli presented before the Imperial Academy of Sciences in Petersburg. The contents and results of this paper constitute the Petersburg paradox.[6]

The paradox can be illustrated as follows. Suppose you are invited to participate in a game of coin tossing. The rules of the game are, your secretary tosses a coin and continues to do so until a head occurs.

[5] David Durand, *Journal of Finance*, vol. 12, no. 3, 1957, pp. 348–363.

[6] The growth-stock paradox is also known as the Petersburg paradox. The paradox was pointed out by Daniel Bernoulli in his famous paper, "Specimen Theorial Noval de Mensura Sortis," St. Petersburg, 1738; "Exposition of a New Theory on the Measurement of Risk," trans. Louise Sommer, *Econometrica*, vol. 22, 1954, pp. 23–36.

If a head occurs on the very first toss, then she will pay you one dollar. If a head occurs on the second toss, then she will pay you two dollars. If the head occurs on the nth toss, then she will pay you $2^{(n-1)}$; that is, the payoff is doubled with each additional throw. The game and the payoffs are illustrated in Table 11.2. The question is, How much are you willing to pay for the privilege of playing this game?

Table 11.2 ILLUSTRATION OF THE
GROWTH-STOCK PARADOX

Outcome of toss	Probability of head	Payoff ($)
H	1 : 2	1
TH	1 : 4	2
TTH	1 : 8	4
TTTH	1 : 16	8
TTTTH	1 : 32	16
⋮	⋮	⋮

The expected value of the game equals infinity. But as a rational investor, are you willing to pay an infinite price for the privilege of entering this game? The expected value is defined as the payoff in the event an outcome does occur, multiplied by the probability that particular outcome will occur.

$$1/2(\$1) + 1/4(\$2) + 1/8(\$4) + 1/16(\$8) + 1/32(\$16)$$
$$+ \cdots + (1/2)^n(\$2)^{n-1} + \cdots \qquad (11.17)$$

Most scholars will argue that no rational person will pay an infinite amount to enter such a game.

Durand notes that the various attempts to resolve the paradox can be classified into three broad groups. The first group consists of those persons who deny the basic assumptions of the game. The game is unrealistic because the game must end in some finite time: at least one of the participants will ultimately die, heads or no heads. Another assumption concerns the solvency of the person making the payoff. This solvency is open to question. After 35 tails, the liability is 2^{34} or $17.18 billion. After three more tosses, the liability is 2^{37}, or more than $137 billion. Hence, even if the game stops after 100 tosses, the stakes, though finite, are staggeringly large.

The second group consists of those persons who argue from additional assumptions. The value of the game is less than its mathematical expectation. If value is assessed in terms of utility (i.e., usefulness), then the worth of the game rises as the number of allowable tosses rises from one up to some larger number. However, as the number of tosses continues to increase, the worth of the game fails to rise more. This is true because the utility of money is proportional to the quantity of money only up to a unique amount and is constant for all larger sums. In other words, ownership of $137 billion will not make many investors very much happier than ownership of only $17 billion.[7] The utility and, hence, the value of the payments cease to increase very much after a given number of tosses.

The third group consists of those persons who argue from the viewpoint of gambler's ruin. For example, the worth of a hazardous venture—be it a dice game, business promotion, or risky security— depends not only on the inherent odds and probability of payoff, but also on the proportion of the risk taker's resources that must be committed, just as the prudent gambler can demand odds stacked in his favor as the price for betting more than an infinitesimal proportion of his assets in a risky issue.

So how, then, does the Petersburg paradox and its solutions relate to growth-stock appraisal? Following the rules of the game as outlined in Table 11.2, one can develop the formula

$$(1/2)^1(\$2)^0 + (1/2)^2(\$2)^1 + (1/2)^3(\$2)^2 + \cdots + (1/2)^n(\$2)^{n-1} + \cdots. \tag{11.18}$$

If $D_0 = \$1$, then the dividend-capitalization formula, (11.1), is similar to the series in the original Petersburg problem.

$$D\left[\frac{1}{(1+k)} + \frac{(1+g)}{(1+k)^2} + \frac{(1+g)^2}{(1+k)^3} + \cdots + \frac{(1+g)^{n-1}}{(1+k)^n} + \cdots\right] \tag{11.19}$$

If the rate of discount equals the rate of growth of dividends, and this process is to continue indefinitely, then the mathematical expectation for the value of the stock is infinity. The same will be true if g exceeds k. But few growth stocks sell at a price of infinity dollars per share! However, this does not necessarily mean that the mathematical theory is wrong and must be discarded.

The three broad groups of arguments set forth above, used either individually or together, can explain why the present value of any dividend stream will be finite, no matter how large the current and temporary rate of growth. In fact, there are so many ways to accomplish the goal of scaling down the sum of the present value series, that there is no clear basis for arriving at any precise valuation. The conclusion is that conventional discount formulas do *not* necessarily provide completely reliable evaluations in all cases, particularly for growth shares.

Durand concludes his discussion of growth stocks and the Petersburg paradox by noting "...as quality deteriorates or duration lengthens, the approximations become rougher and rougher. Growth stocks

---

[7] Your author would be equally happy with only $1 billion (tax-free).

represent the ultimate in risky investments of long duration. The fact that the Petersburg Problem has not yielded a unique and generally acceptable solution to more than 200 years of attack by some of the world's great intellects suggests that the growth-stock problem offers no great hope of a satisfactory solution."[8]

11.2 Dividends vs. Earnings

It is well known that many wealthy investors and successful stock market analysts capitalize earnings, not dividends. What is the difference? Which is correct?

If used properly, there is no difference; an earnings-capitalization model is equivalent to capitalizing dividends. Equivalence between the dividend-capitalization model—complete with all its assumptions concerning infinite time horizon, and dividends growing at some identifiable rate from now to infinity—can be shown as follows. From (11.3), we restate the dividend-capitalization model:

$$P = D/(k - g) \qquad\qquad (11.20)$$

where all terms are the same as defined previously. But since dividends are paid out of earnings, we can write

$$P = (1 - b)\pi/(k - g) \qquad\qquad (11.21)$$

where π = net income (i.e., earnings) available for distribution to common shareholders and b = rate of retention of net income available for payout. Then, using the rate of return on shareholder investment (i.e., equity yield), (k) as the decision variable, we can express the yield in terms of either earnings or dividends. Thus, solving for k from (11.20), we get k expressed as a dividend yield plus a growth term,

$$(k - g) = D/P; \qquad k = (D/P) + g \qquad\qquad (11.22)$$

or else solving for k from (11.21), we get k expressed as an earnings yield plus an adjusted growth term.

$$(k - g) = (1 - b)\pi/P; \qquad k = (1 - b)\pi/P + g$$
$$= (\pi/P) + \left[g - \left(\frac{b\pi}{P}\right)\right] \qquad (11.23)$$

Statement (11.22) says that the rate of return received by the shareholder investor equals a current dividend yield (D/P) a premium plus due to growth. Alternatively, statement (11.23) says that the rate of

---

[8] David Durand *Ibid.*, reprinted in Wu and Zakon (eds.), *Elements of Investments, Selected Readings*, Holt, Rinehart and Winston, Inc., New York, 1965, pp. 179–193.

return received by the shareholder equals an earnings yield (π/P) plus a premium due to adjusted growth. Both statements are equivalent because both are based on the same formulation: the present worth of future dividends.

Since b equals the fraction of profits retained and π equals total earnings available, then $b\pi$ equals total earnings retained (and reinvested) in the operations of the business. These earnings are properly subtracted from g because they are already counted once in growth (i.e., no double-counting allowed).

Therefore, either an earnings yield or a dividend yield can be used. Both concepts lead to identical results, if properly adjusted to account for growth.

11.3 Price Equals a Multiple of Earnings

This is the classic model for equity valuation. The best exposition on the model is presented by Graham and Dodd: "The standard method of valuation of individual enterprises consists of capitalizing the future expected earnings and/or dividends at an appropriate rate of return. The average earnings will be estimated for a period running ordinarily between five and ten years.... The capitalization rate, or multiplier, applied to earnings and dividends, will vary with the quality of the enterprise and will thereby give recognition to the longer term profit possibilities which cannot be established with precision...."[9] The price-earnings model can be stated precisely as

$$P = mE \qquad\qquad (11.24)$$

where

P = warranted price of a share of stock
m = the multiple appropriate for the quality and character of firm under analysis
E = future expected earnings of the firm

The price-earnings model emphasizes the fact that price appreciation of a share of stock can be accomplished via two alternate routes: (1) from an increase in earnings per share or (2) from an increase in the multiple applied to such earnings. A stock will appreciate in price if its per-share earnings improves while the P/E multiple remains the same. Alternatively, price will rise if earnings are flat while the P/E multiple rises. Both routes provide a rise in the stock's price. To obtain a sharp

---

[9] Benjamin Graham, David L. Dodd, and S. Cottle, *Security Analysis— Principles and Technique*, McGraw-Hill, Inc., New York, 1962, pp. 422–423, 443.

rise in price, investors should seek out stocks which have both characteristics simultaneously—where earnings are growing while quality
status is also improving.

However popular, the price-earnings model, as any model, has
several deficiencies. The price-earnings formula, statement (11.24),
masks many important interactions and relationships between corporate
economic variables. In other words, the multiple (m) hides a multitude
of sins. For example, there can be causal interaction between the multiple (m) and earnings (E). The multiple implicitly includes an assumed
rate of growth of earnings (or dividends). Use of the formula can
incorrectly lead to overemphasis on predicting future corporate
earnings. Recall from Chapter 9 that the state of the aggregate economy
has much influence over market value of equity shares.

To illustrate some of the deficiencies, reconsider statement (11.23).

$$k = (\pi/P) + g - (b\pi/P)$$
$$= (\pi/P)(1 - b) + g \tag{11.25}$$

The price-earnings ratio can be solved directly from (11.25).

$$\pi/P = k - g + (b\pi/P)$$
$$= (k - g)/(1 - b) \tag{11.26}$$

$$P/\pi = \left[\frac{1}{k - g + (b\pi/P)}\right] = \frac{(1 - b)}{(k - g)} \tag{11.27}$$

That is, price equals a multiple of earnings

$$P = m\pi \tag{11.28}$$

where

$$m = \frac{1}{k - g + (b\pi/P)} = \frac{(1 - b)}{(k - g)}$$

$$\pi = \text{earnings}$$

However, statement (11.28) can be misleading because interaction
among the various factors, k, g, b, and π, is masked by m. At first
glance, it might appear that if the firm pays small dividends so that b is
close to unity, the multiple is minimum, thereby causing (other things
the same) share price to be small. At the other extreme, using this same
reasoning, if the firm adopts a policy of 100 percent payout so that b
equals zero, then m is maximum, causing price to be large. In other
words, an unsophisticated analyst may examine statement (11.28) and
conclude, "Share price varies inversely with rate of retention of earnings; price is high if retention is small; hence, to cause price to rise, dividends should be increased." The analysis presented in Chapter 8 shows
that this reasoning is wrong.

Looking at the interactions between variables, the reason for retaining income and not increasing payout is to reinvest at rates more profitable than obtainable by shareholders directly. Thus, a rise in b should be accompanied by a rise in g. And, since k is an increasing function of g, then all three factors in the denominator of (11.28) change if b is changed. Since increases in g tend to offset increases in the other two factors (g is subtracted), the ultimate effect depends upon the relative amounts of change. Thus, if retention is increased (dividends cut), then, depending upon the size of increase in g, price per share can (1) rise, (2) remain the same, or (3) fall. Each result can, and has, occurred.

11.4 Some Statistical Models for Calculating Price/Earnings and Earnings/Price Ratios

If the earnings multiple is known (or assumed), then the lion's share of attention can be allocated to the estimation of future earnings. Indeed, as a practical matter, the art of security analysis was for many years perpetuated in this way[10]: great attention was paid to corporate accounting procedures, inventory valuation methods, etc., so as to calculate the precise value of earnings. Then, this precise value was multiplied by an "appropriate" multiple to determine price. Security analysis, therefore, was viewed as consisting of two parts: (1) estimation of earnings and (2) estimation of the appropriate multiple.

Many different formulations have been proposed and used to calculate price-earnings ratios and their reciprocal (earnings-price ratios). The basic idea underlying the design of most of these models is to hypothesize those corporate (or other) factors which are deemed to be most important in explaining earnings multiples, and then to use these factors in a statistical regression model. For example, at the Bank of New York, when the question was asked, "What makes stock prices?", a vice president and economist of the bank, and an assistant secretary together answered: "growth, stability, and payout of earnings."[11] Thus a linear regression model was formulated:

$$(P/E)_N = a_0 + a_1(g) + a_2(D/E) + a_3(\sigma) + e \qquad \textbf{(11.29)}$$

---

[10] Recall from Chapter 9 that more recent studies show aggregate market factors exhibit great influence on share price, not corporate earnings alone. Therefore, the current trend in security analysis is toward including macroeconomic factors as well as corporate factors in calculating the worth of a share and is away from estimating earnings for next year.

[11] Volkert Whitbeck and Manown Kisor, Jr., "A New Tool in Investment Decision-Making," *Financial Analysts Journal*, vol. 19, no. 3, 1963, pp. 55–62. Also, see David Ahlers' extension of the Whitbeck/Kisor model. David M. Ahlers, "SEM: A Security Evaluation Model," in K. Cohen and F. Hammer (eds.), *Analytical Methods in Banking*, Richard D. Irwin, Inc., Homewood, Ill., 1966.

where

$(P/E)_N$ = normalized P/E ratio (normalized earnings are employed: That level of net income which will prevail currently if the economy is experiencing mid-cycle business conditions)

g = projected rate of growth in per share earnings (normalized) over the next 5 years

(D/E) = payout of earnings. The payout factor is calculated by dividing the sum of the past 10 years dividends by the sum of earnings over the same period in order to normalize

σ = the percentage range about trend within which earnings are expected to fluctuate over the next 5 years

e = a random error term whose expected value is zero

a_i = constant coefficients of regression

The price-earnings ratio as stated in the Whitbeck-Kisor model, (11.29), expresses a theoretical value, not necessarily an actual current market value. Whitbeck and Kisor examined and answered the question, "What makes stock prices?" as of any particular point in time. Actual market price, on the other hand, is a succession of such moments. Therefore, the average relationships expressed in (11.29) are expected to change from day to day; actual market prices are expected to converge towards the theoretical value at a rate faster than the theoretical value itself will change. As of any particular point in time, the regression (11.29) can be calculated using a cross-section of admissable companies. The actual sample used at the Bank of New York was 135 stocks of general investment interest to the bank.

Assuming that the model, (11.29), is correctly specified, then the empirical regression ought to result in (1) the coefficient a_1 being positive because, ceteris paribus, larger growth warrants larger price, (2) the coefficient a_2 being positive, if the assumption is made that, other things the same, large dividend payout is worth more than small dividend payout, and (3) the coefficient a_3 being negative because, ceteris paribus, large deviations about expectations (i.e., great instability) signify added risk, and as risk rises, value declines.

However, we recognize that the model may not be correctly specified. Some important factors, as discussed in Chapter 8, may be omitted. Also, the three variables, g, D/E, and σ may be mutually correlated, thereby giving rise to a statistical ailment known as multicolinearity. All the firms included in the sample may not belong to the same population, causing another statistical problem known as heteroskedasticity. Finally, the correct model may be nonlinear (e.g. logarithmic) instead of linear.

Whitbeck and Kisor recognize these possibilities and have since experimented with other forms of the model (11.29) and completely different models as well. For example, they have a model "B" which includes a term a_4M, where M is a dummy variable taking on a value of 7, when the stock is listed on the New York Stock Exchange; 5, when the stock is listed on the American Exchange; 4, when it is traded over-the-counter; and 3, when it is an American Depository Receipt for stock of a foreign corporation. They have a model "L" which is a logarithmic formulation of the price equation, treating the entire calculated value of price-earnings ratio from model B as a single complex variable. Then they proceed to transpose the normal earnings from the denominator of the dependent variable to the right-hand side as an independent explanatory variable and in this way calculate price. In other words, security valuation models used in actual practice are continuously being updated and refined.

After the coefficients (a_i) are calculated from the regression stated in (11.29), then, to assess the worth of any particular security contained in the sample, values for that particular company, g, D/E, and σ are inserted into the equation and the theoretical, normalized P/E ratio is calculated.

If the actual P/E ratio exceeds the theoretical (calculated) value, then the implication is *sell* because the security is "overvalued" at current market prices. This implication is true because the actual multiple is hypothesized move toward its theoretical value at a rate faster than the theoretical value will change. And, since the current value exceeds the theoretical value, within a relatively short time in the future, the actual value will proceed down towards its theoretical value.

Conversely, if the actual P/E ratio is less than the calculated (theoretical) value, then the implication is *buy* because the security is "undervalued" at current market prices. By experimental analysis, Whitbeck and Kisor found that if the ratio of actual to calculated is .85 or less, then the security is undervalued. If the ratio of actual to calculated is 1.15 or greater, then the security is overvalued.

In this way, the decision is made to buy, sell, or hold any particular security as of any particular time.

Haskell Benishay,[12] writing in 1961, designed a model to examine empirically what factors determine the differences in rates of return on corporate equities. Benishay hypothesized the earnings-price ratio as being determined by a combination of seven variables.

$$E/P = f(X_1, X_2, X_3, X_4, X_5, X_6, X_7) \tag{11.30}$$

where

> $X_1 =$ the rate of growth of earnings over the past 9 years, up to and including the cross-section year

---

[12] Haskell Benishay, "Variability in Earnings-Price Ratios of Corporate Equities," *American Economic Review*, vol. 51, March 1961, pp. 81–94.

$X_2 =$ the rate of growth in the market value of the common equity over the past 9-year period

$X_3 =$ the logarithms of the average dividend pay-out rate for the 3 years, up to and including the cross-section year

$X_4 =$ the expected stability of the future income stream; the mean value of earnings for the past 9 years, divided by the standard deviation of earnings around its trend

$X_5 =$ expected stability of the equity value; similar to X_4, with equity value substituted for earnings

$X_6 =$ the size of the firm and the liquidity of its shares, both represented by the market value of the equity

$X_7 =$ the debt-equity ratio of the firm.

The first three variables, X_1 through X_3 in (11.30), are what Benishay calls "corrective" variables. The purpose of the correction is to account for the variation in measured (i.e., actual market) yield that does *not* represent variation in true (i.e. theoretical expected) yield. For example, if the current earnings and future expected earnings are both $5 per share and the current price per share is $50, then both the measured and true yields are 10 percent. But if the expected future earnings per period are $10 instead of $5, then the true yield is 20 percent. The measured yield remains at 10 percent.

The last four variables, X_4 through X_7 are what Benishay calls "risk variables." These variables are intended to explain the way by which risk affects the worth of equity ownership.

Benishay presents theoretical justification for inclusion of these particular variables, as well as empirical evidence to support validity of the model. But even so, Benishay's model falls short of universal acceptance.[13]

Friend and Puckett[14] set out to find empirical evidence concerning the questions, "Are stockholders indifferent between current dividends and retained earnings? Is a dollar of dividends worth the same as a dollar of retained earnings?"

They wrote, "...it is our opinion that those statistical studies purporting to show strong market preference for dividends are in error."

---

[13] For some critical comments on Benishay's model and a reply, see (1) Myron J. Gordon, "Variability in Earnings-Price Ratios: Comment," *The American Economic Review*, vol. LII, no. 1, March 1962, pp. 203–209; and (2) Haskel Benishay, "Variability in Earnings-Price Ratios: Reply," *The American Economic Review*, vol. LII, no. 1, March 1962, pp. 209–216.

[14] Irwin Friend and Marshall Puckett, "Dividends and Stock Prices," *American Economic Review*, vol. LIV, September 1964, pp. 656–682; reprinted in James Van Horne (ed.), *Foundations for Financial Management, A Book of Readings*, Richard D. Irwin, Inc., Homewood, Ill., 1966, pp. 535–561.

Several reasons are cited by Friend and Puckett for these beliefs. Some reasons are: omitted variables in the regression equations (e.g., risk, and growth), regression weights influenced greatly by extreme values, random variations in income (short-run economic and accounting factors), income measurement errors (diverse accounting procedures), and least-squares bias. The regression equation can fail to take into account the fact that dividend payout differences between companies are, at least in part, the result rather than the cause of differences in price-earnings ratios. That is, if management regards a market price-earnings ratio as high, then management can order high payout and external stock financing. If management regards capitalization ratios as low, it may place heavier reliance on internal financing and consequently low payout. Also, management can be motivated by a desire to maintain only dividend-price ratios close to the average for the industry.

To test the hypothesis put forth, Friend and Puckett started by "normalizing" earnings. That is, price and dividends are always taken as normal, and short-run earnings abnormalities sum to zero over the sample of companies under analysis. Their model assumes the dividend-price ratio is always normal, but the earnings-price ratio is subject to short-run fluctuations. Their precise method for normalizing earnings is by calculating a linear underlying time trend.[15]

$$\frac{(E/P)_{it}}{(E/P)_{kt}} = a_i + b_i t + e_{it} \qquad (11.31)$$

where

$(E/P)_{it}$ = earnings-price ratio for shares of company i, measured as of time t

$(E/P)_{kt}$ = average earnings-price ratio for the entire sample of companies under analysis as of time t

Then, after having calculated the constants of regression (a_i and b_i), the normal value of earnings-price ratio for the shares can be calculated

$$(E/P)_{it} = (a_i + b_i t)(E/P)_{kt} \qquad (11.32)$$

where $(E/P)_{it}$ = normalized earnings-price ratio for shares of company i.

From $(E/P)_{it}$, normalized earnings can be calculated as

$$E_i = P_i (E/P)_{it} \qquad (11.33)$$

where E_i = normalized earnings per share, P_i = per share price, and $(E/P)_{it}$ is defined above.

---

[15] The regression is assigned a linear form by Friend and Puckett on grounds of empirical scatter diagrams.

Finally, normalized retained earnings are calculated by subtracting observed dividends from normalized earnings. The influence of dividend payout on price is subjected to time-series analysis through the formula

$$\frac{(D/E)_{it}}{(D/E)_{kt}} = a_i + b_i t + e_{it} \tag{11.34}$$

By comparing the relative earnings yields, (11.31), with the payout ratios, (11.34), insights can be obtained concerning whether time-series changes in E/P ratios are consistently associated with time-series changes in dividend payout ratios.

Empirical results are mixed. But on the whole, Friend and Puckett conclude, "Our analysis suggests that there is little basis for the customary view that in the stock market generally, except for unusual growth stocks, a dollar of dividends has several times the impact on price of a dollar of retained earnings."[16]

Arditti[17] addresses himself to the question of identifying the determinants of the required return on equity capital. Arditti attempts to measure the relation of this return with various types of investment risks. Arditti's model hypothesizes the required return on equity capital to be a function of five variables.

$$\rho = a_0 + a_1 X_1 + a_2 X_2 + a_3 X_3 + a_4 X_4 + a_5 X_5 \tag{11.35}$$

where

ρ = the required return on equity investment
X_1 = variance of the distribution of required return
X_2 = skewness of the distribution of returns
X_3 = correlation coefficient between the stock's return and return from all other stocks which comprise the shareholder's portfolio
X_4 = debt-equity ratio of the firm
X_5 = the dividend-earnings ratio of the firm

Using reasoning similar to that above for the Whitbeck-Kisor model, and assuming that the model (11.35) *is* specified correctly, the empirical regression ought to result in: (1) the coefficient a_i being positive because, ceteris paribus, larger variance means greater risk and, therefore, merits larger required return, (2) the coefficient a_2 being negative (for positive skewness) because greater skewness means larger chances for exceptionally large returns and, therefore, merits smaller worth, (3) the coefficient a_3 being positive (for negative correlation)

---

[16] Friend and Puckett, *Ibid.* Also see pp. 483–493 below.
[17] Fred D. Arditti, "Risk and the Required Return on Equity," *The Journal of Finance*, vol. 22, March 1967, pp. 19–36.

because, other things the same, larger negative correlation means smaller total risks and, therefore, merits smaller required return, (4) the coefficient a_4 being positive because, other things the same, larger ratios of debt to equity mean larger financial risks and, therefore, merits larger required returns to equity, and (5) the coefficient a_5 being negative, if one assumes that investors prefer high dividend payout, or zero, if one assumes that dividends do not matter.

Empirical results using all the firms listed in Standard & Poor's Composite Index of industrials, railroads, and utilities—over the years 1946 through 1963—indicated that in general (1) the coefficient a_1 was significant (at the .01 level) and positive as expected, (2) the coefficient a_2 was significant (at the .01 level) and negative as expected, (3) the coefficient a_3 was nowhere significant, (4) coefficient a_4 was significant but negative instead of positive, and (5) coefficient a_5 was significant and negative, not zero.

Arditti quarrels with his own results. For example, he writes: "The debt-equity ratio appeared in all regressions with a negative sign. If one were to draw conclusions strictly from these results he would say that shareholders like debt and are therefore willing to accept a lower return from firms which carry debt. *This is difficult to accept.*"[18]

However, we have found in the analysis of Chapter 8 that financing growth via additional debt instead of additional equity can be profitable to shareholders.[19] Arditti's empirical results may be both correct and explainable.

Professor James E. Walter emphasizes the influence of two factors, dividend policy and corporate profitability, on the market price of a share of common stock.[20] Walter's formula is

$$P = \frac{D + (r/k)(E - D)}{k} \tag{11.36}$$

where

$$P = \text{market price per share of common stock}$$
$$D = \text{dividends per share}$$
$$r = \text{rate of return on corporate investment}$$
$$k = \text{market capitalization rate}$$
$$E = \text{earnings per share}$$

---

[18] Arditti, *Ibid.*, p. 36.

[19] See Chapter 8, equations (8.72) through (8.98).

[20] James E. Walter, "Dividend Policies and Common Stock Prices," *Journal of Finance*, vol. 11, March 1956, pp. 29–41; and James C. Van Horne, *Financial Management and Policy*, Prentice Hall, Inc., Englewood Cliffs, N.J., 1968, pp. 180–182.

According to Eq. (11.36), so long as r exceeds k, price per share will rise as dividend payments fall. For example, if r equals 20 percent, $k = .10$, $E = \$2.00$, and $D = \$.50$, then the market price per share is $35.

$$P = \frac{.50 + (.20/.10)(\$2 - \$.50)}{.10} = \$35 \qquad (11.37)$$

If D equals zero, then using the same other values as before, the share will rise to $40.

$$P = \frac{(.20/.10)(\$2)}{.10} = \$40 \qquad (11.38)$$

Conversely, if D equals 100 percent, then market price will fall to $20.

$$P = \frac{2 + (.20/.10)(\$0)}{.10} = \$20 \qquad (11.39)$$

Therefore, one may be tempted to try to use formula (11.36) to maximize price per share with respect to dividend payments.

$$\partial P/\partial D = (1/k) - (r/k^2) = 0; \qquad r = k \qquad (11.40)$$

The results from (11.40) imply that $r = k$ satisfies the necessary condition; but the test fails to show whether a maximum or minimum price has been achieved because no second derivative exists. Put a different way, by substituting $r = k$ back into formula (11.36), dividends subtract out so that price equals discounted earnings.

$$P = E/k \qquad (11.41)$$

The reduced formula (11.41) states that dividends are not relevant to the question of maximizing share price. Note that according to the formula (11.36), if r is less than k, price per share rises as dividend payments rise. Recall from our previous analyses in Chapter 8 that if a firm earns less from business operations than the market rate of discount, then the optimal strategy is to liquidate the business and invest the proceeds at the ever-obtainable market rate of discount.

In 1959, James E. Walter[21] undertook a study to find out the linear combination of financial characteristics that best "discriminates" large industrial corporations with low ratios of earnings (per share) to (common stock) price from those firms having high ratios. By best discriminates, Walter means that the chance of erroneous classification is approximately minimal. Walter uses the *Fortune* list of 500 industrial

---

[21] James E. Walter, "A Discriminant Function for Earnings Price Ratios of Large Industrial Corporations," *The Review of Economics and Statistics*, vol. XLI, no. 1, February 1959, pp. 44–52.

firms and a linear discriminant function containing six discriminating variables.

$$Z = k_1 X_1 + \cdots + k_6 X_6 \tag{11.42}$$

where

$$Z = \text{earnings-price ratio for the firm}$$
$$X_1 = \text{dividend policy of the firm}$$
$$X_2, X_5 \text{ (together)} = \text{the willingness and ability of the firm to grow and the profitability of that growth}$$
$$X_3, X_4 \text{ (together)} = \text{the solvency and/or liquidity of the firm}$$
$$X_6 = \text{the relative stability of common stock price over a 12-year period (\textit{Value Line Index of Stability})}$$

More precisely,

$$X_1 = \sum_{t=1952}^{1955} D_{ti} \bigg/ \sum_{t=1952}^{1955} E_{ti} \tag{11.43}$$

$$X_2 = [(E_{t+3,i} - E_{t-1,i}) + .5(I_{t+3,i} - I_{t-1,i})] \bigg/ [.5 \sum_{t=1952}^{1955} C_{ti} + (A_{t+3,i} - A_{t-1,i})] \tag{11.44}$$

$$X_3 = \sum_{t=1952}^{1955} A_{ti} \bigg/ \sum_{t=1952}^{1955} L_{ti} \tag{11.45}$$

$$X_4 = \sum_{t=1952}^{1955} I_{ti} \bigg/ \sum_{t=1952}^{1955} (E + .5I)_{ti} \tag{11.46}$$

$$X_5 = \left[\sum_{t=1952}^{1955} S_{ti} \bigg/ \sum_{t=1948}^{1951} S_{ti} \right] \times 100 \tag{11.47}$$

where

$$D = \text{total dividends paid out}$$
$$E = \text{net earnings}$$
$$I = \text{total interest paid by the company}$$
$$C = \text{capital expenditures}$$
$$A = \text{current assets}$$
$$L = \text{current liabilities}$$
$$S = \text{annual sales}$$
$$t \text{ denotes the } t\text{th year}$$
$$i \text{ denotes the } i\text{th company}$$

Walter's empirical results showed that it is possible to use financial characteristics to distinguish firms with small E/P ratios from firms with large E/P ratios. Walter draws no conclusion concerning the optimal number of variables necessary to accomplish the distinction. Of the six variables which he used, dividend payout (X_1) and stability of price (X_6) were assigned the largest weights in the discriminant function. The remaining variables, X_2 through X_5, were less clearly differentiated between groups.

11.5 Some Growth-Stock Models

This section discusses two models which are concerned primarily with growth stocks. The models were published originally by Professor Burton Malkiel and Professor Charles Holt.

Malkiel's Model was published in 1963. After an extensive study of equity yields, growth and structure of share prices, Professor Malkiel summarized his findings in the following model.[22]

$$P = \frac{D(1 + g)}{(1 + \bar{r})} + \frac{D(1 + g)^2}{(1 + \bar{r})^2} + \cdots + \frac{D(1 + g)^N}{(1 + \bar{r})^N} + \frac{\bar{m}_s E(1 + g)^N}{(1 + \bar{r})^N}$$

$$(11.48)$$

where

P = the present value of the future stream of receipts, i.e., the value of the common share today

D = dividends per share in the past fiscal year. Dividends are assumed to be paid out annually as of the end of each fiscal year

g = the expected growth rate of earning per share and dividends per share over the next N years

$\bar{m}_s$ = the standard multiple of earnings (i.e., the multiple of a nongrowth share). The subscript s refers to the earnings of the standard (nongrowth) share

$\bar{r}$ = the apparent marginal efficiency of a representative share

E = current earnings of the growth shares

The reader should compare Malkiel's model, Eq. (11.48), with the dividend-capitalization model, Eq. (11.1).

Malkiel points out that (1) the warranted price-earnings ratio (m) that can be paid for a growth stock will always exceed the standard earnings multiple ($\bar{m}_s$) and (2) the premium over the standard earnings multiple is an increasing function of the rate of growth itself (g). The analysis can proceed as follows.

Summing the factors in (11.48) in a way similar to the simplification of (11.1), and dividing through by E, the current price-earnings ratio can be calculated.

$$(P/E) = m = \frac{(D/E)(1 + g)}{(\bar{r} - g)}\left\{1 - \left[\frac{(1 + g)}{(1 + \bar{r})}\right]^n\right\} + \frac{\bar{m}_s(1 + g)^N}{(1 + \bar{r})^N}$$

$$(11.49)$$

Note that it may appear from (11.49) that the multiple changes as the dividend payout changes, $(\partial m/\partial D) > 0$; but Malkiel explicitly notes

---

[22] Burton G. Malkiel, "Equity Yields, Growth, and the Structure of Share Prices," *The American Economic Review*, vol. LIII, no. 5, December 1963.

that the formula omits the possible relationship between dividend payments per share and the ability to achieve future earnings growth per share. Malkiel writes, "It could well be that $\partial m/\partial D = 0$ because, while the effect of a large dividend per share would tend to increase m, the lower terminal value per share might reduce m by an exactly equal amount."[23]

In the special case of a growth stock which pays *no* dividends, $D = 0$ causing the multiple in (11.49) to reduce to

$$m = \bar{m}_s \frac{(1 + g)^N}{(1 + \bar{r})^N} \qquad (11.50)$$

Equation (11.50) states that the multiple of the growth stock (m) equals the standard multiple ($\bar{m}_s$) times some factor which is always greater than unity. The price of a share of growth stock can then be written

$$P = \left[\bar{m}_s \frac{(1 + g)^N}{(1 + \bar{r})^N}\right] E \qquad (11.51)$$

Hence, the price of a growth stock which pays no dividends can be stated in terms of the price-earnings ratio for a representative standard share. [NOTE: Beware of the growth-stock paradox and infinite price.]

Based on the above formulations, Malkiel draws several conclusions. He writes, "We conclude, then, that in one important respect growth stocks are intrinsically different from standard issues. When the level of share prices changes, the prices of growth stocks must fluctuate more than proportionately if the structure of share prices is to remain unchanged....Growth stocks are inherently more volatile than standard issues."[24]

Professor Charles Holt,[25] writing in 1962, called attention to the point that a company's high rate of growth can come to an end at any time. When growth stops, share price falls. The object of analysis, therefore, is to calculate the time duration of growth.

Holt's model assumes that the growth in earnings per share (adjusted for stock dividends and splits) of a company will continue at a constant high rate until some point in time when the rate will drop abruptly to the average rate for nongrowth companies. Then, under this assumption, the duration of growth for a company is defined as the time duration of the high growth rate. The time duration of growth can be calculated as follows.

[23] Malkiel, *Ibid.*

[24] Malkiel, *Ibid.*

[25] Charles Holt, "The Influence of Growth Duration on Share Prices," *Journal of Finance*, vol. 17, no. 3, 1962, pp. 465–475.

First, earnings per share as of the end of future year t are hypo-thesized to be proportional to (1) the current level of earnings per share, (2) the annual rate of growth of current earnings per share, (3) the dividend yield, and (4) the number of years in the interim time.

$$E_t \approx E_0[1 + (\Delta E)/E + (D/P)]^t \qquad (11.52)$$

where

E_t = total earnings per share at the end of year t
E_0 = total current earnings per share
$(\Delta E)/E$ = the percent per annum growth rate of earnings per share
(D/P) = the constant percent per annum dividend yield (i.e., ratio of dividends to market price)
t = time duration of growth

To consider the warranted price-earnings ratio for growth shares in relation to the warranted price-earnings ratio for standard (non-growth) shares, Holt writes the ratio

$$\frac{(P_0/E_0)_{growth}}{(P_0/E_0)_{standard}} \approx \left\{\frac{1 + [(\Delta E)/E]_g + (D/P)_g}{1 + [(\Delta E)/E]_s + (D/P)_s}\right\}^t \qquad (11.53)$$

where the subscript g indicates growth stock, the subscript s indicates standard shares, and other terms are the same as defined previously.

Then, the time duration of growth (t) can be calculated by taking the logarithm of both sides of (11.53) or else by plotting a graph.

$$t = \frac{\log (m_g/m_s)}{\log \{[1 + (\Delta E/E)_g + (D/P)_g]/[1 + (\Delta E/E)_s + (D/P)_s]\}} \qquad (11.54)$$

where m_g = current multiple for the growth stock and m_s = current multiple for the standard share.

To illustrate application of (11.54), suppose the following data are given.

$$m_g = 45, \quad [(\Delta E)/E]_g = .30, \quad (D/P)_g = .01 \quad (11.55)$$

$$m_s = 15, \quad [(\Delta E)/E]_s = .05, \quad (D/P)_s = .05 \quad (11.56)$$

Then substitution of these values into (11.54) indicates that $t = 6$. In words, the market is valuing the growth stock as if its present high rate of growth of 30 percent will continue for 6 years and then decline sharply to the normal (market) level of 5 percent per year. The time duration of the high rate of growth in this case is 6 years.

Alternatively, application of (11.54) using the data given above can proceed as follows. A growth rate of 30 percent is 25 percentage points larger than the normal (stated market) rate of 5 percent. Considering that this high rate is forecast (by the model) to persist for 6 years, the earnings per share of the growth stock will improve by almost a factor of four. That is

$$(1 + .25)^6 = 3.82 \tag{11.57}$$

Finally, if independent estimates are made for the time duration of growth, Holt's model can be used to calculate the warranted price-earnings ratio for the growth stock. That is, knowing the value of all factors on the right-hand side of (11.53), including t, we can write

$$(P_0/E_0)_{\text{growth}} = m_s \left\{ \frac{1 + [(\Delta E)/E]_g + (D/P)_g}{1 + [(\Delta E)/E]_s + (D/P)_s} \right\}^t \tag{11.58}$$

where all terms are the same as defined previously. Statement (11.58) is the price-earnings ratio warranted by the assumed duration of growth. This warranted value can be compared with the actual current price-earnings ratio, and buy-sell decisions can be made accordingly.

11.6 The Extended-Dividend-Capitalization Model

This model, which represents an attempt to integrate stock valuation with the capital budgeting decision was developed by Professors Eugene Lerner and Willard Carleton.[26] Three principal notions characterize the L-C model. They are (1) an earnings opportunity schedule, (2) a financial constraint, and (3) a security valuation model.

The L-C model starts where the dividend-capitalization model, (11.59), ends.

$$P = D/(k - g) \tag{11.59}$$

Since dividends must be paid from earnings, then assuming no debt and ignoring taxes, (11.59) is the same as

$$P = \frac{(1 - b)rA}{k - rb} \tag{11.60}$$

Solving (11.60) for r, we get

$$r = \frac{kP}{b(P - A) + A} \tag{11.61}$$

where

P = market price of all shares outstanding
b = rate of retention of corporate profits

---

[26] Eugene M. Lerner and Willard T. Carleton, *A Theory of Financial Analysis*, Harcourt, Brace & World, Inc., New York, 1966.

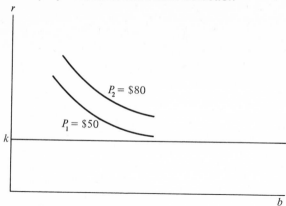

Figure 11.1. Isoprice curves.

r = rate of return on corporate assets
A = book value of total assets
k = market rate of discount of future stream of dividends
rb = rate of growth of dividends (assuming no debt)

Then for given levels of A and k, isoprice curves can be plotted using alternative combinations of b and r in (11.61). These isoprice curves are illustrated in Figure 11.1. Figure 11.1 shows how alternative combinations of r and b can result in the same price per share.

However, no share price ever reaches infinity dollars. Aside from the growth-stock paradox, constraints in product, factor, and financial markets all interact to limit the maximum permissible price. Lerner and Carleton hypothesize that constraints in product and factor markets behave according to an L-C function and that constraints in financial markets behave according to an F-C function.

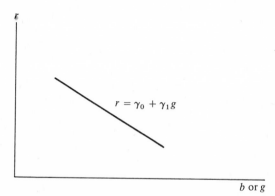

Figure 11.2. Earnings opportunity constraint.

The earnings opportunity constraint (or L-C function) expresses the relationship between corporate growth and corporate profitability. This function is depicted in Figure 11.2.

$$r = \pi/A = \gamma_0 + \gamma_1 g \tag{11.62}$$

where

r = rate of return on corporate assets
π = income (before taxes and fixed charges; after depreciation)
A = level of total assets (book value)
γ_0 = some positive constant (intercept value)
γ_1 = a negative constant, depending upon the slope of the demand schedule, the slope of the cost schedule, and the ratio of output-to-capital
g = rate of growth of corporate output

The hypothesis underlying the formulation of the L-C function, Equation (11.62), is that profits are a linear homogeneous function of two factors: level of assets and rate of change in level of assets. The detailed examination required to arrive at this conclusion begins with an analysis of profits for the firm. Thus, if all produced goods and services are sold, the accounting profits for one time period will be

$$\pi = (p - c)Q \tag{11.63}$$

where

π = average profits
p = average revenue per unit of output
c = average cost per unit of output
Q = average flow of output into the market

Three assumptions are now invoked. They are

1. Revenues fall as output rises, $(\partial p/\partial Q) < 0$. This decline in revenues occurs because of product market characteristics (e.g., the relative inelasticity of demand facing the typical giant industrial corporation whose securities are traded on the New York Stock Exchange, or the effects of other firms that produce substitute or complement products).
2. Costs rise as output increases, $(\partial c/\partial Q) > 0$. This rise in costs occurs because of factor market characteristics such as upward-sloping cost schedules (due to the necessity for large firms to bid away labor and capital from alternative employment when expansion of output is desired), or because of constraints such as limited technology or inefficiencies that occur when full employment of production capacity is approached.
3. Output is directly related to assets, $Q = \lambda A$, where λ = ratio of output to capital and A = total assets. The ratio λ is assumed to be constant for a firm.

Using these three assumptions along with the profit equation (11.63), the hypothesis underlying the earnings opportunity schedule asserts that because increased output will be accompanied by both increased costs and reduced revenues, profits will fall if either the rate of growth of assets or the level of assets increases. Specifically, growing firms will experience a secular decline in their rate of return.

However, the real-world marketplace may not conform to assumptions such as those listed above. In an actual economy, growth in national income, rising levels of technology, increasing supply of knowledgeable and skilled labor, increasing variety and quality of goods and services, more and different physical capital, increased competition among buyers and sellers, and changes in consumer tastes all interact to violate each of the three outlined assumptions. Considering these violations, Lerner and Carleton argue that instead of a secular decline in the rate of return on assets, corporate profitability should remain constant so long as assets are maintained at some fixed level.

The above reasoning is expressed mathematically by Lerner and Carleton as

$$\pi_t = a_0 A_t + a_1 \left(\frac{dA_t}{dt} \right) \tag{11.64}$$

where a_0 and a_1 represent constants of proportionality, dA_t/dt represents the rate of change of assets over time, and other terms are as defined previously. Equation (11.64) indicates that if assets are maintained at some fixed level, then $dA_t/dt = 0$ so that $\pi_t/A_t = a_0$. Then a_0 is the rate of return on assets (r) and a measure of corporate profitability. For a given level of assets, then, r should equal a constant, altered by some fraction of the rate of change of that level. On the basis of the above considerations, the L-C function is finally hypothesized to be

$$r = \gamma_0 + \gamma_1 \frac{\Delta A}{A} + u \tag{11.65}$$

where

r = rate of return on assets

γ_0 = a positive constant which reflects, as of any particular point in time, the effects of the three assumptions outlined above, as well as the period-by-period shifts that can occur over time to alter the assumptions

γ_1 = a negative constant which reflects the assumptions of relatively inelastic demand and upward sloping cost schedules, which cause revenues to decline and costs to rise as assets and output both increase

$\Delta A/A$ = percentage change in assets. This represents the rate of growth of corporate assets for one time interval. If $Q = \lambda A$

as specified in one of the assumptions, then $\Delta A/A$ also equals the rate of growth of output $(\Delta Q/Q)$ for that time interval, assuming $\lambda =$ constant

$u =$ a Gaussian random-error term with zero mean and finite variance

Consequently, the earnings opportunity schedule facing the firm is hypothesized to be a downward-sloping function that can shift its relative position over time. This function specifies the maximum rate of profit that a firm can earn for a given rate of growth.

The financial constraint in the L-C model expresses the relationship between the cost of borrowing and financial risk. The F-C function is intended to describe supply, demand, and risk conditions that prevail in financial markets. The hypothesis underlying specification of the financial constraint is that the cost of debt is proportional to the financial risk exposure that a company offers the debtholder. The F-C function is written

$$i = \delta(L/E) \qquad\qquad \textbf{(11.66)}$$

where

$i =$ rate of interest paid on total debt
$\delta =$ a constant of proportionality
$L =$ total liabilities (debt)
$E =$ total equity (shares)
$L/E =$ ratio of debt to equity

Equation (11.66) contains four requirements: (1) equity must be positive in order for "cost of debt" to be a meaningful phrase. This is so, in view of the fact that few debt funds will be forthcoming in the absence of prior equity funds, (2) debt can be zero, in which case the cost of debt is zero, (3) increasing debt, relative to equity, exposes the debtholder to increasing financial risk, thereby raising the cost of debt. Of course, Lerner and Carleton recognize that the precise functional relationship between i and L/E can be nonlinear instead of linear as indicated in equation (11.66); nevertheless, the conceptual treatment is the same as indicated here, and (4) increasing equity, relative to debt, exposes the debtholder to less risk, thereby lowering the cost of debt.

Other factors that influence the cost and supply of funds, such as the risk-return preferences of both borrowers and lenders, level of the aggregate interest rate, size and stability of the firm, and the quality of management, all are assumed to be constant. Thus, the particular formulation for the financial constraint is not rigid but rather reduces to some functional relationship between the cost of debt and the financial risk exposure of the firm. To emphasize the tentative and conceptual nature of equation (11.66), Lerner and Carleton suggest, but do not explore, the alternative possibility

$$i = \delta(L/E)/r, \qquad\qquad \textbf{(11.67)}$$

where all terms are as defined previously.

Equation (11.67) indicates that in addition to the previous considerations, the cost of debt can be inversely proportional to the rate of return earned on corporate assets. This will be true if more profitable firms exhibit less financial risk than less profitable firms. The L-C and F-C functions together define the two constraints that limit the profitable growth of a corporation.

Lerner and Carleton proceed to develop a more complete specification for k, the rate of discount in the security valuation model, and then maximize share price subject to the two operating constraints. The rationale underlying the specification for k can be summarized as follows. Let the risk adjusted rate of discount, k, be expressed as a certainty-equivalent return function (see page 396).

$$\text{Utility}(k) = E(k) - A\text{var}(k) \qquad\qquad \textbf{(11.68)}$$

where

$$\begin{aligned}
\text{Utility}(k) &= \text{certainty-equivalent return function} \\
E(k) &= \text{expected rate of return on shareholder investment} \\
A > 0 &= \text{a constant denoting aversion to risk} \\
\text{var}(k) &= \text{a measure of the risk that is associated with the} \\
& \quad\; \text{stated expected rate of return}
\end{aligned}$$

[Note: Compare (11.68) with (12.35).] Then since k is a function of growth, g, one can infer that $\text{var}(k)$ is proportional to $\text{var}(g)$. The implication for financial analysis is that the denominator of equation (11.59) can be written as the rate that applies to long-term government securities, minus a certainty-equivalent growth rate. That is,

$$(k - g) = [\alpha + s\text{var}(g)] - E(g) = \alpha - CE(g) \qquad \textbf{(11.69)}$$

where

$$\begin{aligned}
\alpha &= \text{alternative yield available from a safe, long-term invest-} \\
& \quad\; \text{ment (e.g. government bonds)} \\
s &= \text{investor's risk-aversion coefficient} \\
g &= E(g) = \text{mean growth rate of the expected future income} \\
& \quad\qquad\;\; \text{stream} \\
\text{var}(g) &= \text{variance of expected growth rate} = \text{measure of risk} \\
CE(g) &= \text{certainty-equivalent growth rate} \\
&= E(g) - s\text{var}(g)
\end{aligned}$$

Further, using the L-C function, equation (11.65), in the form

$$g = \frac{r - \gamma_0 - u}{\gamma_1} \tag{11.70}$$

where all the terms are as defined previously, one can write

$$
\begin{aligned}
\text{var}(g) &= E[g - E(g)]^2 \\
&= E\left[\frac{(r - \gamma_0 - u)}{\gamma_1} - \frac{(r - \gamma_0)}{\gamma_1}\right]^2 \\
&= \frac{\text{var}(u)}{\gamma_1^2} = u^2/\gamma_1^2
\end{aligned}
\tag{11.71}
$$

Now, using economic theory[27] to reason that

$$\text{var}(u) = c(g)^2 \tag{11.72}$$

where c = a constant of proportionality, Lerner and Carleton specify the discount rate to be

$$k = \alpha + \frac{\Psi}{\gamma_1^2}(g)^2 \tag{11.73}$$

where Ψ = a constant of proportionality that includes risk aversion preferences of investors.

Finally, the complete L-C model can be stated as follows. Using equations (11.59), (11.73), (11.74), and (11.75), the dividend-capitalization model becomes[28]

$$P = \frac{D}{k - g} = \frac{(1 - b)[r + (r - i)L/E]E}{\alpha + (\Psi/\gamma_1^2)(g)^2 - g} \tag{11.76}$$

---

[27] See Lerner and Carleton, *op. cit.*, p. 142.

[28]

$$D = (1 - T)(1 - b)\pi \tag{11.74}$$

where

    D = total dividends paid to shareholders
    T = corporate tax rate, assumed to be zero for simplicity
    π = total profits available for distribution among common shares
    b = rate of retention of profits, which is a corporate policy decision variable

$$
\begin{aligned}
\pi &= rA - iL \\
&= r(E + L - iL \\
&= [r + (r - i)L/E]E
\end{aligned}
\tag{11.75}
$$

where

    rA = total profits before interest and taxes
    iL = total interest paid on the debt outstanding

Since from equation (11.77) we get[29]

$$b = \frac{g}{r + (r - i)L/E} \qquad (11.78)$$

equation (11.76) reduces further to

$$P = \frac{[r + (r - i)L/E - g]E}{\alpha + (\Psi/\gamma_1^2)(g)^2 - g} \qquad (11.79)$$

Since corporate managers must act within constraints imposed upon them by product, factor, and financial markets, and since managers should act in the best interests of the shareholders, one of the goals of management can be to maximize the market value of the firm. Hence Lerner and Carleton proceed to maximize share price subject to constraints (11.65) and (11.66). This is achieved by substituting the two constraints directly into equation (11.79) and differentiating. This substitution yields the complete Lerner-Carleton model:

$$P = \frac{[\{r + [r - \delta(L/E)]L/E\} - (r - \gamma_0)/\gamma_1]E}{\alpha + (\Psi/\gamma^2)[(r - \gamma_0)/\gamma_1]^2 - [(r - \gamma_0)/\gamma_1]} \qquad (11.80)$$

Then, in order to answer some strategic questions in corporation finance [for example, to determine the optimal level of capital budget (r), the optimal capital structure mix (L/E), the optimal rate of growth of production (g), the optimal rate of retention (b), and the cost of equity capital (k)], Lerner and Carleton proceed to maximize price by taking $\delta P/\delta r = 0$ and $\delta P/\delta(L/E) = 0$ for equation (11.80) and then solving these two differential equations simultaneously for values of r and L/E. Using the two constraints (11.65) and (11.66) and the previously determined values for r and L/E, values can be calculated for g and b. Finally, since α is exogenous, equation (11.73) can be used to calculate the cost of capital (k). In this manner, the complete L-C model is solved.

29

$$g = b[r + (r - i)L/E] \qquad (11.77)$$

If $L = 0$ (assuming no debt, for simplicity), then equation (11.77) reduces to $g = br$.

A BIBLIOGRAPHY FOR STOCK VALUATION MODELS

The purpose of this appendix is to list some representative models that have appeared in the literature. For convenience, the models can be placed in one of three categories and identified by the name of the author(s) proposing the model. The authors and categories are

1. General models for the valuation of corporate assets
   Durand
   Modigliani and Miller
   Lintner
2. Theoretical/empirical models for the valuation of equity investment

J. B. Williams	Solomon
Robichek and Myers	Miller and Modigliani
Gordon and Shapiro	Gordon
Walter	Lerner and Carleton

3. Statistical models for estimating relative change in price

Whitbeck and Kisor	Graham and Dodd
Ahlers	Walter
Benishay	Holt
Friend and Puckett	Malkiel
Miller and Modigliani	Sharpe
Arditti	Lintner
King	Bower and Bower
Fama	Renwick

In addition to equity valuation models, there are portfolio models as discussed in Part IV of the book.

Arditti, Fred D., "Risk and the Required Return on Equity," *The Journal of Finance*, vol. 22, March 1967, pp. 19–36.

Benishay, Haskel, "Variability in Earnings–Price Ratios of Corporate Equities," *American Economic Review*, vol. 51, March 1961, pp. 81–94.

Bower, Richard S. and Dorothy H. Bower, "Risk and the Valuation of Common Stock," *Journal of Political Economy*, vol. 77, no. 3, June 1969, pp. 349–362.

Durand, D., "Costs of Debt and Equity Funds: Trends and Problems," reprinted in Solomon, *The Management of Corporate Capital*, The Free Press of New York, 1964, pp. 91–116.

Fama, Eugene F., "Mandelbrot and the Stable Paretian Hypothesis," printed in Cootner, *The Random Character of Stock Market Prices*, The MIT Press, Cambridge, Mass., 1964.

———, "The Behavior of Stock Market Prices," *Journal of Business*, vol. XXVIII, no. 1, January 1965.

———, "Portfolio Analysis in a Stable Paretian Market," *Management Science*, vol. 11, no. 3, January 1965, pp. 404–419.

———, "Tomorrow on the New York Stock Exchange," *Journal of Business*, vol. 38, no. 3, July 1965, pp. 285–299.

———, "Risk, Return and Equilibrium: Some Clarifying Comments," *The Journal of Finance*, vol. XXIII, no. 1, March 1968, pp. 29–40.

Friend, Irwin, and Marshall Puckett, "Dividends and Stock Prices," *American Economic Review*, vol. LIV, September 1964, pp. 656–682.

Gordon, M. J., *The Investment, Financing and Valuation of the Corporation*, Richard D. Irwin, Inc., Homewood, Ill., 1962.

———, "Variability in Earnings—Price Ratios: Comment," *The American Economic Review*, vol. LII, no. 1, March 1962, pp. 203–208.

———, "The Savings Investment and Valuation of a Corporation," *Review of Economics and Statistics*, vol. XLIV, February 1962.

Gordon, M. J., and Eli Shapiro, "Capital Equipment Analysis: The Required Rate of Profit," *Management Science*, vol. 3, October 1956.

Graham, Benjamin, David L. Dodd, and Sidney Cottle, *Security Analysis, Principles and Technique*, McGraw-Hill, Inc., New York, 1965.

Holt, Charles C., "The Influence of Growth Duration on Share Prices," *The Journal of Finance*, vol. XVII, no. 3, September 1962.

King, Benjamin F., "Market and Industry Factors in Stock Price Behavior," *The Journal of Business*, vol. XXXIX, no. 1, January 1966, pp. 139–167.

Lerner, Eugene M., and Willard T. Carleton, *A Theory of Financial Analysis*, Harcourt, Brace & World, Inc., New York, 1966; also see Renwick, Fred B., "Economic Growth and Distributions of Change in Stock Market Prices," *Industrial Management Review*, Spring Issue 1968, pp. 39–67.

Lintner, John, "Dividends, Earnings, Leverage, Stock Prices and the Supply of Capital to Corporations," *The Review of Economics and Statistics*, vol. XLIV, no. 3, August 1962.

———, "The Valuation of Risk Assets and the Selection of Risky Investments in Stock Portfolios and Capital Budgets," *The Review of Economics and Statistics*, vol. XLVII, no. 1, February 1965, pp. 13–37.

———, "Security Prices, Risk & Maximal Gains from Diversification," *Journal of Finance*, vol. 38, no. 4, December 1965, pp. 587–615.

Malkiel, Burton G., "Equity Yields, Growth and the Structure of Share Prices," *American Economic Review*, vol. LIII, no. 5, December 1963; also see "Reply," *A.E.R.*, vol. LIV, December 1964, pp. 1042–51.

————, "How Yield Curve Analysis Can Help Bond Portfolio Managers," *The Institutional Investor*, May 1967.

Miller, M. H., and F. Modigliani, "Dividend Policy, Growth, and the Valuation of Shares," *Journal of Business*, vol. XXXIV, no. 4, October 1961.

————, "Some Estimates of the Cost of Capital to the Electric Utility Industry, 1954–57," *The American Economic Review*, vol. LVI, no. 3, June 1966, pp. 333–391.

Modigliani, F., and M. Miller, "The Cost of Capital, Corporation Finance, and the Theory of Investment," *The American Economic Review*, vol. XLVIII, no. 3, June 1958, pp. 261–297.

Robichek, A., and S. Myers, "Risk Adjusted Discount Rates," *The Journal of Finance*, vol. XXI, no. 4, December 1966.

Renwick, Fred B., "Theory of Investment Behavior & Empirical Analysis of Stock Market Price Relatives," *Management Science*, vol. 15, no. 1, September 1968, pp. 57–71.

————, "Asset Management and Investor Portfolio Behavior, Theory and Practice," *Journal of Finance*, Supplement, May 1969.

Solomon, Ezra, *The Theory of Financial Management*, Columbia University Press, New York, 1963.

Sharpe, W. F., "Capital Asset Prices: A Theory of Market Equilibrium Under Conditions of Risk," *The Journal of Finance*, vol. XIX, no. 3, September 1964, pp. 425–442.

————, "Risk Aversion in the Stock Market: Some Empirical Evidence," *Journal of Finance*, vol. XX, no. 3, September 1965, pp. 416–422.

Walter, James E., "Dividend Policies and Common Stock Prices," *Journal of Finance*, vol. 11, March 1956, pp. 29–41.

————, "A Discriminant Function for Earnings–Price Ratios of Large Industrial Corporations," *The Review of Economics and Statistics*, vol. XLI, no. 1, February 1959.

Whitbeck, V. S., and M. Kisor, Jr., "A New Tool in Investment Decision-Making," *Financial Analysts Journal*, vol. 19, no. 3, May–June 1963. Also see the extension by D. M. Ahlers, "Sem: A Security Evaluation Model," Kalman J. Cohen and Frederick S. Hammer (eds.), *Analytical Methods in Banking*, Richard D. Irwin, Inc., Homewood, Ill., 1966.

Williams, J. B., *The Theory of Investment Value*, North Holland Publishing Company, Amsterdam, 1964.

    Also Shannon P. Pratt, "Bibliography on Risks and Rates of

Return for Common Stocks," *Financial Analysts Journal*, May–June 1968, pp. 151–166.

QUESTIONS FOR STUDY

1. Contrast briefly the Lerner-Carleton approach to security analysis with any one of the following approaches:
   (a) Whitbeck/Kisor/Ahlers
   (b) Graham and Dodd
   (c) Walters
2. Two major differences between Gordon's model $[P = D/(k - g)]$ and Graham and Dodd's model $(P = mE)$ are
   (a) Gordon's model does not work when current dividends are zero.
   (b) Graham and Dodd's model allows the analyst to use earnings estimates 3–5 years in the future, whereas Gordon's model requires estimates of dividend payments from now to infinity. True or false? Explain.
3. Outline the relative advantages and the relative disadvantages of using the Lerner-Carleton framework for financial analysis.
4. The Bank of New York model (as reported in the *Financial Analysts Journal*, vol. 19, no. 3, May–June 1963) is a good practical model for finding undervalued stocks because it allows the analyst to exercise his judgment of economic conditions over the next 3–5 years. True or false? Explain.
5. In what way does the financial constraint (i.e., the F-C function) influence share price?
6. Use the Lerner-Carleton model to explain
   (a) share price behavior for a given corporation
   (b) differences in price of common stock for different corporations
   (c) the terms upon which additional financing (debt or equity) can be obtained (include a discussion of rate of return on equity, risk, and overall profitability)
7. In the model $P = D/(k - g)$, how would you arrive at an estimate of dividends (D), rate of discount (k), and rate of growth (g) to determine price (P)?
8. Given the following characteristics about a company:
   (a) rate of return on assets = 20 percent
   (b) rate of retention = 50 percent
   (c) level of assets = $20 per share
   (d) share price = $40 per share
   Compute:
   (a) rate of growth of dividends = _____ percent
   (b) current dividend payment = $_____ per share
   (c) current earnings of the firm = $_____ per share
   (d) dividend yield = _____ percent

    (e) rate of growth of earnings   = _____ percent

    (f) the rate of capitalization (k) = _____ percent

9. Explain the significance of the earnings opportunity schedule.

10. If ABQ company earns $5.00 per share, has an equity capitalization rate of 10 percent, a return on investment of 8 percent, no debt in its capital structure, and is expected to pay out 20 percent of its income, then, using the Lerner-Carleton model,

    (a) compute the total market value of the firm if there are one million shares outstanding

    (b) compute the optimal rate of growth of sales and the expected rate of increase in share price

    (c) in what way would you alter your answer to both (a) and (b) above if, instead of no debt, the firm is financed with 60 per cent equity and 40 percent debt. Assume the debt to be 5 percent debentures.

Principles for Analysis and Management of Financial Assets

Part IV

This chapter is concerned with personal utility for money. Over the years, investors have demonstrated resourcefulness and expertise in articulating requirements for income and/or capital gains from investments. Basically, most investors always want more, now. But markets for money and capital operate so that larger returns now (or later) are usually available only with a tradeoff of accepting higher risks. Many investors, especially investors who live on fixed incomes, abhor risk. Therefore optimal management of money and capital assets requires articulation of *risk policy* as well as statements concerning *required returns*.

Specific statements declaring policy for risk are crucial for optimal management of assets. These statements help to avoid errors of rejecting assets (or portfolios) on the grounds that the assets are too risky,

Risk Policy and Investment Objectives 12

when, in fact, if the potential rewards are sufficiently large, the investor subjectively may be willing to accept these larger risks. Articulation of policy for risk, therefore, helps to avoid errors of incorrectly rejecting investment opportunities which in fact might maximize personal satisfaction. At the other extreme, an explicit statement of preference for risk helps to avoid errors of incorrectly accepting inferior (i.e., dominated) assets on the grounds that these assets are not risky, when in fact higher returns may be available at the same or perhaps even smaller risks. In short, because assets are analyzed and purchased (or sold) because of their risk-return characteristics, investors need explicit statements on policy for risk as well as statements on requirements for income and capital gains.

12.1 Criteria for Selection of Assets

In developing these ideas, we can note that the present day theory of portfolio management prescribes a way of thinking about opportunities for investment. Instead of extensive evaluation of a single asset

379

in isolation as performed earlier in Chapters 4, 5, and 6, modern portfolio analysis prescribes that investment policy can and should be formulated in the following manner: purchase an available asset if and only if that asset, when added to an existing portfolio, will cause a rise in overall personal satisfactions obtained from owning that portfolio. A rise in total personal satisfaction can occur in one of three ways: (1) the new asset can cause a net increase in total present expected return on the entire portfolio, (2) the new asset can cause a net decline in total risk exposure on the entire portfolio, or (3) there can be some subjectively acceptable tradeoff between change in total risk and change in total expected return on the portfolio.

More specifically, invoking the theory of utility from economics, we can recognize that risk-averse investors always desire larger expected returns but, at the same time, always experience a rise in pain from exposure to more risk. On this basis, therefore, policy for investing can be formulated according to criteria outlined in the following four paragraphs.

If, by including a proposed investment in an existing portfolio, the net change in expected return for the portfolio is positive, while the corresponding net change in investment risk is zero or lower, then the proposal for investment can be accepted unconditionally. Stated a different way, proposals for investment can be accepted enthusiastically if the change in parameters on the existing portfolio lie in (or along a boundary axis of) the fourth quadrant on risk-return dimension as indicated in Figure 12.1. For unconditional acceptance, therefore, the proposed investment must offer a risk-return combination such that the new portfolio has (1) lower risk than the original portfolio, even though the total expected return may not change, (2) higher return than the original portfolio, even though the total risk may not change, or (3) lower risk as well as higher return when compared with the original portfolio.

If the net change in portfolio parameters is located at the origin, point (0,0) in Figure 12.1, the proposed investment can be rejected on the grounds that the new asset makes no positive contribution toward either raising expected return or lowering risk.

If the net change in portfolio parameters is located in either the first or the third quadrants in Figure 12.1 (that is, the proposed investment causes a rise in risk but also an increase in expected return or else a decline in expected return, but also a decline in risk, respectively), then the investment decision depends upon subjective risk-preference codes (or loci of constant expected utility) of the individual investor. A given proposal can be rejected by one investor and can be accepted by another investor. If the increase in personal satisfactions (caused by either the increase in expected return in the case of quadrant 1, or else

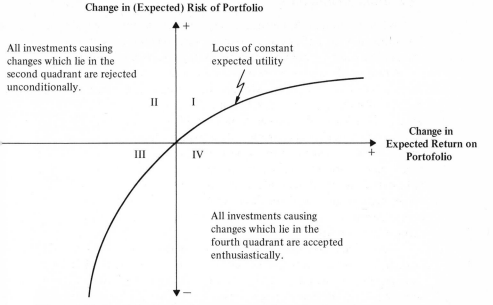

Change in (Expected) Risk of Portfolio

All investments causing changes which lie in the second quadrant are rejected unconditionally.

Locus of constant expected utility

II   I

III   IV

Change in Expected Return on Portofolio

All investments causing changes which lie in the fourth quadrant are accepted enthusiastically.

Figure 12.1.   Criteria for investment policy: Regions for acceptability of Investment. (After Renwick, "Asset Management and Investor Portfolio Behavior: Theory and Practice," *The Journal of Finance*, Vol. XXIV, No. 2, May, 1969, pp. 181–206.)

the decline in risk in the case of quadrant 3) more than offsets the decrease in personal satisfactions (caused by either the increase in risk in the case of quadrant 1, or the decrease in expected return in the case of quadrant 3), then the policy is to adopt the proposal. Investment policy and portfolio behavior, therefore, logically and rationally depend upon subjective risk preferences of the investing public. Policy for risk is crucial to the optimal management of assets.

If investors are indifferent to substituting some units of risk for some units of expected return, then those proposals which cause portfolio parameters to lie to the right of the locus of constant expected utility (as shown in quadrants 1 and 3 in Figure 12.1) will be adopted. All other investments will be rejected. In particular, all investments in quadrant 2 will be rejected unconditionally. These maxims describe behavior and attitudes towards risky investment portfolios.

To use the notions expressed in Figure 12.1 as a normative guide to asset management, two concepts are necessary. They are (1) the expected utility for money and (2) the risk-return parameters of a portfolio. The first concept, utility, is discussed in the remainder of this chapter. The second concept, portfolio risk, is discussed in the following chapter.

12.2 Subjective Utility

What is utility? Subjective utility implies personal satisfaction. The ultimate worth of any asset, risky or not, depends in part upon the personal satisfaction derived from ownership and/or use thereof.

Goods and services have value because of their usefulness as well as because of their scarcity. Money, for example, has value not only because of its scarcity, but also because of its use in exchange for other goods and services. Roast beef, to take another example, has value not because of its use in exchange for other commodities but because of its use in personal consumption. Roast beef is also scarce. Scarcity is a necessary condition for value. Air, to take a third example, even though required to sustain human life, commands no price (i.e., has no dollar value) because air is available everywhere in unlimited quantities. Asset value, therefore, is determined by at least two factors: personal satisfaction and scarcity.

How much an asset is worth is ultimately based on subjective evaluation; hence, anticipated returns from investments should be assessed and evaluated in accord with the utility derived therefrom. In selecting from alternative assets, many or all of which are risky, it is helpful to use utility scores to sort and rank these available alternatives.[1] In this chapter, we shall focus attention on the notions and axioms underlying the construction and use of utility scores. The following outline will guide us through the chapter.

1. Factors affecting subjective utility

----

[1] The literature concerning utility theory and measurement is vast. For reference, some important articles are (1) Kenneth J. Arrow, "Alternative Approaches to the Theory of Choice in Risk-Taking Situations," *Econometrica*, vol. 19, October 1951; (2) A. A. Alchian, "The Meaning of Utility Measurement," *American Economic Review*, vol. XLIII, March 1953; (3) M. Friedman, and L. J. Savage, "The Expected Utility-Hypothesis and the Measurability of Utility," *Journal of Political Economy*, vol. LX, December 1952; (4) Ward Edwards, "Probability-Preferences in Gambling," *The American Journal of Psychology*, vol. 66, July 1953; (5) I. N. Herstein, and John Milnor, "An Axiomatic Approach to Measurable Utility," *Econometrica*, vol. 21, April 1953; (6) H. Markowitz, "The Utility of Wealth," *Journal of Political Economy*, vol. LX, April 1952, pp. 151–158; (7) Frederick Mosteller, and Philip Nogee, "An Experimental Measurement of Utility," *Journal of Political Economy*, vol. LIX, no. 5, October 1951; (8) Paul A. Samuelson, "Probability, Utility, and the Independence Axiom," *Econometrica*, vol. 20, October 1952; and (9) Robert H. Strotz, "Cardinal Utility," *Papers and Proceedings of the Sixty-Fifth Annual Meeting of the American Economic Association, American Economic Review*, vol. 43, May 1953, and the comment by W. J. Baumol; (10) A broad survey of modern utility theory is contained in S. A. Ozga, *Expectations in Economic Theory*, Weidenfeld and Nicholson, London, 1965.

2. Shape of the utility function
3. Axioms for calculating utility curves
4. Certainty-equivalent returns
5. Aversion to risk and risk premiums
6. Constant expected utility and indifference curves

12.3 Factors Affecting Subjective Utility

The amount of satisfaction derived from owning a particular risky asset (or set of risky assets) depends upon the personal preferences and circumstances of the investor. We can hypothesize subjective utility to be determined by four factors: wealth, return, risk, and time. For example, a gain of $1000 is most likely more significant to a pauper than to a rich man, though both gain the same absolute amount. On preliminary examination, therefore, wealth appears to be an important factor in determining utility for money. Another factor is time. Income anticipated 50 years hence may be quite valuable today to say a life insurance institutional investor or to a pension fund administrator. But that same income, no matter how large the absolute amount may be, can have very little value today to a 60-year old private individual investor.[2] Fifty years hence can be beyond the planning horizon of a private investor who is already 60 years old. In addition to time and wealth as being codeterminants of utility for money, there are also (1) return: the amount of profit (or loss) expected on the potential investment and (2) risk: the possibilities associated with actually achieving that expected profit (or loss). Statement (12.1) expresses the functional form of the relationship of these four factors of subjective utility.

$$U(R) = f(W,R,p,T) \tag{12.1}$$

where

$U(R)$ = ordinal subjective utility for money (or risk)
W = present wealth (with certainty)
R = uncertain (risky) additional after-tax return (wealth) expected at some given future date as a consequence of investing some proportion of W today
p = a set of probabilities (risk) associated with the expected return R

$$\sum_{i=1}^{N} p_i = 1.00$$

T = the time period of the investment

---

[2] Barring, of course, special actions such as selling the rights thereto to the long-term institutional investor or establishing an estate for heirs.

Because statement (12.1) is in functional form only, further discussion is needed. We should examine the influence on utility when each factor stated in (12.1) is varied, one at a time, holding all other things constant.

Utility vs. Present Wealth. For a stated amount of additional income (R), subjective utility for that income tends to vary inversely with the level of current wealth. Daniel Bernoulli, several centuries ago, hypothesized this fact and noted that the requirement can be fulfilled by a logarithmic form such as [3]

$$U(R) = b \log (R/W) = b[\log (R) - \log (W)] \qquad (12.2)$$

where $b =$ some constant of proportionality, R and W are both positive dollar amounts, and other terms are the same as specified above. Statement (12.2) says precisely that a return of $R = \$1000$ provides greater utility to a less wealthy investor than it does to a more wealthy investor. Utility for money declines as wealth rises.

$$\partial U(R)/\partial (W) < 0 \qquad (12.3)$$

Utility vs. Return. For any given level of wealth, we shall assume that utility must always rise (i.e., utility never remains the same nor declines) with (prospects of) additional wealth. In other words, we shall assume that rational investors always prefer more money instead of less money. Investors are never worse off for having more money. Under this assumption, the rate of change of utility with respect to return always must be positive.

$$\partial U(R)/\partial R > 0 \qquad (12.4)$$

But statement (12.4) is incomplete. Considering the entire range of returns possible in the money and capital markets (i.e., possible losses as well as possible profits), a given increment in return (ΔR) can cause a different increment in utility ($\Delta U(R)$), depending upon the level around which the given increment occurs. That is, the rate of change of utility with respect to return, though positive, is not necessarily constant over the entire range of possible returns. For example, a $1000 net change in return can cause a different increment in utility, if the change occurs

[3] Daniel Bernoulli, "Exposition of a New Theory on the Measurement of Risk," (trans. from Latin into English by Dr. Louise Sommer), *Econometrica*, vol. 22, no. 1, January 1954, pp. 23–36. Translation of "Specimen Theoriae Novae de Mensura Sortis," St. Petersburg, 1738. Also, see the references at the end of Bernoulli's paper.

around possible losses instead of occurring around possible profits. The resultant increment in utility can be different for the former $1000 net increment than for the latter $1000 increment. Therefore, we can write

$$\partial U(R)/\partial R \neq \text{Constant, necessarily} \qquad \textbf{(12.5)}$$

Also, because rising returns cause wealth to rise then, recognizing (12.4) as well as (12.5), we can note that rising returns must cause rising utility. But the *rate* of rise of utility must be decreasing because the increasing wealth will tend to slow the rate of increase of utility. More precisely

$$\frac{\partial}{\partial R}[\partial U(R)/\partial R] = \frac{\partial^2 U(R)}{\partial R^2} < 0 \qquad \textbf{(12.6)}$$

In other words, given a sufficiently wide range of possible returns, so that the wealth of the investor is affected significantly, the utility function will be concave downward over that range of possible returns.

Utility vs. Risk. Still holding other things constant, we shall assume that utility for additional money always varies inversely with risk (no matter how risk is defined). That is, we shall assume that utility always declines as risk rises. More precisely, the rate of change of utility with respect to risk is always negative.

$$\partial U(R)/\partial \text{Risk} < 0 \qquad \textbf{(12.7)}$$

But statement (12.7) is not *always* true. Statement (12.7) assumes aversion to risk on the part of investors. All investors need not be averse to risk. Some (irrational) investors may prefer to ignore risk. Ignoring risk is the same as risk neutrality. For risk neutral investors, we can write

$$\partial U(R)/\partial \text{Risk} = 0 \qquad \textbf{(12.8)}$$

Statement (12.8) says that changing risk has no influence on the utility of risk neutral investors. Given two risky assets, both of which have the same expected return, a risk neutral investor will be indifferent between the two assets. Risk neutral investors choose between assets on the basis of expected returns alone. Rationality requires preference for certainty.

A third type of attitude exhibited by some investors is risk seeking or gambling. Risk seeking is the opposite of risk aversion. Risk seekers (or gamblers) prefer risk. Given two risky assets, both of which have the same expected return, a risk seeking gambler will prefer the more risky of the two assets. A rational, risk averse investor will prefer the less risky of the two assets. A risk neutral investor will be indifferent between the two. Therefore, since rising risk will cause a rise in utility for risk seekers, we can write

$$\partial U(R)/\partial \text{Risk} > 0 \qquad (12.9)$$

Finally, there can exist a hybrid type of behavior, e.g., risk aversion to possibilities of loss, risk neutrality to possibilities of relatively small profits, and risk seeking (or perhaps smaller levels of aversion) to possibilities of relatively large profits. Throughout the analysis to follow, we shall assume risk aversion as stated in (12.7).

More remains to consider between utility and risk. We have indicated previously that financial markets operate in a way so that expected returns tend to rise as risk rises.[4]

$$\partial R/\partial \text{Risk} > 0 \qquad (12.10)$$

Because larger returns cause a rise in utility but larger risks cause a decline in utility, and because larger returns can be obtained only at the expense of larger risks, we can say that utility rises with return as stated in (12.4). But because of risk, the rate of rise will decline over the range of relevant returns. We, therefore, have reason for restating (12.6).

$$\partial^2 U(R)/\partial R^2 < 0 \qquad (12.11)$$

Statement (12.11) says that aversion to risk implies a utility function which is concave downward. But also, as in (12.6) we can note that the second derivative of utility need not necessarily be constant over the entire range of possible returns. Utility must always rise as expected returns rise, but the rate of increase can vary within the range of returns under consideration.

$$\partial^2 U(R)/\partial R^2 \neq \text{Constant, necessarily} \qquad (12.12)$$

Utility vs. Time. Utility for additional money varies inversely with time. As expected returns go deeper into time, utility for those returns declines. Many investors are impatient. Not only do investors prefer more money, they usually prefer more money now. The sooner the better. Therefore, we can write

$$\partial U(R)/\partial T < 0 \qquad (12.13)$$

Statement (12.13) is one reason for invoking criteria such as net present value and internal rate of return as we did in earlier chapters to

---

[4] We shall elaborate on this statement in the next chapter.

arrive at capital budgeting decisions. However, statement (12.13) is not a universal truism. Some investors prefer more money later rather than now. For example, a relatively young investor with large current income may rationally prefer additional money later, upon anticipated retirement, instead of now. Indeed, forests must be financed today if wood for lumber is to be available 100 years hence; but according to the net present value criterion, an investment which offers payoff 100 years hence can rank near the bottom of a list of alternative opportunities. Net present value can fail to lead to planting of the forest. Hence, for some projects, utility can conceivably *rise* as time lengthens.

$$\partial U(R)/\partial T > 0 \qquad\qquad (12.14)$$

Throughout the analysis to follow, we shall assume time preference as stated in (12.3).

SUMMARY. To summarize, each factor affecting utility as stated in (12.1) has been considered alone, holding everything else constant while varying that single factor. Real-world analysis will permit no such simplifications. In the practicality of the real world, all four factors can and do vary and interact together. For example, risk increases with time because possibilities for unforeseen contingencies and random catastrophes rise as time deepens. Returns on investment also rise both with risk (otherwise no one would purchase risky assets) and with time (because of the phenomenon of compound interest). Wealth varies in all three—returns, time and risk—with the result that utility in the real world of asset management becomes complex to define and articulate. But define it we must! Toward that end, we shall turn next to some considerations for defining and calculating utility curves that are more precise than the functional statement (12.1).

12.4 What Is the Shape of the Utility Function?

Since subjective utility is determined by wealth, time, risk, and return (as discussed in the preceding section), the precise shape of the utility function is determined by these four factors. However, analysis in four-dimensional sample space can become (unnecessarily?) complex. As with Occum's Razor, we must never use a more complex model if a simpler model will suffice. To reduce the problem to workable dimensions we can (1) hold wealth constant, (2) collapse the time dimension into equivalent present lump sums, and (3) work with the two dimensions of risk and return.[5]

Risk and return interact. More risky investments require larger returns to induce investors to purchase them. Less risky returns can approach the risk-free rate of discount. Hence, the shape of the utility function for money as studied generally is determined by alternative combinations of expected return and risk, assuming other things equal and constant.

A number of such functions have previously appeared in the literature.[6] A common assumption is that the utility function can be approximated by a section of a quadratic curve (i.e., the increasing section of a parabola). Quadratic utility forms the basis for Markowitz-type analysis. A quadratic utility function is written in the form

$$U = aR - bR^2 \tag{12.15}$$

where U = ordinal utility, R = return, and a and b are both positive constants determined subjectively by the risk preference of the investor. However, forms other than the quadratic have been proposed also.

Bernoulli, for example, expresses the total utility of money as a logarithmic function.[7]

$$\frac{dU(W)}{dW} = \frac{a}{W}; \qquad U(W) = a \log (W) + b \tag{12.16}$$

where $U(W)$ = utility for money, a and b are unspecified constants, and W = total amount of the risk takers' wealth.

---

[5] Concerning joint time-risk preference, individuals often must choose between monetary rewards that are not only uncertain but are distributed over time. In these situations, time and risk preference must be jointly encoded. The description of joint time-risk preference is a problem that permits many solutions. The analysis in Chapters 4 and 5 employed the idea of reducing any time stream to a present value, using the time value of money. Now we shall apply a utility function to this present value to calculate which among alternative present values is most desirable.

[6] See (1) H. M. Markowitz, "The Utility of Wealth," *Journal of Political Economy*, vol. LX, April 1952, pp. 151–158; (2) D. E. Farrar, *The Investment Decision Under Uncertainty*, Prentice-Hall, Inc., Englewood Cliffs, N.J., 1962; (3) F. T. Dolbear, "Individual Choice under Uncertainty," *Yale Economic Essays*, Fall 1963; (4) J. W. Pratt, "Risk Aversion in the Small and in the Large," *Econometrica*, vol. 32, January-April 1964; (5) James Tobin, "The Theory of Portfolio Selection," in F. H. Hahn and F. P. R. Brechling (eds.), *The Theory of Interest Rates*, St. Martin's Press, New York, 1965, pp. 18–22; (6) K. Borch, "A Note on Utility and Attitudes to Risk," *Management Science*, vol. 9, July 1963, pp. 697–700.

[7] D. Bernoulli, *op. cit.*

Gabriel Cramer, a distinguished French mathematician (1704–1752), expresses utility for money as being proportional to the square root of the total dollar sum.[8]

$$U(W) \approx \sqrt{W} \qquad (12.17)$$

Some other forms for utility are summarized in Appendix 1 for Chapter 12.

Since, for normative purposes, the utility function must have a good fit only over the range of expected returns under consideration, segments of a multitude of functions can be used. Theoretical considerations give some indications and guidance as to the choice of a particular function. These considerations are set forth below.

12.5 Axioms for Calculating Utility Curves

To calculate utility curves for the purpose of formulating policy for risk, investors must subscribe to a particular set of axioms. Five axioms are important. A sixth axiom is relevant. These six axioms are described below. The notions key to understanding the discussions are *transitivity* and *certainty equivalence*.

AXIOM 1: Transitivity. To define and calculate utility, investors must subscribe to transitivity in the return dimension. Given several alternative returns possible from a potential investment, this first axiom requires that investors be able to rank the order of preference for all those returns. The assumption underlying this ranking is that all other things (including risks) are held equal and constant.

When thinking of dollars, this first axiom can be easy to apply. For example, axiom 1 states that if a given investment offers prospects of $7500, $5000, or $10,000, then the rank order preference must be $10,000 first, $7500 second, and $5000 third. This particular ranking must occur because, by statement (12.4), for a given level of risk, $10,000 provides greater utility than either $7500 or $5000. Transitivity means that if $10,000 is preferred to $7500, *and* if $7500 is preferred to $5000, then $10,000 must be preferred to $5000. For transitivity to be violated, the $5000 return would have to be preferred over the $10,000 return.

Transitivity does not always hold. One typical example is where ordering has been completed within two or more dimensions, but the final preference extends over all dimensions. To illustrate, an ordering of three assets within the return dimension might be A to B to C, with

---

[8] Cramer's theory is discussed by Bernoulli. See D. Bernoulli, *op. cit.*

A being preferred to *C* so that transitivity holds within the return dimension. Now those same three assets ranked and ordered in the risk dimension might be *B* to *C* to *A*, with *C* being preferred to *A*. The conclusion is that *A* is preferred to *C* in one dimension (return), but *C* is preferred to A in another dimension (risk). Confusion of this type (i.e., changing dimensions) occurs frequently when applied in human terms.

For example, Caroline may have more money than Betty-Jo, and Betty-Jo may have more money than Annie, but Andrew (who maximizes wealth, usually) may prefer Annie to Caroline, even though he rationally prefers Caroline to Betty-Jo and Betty-Jo to Annie. Annie, though relatively poor, can have other irresistible attributes.

In the logic of investments, assets are bought and sold on the basis of monetary rationality. No such (inadvertent?) swaps as between Annie and Caroline are permissible. Given equal risks, if $10,000 is preferred to $7500, and $7500 is preferred to $5000, then $10,000 *must* be preferred to $5000, always.

Axiom 1 and Ordinal Utility. Note that utility is to be used primarily to express preference among ordering. That is, we are constructing *ordinal utility*. Our measure of utility, which actually will be utils (i.e., one util equals one unit of satisfaction), will give no indication of whether the difference in preferences between *A* and *B* is greater or less than the difference in preferences for *B* and *C*. We shall only know that *A* is preferred over *B*, and *B* is preferred over *C*. Therefore, the utility function shall be unique only up to a positive linear transformation. That is, the two functions U_1 and U_2 both represent the same preference ordering and therefore are equally useful for purposes of establishing risk policy.

$$U_1 = U(R) \quad \text{and} \quad U_2 = A + B[U(R)] \quad (12.18)$$

where *A* and *B* are constants, $B > 0$, and $U(R)$ = utility, a function of money return.

It may be worthwhile to note here that the two functions U_3 and U_4 can, in general, represent *different* preference ordering.

$$U_3 = U(R) \quad \text{and} \quad U_4 = U(B + R) \quad (12.19)$$

where all terms are the same as defined above. If *B* is interpreted to mean initial wealth, then $U(B + R)$ means that initial wealth influences the utility of expected return *R*. But $B[U(R)]$ means that the selection decision (i.e., utility) is made solely on the basis of *R*, and the resultant utility is then "blown up" (i.e., multiplied) *B* times. Note also that, since the utility function must be specified for the entire range of relevant returns, either part of statement (12.18) can be scaled, without loss of generality, to be contained with a standardized interval (0,1).

Stated in this way, utility of return can be interpreted as a cumulative probability distribution.

$$.00 \leq U(R) \leq 1.00 \tag{12.20}$$

Such an interpretation of utility may facilitate analysis on some occasions.

A X I O M 2 : Certainty Equivalence.   Axiom 2 and certainty equivalence can be explained as follows. Since $10,000 is always preferred over $7500, and $7500 is always preferred over $5000, then, if the investor is offered a choice between (1) $7500 for sure and (2) a lottery where the prizes are $10,000 with probability p or $5000 with probability $(1 - p)$, there must be *some* value of p for which indifference between the two choices occurs. The reason indifference *must* occur can be explained as follows.

   If p equals unity, then the outcome from the lottery certainly will be $10,000; hence, the investor will choose the lottery because he prefers $10,000 over $7500. At the other extreme (if p equals zero) the outcome from the lottery certainly will be $5000; the investor will choose the $7500 for sure because $7500 is preferred over $5000. Since the selection changed from choice 2 (the lottery) to choice 1 (the certain return) as p was varied from 1.00 down to zero, then there must be some value of p (between 1.00 and .00) at which the investor is indifferent between the two choices. For this value of p, choice 1 (the guaranteed or certain return) is the *certainty equivalent* of the risky alternative. Put another way, the appropriate value of p has been stated by the investor as the indication that $7500 is the certainty equivalent of a lottery on $10,000 and $5000 with probability p of winning $10,000.[9]

   A certainty-equivalent return function is an important concept in measuring utility for money. One reason for its importance is that certainty equivalence enables us to evaluate an asset (or a portfolio of assets) in a single meaningful monetary (*not* utility) number. We can ask, "What amount of money received for certain will have the same utility as this risky asset?" Thus, the certain equivalent is the amount of money shown by the utility curve to have the same utility as the asset. To calculate certainty-equivalent returns and corresponding utility curves, we can proceed as follows.

Calculating Utility, Using Certainty-Equivalent Returns.   To illustrate the use of certainty equivalents in the calculation of utility curves,

---

[9] Note: this is the "betting odds" concept of probability, not long-run relative frequency. Refer to Appendix 1 of Chapter 6 for a review of some alternative meanings and concepts of probability.

suppose we let $R_2 = \$10,000$ and $R_1 = \$5000$ cover the entire range of possible returns on investment.[10] The object is to calculate the amount of utility for all returns between \$5000 and \$10,000, inclusive. We can begin by specifying a scale for utility.

Since utility is measured *ordinally* (i.e., only more or less, not how much more), the utility of \$10,000 [$U(\$10,000)$] and the utility of \$5000 [$U(\$5000)$] can be set arbitrarily (i.e., subjectively). Utilities for all returns between \$10,000 and \$5000 then will be scaled proportionately. This is another way of interpreting and applying statement (12.20). So we can arbitrarily set

$$U(\$5000) = 5 \text{ utils} \qquad (12.21)$$

$$U(\$10,000) = 12 \text{ utils} \qquad (12.22)$$

Then R_1 and R_2 can be plotted as shown in Figure 12.2.

Continuing toward the objective of calculating subjective utility for all returns between \$5000 and \$10,000, we can set up lotteries and determine certainty equivalents as follows. Select any return between \$5000 and \$10,000, let us say \$8000, and offer the investor a choice between \$8000 for sure or a lottery involving payoff \$10,000 with chances p or payoff \$5000 with chances $(1 - p)$. When p equals unity then the lottery must be preferable because \$10,000 must provide larger utility than \$8000. As p declines, the choice must change from the lottery to the \$8000 with certainty because, by axiom 1, \$8000 must provide larger utility than lesser amounts.

If the investor (subjectively) declares indifference between the two choices at p equal to $3:5$ (i.e., three chances in five of winning \$10,000 from the lottery), then the investor is exhibiting *neutrality* towards risk. This is so because at $p = 3:5$, the expected value of the lottery equals the value of the certainty return—\$8000.

Expected value of lottery $= (3/5)(\$10,000) + (2/5)(\$5000) = \$8000$
$$(12.23)$$

$$
\begin{aligned}
U(\$8000) &= U(\text{lottery}) \\
&= (3/5)U(\$10,000) + (2/5)U(\$5000) \\
&= (3/5)(12) + (2/5)(5) \\
&= 9.2 \text{ utils}
\end{aligned}
\qquad (12.24)
$$

If the investor (subjectively) declares indifference between the two choices at p equal to $4:5$ instead of $3:5$, then he is exhibiting *risk averse*

---

[10] This method of calculating utility is put forth in Milton Friedman and Leonard J. Savage, "Utility Analysis of Choices involving Risk," *The Journal of Political Economy*, vol. LVI, no. 4, August 1948, pp. 279–304.

Utility
(Utils)

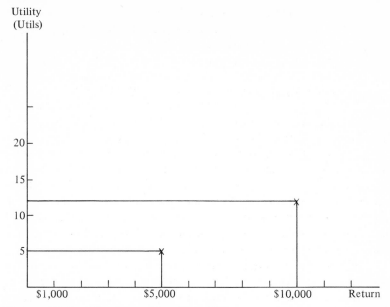

Figure 12.2.   Plotting subjective utility.

behavior because with $p = 4:5$, the expected value of the lottery is
$9000. The investor is expressing the same utility for (i.e., is indifferent
between) $8000 with certainty as for $9000 with risk. If indifference had
occurred at even larger p (i.e., p greater than .80) then the investor would
be expressing even more aversion (i.e., dislike) for risk.

$$\text{Expected value of lottery} = (4/5)(\$10,000) + (1/5)(\$5000) = \$9000$$
(12.25)

$$
\begin{aligned}
U(\$8000) &= U(\text{lottery}) \\
&= (4/5)U(\$10,000) + (1/5)U(\$5000) \\
&= (4/5)(12) + (1/5)(5) \\
&= 10.6 \text{ utils}
\end{aligned}
$$
(12.26)

    If the investor (subjectively) declares indifference between the two
choices of p equal to $1:4$ instead of $3:5$ (i.e., one chance in four of
winning the $10,000 prize from the lottery), then he is exhibiting *risk
seeking* behavior because with $p = 1:4$, the expected value of the lottery
is $6250. Under these conditions, the investor is expressing the same
utility for $8000 with certainty as for $6250 with risk. If indifference had
occurred at even smaller p (i.e., p less than .25), then he would be expressing even more liking (pleasure) for risk.

$$\text{Expected value of lottery} = (1/4)(\$10,000) + (3/4)(\$5000) = \$6250$$
(12.27)

$$U(\$8000) = U(\text{lottery})$$
$$= (1/4)U(\$10,000) + (3/4)U(\$5000)$$
$$= (1/4)(12) + (1/5)(5) \quad\quad (12.28)$$
$$= 3.4 \text{ utils}$$

To complete the calculations, other certain returns between \$5000 and \$10,000 can be selected, and the decision process outlined above is repeated. Just as the utility for \$8000 was calculated, utilities can be calculated for \$5000, \$6000, \$5820, etc. Finally, we can trace out one of the curves shown in Figure 12.3. These three curves represent utility for money in the range of all possible returns under consideration.

Utility curve 1 in Figure 12.3 represents utility of investors who are averse to risk because the certainty-equivalent return is less than the expected value of the lottery. Curve 2 represents indifference (i.e., ignoring) the risk and curve 3 represents risk seeking behavior. These curves result from application of the "standard gamble approach."[11]

The notion of certainty equivalence is important in quantifying subjective utility for money. One reason for the importance of certainty equivalence is that utility numbers per se give no indication of *strength* of the preference. Numerical magnitude of utility can be no help in measuring strength because, if we add 100 to all utility numbers calculated, we will derive exactly the same preference ordering. The only difference will be much smaller percentage differences in utility numbers. To measure strength of preference, it is helpful to use the concept of certainty equivalence.

To illustrate further how the notions of certainty equivalence and expected utility can be applied to the analysis of risky alternative investments, consider the two lotteries shown in Table 12.1. The expected value of each lottery and its associated expected utility can be calculated as follows.

Expected value of L_1 = .2(\$300) + .3(\$200) + .5(\$.0) = \$120
Expected value of L_2 = .1(\$400) + .2(\$150) + .7(\$60) = \$112

Table 12.1   TWO LOTTERIES

Probability	Lottery L_1 Money (\$)	Utility	Probability	Lottery L_2 Money (\$)	Utility
.2	300	.90	.1	400	.95
.3	200	.42	.2	150	.40
.5	0	.00	.7	60	.35

[11] See John von Neumann and Oskar Morgenstern, *Theory of Games and Economic Behavior*, 2nd ed., Princeton University Press, Princeton, N.J., 1947, Chap. III and Appendix, "The Axiomatic Treatment of Utility."

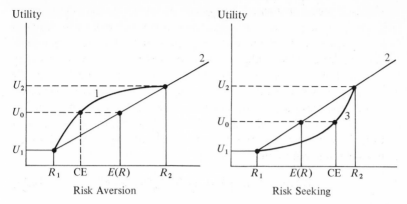

Figure 12.3. Three types of investment behavior. The certainty-equivalent return provides the same utility as the expected risky return.

    Investors who are indifferent to risk will prefer lottery L_1 because its expected value exceeds the expected value of lottery L_2 by $8. To determine the preference of the individual who has utility for money as stated in Table 12.1, we must first calculate the utility of each possible prize in each lottery. Then, using the stated utility for money, we can calculate the expected value of the utility for each lottery. These calculations are shown below.

    Expected utility of L_1 = .2(.90) + .3(.42) + .5(.0) = .306
    Expected utility of L_2 = .1(.95) + .20(.40) + .7(.35) = .42

Thus, an individual whose utility curve is so stated will prefer lottery L_2 in spite of its lower expected value.

    Next, to calculate the certain-equivalent return of the lotteries, we can ask, what amount of money received for certain will have the same utility as the two lotteries? The certain-equivalent is the amount of money shown by the utility curve to have the same utility as the lottery. Thus, interpolating from the utility numbers stated in Table 12.1, we see that the calculated utility of .306 (for lottery L_1) corresponds to a certain equivalent of less than $60, while the calculated utility of .42 (for lottery L_2) means a certainty equivalent of $200. This means that an investor will be justly indifferent to receiving a little less than $60 for certain or lottery L_1 instead. Also, an investor with the utility preferences stated in Table 12.1 will be indifferent to receiving $200 for certain or lottery L_2 instead. It is slightly inaccurate but intuitively satisfying to say that lottery L_2 is worth approximately $140 more to this particular investor than in lottery L_1. This is despite the fact that the expected value of lottery L_1 exceeds the expected value of lottery L_2 by $8.

Certainty-Equivalent Return Function. A certainty-equivalent return function is a precise way of expressing policy for risk. The function has all the properties outlined and discussed above for utility functions. In fact, a certainty-equivalent return function can be used as a utility function. If risk equals zero, then the certainty equivalent (i.e., utility of return) varies directly with expected return. As risk increases, however, the certainty-equivalent return decreases, denoting aversion to risk. One widely used utility schedule is a quadratic function of return.[12] Over the range of relevant returns, the form of a quadratic utility schedule is hypothesized to be

$$U(R) = C.E.(R) = A_0 + A_1R + A_2R^2 \qquad (12.29)$$

where

$$U(R) = \text{utility of return}$$
$$C.E.(R) = \text{certainty-equivalent return}$$
$$A_0, A_1, A_2 = \text{constants denoting aversion to risk}$$

In the special case of Figure 12.2, the utility curve can be approximated over the range $5000 \leq R \leq $10,000$ by (12.29) if the constants are

$$A_0 = -13.62$$
$$A_1 = 4.895 \times 10^{-3} \qquad (12.30)$$
$$A_2 = -.233 \times 10^{-6}$$

That is, using the constants stated in (12.30), statement (12.29) is the equation which fits the data plotted in Figure 12.3, investment behavior type 1.

Note that because utility functions are used only to indicate *order* of preference, linear transformations of the utility function in no way affect the end results of their use. This is another way of stating (12.18). Thus, (12.29) will be unaffected if we divide both sides of the equation by the constant A_1 to obtain

$$A_0' = -2782$$
$$A_1' = 1 \qquad (12.31)$$
$$A_2' = -47.6 \times 10^{-6}$$

and then ignore the constant A_0', because a constant adds nothing to the determination of rank order. The quadratic utility function over the range $5000 \leq R \leq $10,000$ is

$$U(R) = C.E.(R) = R - AR^2 \qquad (12.32)$$

---

[12] See Markowitz, *op. cit.*

where $A = 47.6 \times 10^{-6}$. The constant A is called a *coefficient of risk aversion*. If A equals zero, then the investor is neutral to risk. If A is large, the investor is highly averse to risk. In other words, the quadratic utility schedule implies that R^2 is proportional to risk (i.e., standard error, or variance) of prediction.[13]

The certainty-equivalent return is affected by changes in risk policy as well as by changes in magnitudes of outcomes. That is, the risk policy parameter (A) helps to determine the certainty equivalent. If $A = 0$, then risk neutrality is being exhibited. If risk is ignored, then utility is directly proportional to the expected value of return alone. But as A increases, indicating rising aversion to risk, then the relative amount of risk present (σ^2) becomes important in determining utility and hence value of the prospective asset.

AXIOM 3.   This axiom states that the certain equivalent of a lottery always can be substituted for the lottery in any situation and without changing the preferences of the decision maker. This third axiom can be called a "did you really mean it?" axiom. It is another way of interpreting statement (12.32). Indifference implies equal utility. Therefore, either the left-hand side or the right-hand side of the equation can be used.

---

[13] This assertion can be shown as follows.

Hypothesis. If the utility function for money is quadratic

$$U(R) = R - AR^2 \tag{12.33}$$

then the expected value of utility can be written

$$E[U(R)] = E(R - AR^2) \tag{12.34}$$

where $A > 0$.

Then, using the theorems from Appendix 2 of Chapter 6, we can write

$$\begin{aligned} E[U(R)] &= E(R) - AE(R^2) \\ &= \mu - A(\mu^2 + \sigma^2) \end{aligned} \tag{12.35}$$

where μ and σ both are positive. The latter part of (12.35) is true because, from Chapter 6, statement (6.75),

$$E(R^2) = \mu^2 + \text{var}(R) \tag{6.75}$$

That is, in the special case when a quadratic function of return can be used to state certainty-equivalent return, then utility is a function of expected return and standard deviation of return.

$$C.E. = E[U(R)] = f(\mu, \sigma) \tag{12.36}$$

where

    $C.E.$ = certainty-equivalent return
      μ = mean value of probability distribution of possible returns
      σ = standard error of predicted returns (i.e., risk)

When incorporated into investment (portfolio) analysis, the goal of maximizing expected utility can be achieved by working with and maximizing certainty-equivalent returns. That is, all risky returns can be transformed into certainty-equivalent returns according to the personal preferences of the individual investor. Therefore, communication of the policy for risk can lead to a greater improvement in the decision process and also to improvement in the analytical technique.

AXIOM 4.   The fourth axiom for calculating and using utility curves involves transitivity in the risk dimension. The fourth axiom states that if an investor prefers asset A to asset B and if two lotteries are presented, each lottery offering both assets but with different probabilities, then the investor must prefer the lottery that yields A with the higher probability. For example, if two lotteries each offer $10,000 and $5000 but with probabilities of

$$pr(\$10,000) \text{ from } L_1 = 1/5 \qquad (12.37)$$

$$pr(\$10,000) \text{ from } L_2 = 3/4 \qquad (12.38)$$

then the investor must prefer (i.e., have larger utility for the lottery that offers $10,000 with the higher probability (i.e., lower risk) lottery L_2.

AXIOM 5.   The fifth axiom says that a lottery (or portfolio) whose prizes (or returns) are themselves lotteries (e.g., each possible return has its own probability distribution) is equivalent to a lottery that produces the same ultimate prizes with probability computed according to the laws of probability. This can be termed a "no fun in gambling" axiom; investments are accepted in anticipation of profit, *not* merely for the sake of playing the game.

AXIOM 6: Exponential Utility Curves.   In some cases investors subscribe to a sixth axiom. Axiom 6 is illustrated by a situation where all prizes in a lottery are increased by the same amount (Δ). Then the axiom says that the certain equivalent of the lottery will also increase by that same amount (Δ).

Since the increment (Δ) will be received with certainty, regardless of the outcome of the lottery, the axiom may sound persuasive; however, the same increment (Δ) can have different utility, depending on the level of return and/or the wealth of the investor. Therefore, axiom 6 is not a necessary condition to establish utility.

If investors *are* in fact governed by axiom 6, then analysis for risk policy is relatively easy because the utility curve can then be specified as either linear or exponential in form. In either of these two cases, the mathematical form facilitates analysis. It would be convenient if the real-world marketplace would accommodate these simplifying theoretical assumptions!

Stochastic Dominance. There is one important case in which risk preference need not be measured at all. That is the case where the choice between two alternatives is clear regardless of preference for risk. Portfolio P_1 stochastically dominates portfolio P_2 if the probability of receiving a monetary return in excess of c is higher for P_1 than for P_2 for any value of c. If one security (or portfolio) stochastically dominates all others, then that portfolio is preferred by investors regardless of attitudes toward risk; there is no need to use a utility function.

Summary. To summarize, we can list the five axioms for calculating utility curves.

1. Transitivity of rank order preferences of all possible payoffs within the lottery.
2. Equivalence between certain return (certainty-equivalent return) and a lottery with stated payoffs and stated probabilities. There must be some p at which this indifference occurs.
3. Given the p, the investor must be indifferent between receiving the certain equivalent income and the lottery.
4. Transitivity of probabilities.
5. Transitivity of lotteries.

Three basic methods of converting the responses into a utility plot are to[14]

1. Obtain certainty equivalent responses for a risky alternative where two possible (extreme value) outcomes are always kept the same.
2. Compute segments of a utility plot (e.g., as in method 1 above) and then overlap these segments.
3. Assume a mathematical form for the utility function and then search for the best fit of this function.

---

[14] Another, different approach called the state description approach, originated with Arrow and has been employed by Debreu, Diamond, and Hirschleifer, among others. See (1) K. J. Arrow, "The Role of Securities in the Optimal Allocation of Risk Bearing," *Review of Economic Studies*, vol. 31, April 1964, pp. 91–96; (2) G. Debreu, *Theory of Value*, John Wiley & Sons, Inc., New York, 1959; (3) P. A. Diamond, "The Role of a Stock Market in a General Equilibrium Model with Technological Uncertainty," *American Economic Review*, vol. 57, September 1967, pp. 759–776; (4) J. Hirshleifer, "Investment Decision under Uncertainty," *Quarterly Journal of Economics*, vol. 79, November 1965, pp. 509–536, and vol. 80, May 1966, pp. 252–277.

12.6 Aversion to Risk and Risk Premiums

We concluded from Figure 12.3 and statements (12.7) through (12.12) that rational investment behavior always requires aversion to risk. Other things the same, no rational investor will prefer risk instead of certainty. However, over the entire range of possible returns, the *amount* of aversion need not necessarily be constant. This condition provides three possible cases for analysis. Over the range of available investment returns, there can be

1. Constant aversion to risk.
2. Decreasing aversion to risk.
3. Increasing aversion to risk.

Of course, a real-life situation over a wide range of available returns can consist of a combination of all three pure cases.

To perform the required analysis, we need to introduce a new concept: *risk premium*. The risk premium required by an investor can be viewed as a measure of the amount of risk aversion. Large required premiums imply great aversion to risk; small required premiums imply little aversion to risk.

A risk premium can be thought of as the amount the investor must be paid in order for him to risk a sum equal to his cash equivalent. A risk premium is the difference between a risky return and a guaranteed return. For risk averse investors, risk premiums must always be positive (i.e., never zero or negative) because investors who are averse to risk always prefer certainty over risks.

To illustrate, if a guaranteed return of 6 percent can be obtained on a $10,000 investment, then any risky alternative investment must offer more than 6 percent, perhaps 15 percent. Then the difference, 9 percent in this case, is the premium paid for bearing risk. The important question is, "Is 9 percent large enough?" The answer depends upon subjective utility and policy for risk. We need an analytic definition of risk premium stated in terms of subjective utility.

Pratt defined both risk aversion and risk premium in terms of utility.[15] Following Pratt, if we let $U(R)$ be a utility function for money, then a useful measure of risk aversion is the function

$$r(R) = -U''(R)/U'(R) > 0 \qquad (12.39)$$

where

$r(R)$ = a measure of local risk aversion

$U'(R)$ = rate of change of utility as expected return changes, i.e., the first derivative with respect to R of $U(R)$; $U'(R) > 0$ for all rational investors

---

[15] John W. Pratt, "Risk Aversion in the Small and Large," *Econometrica*, vol. XXXII, January–April 1964, pp. 122–136.

$U''(R)$ = acceleration (second derivative) of change in utility as expected return changes: $U''(R) < 0$ for risk averse investors

For a complete discussion of (12.39), the reader is referred to the original literature. However, we can make the following observations from (12.39).

In the context of (12.39), the required risk premium (risk aversion) *declines* as the marginal utility for money [$U'(R)$] increases. $U'(R)$ can increase by relatively large amounts if relatively large returns are involved. But (12.39) also states that risk aversion (risk premium) *rises* as the amount of concavity (i.e., acceleration) of $U(R)$ increases. That is, interpreting $U''(R)$ as the rate of change of marginal utility, then, if $U''(R)$ is relatively large, then a relatively large premium can be required for accepting the risk under consideration. If the magnitude of rate of change of marginal utility is relatively small and the marginal utility itself is relatively large (e.g., if relatively huge profits are possible and are "worth the risks involved") then the ratio stated in (12.39) can be relatively small, requiring a relatively small premium for accepting the risks. Statement (12.39) describes relative amounts of aversion to risk and is indicative of premiums required by risk averse investors to accept risk.

Since (12.39) is proportional to risk aversion and risk premium, then *constant* risk aversion implies constant risk premiums throughout the range of returns under consideration.

$$r'(R) = d[r(R)]/dR = \text{Constant for all relevant } R \qquad \textbf{(12.40)}$$

Since risk premium is defined as the difference between the cash equivalent (i.e., certainty-equivalent value) and the expected value of the risky return, constant risk premium means that this difference must remain constant when considering the entire range of possible returns. The situation implies that the investor is no more (or no less) averse to risk when large sums of money are involved than when smaller sums of money are involved. Also, under constant risk aversion, the investor is equally averse to risk when considering possible profits as he is when considering possible losses. There may be some range of potential returns over which constant risk aversion applies in the real-world, but then again there may not. The real-life situation depends upon the particular set of alternatives available and the personal preferences of the investor.

Declining (but always positive) aversion to risk implies decreasing risk premiums throughout the range of relevant returns.

$$r'(R) = d[r(R)]/dR < 0 \qquad \textbf{(12.41)}$$

Decreasing aversion to risk means that though averse, the amount of aversion decreases as potential payoffs rise. Hence, over the range of possible returns, the risk premium declines as the expected return rises. This behavior is typical of investors who are highly averse to risk (i.e., require large risk premiums) if losses on investment are possible. But at the same time, these investors are *not* quite so averse to taking bigger chances at possibly doubling their money (especially if at worse they will break even). One can infer from these statements that risk premiums can decrease with wealth.

Increasing aversion to risk implies that risk premiums rise monotonically over the range of possible returns.

$$r'(R) = d[r(R)]/dr > 0 \qquad \text{(12.42)}$$

Increasing aversion to risk means that the amount of aversion and, hence, risk premiums *increase* as the expected return on investment rises. Quadratic utility functions as stated in (12.29) exhibit this property of increasing aversion to risk. To illustrate, take the quadratic utility function

$$U(R) = A_0 + A_1 R + A_2 R^2 \qquad \text{(12.43)}$$

where A_0 and A_1 both are positive constants and A_2 is a negative constant, then

$$U'(R) = A_1 + A_2 R > 0 \qquad \text{(12.44)}$$

and

$$U''(R) = A_2 < 0 \qquad \text{(12.45)}$$

Therefore, by (12.39), a measure of risk aversion can be written as

$$\begin{aligned} r(R) &= -[U''(R)/U'(R)] \\ &= -A_2/(A_1 + A_2 R) > 0 \end{aligned} \qquad \text{(12.46)}$$

The risk premium as stated in (12.46) is positive as required. The rate of change of aversion to risk over the range of relevant returns can be written:

$$\begin{aligned} r'(R) &= -A_2[-1(A_1 + A_2 R)^{-2}](A_2) \\ &= [A_2/(A_1 + A_2 R)]^2 > 0 \end{aligned} \qquad \text{(12.47)}$$

Since the term inside the brackets of (12.47) is to be squared, its results are always positive. Therefore, for a quadratic utility function, $r'(R)$ is always positive, implying an increasing risk premium over the entire range of relevant returns. Quadratic utility functions may be useful for describing behavior of some investors but can be highly inappropriate for describing risk policy for other investors. Since quadratic functions are used extensively in the literature, we shall sheepishly follow the practice, despite their shortcomings.

12.7 Constant Expected Utility: Indifference Curves

The purpose of this section is to show some relationships which must exist between risk and return, if utility is to remain constant while substituting return for risk. Constant utility implies indifference between one risk-return pair and some alternative risk-return pair.

The analysis will proceed assuming a quadratic certainty equivalent utility function. Let

$$U(R) = aR - bR^2 \tag{12.48}$$

where

$U(R)$ = utility for return
R = return
a and b = positive constants determined subjectively by the risk preferences of the investor

Now, if expected utility is to be always constant, we can write

$$E[U(R)] = E(aR) - E(bR^2) = \text{Constant} \tag{12.49}$$

Taking expected values we get

$$aE(R) - b\{[E(R)]^2 + \sigma^2(R)\} = \text{Constant} \tag{12.50}$$

or, equivalently,

$$a\mu - b\mu^2 - b\sigma^2 = \text{Constant} \tag{12.51}$$

Then to calculate the relationship between expected return (μ) and risk [$\sigma(R)$] which is necessary to afford constant expected utility, we can differentiate (12.51) with respect to risk.

$$\frac{d(a\mu)}{d\sigma} - \frac{d(b\mu^2)}{d\sigma} - \frac{d(b\sigma^2)}{d\sigma} = \frac{d(\text{Constant})}{d\sigma} \tag{12.52}$$

$$a\left(\frac{d\mu}{d\sigma}\right) - 2b\mu\left(\frac{d\mu}{d\sigma}\right) - 2b\sigma = 0 \tag{12.53}$$

Solving (12.53) for ($d\mu/d\sigma$), we get

$$(a - 2b\mu)\frac{d\mu}{d\sigma} = 2b\sigma \tag{12.54}$$

$$\frac{d\mu}{d\sigma} = 2b\sigma/(a - 2b\mu) > 0 \tag{12.55}$$

The denominator of (12.55), $\{a - 2b[E(R)]\}$ = marginal utility of return at $E(R)$ and, by equation (12.4) is positive. Hence, for b positive,

$(d\mu/d\sigma)$ is positive (i.e., the slope of the indifference curve in the μ, σ plane is always positive). Similar results are obtained if $d\sigma/d\mu$ is taken.[16]

To study the acceleration (curvature) of the indifference curve in the μ, σ plane, second derivatives must be taken. The second derivative is positive for aversion to risk, which causes the general shape of the indifference curve to be as shown in Figure 12.4.[17] In Figure 12.4, the two assets, A and B, both provide the same level of utility.

---

[16] The equations are as follows

$$\frac{d(a\mu)}{d\mu} - \frac{d(b\mu^2)}{d\mu} - \frac{d(b\sigma^2)}{d\mu} = \frac{d(\text{constant})}{d\mu} \tag{12.56}$$

$$a - 2b\mu - 2b\sigma\left(\frac{d\sigma}{d\mu}\right) = 0 \tag{12.57}$$

$$(a - 2b\mu) = 2b\sigma\left(\frac{d\sigma}{d\mu}\right) \tag{12.58}$$

$$\frac{d\sigma}{d\mu} = [(a - 2b\mu)/2b\sigma] > 0 \tag{12.59}$$

[17] The second derivative (acceleration) is positive (for b positive). This can be shown as follows.

$$\frac{d}{d\sigma(R)}\left\{\frac{d[E(R)]}{d[\sigma(R)]}\right\} = \frac{\{[a - 2bE(R)][+2b]\}\left([2b\sigma(R)]\left\{- 2b\frac{d[E(R)]}{d[\sigma(R)]}\right\}\right)}{[a - 2bE(R)]^2}$$

$$= \frac{\{2b[a - 2bE(R)]\} - \left\{2b[-2b\sigma(R)]\frac{d[E(R)]}{d[\sigma(R)]}\right\}}{[a - 2bE(R)]^2}$$

$$= \left[\frac{2b}{a - 2bE(R)}\right] - \left\{\frac{2b[-2b\sigma(R)]\left[\frac{a - 2bE(R)}{a - 2bE(R)}\right]\frac{d[E(R)]}{d\sigma(R)}}{[a - 2bE(R)]^2}\right\} \tag{12.60}$$

$$= \left[\frac{2b}{a - 2bE(R)}\right] - \left\{\frac{- 2b[a - 2bE(R)]\left[\frac{dE(R)}{d\sigma(R)}\right]^2}{[a - 2bE(R)]^2}\right\}$$

$$= \left[\frac{2b}{a - 2bE(R)}\right] + \left\{\frac{2b\left[\frac{dE(R)}{d\sigma(R)}\right]^2}{a - 2bE(R)}\right\}$$

$$\frac{d^2E(R)}{d[\sigma(R)]^2} = \frac{2b\left\{1 + \left[\frac{dE(R)}{d(R)}\right]^2\right\}}{a - 2bE(R)} > 0 \tag{12.61}$$

because $b > 0$ and $[a - 2bE(R)] > 0$.

See James Tobin, "The Theory of Portfolio Selection," in F. Hahn & F. Brechling, *The Theory of Interest Rates*, The Macmillan Company, New York, 1965, pp. 18–22.

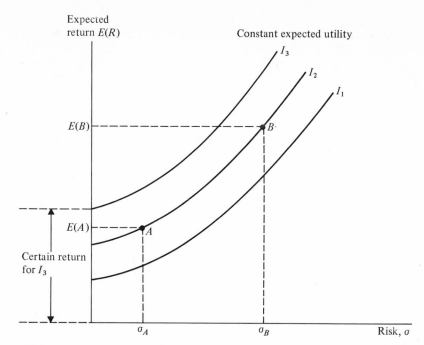

Figure 12.4. Indifference curves: Loci of constant expected quadratic utility. Quadratic certainty-equivalent return.

SOME POSSIBLE ANALYTIC FORMS FOR UTILITY FUNCTIONS

1. Quadratic or cubic

$$U(R) = A_0 + A_1R + A_2R^2 \qquad (12.62a)$$

$$U(R) = A_0 + A_1R + A_2R^2 + A_3R^3 \qquad (12.62b)$$

2. Logarithmic form 1

$$U(R) = A_0 + A_1\{\ln [(R + A_2)/W]\}, \qquad (R + A_2) > 0$$
$$W \geq 1$$
$$(12.63)$$

3. Logarithmic form 2

$$U(R) = A_0 + A_1\{\ln [(R + A_2 - A_3|R|)/W]\},$$
$$(R + A_2) > A_3|R|, \qquad W \geq 1$$
$$(12.64)$$

4. Radical (square root) form

$$U(R) = A_0 + A_1[(R + A_2)/W]^{1/n} \qquad (12.65)$$

where

$$(R + A_2) > 0$$
$$W \geq 1$$
$$n \geq 2$$

5. Exponential forms

$$U(R) = A_0 + A_1 \exp -\{\psi[\phi(R)]\} \qquad (12.66a)$$

$$U(R) = \frac{A_0 + R - e^{-\Psi R}}{A_1 - e^{-\Psi}} \qquad (12.66b)$$

$$U(R) = \frac{R + e^{\Psi R} - A_0}{e^{\Psi}} \qquad (12.66c)$$

where

ψ = coefficient of risk aversion

$\phi(R)$ = either of forms (12.62), (12.63), (12.64), or (12.65) above.

406

RELATING UTILITY FUNCTIONS TO RISK-RETURN PARAMETERS OF INVESTMENT PORTFOLIOS

The purpose of this appendix is to show how utility functions can be expressed as moments of a probability distribution stated in terms of expected return and risk on investment. The method involves expanding the utility function into a Taylor series.

TAYLOR EXPANSION OF A UTILITY FUNCTION. To express any function $[f(R)]$ (transcendental or not) as a polynomial of degree n, we can use a Taylor series expansion of $f(R)$ about any constant $(R = \mu)$. That is, if we are concerned with value of return (R) near the mean (μ), then we can write an approximating polynomial in powers of $(R - \mu)$. Thus,

$$f_n(R) = a_0 + a_1(R - \mu) + a_2(R - \mu)^2 + \cdots + a_n(R - \mu)^n$$
$$(12.67)$$

The objective is to calculate the coefficients $a_0, a_1, \ldots, a_n$. The coefficients must be calculated so that the polynomial (12.67) and its first n derivatives agree with the function stated originally. That is, the first n derivatives of the polynomial (12.67) must agree with the corresponding derivatives of the given function, when evaluated at R equals μ. So we are led to the series

$$f(\mu) + f'(\mu)(R - \mu) + \frac{f''(\mu)}{2!}(R - \mu)^2 + \frac{f'''(\mu)}{3!}(R - \mu)^3 + \cdots$$
$$+ \frac{f^n(\mu)}{n!}(R - \mu)^n + \cdots \qquad (12.68)$$

where $f^n(\mu)$ denotes the value of the nth derivative of the function $f(R)$ evaluated at $R = \mu$, and $n!$ represents factorial n.

Statement (12.68) is known as the Taylor series expansion of $f(R)$ about $R = \mu$. Evaluation of the function is illustrated below.

EXPANSION OF A QUADRATIC UTILITY FUNCTION INTO A TAYLOR SERIES. Suppose we have a quadratic utility function,

$$U(R) = f(R) = R - AR^2 \qquad (12.69)$$

then the first three derivatives can be written as follows:

$$f'(R) = 1 - 2AR \qquad (12.70)$$

$$f''(R) = -2A \qquad (12.71)$$

$$f''' = 0 \qquad (12.72)$$

407

Now the Taylor series expansion of $f(R)$ is written

$$f_n(R) = a_0 + a_1(R - \mu) + a_2(R - \mu)^2 + a_3(R - \mu)^2 + \cdots \tag{12.73}$$

where μ = mean of the probability distribution of expected returns. The constants in (12.73) are written as follows

$$a_0 = f(\mu) = \mu - A\mu^2 \tag{12.74}$$

$$a_1 = f'(\mu) = 1 - 2A\mu \tag{12.75}$$

$$a_2 = [f''(\mu)/2] = -A \tag{12.76}$$

Substituting the constants into (12.73) we get

$$f_n(R) = (\mu - A\mu^2) + (1 - 2A\mu)(R - \mu) + (-A)(R - \mu)^2 \tag{12.77}$$

Therefore, taking expectations from (12.77), we get

$$\begin{aligned} E[U(R)] &= E[f_n(R)] \\ &= E(\mu - A\mu^2) + E[(1 - 2A\mu)(R - \mu)] + E[(-A)(R - \mu)^2] \\ &= [\mu - AE(\mu^2)] + 0 + [(-A)E(R - \mu)^2] \end{aligned} \tag{12.78}$$

But since the mean-value (μ) of the distribution is an expected constant, (12.78) can be written as

$$\begin{aligned} E[U(R)] &= \mu - A\mu^2 - A\mathrm{var}(R) \\ &= \mu - A[\mu^2 + \mathrm{var}(R)] \end{aligned} \tag{12.79}$$

Statement (12.79) is the expected quadratic utility of return, expressed in terms of the mean and variance of the probability distribution of expected returns, where A equals the coefficient of aversion to risk.

QUESTIONS FOR STUDY

1. Explain the Friedman-Savage (standard gamble) experiment for calculating the subjective utility function for investors who are averse to risk.
2. One of the Friedman-Savage conclusions is that investors generally behave as if they have a consistent set of preferences, and these preferences can be completely described by attaching a numerical value—designated "utility"—to alternatives each of which is regarded as certain. Describe and illustrate how such numerical values can be obtained.
3. Explain how you might devise an experiment to calculate the utility function for an investor of your choice. Choose (a) an institutional investor and (b) an individual investor.

4. Sketch a graph of the following utility functions:
   (a) $U(r) = A + B \log (R + C)$
   $\qquad R =$ minus $40 million to plus $150 million
   (b) $U(r) = A + B \log (R + C - D|R|)$
   $\qquad R =$ minus $400 million to plus $800 million
   $\qquad$ Assume appropriate values for the other constants, A, B, C, D.

5. Plot a family of utility curves for various values for the arguments in the utility functions specified below.
   $$U_1 = f(W, X, X^2) \qquad \text{quadratic}$$
   $$U_2 = f(W, \sqrt{X}) \qquad \text{square root}$$
   $$U_3 = f(W, \log X) \qquad \text{logarithmic}$$
   $$U_4 = f(W, e^x) \qquad \text{exponential}$$

6. Show that all the conditions necessary for a utility curve, including the requirement of constant or monotonically decreasing risk premiums, are satisfied by the logarithmic function, $U(R) = A + B \log (R + c)$, where $(R + c) > 0$.

7. Show that for a quadratic utility function
   (a) utility rises as return rises (over the relevant range of expected return).
   (b) the rate of change of marginal utility (second derivative of utility) is always at a decreasing rate (over the relevant range of expected returns).
   (c) utility falls as risk rises.

8. Calculate the quadratic curve for Figure 12.2, using utility limits of zero and 1, instead of 5 and 12. [See equations (12.30).]

9. Explain the practical significance of axioms 4 and 5.

10. Explain the meaning of the following concepts:
    (a) increasing aversion to risk
    (b) decreasing aversion to risk
    (c) constant aversion to risk
    (d) risk premium

11. Calculate a Taylor series expansion for a square root utility function. (See equation 12.79, Appendix 2 for Chapter 12.)

12. Describe the locus of constant expected utility (i.e., compute the indifference curves of Figure 12.4) when a square root function describes utility. Note that skewness becomes important for a square root utility.

13. Explain the difference between a risk-aversion parameter and a risk premium.

From chapter 12, we found that analysis for the optimal management of assets can be divided into two parts: (1) there is the individual (or institutional) investor, who has the task of specifying required returns and policy for accepting (or rejecting) risk. The required specification usually depends upon subjective attitudes and behavior towards risk and upon utility for money. (2) There is the market, complete with all its opportunities available for investment. Some investment opportunities in the market can dominate others. Dominant opportunities are unequivocally superior.[1]

But many real-world opportunities may be neither clearly dominant nor clearly inferior. Many real-world opportunities can offer more risk than is necessary to obtain a given return. In one sense, these opportunities can be labeled "clearly inferior" because alternative opportunities exist which are more "efficient." Efficient alternatives offer the same returns, but at lower risks and, therefore, provide larger utility. Risk preferences and utility were discussed in the preceding chapter; analysis of efficient opportunities is discussed here.

Portfolio Analysis: Efficient Diversification and Optimal Investments

13

The analysis in Chapter 13 proceeds in two dimensions: risk and expected return. We shall find that it is possible to obtain real-world investments which satisfy the conditions of utility as set forth in the preceding chapter. Many real-world investment returns do rise with increasing risk.

13.1 The Portfolio Problem

The portfolio problem can be set forth in a generalized way as follows. Consider an array of assets for potential investment. The assets can be labeled $A_1, A_2, \ldots, A_n$. The collection of assets can be (1) the

-----
[1] Refer to Figure 6.1.

product mix for a diversified conglomerate business operation, (2) a mix of alternative media for advertising, or (3) a set of bonds and common stocks. One possible portfolio might include a collection of assets such as:

1. Cash—Foreign and/or domestic currency.
2. Time deposits—Insured savings accounts, certificates of deposit, and savings and loan shares.
3. Bonds—Corporate debt and federal, state, or local government obligations.
4. Common stocks—Stocks traded on the NYSE, AMEX, and over-the-counter or regional exchanges.
5. Physical assets—Real estate and business plant and equipment.
6. Human capital—Education and health.
7. Professional practice.

Then, given a set of assets to be considered for investment, the questions to be answered are (1) what particular assets from the overall available set should be selected for investment and (2) after the selection of individual items, what proportion of the money available should be allocated to each item?

Answers to the portfolio problem depend partly upon personal preference as discussed in the preceding chapter. This is so, because one ultimate objective of asset management is to maximize utility. But utility can be maximized only within the set of available opportunities—the assets themselves. The available assets can be considered either alone or together in various combinations with one another. We shall proceed toward maximizing utility via an analysis of potential portfolios.

The approach follows two steps. First, the basic principles of diversification are discussed. Three situations are used to illustrate the principles: (1) hold either risky or riskless assets (*no* diversification), (2) hold both risky and riskless assets, and (3) hold various proportions of two risky assets. Second, the fundamental principles are expanded and applied to portfolios which contain any number of assets and which operate under any number of constraints.

13.2 Diversification

"Don't put all your eggs in one basket!" So goes the advice of an ancient expert on broken eggs. The same advice is often made to prudent investors. Diversification represents a fundamental principle of successful portfolio management. The principle is to reduce the risks in investment by diversifying over several assets. In other words, assuming that risk is inherent in most available opportunities for investment and that these risks cannot be avoided, then one rational act is to reduce the inherent risk (to its minimum possible value?) and subsequently get paid appropriately for accepting the residual. The object of diversifying is not necessarily to avoid risk but to find, accept, and get paid for an acceptable type and level of risk.

The logic behind spreading one's eggs over many baskets is rooted in years of experience on a farm. If disaster befalls a lone basket which contains all the eggs, then every egg can be broken; every dollar can be lost and financial disaster can occur. Advice to diversify, therefore, is conservative. Diversification limits risk. But there is a price to pay for safety because diversification also limits return. That is, if all the eggs are in a single basket, and that particular basket happens to be precisely the right basket at precisely the right time (i.e., your particular invest- ment happens to be a "winner"), then astronomical profits can result. Therefore, the conclusion is that diversification can be viewed as "good" in that it limits risks, but at the same time diversification can be viewed as "bad" in that it can limit profits. Optimal diversification means obtaining the best possible tradeoff between safety (i.e., risk) and return. More precisely, optimal diversification means minimizing risk (or, stated positively, maximizing safety) for a given required (i.e., expected) return. Optimal diversification also means maximizing expected return for a given acceptable level of risk. Efficient manage- ment of assets means obtaining optimal diversification. The essential characteristics and impact of optimal diversification on investment results (i.e., the variations of portfolio returns as risk levels vary) are · illustrated in the cases of the following example.

To Diversify or Not To Diversify?   Suppose $100,000 in cash is avail- able to you for a 1-year investment. The first question is, What assets are to be considered? For simplicity, consider only three assets:

1. Cash, with certainty of zero return.
2. A guaranteed 1-year loan made to some borrower in the market- place.
3. A long-term government bond (e.g., a consol).

The expected returns from the three potential investments are

$$\text{Expected return from cash} = E(R_{\text{cash}}) = R_c = .00 \qquad \textbf{(13.1)}$$

$$\text{Expected guaranteed return} = E(R_{\text{guaranteed}}) = R_G > .00$$
$$\textbf{(13.2)}$$

$$\text{Expected return from the consol} = E(R_{\text{bond}})$$
$$= E(C/P_0) + E[(P_1 - P_0)/P_0]$$
$$= (C/P_0) + (1/P_0)E(P_1) - 1.00$$
$$\textbf{(13.3)}$$

where

$$C/P_0 = \text{coupon (current) yield}$$
$$(P_1 - P_0)/P_0 = \text{capital gain (or loss) obtained upon sale of the}$$
$$\text{consol one year hence}$$

The risks (i.e., errors of prediction) associated with those three investments are

$$\text{Risk from cash} = \sigma(R_c) = .00 \tag{13.4}$$

$$\text{Risk from guaranteed return} = \sigma(R_G) = .00 \tag{13.5}$$

$$\text{Risk from bond} = \sigma(R_B) = \{\text{var}(C/P_0) + \text{var}[(P_1 - P_0)/P_0]\}^{1/2}$$
$$= [(1/P_0)^2\text{var}(P_1)]^{1/2} \tag{13.6}$$
$$= (1/P_0)\sigma(P_1) \geq .00$$

Note that in stating the risk incurred from investing in the bond, we assume that the current yield will be paid for sure (i.e., no chance of default on interest income), which causes $\text{var}(C/P_0)$ to equal zero. All covariances equal zero. Hence (13.6) says that risk of investment in long-term bonds emanates from error of estimate (i.e., inability to predict) sale price (P_1) 1 year hence. This prediction and corresponding error can inherently capture notions such as (1) probability that the bond will become worthless and (2) poor marketability. If the error of prediction equals zero, then $\sigma(P_1)$ equals zero and investment in the consol is not risky. However, as the inability to predict increases, $\sigma(P_1)$ increases, causing risk $[\sigma(R_B)]$ to increase.

The next question to be answered is, Given the three available assets, which one (or ones) should be selected? What should be the diversification? The answer involves portfolio analysis.

To begin, the criterion of maximizing utility directs us to rank asset A_2, the guaranteed loan, ahead of asset A_1, cash, because both assets have the same risk, $\sigma(R_G) = \sigma(R_C) = .00$. But the guaranteed lending rate exceeds the return obtained from holding cash. The return from cash is assumed to be zero.

$$R_G > R_C = .00 \tag{13.7}$$

Therefore the guaranteed loan is preferred over cash.

But what about investment in the bond? The bond is risky. As stated in (13.3), if the sale price one year hence (P_1) is sufficiently small, then losses can result from investing in the bond. To be precise (but ignoring taxes and transactions costs) losses are expected if the expected sale price is less than the present price, less coupon income.

$$(C/P_0) + (1/P_0)E(P_1) < 1.00 \tag{13.8}$$

or

$$E(P_1) < (P_0 - C) \tag{13.9}$$

Therefore, the choice between the guaranteed loan and the bond (or some of each) depends upon expectations concerning future prices of bonds and chances for error in those expectations. The analysis can proceed as follows. Two options are possible: (1) not to diversify or (2) diversify.

CASE 1: Not to Diversify. In the special case when the returns expected from one asset dominate the returns expected from the alternative asset, then the entire amount ($100,000 in this case) can be allocated optimally to the single asset, the dominant asset. Dominance can occur in either of two possible conditions. For the two assets at hand, the first possibility is that future sale price of the bond is believed to be known with certainty [i.e., $\sigma(R_B) = .00$], and also that price is sufficiently large so that the expected return on the bond exceeds the guaranteed return.

$$E(R_B) = R_B = [(C/P_0) + (P_1/P_0) - 1.00] > R_G > .00 \tag{13.10}$$

$$\sigma(R_B) = (1/P_0)\sigma(P_1) = .00 \tag{13.11}$$

In this situation, 100 percent investment in the (riskless) bond is the most profitable strategy.

The second possibility is that the future sale price of the bond is predicted, not with certainty but with error; but, even considering the error, the smallest return likely from the bond exceeds the guaranteed alternative lending rate.

$$\sigma(R_B) > .00 \tag{13.12}$$

$$[E(R_B) - \delta\sigma(R_B)] > R_G > .00 \tag{13.13}$$

where δ = a constant.[2]

Statement (13.13) requires the expected return on investment from the bonds to exceed the guaranteed lending rate by an amount at least equal to $\delta\sigma(R_B)$.

$$E(R_B) > [R_G + \delta\sigma(R_B)] = K \tag{13.14}$$

where K = a constant. In this second situation, 100 percent investment in bonds is the most profitable strategy. No diversification is needed.

Note that in the special case when the forecast error equals zero, statement (13.14) is the same as (13.10). In either case, the investment

---

[2] The constant δ denotes the number of standard deviation units to the left of the mean that are considered relevant. For example, if the errors of prediction are distributed normally, then $\delta = 3.00$ will provide small chances (probability equals one-half of three-tenths of 1 percent or 15 chances in 10,000) that the return will fall below the point stated in (13.13).

decision depends upon future price of bonds which, in turn, depends upon future long-term yields available in the marketplace as discussed in Chapter 9.

To review, bond prices vary inversely with yields. With a consol, for example,

$$P = C/i \qquad (13.15)$$

where

P = market price (i.e., present value) of consol
C = periodic coupon (interest) income stream forever
i = rate of return or yield[3]

Therefore current price (P_0) depends upon present yields (i_0) and future price (P_1) depends upon future yields (i_1).

$$P_0 = C/i_0, \qquad P_1 = C/i_1 \qquad (13.16)$$

We can conclude that the investment decision, whether to diversify or not, depends upon the level and predictability of either future price (P_1) or future yield (i_1). The precise conditions and minimum requirements for a decision can be derived and stated as follows.

First, solve equation (13.10) for either i_1 (in terms of R_G and i_0) or else for i_0 (in terms of R_G and i_1). Thus, after substituting (13.16) into (13.10) we calculate the minimum return required on the bond, stated in terms of bond yields.

$$\{i_0 + (i_0/C)[C(1/i_1)] - 1.00\} > R_G \qquad (13.17)$$

Equation (13.17) can be solved for either i_1 or i_0[4]

$$i_1 < [i_0/(1 + i_0 + R_G)] \qquad \text{or} \qquad i_0 > \{(1 + R_G)[i_1/(1 + i_1)]\} \qquad (13.18)$$

Note that neither of the two statements in (13.18) necessarily implies a cause-effect relationship between the three factors i_0, i_1, and R_G.

---

[3] See equation (4.38).
[4] The solution of equation (13.17) can be shown as follows. Solving (13.17) for i_1, we get

$$i_0 + (i_0/i_1) > (1 + R_G) \qquad (13.19)$$

$$(i_0/i_1) > (1 + R_G - i_0) \qquad (13.20)$$

$$i_1 < i_0/(1 + R_G - i_0) \qquad (13.21)$$

Solving (13.17) for i_0, we get

$$[1 + (1/i_1)]i_0 > (1 + R_G) \qquad (13.22)$$

$$[(1 + i_1)/i_1]i_0 > (1 + R_G) \qquad (13.23)$$

$$i_0 > [(1 + R_G)i_1/(1 + i_1)] \qquad (13.24)$$

Indeed, the assumption is: i_0 and R_G are known and stated, today. Exogenous expectations are stated for i_1.

Second, sufficient conditions for bonds to dominate the guaranteed investment can be stated as follows.

In terms of i_1, condition (13.18) indicates that if long-term yields on bonds are believed with certainty to fall to levels below $i_0/(1 - i_0 + R_G)$, then consol prices will rise sufficiently high so that (ignoring taxes and transactions costs) capital gains and current income will cause consols to be a better investment than the best guaranteed (i.e., risk-free) alternative. If there is error associated with expectations for the level of i_1, then, for R_G, substitute $K = [R_G + \delta\sigma(R_B)]$ as stated in 13.14).

EXAMPLE. To illustrate the calculations using actual numbers, suppose the following data are given:

$$i_0 = 6 \text{ percent}, \qquad R_G = 10 \text{ percent} \qquad \textbf{(13.25)}$$

Then optimal investment will be 100 percent bonds if i_1 is believed for sure to be less than 5.77 percent; otherwise, the optimal investment is the risk-free 1-year loan.

$$i_1 < .06/(1.00 - .06 + .10) = .0577 \qquad \textbf{(13.26)}$$

If there is error associated with beliefs for the level of i_1 (possibly a normally distributed error so that $\delta = 3.00$), then for bonds to dominate the guaranteed 10 percent, long-term yields must fall to levels which become lower as the error increases.

$$i_1 < .06/[1.04 + 3\sigma(R_B)] \qquad \textbf{(13.27)}$$

For example, if i_1 is believed with error of $\sigma(R_B) = .01$ to be equal to 5 percent (remember, the present rate is 6 percent), then even with error, the bond will dominate the loan.

$$i_1 < .06/[1.04 + 3(.01)] = .056 = 5.6 \text{ percent} \qquad \textbf{(13.28)}$$

If the best alternative available is cash with a yield of zero then long-term yields can actually rise from 6.00 percent to 6.38 percent, with bond prices falling, so that capital losses neutralize some of the coupon income.

$$i_1 < .06/(1.00 - .06 + .00) = .0638 \qquad \textbf{(13.29)}$$

Hence, the optimal investment depends upon a combination of the level of future yields (i_1) relative to present yields (i_0), along with the most profitable present guaranteed alternative opportunity. Observe from statement (13.17) that as the guaranteed alternative return (R_G) rises, the future yield (i_1) must fall to even lower levels (i.e., capital gains must be even larger) if long-term bonds are to attract investment dollars today.

Sufficient conditions for bonds to dominate the guaranteed investment can be stated in terms of i_0 instead of i_1. In terms of prevailing yields (i_0) condition (13.18) indicates that if long-term yields on bonds presently exceed $(1 + R_G)[i_1/(1 + i_1)]$, then consol prices will rise sufficiently so that 100 percent investment in consols will be superior to 100 percent investment in the best risk-free alternative.

To illustrate, suppose the following data are given:

$$i_1 = 5 \text{ percent}; \quad \sigma(R_B) = \sigma(P_1) = \sigma(C/i_1) = .00; R_G = 9 \text{ percent} \tag{13.30}$$

Then optimal investment will be 100 percent in bonds if long-term yields presently exceed 5.19 percent.

$$i_0 > \{(1.00 + .09)[.05/(1.00 + .05)]\} = .0519 \tag{13.31}$$

If i_1 is believed to be 5 percent but with an error of $\sigma(R_B) = .04$, then, for bonds to dominate the guaranteed loan, i_0 must exceed 5.76 percent.[5]

$$i_0 > [1.09 + 3(.04)](.05/1.05) = .0576 \tag{13.32}$$

Statement (13.32) says that if long-term yields presently are 5.9 percent (or higher), and i_1 is believed to be 5 percent, with error $\sigma = .04$, then the long-term bonds are superior to the 9 percent alternative. This is true because capital gains resulting from the fall in bond yields (from 5.9 percent to 5.0 percent) will more than compensate for the difference between 5.9 percent obtained and 9 percent foregone.

$$[.059 + (.059/.050) - 1.00] = .24 > R_G = .09 \tag{13.33}$$

To study how the value of the guaranteed return will affect the investment decision, we can note that if the best available alternative for investment is cash with a yield of zero, and if i_1 is known to be 5 percent, then i_0 must be larger than 4.76 percent to make a one-year investment in long-term bonds preferable to cash.

$$i_0 > \{(1.00 + .00)[.05/(1.00 + .05)]\} = .0476 \tag{13.34}$$

SUMMARY. A summary of the above analysis can be expressed as follows. If investors believe (for sure) that present long-term interest

---

[5] This calculation assumes that 99.7 percent of the possible outcomes will be captured within three standard deviation units of the expected value. This is as per the normal distribution. If the distribution of errors of forecast has finite variance but unknown shape, then the Tchebycheff theorem as discussed in Appendix 2 for Chapter 6 can be applied.

rates are abnormally high (i.e., prices of long-term bonds are abnormally low) and, therefore, will fall (i.e., causing bond prices to rise) soon, then investors can profit by holding bonds instead of cash. Alternatively, if investors believe that current interest rates are abnormally low (i.e., bond prices are abnormally high) and will therefore soon rise (causing bond prices to fall), then investors can profit (i.e., avoid capital losses) by holding cash instead of bonds.

In the Keynesian world with inelasticity of expectations of future interest rates and certainty, rational investors will hold either cash or bonds, not both.[6] Even if the Keynesian world is extended, as we did above, to allow for risk and uncertainty, then, under some conditions, investors can maximize utility by holding either cash or bonds, not both. However, in situations where risk and uncertainty are large, and dominance fails to hold, then rational investors can hedge by holding both cash *and* bonds. This possibility of hedging is examined next.

CASE 2: To Diversify.   Continuing with the two assets A_2 and A_3 as hypothesized above, we can ask "Under what conditions is diversification advisable?" The answer can be stated simply. Other things being the same, higher returns are always preferred over lower returns; hence if the (ex-post) return on bonds will exceed the (ex-post) guaranteed return, then bonds are preferred. But bonds are risky because of the inability to precisely predict future yields (i_1). That is, from (13.10), (13.11), and (13.13), the expected return from the bonds is related linearly to the expected sale price one year hence. The error of predicting that return [$\sigma(R_B)$] is linearly related to the error of predicting the price [$\sigma(P_1)$].

$$
\begin{aligned}
E(R_B) &= (C/P_0 - 1.00) + (1/P_0)E(P_1) \\
&= (C/P_0 - 1.00) + (C/P_0)E(1/i_1) \qquad \textbf{(13.35)} \\
&= \alpha + \beta E(1/i_1)
\end{aligned}
$$

where

$$
\begin{aligned}
\alpha &= \text{Constant} = [(C/P_0) - 1.00] \\
\beta &= \text{Constant} = C/P_0
\end{aligned}
$$

$$
\begin{aligned}
\sigma(R_B) &= [(1/P_0)^2\text{var}(P_1)]^{1/2} \\
&= [(1/P_0)^2\text{var}(C/i_1)]^{1/2} \\
&= [(C/P_0)^2\text{var}(1/i_1)]^{1/2} \qquad \textbf{(13.36)} \\
&= (C/P_0)\sigma(1/i_1) \\
&= \beta\sigma(1/i_1)
\end{aligned}
$$

---

[6] John Maynard Keynes, *General Theory of Employment, Interest, and Money*, Harcourt, Brace & World, Inc., New York, 1936. Also see J. Tobin, "Liquidity Preference as Behavior Towards Risk," *The Review of Economics and Statistics*, vol. 25, February 1958, pp. 65–86.

The conditions necessary for diversification to be profitable are (1) error $\sigma(R_B)$ sufficiently large and (2) expected return $[E(R_B)]$ of an appropriate level, so that some of the returns possible from the bonds will exceed the alternative lending rate, but, at the same time, other of the returns possible from the bonds will fall below the alternative lending rate. This situation is pictured in Figure 13.1. For diversification to increase utility, the guaranteed return (R_G) must fall somewhere within the range of possible returns from the bond. If it were otherwise, the situation would be as explained in case 1. Stated in terms of the risky bond investment, diversification will cause a rise in utility when the distribution of expected returns from investment in bonds overlaps the alternative guaranteed return. One sufficient condition for overlap to occur is shown in Figure 13.1. Otherwise, stochastic dominance occurs. The conditions for dominance are either

$$E(R_B) \geq R_G + \delta\sigma(R_B) \qquad (13.37)$$

or

$$E(R_B) \leq R_G - \delta\sigma(R_B) \qquad (13.38)$$

Given the situation shown in Figure 13.1, the reason for wanting to diversify can be stated as follows. The guaranteed return can be obtained for sure. The risky return can exceed the guaranteed return, but then it may not. Let us see what happens to risk and return on the portfolio if the entire \$100,000 is allocated between the two alternative opportunities. Spreading the eggs over both baskets, we can write the expected return on the combination of two assets

$$E(R_p) = [X_1 E(R_{\text{guaranteed}})] + [X_2 E(R_{\text{bond}})] \qquad (13.39)$$

where

$E(R_p)$ = expected return on the total portfolio of two assets
X_1 = proportion of total investment allocated to the risk-free asset
X_2 = proportion of total investment allocated to the risky security

Note the constraints that all money must be invested, and there is no short selling.

$$X_1 + X_2 = 1.00; \qquad X_1 \geq 0; \qquad X_2 \geq 0 \qquad (13.40)$$

The return expected on the portfolio can be stated in terms of X_2 alone because of condition (13.40). That is, substituting $X_2 = (1 - X_1)$ into (13.39), we can write a statement which shows that the expected return on the portfolio is related linearly to the proportion of money invested in the risky asset.

$$
\begin{aligned}
E(R_p) &= [(1 - X_2)E(R_G)] + X_2 E(R_B) \\
&= E(R_G) + [E(R_B) - E(R_G)]X_2 \qquad (13.41) \\
&= \alpha + \beta X_2
\end{aligned}
$$

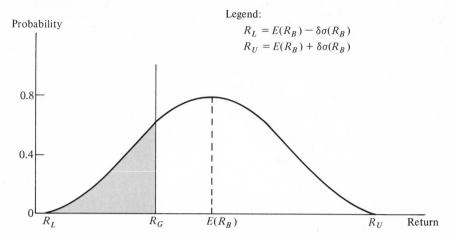

Figure 13.1. Necessary condition for diversification.

where α = constant = R_G and β = constant = $[E(R_B) - R_G]$. Statement (13.41) is a very important relationship which shall be used again later.

Next, the prediction error of the portfolio (risk) is linearly related to the prediction error of the risky asset.

$$\sigma(R_p) = [X_1^2 \text{var}(R_G) + X_2^2 \text{var}(R_B) + 2X_1 X_2 \text{cov}(R_G, R_B)]^{1/2}$$
$$= [.00 + X_2^2 \text{var}(R_B) + .00]^{1/2} \qquad (13.42)$$
$$= X_2 \sigma(R_B)$$

Statement (13.42) shows that since X_2 is constant for any particular portfolio, but is at most equal to 100 percent, the risk associated with any combination of the two assets being analyzed is linearly related to the risk inherent to the risky asset. However, the risk of the combination is less than (or at most equal to) the risk of the risky asset alone. Stated precisely,

$$\sigma(R_p) \leq \sigma(R_B) \text{ because } X_2 \leq 1.00 \qquad (13.43)$$

The risk and expected return of the portfolio, therefore, are stated in (13.42) and (13.41), respectively.

Return vs. Risk. Now comes the important question. In what way does expected return vary with risk? Will expected return increase if risk increases as required by risk-averse investors?[7] The answer is, not

---

[7] Refer to Chapter 12 for a review of the characteristics of risk averse investors.

only does expected return increase with risk; the increase is *linear*. This result can be shown by solving (13.42) for X_2 and then substituting the result into (13.41). Hence, we get a precise statement of the relationship between portfolio risk and portfolio return.

$$E(R_p) = E(R_G) + \{[E(R_B) - R_G]/\sigma(R_B)\}\sigma(R_p)$$
$$= \alpha + \beta\sigma(R_p) \tag{13.44}$$

where $\alpha = $ constant $= R_G$ and $\beta = $ constant $= [E(R_p) - E(R_G)]/\sigma(R_B)$. Applying (6.70) from Chapter 6, we can write

$$\frac{[\sigma(R_P)][\sigma(R_B)]}{\text{var}(R_B)} = \frac{\text{cov}(R_P,R_B)}{\rho\text{var}(R_B)} = \frac{\sigma(R_P)}{\sigma(R_B)} \tag{13.44a}$$

so that (13.44) simplifies to

$$E(R_P) = E(R_G) + \left[\frac{E(R_B) - R_G}{\rho\text{var}(R_B)}\right]\text{cov}(R_P,R_B)$$
$$= \alpha + \beta\text{cov}(R_B,R_B) \tag{13.44b}$$

where

$\alpha = R_G = $ guaranteed return

$\beta = \left[\dfrac{E(R_B) - R_G}{\rho\text{var}(R_B)}\right] = $ constant $= $ risk premium per unit of risk

$\rho = $ coefficient of correlation between portfolio returns and risky asset returns.

Recalling from Chapter 12 that risk premium means the difference between a risky return and a guaranteed return, the constant β in statements (13.44) and (13.44b) can be interpreted as the risk premium per unit of risk offered by the risky asset. In the next chapter, we shall explore further this notion of risk premium per unit of risk. The fundamental idea underlying the significance of the constant (β) is simple: other things the same, assets which offer high ratios of premium to risk are superior to (i.e., have better performance than) assets which have lower ratios of premium to risk.

The linear relationship between risk and expected return as stated in (13.44) can be plotted on a risk-return diagram as shown in Figure 13.3. Statement (13.44) is the equation of the straight line connecting points A_2 and A_3 in Figure 13.2. The line describes the risk-return values of all possible combinations of assets A_2 with A_3. This characteristic line can be explained as follows.

As X_2 varies from 100 percent down to .00 percent, the risk of the portfolio $[\sigma(R_p)]$ varies from its maximum value $[\sigma(R_B)]$ down to its minimum value, zero. As stated in (13.42), this variation in risk is linear. While the risk of the portfolio is declining, the expected return on the

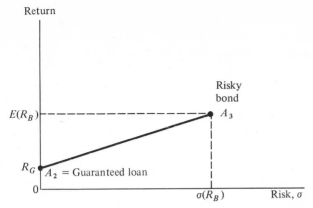

Figure 13.2. Combination of risk-free investment with risky investment.

portfolio is also declining. Recall that we said earlier "diversification can be viewed as 'good' in that it limits risks; but at the same time diversification might be viewed as 'bad' in that it *might* limit profits."[8] With maximum risk $[\sigma(R_p) = \sigma(R_B)]$ expected return is maximum, $E(R_p) = E(R_B)$. As X_2 declines from 1.00 down toward .00, risk declines *linearly* toward zero and expected return declines toward its minimum value, the guaranteed lending rate. Sharpe has found and reported empirical evidence that investors behave in accordance with (13.44).[9]

EXAMPLE. To illustrate the conclusions stated above, suppose the following data are given:

$$E(R_B) = 20 \text{ percent;} \quad \sigma(R_B) = .27; \quad R_G = 8 \text{ percent} \tag{13.45}$$

Then the portfolio risk depends upon the proportion of money allocated to risky bonds. The expected return on the portfolio is linearly related to the portfolio risk.

$$\sigma(R_p) = .27X_2 \tag{13.46}$$

$$E(R_p) = .08 + [(.20 - .08)/(.27)]\sigma(R_p) \\ = .08 + .444\sigma(R_p) \tag{13.47}$$

---

[8] The word "might" is italicized here because, depending upon covariance, as we shall see shortly, expected returns can rise while risks fall.
[9] See William F. Sharpe, "Risk Aversion in the Stock Market," *Journal of Finance*, vol. 20, September, 1965, pp. 416–422.

Statement (13.47) is an important result which can be stated in several ways. First, considering alternative risky (but nondominant) assets, the "best" asset is the asset for which the line shown in Figure 13.2 is steepest. That is, the risky asset which provides the greatest ratio of risk premium to risk $[E(R_B - R_G)/\sigma(R_B)]$ will allow expected return to rise at a faster (even though constant) rate than some alternative asset. This faster rise in expected return will in turn allow higher levels of utility to be achieved, as explained in Chapter 12.

Second, after having selected from among alternative risky assets and considering guaranteed opportunities for lending or borrowing (i.e., opportunities which involve some risk-free rate of return), all possible patterns of diversification between the risk-free opportunity and the risky asset (i.e., X_2 anywhere between .00 and 100 percent) must lie along the same straight line. Any actual portfolio which lies below or to the right of the line in Figure 13.2 is inferior and inefficient because, *for the same return*, a portfolio on the line is less risky.

Third, given that all efficient portfolios lie on the line shown in Figure 13.2 and since the equation of the line is known (i.e., can be calculated if R_G is known), any single efficient portfolio completely determines all other efficient portfolios. Restated, the straight line of Figure 13.2 implies that all efficient portfolios are perfectly correlated with each other because knowledge of the risk-return parameters of any one, given the linear relationship, implies knowledge of the risk-return parameters of all others. The optimal portfolio is the efficient portfolio which maximizes the subjective utility function.

13.3 Generalized Rationale for Diversification

Diversification reduces risk. For a given level of return, the greater the reduction in risk, the more effective is the diversification. The analysis outlined above for case 2 showed how portfolio risk and return behave when diversification is made between a risky asset and a risk-free asset. For case 2, expected return varies linearly with risk.

Now we shall expand the analysis by considering diversification between *any* pair of securities, risky or not. For simplicity of discussion, we shall limit the considerations to two assets. The general principles hold for any number of assets.

Consider two assets, A_3 and A_4, both of which may be risky. The purpose of portfolio analysis is to help decide the best allocation of money between these two assets. Suppose that security analysis of the two assets concludes that neither asset dominates the other (thereby ruling out the strategy of no diversification), but that asset A_4 offers higher expected returns (and higher risks) than asset A_3. Also, the expected returns from the two potential investments can be correlated,

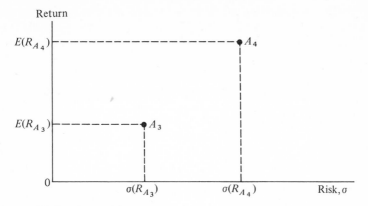

Figure 13.3.   Two risky assets.

but then again the returns may not be correlated.[10] In either situation, the input data from the security analyst can be plotted on a risk-return diagram as shown in Figure 13.3 and summarized as follows.

$$E(R_{A_4}) = \mu_4 > E(R_{A_3}) = \mu_3 > .00 \qquad \textbf{(13.49)}$$

$$\sigma(R_{A_4}) = \sigma_4 > \sigma(R_{A_3}) = \sigma_3 > .00 \qquad \textbf{(13.50)}$$

$$\mathrm{cov}(R_{A_3}, R_{A_4}) = \sigma_{3,4} = \sigma_{4,3} \qquad \textbf{(13.51)}$$

where

$E(R_A)$ = expected return on investment from asset A
μ = mean value of a probability distribution of possible returns
$\sigma(R_A)$ = standard error of estimate of the expected return
$\sigma_{3,4}$ = covariance of expected return from asset A_3 with return on investment from asset A_4

---

[10] Recall from equation (6.70) in Chapter 6 that two stochastic variates can be (but not necessarily must be) correlated. If correlation is present between the two expected returns, then the coefficient of correlation is measured by

$$\rho_{A3,A4} = \frac{\mathrm{cov}(R_{A3}, R_{A4})}{[\sigma(R_{A3})][\sigma(R_{A4})]} \qquad \textbf{(13.48)}$$

where

$\rho_{A3,A4}$ = coefficient of correlation between returns expected from asset A_3 and asset A_4
$\sigma(R_{A3})$ = standard error of estimate of return anticipated from asset A_3
$\sigma(R_{A4})$ = standard error of estimate of return anticipated from asset A_4
$\mathrm{cov}(R_{A3}, R_{A4})$ = covariance of return expected from A_3 with the return expected from A_4

Then, the task confronting us is to study the relationship between risk of the portfolio and expected return of the portfolio. We know now that diversification should reduce risk, but it remains to be seen how expected return behaves as risk is changed.

Proceeding as before in (13.39) and (13.42), we can write the expected return and risk of the portfolio containing some of both assets

$$\begin{aligned} E(R_p) &= X_3\mu_3 + X_4\mu_4 \\ &= (1 - X_4)\mu_3 + X_4\mu_4 \\ &= \mu_3 + (\mu_4 - \mu_3)X_4 \end{aligned} \tag{13.52}$$

$$X_3 + X_4 = 1 \tag{13.53}$$

$$\begin{aligned} \text{Risk} = [\text{var}(R_p)]^{1/2} &= [X_3^2\sigma_3^2 + X_4^2\sigma_4^2 + 2X_3X_4\text{cov}(R_3,R_4)]^{1/2} \\ &= (X_3^2\sigma_3^2 + 2X_3X_4\rho\sigma_3\sigma_4 + X_4^2\sigma_4^2)^{1/2} \end{aligned}$$
$$\tag{13.54}$$

Equation (13.52) states that the expected return on the portfolio is related linearly to X_4. Equation (13.54) notes that the risk of the portfolio depends not only on the risk of the two individual assets alone (σ_3 and σ_4) but also depends upon the *covariance* (or, equivalently, correlation) between expected returns from the two assets. Since the coefficient of correlation (ρ) can range from an upper limit of $+1$ down through zero to a lower limit of -1, three important possibilities for correlation emerge for analysis. Each of these three situations is discussed below.

SITUATION 1: Perfect Negative Correlation. If the returns from two risky assets are perfectly correlated negatively, then ρ equals -1, and any deviation of one return away from its expected value will be accompanied by a corresponding *known* deviation of the other return away from its expected value. Since the correlation is negative, the deviation of one return will be in the opposite direction from the deviation of the other return.

Correlation (covariance), by definition, means that the two returns tend to move together. So given one change, along with the correlation, the other change can be predicted. If correlation is positive, then the two returns tend to move in the same direction (i.e., they both tend to rise or fall together.) If correlation is negative, then the two returns tend to move in opposite directions (i.e., when one return rises, the other falls). No cause-effect relationship is implied by statistical correlation. Refer to equation (6.76) in Chapter 6.

Perfect diversification can be achieved in the happy event of having two assets whose returns are perfectly correlated, negatively. Perfect diversification means that the error of prediction of expected return on the overall portfolio can be reduced to zero. If $\sigma(R_p)$ equals zero, then, as illustrated in case 1 above, risk equals zero, and the expected return is known with certainty.

To show that risk can be reduced to zero in the situation of perfect negative correlation, we can proceed as follows. First, substitute -1 for ρ in (13.54). Then, introducing the constraint $X_4 = (1 - X_3)$ from (13.53), the risk of the portfolio is

$$\begin{aligned} \sigma(R_p) &= (X_3^2\sigma_3^2 - 2X_3X_4\sigma_3\sigma_4 + X_4^2\sigma_4^2)^{1/2} \\ &= [(1 - X_4)^2\sigma_3^2 - 2(1 - X_4)X_4\sigma_3\sigma_4^2 + X_4^2\sigma_4^2]^{1/2} \end{aligned}$$

$$(13.55)$$

Statement (13.55) can be simplified by factoring the binomial perfect square on the right-hand side of (13.55) and then extracting the square-root. Hence, we get

$$\begin{aligned} \sigma(R_p) &= \{[(1 - X_4)\sigma_3 - X_4\sigma_4]^2\}^{1/2} \\ &= (1 - X_4)\sigma_3 - X_4\sigma_4 \\ &= \sigma_3 - (\sigma_3 + \sigma_4)X_4 \\ &= \alpha - \beta X_4 \geq 0 \end{aligned}$$

$$(13.56)$$

where $\alpha = \text{constant} = \sigma_3$, $\beta = \text{constant} = (\sigma_3 + \sigma_4)$ and $\sigma(R_p)$ is nonnegative.

Verbally, (13.56) says that for the case of perfect negative correlation between the returns of two risky assets, the risk (i.e., the standard error of estimate of the overall expected return) of a portfolio, consisting of some of each of these two assets, varies *linearly* with the proportion of money allocated to the more risky of the two assets. If X_4 equals 100 percent, then risk of the portfolio equals σ_4, the error of prediction of the return expected from asset A_4. As X_4 declines, $\sigma(R_p)$ declines at a constant (i.e., linear) rate down toward zero.

$$\frac{\partial\sigma(R_p)}{\partial X_4} = -(\sigma_3 + \sigma_4) = \text{constant} \qquad (13.57)$$

If $\sigma(R_p)$ equals zero, then risk, by definition equals zero, and diversification is perfect. The diversification which provides zero risk can be solved from (13.56).

The risk of the diversified portfolio equals zero when

$$(\sigma_3 + \sigma_4)X_4 = \sigma_3 \qquad (13.58)$$

or

$$\begin{aligned} X_{4\text{critical}} &= \sigma_3/(\sigma_3 + \sigma_4); \\ X_{3\text{critical}} &= (1 - X_{4\text{critical}}) = \sigma_4/(\sigma_3 + \sigma_4) \end{aligned} \qquad (13.59)$$

Restated, if actual (ex-post) returns on asset A_2 fall below expectations by a given amount, then, since $\rho = -1$, it is possible to diversify in a way so that actual (ex-post) returns on asset A_1 will exceed expectations by the same amount as A_2 fell short, causing the error in (i.e., difference between) total expected (ex-ante) returns and realized (ex-post) portfolio returns to equal zero. Perfect diversification occurs when money is allocated between the two assets in proportions stated in (13.59).

Proceeding with the analysis of risk as X_4 varies, (13.56) indicates that if X_4 equals zero (i.e., 100 percent investment in asset A_3), then $\sigma(R_p) = \sigma_3$. As X_4 increases from zero up to the critical amount stated in (13.59), then by (13.56), risk declines linearly from σ_3 down to zero.

Let us turn next to an analysis of behavior of $E(R_p)$ as X_4 and $\sigma(R_p)$ vary. To describe the relationship between $\sigma(R_p)$ and $E(R_p)$ for all levels of diversification when $\rho = -1$, we can solve (13.56) for X_4, substitute that value into (13.52), and simplify.

$$X_4 = [\sigma_3 - \sigma(R_p)]/(\sigma_3 + \sigma_4); \qquad\qquad .00 \le X_4 \le \sigma_3/(\sigma_3 + \sigma_4)$$
$$\text{(13.60)}$$

$$X_4 = [\sigma_3 + \sigma(R_p)]/(\sigma_3 + \sigma_4); \qquad \sigma_3/(\sigma_3 + \sigma_4) < X_4 \le 1.00$$
$$\text{(13.61)}$$

$$E(R_p) = \mu_3 + (\mu_4 - \mu_3)[\sigma_3 \pm \sigma(R_p)]/(\sigma_3 + \sigma_4) \qquad \text{(13.62)}$$

The plus (or minus) sign in (13.62) is taken depending upon whether X_4 is above (or below) its critical value as stated in (13.59), (13.60), and (13.61).

Statement (13.62) shows a *linear* relationship between expected return on the portfolio and risk of the portfolio. The linear relationship between risk and return can be stated more explicitly as follows

$$E(R_p) = \mu_3 + (\mu_4\sigma_3 - \mu_3\sigma_3)/(\sigma_3 + \sigma_4) \pm [(\mu_4 - \mu_3)/(\sigma_3 + \sigma_4)]\sigma(R_p)$$
$$= \alpha \pm \beta\sigma(R_p)$$
$$\text{(13.63)}$$

where

$$\alpha = \text{positive constant} = \mu_3 + (\mu_4\sigma_3 - \mu_3\sigma_3)/(\sigma_3 + \sigma_4)$$
$$\beta = \text{positive constant} = (\mu_4 - \mu_3)/(\sigma_3 + \sigma_4)$$

When critical diversification is applied, risk equals zero, and the expected return on the portfolio equals the constant α, as stated in (13.63). That is, when $\sigma(R_p) = 0$, and X_3, X_4 are as stated in (13.59), then from (13.52) we get

$$E(R_p) = (\mu_3\sigma_4 + \mu_4\sigma_3)/(\sigma_3 + \sigma_4) \qquad \text{(13.64)}$$

As X_4 increases from .00 up to its critical value, portfolio risk declines linearly from $\sigma(R_p) = \sigma_3$ down to zero, causing the expected return on the portfolio to *rise* from μ_3 up to the value stated in (13.64). When X_4 is in the interval below the critical value (as stated in 13.60), the portfolio risk declines linearly as X_4 rises, and portfolio return rises. That is, using the minus sign from (13.63), we get

$$\frac{\partial E(R_p)}{\partial \sigma(R_p)} = -\beta \qquad (13.65)$$

Equation (13.65) says that risk and return vary inversely within the interval under analysis. As X_4 continues to increase from its critical value up to 100 percent, as stated in (13.61), the expected return on the portfolio increases linearly from the value stated in (13.64) up to $E(R_p)$ = μ_4. Within this interval of diversification, expected return increases linearly as risk increases.

$$\frac{\partial E(R_p)}{\partial \sigma(R_p)} = \beta \qquad (13.66)$$

EXAMPLE. To illustrate the analysis outlined above, suppose the following data are given

$$\begin{aligned} E(R_{A_3}) &= 16 \text{ percent}; & \sigma_3 &= .27 \\ E(R_{A_4}) &= 45 \text{ percent}; & \sigma_4 &= .52 \\ \rho &= -1.00 \end{aligned} \qquad (13.67)$$

Then the expected returns and risk of all possible diversifications between the two assets are described by the following statements: The return expected on the portfolio is

$$\begin{aligned} E(R_p) &= .16 + [(.45)(.27) - (.16)(.27)]/(.27 + .52) \\ &\quad \pm [(.45 - .16)/(.27 + .52)]\sigma(R_p) \\ &= .259 \pm .367\sigma(R_p) \end{aligned} \qquad (13.68)$$

The risk of the portfolio is

$$\begin{aligned} \sigma(R_p) &= \{[.27 - (.27 + .52)X_4]^2\}^{1/2} \\ &= [(.27 - .79X_4)^2]^{1/2} \end{aligned} \qquad (13.69)$$

$$X_{4\text{critical}} = .27/(.27 + .52) = .342 = 34.2 \text{ percent} \qquad (13.70)$$

$$X_{3\text{critical}} = .52/(.27 + .52) = .658 = 65.8 \text{ percent} \qquad (13.71)$$

The return expected at critical diversification is

$$E[R_p|\sigma(R_p) = 0] = .259 = 25.9 \text{ percent} \qquad (13.72)$$

Hence, for the data given, 100 percent investment in asset A_4 yields an expected return of 45 percent, with risk .52. However, perfect diversification between the two assets can be achieved by allocating 34.2 percent of the available funds to asset A_3 and the remaining 65.8 percent to

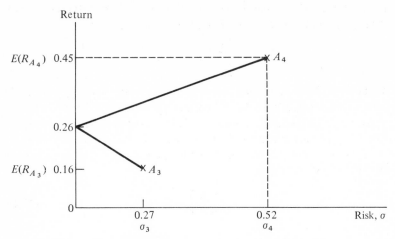

Figure 13.4. Diversification when rho equals minus one.

asset A_4. For perfect diversification, expected return on the portfolio is 25.9 percent, with risk equal zero. These results are plotted on the diagram of Figure 13.4.

SITUATION 2: No Correlation. If the returns anticipated from two risky assets are statistically uncorrelated, then diversification still reduces risk. Zero correlation means that the errors of forecast of the two returns are independent of each other. Given are the expectations for both returns, μ_3 and μ_4, with error, σ_3 and σ_4, respectively. If the actual (ex-post) return for asset A_3 falls below its expectation, then, with zero correlation between $E(R_3)$ and $E(R_4)$, the actual (ex-post) return for asset A_4 is statistically independent of the fact that the return from A_3 fell below expectations. With zero correlation, knowledge of how one return varies (i.e., either above or below expectations) is of no benefit in predicting how the other return will vary. But even so, diversification reduces risk.

Reduction of risk in this situation can be shown as follows. First, substitute $\rho = 0$ in statement (13.54). Then, introducing the constraint $X_4 = (1 - X_3)$ from (13.53), the risk of the portfolio of uncorrelated returns is

$$
\begin{aligned}
\sigma(R_p) &= (X_3^2\sigma_3^2 + X_4^2\sigma_4^2)^{1/2} \\
&= [(1 - X_4)^2\sigma_3^2 + X_4^2\sigma_4^2]^{1/2} \qquad\qquad \textbf{(13.73)} \\
&= [\sigma_3^2 - 2\sigma_3^2 X_4 + (\sigma_3^2 + \sigma_4^2)X_4^2]^{1/2} > 0
\end{aligned}
$$

Statement (13.73) is a formidable-looking structure which shows that if returns are uncorrelated, then risk of the portfolio is related in a *nonlinear* way to the diversification between the two assets. If 100 percent of the available money is allocated to asset A_4, then $X_4 = 1.00$, and (13.73) reduces to $\sigma(R_p) = \sigma_4$. At the other extreme, if 100 percent of the available money is allocated to asset A_3, then $X_4 = .00$, and (13.73) reduces to $\sigma(R_p) = \sigma_3$. At minimum risk, the rate of change of portfolio risk, $\sigma(R_p)$, with respect to X_4 must equal zero. Solving (13.73) for these conditions of minimum risk, we get

$$\frac{\partial \sigma(R_p)}{\partial X_4} = (1/2) \left\{ \frac{-2\sigma_3^2 + 2(\sigma_3^2 + \sigma_4^2)X_4}{[\sigma_3^2 - (2\sigma_3^2)X_4 + (\sigma_3^2 + \sigma_4^2)X_4^2]^{1/2}} \right\} = 0$$

(13.74)

For (13.74) to equal zero, the numerator must equal zero because the denominator is always positive. Hence, solution for this condition of minimum risk yields the value of X_4 for critical diversification.

$$2(\sigma_3^2 + \sigma_4^2)X_4 = 2\sigma_3^2 \qquad (13.75)$$

$$X_{4\text{critical}} = \sigma_3^2/(\sigma_3^2 + \sigma_4^2);$$
$$X_{3\text{critical}} = (1 - X_{4\text{critical}}) = \sigma_4^2/(\sigma_3^2 + \sigma_4^2) \qquad (13.76)$$

The reader should compare (13.76) with (13.59). The precise value of the minimum risk can be calculated by substituting the critical value for X_4 from (13.76) into (13.73).

One way of deriving further insights to the relationship between diversification and risk when rho equals zero is to solve equation (13.73) for X_4. Since (13.73) is quadratic in X_4 (after squaring both sides), the standard quadratic formula can be applied directly, giving

$$X_4 = \frac{(2\sigma_3^2) \pm \{4\sigma_3^4 - 4(\sigma_3^2 + \sigma_4^2)[\sigma_3^2 - \sigma^2(R_p)]\}^{1/2}}{2(\sigma_3^2 + \sigma_4^2)}$$

$$= \frac{\sigma_3^2 \pm \sqrt{\{[(\sigma_3^2 + \sigma_4^2)\sigma^2(R_p)] - \sigma_3^2\sigma_4^2\}}}{(\sigma_3^2 + \sigma_4^2)}$$

(13.77)

Since X_4 must remain within the range between 1.00 and .00, the quantity underneath the square-root sign in (13.77) must be positive always. This condition can be stated

$$(\sigma_3^2 + \sigma_4^2)\text{var}(R_p) \geq \sigma_3^2\sigma_4^2 \qquad (13.78)$$

Therefore, the lower bound on the risk of a portfolio wherein the two returns are uncorrelated occurs when

$$\sigma(R_p) = [\sigma_3\sigma_4/(\sigma_3^2 + \sigma_4^2)^{1/2}] \qquad (13.79)$$

Hence, when $\rho = 0$, diversification cannot reduce risk to zero, but diversification can reduce risk to levels smaller than the risk of the least risky asset in the portfolio. That is, since

$$\sigma_4/(\sigma_3^2 + \sigma_4^2)^{1/2} = \text{constant} = C < 1.00 \qquad (13.80)$$

then σ_3, from equation (13.79), multiplied by C is less than σ_3 alone.

The relationship between expected return on the portfolio and risk can be stated in a way analogous to (13.63). At minimum risk, the expected return is

$$E(R_p)_{\text{critical}} = \mu_3 + (\mu_4 - \mu_3)X_{4\text{critical}}$$
$$= \mu_3 + (\mu_4 - \mu_3)[\sigma_3^2/(\sigma_3^2 + \sigma_4^2)] \qquad \textbf{(13.81)}$$
$$= (\mu_3\sigma_4^2 + \mu_4\sigma_3^2)/(\sigma_3^2 + \sigma_4^2)$$

EXAMPLE. To illustrate the relationship between expected return and risk on the portfolios for various combinations of diversification, when the individual expected returns are uncorrelated, the same data as stated in (13.67) can be used, except rho equals zero. Using these two assets, critical diversification is achieved when

$$X_{4\text{critical}} = (.27)^2/[(.27)^2 + (.52)^2] = .2123 = 21.23 \text{ percent}$$
$$X_{3\text{critical}} = (.52)^2/[(.27)^2 + (.52)^2] = .7877 = 78.77 \text{ percent} \qquad \textbf{(13.82)}$$

At critical diversification, the expected return and risk for the portfolio are

$$E(R_p) = [.16(.52)^2 + .45(.27)^2]/[(.27)^2 + (.52)^2]$$
$$= (.07608)/(.3433) = .222 \qquad \textbf{(13.83)}$$

$$\sigma(R_p) = [(.7877)^2(.27)^2 + (.2123)^2(.52)^2]^{1/2}$$
$$= (.04523 + .01219)^{1/2} \qquad \textbf{(13.84)}$$
$$= (.05752)^{1/2} = .24$$

These results are plotted in Figure 13.5. As diversification changes from 100 percent investment in the most profitable (but most risky) opportunity, risk declines in a nonlinear way from .52 down to a minimum of .24, along with a corresponding nonlinear decline in expected return from 45 percent down to 22 percent. As still larger proportions of

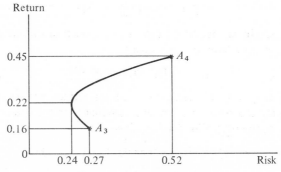

Figure 13.5. Diversification when rho equals zero.

money are allocated to asset A_3, return continues to decline (from .22 down to .16), but risk rises (from .24 up to .27). Diversifications in the range $.00 \leq X_4 < 21.23$ percent, therefore, will be avoided by rational risk averse investors who have quadratic utility schedules. All optimal portfolios lie on the curve in the interval 21.23 percent $\leq X_4 \leq 100$ percent.

SITUATION 3: Perfect Positive Correlation. The situation of perfect positive correlation between the expected returns from two risky assets is the easiest of the three situations to analyze. Perfect positive correlation means that $\rho = +1$, so that the risk of the portfolio, stated in (13.54), reduces to a relationship which is linear with diversification.

$$
\begin{aligned}
\sigma(R_p) &= [X_3^2\sigma_3^2 + 2X_3X_3\sigma_3\sigma_4 + X_4^2\sigma_4^2]^{1/2} \\
&= [(1 - X_4)^2\sigma_3^2 + 2(1\ \delta\ X_4)X_4\sigma_3\sigma_4 + X_4^2\sigma_4^2]^{1/2} \\
&= \{[(1 - X_4)\sigma_3 + X_4\sigma_4]^2\}^{1/2} \qquad \textbf{(13.85)} \\
&= \sigma_3 + (\sigma_4 - \sigma_3)X_4 \\
&= \alpha + \beta X_4 > 0
\end{aligned}
$$

where α = a positive constant = σ_3 and β = a positive constant = $(\sigma_4 - \sigma_3)$. In other words, (13.85) says that portfolio risk rises linearly over the entire range of X_4. Hence, if returns from assets are perfectly positively correlated, there is no such thing as critical diversification to provide minimum risk. Statement (13.85) shows that if $\rho = +1$, the smallest risk occurs if $X_4 = 0$ so that $\sigma(R_p) = \sigma_3$; i.e., no diversification.

We said earlier that "optimal diversification means obtaining the best possible tradeoff between risk and return." In the context of the preceding analysis, we can now note the difference between *critical* diversification and *optimal* diversification. Critical diversification is that value for X_4 which results in minimum risk (regardless of return). Optimal diversification is that value for X_4 which results in maximum utility for the investor who owns the portfolio. Maximum utility occurs when there is the right tradeoff between return and risk, not necessarily absolute minimum risk. Therefore, even in the situation when the returns from two risky assets are perfectly positively correlated, diversification can be valuable because risks can be lowered (though not minimized).

A linear relationship between risk and diversification as stated in (13.85) implies a linear relationship between risk and return on the portfolio. This is true because return is related linearly to diversification between the two assets. That is, solving for X_4 from (13.85) and substituting that value into (13.52), we get the desired relationship between expected return and risk.

$$
\begin{aligned}
E(R_p) &= \mu_3 + (\mu_4 - \mu_3)X_4 \\
&= \mu_3 + (\mu_4 - \mu_3)[\sigma(R_p) - \sigma_3]/(\sigma_4 - \sigma_3) \\
&= [(\mu_3\sigma_4 - \mu_4\sigma_3)/(\sigma_4 - \sigma_3)] + [(\mu_4 - \mu_3)/(\sigma_4 - \sigma_3)]\sigma(R_p) \\
&= \alpha + \beta\sigma(R_p)
\end{aligned}
$$

(13.86)

where α = a constant = $(\mu_3\sigma_4 - \mu_4\sigma_3)/(\sigma_4 - \sigma_3)$ and β = a positive constant = $(\mu_4 - \mu_3)/(\sigma_4 - \sigma_3)$. Statement (13.86) shows that when the returns from two risky assets are perfectly positively correlated, the expected return on the portfolio rises linearly with risk of the portfolio.

$$
\frac{\partial E(R_p)}{\partial \sigma(R_p)} = [(\mu_4 - \mu_3)/(\sigma_4 - \sigma_3)] > 0
$$

(13.87)

Since the overall level of expected returns is determined by α in (13.86) (β determines the slope of the linear relationship), and since utility always rises with anticipation of larger return, we can state that if alternative pairs of assets are being compared, then, other things the same, that pair which offers the highest value of α will also provide the largest utility. That is, given equal values of β for two alternative portfolios, then, from (13.86),

$$
\mu_3\sigma_4 > \mu_4\sigma_3
$$

(13.88)

provides larger utility than does a portfolio wherein

$$
\mu_3\sigma_4 \leq \mu_4\sigma_3
$$

(13.89)

SUMMARY. Risk and return are related when considering non-dominant assets. Under the maxims governing investor preference, ceteris paribus, higher returns are always preferred over lower returns. But in the marketplace of real-world opportunities for investment, higher risks usually accompany higher expected returns, causing utility for higher returns to rise but rise at a declining rate (assuming rational aversion to added risk). Conceivably, therefore, there is some rate of substitution of added return for added risk which will leave the investor indifferent between alternative combinations of risk and return. The rationale underlying diversification is to identify and state these alternative combinations. That particular combination of risk and return (i.e., that particular portfolio) which coincides with the highest level of indifference is the optimal portfolio for that particular investor.[11]

[11] For further reading, see Paul A. Samuelson, "General Proof that Diversification Pays," *Journal of Financial and Quantitative Analysis*, vol. 2, March 1967, pp. 1–13. For work on equilibrium in Capital Markets, see

We shall turn next to an analysis of some specific data. The purpose of the following analysis is to demonstrate the use of the Markowitz and Sharpe/Linter models for portfolio analysis and asset management.

13.4 General Solutions to the Portfolio Problem

In this section, we shall discuss and apply methods set forth initially in the pathbreaking work of Harry Markowitz.[12] Later, we shall incorporate refinements set forth by William Sharpe.[13]

Calculation of Markowitz-Efficient Portfolios. Consider n securities, each with some expected return $[E(R)]$ and error of expectation $[\sigma(R_i)]$ where all returns and errors are positive and finite.[14] Also, for now, assume that the correlation (covariance) between all pairs of expected returns is known. This latter assumption will be modified as the analysis proceeds. Then the questions to be answered are, Which of the n available opportunities are the best to exploit? Which particular securities should be selected, and what proportion of money should be allocated

---

(1) William F. Sharpe, "Capital Asset Prices: A Theory of Market Equilibrium under Conditions of Risk," *Journal of Finance*, vol. 19, September 1964, pp. 435–442; (2) John Lintner, "Security Prices, Risk, and Maximal Gains from Diversification," *Journal of Finance*, vol. 20, December, 1965, pp. 587–615; (3) John Lintner, "The Valuation of Risk Assets and the Selection of Risky Investments in Stock Portfolios and Capital Budgets," *Review of Economics and Statistics*, vol. 47, February 1965, pp. 13–37; (4) Eugene F. Fama, "Risk, Return, and Equilibrium: Some Clarifying Comments," *The Journal of Finance*, vol. XXIII, no. 1, March 1968, pp. 29–40; (5) Jan Mossin, "Equilibrium in a Capital Asset Market," *Econometrica*, vol. XXXIV, October 1966, pp. 768–783; (6) Jan Mossin, "Optimal Multiperiod Portfolio Policies," *Journal of Business*, vol. XLI, April 1968, pp. 215–229.

[12] See (1) Harry M. Markowitz, "Portfolio Selection," *Journal of Finance*, vol. VII, March 1952, pp. 77–91; and (2) H. M. Markowitz, "Portfolio Selection: Efficient Diversification of Investments, Cowles Foundation Monograph No. 16, John Wiley & Sons, Inc., New York, 1959.

[13] See (1) William F. Sharpe, "A Simplified Model for Portfolio Analysis," *Management Science*, Vol. IX, January 1963, pp 277-293, (2) William F. Sharpe, "A Linear Programming Algorithm for Mutual Fund Portfolio Selection," *Management Science*, vol. XIII, March 1967, pp. 499–510; and (3) William F. Sharpe, *Portfolio Theory and Capital Markets*, McGraw-Hill, Inc., New York, 1970.

[14] Recall from Chapter 10 that the assumption of finite variance may *not* be accepted universally. See, for example, (1) Eugene Fama, "Portfolio Analysis in a Stable Paretian Market," *Management Science*, vol. 11, no. 3, January 1965, pp. 404–419; and (2) Paul A. Samuelson, "Efficient Portfolio Selection for Pareto-Levy Investments," *The Journal of Financial and Quantitative Analysis*, June 1967, pp. 107–122.

to each security? The answer, as we shall see, is that there is no single portfolio which is best in the context of both risk and return. Many diversifications can be calculated, each of which offers the smallest possible risk for a given level of return.

More specifically, consider shares of the companies listed in Table 13.1. Suppose a security analysis has been completed and the results show the same expected returns and risks for the 30 assets as those in Table 13.1. One interesting (but nonrelevant) question at this point is, How are the data on Table 13.1 obtained? In practice, such data should be obtained through methods of security analysis as discussed previously in the chapters of Part III. For purposes of illustration of methods of portfolio analysis (in contrast with methods of security analysis), the data in Table 13.1 were calculated in a naive way using Standard & Poor's Compustat tape. The procedure was as follows. First specify a 10-year span of time for which the necessary data are on the tape (closing prices and dividends). Then, for each company for each year, calculate the rate of return on investment—dividend yield plus capital gain.

$$R_{it} = D_{t+1}/P_t + (P_{t+1} - P_t)/P_t \qquad \textbf{(13.90)}$$

Next, calculate the arithmetic average of the ten returns along with the variance about the average

$$E(R_i) = \sum_{t=1}^{10} (R_{it})/10 \qquad \textbf{(13.91)}$$

$$\mathrm{var}(R_i) = \sum_{t=1}^{10} [R_{it} - E(R_i)]^2/9 \qquad \textbf{(13.92)}$$

The resultant mean and variance specify one rational way, a naive way, of formulating the expectation necessary to solve the Markowitz model. That is, to formulate expectations concerning the return and variance of, for example, Zenith Radio, we sample from the (hopefully stationary) probability distribution previously established. The best estimate of the expected return is the mean of the probability distribution, 50.5 percent, with variance of .520. Stated differently, assuming that a sample size of 10 is sufficiently large to estimate mean and variance, then if one additional observation, observation number 11, is added (ex-post) to the existing sample, neither the mean nor the variance will change. The best (ex-ante) estimate of the value of observation number 11 is .505.[15]

---

[15] For a theoretical exposition on the estimation of risk and return in a form suitable for the Markowitz/Sharpe models, see Joel Fried, "Forecasting and Probability Distributions for Models of Portfolio Selection," *The Journal of Finance*, vol. XXV, no. 3, June 1970, pp. 539–554.

Table 13.1   EMPIRICAL DATA FOR ANALYSIS

Name of Security (1)	Expected Return $E(R)$ (2)	Risk var(R) (3)	$\sigma(R)$ (4)
1. Zenith Radio	.505	.520	.721
2. Interstate Hosts Inc.	.519	.549	.741
3. Northwest Airlines	.537	.625	.791
4. Polaroid Corp.	.544	.334	.578
5. Leesona Corp.	.547	1.577	1.119
6. Lukens Steel	.541	1.058	1.030
7. Xerox Corp.	.659	.482	.694
8. Control Data Co.	.852	1.145	1.070
9. Great American Insurance	.972	6.645	2.580
10. Fairchild Camera	1.022	3.809	1.952
11. St. Paul Fire and Casualty	.402	.763	.874
12. E. J. Korvette Inc.	.412	.914	.956
13. Hoover Co.	.415	.742	.861
14. Holiday Inns of America	.417	.381	.617
15. Motorola, Inc.	.419	.502	.709
16. Crown Cork and Seal Co. Inc.	.426	.507	.712
17. Brunswick Corp.	.427	.520	.721
18. Jim Walter Corp.	.441	.811	.901
19. Admiral Corp.	.443	1.321	1.150
20. Holt, Rinehart and Winston, Inc.	.450	.267	.517
21. U.S. Steel	.083	.125	.354
22. Owens Illinois	.113	.039	.198
23. Std. Oil (Calif.)	.121	.024	.155
24. A.T. and T.	.125	.032	.179
25. F. W. Woolworth	.141	.053	.230
26. American Tobacco	.148	.058	.241
27. Texaco	.158	.024	.155
28. General Motors	.163	.070	.265
29. General Foods Corp.	.187	.052	.228
30. Sears	.198	.073	.270

Perusal of columns (2) and (4) of Table 13.1 indicates that some shares are inferior to others in that they offer higher risks for the same or lower expected returns. For example, Xerox Corporation (item 7) offers a higher return at lower risk than Lukens Steel (item 6). Also, Texaco (item 27) offers approximately the same return as General Motors (item 28) but with approximately half the error of estimate.

To see the differences better, the data from Table 13.1 can be plotted on a risk-return diagram as shown in Figure 13.6. From Figure 13.6, it is easier to see and pick out individual securities which offer higher

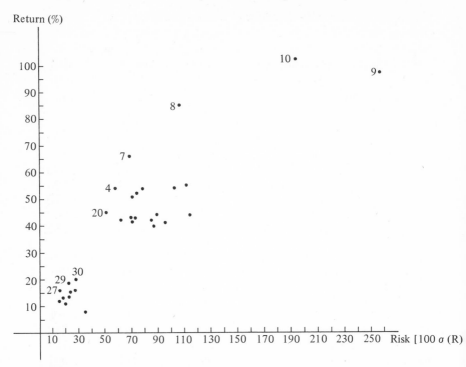

Figure 13.6. Plot of empirical data. (*Numbers refer to securities listed on Table 13.1. Points not numbered [except 9] represent inferior opportunities.*)

returns at the same (or smaller) risk. For example, the two points in the upper right-hand corner of Figure 13.6, Great American Insurance and Fairchild Camera, offer the highest possible returns from the group but also contain the largest risks. The lower risk cluster (in the lower left-hand part of quadrant 1 in Figure 13.6) offers lower expected returns.

Since the object of diversifying is to reduce risk, we can start by defining the risk of a portfolio which contains n securities. The square of that risk is proportional to the sum of squares of each individual risk. Each individual risk is weighted by the square of the percentage of the portfolio invested in that particular risk. Then twice the weighted sums of covariances between all possible pairs of securities is added to calculate the total risk of the portfolio. Stated unambiguously,

$$\text{var}(R_p) = \sum_{i=1}^{n} X_i^2 \text{var}(R_i) + 2 \sum_{j=1}^{(n-1)} \sum_{k=(j+1)}^{n} X_j X_k \text{cov}(R_j, R_k)$$

$$(13.93)$$

where all terms at the same as defined previously. Statement (13.93) is the objective function to be minimized.

The rationale underlying the minimization of risk is that reducing risk results in raising utility, as explained above in Chapter 12. Minimizing variance provides the same results as minimizing standard deviation.[16] There can be constraints. Previously, we recognized constraints of nonnegativity (no short selling) and full accounting for the money available.

$$X_i = \geq 0 \tag{13.98}$$

$$\sum_{i=1}^{n} X_i = 100 \text{ percent} \tag{13.99}$$

There also can be legal and management policy constraints which limit the total proportion of money allocated to any single asset.

$$X_i \leq C_i \tag{13.100}$$

where C_i = some constant specified exogenously by law or by management. For example, C_i may be 10 percent of the market value of the stock outstanding for company i. Finally, there can be some lower limit on the acceptable return on the portfolio

$$E(R_p) = \sum_{i=1}^{n} X_i E(R_i) \geq C \tag{13.101}$$

where C = some constant specified exogenously by the investor. C is a minimum return acceptable. For example, C can be the riskless rate of return. The objective, therefore, is to select (i.e., calculate) that diversification which minimizes risk (13.93), subject to constraints such as (13.98) through (13.101).

The portfolio problem as set forth above is basically an extremal problem with constraints. In general, there can be many equations of constraint. In the case outlined above, there are four such constraints,

---

[16] *Proof.* Let y_1 equal any twice differentiable analytic function of y and let y_2 equal the square root of y_1

$$y_1 = f(x) \tag{13.94}$$

$$y_2 = [f(x)]^{1/2} \tag{13.95}$$

Then the minima occur at $x = a$ when the first derivative equals zero at that point, provided that the second derivative is positive when $x = a$. Thus

$$\frac{dy_1}{dx} = f'(x) = 0 \tag{13.96}$$

$$\frac{dy_2}{dx} = \frac{f'(x)}{2[f(x)]^{1/2}} = 0 \tag{13.97}$$

In either case (y_1) or its square root (y_2), $f'(x) = 0$.

statements (13.98) through (13.101). Each constraint can involve one or more of the n variables. In the case outlined above, the n variables constitute $X_1, X_2, \ldots, X_n$. It is of no consequence whether the equation of constraint has the general form $G(x,y,z) = 0$ or $G(x,y,z) = k$, where k is a specified constant, for the latter form of constraint can be written $G(x,y,z) - k = 0$. In the case outlined above, there is a single *equation* of constraint, statement (13.99). The other constraints are *inequalities*, signifying that any value above (or below) the specified limit is acceptable. There are various methods for solving extremal problems with constraints. However, a discussion of these methods takes us away from the main topic under discussion: optimal diversification.[17]

To summarize, the inputs to the Markowitz model are

1. Expected return on each security under consideration (R_i).
2. Risk (i.e., error of prediction) of each expected return [var(R_i)].
3. Covariation (i.e., either covariance or coefficient of correlation) between expected returns of all pairs of securities under consideration, cov(R_i,R_j) or else ρ_{R_i,R_j}.
4. Operating constraints imposed on the selection of the portfolio.

Stochastic Dominance and Removal of Inferior Sets. Continuing toward the objective of diversifying among the 30 securities listed in Table 13.1, we can perform a preliminary screening by removing inferior opportunities. That is to say, if any one of the 30 possible returns has a μ_i,σ_i combination such that the lower tail of its probability distribution $[(\mu_i - \delta\sigma_i)]$ exceeds the limits of the upper tail of some alternative security $[(\mu_j + \delta\sigma_j)]$, where δ equals some positive constant as stated in Tchebycheff's Theorem in Appendix 2 of Chapter 6, then that alternative security is unconditionally inferior and should be removed from the set of possibilities. Its removal is justified because, since it is unconditionally inferior, no combination of it with the superior asset will be preferred over the superior asset alone. The superior asset dominates, regardless of its dispersion.

Aside from being dominant or inferior, expected returns can be either efficient or inefficient. An inefficient security is one which has a

---

[17] If the constraints are expressed as equations instead of inequalities, then three general methods of solution are (1) the method of direct elimination, (2) the method of implicit functions, and (3) Lagrange's method. One great advantage of Lagrange's method over the method of implicit functions or the method of direct elimination is that Lagrange's method enables the analyst to avoid making a choice of independent variables. For further reading on methods of solving extremal problems with constraints see any good text on calculus or optimization procedures.

higher level of risk for a given return than some alternative security. An inefficient security is one which offers a lower return for a given level of risk than some alternative security. Inspection of Figure 13.6 shows that among the *individual* assets, eight are Markowitz-efficient. They are 10, 8, 7, 4, 20, 30, 29, and 27. The others are inefficient. In combination, however, the risk-return characteristics of a portfolio depend upon the covariance between the alternative pairs of returns. We shall turn next to considerations for calculating an efficiency frontier involving combinations of securities. For simplicity of explanation, we shall limit the discussion to three securities; the general principles hold for any number of securities.

Calculation of the Efficiency Frontier. Consider the three securities with expected return and variance of return as shown in Table 13.2. The actual securities happen to be Xerox Corporation, Holt, Rinehart and Winston, Inc. (HRW), and General Motors (GM). Suppose that the data tabulated in Table 13.2 are calculated from subjective estimates of possible returns on investment from each security.[18] To further clarify the differences between the three alternative securities, the data in Table 13.2 can be plotted on a risk-return diagram as shown in Figure 13.7. Xerox (7) offers the highest expected return (and highest risk). General Motors (28) offers the smallest expected return (and smallest risk). HRW (20) is in between. The objective is to diversify among the three securities.

---

[18] Actually, the data tabulated in Table 13.2 consist of average annual returns (dividend yields plus capital gains) for the years $R_1 = 1964–1965$ back through time to $R_{10} = 1955–1956$ as shown on Table 13.3. The data are taken from compustat tape. Equations (13.102) through (13.105) are used to calculate the data

$$E(R_i) = \sum_{t=-10}^{t=-1} [(D_{t+1}/P_t) + (P_{t+1} - P_t)/P_t]/n \qquad \text{(13.102)}$$

$$\text{var}(R_i) = \sum_{t=-10}^{t=-1} [R_{i,t} - E(R_i)]^2/(n-1) \qquad \text{(13.103)}$$

$$\text{cov}(R_i,R_j) = \sum_{t=-10}^{t=-1} [R_{i,t} - E(R_i)][R_{j,t} - E(R_j)]/(n-1)$$
$$\text{(13.104)}$$

$$\rho_{R_i,R_j} = \frac{\text{cov}(R_i,R_j)}{\{[\text{var}(R_i)][\text{var}(R_j)]\}^{1/2}} \qquad \text{(13.105)}$$

Note the difference between statistics for the universe and statistics for a sample. For the sample, we divide by degrees of freedom instead of size of sample.

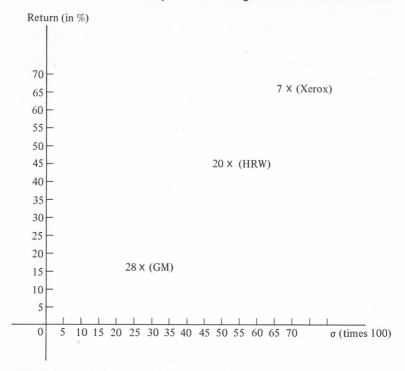

Figure 13.7. Three securities plotted.

The rationale underlying the desire to diversify efficiently can be explained as follows. Security 1 offers the highest expected return, 66 percent. But security 1 also offers the largest risk, variance = .482. By diversifying, the risk can be reduced, but some expected return must be sacrificed also. If diversification between the two securities with highest returns is selected, then the expected return on the combination is

$$E(R_p) = .66X_1 + .45X_2 \qquad \textbf{(13.106)}$$

Table 13.2 THREE SECURITIES FOR A PORTFOLIO

Security	Expected return R_i (%)	Variance of return var(R_i)
(1) Xerox Corp.	66	.482
(2) Holt, Rinehart and Winston	45	.267
(3) General Motors	16	.070

$$\text{cov}_{1,2} = -.099 \qquad \rho_{1,2} = -.275$$
$$\text{cov}_{1,3} = +.072 \qquad \rho_{1,3} = +.389$$
$$\text{cov}_{2,3} = -.008 \qquad \rho_{2,3} = -.062$$

Table 13.3   SUPPORTING DATA FOR THREE SECURITIES

Subjective estimate of possible return	Security 1 (Xerox Corp.)	Security 2 (Holt, Rinehart Winston, Inc.)	Security 3 (General Motors)
R_1	1.054	.625	.111
R_2	.165	.230	.301
R_3	1.689	−.183	.421
R_4	−.012	−.243	.072
R_5	1.177	.135	.464
R_6	1.454	.231	−.217
R_7	.338	1.354	.141
R_8	1.017	.945	.537
R_9	−.092	.479	−.193
R_{10}	−.197	.926	−.005
Expected Return $E(R)$	.659	.450	.163
Variance of Returns $\text{var}(R)$	.482	.267	.070

$$\text{cov(GM-HRW)} = -.0085$$
$$\text{cov(GM-Xerox)} = +.0716$$
$$\text{cov(HRW-Xerox)} = -.0988$$
$$\rho_{\text{GM-HRW}} = -.008487/[(.070)(.2667)]^{1/2}$$
$$= -.0621$$
$$\rho_{\text{GM-XEROX}} = +.07155/[(.070)(.4822)]^{1/2}$$
$$= +.3894$$
$$\rho_{\text{HRW-XEROX}} = -.09875/[(.2667)(.4822)]^{1/2}$$
$$= -.2754$$

where

X_1 = proportion of total investment allocated to security 1
X_2 = proportion of total investment allocated to security 2

$$X_1 + X_2 = 100 \text{ percent} \qquad \textbf{(13.107)}$$
$$X_1 \geq 0, \ X_2 \geq 0 \qquad \textbf{(13.108)}$$

The variance of return expected on that combination is

$$\text{var}(R_p) = .482X_1^2 + .267X_2^2 - (2)(.099)X_1X_2 \qquad \textbf{(13.109)}$$

The solution to the portfolio problem starts with solving the system of equations (13.106) through (13.109). The objective is to maximize expected return [(13.106)], subject to constraints (13.107), (13.108), and letting var (R_p) equal some (realizable) constant, specified exogenously. This result will lead to the same allocation of resources as minimizing variance [(13.109)], subject to constraints (13.107), (13.108), and letting expected return equal to some (realizable) constant, specified exogenously.

One way to solve the problem is by the method of Lagrangian multipliers. The method is named for Joseph Louis Lagrange, an eighteenth century mathematician, and can be illustrated as follows.

To find the extremal values of any function $F(t,y,z)$, subject to any constraint $G(t,y,z) = C$, first form the function $\phi = F(t,y,z) + \lambda G(t,y,z)$, where λ is a constant whose value is to be determined.

Second, treat t, y, and z as independent variables and write the conditions

$$\frac{\partial \phi}{\partial t} = 0, \qquad \frac{\partial \phi}{\partial y} = 0, \qquad \frac{\partial \phi}{\partial z} = 0$$

Third, solve these three equations along with the equation of constraint $G(t,y,z) = C$ in order to find the values of the four quantities, t, y, z, and λ.

Then, using only one constraint [(13.107)], for simplicity of exposition, we can write

$$\begin{aligned} \phi &= \text{var}(R_p) + \lambda(X_1 + X_2) \\ &= X_1^2(.482) + X_2^2(.267) + 2X_1X_2(-.099) + \lambda(X_1 + X_2) \end{aligned}$$

(13.110)

$$\frac{\partial \phi}{\partial X_1} = 2(.482)X_1 + 2(-.099)X_2 + \lambda = 0$$

$$\frac{\partial \phi}{\partial X_2} = 2(-.099)X_1 + 2(.267)X_2 + \lambda = 0$$

(13.111)

$$X_1 + X_2 = 1$$

$$\begin{aligned} .964X_1 - .198X_2 + \lambda &= 0 \\ -.198X_1 + .534X_2 + \lambda &= 0 \\ X_1 &= 1 - X_2 \end{aligned}$$

(13.112)

Solving the three equations in (13.112) simultaneously, we get

$$X_2 = 61.4 \text{ percent}, \qquad X_1 = 38.6 \text{ percent}, \qquad \lambda = -.2511$$

(13.113)

Then

$$\begin{aligned} \text{var}(R_p) &= (.386)^2(.482) + (.614)^2(.267) + 2(.386)(.614)(-.099) \\ &= .07182 + .1006 - .0469 \\ &= .1255 \end{aligned}$$

(13.114)

and

$$\begin{aligned} E(R_p) &= (.66)(.386) + (.45)(.614) \\ &= .2548 + .2763 \\ &= .5311 \end{aligned}$$

(13.115)

That is to say, an investor can diversify among the two assets under analysis and obtain a risk (variance) as low as .126 with expected return

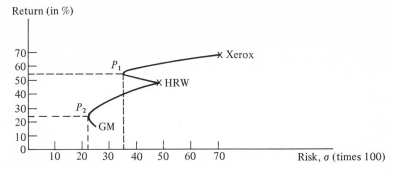

Figure 13.8. Portfolios of two securities. (*Portfolio P_1 is specified by equations 13.14 and 13.15. Portfolio P_2 is specified by equations (13.19) and (13.20).)*

of approximately 53 percent. Higher returns, with commensurately higher variance can be obtained, (up to a limit of 66 percent) by increasing the proportion X_1 from 38.6 percent up toward 100 percent.

If a variance of .126 is still too large to suit subjective risk preferences, then security 3 can be substituted for security 1 and the minimization procedure repeated. Repetition yields

$$\phi = \text{var}(R_p) + \lambda(X_2 + X_3)$$
$$= .267X_2^2 + .070X_3^2 + 2(-.008)X_2X_3 + \lambda(X_2 + X_3) \tag{13.116}$$

$$\frac{\partial \phi}{\partial X_2} = 2(.267)X_2 - 2(.008)X_3 + \lambda = 0 \tag{13.117}$$

$$\frac{\partial \phi}{\partial X_3} = 2(-.008)X_2 + 2(.070)X_3 + \lambda = 0$$

$$X_2 + X_3 = 1.00$$

$$X_3 = .834, \qquad X_2 = .166, \qquad \lambda = -.042 \tag{13.118}$$

so that portfolio risk and expected return are

$$\text{var}(R_p) = (.267)(.166)^2 + (.070)(.834)^2 + 2(-.008)(.166)(.834)$$
$$= .007367 + .04869 - .002215$$
$$= .05383 \tag{13.119}$$

and

$$E(R_p) = (.45)(.166) + (.16)(.834)$$
$$= .075 + .134 \tag{13.120}$$
$$= .209$$

The efficiency frontier bounding all portfolios consisting of the combinations of the two securities is shown in Figure 13.8.

While an economic interpretation of the Lagrangian multipliers is not necessary to the solution of the problem, such an interpretation can be worthy of note. In the case where two constraints are used

$$E(R_p) = \sum_{i=1}^{n} X_i E(R_i) = C \qquad (13.121)$$

and

$$\sum_{i=1}^{n} X_i = 1 \qquad (13.122)$$

where all terms are defined above, the function ϕ can be stated

$$\phi = \text{var}(R_p) + \lambda_1 \left[\sum_{i=1}^{n} X_i E(R_i) - C \right] + \lambda_2 \left(\sum_{i=1}^{n} X_i - 1 \right) \qquad (13.123)$$

and the equations $\partial\phi/\partial X_1 = 0$, $\partial\phi/\partial X_2 = 0$, $\cdots \partial\phi/\partial X_n = 0$ can be solved simultaneously along with the two constraints, (13.121) and (13.122). In this particular case, λ_1 represents the marginal variance of expected returns.

$$\lambda_1 = -\partial\text{var}(R_p)/\partial E(R_p) \qquad (13.124)$$

That is, at any level of expected return, an increment (Δ) in expected return can be obtained by increasing variance by an amount $-\lambda_1\Delta$.

Interpretation of λ_2 in a meaningful way requires a restatement of the problem. If, instead of letting $\sum X_i = 1$ (i.e., deal with percentages of investible funds), we let $\sum X_i = A$ (where A is a dollar amount of assets to be invested), then $\lambda_2 = \partial\text{var}(R_p)/\partial A$. That is to say, λ_2 can be interpreted as the marginal risk of increased (or decreased) investment.[19]

Observe that the Markowitz model is in essence a one-period model. That is, we can formulate expectations regarding future returns on investment, crank through the procedure, purchase the optimally diversified portfolio, and hold the portfolio until the end of the period. If expectations are revised at the end of the period (or before), the entire procedure must be repeated and perhaps a new portfolio purchased.

Conceptually, the one-period model can be tenable. That is to say, if the goal of portfolio management is defined as the selection of a portfolio so as to maximize wealth at the end of a number of years, assuming reinvestment of all returns, then it is sufficient to maximize returns (or, equivalently, minimize risk) during each year within the overall span of time. Indeed, to maximize returns during every time period is, in one sense, minimizing risk (i.e., minimizing probability of failure) over time. Stated differently, given a 10-year planning horizon, the

---

[19] See A. D. Martin, Jr., "Mathematical Programming of Portfolio Selections," *Management Science*, vol. 1, no. 2, January 1955.

chances of achieving the final wealth goal are higher if returns are maximized each year during the 10-year time span than the chances would be if some alternative strategy is adopted.[20] The problem of portfolio turnover can be mitigated by imposing additional constraints. That is, one can consider limiting any changes to different diversifications, holding the same securities, or swapping a new (more desirable) security for an existing (least desirable) security as described in Figure 12.1.[21]

Addition of a Guaranteed Loan.   Consider the minimum risk portfolio of shares of Xerox with shares of Holt, Rinehart and Winston, Inc., as calculated previously in (13.114) and (13.115). The expected return and risk of this portfolio are

$$E(R_p) = 53.11 \text{ percent}, \quad \sigma(R_p) = \sqrt{.1253} = .354$$

$$(13.125)$$

Even with this minimum value for risk, losses are possible. To reduce risk even further, consider adding a guaranteed (risk-free) investment to the two-stock portfolio.

$$R_G = 8 \text{ percent}, \quad \sigma(R_G) = .00 \qquad (13.126)$$

Then copying (13.44) and (13.42), we get

$$
\begin{aligned}
E(R_p) &= R_G + \{[E(R_B) - R_G]/\sigma(R_B)\}\sigma(R_p) \\
&= .08 + [(.5311 - .08)/(.354)]\sigma(R_p) \\
&= .08 + 1.2743\sigma(R_p) \\
&= .08 + .4511 X_2
\end{aligned}
$$

$$(13.127)$$

$$
\begin{aligned}
\sigma(R_p) &= X_2\sigma(R_B) \\
&= .354 X_2
\end{aligned}
$$

$$(13.128)$$

Hence *any* combination of risk and return along the straight line shown in Figure 13.9 can be obtained. One simply alters X_2. *All* investments which lie to the right and below the line are inefficient.

Calculation of Efficient Portfolios Using Sharpe's Single-Index (Diagonal) Model.   Recall from the preceding section that the inputs required

---

[20] See, for example, Henry A. Latane, "Criteria for Choice Among Risky Ventures," *The Journal of Political Economy*, vol. LXVII, no. 2, April 1959, pp. 144–155.

[21] Grubel extends application of the Markowitz model to long-term asset holdings that are diversified among foreign currencies. See Herbert G. Grubel, "Internationally Diversified Portfolios: Welfare Gains and Capital Flows," *The American Economic Review*, vol. LVIII, no. 5, part 1, December 1968, pp. 1299–1303.

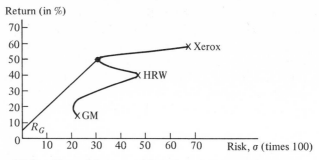

Figure 13.9. Two risky securities plus guaranteed return.

for use of the Markowitz model include covariance (or coefficient of correlation) between expected returns of all pairs of securities under consideration. In practice, this requirement can be difficult to meet. Security analysts, if pressed hard, may give estimates of probable error associated with their forecast of expected return on investment in a given security. But to give estimates of possible covariance of expected returns with returns from all other securities—perhaps securities of firms with which the analyst is not familiar—may be not only a heroic but impossible task. The ability to drop the requirement to know covariance is a giant step forward toward making the portfolio model more operational. Such a procedure was developed and tested by Professor Sharpe.

Correlation of Asset Yields with Market Yields.   Instead of formulating expectations according to the scheme used to illustrate the Markowitz portfolios, we can proceed as follows. Since it is well known that most asset yields are correlated one with another, and since all yields in the aggregate constitute the market, then yields of individual assets ought to be correlated with market yields.[22] If this is true, then advantage can be taken of such correlation to bypass the need to calculate covariance directly.

Stated a different way, since the return from asset 1 varies with the market and the return from asset 2 also varies with the market,

---

[22] There can be some concern over which particular index of the market provides best results. Keith Smith investigated eight different indexes and concluded that a stock price index yields better results than an economic index. The indexes examined by Smith are the (1) *Dow-Jones Industrial Average*, (2) *Standard & Poor's 425 Industrials*, (3) *New York Stock Exchange Composite Index*, (4) Gross National Product (GNP), (5) Consumer Price Index (CPI), (6) Federal Reserve Board Index of Industrial Production (FRB), (7) *Business Week* Index, and (8) money supply. See Keith V. Smith, "Stock Price and Economic Indexes for Generating Efficient Portfolios," *The Journal of Business*, vol. 42, no. 3, July 1969.

then by capturing the relationship of the returns of the two assets with the market, we implicitly capture the covariance relationship of the return from one asset with the other. Put more precisely, from equation (6.76) in Chapter 6, if

$$\rho_{1,M} = \beta_{1,M}[\sigma(R_M)/\sigma(R_1)] \tag{13.129}$$

$$\rho_{2,M} = \beta_{2,M}[\sigma(R_M)/\sigma(R_2)] \tag{13.130}$$

then

$$\rho_{1,M} = k\rho_{2,M} \tag{13.131}$$

where $k = \dfrac{\beta_{1,M}}{\beta_{2,M}} \cdot \dfrac{\sigma(R_2)}{\sigma(R_1)} = $ constant, and $\sigma(R_M)$ is the standard error of estimate of returns offered by the market. That is, the two correlations, $\rho_{1,M}$ and $\rho_{2,M}$, are proportional to one another.

An interpretation of covariance [correlation] in the context of regression analysis can be explained as follows. Consider the regression of R_1 on R_M as stated in (13.132). Then there will be (i.e., can be calculated) a total variance of deviations from this regression line (13.134). A similar regression of R_2 on R_M as stated in (13.133) will yield a corresponding variance of deviations from its regression line (13.135). In each case, the regression lines have slope B_1 and B_2 respectively, and $\text{var}(e_1)$ and $\text{var}(e_2)$ are estimates of the variance about the regression line in each case.

$$R_1 = A_1 + B_1(R_M) + e_1 \tag{13.132}$$

$$R_2 = A_2 + B_2(R_M) + e_2 \tag{13.133}$$

where

$R_i = $ price (or expected return) of asset i
$A_i, B_i = $ parameters correlating the asset with the market (e.g., constants of regression)
$R_M = $ price (or expected return) offered by the market
$e_i = $ a stochastic error term associated with the estimate

$$\text{var}(R_1) = B_1^2\text{var}(R_M) + \text{var}(e_1) \tag{13.134}$$

$$\text{var}(R_2) = B_2^2\text{var}(R_M) + \text{var}(e_2) \tag{13.135}$$

Next, instead of taking sample size S_1 for R_1 and calculating a regression, and then taking a sample size S_2 for R_2 and plotting a separate regression, now pool the two samples S_1 and S_2 and then calculate a single regression on R_M. If the (weighted) sum of the original (separate) dispersions is significantly different from the dispersion of total sample, we can conclude that the procedure of bringing all the returns together has had a significant effect on the risk of the portfolio.

This effect, if significant, is attributable to covariation of errors of estimate.

The expected return on a portfolio consisting of n securities, all of which are correlated with the market, can be written as a function of the market return alone.

$$E(R_p) = \sum_{i=1}^{N} E(X_i R_i) = \sum_{i=1}^{N} X_i E(A_i + B_i R_M + e_i)$$

$$= \sum_{i=1}^{N} X_i E(A_i + e_i) + \left(\sum_{i=1}^{N} X_i B_i\right) E(R_M) \qquad \textbf{(13.136)}$$

$$= A + B[E(R_M)]$$

where

$$A = \sum_{i=1}^{N} X_i A_i = \text{Constant}$$

$$B = \sum_{i=1}^{N} X_i B_i = \text{Constant}$$

$$E(R_M) = \text{expected return offered by the market}$$

The risk of the portfolio also can be written as a function of the market risk and prediction (regression) errors alone. Covariance is captured implicitly.

$$\text{var}(R_p) = \sum_{i=1}^{n} X_i^2 \text{var}(R_i) + 2 \sum_{j=1}^{(n-1)} \sum_{k=(j+1)}^{n} X_j X_k \text{cov}(R_j R_k)$$

$$= \sum_{i=1}^{N} X_i^2 \text{var}(A_i + B_i R_M + e_i) \qquad \textbf{(13.137)}$$

$$+ 2 \sum_{j=1}^{(n-1)} \sum_{k=(j+1)}^{n} X_j X_k \text{cov}[(A_j + B_j R_M + e_j),$$

$$(A_k + B_k R_M + e_k)]$$

$$= \left(\sum_{i=1}^{n} X_i^2 B_i^2\right) \text{var}(R_M) + \left[\sum_{i=1}^{n} X_i^2 \text{var}(e_i)\right]$$

$$+ \left(2 \sum_{j=1}^{(n-1)} \sum_{k=(j+1)}^{n} X_j X_k B_j B_k\right) \text{var}(R_M)$$

$$= \alpha_1 \text{var}(R_M) + \sum_{i=1}^{n} X_i^2 \text{var}(e_i)$$

where

$$\alpha_1 = \sum_{i=1}^{n} X_i^2 B_i^2 + 2 \sum_{(j=1)}^{(n-1)} \sum_{k=(j+1)}^{n} X_j X_k B_j B_k$$

Statements (13.136) and (13.137) assume

$$E(e_i) = 0 \qquad \textbf{(13.138)}$$

$$\text{var}(e_i) = \sigma_i^2 < \infty \tag{13.139}$$

$$\text{cov}(e_i, R_M) = 0 \tag{13.140}$$

$$\text{cov}(e_j, e_k) = 0 \tag{13.141}$$

$$\text{cov}(R_M, R_M) = \text{var}(R_M) \tag{13.142}$$

Note if R_1 from (13.132) is interpreted to be expected return then

$$R_1 = \ln(P_{t+1}/P_t) \tag{13.143}$$

where

R_1 = yield for holding security *1* for one time period, assuming continuous compounding[23]
P_t = price of asset as of time t
P_{t+1} = price of asset as of time $(t + 1)$

The constant A in equation (13.136) can be interpreted as an investment in "basic securities" and can be diversified away.[24] However, in the light of Figure 13.9 and the discussion associated with equations (13.44) and (13.44b), it might appear that A should be maximized instead of being diversified away.

The risk of the portfolio containing n securities therefore can be stated in terms of error of estimate of market returns.

Illustration of Portfolio Optimization Utilizing Correlations with the Market. Reconsider diversification between the three securities with data as tabulated in Table 13.3. This time, however, introduce the

---

[23] Refer to statement (10.8).

[24] *Proof.* A is an intercept value on a regression line. That is, using the definition of regression from statement (6.78),

$$(R_{1C} - R_1) = \beta_{1,2}(R_2 - R_2) \tag{6.78}$$

we can write

$$\begin{aligned} R_{1C} &= (R_1 - \beta_{1,2}R_2) + \beta_{1,2}R_2 \\ &= A + \beta_{1,2}R_2 \end{aligned} \tag{13.144}$$

Then for A to equal zero,

$$R_1 = \beta_{1,2}R_2 \tag{13.145}$$

That is, select two securities so that the expected return from security *1* equals $\beta_{1,2}$ times the expected return from the other security. R_2 can equal R_M.

Table 13.4 EMPIRICAL DATA FOR THE MARKET

Subjective Estimate of possible return	S & P 500 composite	1075 stocks
R_1	.255	.286
R_2	.196	.179
R_3	.236	.201
R_4	−.118	−.130
R_5	.295	.347
R_6	.018	.054
R_7	.178	.241
R_8	.577	.631
R_9	−.089	−.075
R_{10}	.108	.109
R_{Average}	.165	.183

market. Two alternative measures of the market are tabulated in Table 13.4.[25] Then, instead of estimating $\rho_{1,2}$, $\rho_{1,3}$, and $\rho_{2,3}$ for the stocks, we now estimate $\rho_{1,M}$, $\rho_{2,M}$, and $\rho_{3,M}$. These data are tabulated in Table 13.5 and are plotted in Figure 13.10.

From the data tabulated on Table 13.5, the mean, sum of squares, and sum of cross products can be calculated as follows.

Means: $\mu_{GM} = .1263;$ $\mu_{\text{Xerox}} = .4208;$ $\mu_{\text{S\&P}} = .1416$ **(13.146)**

Sum of squares: .4999;   1.7966;   .2754   **(13.147)**

Sum of cross products:

$$\sum_{i=1}^{10} [(\ln_i - \mu_i)_{GM}(\ln_i - \mu_i)_{\text{S\&P}}] = .2860 \tag{13.148}$$

$$\sum_{i=1}^{10} [(\ln_i - \mu_i)_{\text{Xerox}}(\ln_i - \mu_i)_{\text{S\&P}}] = .3364$$

To calculate the precise lines of regression in order to express common stock returns in terms of market returns, we can apply the formulas (13.129) and (13.130) in the following way.

$$\beta_{\text{GM-S\&P}} = \rho_{\text{GM-S\&P}} \left[\frac{\text{var(GM)}}{\text{var(S\&P)}} \right]^{1/2} \tag{13.149}$$

$$\beta_{\text{Xerox-S\&P}} = \rho_{\text{Xerox-S\&P}} \left[\frac{\text{var(Xerox)}}{\text{var(S\&P)}} \right]^{1/2} \tag{13.150}$$

---

[25] Refer to footnote 18 for understanding of how the data in Table 13.4 were actually generated. Equation (13.102) was used. All the stocks contained on compustat (annual data) were used to calculate column 2 of Table 13.4.

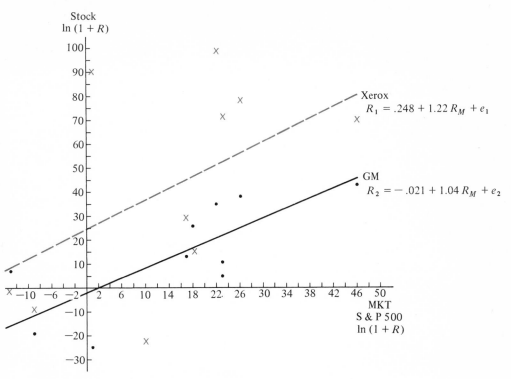

Figure 13.10.   Two linear regressions.

Table 13.5   SECURITY RETURNS VS. THE MARKET RETURNS

(1)	GM R (2)	ln(1 + R) (3)	Xerox R (4)	ln(1 + R) (5)	S and P 500 R (6)	ln(1 + R) (7)
t_{-1}	.111	.104	1.054	.718	.255	.231
t_{-2}	.301	.262	.165	.157	.196	.182
t_{-3}	.421	.351	1.689	.990	.236	.215
t_{-4}	.072	.068	−.012	−.012	−.118	−.126
t_{-5}	.464	.378	1.177	.779	.295	.262
t_{-6}	−.217	−.245	1.454	.896	.018	.010
t_{-7}	.141	.131	.338	.293	.178	.174
t_{-8}	.537	.432	1.017	.703	.577	.457
t_{-9}	−.193	−.213	−.092	−.097	−.089	−.093
t_{-10}	−.005	−.005	−.197	−.219	.108	.104
Mean (μ)		.1263		.4208		.1416
$\sum_{i=1}^{10} (\ln_i - \mu)^2$		.4999		1.7966		.2754

where

$$\rho_{A,B} = \frac{(1/N)[\sum (A)(B)]}{\{[(1/N)\sum (A)^2][(1/N)\sum (B)^2]\}^{1/2}}$$

$$\sum (A)(B) = \text{sums of cross products from (13.148)}$$

$$\sum (A)^2 = \text{sums of squares from (13.147)}$$

Using the data and formulas stated above, the coefficients of correlation between expected return for the individual securities and expected return for the market are

$$\rho_{\text{GM-S\&P}} = \frac{.2860}{\sqrt{(.4999)(.2754)}} = \frac{.2860}{.3711} = .7708 \qquad \textbf{(13.151)}$$

$$\rho_{\text{Xerox-S\&P}} = \frac{.3364}{\sqrt{(1.7966)(.2754)}} = \frac{.3364}{.7035} = .4782 \qquad \textbf{(13.152)}$$

The regression equation is given by the standard formula (13.144). Restated, we get

$$R_{1C} = (\bar{R}_1 - \beta_{1,2}\bar{R}_M) + \beta_{1,2}R_M$$
$$= A + \beta R_M \qquad \textbf{(13.153)}$$

Using (13.149) and (13.150), the slope of each regression line is

$$\beta_{\text{GM-S\&P}} = .7708\left(\frac{.4999}{.2754}\right)^{1/2} = 1.0385 \qquad \textbf{(13.154)}$$

$$\beta_{\text{Xerox-S\&P}} = .4782\left(\frac{1.7966}{.2754}\right)^{1/2} = 1.222 \qquad \textbf{(13.155)}$$

The constant intercept values (A) of the regressions are

$$A_{\text{GM-S\&P}} = .1263 - 1.0385(.1416) = .1263 - .1470$$
$$= -.0207 \qquad \textbf{(13.156)}$$

$$A_{\text{Xerox-S\&P}} = .4208 - 1.222(.1416) = .4208 - .1730$$
$$= .2478 \qquad \textbf{(13.157)}$$

Hence, the precise regression relationships sought are

$$\ln[(D_{t+1} + P_{t+1})/P_t]_{\text{GM}} = -.021 + 1.04 \ln[(D_{t+1} + P_{t+1})/P_t]_{\text{S\&P}}$$
$$\textbf{(13.158)}$$

$$\ln[(D_{t+1} + P_{t+1})/P_t]_{\text{Xerox}} = .248 + 1.22 \ln[(D_{t+1} + P_{t+1})/P_t]_{\text{S\&P}}$$
$$\textbf{(13.159)}$$

Finally, applying statements (13.158) and (13.159), the expected return and risk of the portfolio can be stated [as per (13.136) through (13.142)] and then the mechanical mathematical procedures [described in (13.110) through (13.115)] can be applied so as to minimize risk, subject to constraints of full investments and some minimum desired return.

CHAPTER 13 **APPENDIX**

SOME ADDITIONAL MODELS FOR PORTFOLIO RETURNS

Several alternative models for portfolio analysis have appeared in the literature during recent years. Representative types of these models are summarized in this Appendix. Of significance, are models for

1. Direct maximization of expected utility
2. Maximizing the probability of survival
3. Minimizing the probability of disaster
4. Bond portfolios (diversification by maturity)

Each of these models for portfolio analysis and management is summarized briefly below.

Direct Maximization of Expected Utility. Models in this category are based on either of two assumptions, (1) inelastic expectations regarding market returns or (2) an assumed probability distribution for market conditions. The first was described by Farrar[26]; the second was described by Mao and Sarndal.[27] The Farrar method shall be described first.

Consider a quadratic utility function as hypothesized in Chapter 12, Equation (12.79).

$$E[U(R)] = \mu - \psi[\mu^2 + \text{var}(R)] \qquad (13.160)$$

where $\psi = a$ positive constant, determined by the risk preferences of the investor and is assumed to be known.

The expected return and variance on a portfolio can be written

$$\mu = \sum_{i=1}^{N} X_i E(R_i) \qquad (13.161)$$

$$\text{var}(R) = \sum_{j=1}^{N} \sum_{i=1}^{N} X_i X_j \text{cov}(R_i, R_j) \qquad (13.162)$$

where $\text{cov}(R_i, R_j) = \sigma_{ij}$. When $i = j$, $\sigma_{ij} = \text{var}(R_i)$. Operating constraints can be listed

$$\sum_{i=1}^{N} X_i = 1, \qquad C_1 \le X_i \le C_2 \qquad (13.163)$$

---

[26] Donald E. Farrar, *The Investment Decision under Uncertainty*, Prentice-Hall, Inc., New York, 1962.
[27] James C. T. Mao and Carl Erik Sarndal, "A Decision Theory Approach to Portfolio Selection," *Management Science*, vol. 12, no. 8, April 1966, pp. B327–B331.

456

Then, substitute (13.161) and (13.162) directly into (13.160) and proceed to maximize expected utility (with respect to X_i), subject to the constraints, (13.163). That is to say, maximize a portfolio's expected utility

$$E[U(R_p)] = \sum_{i=1}^{N} X_i\mu_i - \psi\left[\left(\sum_{i=1}^{N} X_i\mu_i\right)^2 + \left(\sum_{j=1}^{N}\sum_{i=1}^{N} X_i\sigma_{ij}X_j\right)\right]$$

(13.164)

where

R_p = return expected on the portfolio. R_p is a weighted sum $\sum X_i\mu_i$ of individual securities, $X_i \geq 0$

$U(R_p)$ = subjective ordinal utility associated with return R_p

X_i = is the proportion of the portfolio which is invested in security i

$$\sum_{i=1}^{N} X_i = 1.00$$

In a more general case, when the states of the world are uncertain, then Mao and Sarndal point out the Markowitz model can be reformulated according to the Bayesian strategy to yield an objective function which can be written

$$E[U(R_p)] = \sum_{i=1}^{N} X_i(p^*\mu_i + q^*\mu_i') - \psi\left\{\left[\sum_{i=1}^{N} X_i(p^*\mu_i + q^*\mu_i')^2\right.\right.$$
$$\left.\left. + \left[\sum_{j=1}^{N}\sum_{i=1}^{N} X_i(p^*\sigma_{ij} + q^*\sigma_{ij}')X_j\right]\right\}$$

(13.165)

where

p^*, q^* = revised (posteriori) probabilities of occurrence of two alternative states of the market (or the economy generally), Θ_1 and Θ_2, respectively. $p^* + q^* = 1.00$

μ_i = expected return on investment under the condition that state Θ_1 occur

μ_i' = expected return on investment under the condition that state Θ_2 occur

σ_{ij} = variance/covariance set under the condition that state Θ_1 occur

σ_{ij}' = variance/covariance set under the condition that state Θ_2 occur

and other terms are the same as defined previously. Statement (13.165) can be expanded to admit the case of m alternative states of nature: $\Theta_1, \Theta_2, \ldots, \Theta_M$.

Maximizing Probability of Survival. Maximizing the probability of survival is similar to minimizing the probability of disaster. Roy[28] and Hannsmann[29] address themselves to these methods. Roy emphasizes minimizing the probability of disaster: "We wish to know what values of X_1, X_2, ..., X_n should be chosen if the outcome associated with... (the risky investment)... is the most safe from our point of view. We should also like to know how secure this most safe position actually is."

Analysis for diversifying for minimizing the probability of disaster can proceed as follows.

Given n securities with μ_i, σ_i, and $\rho_{i,j}$ all known, then expected return and risk for the portfolio are

$$E(R_p) = \sum_{i=1}^{N} X_i \mu_i \tag{13.166}$$

$$\sigma(R_p) = \left\{ \left[\sum_{i=1}^{N} X_i^2 \sigma_i^2 \right] + 2 \left[\sum_{j=1}^{(N-1)} \sum_{i=j+1}^{N} X_i X_j \rho_{i,j} \sigma_i \sigma_j \right] \right\}^{1/2}$$

where $\hspace{11cm}$ (13.167)

$$\sum_{i=1}^{N} X_i = 1.$$

As stated previously, the equations (13.166) and (13.167) trace out an envelope of attainable $E(R_p)$ and $\sigma(R_p)$ combinations, depending on the selected diversification (X_i). The actual (ex-post) return is expected to fall in the neighborhood of $E(R_p)$. Let the disastrous return be d. We wish to diversify so as to assure that the probability of obtaining d or less is minimal. Since it is not possible to calculate the precise probability of d, given $E(R_p)$ and $\sigma(R_p)$, we can state, using the Bienayme-Tchebycheff inequality,[30] the upper bound of this probability. Letting the actual (ex-post) return be R_A, we can write

$$Pr\{|R_A - E(R_p)| \geq [E(R_p) - d]\} \leq [\sigma(R_p)]^2/[E(R_p) - d]^2 \tag{13.168}$$

Then, since

$$Pr\{|R_A - E(R_p)| \geq [E(R_p) - d]\} \approx Pr\{[E(R_p) - R_A] \geq [E(R_p) - d]\} \tag{13.169}$$

we can write

$$Pr(R_A \leq d) \leq [\sigma(R_p)]^2/[E(R_p) - d]^2 \tag{13.170}$$

---

[28] A. D. Roy, "Safety First and the Holding of Assets," *Econometrica*, vol. 20, July 1952, pp. 431–449.

[29] Fred Hannsmann, "Probability of Survival as an Investment Criterion," *Management Science*, vol. 15, no. 1, September 1968, pp. 33–48.

[30] Refer to Appendix 2 for Chapter 6 for a statement of the relevant statistics.

Then minimizing the probability that R_A is less than the disastrous outcome d, $[Pr(R_A \leq d)]$, is the same as minimizing the ratio $[\sigma(R_p)]^2/[E(R_p) - d]^2$, which is equivalent to maximizing $[E(R_p) - d]$ $/\sigma(R_p)$, the slope of the capital market line.[31] The analysis for diversification, therefore, focuses on maximizing $[E(R_p) - d]/\sigma(R_p)$. This is what Roy calls the principle of "safety first."

To calculate the smallest upper bound of the probability that d, or worse, will occur, consider a straight line of slope (h).

$$h = [E(R_p) - d]/\sigma(R_p) \qquad (13.171)$$

This line, $h[\sigma(R_p)] = [E(R_p) - d]$, is tangent to the envelope traced out by the solution of (13.166) and (13.167). Since on the line we have $[\sigma(R_p)]^2/[E(R_p) - d]^2 = 1/h^2$, the upper bound of the probability that d or worse will occur is $1/h^2$. The objective of analysis, therefore, is to maximize h. That is to say, the optimal diversification is that allocation $[E(R_p), \sigma(R_p)]$ which lies along a straight line having maximum slope in the risk-return plane as shown in Figure 13.9.

Hannsmann addresses himself to the criterion of maximizing the probability of exceeding a specified return. Hannsmann considers cases where the distribution of total return can be approximated by a normal distribution.

If $N(\mu,\sigma)$ designates the standardized cumulative normal distribution, then the probability of exceeding some critical return C is given by

$$Pr(R_p \geq C) = 1 - N[(C - E)/S] \qquad (13.172)$$

where E = expected value of the total return on the portfolio (R_p) and S = standard deviation of the total return. To solve the problem, it is sufficient to *minimize* the function

$$H_{(x_1,\ldots,x_n)} = \left[C - \sum f_i(X_i)\right]/S_{(x_1,\cdots,x_n)} \qquad (13.173)$$

subject to the constraint

$$\sum_{i=1}^{N} X_i = A = \text{total amount (assets) available to invest}$$

$$(13.174)$$

and the nonnegativity constraints

$$X_i \geq 0 \qquad (13.175)$$

where X_i = amount invested in asset i. Following-through the procedures in this way, a rational diversification strategy can be derived. This diversification maximizes the probability of exceeding a stated critical return, C.

---

[31] Refer to Figure 13.9, equations (13.44) and (13.44b), and the discussion associated with footnote 24.

Bond Portfolios. Diversification by date of maturity is possible for bond portfolios. Cheng notes that during any given planning period, a financial manager has a number of possible ways of sequencing bonds of different maturities.[32] For example, given an investment time horizon of 5 years, then one alternative open to an investor is to purchase a series of 1-year bonds.

$$(0,1) \rightarrow (1,1) \rightarrow (2,1) \rightarrow (3,1) \rightarrow (4,1) \qquad \textbf{(13.176)}$$

where the first number in parenthesis in (13.176) indicates the time of purchase, (e.g., 0 indicates today, 1 indicates one year hence, ..., 4 indicates four years hence), and the second number in parenthesis indicates the length of time to maturity of the bond.

Alternatively, the investor can purchase one 3-year bond now and upon its maturity purchase a 2-year bond to cover the required span of five years.

$$(0,3) \rightarrow (3,2) \qquad \textbf{(13.179)}$$

In general, investor tactics can be denoted

$$(k, h) \qquad \textbf{(13.178)}$$

where

$$\sum h_i = n = \text{investment time horizon}$$
$$k_i - k_{i-1} = h_{i-1}$$

and other possible restrictions may be imposed exogenously. For example,

$$p \leq h_i \leq q \qquad \textbf{(13.179)}$$

where p = minimum desirable maturity to be held, q = maximum desirable maturity, and the number of possible tactics is the number of solutions of $\sum h_i = n$. For example, if $1 \leq h_i \leq 2$ and $n = 5$, then there will be eight possible tactics. The reader should list all eight possibilities.

The other side of the picture is the bond market. A market tactic for bonds consists of a set of alternative yield curves. As of any particular time, there exists some (ex-ante) probability distribution for yields to maturity. For example, given one of several alternative sets of business conditions, Θ_1, there will exist a corresponding set of possible yields. Given another alternative set of business conditions, Θ_2, there will exist a different set of possible yields to maturity.

The market tactic implies that the market is free to take on one of any number of different possible yield curves, and that the actual (ex-post) future yields will vary, depending upon which particular tactic is

---

[32] Pao Lun Cheng, "Optimal Bond Portfolio Selection," *Management Science*, vol. 8, no. 4, July 1962, pp. 490–499.

chosen by the market. The objective of diversifying among bonds is to select a mixed investment tactic so that minimum risk is achieved when the (ex-ante) market tactic is uncertain.

To illustrate diversification with bonds, consider an investor tactic such as (13.176). Call this tactic $(\tilde{G}_i)$ and treat it as if it is an asset or a security associated with an expected yield $E(\tilde{G}_i)$, or μ_i for short, and variance $\text{var}(\tilde{G}_i)$, or V_i for short. Then the expected return on an investment in many (w) such tactics can be written

$$E(R_p) = x_1\mu_1 + x_2\mu_2 + \cdots + x_i\mu_i + \cdots + x_w\mu_w$$

$$(13.180)$$

where $E(R_p)$ is the rate of growth expected of the portfolio by the financial manager, and

$$x_1 + x_2 + \cdots + x_i + \cdots + x_w = 1 \qquad (13.181)$$

where $x_i \geq 0, (i = 1, 2, \ldots, w)$ and x_i is the fraction of total assets to be invested in the pure tactic $\tilde{G}_i$.

The variance (risk) of the investment portfolio can be written in terms of the variance-covariance matrix and the diversification proportions.

$$V = (x_1, x_2, \ldots, x_i, \ldots, x_w) \begin{bmatrix} V_{11} & V_{12} & \cdots & V_{1i} & \cdots & V_{1w} \\ V_{21} & V_{22} & \cdots & V_{2i} & \cdots & V_{2w} \\ \vdots & \vdots & & \vdots & & \vdots \\ V_{i1} & V_{i2} & \cdots & V_{ii} & \cdots & V_{iw} \\ \vdots & \vdots & & \vdots & & \vdots \\ V_{w1} & V_{w2} & \cdots & V_{wi} & \cdots & V_{ww} \end{bmatrix} \begin{bmatrix} x_1 \\ x_2 \\ \vdots \\ x_i \\ \vdots \\ x_w \end{bmatrix}$$

$$(13.82)$$

where V is the variance of the portfolio, and V_{ij} are variances and covariances with and among the w investor tactics. The individual variances (V_{ij}) are calculated in the same way Markowitz calculates variance for expected return on equity issues. The only difference here is that an investment tactic is treated as a security. The variance for an investor tactic is the second moment about the mean of the probability distribution of possible returns—the mean square error of estimate of yield for that particular strategy. Then the optimal diversification (i.e., best values for $x_1, x_2, \ldots, x_w$) can be calculated in the usual way [33]

---

[33] See (1) A. D. Martin, Jr., "Mathematical Programming of Portfolio Selection," *Management Science*, vol. 1, no. 2, January 1955, pp. 152–166); (2) Markowitz, *op. cit.*, p. 187; and (3) Sharpe, *op. cit.*

described previously by minimizing the objective function, (13.182), given the constraints stated in (13.181) and (13.180). Recall from the previous discussions (e.g. footnote 17) that several alternative techniques can be applied to solve the minimization. Martin, for example, used Lagrangian multipliers. So did Sharpe. Markowitz used quadratic programming. Cheng's technique follows Markowitz.

The values for X_i so calculated are the optimal fractions of total investment to be allocated to each of the available investor tactics for bond portfolios.

QUESTIONS FOR STUDY

1. Outline briefly the difference between the jobs of the security analyst and the portfolio manager.
2. Explain the principle of diversification and illustrate how you would diversify a portfolio.
3. Explain why the Sharpe model for portfolio is superior (or inferior) to the original Markowitz model.
4. Explain the advantages and disadvantages of using variance of expected return as an operational measure of risk. Suggest some alternative measures of risk.
5. Suppose you have $30 million available for investment purposes. In the light of the chapter just finished, present some notes on the analysis you would undertake prior to committing this money to a
   (a) Bond portfolio
   (b) Stock portfolio
   (c) Portfolio consisting of both bonds and stock
   Be sure to justify each factor you introduce as being important in the analysis. That is, note specific reasons why your analysis is appropriate.
6. The Markowitz model requires analysis of historical data in order to select a portfolio. True or false? Explain.
7. (a) What is an efficient portfolio?
   (b) Are efficient portfolios more risky or less risky than inefficient portfolios?
   Explain your answer.
8. In view of the fact that the $E\text{-}V$ theory of diversification ignores crucial factors such as (1) portfolio liquidity requirements, (2) marketability of the securities, (3) length of time of uninterrupted dividend payments, (4) corporate financial structure (e.g., ratio of debt to equity), (5) quality rating of the firm, and (6) quality of management, we can conclude that the $E\text{-}V$ theory is not a practical guide to portfolio selection. True or false? Explain.
9. Explain why Sharpe's model has no term involving covariance among securities.

10. *Given.* $100,000 and two securities. Both securities offer the same expected return, both have the same variance of expected return, with a positive covariance of .02.

$$E(R_1) = E(R_2) = 20 \text{ percent}$$
$$\text{var}(R_1) = \text{var}(R_2) = .06$$
$$\text{cov}(R_1, R_2) = .02$$

A client wants to invest $50,000 in each of the two securities, but an investment counsellor points out that there is positive covariance which raises the risk. So the client's optimal strategy is to invest the entire $100,000 in one security.

Question. Is the advice of the investment counsellor correct or incorrect?

11. Explain which of the two following alternatives you would select and why?
    (a) Invest $10 in a single stock whose expected return is 45 percent and variance of return is .015.
    (b) Invest $5 in a stock with an expected return of 60 percent and standard derivation of return of .300. Simultaneously, invest another $5 in a stock with an expected return of 30 percent and standard derivation of return of .100. The covariance of return between the two stocks is $-.010$.

12. *Given.* $1000 for investment and two securities S_1 and S_2 whose data are shown in Table 13.6. How much would you invest in each security if you want to minimize risk? What return do you expect from the minimum-risk portfolio? Is it advisable to invest in the minimum-risk portfolio?

Table 13.6   DATA FOR TWO SECURITIES

Security	k_i (%)	Variance	Covariance
1	20	.02	$-.04$
2	40	.09	$-.04$

13. Explain the meaning of the term "systematic risk." How does systematic risk differ from unsystematic risk? Refer to equations (13.137) and (13.44b).

14. Explain the concept and the advantages of Sharpe's diagonal model (a single-index formulation of a Markowitz portfolio). What problems are caused by the fact that market returns (by definition) include returns from every individual security?

15. Describe the input data required and explain how you would obtain it in order to select a portfolio for a client investor.

16. Explain Sharpe's borrowing and lending portfolios. (Reference: William F. Sharpe, "A Simplified Model for Portfolio Analysis," *Management Science*, vol. IX, January 1963, pp. 277–293).

In the first thirteen chapters we covered the basic elements of analysis for financial decision making. In this chapter, we shall look back over time and ask some questions, How well did we do? Could we have done better? How does our investment performance compare with other performances?

Initially, the measurement of performance might seem to be a relatively simple matter. It might appear that the only requirements are to observe where we were at the beginning of the period, to look at where we are presently (at the end of the period), and to measure the improvement or decline in investment value. Let us see if the process is as simple as all of that.

Evaluation of Investment Performance 14

14.1 Measuring Investment Performance

Consider the three portfolios listed in Table 14.1. Each portfolio has achieved some actual (i.e., realized) return (R_i). As of the date of purchase of the portfolios, there was some expected return $[E(R_i)]$ and risk $[\sigma(R_i)]$. The objective now is to evaluate those three portfolios. Qualitatively, which of the three portfolios should be scored superior? Which portfolio was mediocre and which one was poor? We want to know how well did we do; could we have done better?

Most performance measures discussed in the literature are based primarily on statistical properties and linear or rank correlations between portfolio returns and market returns. Instead of focusing attention on statistical methods of analysis however, let us consider the criteria by which performance ought to be judged. There must be some criteria for ranking good, better, or best and some explanation as to why such a ranking is recommended. Otherwise, procedures for evaluation of investment performance are little more than purposeless exercises in statistics.

Table 14.1 PORTFOLIOS FOR TEST AND EVALUATION

Item	Portfolio 1	Portfolio 2	Portfolio 3
1	Avon Products	American Tobacco	Crown Zellerbach
2	Crown Cork and Seal	General Motors	B. F. Goodrich
3	Fairchild Camera	Johns-Manville	Lily-Tulip Cup
4	Leesona Corporation	Owens Illinois Inc.	Lone Star Cement
5	Lukens Steel	Procter and Gamble	National Gypsum
6	Magnavox Company	Std. Oil (Calif.)	National Lead Company
7	Northwest Airlines	Texaco Incorporated	Neisner Brothers
8	Polaroid Corporation	Union Carbide	Pittsburgh Plate Glass
9	Texas Instruments	U.S. Steel	Sun Oil Company
10	Xerox Corporation	F. W. Woolworth	U.S. Borax and Chemical

The ultimate criterion on which to base performance measures is the criterion by which the original purchase was made, *subjective utility*. Understanding that a portfolio is purchased for the purpose of maximizing utility of the owner, then the ultimate criterion of performance is to test whether the portfolio selected (ex-ante) was in fact the optimal (ex-post) portfolio to have held, so that subjective utility was in fact maximized.

But such a conceptual measure is difficult to construct in actual practice. The difficulty stems from the multidimensional nature of each of the variables under consideration: utility, risk, and return. Therefore, no matter what particular criteria are used, there will be no single universally accepted measure of performance applicable to all investment portfolios. For example, in the discussion of transitivity in Chapter 12, we saw that one can calculate a rank order of performance *in a single dimension* for a set of portfolios. The calculations can be repeated to effect rankings in other dimensions. But there is no guarantee that a given portfolio will occupy the same rank in all dimensions. Most likely it will not. If a portfolio ranks high in (ex-post) return, then quite likely it will rank low (i.e., will have been high) in risk exposure. Therefore, instead of deriving a single composite unique measure of investment performance, one practical alternative is to prepare a checklist of criteria for measuring investment performance and leave the final evaluation up to subjective judgment.

A checklist of criteria for measuring investment performance might include the following items:

1. Best possible securities
2. Efficiency (reward-risk ratio)
3. Optimal allocation between risky assets and risk-free assets
4. Timing
5. Statistically significant differences in performance on all counts

Before proceeding with a detailed study of alternative measures of performance, it may be profitable first to formulate some notions of *why* performance needs to be measured. What are we attempting to measure? In fact, what *is* investment performance?

Performance can be measured for three basic purposes:

1. Description of historical results
2. Prediction of future results
3. Normative guide to forming policy for future investments

These purposes are discussed in the following paragraphs.

14.2 Some Measures of Historical Performance

Description involves history. How well (or poorly) was the job performed? Given (ex-ante) expectations, how close did the (ex-post) results come? If ex-post returns far exceeded expectations, then one might be well advised to look for special causes to explain why expectations were in fact exceeded. If ex-post results fell far below expectations, then one might again search for special causes to explain why. If ex-post results fell within the range of expectations, then performance can possibly be rated as good, provided that the ex-ante expectations were well formulated in the first place.

Description based on historical results can be important. Job promotions and the career of an asset manager can depend upon the validity as well as the accuracy of such historical measures. Validity means, for example, that if the portfolio was particularly difficult (i.e., hard to predict), then a bonus can be forthcoming for a rating of "satisfactory performance." But, if the portfolio was relatively easy to predict and obtain, then a rating of satisfactory may be only mediocre and, therefore, may incur demerits.

Description, as defined above, tests the accuracy of forecasts. How close are ex-post results to ex-ante expectations? Did the portfolio do the job as intended? For good performance, there should be no significant surprises when ex-post results are compared with ex-ante expectations.[1]

In the context of historical statistical comparisons, there are two "error" terms to consider: (1) the ex-ante error or probability distribution expressing possible future outcomes; this error is the risk of the investment portfolio, and (2) the ex-post error or root-mean-square deviation of realized returns away from expected returns. This second error measures the accuracy of prediction. The two errors can be stated as follows.

$$e_1^2 = \frac{1}{N} \sum_{i=1}^{N} [R_i - E(R)]^2 \qquad (14.2)$$

where

$e_1^2 =$ variance of (ex-ante) probability distribution of possible returns = risk of portfolio

$R_i =$ ith probable (ex-ante) return

$E(R) =$ ex-ante expected return on the investment portfolio

$$e_2^2 = \frac{1}{\tau} \sum_{t=1}^{\tau} [R_{At} - R_{Pt}]^2 \qquad (14.3)$$

---

[1] In the context of information theory as noted in Chapter 10, the information content of the actual outcome from investment should be relatively small if performance is good. Stated quantitatively, (14.1) should be approximately minimal.

$$I(q:p) = \sum_{i=1}^{N} q_i(\log_2 q_i - \log_2 p_i) \qquad (14.1)$$

where all terms are the same as defined in (10.17).

where

e_2^2 = mean square error of forecast
R_{At} = actual realized return (ex-post) as of time t
R_{Pt} = predicted return (ex-ante) for time t
τ = total number of prediction intervals under evaluation

If performance is good, then there should be no significant differ-ence over time between e_2 and e_1 as defined in (14.2) and (14.3). If e_2 is significantly larger than e_1, then performance is poor, because addi-tional, unanticipated risk in the form of unpredicted large dispersion is being borne without the required compensation. If e_2 is significantly smaller than e_1, then performance is also poor, because the portfolio held is in fact less risky than originally believed, causing lower utility than could have been achieved otherwise.

In one sense, therefore, the measurement of investment perform-ance can be viewed as measuring the accuracy of forecasts of expected returns on investment. To answer the questions, Did the portfolio perform as it was supposed to? Was the portfolio in fact optimal?, we must know what the portfolio was supposed to do (i.e., ex-ante expec-tations $[E(R_p)$ and $\sigma(R_p)]$ must be known) and subjective risk policy $[U = U(R,\sigma)$, or the risk premium demanded] must be known in advance. Given ex-ante expectations (expected return and diversifica-tion) and risk policy, measuring performance becomes synonymous with measuring deviations of ex-post realizations from ex-ante expecta-tions. All actual outcomes that lie within the tolerance limits calculated ex-ante are indicative that the portfolio performed within expectations.

But there remain several obstacles to practical application of the notions set forth above. Measures such as described above actually measure the analyst's ability to predict portfolio returns. Given perfect predictions always, the performance always will be rated excellent. No bonus is given for difficult predictions (e.g., price of shares of a firm operating in high technology); no penalty is incurred for easy predic-tions (e.g., price of shares of a relatively stable public utility firm).

What actually needs measuring is not so much the accuracy of the analysts' forecast but the accuracy of the analyst as compared with some alternative forecast, perhaps even a naive forecast. If there is no significant difference between the magnitude of errors produced by the analyst and the magnitude of errors produced by a naive (mechanical) model, then, to reduce costs, use the cheaper of the two: the analyst or the mechanical model. The analyst may not need firing, though, even if he is more expensive that the model; the analyst may be needed to monitor the mechanical model. Hence, some relative measures of performance can be worthwhile.

Some Relative Measures of Historical Performance. Several indexes of relative forecasting accuracy can be formulated. Three specific possibilities are[2]

1.
$$RM_1 = \frac{e_A}{e_m} = \frac{E(R_{At} - R_{Pt})^2}{E(R_{At} - R_{A,t-1})^2}$$ (14.4)

where

RM_1 = relative measure 1
e_A = mean square error of analyst's forecast
e_m = mean square error using a mechanical model to forecast
R_{t-1} = mechanical model prediction of "no change"; the predicted return for the next time period is the same as the actual return realized last time.

Relative measure 1 expresses the analyst's error of forecast as a percent of the mechanical model's error of forecast. The model is naive in that it always predicts the next return to be the same as the last most recent return. For good performance, the ratio RM_1 should be less than unity.

2.
$$RM_2 = \frac{e_A}{\text{var}(R_A)} = \frac{E[R_{At} - R_{Pt}]^2}{E[R_{At} - E(R_{At})]^2}$$ (14.5)

where

RM_2 = relative measure 2
e_A = mean square error of analyst's forecast
$\text{var}(R_A)$ = mean square error using a mechanical model which assumes that the naive projection is always the mean of the series (or distribution) of returns actually realized. This index is one of the "inequality indexes" proposed by H. Theil.[3]

Relative measure 2 is similar to relative measure 1 in that the ratio measures the analyst's error of forecast as a percent of the model's error of forecast. But for RM_2, the model always predicts the next return to be the same as the average return (e.g., a trend-line return) realized over the recent past. The important point here is that no matter what particular mechanical model is assumed, the analyst's error can be measured as a percent of the model's error. For good performance, the ratio RM_2 should be less than unity.

[2] See Jacob Mincer, "Measuring the Accuracy of Forecasts," *The New York Statistician*, vol. 19, no. 4, March–April 1968.

[3] H. Theil, *Applied Economic Forecasting*, Rand McNally and Company, Skokie, Ill., 1966.

3. $$RM_3 = \frac{e^c_A}{\text{var}(R_A)} = 1 - r^2_{A,P} \qquad (14.6)$$

where

RM_3 = relative measure 3

e^c_A = linearly corrected mean square error of analyst's forecast

$r^2_{A,P}$ = coefficient of determination between predicted and actual values.

$\text{var}(R_A)$ is the same as defined above

Relative measure 3 is derived by "correcting" the analyst's forecast. That is, (1) if we use a naive model whose forecast is the historical mean value of the time series of realized returns, and (2) if we regress the predictions made by the analyst on the predictions made by the naive model, then (3) the equation of regression allows a "linearly corrected forecast" from the analyst.

As discussed in Appendix 2 of Chapter 6, [equation (6.81)] the coefficient of determination $(r^2_{A,P})$ compares the mean square error resulting from the linearly corrected forecast with the mean square error obtained from the naive projection. If the analyst's predictions have little correlation with the predictions from the model (e.g., if the analyst is usually correct and the model is correct only by chance), then $r^2_{A,P}$ will be small and RM_3 will be close to unity.

Allowing for Difficulty of Forecasts.   The three relative measures discussed above all fail to ensure criteria of uniform quality of performance. To illustrate, consider two industry analysts, one who must forecast returns from public utility stocks, bonds, or blue chips (i.e., analyst 1 must predict time series which are relatively smooth), and the other analyst must forecast returns from electronics and computer stocks (e.g., predicting time series which can fluctuate wildly and erratically on account of fast growth, high technology and rapid economic depreciation). Then relative measure 1 discussed above can give unfair advantage to the second analyst who should be able to do better than use last period's value as the prediction for next period. Relative measure 2 can give unfair advantage to the first analyst who should be able to do better than use the mean of the historical time series as the prediction for next period's outcome. RM_3 is an inferior measure to RM_2, because RM_3 does *not* penalize either analyst for systematic bias. Forecasts which are statistically biased and inefficient receive the same score, according to RM_3, as unbiased and efficient forecasts, so long as the former are a linear transformation of the latter.

Using another example to illustrate why allowance should be made for the differences in difficulty of forecasts (i.e., *quality* of forecast), consider two asset managers, A and B. Suppose manager A has access to only publicly available information and calculates his expectations and risks accordingly (and actually achieves these expectations), while manager *B* has access to additional, inside, information and achieves his results accordingly. Then which manager merits the better performance score?

The final answer to the question stated above depends upon the rules of the game. For example, if the inside information is the same as privileged information obtained as special knowledge while acting in an official capacity relating to the future operations of the firm, then use of this inside information for personal profit can be illegal. Under these conditions, the rules of the game call for at least censure (or, at most, prison) for manager *B*. But if the inside information is the same as privileged information obtained from application of superior knowledge of the behavior of the capital markets and/or superior synthesis of publicly available data, perhaps through the use of high speed digital computers, then this inside information is legitimate and its use merits an unqualified rating of outstanding.

Note that, instead of focusing all the attention on accuracy of forecasting returns, the concept of *quality* of forecasts is important for the valid measurement of investment performance. Naive benchmarks, such as the relative measures discussed above, are helpful to judge investment performance, but these measures by no means provide complete solutions to the problem of measuring performance. Even optimal forecasting methods have doubtful validity in the securities markets over short periods of time because of the random character of stock market prices as discussed in Chapter 10. Over longer periods (e.g., one year and longer) optimal extrapolations and/or correlations with fundamental macro and microeconomic variables can prove useful.[4] In any case, measuring investment performance requires additional considerations. Some of these considerations are outlined below.

Testing for the Best Possible Securities. Our checklist of criteria for measuring investment performance outlined above included examination of particular securities held during the review period, in light of

---

[4] A "best extrapolation" is an extrapolation which produces the smallest error of forecast. For an analysis of optimal extrapolation as defined by the minimum mean square error criterion, see, for example, A. M. Yagham, *Stationary Random Functions*, Prentice-Hall, Inc., Englewood Cliffs, N.J., 1962. Also, see, Victor Zarnowitz, *An Appraisal of Short-Term Economic Forecasts*, Occasional Paper 104, National Bureau of Economic Research, New York, 1967.

Some evidence using economic variables is presented below in Section 14.6.

ex-post knowledge. In one sense, this type of evaluating measures the ability of the asset manager to select (ex-ante) the best possible securities and then to diversify among these, considering his operating constraints. In other words, to assess whether the best possible securities were in fact selected, an ex-post analysis of all possible securities must be undertaken. Several formal methods of analysis and corresponding indexes of performance have been proposed in the literature. For example, Cohen and Fitch proposed an index called the Average Investment Performance Index (AIPI).[5] Professor Lawrence Fisher developed link relatives and market indexes to enable comparisons between a portfolio to be evaluated and a standard market portfolio.[6]

The AIPI measures the average return realized during a particular period of time from some specified universe of securities. The index is calculated assuming that, exercising no particular skill in portfolio selection, any one of the many possible available portfolios could have been held. The AIPI implies random selection among portfolios which include

1. Any *number* of securities, from one up to and including the maximum number contained in the universe. (e.g., $N = 1, 2, \ldots,$ 1500).
2. All possible *names* of companies to match the number of securities selected in item 1 above
3. All possible (discrete) *diversifications* within the number of securities selected in item 1 above.

As a final result, the AIPI is equivalent to an unweighted arithmetic average of all actual returns in the given universe of securities.

$$\text{AIPI} = (1/N) \sum_{i=1}^{N} \{[P_i(t + 1) - P_i(t)]/P_i(t)\} \qquad \textbf{(14.7)}$$

where

N = number of stocks in the universe (e.g., all stocks traded on the New York Stock Exchange)
$P_i(t + 1)$ = price of the ith stock at time $t + 1$
$P_i(t)$ = price of the ith stock at time t

Along with the mean value calculated in (14.7), the variance of returns from all possible random portfolios also can be calculated. Then, given a mean and a variance of the probability distribution of

---

[5] Kalman J. Cohen and Bruce P. Fitch, "The Average Investment Performance Index," *Management Science*, vol. 12, no. 6, February 1966, pp. B195–B215.

[6] Lawrence Fisher, "Some New Stock Market Indexes," *The Journal of Business*, vol. XXXIX, no. 1, part II, January 1966, pp. 191–225.

ex-post returns from all portfolios that could have been held during the review period, a comparison is made with the portfolio actually held. For example, if the mean and variance as calculated by the AIPI are used to construct percentile rankings of (ex-post) return realized on all random portfolios, then a table such as 14.2 can be prepared. To evaluate a given portfolio, its (ex-post) return is classified into the appropriate percentile rank listed on Table 14.2. A rating of 0, for example, indicates that the portfolio being evaluated realized a return (ex-post) which is smaller than the return realized on 90 percent of the portfolios available in the marketplace. A rating of 5 indicates the portfolio being evaluated realized a return which is greater than the return realized by 50 percent of all available portfolios.

Values of the AIPI also can be linked across successive periods of time. As described above, the AIPI and the variance of returns from random portfolios can be used for rating the investment results achieved by actual portfolios.

A Word of Caution.   The operating constraints imposed on an actual portfolio can be very important in measuring its performance. Standard measures of performance such as those discussed above often ignore real-world operating constraints imposed on particular portfolios and, therefore, often are inappropriate as standards for performance of these particular portfolios.

To illustrate, consider three possible constraints: (1) size of portfolio to be evaluated, (2) total market value of each asset contained in the portfolio, and (3) timing of cash flows into and out of the portfolio being evaluated. All three of these possible constraints can affect performance. In addition, there can be legal and/or managerial policy constraints. For example, legal constraints may prohibit a financial

Table 14.2 PERCENTILE RANKINGS FOR
MEASURING PERFORMANCE

Rating	Percentiles between which R_i occurs
	% %
0	$0 \le R_i < 10$
1	$10 \le R_i < 20$
2	$20 \le R_i < 30$
3	$30 \le R_i < 40$
4	$40 \le R_i < 50$
5	$50 \le R_i < 60$
6	$60 \le R_i < 70$
7	$70 \le R_i < 80$
8	$80 \le R_i < 90$
9	$90 \le R_i \le 100$

institution from purchasing common stock. Buying on margin, or short selling, may be prohibited.

Considering timing of cash flows, if a relatively large amount of purchases are made at market highs, and a relatively large amount of liquidations are made consistently at market lows, then losses will occur. Conversely, if purchases are made consistently at market lows and sales are made at market highs, then large returns will result, because capital gains can be taken. But since either extreme implies some ability to predict turning points in the market, and since no one has demonstrated consistent ability to predict turning points, then performance measures based on timing strategies can have doubtful value.[7] In other words, when evaluating performance in terms of timing strategy, any apparent success in predicting highs and lows in the stock market can be due solely to chance. If constraints are imposed exogenously upon the portfolio manager so that he has little or no control over when to buy and/or when to sell, then this exogenous constraint can be the cause of his buying when the market was by chance high and/ or selling when the market was by chance low.

Size constraints, particularly on some large institutional portfolios, can act to limit large realized returns. For example, if shares of Avon Products appear to be a good buy at current prices, and an order is placed for 40 percent of the shares outstanding for Avon, then, most likely, share prices will rise because of demand and supply. A similar situation holds on the sell side. One percent of a large portfolio (a $1 billion portfolio) can even exceed the total market value of equity outstanding for many small companies. Large portfolios, therefore, can and do behave differently from small portfolios. A $10,000 personal portfolio can be either in or out of the market with relative ease and with relative speed; not so with a $1 billion pension fund. If the market is expected to go down, then, at best, a pension fund may adopt a strategy of minimizing losses while a small private portfolio can get out of the stock market entirely and hold cash or else sell short at high prices in anticipation of buying later when prices are lower.

In other words, there is no single measure of performance universally applicable to all portfolios. To have one universal measure of performance to apply to all investment portfolios, regardless of size or purpose, or operating constraints, is as naive as having one universal standard for beauty. Beauty may mean roses to some people, but

---

[7] Dietz discusses timing measures. See Peter O. Dietz, *Measuring Pension Fund Performance*, Columbia University and The Free Press, New York, 1966. Also, see Peter O. Dietz, "Measurement of Performance of Security Portfolios—Components of a Measurement Model: Rate of Return, Risk, and Timing," *The Journal of Finance*, vol. xiii, no. 2, May 1968, pp. 267–275.

chrysanthemums are also beautiful. A large institutional portfolio and a small personal portfolio both can enjoy excellent performance, but the standards can be different.

14.3 Measuring Efficiency of Investment Portfolios

Efficiency measures for investment performance attempt to collapse the two dimensions, return and risk, into a single dimension: return per unit of risk, or ratio of "reward to risk."

The idea underlying such a ratio emanates from the linear relationship between return and risk in capital markets. That is to say, from equations (13.44), (13.44b), and (13.170) in Chapter 13, we can write statements expressing the relationship between risk and return of (efficient) portfolios.

$$E(R_p) = \alpha \;\; + \beta_1 \sigma(R_p) \tag{14.8}$$

$$= R_G + \left[\frac{E(R_p) - E(R_G)}{\sigma(R_B)} \right] \sigma(R_p) \tag{14.9}$$

$$= R_G + \left[\frac{E(R_B) - R_G}{\rho \mathrm{var}(R_B)} \right] \mathrm{cov}(R_p, R_B) \tag{14.10}$$

$$= R_G + [E(R_B) - R_G]\beta_2 \tag{14.11}$$

$$= \text{risk-free return} + \text{risk premium} \tag{14.12}$$

where

$E(R_p)$ = expected (ex-ante) return on a portfolio (to be evaluated)

α = constant (e.g., expected return when risk equals zero)

β_1 = risk premium per unit of risk

$\sigma(R_p)$ = ex-ante risk (standard error of expected return) on the portfolio being evaluated

$E(R_G) = R_G$ = guaranteed return

$\sigma(R_B) = \sqrt{\mathrm{var}(R_B)}$ = risk of the risky asset (assuming diversification between a risk free return, R_G, and a risky return, R_B.

$E(R_B)$ = expected (ex-ante) return from the risky asset

ρ = coefficient of correlation between expected return on the portfolio and expected return from the risky asset alone

$\mathrm{cov}(R_p, R_B)$ = covariance between portfolio expected return and expected return from the risky asset

$\beta_2 = [\mathrm{cov}(R_p, R_B)]/[\rho \mathrm{var}(R_B)]$

Equations (14.8) and (14.9) state that for a given level of (ex-ante) risk, $[\sigma(R_p)]/[\sigma(R_B)]$, portfolio performance varies directly with the premium expected, $[E(R_p) - A]$. Put differently, performance is measured by the slope of the capital market line, β_1, in equation (14.8). The idea is to calculate the ratio of reward, $(R_p - R_G)$, to risk, $\sigma(R_B)$. This way of measuring performance has been proposed by several scholars.[8] However, there is nowhere near unanimous agreement that β_1 is universally applicable.[9] Some difficulties with practical application of (14.9) can be listed as follows.

First, the measure β_1 has the problem of ordinal ranking instead of cardinal ranking of performance. That is to say, even if portfolios can be ranked according to risk-premiums calculated by (14.9), there is no indication of *how much* better the top ranking portfolio is than the second ranking portfolio. There may be no significant difference between the top two portfolios. Number two might be number two solely because of chance; not necessarily because of inferior skills at analysis and selection.

Second, recalling the discussion which concerns the use of expert knowledge and inside information to obtain larger values for α, then universal application of (14.8) or (14.9) across all quality classes of investment managers can lead to incorrect evaluation of true performance.

Third, and probably the most bothersome problem with application of (14.9) is that for correct evaluation, ex-ante values are required for expected return $[E(R_p)]$ as well as for risk $[\sigma(R_p)]$. In most practical

---

[8] W. J. Sharpe, "Mutual Fund Performance," *The Journal of Business*, vol. XXXIX, January 1966, pp. 119–138; and "Risk Aversion in the Stock Market: Some Empirical Evidence," *The Journal of Finance*, vol. XX, no. 3, September 1965, pp. 416–422. A measure similar to the reward/risk ratio is Treynor's index of volatility. See Jack L. Treynor, "How to Rate Management of Investment Funds," *Harvard Business Review*, vol. XLIII, January–February 1965, pp. 63–75; and J. L. Treynor and Kay K. Mazuy, "Can Mutual Funds Outguess the Market?" *Harvard Business Review*, vol. 44, no. 4, July–August, 1966, pp. 131–136.

[9] See (1) Ira Horowitz, "The 'Reward-to-Variability' Ratio and Mutual Fund Performance," *The Journal of Business*, vol. XXXIX, no. 4, October 1966, pp. 485–488; (2) Kalman J. Cohen and Jerry A. Pogue, "An Empirical Evaluation of Alternative Portfolio-Selection Models," *The Journal of Business*, vol. 40, no. 2, April 1967, pp. 166–193; (3) Irwin Friend and Douglas Vickers, "Evaluation of Alternative Portfolio-Selection Models," *The Journal of Business*, vol. 41, no. 2, April 1968, pp. 174–179; (4) Kalman J. Cohen and Jerry A. Pogue, "Some Comments Concerning Mutual Fund Versus Random Portfolio Performance," *The Journal of Business*, vol. 41, no. 2, April 1968, pp. 180–190; and (5) Irwin Friend and Marshall Blume, "Measurement of Portfolio Performance under Uncertainty," *The American Economic Review*, September 1970.

situations, neither of these values is known by the performance evalua-
tor outside the investment firm. As a practical expedient, many scholars
use ex-post variability of historical returns as a surrogate for $\sigma(R_p)$.
However, as noted above in the discussion of RM_2, ex-post variability
may be an inferior measure error of predicting future returns. Specifically, the estimate of $\sigma(R_p)$ in (14.9) is likely to be biased upward if
historical variance is used, except in the trivial case when there are no
(economic) variables that can explain the behavior of $E(R_p)$.[10]

Beta two, from equations (14.10) and (14.11), has been used
extensively as a measure of performance.[11] Application of β_2 is made in
the context of a "market portfolio." That is to say, from (14.10) let

$$E(R_B) = E(R_M) = \text{expected return offered by the market} \qquad \textbf{(14.13)}$$
$$\text{generally}$$

$$\text{Var}(R_B) = \text{Var}(R_M) = \text{risk associated with the market} \qquad \textbf{(14.14)}$$

Then if the portfolio being evaluated *is* the market, then rho equals
unity and

$$\text{cov}(R_p, R_M) = \text{cov}(R_M, R_M) = \text{var}(R_M) \qquad \textbf{(14.15)}$$

so that β_2 is standardized at unity. Performance of all portfolios then
can be measured by the beta coefficient and excess return as stated in
(14.11). Any *efficient* portfolio will be perfectly positively correlated
with market returns [see (13.86)], hence rho in (14.10) equals unity.

Equation (14.10) mitigates the problem of having to know ex-ante
expectations, for given the ex-post results of the market, $[E(R_M)$ and
$\text{var}(R_M)]$, then ex-ante expectations for $E(R_p)$ can be stated, using
historical values of covariance with the market and assuming stability.
Using such a scheme, Jensen measures portfolio performance as the
difference between ex-post realized return on the portfolio and ex-ante
expected return.[12]

$$\delta_j = R_j - [R_G + (R_M - R_G)\beta_j] \qquad \textbf{(14.16)}$$

---

[10] See Joel Fried, "Forecasting and Probability Distributions for Models
of Portfolio Selection," *The Journal of Finance*, vol. XXV, no. 3, June 1970,
pp. 539–554.

[11] See (1) Michael Jensen, "Risk, the Pricing of Capital Assets and the
Evaluation of Investment Portfolios," *The Journal of Business*, vol. 42,
no. 2, April 1969, pp. 167–247; (2) Irwin Friend, Marshall Blume, Jean
Crockett, *Mutual Funds and other Institutional Investors: A New Perspective*,
McGraw-Hill Book Company, New York, 1970; (3) James H. Lorie,
Kalman J. Cohen, Joel Dean, David Durand, Eugene F. Fama, Lawrence
Fisher and Eli Shapiro, *Measuring the Investment Performance of Pension
Funds for the Purpose of Inter-Fund Comparison*, Park Ridge, Illinois:
Bank Administration Institute, 1968.

[12] See Jensen, *ibid.*

where

       δ_j = performance measure of portfolio j

       R_j = ex-post (realized) rate of return on portfolio j

      R_G = guaranteed (riskless) rate of interest

     R_M = ex-post (realized) rate of return on a market portfolio

      β_j = the systematic risk as defined in (14.11) for portfolio j.

Testing for Optimality. After having verified the accuracy of the forecasts, and the efficiency of the portfolio, we can return to the original premise that the portfolio was purchased for the purpose of maximizing utility of the owner. Here, again, it is necessary to compare ex-post realizations with ex-ante expectations. The expectations may have been realized (performance is rated good, as discussed above); the portfolio could have rested along the efficiency frontier. But, using 20:20 hindsight, the wrong set of expectations may have been held. In terms of market opportunities, instead of diversifying between Xerox and General Motors, the diversification perhaps should have been between bonds and several over-the-counter securities, or vice versa. Or, even admitting that Xerox and General Motors were the two correct stocks to have bought, tests need to be made to assure that the particular diversification held was in fact optimal. Farrar used as a test of optimality of diversification the mean square deviation of actual diversification from optimal diversification.[13]

$$e^2 = [(1/N) \sum_{i=1}^{N} (X_{i_{Act}} - X_{i_{Opt}})^2] \tag{14.17}$$

where

       e^2 = average error in diversification

      N = total number of securities contained in the portfolio

   $X_{i_{Act}}$ = actual proportion of the total investment allocated to the ith security

   $X_{i_{Opt}}$ = proportion of the total investment allocated to the ith security so that utility is maximized

The smaller the error stated in (14.17), the better the investment performance. Perfect performance yields zero error.

---

[13] See Donald E. Farrar, *The Investment Decision Under Uncertainty*, Prentice-Hall, Inc., Englewood Cliffs, N.J., 1962. Also see (1) Irwin Friend, F. E. Brown, Edward S. Herman, and Douglas Vickers, "A Study of Mutual Funds," U.S. Government Printing Office, 1962, Washington, D.C., pp. 16–21 and 294–358; and (2) Irwin Friend and Douglas Vickers, "Portfolio Selection and Investment Performance," *The Journal of Finance*, vol. XX, no. 3, September 1965, pp. 391–415.

Table 14.3 DATA FOR SELECTED PORTFOLIOS*

Year	Portfolio 1		Portfolio 2		Portfolio 3	
	Rates of return	Log of price relative	Rates of return	Log of price relative	Rates of return	Log of price relative
1966–67	.203	.185	.030	.030	.100	.095
1965–66	.539	.431	−.047	−.048	.001	.001
1964–65	.857	.619	.100	.095	.030	.030
1963–64	.250	.223	.185	.170	.132	.124
1962–63	.282	.248	.098	.094	.024	.024
1961–62	−.094	−.099	−.066	−.068	−.152	−.165
1960–61	.438	.363	.228	.205	.079	.076
1959–60	.316	.275	.064	.062	−.117	−.124
1958–59	1.205	.791	.258	.230	.174	.160
1957–58	.712	.538	.173	.160	.049	.048
1956–57	.205	.187	−.024	−.024	.015	.015
Arithmetic average	.447	.342	.091	.082	.030	.026
Sum of squares	1.315	.595	.124	.105	.095	.095
Standard deviation	.363	.194	.111	.103	.097	.098

* Source for rates of return: Moody's industrial and transportation manuals, year end closing prices and dividends.

14.4 Statistically Significant Performance

Returning to the three portfolios selected on Table 14.1, we can ask, Is there any significant difference between the realized returns from these three portfolios? Actual data for each of the three portfolios are listed in Table 14.3. Table 14.3 shows that the (arithmetic) average returns on the three portfolios being evaluated are 44.7 percent, 9.1 percent, and 3.0 percent respectively. The corresponding standard errors of those returns are .363, .111, and .097, respectively. We can ask: is there any significant difference between the returns achieved by these three portfolios?

One method of testing for significant difference between means is analysis of variance.[14] Then, performing an analysis of variance test on the data listed in Table 14.3, results as shown in Table 14.4 are obtained.[15] The F ratios indicate significant differences (at the .005 level or smaller) between portfolios 1 and 2 and portfolios 1 and 3. However, the apparent differences between portfolios 2 and 3 (mean return over the 11-year time period of 3 percent for portfolio 3 as compared with 9.1 percent for portfolio 2, as shown in Table 14.4) could have occurred by chance, with a high probability (at the .200 level of significance, or one chance in five). Therefore, one should expect, with relatively high probability of success, to be able to distinguish portfolio 1 from both 2 and 3 and, at the same time, not necessarily be able to distinguish portfolio 2 from portfolio 3. That is to say, since it is unlikely that portfolio 1 achieved 44.7 percent by chance, then one is justified in looking for the causes of such high performance.

14.5 Historical Performance as a Guide to Future Performance?

Prediction of performance (in contrast with prediction of expected return) involves forecasting future performance. Given outstanding (or poor) past performance, is there any guarantee that future performance will be outstanding (or poor)? Sharpe presented some empirical evidence on this question and found that for some mutual funds, performance

---

[14] See any good statistics text for the procedures and assumptions underlying the validity of the method. One such text is H. C. Fryer, *Concepts and Methods of Experimental Statistics*, Allyn & Bacon, Inc., Boston, 1966.

[15] The natural logarithm of price relatives is taken as the particular statistic in the analysis of variance test. The reason for this is to affect approximate normality according to the Bachlier-Osborne arguments as summarized in Chapter 10. Recall from Chapter 10 that there is controversy over whether this statistic is appoximately normal or whether it is stable paretian. Also, see equation (10.5).

Table 14.4 ANALYSIS OF VARIANCE FOR VERIFYING SIGNIFICANT DIFFERENCE IN PERFORMANCE (EACH PAIR OF PORTFOLIOS: 1956–1966) *

Source of variation	DF	Portfolios 1 and 2			Portfolios 1 and 3			Portfolios 2 and 3		
		Sum of squares	Mean square	$F_{(1,20)}$	Sum of squares	Mean square	$F_{(1,20)}$	Sum of squares	Mean square	$F_{(1,20)}$
Between portfolios	1	.37094	.37094	10.594	.54958	.54958	15.911	.01750	.01750	1.748
Within portfolios	20	.70031	.03502		.69081	.03454		.20026	.01003	
Total about x	21	1.07124			1.24039			.21776		

* $F_{(1,20)}$ Book (for reference)

Probability	.250	.200	.010	.005
$F_{(1,20)}$	1.40	1.76	8.10	9.94

ranking for one time period did tend to be correlated with corresponding rankings for the next time period.[16]

If there is a high correlation between performance in successive time periods (i.e., large serial correlation between change in performance from one time period to the next), then the performance measure has value as a predictive tool. If performance is rated good for the current time period, then with large serial correlation between successive time periods, chances are high that using the same procedures, performance will be good again during the next time period.

But if performance is bad, then measures like these are of little help, because these measures say that performance will continue to be bad. These measures do not tell you what you are doing wrong or how to alter policy for investment so as to improve performance. To use past mistakes as a guide to future performance, we need a measure of performance which can be used as a normative guide to investment policy.

14.6 Toward a Normative Theory of Investment Performance

A *normative theory* of performance measures provides insights into the causes of superior (or inferior) performance so that the asset manager can know what the results will be later if particular actions are undertaken now.

To use performance measures as a normative guide to future investments, the measure must capture some behavioral characteristics of the securities held. That is, instead of making measurements in terms of realized returns alone, the measurements must be made on the causal factors underlying return. The implication is that these particular measures are rooted in theory of what makes good performance good. Nerlove, for example, lists seven factors as being important[17]:

1. Growth of sales.
2. Retention of earnings.
3. Growth in earnings (considerably less important than either growth in sales or retention of earnings).
4. Dividends (over the long run but not over short periods).

---

[16] William F. Sharpe, "Mutual Fund Performance," *The Journal of Business*, vol. XXXIX, no. 1, part II, January 1966, pp. 119–138.

[17] Marc Nerlove, "Factors Affecting Differences Among Rates of Return on Investments in Individual Common Stocks," *Review of Economics and Statistics*, vol. 50, no. 3, August, 1968, pp. 122–136. Also, see G. R. Fisher, "Some Factors Influencing Share Prices," *Economic Journal*, vol. LXXI, March 1961, pp. 121–141.

5. Leverage.
6. General nature of the final products produced by the firm.
7. Proportion of fixed plant included in total assets.

Nerlove examined other variables such as asset growth, inventory turnover, cash flow, share turnover, quick ratios, and current ratios. But he found that none of these have any appreciable effect on relative investment performance.

Renwick, in a much more modest study, performed without benefit of knowledge of Nerlove's heroic undertaking, found that any three of the following four variables are sufficient to distinguish outstanding investment performance from poor investment performance.[18]

X_1 = profitability of the firm (net operating income divided by total assets)
X_2 = rate of growth of sales
X_3 = rate of retention of corporate profits (i.e., dividend payout)
X_4 = finance of corporate assets (leverage)

The basic idea underlying the Renwick study can be explained as follows. If one wants to know the causes of good performance and the causes of bad performance, then one can obtain several portfolios having the desired effect and study their characteristics. Toward this end, portfolios 1, 2, and 3 in Table 14.1 were selected for study and comparison. The method of selecting the three portfolios was as follows.

Using a 10-year time span from the Compustat tape, calculate the return on investment (dividend yield plus capital gain) for each year, for each company. Next, after calculating the arithmetic average 10 year return for each company on the tape, rank all companies. Portfolio 1 was selected from those companies ranking highest on the list; portfolio 3 was selected from those companies ranking lowest on the list; and the control group, portfolio 2 was selected arbitrarily from the Dow-Jones 30 industrials. Hence, the experiment was designed specifically to investigate the causes of superior performance.

Given that portfolio 1 is statistically different from portfolios 2 and 3 in Table 14.3, and assuming that the differences in 10-year performance did not occur by chance, we should be able to use fundamental factors to distinguish portfolio 1 from both 2 and 3, and, at the same time, not necessarily be able to distinguish portfolio 2 from portfolio 3. If the assumptions and logic underlying the experiment are

---

[18] Fred B. Renwick, "Asset Management and Investor Portfolio Behavior: Theory and Practice," *The Journal of Finance*, vol. XXIV, no. 2, May 1969, pp. 181–206.

Table 14.5 PORTFOLIOS*

Mean values each year for each explanatory variable

Variable (1)	Portfolio (2)	1956 (3)	1957 (4)	1958 (5)	1959 (6)	1960 (7)	1961 (8)	1962 (9)	1963 (10)	1964 (11)	1965 (12)	1966 (13)	1967 (14)	Grand mean (15)	Grand variance (16)
X_1 = rate of return on assets = net operating income divided by total assets	1	.232	.248	.210	.231	.246	.226	.233	.230	.257	.265	.279	.242	.242	.010
	2	.200	.195	.166	.180	.172	.162	.172	.177	.180	.185	.150	.137	.173	.004
	3	.235	.207	.179	.203	.191	.183	.171	.170	.177	.165	.104	.088	.173	.004
X_2 = rate of growth of output = percentage change in sales	1		.146	.073	.289	.268	.121	.188	.160	.276	.258	.191	.091	.187	.009
	2		.057	−.019	.099	.048	.027	.063	.047	.083	.094	.082	.068	.059	.001
	3		.010	−.018	.134	.024	.029	.048	.058	.077	.087	.042	.018	.046	.001
X_3 = rate of retention of income available for common equity	1	.868	.783	.754	.790	.698	.758	.647	.690	.739	.798	.777	.774	.756	.029
	2	.436	.409	.359	.449	.436	.363	.377	.419	.460	.491	.491	.436	.427	.007
	3	.551	.389	.175	.470	.106	.387	.590	.442	.512	.521	.463	.419	.419	.021
X_4 = ratio of total liabilities to total equity	1	.715	.719	.709	.765	.681	.706	.714	.705	.727	.761	.733	.665	.717	.052
	2	.379	.379	.388	.360	.350	.356	.341	.318	.317	.346	.632	.666	.403	.029
	3	.381	.437	.361	.344	.328	.399	.353	.337	.355	.433	.527	.608	.405	.032

* Source of original Data: Moody's *Industrial Manual* and Moody's *Transportation Manual*.

correct, then there ought to be a high probability of successful discrimination between the two extreme groups, portfolio 1 and 3. The experiment, therefore, has a control group, portfolios 2 and 3, between which there is no statistically significant difference and an experimental group, portfolio 1, which is significantly different (statistically) from the control group.

Test Results Using Discriminant Analysis.   Mean values for each of the four explanatory variables for each portfolio are listed in Table 14.5. For X_1, X_3, and X_4, the data are taken from balance sheets and income statements for each company as of the current year. Since equal dollars are assumed to be invested in each security, simple arithmetic averages are taken for data on the ten stocks in each portfolio, each year. For X_2, because of the selfimposed desire to avoid the need for forecasting, data are taken for the current year and compared with the previous year to compute a percentage change. But, because the theory explicitly calls for future rates of growth, one implicit assumption here is that historical growth rates contain information concerning future growth.[19] Also, because 1956 was the starting year for the analysis, column 3 in Table 14.5 remains blank. The grand totals, columns (15) and (16), are computed using the entire 12-year time span, 1956–1967, as the sample observation (11 years, 1957–1967 in the case of X_2). These data in Table 14.5, then, along with corresponding sums of squares and sums of cross products are used for the discrimination.[20]

The complete output from the analyses is too voluminous to be included here. However, some typical discriminant functions are shown in Table 14.6 for various combinations of variables for 1966. These results are representative of the total output. Using either the Fisher or Rao method, the discrimination is significant. The F ratios, though significant at the .01 level for classification using only two variables,

---

[19] This assumption needs further empirical evidence. For indirect evidence see J. G. Cragg and Burton G. Malkiel, "The Consensus and Accuracy of Some Predictions of the Growth of Corporate Earnings," *The Journal of Finance*, vol. XXIII, no. 1, March 1968, pp. 67–84.

[20] The method used for the remaining tests was discriminant analysis. See C. R. Rao, *Advanced Statistical Methods in Biometric Research*, John Wiley & Sons, Inc., New York, 1952; and R. A. Fisher, "The Use of Multiple Measurements in Taxonomic Problems," *Ann. Eugenics*, vol. 7, 1936, pp. 179–188. For a discriminant analysis similar to the one used here, see James E. Walter, "A Discriminant Function for Earnings-Price Ratios of Large Industrial Corporations," *The Review of Economics and Statistics*, vol. XLI, no. 1, February 1959. For alternative methods of defining identifiable classes, see H. Friedman and J. Rubin, "On Some Invariant Criteria for Grouping Data," *Journal of the American Statistical Association*, vol. 62, no. 320, December 1967, pp. 1159–1178.

Table 14.6 SELECTED DISCRIMINANT SCORES: PORTFOLIOS 1 AND 3 (1966)

Fisher's Discriminant Scores

	λ_1	λ_2	λ_3	λ_4	Score for portfolio		Midpoint	Statistical significance Snedecor F-ratio
					1	3		
2 Variables X_3, X_4	.379	.186			.431	.273	.352	$6.68 = F_{(2,17)}$
3 Variables X_1, X_3, X_4	3.002	.852	.730		2.034	1.092	1.563	$25.13 = F_{(3,16)}$
4 Variables X_1, X_2, X_3, X_4	2.105	.035	.447	.390	1.227	.633	.930	$11.13 = F_{(4,15)}$

Rao's Discriminant Scores

		λ_1	λ_2	λ_3	λ_4	c	Score for portfolio		Chi-square
							1	3	
2 Variables X_3, X_4	L1	.979	.601			−.600	.600	.170	$9.86 = \chi^2(2)$
	L2	.599	.415			−.248	.522	.248	
3 Variables X_1, X_3, X_4	L1	6.145	1.938	1.709		−2.236	2.236	.202	$28.75 = \chi^2(3)$
	L2	3.143	1.086	.980		−.673	1.765	.673	
4 Variables X_1, X_2, X_3, X_4	L1	4.258	.425	1.045	.912	−1.375	1.375	1.016	$12.32 = \chi^2(4)$
	L2	2.153	−.261	.598	.523	−.383	.052	.383	

For Reference: Probability .01

$\chi^2(2) = 9.210$ $\chi^2(3) = 11.345$ $\chi^2(4) = 13.27$
$F_{(2,17)} = 6.11$ $F_{(3,16)} = 5.29$ $F_{(4,15)} = 4.89$

Probability .005

$\chi^2(2) = 10.60$ $\chi^2(3) = 12.84$ $\chi^2(4) = 14.86$
$F_{(2,17)} = 7.35$ $F_{(3,16)} = 6.30$ $F_{(4,15)} = 5.80$

Table 14.7 PORTFOLIOS: TEST OF SIGNIFICANCE OF DISCRIMINATION*

Port-folios	Variables	1957			1958			1959			1960		
		T^2	F	χ^2	T^2	F	χ^2	T^2	F	χ^2	T^2	F	χ^2
1 vs. 2	X_1, X_2	1.986	.94	1.78	1.730	.82	1.56	3.391	1.60	2.93	14.660	6.92	10.13
	X_1, X_2, X_3	30.691	9.09	16.42	30.236	8.96	16.26	36.803	10.90	18.37	15.325	4.54	10.16
	X_1, X_2, X_4	10.267	3.04	7.45	11.718	3.47	8.27	20.214	5.99	12.42	32.266	9.56	16.94
	X_1, X_2, X_3, X_4	48.135	10.03		48.830	10.17		82.785	17.25		45.333	9.44	
	X_1, X_3	29.081	13.73	16.35	24.575	11.60	14.64	33.666	15.90	17.93	9.951	4.70	7.48
	X_1, X_4	10.253	4.84	7.66	11.335	5.35	8.30	20.112	9.50	12.75	14.927	7.05	10.27
	X_1, X_3, X_4	33.381	9.89	17.31	32.619	9.66	17.06	41.645	12.34	19.77	23.366	6.92	13.73
	X_2, X_3	28.991	13.69	16.31	24.361	11.50	14.55	34.144	16.12	18.08	15.612	7.37	10.62
	X_2, X_4	10.830	5.11	8.01	11.908	5.62	8.63	21.467	10.14	13.35	19.408	9.17	12.44
	X_2, X_3, X_4	33.275	9.86	17.27	32.689	9.69	17.08	41.745	12.37	19.80	28.072	8.32	15.51
	X_3, X_4	34.294	16.19	18.13	31.545	14.90	17.21	50.343	23.77	22.68	15.492	7.32	10.56
1 vs. 3	X_1, X_2	4.762	2.25	3.99	1.561	.74	1.41	2.029	.96	1.82	15.932	7.52	10.78
	X_1, X_2, X_3	17.614	5.22	11.26	14.125	4.19	9.56	10.428	3.09	7.54	16.168	4.79	10.58
	X_1, X_2, X_4	7.255	2.15	5.59	14.763	4.37	9.88	25.356	7.51	14.50	47.139	13.97	21.22
	X_1, X_2, X_3, X_4	22.031	4.59		36.900	7.69		56.126	11.69		51.590	10.75	
	X_1, X_3	14.874	7.02	10.24	13.034	6.16	9.26	10.411	4.92	7.76	3.226	1.52	2.80
	X_1, X_4	4.294	2.03	3.64	14.647	6.92	10.12	25.355	11.97	14.94	18.987	8.97	12.24
	X_1, X_3, X_4	16.908	5.01	10.93	25.354	7.51	14.50	32.646	9.67	17.07	19.184	5.68	11.97
	X_2, X_3	18.342	8.66	11.94	13.137	6.20	9.32	11.988	5.66	8.68	12.618	5.96	9.03
	X_2, X_4	7.657	3.62	6.03	15.787	7.45	10.70	25.431	12.01	14.97	28.050	13.25	15.97
	X_2, X_3, X_4	20.027	5.93	12.34	25.749	7.63	14.65	32.444	9.61	17.00	28.681	8.50	15.72
	X_3, X_4	17.611	8.32	11.60	27.105	12.80	15.62	35.167	16.61	18.41	12.070	5.70	8.72

Portfolios	Variables	1961			1962			1963			1964		
		T^2	F	χ^2	T^2	F	χ^2	T^2	F	χ^2	T^2	F	χ^2
2 vs. 3	X_1, X_2	4.495	2.12	3.79	.189	.09	.18	1.119	.53	1.02	1.612	.76	1.46
	X_1, X_2, X_3	4.919	1.46	3.99	2.824	.84	2.40	1.148	.34	1.02	3.486	1.03	2.92
	X_1, X_2, X_4	4.586	1.36	3.75	.416	.12	.38	1.150	.34	1.02	1.901	.56	1.66
	X_1, X_2, X_3, X_4	5.372	1.12		5.397	1.23		1.164	.24		6.076	1.27	
	X_1, X_3	.268	.13	.25	2.787	1.32	2.45	.626	.30	.58	2.039	.96	1.82
	X_1, X_4	.275	.13	.26	.409	.19	.38	.638	.30	.59	.468	.22	.44
	X_1, X_3, X_4	.372	.11	.34	3.234	.96	2.73	.741	.22	.67	2.158	.64	1.87
	X_2, X_3	5.039	2.38	4.20	1.613	.76	1.46	1.000	.47	.91	1.447	.68	1.31
	X_2, X_4	6.698	3.16	5.38	.124	.06	.12	1.002	.47	.92	1.491	.70	1.35
	X_2, X_3, X_4	9.699	2.87	7.11	1.768	.52	1.55	1.109	.33	.99	1.507	.45	1.33
	X_3, X_4	.289	.14	.27	1.489	.70	1.35	.112	.05	.11	.883	.42	.81
1 vs. 2	X_1, X_2	3.837	1.81	3.28	2.310	1.09	2.05	3.855	1.82	3.30	12.562	5.93	9.00
	X_1, X_2, X_3	36.725	10.88	18.35	5.729	1.70	4.56	20.109	5.96	12.38	31.036	9.20	16.54
	X_1, X_2, X_4	13.945	4.13	9.47	14.699	4.36	9.85	18.170	5.38	11.51	19.471	5.77	12.10
	X_1, X_2, X_3, X_4	69.548	14.49	18.88	18.432	3.84		52.366	10.91		71.702	14.94	
	X_1, X_3	36.641	17.30		5.663	2.67	4.65	19.784	9.34	12.61	21.748	10.27	13.47
	X_1, X_4	12.475	5.90	8.95	11.933	5.64	8.65	17.761	8.39	11.67	16.775	7.92	11.19
	X_1, X_3, X_4	57.684	17.09	23.70	12.407	3.68	8.65	36.163	10.72	18.18	29.472	8.73	16.00
	X_2, X_3	30.296	14.31	16.78	5.955	2.81	4.86	21.955	10.37	13.56	33.483	15.81	17.87
	X_2, X_4	7.994	3.78	6.25	11.222	5.30	8.24	19.994	9.44	12.70	27.676	13.07	15.83
	X_2, X_3, X_4	41.481	12.29	19.72	12.035	3.57	8.45	36.881	10.93	18.39	41.855	12.40	19.83
	X_3, X_4	37.266	17.60	19.07	14.409	6.80	10.00	32.373	15.29	17.49	28.871	13.63	16.27

Table 14.7 (Continued)

Port-folios	Variables	1961 T²	F	χ²	1962 T²	F	χ²	1963 T²	F	χ²	1964 T²	F	χ²
1 vs. 3	X_1, X_2	2.044	.97	1.83	2.880	1.36	2.52	3.537	1.67	3.05	11.928	5.63	8.64
	X_1, X_2, X_3	25.946	7.69	14.73	2.981	.88	2.53	13.461	3.99	9.21	21.026	6.23	12.77
	X_1, X_2, X_4	5.762	1.71	4.58	17.025	5.04	10.98	21.834	6.47	13.11	17.534	5.20	11.22
	X_1, X_2, X_3, X_4	37.473	7.81		17.695	3.69		44.061	9.18		34.668	7.22	
	X_1, X_3	25.121	11.86	14.85	2.162	1.01	1.93	13.119	6.19	9.31	12.079	5.70	8.73
	X_1, X_4	5.329	2.52	4.41	12.646	5.97	9.05	21.793	10.29	13.49	16.136	7.62	10.88
	X_1, X_3, X_4	28.143	8.34	15.53	12.647	3.75	8.78	36.641	10.86	18.32	22.210	6.58	13.26
	X_2, X_3	25.056	11.83	14.83	2.406	1.14	2.13	12.969	6.12	9.22	21.952	10.37	13.55
	X_2, X_4	5.273	2.49	4.37	11.206	5.29	8.23	18.574	8.77	12.05	26.243	12.39	15.29
	X_2, X_3, X_4	27.482	8.14	15.29	11.260	3.34	8.02	29.415	8.72	15.98	32.719	9.69	17.09
	X_3, X_4	28.444	13.43	16.11	7.813	3.69	6.13	24.309	11.48	14.53	16.277	7.69	10.95
2 vs. 3	X_1, X_2	.466	.22	.43	.256	.12	.24	.392	.19	.37	.048	.02	4.49
	X_1, X_2, X_3	.603	.18	.54	1.767	.52	1.54	.481	.14	.44	.810	.24	.73
	X_1, X_2, X_4	.524	.15	.47	.256	.08	.23	.808	.24	.72	.666	.20	.60
	X_1, X_2, X_3, X_4	.968	.20		2.251	.47		.991	.21		1.023	.21	
	X_1, X_3	.499	.24	.47	1.466	.69	1.33	.146	.07	.14	.766	.30	.71
	X_1, X_4	.457	.22	.43	.024	.01	2.23	.103	.05	9.66	.323	.15	.30
	X_1, X_3, X_4	.508	.15	.46	1.571	.47	1.38	.282	.08	.26	.931	.28	.83
	X_2, X_3	.095	.04	8.92	1.190	.56	1.09	1.323	.62	1.21	.666	.31	.62
	X_2, X_4	.167	.08	.16	.242	.11	.23	.460	.22	.43	.345	.16	.32
	X_2, X_3, X_4	.215	.06	.20	1.237	.37	1.10	3.045	.90	2.58	.834	.25	.75
	X_3, X_4	.219	.10	.21	1.223	.58	1.12	.246	.12	.23	.881	.42	.81

Port-folios	Variables	1965 T^2	1965 F	1965 χ^2	1966 T^2	1966 F	1966 χ^2	1967 T^2	1967 F	1967 χ^2	Grand Totals T^2	Grand Totals F	Grand Totals χ^2
1 vs. 2	X_1, X_2	11.000	5.19	8.11	8.282	3.91	6.43	2.951	1.39	2.58	17.59	8.30	11.59
	X_1, X_2, X_3	109.512	32.45	32.30	54.360	16.11	22.96	26.362	7.81	14.88	60.00	17.75	24.17
	X_1, X_2, X_4	22.995	6.81	13.58	9.969	2.95	7.27	2.981	.88	2.53	29.04	8.60	15.85
	X_1, X_2, X_3, X_4	125.604	26.17		54.555	11.37		27.839	5.80		86.80	18.08	
	X_1, X_3	101.084	47.73	32.12	51.720	24.42	23.02	25.275	11.94	14.91	56.05	26.47	24.04
	X_1, X_4	18.751	8.85	12.13	8.199	3.87	6.38	2.981	1.41	2.61	19.50	9.21	12.48
	X_1, X_3, X_4	125.823	37.28	34.29	65.267	19.34	25.27	25.362	7.51	14.51	78.42	23.24	27.69
	X_2, X_3	123.588	58.36	35.06	36.088	17.04	18.70	18.941	8.94	12.22	122.90	58.03	34.98
	X_2, X_4	28.895	13.64	16.28	3.875	1.83	3.31	.166	.08	.16	42.59	20.11	20.63
	X_2, X_3, X_4	148.034	43.86	36.66	43.828	12.99	20.36	18.975	5.62	11.88	174.22	51.62	39.08
	X_3, X_4	49.850	23.54	22.56	23.222	10.97	14.09	15.310	7.23	10.46	49.11	23.19	22.37
1 vs. 3	X_1, X_2	13.224	6.24	9.36	18.598	8.78	12.06	9.260	4.37	7.06	22.39	10.58	13.74
	X_1, X_2, X_3	33.532	9.94	17.36	37.870	11.22	18.69	33.732	9.99	17.42	47.64	14.11	21.35
	X_1, X_2, X_4	17.824	5.28	11.36	39.683	11.76	19.22	20.587	6.10	12.58	32.32	9.58	16.96
	X_1, X_2, X_3, X_4	36.594	7.62		53.42	11.13		42.529	8.86		73.39	15.29	
	X_1, X_3	32.058	15.14	17.39	37.504	17.71	19.14	28.857	13.63	16.26	33.43	15.79	17.85
	X_1, X_4	14.892	7.03	10.25	37.271	17.60	19.07	18.384	8.68	11.96	22.87	10.80	13.94
	X_1, X_3, X_4	41.055	12.16	19.60	84.798	25.13	28.75	48.741	14.44	21.62	56.10	16.62	23.35
	X_2, X_3	39.567	18.68	19.76	19.299	9.11	12.39	16.481	7.78	11.05	70.60	33.34	27.09
	X_2, X_4	22.026	10.40	13.59	13.126	6.20	9.31	4.875	2.30	4.07	66.33	31.32	26.25
	X_2, X_3, X_4	48.107	14.25	21.46	33.858	10.03	17.46	24.440	7.24	14.15	130.92	38.79	34.87
	X_3, X_4	17.612	8.32	11.60	14.140	6.68	9.86	11.320	5.35	8.29	43.22	20.41	20.81

Table 14.7 (Continued)

Port-folios	Variables	1965			1966			1967			Grand Totals		
		T^2	F	χ^2	T^2	F	χ^2	T^2	F	χ^2	T^2	F	χ^2
2 vs. 3	X_1, X_2	.507	.24	.47	5.423	2.56	4.48	6.653	3.14	5.35	1.86	.88	1.67
	X_1, X_2, X_3	.509	.15	.46	5.560	1.65	4.44	8.000	2.37	6.07	1.96	.58	1.71
	X_1, X_2, X_4	1.474	.44	1.30	5.470	1.62	4.38	7.125	2.11	5.50	1.87	.55	1.63
	X_1, X_2, X_3, X_4	1.621	.34	.46	5.580	1.16		8.366	1.74		1.96	.41	
	X_1, X_3	.504	.24	.47	2.878	1.36	2.52	1.945	.92	1.74	.03	.01	.03
	X_1, X_4	1.329	.63	1.21	2.259	1.07	2.01	1.902	.90	1.71	.00	.00	.00
	X_1, X_3, X_4	1.361	.40	1.20	2.968	.88	2.52	1.986	.59	1.73	.03	.01	.03
	X_2, X_3	.146	.07	.14	4.180	1.97	3.55	2.383	1.13	2.11	2.56	1.21	2.26
	X_2, X_4	.902	.43	.83	2.710	1.28	2.38	2.397	1.13	2.13	2.10	.99	1.87
	X_2, X_3, X_4	.926	.27	.83	4.192	1.24	3.45	2.498	.74	2.14	3.11	.92	2.63
	X_3, X_4	1.003	.47	.92	.795	.38	.73	.183	.09	.17	.03	.01	.03

* Definitions for the statistics are as follows:
Hotelling's T^2 is multiplied by a constant factor to compute the Snedecor F ratio as follows.

$$\left\{\frac{n_1 + n_2 - p - 1}{p(n_1 + n_2 - 2)}\right\} T^2 = F(p, n_1 + n_2 - p - 1)$$

where

n_1 = number of observations in first universe = 10
n_2 = number of observations in second universe = 10
p = number of measurements taken on each observation = 2, 3, or 4
T^2 = Hotelling's T-square
F = Snedecor F-ratio

Chi-square is defined by Rao in terms of Wilks's lambda criterion as follows:

$$\chi^2(\nu) = -m \log_e \Lambda$$

where

χ^2 = Chi-square
ν = degrees of freedom = $p^*(k - 1)$
p = number of measurements taken on each observation = 2, 3, or 4
k = number of populations to be distinguished = 2
$m = N - 1 - (p + k)/2$
N = total number of observations on all populations = 22
Λ = Wilks's lambda

increase further when the third variable (X_1) is added to the model. When the fourth variable (X_2) is included, the F ratios decline, but are still higher than the corresponding F for the two-variable case, indicating that the best results are obtained by omitting growth and using three variables: rate of return on corporate assets, capital structure, and rate of retention. These particular results seem proper because, given four variables with three degrees of freedom, the model is completely specified by any three of the four variables. And since growth truly requires forecasting whereas current values are taken for the other three variables, then growth is the logical candidate to omit from the discriminant analysis model.

Table 14.7 contains a tabulation of results from the test of significance from all possible combinations of variables, including historical growth, for all three portfolios. As predicted, it is possible to identify and separate portfolio 1 from both portfolios 2 and 3, while portfolios 2 and 3 show no significant difference. The discriminant coefficients, scores, and level of significance all vary from year to year but are always consistent. Portfolio 1 is always ranked significantly higher than the other two portfolios.

One can conclude, therefore, that the job of asset management, though interdisciplinary and frustrating, can be performed. It appears that through the use of a judicious combination of expert judgment and objective analysis, one can achieve superior returns consistently, without forecasting, and with small probability of incorrect classification.

QUESTIONS FOR STUDY

1. Explain how you would evaluate the performance of a common stock portfolio.
2. How would you estimate the risk premium on common stocks and on corporate bonds?
3. Explain how Fisher's indexes differ from
    (a) Dow-Jones Industrial Index
    (b) Standard and Poor's 500 Stock Composite Index
    (c) New York Stock Exchange Index
    (e) Cohen and Fitch's AIPI
4. Explain the difference between an index of volatility (as a measure of portfolio performance) and a reward-to-variability ratio.
5. Why is it necessary to measure investment performance?
6. Explain the difference between evaluating a security analyst, a portfolio manager, and investment performance itself.
7. What makes good performance good?
8. Do scientific methods of analysis result in improved investment performance?
9. Write a 10-page paper discussing how to improve portfolio performance.

Appendix

Table for Compound Interest Factors

Column 1 Year $=$ Number of time periods.
      2 S/P $=$ Compound amount factor, given P.
      3 P/S $=$ Present worth factor, given S.
      4 S/R $=$ Compound amount factor, given R.
      5 P/R $=$ Present worth factor, given R.
      6 R/S $=$ Sinking fund deposit factor, given S.
      7 R/P $=$ Capital recovery factor, given P.

INTEREST RATE IS 0.06000

YEAR	S/P	P/S	S/R	P/R	R/S	R/P
1	1.06000	0.94339	1.00000	0.94339	1.00000	1.06001
2	1.12361	0.88999	2.06000	1.83338	0.48544	0.54544
3	1.19103	0.83961	3.18361	2.67298	0.31411	0.37411
4	1.26250	0.79208	4.37465	3.46506	0.22859	0.28860
5	1.33826	0.74724	5.63714	4.21230	0.17739	0.23740
6	1.41856	0.70494	6.97540	4.91724	0.14336	0.20337
7	1.50368	0.66504	8.39396	5.58228	0.11913	0.17914
8	1.59391	0.62739	9.89763	6.20966	0.10103	0.16104
9	1.68955	0.59187	11.49154	6.80154	0.08702	0.14703
10	1.79093	0.55837	13.18109	7.35991	0.07587	0.13587
11	1.89840	0.52676	14.97202	7.88667	0.06679	0.12680
12	2.01231	0.49694	16.87041	8.38361	0.05928	0.11928
13	2.13306	0.46881	18.88272	8.85242	0.05296	0.11296
14	2.26105	0.44227	21.01578	9.29469	0.04758	0.10759
15	2.39673	0.41724	23.27682	9.71192	0.04296	0.10297
16	2.54054	0.39362	25.67355	10.10554	0.03895	0.09896
17	2.69299	0.37133	28.21409	10.47688	0.03544	0.09545
18	2.85458	0.35031	30.90708	10.82719	0.03236	0.09236
19	3.02587	0.33048	33.76165	11.15767	0.02962	0.08962
20	3.20743	0.31178	36.78752	11.46945	0.02718	0.08719
21	3.39990	0.29413	39.99494	11.76358	0.02500	0.08501
22	3.60391	0.27748	43.39484	12.04105	0.02304	0.08305
23	3.82016	0.26177	46.99874	12.30282	0.02128	0.08128
24	4.04939	0.24695	50.81890	12.54977	0.01968	0.07968
25	4.29237	0.23297	54.86828	12.78274	0.01823	0.07823
26	4.54994	0.21978	59.16065	13.00253	0.01690	0.07691
27	4.82295	0.20734	63.71058	13.20987	0.01570	0.07570
28	5.11236	0.19560	68.53353	13.40547	0.01459	0.07460
29	5.41912	0.18453	73.64588	13.59000	0.01358	0.07358
30	5.74430	0.17409	79.06501	13.76409	0.01265	0.07265
31	6.08898	0.16423	84.80931	13.92832	0.01179	0.07180
32	6.45435	0.15493	90.89828	14.08326	0.01100	0.07101
33	6.84164	0.14616	97.35263	14.22942	0.01027	0.07028
34	7.25218	0.13789	104.19425	14.36731	0.00960	0.06960
35	7.68734	0.13008	111.44642	14.49739	0.00897	0.06898
36	8.14862	0.12272	119.13377	14.62011	0.00839	0.06840
37	8.63758	0.11577	127.28236	14.73588	0.00786	0.06786
38	9.15588	0.10922	135.91998	14.84510	0.00736	0.06736
39	9.70527	0.10304	145.07580	14.94814	0.00689	0.06690
40	10.28764	0.09720	154.78109	15.04535	0.00646	0.06647
41	10.90495	0.09170	165.06872	15.13705	0.00606	0.06606
42	11.55930	0.08651	175.97366	15.22356	0.00568	0.06569
43	12.25291	0.08161	187.53295	15.30517	0.00533	0.06534
44	12.98815	0.07699	199.78585	15.38216	0.00501	0.06501
45	13.76750	0.07263	212.77398	15.45480	0.00470	0.06470
46	14.59362	0.06852	226.54150	15.52332	0.00441	0.06442
47	15.46931	0.06464	241.13510	15.58797	0.00415	0.06415
48	16.39755	0.06098	256.60443	15.64895	0.00390	0.06390
49	17.38148	0.05753	273.00195	15.70648	0.00366	0.06367
50	18.42446	0.05428	290.38342	15.76076	0.00344	0.06345

EFFECTIVE ANNUAL INTEREST RATE IS   0.06184

Effective annual interest rate is the equivalent annual rate if the stated nominal rate is compounded continuously.

INTEREST RATE IS 0.07000

YEAR	S/P	P/S	S/R	P/R	R/S	R/P
1	1.07000	0.93458	1.00000	0.93457	1.00000	1.07001
2	1.14491	0.87343	2.07000	1.80800	0.48309	0.55310
3	1.22506	0.81629	3.21491	2.62429	0.31105	0.38106
4	1.31082	0.76288	4.43997	3.38717	0.22523	0.29523
5	1.40258	0.71297	5.75079	4.10014	0.17389	0.24389
6	1.50077	0.66632	7.15337	4.76646	0.13979	0.20980
7	1.60583	0.62273	8.65415	5.38919	0.11555	0.18556
8	1.71825	0.58199	10.25998	5.97118	0.09747	0.16747
9	1.83854	0.54391	11.97823	6.51509	0.08348	0.15349
10	1.96724	0.50833	13.81676	7.02341	0.07238	0.14238
11	2.10496	0.47507	15.78400	7.49848	0.06336	0.13336
12	2.25232	0.44399	17.88896	7.94247	0.05590	0.12591
13	2.40999	0.41494	20.14127	8.35741	0.04965	0.11965
14	2.57870	0.38779	22.55126	8.74520	0.04434	0.11435
15	2.75922	0.36242	25.12996	9.10762	0.03979	0.10980
16	2.95238	0.33871	27.88918	9.44633	0.03586	0.10586
17	3.15906	0.31655	30.84156	9.76288	0.03242	0.10243
18	3.38021	0.29584	34.00062	10.05872	0.02941	0.09942
19	3.61684	0.27648	37.38083	10.33520	0.02675	0.09676
20	3.87004	0.25840	40.99768	10.59360	0.02439	0.09440
21	4.14096	0.24149	44.86771	10.83509	0.02229	0.09229
22	4.43085	0.22569	49.00867	11.06078	0.02040	0.09041
23	4.74103	0.21092	53.43952	11.27170	0.01871	0.08872
24	5.07293	0.19712	58.18054	11.46883	0.01719	0.08719
25	5.42806	0.18423	63.25347	11.65305	0.01581	0.08581
26	5.80805	0.17217	68.68154	11.82523	0.01456	0.08456
27	6.21464	0.16091	74.48959	11.98614	0.01342	0.08343
28	6.64970	0.15038	80.70423	12.13652	0.01239	0.08240
29	7.11521	0.14054	87.35392	12.27707	0.01145	0.08145
30	7.61331	0.13135	94.46911	12.40841	0.01059	0.08059
31	8.14628	0.12276	102.08242	12.53117	0.00980	0.07980
32	8.71656	0.11472	110.22871	12.64590	0.00907	0.07908
33	9.32676	0.10722	118.94523	12.75311	0.00841	0.07841
34	9.97968	0.10020	128.27200	12.85332	0.00780	0.07780
35	10.67831	0.09365	138.25167	12.94696	0.00723	0.07724
36	11.42584	0.08752	148.92999	13.03449	0.00671	0.07672
37	12.22571	0.08179	160.35583	13.11628	0.00624	0.07624
38	13.08157	0.07644	172.58151	13.19272	0.00579	0.07580
39	13.99734	0.07144	185.66308	13.26416	0.00539	0.07539
40	14.97723	0.06677	199.66043	13.33093	0.00501	0.07501
41	16.02571	0.06240	214.63763	13.39333	0.00466	0.07466
42	17.14758	0.05832	230.66329	13.45165	0.00434	0.07434
43	18.34800	0.05450	247.81088	13.50615	0.00404	0.07404
44	19.63245	0.05094	266.15887	13.55709	0.00376	0.07376
45	21.00682	0.04760	285.79132	13.60469	0.00350	0.07350
46	22.47740	0.04449	306.79815	13.64918	0.00326	0.07326
47	24.05093	0.04158	329.27551	13.69076	0.00304	0.07304
48	25.73461	0.03886	353.32641	13.72962	0.00283	0.07284
49	27.53616	0.03632	379.06103	13.76593	0.00264	0.07264
50	29.46383	0.03394	406.59716	13.79987	0.00246	0.07246

EFFECTIVE ANNUAL INTEREST RATE IS 0.07251

Effective annual interest rate is the equivalent annual rate if the stated nominal rate is compounded continuously.

INTERESTᅠRATEᅠISᅠ0.08000

YEAR	S/P	P/S	S/R	P/R	R/S	R/P
1	1.08000	0.92592	1.00000	0.92592	1.00000	1.08001
2	1.16641	0.85733	2.08000	1.78325	0.48077	0.56077
3	1.25973	0.79382	3.24641	2.57707	0.30803	0.38804
4	1.36051	0.73502	4.50614	3.31209	0.22192	0.30192
5	1.46936	0.68057	5.86666	3.99266	0.17045	0.25046
6	1.58692	0.63015	7.33601	4.62281	0.13631	0.21632
7	1.71388	0.58347	8.92293	5.20628	0.11207	0.19208
8	1.85100	0.54025	10.63681	5.74653	0.09401	0.17402
9	1.99909	0.50023	12.48781	6.24675	0.08008	0.16008
10	2.15902	0.46317	14.48689	6.70993	0.06903	0.14903
11	2.33176	0.42886	16.64591	7.13879	0.06007	0.14008
12	2.51831	0.39709	18.97767	7.53588	0.05269	0.13270
13	2.71978	0.36768	21.49597	7.90356	0.04652	0.12653
14	2.93738	0.34044	24.21575	8.24399	0.04130	0.12130
15	3.17239	0.31522	27.15313	8.55921	0.03683	0.11683
16	3.42619	0.29187	30.32552	8.85108	0.03298	0.11298
17	3.70030	0.27025	33.75170	9.12133	0.02963	0.10963
18	3.99635	0.25023	37.45201	9.37156	0.02670	0.10671
19	4.31608	0.23169	41.44835	9.60325	0.02413	0.10413
20	4.66138	0.21453	45.76442	9.81778	0.02185	0.10186
21	5.03432	0.19864	50.42580	10.01642	0.01983	0.09984
22	5.43709	0.18392	55.46012	10.20034	0.01803	0.09804
23	5.87208	0.17030	60.89720	10.37063	0.01642	0.09643
24	6.34187	0.15768	66.76928	10.52832	0.01498	0.09498
25	6.84926	0.14600	73.11116	10.67432	0.01368	0.09368
26	7.39723	0.13519	79.96040	10.80950	0.01251	0.09251
27	7.98904	0.12517	87.35762	10.93467	0.01145	0.09145
28	8.62821	0.11590	95.34664	11.05057	0.01049	0.09049
29	9.31851	0.10731	103.97486	11.15789	0.00962	0.08962
30	10.06403	0.09936	113.29335	11.25725	0.00883	0.08883
31	10.86920	0.09200	123.35737	11.34925	0.00811	0.08811
32	11.73880	0.08519	134.22659	11.43444	0.00745	0.08746
33	12.67796	0.07888	145.96539	11.51332	0.00685	0.08686
34	13.69226	0.07303	158.64334	11.58635	0.00630	0.08631
35	14.78770	0.06762	172.33557	11.65398	0.00580	0.08581
36	15.97079	0.06261	187.12326	11.71659	0.00534	0.08535
37	17.24853	0.05798	203.09402	11.77457	0.00492	0.08493
38	18.62850	0.05368	220.34259	11.82825	0.00454	0.08454
39	20.11888	0.04970	238.97106	11.87795	0.00418	0.08419
40	21.72848	0.04602	259.08990	11.92397	0.00386	0.08386
41	23.46687	0.04261	280.81836	11.96659	0.00356	0.08357
42	25.34434	0.03946	304.28527	12.00604	0.00329	0.08329
43	27.37201	0.03653	329.62957	12.04258	0.00303	0.08304
44	29.56190	0.03383	357.00152	12.07641	0.00280	0.08281
45	31.92700	0.03132	386.56347	12.10773	0.00259	0.08259
46	34.48132	0.02900	418.49047	12.13673	0.00239	0.08239
47	37.23999	0.02685	452.97174	12.16358	0.00221	0.08221
48	40.21937	0.02486	490.21167	12.18844	0.00204	0.08204
49	43.43712	0.02302	530.43103	12.21146	0.00189	0.08189
50	46.91230	0.02132	573.86816	12.23278	0.00174	0.08175

EFFECTIVEᅠANNUALᅠINTERESTᅠRATEᅠISᅠᅠᅠ0.08329

Effective annual interest rate is the equivalent annual rate if the stated nominal rate is compounded continuously.

YEAR	S/P	P/S	S/R	P/R	R/S	R/P
1	1.09000	0.91743	1.00000	0.91742	1.00000	1.09001
2	1.18811	0.84167	2.09000	1.75910	0.47847	0.56847
3	1.29505	0.77217	3.27811	2.53127	0.30505	0.39506
4	1.41161	0.70841	4.57316	3.23968	0.21867	0.30867
5	1.53866	0.64992	5.98477	3.88960	0.16709	0.25710
6	1.67715	0.59625	7.52342	4.48585	0.13292	0.22292
7	1.82810	0.54702	9.20057	5.03287	0.10869	0.19869
8	1.99263	0.50185	11.02866	5.53471	0.09067	0.18068
9	2.17198	0.46041	13.02130	5.99512	0.07680	0.16680
10	2.36747	0.42239	15.19328	6.41751	0.06582	0.15582
11	2.58055	0.38751	17.56074	6.80503	0.05695	0.14695
12	2.81282	0.35552	20.14130	7.16054	0.04965	0.13965
13	3.06598	0.32616	22.95412	7.48670	0.04357	0.13357
14	3.34194	0.29923	26.02010	7.78593	0.03843	0.12844
15	3.64273	0.27452	29.36203	8.06045	0.03406	0.12406
16	3.97059	0.25185	33.00476	8.31230	0.03030	0.12030
17	4.32797	0.23106	36.97534	8.54335	0.02705	0.11705
18	4.71750	0.21198	41.30330	8.75533	0.02421	0.11422
19	5.14210	0.19447	46.02081	8.94980	0.02173	0.11173
20	5.60492	0.17841	51.16291	9.12822	0.01955	0.10955
21	6.10939	0.16368	56.76782	9.29190	0.01762	0.10762
22	6.65926	0.15017	62.87721	9.44207	0.01590	0.10591
23	7.25863	0.13777	69.53646	9.57983	0.01438	0.10439
24	7.91194	0.12639	76.79508	9.70623	0.01302	0.10303
25	8.62405	0.11595	84.70701	9.82218	0.01181	0.10181
26	9.40026	0.10638	93.33107	9.92856	0.01071	0.10072
27	10.24633	0.09760	102.73132	10.02616	0.00973	0.09974
28	11.16855	0.08954	112.97764	10.11569	0.00885	0.09886
29	12.17377	0.08214	124.14619	10.19784	0.00806	0.09806
30	13.26947	0.07536	136.31997	10.27320	0.00734	0.09734
31	14.46379	0.06914	149.58944	10.34234	0.00668	0.09669
32	15.76560	0.06343	164.05322	10.40577	0.00610	0.09610
33	17.18459	0.05819	179.81881	10.46396	0.00556	0.09557
34	18.73128	0.05339	197.00338	10.51734	0.00508	0.09508
35	20.41719	0.04898	215.73468	10.56632	0.00464	0.09464
36	22.25484	0.04493	236.15185	10.61126	0.00423	0.09424
37	24.25788	0.04122	258.40667	10.65248	0.00387	0.09387
38	26.44121	0.03782	282.66455	10.69030	0.00354	0.09354
39	28.82105	0.03470	309.10571	10.72500	0.00324	0.09324
40	31.41509	0.03183	337.92675	10.75683	0.00296	0.09296
41	34.24260	0.02920	369.34185	10.78603	0.00271	0.09271
42	37.32460	0.02679	403.58441	10.81282	0.00248	0.09248
43	40.68400	0.02458	440.90899	10.83740	0.00227	0.09227
44	44.34576	0.02255	481.59295	10.85995	0.00208	0.09208
45	48.33709	0.02069	525.93872	10.88064	0.00190	0.09191
46	52.68767	0.01898	574.27575	10.89962	0.00174	0.09175
47	57.42982	0.01741	626.96338	10.91703	0.00159	0.09160
48	62.59879	0.01597	684.39331	10.93301	0.00146	0.09147
49	68.23300	0.01466	746.99206	10.94767	0.00134	0.09134
50	74.37429	0.01345	815.22485	10.96111	0.00123	0.09123

EFFECTIVE ANNUAL INTEREST RATE IS   0.09417

Effective annual interest rate is the equivalent annual rate if the stated nominal rate is compounded continuously.

Appendix   **499**

```
                            INTEREST RATE IS   0.10000
YEAR       S/P           P/S          S/R           P/R          R/S          R/P

  1      1.10000       0.90909       1.00000      0.90909      1.00000      1.10001
  2      1.21001       0.82644       2.10000      1.73552      0.47619      0.57619
  3      1.33102       0.75130       3.31001      2.48683      0.30211      0.40212
  4      1.46413       0.68300       4.64103      3.16983      0.21547      0.31547
  5      1.61055       0.62091       6.10516      3.79074      0.16380      0.26380
  6      1.77161       0.56446       7.71570      4.35519      0.12961      0.22961
  7      1.94878       0.51314       9.48731      4.86834      0.10540      0.20541
  8      2.14367       0.46649      11.43609      5.33483      0.08744      0.18745
  9      2.35804       0.42408      13.57975      5.75891      0.07364      0.17364
 10      2.59386       0.38553      15.93779      6.14443      0.06274      0.16275
 11      2.85326       0.35048      18.53165      6.49491      0.05396      0.15397
 12      3.13860       0.31861      21.38491      6.81352      0.04676      0.14677
 13      3.45247       0.28965      24.52350      7.10317      0.04078      0.14078
 14      3.79774       0.26331      27.97597      7.36649      0.03574      0.13575
 15      4.17753       0.23938      31.77370      7.60586      0.03147      0.13148
 16      4.59530       0.21761      35.95124      7.82348      0.02782      0.12782
 17      5.05486       0.19783      40.54653      8.02131      0.02466      0.12467
 18      5.56037       0.17984      45.60139      8.20115      0.02193      0.12193
 19      6.11643       0.16349      51.16175      8.36464      0.01955      0.11955
 20      6.72810       0.14863      57.27817      8.51327      0.01746      0.11746
 21      7.40095       0.13512      64.00628      8.64839      0.01562      0.11563
 22      8.14108       0.12283      71.40722      8.77123      0.01400      0.11401
 23      8.95522       0.11167      79.54829      8.88289      0.01257      0.11258
 24      9.85079       0.10151      88.50350      8.98441      0.01130      0.11130
 25     10.83592       0.09229      98.35429      9.07669      0.01017      0.11017
 26     11.91956       0.08390     109.19021      9.16059      0.00916      0.10916
 27     13.11158       0.07627     121.10977      9.23686      0.00826      0.10826
 28     14.42280       0.06933     134.22134      9.30619      0.00745      0.10746
 29     15.86515       0.06303     148.64413      9.36922      0.00673      0.10673
 30     17.45174       0.05730     164.50927      9.42652      0.00608      0.10608
 31     19.19701       0.05209     181.96102      9.47862      0.00550      0.10550
 32     21.11680       0.04736     201.15798      9.52597      0.00497      0.10498
 33     23.22858       0.04305     222.27481      9.56902      0.00450      0.10450
 34     25.55155       0.03914     245.50335      9.60816      0.00407      0.10408
 35     28.10684       0.03558     271.05493      9.64373      0.00369      0.10369
 36     30.91766       0.03234     299.16174      9.67608      0.00334      0.10335
 37     34.00958       0.02940     330.07940      9.70548      0.00303      0.10303
 38     37.41070       0.02673     364.08898      9.73221      0.00275      0.10275
 39     41.15195       0.02430     401.49957      9.75651      0.00249      0.10250
 40     45.26735       0.02209     442.65161      9.77860      0.00226      0.10226
 41     49.79431       0.02008     487.91888      9.79869      0.00205      0.10205
 42     54.77398       0.01826     537.71325      9.81694      0.00186      0.10186
 43     60.25165       0.01660     592.48718      9.83354      0.00169      0.10169
 44     66.27711       0.01509     652.73864      9.84863      0.00153      0.10154
 45     72.90516       0.01372     719.01599      9.86235      0.00139      0.10140
 46     80.19602       0.01247     791.92090      9.87481      0.00126      0.10127
 47     88.21603       0.01134     872.11706      9.88615      0.00115      0.10115
 48     97.03807       0.01031     960.33300      9.89646      0.00104      0.10105
 49    106.74235       0.00937    1057.37109      9.90582      0.00095      0.10095
 50    117.41711       0.00852    1164.11352      9.91434      0.00086      0.10086
```

              EFFECTIVE ANNUAL INTEREST RATE IS   0.10517

Effective annual interest rate is the equivalent annual rate if the stated nominal rate is compounded continuously.

INTEREST RATE IS 0.12000

YEAR	S/P	P/S	S/R	P/R	R/S	R/P
1	1.12000	0.89285	1.00000	0.89285	1.00000	1.12001
2	1.25441	0.79719	2.12000	1.69004	0.47170	0.59170
3	1.40495	0.71177	3.37441	2.40181	0.29635	0.41635
4	1.57355	0.63551	4.77936	3.03732	0.20923	0.32924
5	1.76238	0.56741	6.35290	3.60473	0.15741	0.27741
6	1.97387	0.50662	8.11528	4.11135	0.12322	0.24323
7	2.21075	0.45234	10.08916	4.56368	0.09912	0.21912
8	2.47605	0.40387	12.29990	4.96755	0.08130	0.20131
9	2.77319	0.36060	14.77595	5.32815	0.06768	0.18768
10	3.10598	0.32196	17.54914	5.65011	0.05698	0.17699
11	3.47872	0.28746	20.65512	5.93757	0.04841	0.16842
12	3.89618	0.25666	24.13383	6.19423	0.04144	0.16144
13	4.36374	0.22916	28.03001	6.42339	0.03568	0.15568
14	4.88741	0.20461	32.39375	6.62800	0.03087	0.15088
15	5.47392	0.18268	37.28116	6.81068	0.02682	0.14683
16	6.13082	0.16311	42.75508	6.97379	0.02339	0.14339
17	6.86655	0.14563	48.88590	7.11943	0.02046	0.14046
18	7.69057	0.13003	55.75244	7.24945	0.01794	0.13794
19	8.61347	0.11610	63.44300	7.36555	0.01576	0.13577
20	9.64713	0.10366	72.05647	7.46921	0.01388	0.13388
21	10.80484	0.09255	81.70359	7.56176	0.01224	0.13224
22	12.10147	0.08263	92.50845	7.64439	0.01081	0.13081
23	13.55371	0.07378	104.60989	7.71817	0.00956	0.12956
24	15.18022	0.06588	118.16358	7.78405	0.00846	0.12847
25	17.00192	0.05882	133.34381	7.84287	0.00750	0.12750
26	19.04223	0.05251	150.34570	7.89538	0.00665	0.12666
27	21.32739	0.04689	169.38793	7.94227	0.00590	0.12591
28	23.88678	0.04186	190.71530	7.98413	0.00524	0.12525
29	26.75331	0.03738	214.60208	8.02151	0.00466	0.12466
30	29.96384	0.03337	241.35540	8.05489	0.00414	0.12415
31	33.55965	0.02980	271.31921	8.08468	0.00369	0.12369
32	37.58697	0.02660	304.87884	8.11129	0.00328	0.12328
33	42.09759	0.02375	342.46582	8.13504	0.00292	0.12292
34	47.14951	0.02121	384.56335	8.15625	0.00260	0.12261
35	52.80768	0.01894	431.71289	8.17519	0.00232	0.12232
36	59.14485	0.01691	484.52044	8.19210	0.00206	0.12207
37	66.24253	0.01510	543.66528	8.20719	0.00184	0.12184
38	74.19197	0.01348	609.90783	8.22067	0.00164	0.12164
39	83.09536	0.01203	684.09973	8.23270	0.00146	0.12147
40	93.06721	0.01074	767.19506	8.24345	0.00130	0.12131
41	104.23573	0.00959	860.26220	8.25304	0.00116	0.12117
42	116.74452	0.00857	964.49780	8.26161	0.00104	0.12104
43	130.75445	0.00765	1081.24243	8.26926	0.00092	0.12093
44	146.44561	0.00683	1211.99658	8.27609	0.00083	0.12083
45	164.01980	0.00610	1358.44214	8.28218	0.00074	0.12074
46	183.70297	0.00544	1522.46191	8.28763	0.00066	0.12066
47	205.74823	0.00486	1706.16479	8.29249	0.00059	0.12059
48	230.43902	0.00434	1911.91284	8.29683	0.00052	0.12053
49	258.09283	0.00387	2142.35156	8.30070	0.00047	0.12047
50	289.06524	0.00346	2400.44434	8.30416	0.00042	0.12042

EFFECTIVE ANNUAL INTEREST RATE IS   0.12750

Effective annual interest rate is the equivalent annual rate if the stated nominal rate is compounded continuously.

```
                                    INTEREST RATE IS  0.14000
   YEAR       S/P            P/S            S/R            P/R            R/S            R/P

     1      1.14000        0.87719        1.00000        0.87719        1.00000        1.14001
     2      1.29961        0.76946        2.14000        1.64665        0.46729        0.60729
     3      1.48156        0.67496        3.43961        2.32161        0.29073        0.43074
     4      1.68899        0.59207        4.92117        2.91368        0.20320        0.34321
     5      1.92546        0.51936        6.61016        3.43304        0.15128        0.29129
     6      2.19503        0.45557        8.53561        3.88861        0.11716        0.25716
     7      2.50234        0.39963       10.73064        4.28824        0.09319        0.23320
     8      2.85268        0.35055       13.23298        4.63878        0.07557        0.21557
     9      3.25207        0.30750       16.08567        4.94628        0.06217        0.20217
    10      3.70738        0.26973       19.33773        5.21601        0.05171        0.19172
    11      4.22643        0.23661       23.04511        5.45262        0.04339        0.18340
    12      4.81815        0.20755       27.27154        5.66017        0.03667        0.17667
    13      5.49271        0.18206       32.08968        5.84223        0.03116        0.17117
    14      6.26172        0.15970       37.58238        6.00193        0.02661        0.16661
    15      7.13839        0.14009       43.84410        6.14201        0.02281        0.16281
    16      8.13780        0.12288       50.98249        6.26490        0.01961        0.15962
    17      9.27713        0.10779       59.12027        6.37269        0.01691        0.15692
    18     10.57597        0.09455       68.39741        6.46724        0.01462        0.15463
    19     12.05666        0.08294       78.97337        6.55018        0.01266        0.15267
    20     13.74465        0.07276       91.03002        6.62294        0.01099        0.15099
    21     15.66897        0.06382      104.77467        6.68676        0.00954        0.14955
    22     17.86270        0.05598      120.44363        6.74274        0.00830        0.14831
    23     20.36357        0.04911      138.30633        6.79185        0.00723        0.14724
    24     23.21457        0.04308      158.66989        6.83493        0.00630        0.14631
    25     26.46472        0.03779      181.88443        6.87271        0.00550        0.14550
    26     30.16991        0.03315      208.34912        6.90586        0.00480        0.14480
    27     34.39384        0.02907      238.51901        6.93493        0.00419        0.14420
    28     39.20914        0.02550      272.91284        6.96044        0.00366        0.14367
    29     44.69861        0.02237      312.12194        6.98281        0.00320        0.14321
    30     50.95663        0.01962      356.82049        7.00243        0.00280        0.14281
    31     58.09080        0.01721      407.77710        7.01965        0.00245        0.14246
    32     66.22380        0.01510      465.86779        7.03475        0.00215        0.14215
    33     75.49545        0.01325      532.09155        7.04799        0.00188        0.14188
    34     86.06518        0.01162      607.58703        7.05961        0.00165        0.14165
    35     98.11473        0.01019      693.65222        7.06981        0.00144        0.14145
    36    111.85125        0.00894      791.76672        7.07875        0.00126        0.14127
    37    127.51097        0.00784      903.61792        7.08659        0.00111        0.14111
    38    145.36312        0.00688     1031.12866        7.09347        0.00097        0.14097
    39    165.71466        0.00603     1176.49170        7.09950        0.00085        0.14085
    40    188.91552        0.00529     1342.20630        7.10480        0.00075        0.14075
    41    215.36459        0.00464     1531.12158        7.10944        0.00065        0.14066
    42    245.51669        0.00407     1746.48608        7.11351        0.00057        0.14058
    43    279.89019        0.00357     1992.00244        7.11709        0.00050        0.14051
    44    319.07617        0.00313     2271.89258        7.12022        0.00044        0.14045
    45    363.74841        0.00275     2590.96875        7.12297        0.00039        0.14039
    46    414.67492        0.00241     2954.71680        7.12538        0.00034        0.14034
    47    472.73144        0.00212     3369.39160        7.12750        0.00030        0.14030
    48    538.91613        0.00186     3842.12207        7.12935        0.00026        0.14027
    49    614.36694        0.00163     4381.03809        7.13098        0.00023        0.14023
    50    700.38134        0.00143     4995.40430        7.13241        0.00020        0.14021

               EFFECTIVE ANNUAL INTEREST RATE IS        0.15027
```

Effective annual interest rate is the equivalent annual rate if the stated nominal rate is compounded continuously.

502

Appendix

INTEREST RATE IS   0.16000

YEAR	S/P	P/S	S/R	P/R	R/S	R/P
1	1.16000	0.86207	1.00000	0.86206	1.00000	1.16001
2	1.34561	0.74316	2.16000	1.60522	0.46296	0.62297
3	1.56092	0.64065	3.50561	2.24587	0.28526	0.44526
4	1.81067	0.55228	5.06653	2.79815	0.19737	0.35738
5	2.10039	0.47610	6.87720	3.27425	0.14541	0.30541
6	2.43646	0.41043	8.97758	3.68469	0.11139	0.27139
7	2.82630	0.35382	11.41404	4.03851	0.08761	0.24762
8	3.27852	0.30502	14.24034	4.34352	0.07022	0.23023
9	3.80310	0.26294	17.51886	4.60646	0.05708	0.21709
10	4.41162	0.22667	21.32196	4.83314	0.04690	0.20690
11	5.11750	0.19541	25.73358	5.02855	0.03886	0.19886
12	5.93632	0.16845	30.85108	5.19700	0.03241	0.19242
13	6.88617	0.14522	36.78740	5.34222	0.02718	0.18719
14	7.98798	0.12519	43.67356	5.46741	0.02290	0.18290
15	9.26610	0.10792	51.66154	5.57533	0.01936	0.17936
16	10.74872	0.09303	60.92763	5.66836	0.01641	0.17642
17	12.46857	0.08020	71.67636	5.74856	0.01395	0.17396
18	14.46360	0.06914	84.14492	5.81770	0.01188	0.17189
19	16.77785	0.05960	98.60850	5.87730	0.01014	0.17015
20	19.46239	0.05138	115.38635	5.92868	0.00867	0.16867
21	22.57646	0.04429	134.84872	5.97298	0.00742	0.16742
22	26.18880	0.03818	157.42517	6.01116	0.00635	0.16636
23	30.37914	0.03292	183.61398	6.04408	0.00545	0.16545
24	35.23995	0.02838	213.99310	6.07246	0.00467	0.16468
25	40.87850	0.02446	249.23300	6.09692	0.00401	0.16402
26	47.41927	0.02109	290.11151	6.11801	0.00345	0.16345
27	55.00658	0.01818	337.53076	6.13619	0.00296	0.16297
28	63.80789	0.01567	392.53729	6.15186	0.00255	0.16255
29	74.01747	0.01351	456.34509	6.16537	0.00219	0.16220
30	85.86062	0.01165	530.36255	6.17702	0.00189	0.16189
31	99.59875	0.01004	616.22326	6.18706	0.00162	0.16163
32	115.53503	0.00866	715.82190	6.19571	0.00140	0.16140
33	134.02121	0.00746	831.35693	6.20317	0.00120	0.16121
34	155.46524	0.00643	965.37793	6.20961	0.00104	0.16104
35	180.34042	0.00555	1120.84326	6.21515	0.00089	0.16090
36	209.19577	0.00478	1301.18359	6.21993	0.00077	0.16077
37	242.66809	0.00412	1510.37915	6.22405	0.00066	0.16067
38	281.49615	0.00355	1753.04687	6.22761	0.00057	0.16058
39	326.53692	0.00306	2034.54297	6.23067	0.00049	0.16050
40	378.78442	0.00264	2361.08008	6.23331	0.00042	0.16043
41	439.39172	0.00228	2739.86377	6.23558	0.00036	0.16037
42	509.69653	0.00196	3179.25537	6.23754	0.00031	0.16032
43	591.25048	0.00169	3688.95166	6.23924	0.00027	0.16028
44	685.85339	0.00146	4280.20216	6.24069	0.00023	0.16024
45	795.59326	0.00126	4966.05469	6.24195	0.00020	0.16021
46	922.89209	0.00108	5761.64844	6.24304	0.00017	0.16018
47	1070.55932	0.00093	6684.53907	6.24397	0.00015	0.16015
48	1241.85400	0.00081	7755.09864	6.24477	0.00013	0.16013
49	1440.55664	0.00069	8996.95315	6.24547	0.00011	0.16012
50	1671.05249	0.00060	10437.50783	6.24607	0.00010	0.16010

EFFECTIVE ANNUAL INTEREST RATE IS   0.17351

Effective annual interest rate is the equivalent annual rate if the stated nominal rate is compounded continuously.

INTEREST RATE IS 0.18000

YEAR	S/P	P/S	S/R	P/R	R/S	R/P
1	1.18000	0.84745	1.00000	0.84745	1.00000	1.18001
2	1.39241	0.71818	2.18000	1.56563	0.45872	0.63872
3	1.64305	0.60862	3.57241	2.17426	0.27992	0.45993
4	1.93881	0.51578	5.21547	2.69004	0.19174	0.37174
5	2.28780	0.43710	7.15427	3.12714	0.13978	0.31978
6	2.69962	0.37042	9.44208	3.49756	0.10591	0.28591
7	3.18556	0.31392	12.14169	3.81147	0.08236	0.26237
8	3.75898	0.26603	15.32726	4.07750	0.06524	0.24525
9	4.43562	0.22545	19.08624	4.30295	0.05239	0.23240
10	5.23405	0.19106	23.52185	4.49401	0.04251	0.22252
11	6.17620	0.16191	28.75590	4.65592	0.03478	0.21478
12	7.28795	0.13721	34.93210	4.79313	0.02863	0.20863
13	8.59982	0.11628	42.22005	4.90941	0.02369	0.20369
14	10.14782	0.09854	50.81986	5.00796	0.01968	0.19968
15	11.97448	0.08351	60.96767	5.09147	0.01640	0.19641
16	14.12994	0.07077	72.94215	5.16224	0.01371	0.19371
17	16.67340	0.05998	87.07208	5.22221	0.01148	0.19149
18	19.67470	0.05083	103.74548	5.27304	0.00964	0.18964
19	23.21624	0.04307	123.42018	5.31611	0.00810	0.18811
20	27.39527	0.03650	146.63641	5.35262	0.00682	0.18682
21	32.32655	0.03093	174.03164	5.38355	0.00575	0.18575
22	38.14549	0.02622	206.35821	5.40977	0.00485	0.18485
23	45.01186	0.02222	244.50369	5.43198	0.00409	0.18409
24	53.11421	0.01883	289.51550	5.45081	0.00345	0.18346
25	62.67502	0.01596	342.62970	5.46677	0.00292	0.18292
26	73.95683	0.01352	405.30468	5.48029	0.00247	0.18247
27	87.26942	0.01146	479.26147	5.49175	0.00209	0.18209
28	102.97834	0.00971	566.53100	5.50146	0.00177	0.18177
29	121.51493	0.00823	669.50915	5.50968	0.00149	0.18150
30	143.38821	0.00697	791.02404	5.51666	0.00126	0.18127
31	169.19879	0.00591	934.41223	5.52257	0.00107	0.18108
32	199.65536	0.00501	1103.61084	5.52758	0.00091	0.18091
33	235.59429	0.00424	1303.26611	5.53182	0.00077	0.18077
34	278.00244	0.00360	1538.86035	5.53542	0.00065	0.18065
35	328.04419	0.00305	1816.86255	5.53847	0.00055	0.18056
36	387.09375	0.00258	2144.90674	5.54105	0.00047	0.18047
37	456.77246	0.00219	2532.00049	5.54324	0.00039	0.18040
38	538.99377	0.00186	2988.77246	5.54510	0.00033	0.18034
39	636.01513	0.00157	3527.76563	5.54667	0.00028	0.18029
40	750.50097	0.00133	4163.78126	5.54800	0.00024	0.18025
41	885.59472	0.00113	4914.28126	5.54913	0.00020	0.18021
42	1045.00610	0.00096	5799.87501	5.55009	0.00017	0.18018
43	1233.11230	0.00081	6844.88184	5.55090	0.00015	0.18015
44	1455.07837	0.00069	8077.99220	5.55159	0.00012	0.18013
45	1716.99951	0.00058	9533.07033	5.55217	0.00010	0.18011
46	2026.06762	0.00049	11250.07033	5.55266	0.00009	0.18009
47	2390.76953	0.00042	13276.13479	5.55308	0.00008	0.18008
48	2821.11963	0.00035	15666.90432	5.55344	0.00006	0.18007
49	3328.93457	0.00030	18488.02348	5.55373	0.00005	0.18006
50	3928.15918	0.00025	21816.95708	5.55399	0.00005	0.18005

EFFECTIVE ANNUAL INTEREST RATE IS   0.19722

Effective annual interest rate is the equivalent annual rate if the stated nominal rate is compounded continuously.

YEAR	S/P	P/S	INTEREST RATE IS 0.20000 S/R	P/R	R/S	R/P
1	1.20000	0.83333	1.00000	0.83333	1.00000	1.20001
2	1.44001	0.69444	2.20000	1.52777	0.45454	0.65455
3	1.72802	0.57870	3.64001	2.10646	0.27472	0.47473
4	2.07363	0.48225	5.36804	2.58871	0.18629	0.38629
5	2.48837	0.40187	7.44167	2.99058	0.13438	0.33438
6	2.98606	0.33489	9.93004	3.32547	0.10070	0.30071
7	3.58328	0.27907	12.91609	3.60454	0.07742	0.27743
8	4.29996	0.23256	16.49937	3.83710	0.06061	0.26061
9	5.15997	0.19380	20.79933	4.03090	0.04808	0.24808
10	6.19198	0.16150	25.95929	4.19240	0.03852	0.23853
11	7.43041	0.13458	32.15127	4.32698	0.03110	0.23111
12	8.91653	0.11215	39.58168	4.43914	0.02526	0.22527
13	10.69988	0.09346	48.49821	4.53259	0.02062	0.22062
14	12.83991	0.07788	59.19808	4.61048	0.01689	0.21690
15	15.40795	0.06490	72.03799	4.67538	0.01388	0.21389
16	18.48962	0.05408	87.44593	4.72946	0.01144	0.21144
17	22.18762	0.04507	105.93553	4.77453	0.00944	0.20944
18	26.62526	0.03756	128.12316	4.81209	0.00780	0.20781
19	31.95044	0.03130	154.74841	4.84339	0.00646	0.20647
20	38.34068	0.02608	186.69885	4.86947	0.00536	0.20536
21	46.00900	0.02173	225.03949	4.89121	0.00444	0.20445
22	55.21102	0.01811	271.04846	4.90932	0.00369	0.20369
23	66.25349	0.01509	326.25946	4.92441	0.00307	0.20307
24	79.50451	0.01258	392.51294	4.93699	0.00255	0.20255
25	95.40579	0.01048	472.01739	4.94747	0.00212	0.20212
26	114.48741	0.00873	567.42321	4.95621	0.00176	0.20177
27	137.38546	0.00728	681.91064	4.96348	0.00147	0.20147
28	164.86322	0.00607	819.29602	4.96955	0.00122	0.20123
29	197.83663	0.00505	984.15905	4.97460	0.00102	0.20102
30	237.40490	0.00421	1181.99560	4.97882	0.00085	0.20085
31	284.88708	0.00351	1419.40063	4.98233	0.00070	0.20071
32	341.86584	0.00293	1704.28760	4.98525	0.00059	0.20059
33	410.24066	0.00244	2046.15332	4.98769	0.00049	0.20049
34	492.29077	0.00203	2456.39404	4.98972	0.00041	0.20041
35	590.75134	0.00169	2948.68457	4.99141	0.00034	0.20034
36	708.90442	0.00141	3539.43555	4.99282	0.00028	0.20029
37	850.68872	0.00118	4248.33985	4.99400	0.00024	0.20024
38	1020.83044	0.00098	5099.02735	4.99498	0.00020	0.20020
39	1225.00146	0.00082	6119.85743	4.99580	0.00016	0.20017
40	1470.00781	0.00068	7344.85938	4.99648	0.00014	0.20014
41	1764.01636	0.00057	8814.86721	4.99704	0.00011	0.20012
42	2116.82813	0.00047	10578.88088	4.99752	0.00009	0.20010
43	2540.20410	0.00039	12695.70901	4.99791	0.00008	0.20008
44	3048.25684	0.00033	15235.91213	4.99824	0.00007	0.20007
45	3657.92285	0.00027	18284.16801	4.99851	0.00005	0.20006
46	4389.52540	0.00023	21942.08988	4.99874	0.00005	0.20005
47	5267.45118	0.00019	26331.60942	4.99893	0.00004	0.20004
48	6320.96681	0.00016	31599.06254	4.99909	0.00003	0.20004
49	7585.19044	0.00013	37920.02352	4.99922	0.00003	0.20003
50	9102.26564	0.00011	45505.21102	4.99933	0.00002	0.20003

EFFECTIVE ANNUAL INTEREST RATE IS   0.22140

Effective annual interest rate is the equivalent annual rate if the stated nominal rate is compounded continuously.

Appendix

505

INTEREST RATE IS 0.25000

YEAR	S/P	P/S	S/R	P/R	R/S	R/P
1	1.25000	0.80000	1.00000	0.80000	1.00000	1.25001
2	1.56251	0.64000	2.25000	1.43999	0.44444	0.69445
3	1.95315	0.51199	3.81252	1.95199	0.26229	0.51230
4	2.44144	0.40959	5.76566	2.36158	0.17344	0.42345
5	3.05182	0.32767	8.20710	2.68925	0.12185	0.37185
6	3.81479	0.26214	11.25892	2.95139	0.08882	0.33882
7	4.76850	0.20971	15.07371	3.16110	0.06634	0.31635
8	5.96065	0.16777	19.84221	3.32887	0.05040	0.30040
9	7.45084	0.13421	25.80285	3.46308	0.03876	0.28876
10	9.31358	0.10737	33.25369	3.57045	0.03007	0.28008
11	11.64202	0.08590	42.56727	3.65635	0.02349	0.27350
12	14.55259	0.06872	54.20929	3.72506	0.01845	0.26845
13	18.19080	0.05497	68.76187	3.78003	0.01454	0.26455
14	22.73859	0.04398	86.95266	3.82401	0.01150	0.26151
15	28.42335	0.03518	109.69126	3.85920	0.00912	0.25912
16	35.52932	0.02815	138.11462	3.88734	0.00724	0.25725
17	44.41182	0.02252	173.64395	3.90986	0.00576	0.25576
18	55.51499	0.01801	218.05575	3.92787	0.00459	0.25459
19	69.39401	0.01441	273.57074	3.94228	0.00366	0.25366
20	86.74284	0.01153	342.96472	3.95381	0.00292	0.25292
21	108.42897	0.00922	429.70758	3.96303	0.00233	0.25233
22	135.53674	0.00738	538.13647	3.97041	0.00186	0.25186
23	169.42157	0.00590	673.67321	3.97631	0.00148	0.25149
24	211.77777	0.00472	843.09472	3.98103	0.00119	0.25119
25	264.72326	0.00378	1054.87256	3.98481	0.00095	0.25095
26	330.90533	0.00302	1319.59570	3.98783	0.00076	0.25076
27	413.63324	0.00242	1650.50097	3.99025	0.00061	0.25061
28	517.04358	0.00193	2064.13428	3.99219	0.00048	0.25049
29	646.30688	0.00155	2581.17725	3.99373	0.00039	0.25039
30	807.88672	0.00124	3227.48438	3.99497	0.00031	0.25031
31	1009.86218	0.00099	4035.37061	3.99596	0.00025	0.25025
32	1262.33276	0.00079	5045.23341	3.99675	0.00020	0.25020
33	1577.92187	0.00063	6307.56544	3.99739	0.00016	0.25016
34	1972.40991	0.00051	7885.48731	3.99789	0.00013	0.25013
35	2465.52197	0.00041	9857.89651	3.99830	0.00010	0.25011
36	3081.91406	0.00032	12323.41799	3.99862	0.00008	0.25009
37	3852.40723	0.00026	15405.33010	3.99888	0.00006	0.25007
38	4815.52833	0.00021	19257.73832	3.99909	0.00005	0.25006
39	6019.43262	0.00017	24073.26567	3.99926	0.00004	0.25005
40	7524.32032	0.00013	30092.69926	3.99939	0.00003	0.25004
41	9405.43752	0.00011	37617.02352	3.99950	0.00003	0.25003
42	11756.83986	0.00009	47022.44540	3.99958	0.00002	0.25003
43	14696.10744	0.00007	58779.28915	3.99965	0.00002	0.25002
44	18370.20317	0.00005	73475.39083	3.99970	0.00001	0.25002
45	22962.84380	0.00004	91845.59396	3.99975	0.00001	0.25002
46	28703.66410	0.00003	114808.43768	3.99978	0.00001	0.25001
47	35879.71885	0.00003	143512.09411	3.99981	0.00001	0.25001
48	44849.82041	0.00002	179391.81292	3.99983	0.00001	0.25001
49	56062.49227	0.00002	224241.62536	3.99985	0.00000	0.25001
50	70078.39080	0.00001	280304.12573	3.99987	0.00000	0.25001

EFFECTIVE ANNUAL INTEREST RATE IS   0.28403

Effective annual interest rate is the equivalent annual rate if the stated nominal rate is compounded continuously.

INTEREST RATE IS 0.30000

YEAR	S/P	P/S	S/R	P/R	R/S	R/P
1	1.30000	0.76923	1.00000	0.76923	1.00000	1.30001
2	1.69001	0.59171	2.30000	1.36094	0.43478	0.73479
3	2.19702	0.45516	3.99001	1.81610	0.25063	0.55063
4	2.85614	0.35012	6.18704	2.16622	0.16163	0.46163
5	3.71300	0.26932	9.04318	2.43555	0.11058	0.41059
6	4.82691	0.20717	12.75617	2.64272	0.07839	0.37840
7	6.27501	0.15936	17.58308	2.80208	0.05687	0.35688
8	8.15754	0.12259	23.85808	2.92467	0.04191	0.34192
9	10.60484	0.09430	32.01562	3.01896	0.03123	0.33124
10	13.78634	0.07254	42.62046	3.09150	0.02346	0.32347
11	17.92231	0.05580	56.40679	3.14729	0.01773	0.31773
12	23.29909	0.04292	74.32910	3.19021	0.01345	0.31346
13	30.28892	0.03302	97.62817	3.22323	0.01024	0.31025
14	39.37574	0.02540	127.91708	3.24863	0.00782	0.30782
15	51.18864	0.01954	167.29281	3.26816	0.00598	0.30598
16	66.54548	0.01503	218.48144	3.28319	0.00458	0.30458
17	86.50943	0.01156	285.02685	3.29475	0.00351	0.30351
18	112.46266	0.00889	371.53625	3.30364	0.00269	0.30270
19	146.20199	0.00684	483.99884	3.31048	0.00207	0.30207
20	190.06326	0.00526	630.20080	3.31574	0.00159	0.30159
21	247.08313	0.00405	820.26403	3.31979	0.00122	0.30122
22	321.20922	0.00311	1067.34692	3.32290	0.00094	0.30094
23	417.57348	0.00239	1388.55615	3.32530	0.00072	0.30072
24	542.84741	0.00184	1806.12890	3.32714	0.00055	0.30056
25	705.70422	0.00142	2348.97656	3.32856	0.00043	0.30043
26	917.41870	0.00109	3054.68018	3.32965	0.00033	0.30033
27	1192.64868	0.00084	3972.09863	3.33049	0.00025	0.30026
28	1550.44873	0.00064	5164.74610	3.33113	0.00019	0.30020
29	2015.59057	0.00050	6715.19434	3.33163	0.00015	0.30015
30	2620.27734	0.00038	8730.78517	3.33201	0.00011	0.30012
31	3406.37256	0.00029	11351.06056	3.33230	0.00009	0.30009
32	4428.29981	0.00023	14757.42776	3.33253	0.00007	0.30007
33	5756.81055	0.00017	19185.72660	3.33270	0.00005	0.30006
34	7483.88087	0.00013	24942.53910	3.33283	0.00004	0.30004
35	9729.08010	0.00010	32426.41411	3.33294	0.00003	0.30004
36	12647.84963	0.00008	42155.49227	3.33302	0.00002	0.30003
37	16442.26177	0.00006	54803.32040	3.33308	0.00002	0.30002
38	21375.01957	0.00005	71245.59396	3.33312	0.00001	0.30002
39	27787.62504	0.00004	92620.60955	3.33316	0.00001	0.30002
40	36124.03915	0.00003	120408.18768	3.33319	0.00001	0.30001
41	46961.42196	0.00002	156532.25036	3.33321	0.00001	0.30001
42	61050.06259	0.00002	203493.62536	3.33323	0.00000	0.30001
43	79365.37521	0.00001	264543.68835	3.33324	0.00000	0.30001
44	103175.34396	0.00001	343909.00085	3.33325	0.00000	0.30001
45	134128.43786	0.00001	447084.25085	3.33326	0.00000	0.30001
46	174367.59417	0.00001	581212.62670	3.33326	0.00000	0.30001
47	226678.65667	0.00000	755580.12670	3.33327	0.00000	0.30001
48	294683.31323	0.00000	982258.62646	3.33327	0.00000	0.30001
49	383089.68823	0.00000	1276941.75292	3.33327	0.00000	0.30001
50	498018.37573	0.00000	1660031.50341	3.33327	0.00000	0.30001

EFFECTIVE ANNUAL INTEREST RATE IS   0.34986

Effective annual interest rate is the equivalent annual rate if the stated nominal rate is compounded continuously.

```
                        INTEREST RATE IS  0.35000
YEAR        S/P           P/S           S/R           P/R           R/S           R/P

  1        1.35000       0.74074       1.00000       0.74074       1.00000       1.35001
  2        1.82251       0.54869       2.35000       1.28943       0.42553       0.77554
  3        2.46040       0.40644       4.17252       1.69587       0.23966       0.58967
  4        3.32155       0.30106       6.63292       1.99693       0.15076       0.50077
  5        4.48411       0.22301       9.95447       2.21994       0.10046       0.45046
  6        6.05357       0.16519      14.43858       2.38513       0.06926       0.41926
  7        8.17235       0.12236      20.49215       2.50750       0.04880       0.39880
  8       11.03271       0.09064      28.66450       2.59814       0.03489       0.38489
  9       14.89421       0.06714      39.69721       2.66528       0.02519       0.37520
 10       20.10726       0.04973      54.59142       2.71501       0.01832       0.36832
 11       27.14489       0.03684      74.69868       2.75185       0.01339       0.36339
 12       36.64573       0.02729     101.84356       2.77914       0.00982       0.35982
 13       49.47190       0.02021     138.48928       2.79935       0.00722       0.35723
 14       66.78730       0.01497     187.96118       2.81432       0.00532       0.35533
 15       90.16317       0.01109     254.74847       2.82542       0.00393       0.35393
 16      121.72071       0.00822     344.91168       2.83363       0.00290       0.35290
 17      164.32354       0.00609     466.63232       2.83972       0.00214       0.35215
 18      221.83755       0.00451     630.95593       2.84422       0.00158       0.35159
 19      299.48175       0.00334     852.79333       2.84756       0.00117       0.35118
 20      404.30175       0.00247    1152.27514       2.85004       0.00087       0.35087
 21      545.80932       0.00183    1556.57690       2.85187       0.00064       0.35065
 22      736.84509       0.00136    2102.38623       2.85323       0.00048       0.35048
 23      994.74438       0.00101    2839.23096       2.85423       0.00035       0.35036
 24     1342.90967       0.00074    3833.97510       2.85498       0.00026       0.35027
 25     1812.93432       0.00055    5176.88477       2.85553       0.00019       0.35020
 26     2447.46973       0.00041    6989.81837       2.85594       0.00014       0.35015
 27     3304.09570       0.00030    9437.28908       2.85624       0.00011       0.35011
 28     4460.54493       0.00022   12741.38283       2.85646       0.00008       0.35008
 29     6021.75587       0.00017   17201.92583       2.85663       0.00006       0.35006
 30     8129.39942       0.00012   23223.68363       2.85675       0.00004       0.35005
 31    10974.72658       0.00009   31353.07817       2.85684       0.00003       0.35004
 32    14815.93362       0.00007   42327.80479       2.85691       0.00002       0.35003
 33    20001.57817       0.00005   57143.72666       2.85696       0.00002       0.35002
 34    27002.22660       0.00004   77145.31271       2.85700       0.00001       0.35002
 35    36453.13290       0.00003  104147.53146       2.85703       0.00001       0.35001
 36    49211.89854       0.00002  140600.65661       2.85705       0.00001       0.35001
 37    66436.29705       0.00002  189812.53161       2.85706       0.00001       0.35001
 38    89689.31271       0.00001  256248.81286       2.85707       0.00000       0.35001
 39   121080.94455       0.00001  345938.12573       2.85708       0.00000       0.35001
 40   163459.90667       0.00001  467019.06323       2.85709       0.00000       0.35001
 41   220671.86667       0.00000  630479.00170       2.85709       0.00000       0.35001
 42   297907.75073       0.00000  851150.50170       2.85709       0.00000       0.35001
 43   402176.87573       0.00000 1149058.25292       2.85710       0.00000       0.35001
 44   542940.75170       0.00000 1551235.25292       2.85710       0.00000       0.35001
 45   732972.50170       0.00000 2094175.75341       2.85710       0.00000       0.35001
 46   989516.25170       0.00000 2827148.00585       2.85710       0.00000       0.35001
 47  1335851.75292       0.00000 3816664.50585       2.85710       0.00000       0.35001
 48  1803406.00292       0.00000 5152516.01171       2.85710       0.00000       0.35000
 49  2434606.50683       0.00000 6955921.01171       2.85710       0.00000       0.35000
 50  3286730.50585       0.00000 9390528.02734       2.85710       0.00000       0.35000

              EFFECTIVE ANNUAL INTEREST RATE IS        0.41907
```

Effective annual interest rate is the equivalent annual rate if the stated nominal rate is compounded continuously.

```
                          INTEREST RATE IS  0.40000
YEAR        S/P           P/S           S/R           P/R           R/S           R/P

  1        1.40000       0.71428       1.00000       0.71428       1.00000       1.40001
  2        1.96001       0.51020       2.40000       1.22448       0.41667       0.81667
  3        2.74403       0.36443       4.36002       1.58891       0.22936       0.62936
  4        3.84165       0.26030       7.10404       1.84922       0.14076       0.54077
  5        5.37833       0.18593      10.94569       2.03515       0.09136       0.49136
  6        7.52968       0.13281      16.32402       2.16795       0.06126       0.46126
  7       10.54159       0.09486      23.85370       2.26282       0.04192       0.44193
  8       14.75827       0.06776      34.39528       2.33058       0.02907       0.42908
  9       20.66165       0.04840      49.15355       2.37897       0.02034       0.42035
 10       28.92641       0.03457      69.81520       2.41354       0.01432       0.41433
 11       40.49710       0.02469      98.74160       2.43824       0.01013       0.41013
 12       56.69612       0.01764     139.23867       2.45588       0.00718       0.40719
 13       79.37484       0.01260     195.93481       2.46847       0.00510       0.40511
 14      111.12513       0.00900     275.30963       2.47747       0.00363       0.40364
 15      155.57571       0.00643     386.43469       2.48390       0.00259       0.40259
 16      217.80667       0.00459     542.01025       2.48849       0.00184       0.40185
 17      304.93035       0.00328     759.81689       2.49177       0.00132       0.40132
 18      426.90387       0.00234    1064.74707       2.49411       0.00094       0.40094
 19      597.66736       0.00167    1491.65063       2.49579       0.00067       0.40068
 20      836.73706       0.00120    2089.31836       2.49698       0.00048       0.40048
 21     1171.43579       0.00085    2926.05469       2.49784       0.00034       0.40035
 22     1640.01538       0.00061    4097.49024       2.49845       0.00024       0.40025
 23     2296.02881       0.00044    5737.50391       2.49888       0.00017       0.40018
 24     3214.45068       0.00031    8033.53223       2.49919       0.00012       0.40013
 25     4500.24610       0.00022   11247.98244       2.49941       0.00009       0.40009
 26     6300.36524       0.00016   15748.22658       2.49957       0.00006       0.40007
 27     8820.53908       0.00011   22048.58598       2.49969       0.00005       0.40005
 28    12348.79494       0.00008   30869.12113       2.49977       0.00003       0.40004
 29    17288.37114       0.00006   43217.91416       2.49983       0.00002       0.40003
 30    24203.79692       0.00004   60506.28134       2.49987       0.00002       0.40002
 31    33885.42977       0.00003   84710.07830       2.49990       0.00001       0.40002
 32    47439.75010       0.00002  118595.46896       2.49992       0.00001       0.40001
 33    66415.87521       0.00002  166035.21917       2.49993       0.00001       0.40001
 34    92982.51580       0.00001  232451.03167       2.49994       0.00000       0.40001
 35   130175.95333       0.00001  325433.56323       2.49995       0.00000       0.40001
 36   182246.90667       0.00001  455609.37573       2.49996       0.00000       0.40001
 37   255146.50042       0.00000  637856.25146       2.49996       0.00000       0.40001
 38   357206.31335       0.00000  893002.75170       2.49996       0.00000       0.40001
 39   500090.43823       0.00000 1250209.00292       2.49997       0.00000       0.40001
 40   700128.87646       0.00000 1750299.00341       2.49997       0.00000       0.40001
 41   980183.62646       0.00000 2450428.00683       2.49997       0.00000       0.40001
 42  1372261.50292       0.00000 3430610.50585       2.49997       0.00000       0.40001
 43  1921172.50341       0.00000 4802872.01171       2.49997       0.00000       0.40000
 44  2689650.00683       0.00000 6724043.01367       2.49997       0.00000       0.40000
 45  3765522.50585       0.00000 9413694.02343       2.49997       0.00000       0.40000
 46  5271749.01367       0.00000 13179214.02343      2.49997       0.00000       0.40000
 47  7380472.01367       0.00000 18450960.04687      2.49997       0.00000       0.40000
 48 10332694.02343       0.00000 25831428.04687      2.49997       0.00000       0.40000
 49 14465818.02343       0.00000 36164120.10937      2.49997       0.00000       0.40000
 50 20252212.04687       0.00000 50629928.09374      2.49997       0.00000       0.40000

             EFFECTIVE ANNUAL INTEREST RATE IS      0.49183
```

Effective annual interest rate is the equivalent annual rate if the stated nominal rate is compounded continuously.

INTEREST RATE IS 0.45000

YEAR	S/P	P/S	S/R	P/R	R/S	R/P
1	1.45000	0.68965	1.00000	0.68965	1.00000	1.45001
2	2.10251	0.47562	2.45000	1.16527	0.40816	0.85817
3	3.04865	0.32801	4.55251	1.49329	0.21966	0.66966
4	4.42056	0.22622	7.60117	1.71950	0.13156	0.58156
5	6.40983	0.15601	12.02172	1.87551	0.08318	0.53319
6	9.29428	0.10759	18.43155	1.98311	0.05425	0.50426
7	13.47675	0.07420	27.72583	2.05731	0.03607	0.48607
8	19.54135	0.05117	41.20257	2.10848	0.02427	0.47428
9	28.33504	0.03529	60.74391	2.14377	0.01646	0.46647
10	41.08594	0.02434	89.07894	2.16811	0.01123	0.46123
11	59.57479	0.01679	130.16488	2.18490	0.00768	0.45769
12	86.38371	0.01158	189.73962	2.19647	0.00527	0.45528
13	125.25675	0.00798	276.12329	2.20446	0.00362	0.45363
14	181.62286	0.00551	401.37994	2.20996	0.00249	0.45250
15	263.35394	0.00380	583.00268	2.21376	0.00172	0.45172
16	381.86438	0.00262	846.35644	2.21638	0.00118	0.45119
17	553.70507	0.00181	1228.22070	2.21819	0.00081	0.45082
18	802.87475	0.00125	1781.92529	2.21943	0.00056	0.45057
19	1164.17187	0.00086	2584.79932	2.22029	0.00039	0.45039
20	1688.05444	0.00059	3748.97070	2.22088	0.00027	0.45027
21	2447.68653	0.00041	5437.02442	2.22129	0.00018	0.45019
22	3549.15625	0.00028	7884.70997	2.22157	0.00013	0.45013
23	5146.29200	0.00019	11433.86330	2.22177	0.00009	0.45009
24	7462.14551	0.00013	16580.15238	2.22190	0.00006	0.45007
25	10820.14455	0.00009	24042.29302	2.22199	0.00004	0.45005
26	15689.25588	0.00006	34862.42977	2.22206	0.00003	0.45003
27	22749.49224	0.00004	50551.67979	2.22210	0.00002	0.45002
28	32986.86729	0.00003	73301.15646	2.22213	0.00001	0.45002
29	47831.09384	0.00002	106288.00021	2.22215	0.00001	0.45001
30	69355.29708	0.00001	154119.06292	2.22217	0.00001	0.45001
31	100565.48458	0.00001	223474.31292	2.22218	0.00000	0.45001
32	145820.40661	0.00001	324039.75085	2.22218	0.00000	0.45001
33	211440.21911	0.00000	469860.06335	2.22219	0.00000	0.45001
34	306589.25085	0.00000	681300.12646	2.22219	0.00000	0.45001
35	444555.81323	0.00000	987889.37646	2.22219	0.00000	0.45001
36	644607.87670	0.00000	1432444.75341	2.22220	0.00000	0.45001
37	934684.25170	0.00000	2077052.25341	2.22220	0.00000	0.45001
38	1355296.25292	0.00000	3011736.00585	2.22220	0.00000	0.45001
39	1965185.50292	0.00000	4367032.01171	2.22220	0.00000	0.45000
40	2849527.50683	0.00000	6332215.01171	2.22220	0.00000	0.45000
41	4131827.50683	0.00000	9181742.02343	2.22220	0.00000	0.45000
42	5991168.01367	0.00000	13313566.02343	2.22220	0.00000	0.45000
43	8687220.02343	0.00000	19304728.05468	2.22220	0.00000	0.45000
44	12596508.02343	0.00000	27991948.05468	2.22220	0.00000	0.45000
45	18264992.05468	0.00000	40588448.09374	2.22220	0.00000	0.45000
46	26484316.04687	0.00000	58853424.09374	2.22220	0.00000	0.45000
47	38402376.09374	0.00000	85337728.21874	2.22220	0.00000	0.45000
48	55683616.10937	0.00000	123740080.21874	2.22220	0.00000	0.45000
49	80741488.21874	0.00000	179423648.43749	2.22220	0.00000	0.45000
50	117075520.21874	0.00000	260165120.43749	2.22220	0.00000	0.45000

EFFECTIVE ANNUAL INTEREST RATE IS   0.56831

Effective annual interest rate is the equivalent annual rate if the stated nominal rate is compounded continuously.

```
                              INTEREST RATE IS   0.50000
YEAR        S/P          P/S          S/R          P/R          R/S          R/P
```

YEAR	S/P	P/S	S/R	P/R	R/S	R/P
1	1.50000	0.66666	1.00000	0.66666	1.00000	1.50001
2	2.25001	0.44444	2.50000	1.11111	0.40000	0.90000
3	3.37503	0.29629	4.75002	1.40740	0.21053	0.71053
4	5.06256	0.19753	8.12505	1.60493	0.12308	0.62308
5	7.59386	0.13169	13.18761	1.73661	0.07583	0.57583
6	11.39083	0.08779	20.78147	1.82440	0.04812	0.54812
7	17.08629	0.05853	32.17229	1.88293	0.03108	0.53109
8	25.62952	0.03902	49.25859	1.92195	0.02030	0.52031
9	38.44439	0.02601	74.88810	1.94796	0.01335	0.51336
10	57.66677	0.01734	113.33250	1.96530	0.00882	0.50883
11	86.50041	0.01156	170.99926	1.97686	0.00585	0.50585
12	129.75100	0.00771	257.49963	1.98457	0.00388	0.50389
13	194.62710	0.00514	387.25067	1.98971	0.00258	0.50259
14	291.94152	0.00343	581.87768	1.99313	0.00172	0.50172
15	437.91363	0.00228	873.81933	1.99541	0.00114	0.50115
16	656.87243	0.00152	1311.73291	1.99694	0.00076	0.50077
17	985.31152	0.00101	1968.60498	1.99795	0.00051	0.50051
18	1477.97168	0.00068	2953.91651	1.99863	0.00034	0.50034
19	2216.96436	0.00045	4431.88770	1.99908	0.00023	0.50023
20	3325.45606	0.00030	6648.85157	1.99938	0.00015	0.50015
21	4988.19923	0.00020	9974.30666	1.99958	0.00010	0.50010
22	7482.32130	0.00013	14962.50588	1.99971	0.00007	0.50007
23	11223.51564	0.00009	22444.82427	1.99980	0.00004	0.50005
24	16835.32427	0.00006	33668.33602	1.99986	0.00003	0.50003
25	25253.06254	0.00004	50503.66416	1.99990	0.00002	0.50002
26	37879.71104	0.00003	75756.73455	1.99993	0.00001	0.50002
27	56819.73448	0.00002	113636.43768	1.99995	0.00001	0.50001
28	85229.85958	0.00001	170456.15661	1.99996	0.00001	0.50001
29	127845.15646	0.00001	255685.96911	1.99997	0.00000	0.50001
30	191768.31286	0.00001	383531.12573	1.99997	0.00000	0.50001
31	287653.37585	0.00000	575299.50146	1.99997	0.00000	0.50001
32	431481.31323	0.00000	862952.75170	1.99998	0.00000	0.50001
33	647223.87646	0.00000	1294434.00292	1.99998	0.00000	0.50001
34	970838.74146	0.00000	1941657.75341	1.99998	0.00000	0.50001
35	1456262.50292	0.00000	2912496.50683	1.99998	0.00000	0.50001
36	2184400.50585	0.00000	4368759.01367	1.99998	0.00000	0.50000
37	3276610.00585	0.00000	6553158.01367	1.99998	0.00000	0.50000
38	4914930.01367	0.00000	9829768.02734	1.99998	0.00000	0.50000
39	7372417.01171	0.00000	14744698.02343	1.99998	0.00000	0.50000
40	11058658.02734	0.00000	22117112.04687	1.99998	0.00000	0.50000
41	16588038.02343	0.00000	33175772.04687	1.99998	0.00000	0.50000
42	24882132.05468	0.00000	49763808.09374	1.99998	0.00000	0.50000
43	37323312.10937	0.00000	74645936.18749	1.99998	0.00000	0.50000
44	55985128.10937	0.00000111969232.18749		1.99998	0.00000	0.50000
45	83977952.21874	0.00000167954368.37499		1.99998	0.00000	0.50000
46	125967296.18749	0.00000251932288.43749		1.99998	0.00000	0.50000
47	188951520.43749	0.00000377899584.74999		1.99998	0.00000	0.50000
48	283428160.74999	0.00000566851073.74999		1.99998	0.00000	0.50000
49	425143488.74999	0.00000850279169.74999		1.99998	0.00000	0.50000
50	637717121.49999	0.00000***************		1.99998	0.00000	0.50000

```
         EFFECTIVE ANNUAL INTEREST RATE IS      0.64872
```

Effective annual interest rate is the equivalent annual rate if the stated nominal rate is compounded continuously.

Index